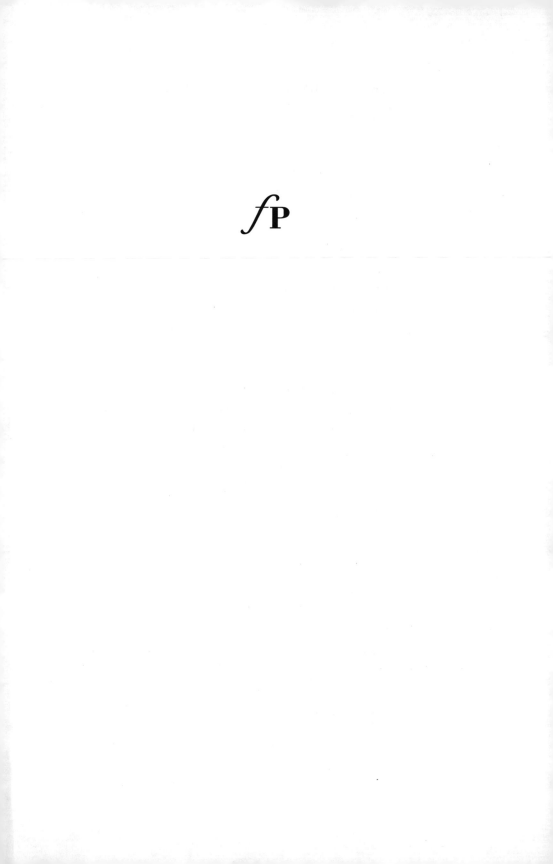

BOOKS BY MARTIN GILBERT

The Churchill Biography

Volume III: The Challenge of War, 1914–1916

Document Volume III (in two parts)

Volume IV: World in Torment, 1917–1922

Document Volume IV (in two parts)

Volume V: The Coming of War, 1922–1939

Document Volume V: The Exchequer Years, 1922–1929

Document Volume V: The Wilderness Years, 1929–1935

Document Volume V: The Coming of War, 1936–1939

Volume VI: Finest Hour, 1939–1941

Churchill War Papers I: At the Admiralty, September 1939–May 1940

Churchill War Papers II: Never Surrender, May–December 1940

Churchill War Papers III: The Ever-Widening War, 1941

Volume VII: Road to Victory, 1941–1945

Volume VIII: Never Despair, 1945–1965

Churchill: A Photographic Portrait

Churchill: A Life

Other Books

The Appeaser (with Richard Gott)

The European Powers, 1900–1945

The Roots of Appeasement

Children's Illustrated Bible Atlas

Atlas of British Charities

Atlas of American History

Atlas of the Arab-Israeli Conflict

Atlas of British History

Atlas of the First World War

Atlas of the Holocaust

The Holocaust: Maps and Photographs

Atlas of Jewish History

Atlas of Russian History

The Jews of Arab Lands: Their History in Maps

The Jews of Russia: Their History in Maps

Jerusalem Illustrated History Atlas

Sir Horace Rumbold: Portrait of a Diplomat

Jerusalem: Rebirth of a City

Jerusalem in the Twentieth Century

Exile and Return: The Struggle for Jewish Statehood

Israel: A History

Auschwitz and the Allies

The Jews of Hope: The Plight of Soviet Jewry Today

Shcharansky: Hero of Our Time

The Holocaust: The Jewish Tragedy

The Boys: Triumph over Adversity

The First World War

The Second World War

D-Day

The Day the War Ended

In Search of Churchill

Empires in Conflict: A History of the Twentieth Century, 1900–1933

Descent into Barbarism: A History of the Twentieth Century, 1934–1951

Challenge to Civilization: A History of the Twentieth Century,
1952–1999

Never Again: A History of the Holocaust

The Jews in the Twentieth Century: An Illustrated History

Letters to Auntie Fori: The 5,000-Year History of the Jewish People and
Their Faith

The Righteous: The Unsung Heroes of the Holocaust

EDITIONS OF DOCUMENTS

Britain and Germany Between the Wars

Plough My Own Furrow: The Life of Lord Allen of Hurtwood

Servant of India: Diaries of the Viceroy's Private Secretary, 1905–1910

CHURCHILL

and

AMERICA

Martin Gilbert

FREE PRESS

New York • London • Toronto • Sydney

fP

FREE PRESS

A Division of Simon & Schuster, Inc.

1230 Avenue of the Americas

New York, NY 10020

For information about special discounts for bulk purchases,
please contact Simon & Schuster Special Sales:
1-800-456-6798 or business@simonandschuster.com

Designed by Dana Sloan

Manufactured in the United States of America

1   3   5   7   9   10   8   6   4   2

Library of Congress Cataloging-in-Publication Data
Gilbert, Martin.
Churchill and America/Martin Gilbert.
p.   cm.
Includes bibliographical references (p.) and index.
1. Churchill, Winston, Sir, 1874–1965—Relations with Americans.   2. Churchill, Winston,
Sir, 1874–1965—Appreciation—America.   3. Churchill, Winston, Sir, 1874–1965—
Knowledge—America.   4. Prime ministers—Great Britain—Biography.
5. Great Britain—Foreign relations—United States.   6. United States—
Foreign relations—Great Britain.   I. Title.
DA566.9.C5 G4445   2005
941.084'092—dc22   2005049412
ISBN-13: 978-0-7432-5992-7
ISBN-10:   0-7432-5992-0

Dedicated to

Mary Soames

who has been a constant encouragement

in my quest to tell her father's story

CONTENTS

✠

LIST OF MAPS

⚜

LIST OF PHOTOGRAPHS

ACKNOWLEDGMENTS

The documentary material used in these pages has come from many archives and private collections. I would like to thank the owners, custodians and archivists of the following collections for access to their holdings and permission to make use of them: the United States Army War College, Carlisle, Pennsylvania; the Robert Hastings Collection; the Library of Congress, Washington, D.C.; the National Archive (formerly Public Record Office), London; the New York Public Library; the Franklin D. Roosevelt Library, Hyde Park, New York; the Harry S. Truman Presidential Museum and Library, Independence, Missouri; the Dwight D. Eisenhower Library, Abilene, Kansas; and the David Satinoff Collection. Special thanks are due to Allen Packwood, Director, and the staff of the Archives Centre at Churchill College, Cambridge, who have always been ready with assistance.

The Library of Congress exhibition "Churchill and the Great Republic", held in 2004, was a source of several important documents. I am grateful to Kimberli Curry, Exhibition Director, for welcoming me to the library before the exhibition opened, and also for her help with the library's photographic collection.

The enthusiasm of the Churchill Centre and its allied Churchill Societies has been a factor in all my Churchill work. I would like to thank in particular its founder and doyen, Richard Langworth, CBE, and its other honorary officers, among them Bill Ives, the Churchill Centre President; Randy Barber (International Churchill Society, Canada), David Boler, Paul Courtenay and Colonel Nigel Knocker, OBE (International Churchill Society, United Kingdom), and their members, for continual encouragement.

It is forty years since I first met Ralph G. Martin, the biographer of

Churchill's mother; his quest for historical materials and zeal for history much influenced me in those early days, and do so still. He has always been a source of encouragement as well as advice.

I am grateful to all those who helped me in my quest for information, and have answered my queries: Jamie Awamleh, Simon Bird, Edwin Black, Shanez Cheytan, Professor Margaret Gilbert, David J. Jhirad, Peter Joy, Morris Massel, Dr. John H. Mather, Sir Anthony Montague Browne, Professor Peter Neary, Professor David Reynolds, Erich Segal, Sir Harry Solomon, Mark Webber and Curt Zoller. The currency conversions are derived from the work of Lawrence H. Officer, professor of economics at the University of Illinois at Chicago.

For help in my search for photographs, I would like to thank Dr. Christopher Dowling of the Imperial War Museum; John R. Hensley, the curator, and staff of the Churchill collections at Westminster College, Fulton, Missouri; Maris Kreizman; R. J. Mahoney, Fellow of the Churchill Memorial and Library at Westminster College; Hilary Roberts, Photograph Archive, Imperial War Museum; and Larry W. Williams. On all matters bibliographical Ronald Cohen has been of the greatest assistance. His enthusiasm for the Churchill canon is infectious.

The support of my publishers, headed by Liz Stein at the Free Press and Andrew Gordon at Simon & Schuster UK, has been important to me, as has been the help of all those at my literary agency, A.P. Watt, among them Caradoc King and Rinku Pattni. The text has been scrutinized to good effect by Susan H. Llewellyn, Erica Hunningher, Esther Goldberg and Kay Thomson.

INTRODUCTION

*Evil would be the counsellors, dark would be the day when
we embarked on that most foolish, futile, and fatal of all
wars — a war with the United States.*

— WINSTON CHURCHILL, 13 May 1901

George Washington was part of his family pedigree. Three of his
ancestors had fought against the British in the American Revolutionary War. His mother was an American, born in Brooklyn in 1854.
He himself was an honorary citizen of the United States. He was Winston Churchill, Britain's wartime leader, whose links with America are
the focus of this book.

The story of Churchill and America spans ninety years. The special
relationship he felt with the United States, and strove to establish—not
always successfully—remains a central aspect of international relations. "Whatever the pathway of the future may bring," he told an
American audience in 1932, "we can face it more safely, more comfortably, and more happily if we travel it together, like good companions.
We have quarrelled in the past, but even in our quarrels great leaders
on both sides were agreed on principles." Churchill added: "Let our
common tongue, our common basic law, our joint heritage of literature and ideals, the red tie of kinship, become the sponge of obliteration of all the unpleasantness of the past."

Churchill spent much of his seventy adult years in close contact
with the United States. He made sixteen journeys across the Atlantic. A
British political opponent once called him "Half alien—and wholly
reprehensible." A First World War colleague said of him: "There's a lot
of Yankee in Winston. He knows how to hustle and how to make others

hustle too." Many Americans were attracted to Churchill's personality. "Unlike most Englishmen," one of his secretaries recalled, "he is naturally at ease among Americans, who seem to understand him better than his own countrymen." President Franklin D. Roosevelt expressed it in a telegram to Churchill during the Second World War: "It is fun being in the same decade as you."

Churchill was proud of his American ancestry. During a discussion at the Truman White House in 1952, to standardize the type of rifle to be used by the two countries' armies, the following exchange took place between Churchill and the senior British officer present:

Field Marshal Slim: "Well, I suppose we could experiment with a bastard rifle, partly American, partly British."

Churchill: "Kindly moderate your language, Field Marshal. It may be recalled that I am myself partly British, partly American."

In two world wars, in both of which Britain's future was endangered, Churchill's was the chief British voice urging, and attaining, the closest possible cooperation with the United States. After the United States had entered the First World War, Churchill told the British War Cabinet that "the intermingling of British and American units on the field of battle and their endurance of losses and suffering together may exert an immeasurable effect upon the future destiny of the English-speaking peoples." As Minister of Munitions he worked to ensure that the two armies would be well mingled and well supplied.

Speaking on 4 July 1918, to a large Anglo-American gathering in London, Churchill, having just returned from the Western Front, declared: "When I have seen during the past few weeks the splendour of American manhood striding forward on all the roads of France and Flanders, I have experienced emotions which words cannot describe." The only recompense Britain sought from American participation in the First World War was the "supreme reconciliation" of Britain and the United States. If the two armies and the two nations "worked well together to secure victory in 1918, Britain and the United States may act permanently together."

Such sentiments were not shared by all Churchill's fellow countrymen. Throughout his life one of Churchill's battles was against the sometimes latent, sometimes strong anti-Americanism that could be found throughout British society. He was always urging his friends, his colleagues, and, as Prime Minister, his War Cabinet, not to alienate the United States, whatever vexations American policy might be causing.

In 1944, as victory came closer, Churchill saw a bolder and brighter future for the Anglo-American relationship than victory alone. In a speech in London at the Royal Albert Hall on 23 November 1944, in celebration of American Thanksgiving Day, he spoke of how "in three or four years the United States has in sober fact become the greatest military, naval, and air power in the world—that, I say to you in this time of war, is itself a subject for profound thanksgiving." But he also spoke of "a greater Thanksgiving Day, which still shines ahead, which beckons the bold and loyal and warm-hearted."

That future Thanksgiving Day would be "when this union of action which has been forced upon us by our common hatred of tyranny, which we have maintained during these dark and fearful days, shall become a lasting union of sympathy and good-feeling and loyalty and hope between all the British and American peoples, wherever they may dwell. Then, indeed," Churchill declared, "there will be a Day of Thanksgiving, and one in which all the world will share."

During the Second World War it is doubtful whether Britain could have sustained itself against the Nazi onslaught, or maintained itself at war, without Churchill's almost daily efforts to win the United States to the British and Allied cause: first as a benign neutral providing vast amounts of war material, and then as an ally willing to put the defeat of Germany before that of Japan. When the Cold War began with the Soviet Union, Churchill told his Foreign Secretary, Anthony Eden: "The similarity and unity which we have with the United States will grow and it is indispensable to our safety." To ensure that unity and safety, Churchill worked closely for the next decade with Presidents Harry S. Truman and Dwight D. Eisenhower.

Truman and Eisenhower were important in Churchill's efforts to forge a common Anglo-American policy and theme, but no world leaders had such a long, constructive, intimate, frustrating, disputatious and affectionate relationship as Winston Churchill and Franklin Roosevelt. Churchill said of the President whom he met so many times and corresponded with so frequently over a period of five years: "I have wooed President Roosevelt as a man might woo a maid." There were many quarrels, but, as Churchill once telegraphed to Roosevelt, using one of his favorite Latin quotations: *"Amantium irae amoris integratio est."* When one of Churchill's secretaries said she did not know what this meant, Churchill told her: "It means the wrath of lovers hots up their love." Roosevelt's staff translated the quotation for him somewhat more prosaically, and more accurately, as "Lovers' quarrels always go with true love."

These pages tell the story of Churchill's lifelong "true love" of the United States. It was a love affair that began with his first visit to New York in 1895 and was still in evidence during his final visit in 1961. At the beginning of 1942 Churchill told King George VI that Britain and the United States "were now 'married' after many months of 'walking out.' " As with all close and sustained relationships, it was replete with ups and downs, uncertainties and disagreements, even anger, but its high points were sustained and remarkable, and of deep benefit to both nations. Churchill's determination to maintain, repair, strengthen and make full use of the ties between the two countries is unique in the annals of Anglo-American relations.

Martin Gilbert
Merton College, Oxford
18 May 2005

Chapter One

⌗

FROM BLENHEIM PALACE
TO BUFFALO BILL

In 1963, in a message sent when he was eighty-eight years old, Churchill remarked with pride to President John F. Kennedy that the story of his association with the United States went back nearly ninety years, "to the day of my father's marriage."[1] That marriage took place in Paris on 15 April 1874. The bridegroom, Lord Randolph Spencer Churchill, was the son of a British duke. The bride, Jennie Jerome, was the daughter of an American millionaire—although at that precise moment Leonard Jerome's fortune had taken a temporary dip.

At the time of their marriage, Jennie was twenty years old and Lord Randolph twenty-five. Their courtship had been short, their love intense, their determination to marry stronger than the doubts of either set of parents. The American ancestry of Jennie Jerome did not impress the aristocratic Churchills, but it was impressive nevertheless. The first member of her family to settle in America was an Englishman, Timothy Jerome, who reached America from the Isle of Wight in 1710, a descendant of Huguenot Protestants who had fled France for Britain three generations earlier.

One of Winston Churchill's great-great-grandfathers, Lieutenant Reuben Murray, had served during the American Revolutionary War in the 17th Connecticut Regiment and the 7th Albany Regiment, New York Militia. Because of this, during a visit to Washington in 1952 Churchill was invested with the Eagle and Diploma of the Society of

---

1. *New York Times,* 10 April 1963.

1

Cincinnatus, which is limited to direct male descendants of officers who served three years in the army and navy during that war.[2]

Two of Churchill's American great-great-great-grandfathers had also fought in the American Revolution: Samuel Jerome was a Militia Sergeant; Major Libbeus Ball had been wounded in action.[3] Major Ball's father, a clergyman, was a cousin of George Washington's mother. Thus Churchill and Washington had a common ancestor.[4] A scrutiny of genealogical tables also reveals that Winston Churchill and Franklin Roosevelt—the President with whom he was to become inextricably involved in the Second World War—were also related, albeit distantly, as eighth cousins, once removed.[5]

In 1849 Leonard Jerome married Clara, the daughter of Ambrose Hall and Anna Baker. They had three daughters, Clarita, Jennie and Leonie; a fourth daughter died at the age of six. Jennie's maternal grandfather, Ambrose Hall, was a respected member of the New York State Assembly. A mystery surrounds the identity of Jennie's grandmother's mother, whose maiden name is not recorded in the Hall genealogies. According to family lore she was "believed to have been" an Iroquois Indian.[6] She came, in fact, from Nova Scotia, where there were no Iroquois, but several Indian tribes lived there, principally the Micmac and Abenaki. Although marriage between Indians and whites was then extremely rare, rape was not: Churchill's great-great-great-grandmother could well have been a half-caste.

Within the Jerome family an Indian likeness was much commented on. Clara Jerome was nicknamed "Sitting Bull," and her sister "Hatchet Face."[7] Clara Jerome's great-granddaughter, Anita Leslie, has

---

2. Randolph S. Churchill and Helmut Gernsheim, editors, *Churchill, His Life in Photographs,* caption 348.

3. Genealogical Table, Richard Harrity and Ralph G. Martin, *Man of the Century, Churchill,* page 23.

4. Genealogical Table: Richard Harrity and Ralph G. Martin, *Man of the Century, Churchill,* page 23.

5. Cornelius Mann, "Two Famous Descendants of John Cooke and Sarah Warren," *New York Genealogical and Biographical Record* 73, no. 3 (New York, July 1942), pages 159–66.

6. Randolph S. Churchill, *Winston S. Churchill,* volume 1, pages 16–17.

7. Ralph G. Martin, *Jennie: The Life of Lady Randolph Churchill, The Romantic Years, 1854–1895,* page 4.

written: "Although told she must never mention her Indian blood, Clara could not forget that it burnt in her veins," adding: "People might not consider the Iroquois strain 'genteel' but there it was, pounding through her heart. . . ."[8] In 1960, five years before his death, Churchill told one of his doctors: ". . . you may not know it, but I am descended from a Seneca Indian squaw who was an ancestor of my mother."[9] The quintessential Englishman was not only half American but also one-sixty-fourth Native American. "For me," writes Churchill's grandson Winston, "physical features speak louder than any entry in a register of births."[10]

Leonard Jerome and his brother Lawrence married two sisters. Lawrence Jerome's son, William Travers Jerome—Churchill's second cousin—was to become a reforming District Attorney of New York who refused to bow to the dictates of Tammany Hall, with its strong political control. In 1906 he sought to be nominated as Governor of New York, but was unsuccessful. The biographer of Churchill's mother, Ralph G. Martin, speculates that if Travers Jerome had won the nomination and the governorship in 1906, "he might well have been nominated by the Democrats for President in 1912 instead of Woodrow Wilson."[11]

After his marriage Leonard Jerome lived in Rochester, New York, a town on Lake Ontario, whose main newspaper, the *Daily American*, he purchased. From Rochester the Jeromes moved in 1850 to Madison Square, New York City, to one of the finest private houses in the city; it included its own six-hundred-seat theater. Becoming a leading stockbroker, Leonard Jerome was known as the "King of Wall Street." A staunch Republican, he was rewarded in 1851 for his political allegiance by being appointed American Consul in Trieste, then a flourishing Austro-Hungarian port on the Adriatic.

With the advent of a Democratic administration in January 1853, Leonard Jerome's appointment in Trieste came to an end, and he returned to New York. In his absence Addison Jerome, one of his seven

---

8. Anita Leslie, *The Fabulous Leonard Jerome,* page 36.
9. Recollections of Professor Rob, letter to the author, 17 November 1986.
10. Winston S. Churchill, "The Indian Blood That Fired My Grandfather," *Sunday Telegraph,* 24 October 1999.
11. Ralph G. Martin, letter to the author, 29 July 2004.

brothers, had been left in charge of the family stockbroker firm, and it had failed. Under Leonard Jerome's efforts the family fortune was restored. On 9 January 1854, his second daughter was born. He named her Jennie, after the opera singer Jenny Lind, whom he much admired.

In 1858 Leonard Jerome purchased a substantial financial interest in the *New York Times,* America's leading newspaper, acquiring a fifth of the shares. A high point in his family's social standing came in 1860, when the Jeromes' ballroom, which could accommodate three hundred people, was the scene of a ball given in honor of the Prince of Wales, Queen Victoria's eldest son, later King Edward VII. The Prince was then nineteen years old. Jennie, who was later to be his friend, was seven. Despite her tears of protest she was not allowed to attend the ball, even as a demure spectator.

With the outbreak of the American Civil War in 1861, Leonard Jerome was active on behalf of the Union. He paid a considerable sum toward the construction of the warship *Meteor.* In 1865, from the window of their house on East Twenty-sixth Street, Jennie and her two sisters watched as the horse-drawn coffin of the assassinated President Abraham Lincoln passed in solemn procession in the street below.[12]

A man of diverse interests, Leonard Jerome was generous to those in need, and a keen investor in stocks and shares, two traits his grandson was to inherit. A prominent member of fashionable society, he was a member of the Union Club, one of the oldest in New York. A keen and accomplished yachtsman, when the Atlantic underwater cable was broken in 1865, he offered his yacht to take the engineer to repair it. He was also a patron of the opera and a lover of horseracing, one of the founders of the American Jockey Club, and the main organizer of flat racing in the United States. With his brother Lawrence, he built a racecourse, Jerome Park, near Fordham in the Bronx, New York. The opening, in 1866, was described by the *New York Tribune* as "the social event of all time," ushering in "a new era in the horse-racing world."[13] Lawrence Jerome was known as one of the wittiest men of his day.

---

12. Anita Leslie, *Jennie: The Life of Lady Randolph Churchill,* page 9.
13. *New York Tribune,* 26 September 1866.

Churchill's mother remembered her uncle having "kept us in transports of laughter."[14]

In 1867 Clara Jerome took her daughters to live in Paris, where she held a salon at which an array of European aristocrats gathered. In the winter she and her husband went to the resort and spa at Pau, in the French Pyrenees. Their first journey to Britain was in the summer of 1871, when Leonard Jerome took his family to Cowes on the Isle of Wight, for the yacht racing. Two years later Mrs. Jerome and her three daughters returned to Cowes, but without her husband. The financial crash of 1873 in the United States had led to a sharp fall in stocks, and Leonard Jerome had to close down his magnificent house on Madison Square and move into a smaller home, living in two rooms instead of twenty until his position on Wall Street, although not his former fortune, was restored. Earlier, however, he had with much prudence settled a sufficiently large sum of money on his wife to secure her financial independence, enabling her to maintain a comfortable lifestyle in Paris.

In August 1873, while Clara Jerome and her daughters were once again at Cowes, the captain and officers of the Royal Navy cruiser *Ariadne* invited them to a shipboard reception. The occasion was to meet both the Prince and Princess of Wales (later King Edward VII and Queen Alexandra) and the Grand Duke Czarevitch and Grand Duchess Czarevna of Russia (later Czar Alexander III and the Empress Maria Feodorovna). The reception was held on August 12. It was at this reception that Jennie met Lord Randolph. Three days later he proposed and she accepted.

All three Jerome girls were to marry Englishmen. The oldest, Clarita, married Moreton Frewen, later a Member of Parliament, known because of his unsuccessful financial ventures as "Mortal Ruin." The youngest, Leonie, married John Leslie, a landowner with estates in Ireland. Jennie was the first of the three sisters to marry. When she wrote to her father of her engagement to Lord Randolph Churchill, he replied with a combination of unease and pride: "I fear he is too swell according to English ideas to gain the consent of his family, though he will have to look a good while among his countrywomen to

---

14. Anita Leslie, *Jennie: The Life of Lady Randolph Churchill,* page 57.

find one equal to you." He would not object to a marriage with some-one who was not an American, Leonard Jerome added, "provided al-ways he is not a Frenchman or any other of those continental cusses."[15]

Lord Randolph Churchill's father, the Eighth Duke of Marlbor-ough, was firmly opposed to the marriage. From Blenheim Palace he made prompt inquiries, from which he learned that Leonard Jerome had been declared bankrupt twenty years earlier. The Duke warned his son: "It is evident that he is of the class of speculators, he has been bankrupt once; and may be so again."[16] Leonard Jerome upheld his family's name as best he could, telling his daughter that he hoped the Duke would give his approval once he learned that decent financial provision could be made for her, "and that our family is entirely re-spectable—which is all that can be said for any American family."[17]

The Duke still hesitated, but only for reasons of the financial set-tlement, on which Leonard Jerome was confident of putting the ducal mind at rest. "I know the great prejudices the English have against Americans socially," he wrote to Jennie, "and I feared that you might be left in a very disagreeable position." He was thrilled, however, by the imminent marriage, telling his daughter that it was the "greatest match any American has made since the Duchess of Leeds."[18] Leonard Jerome was referring to the daughter of a wealthy merchant from Maryland. She married, in 1828, when she was thirty-nine, Francis, Marquess of Carmarthen, who ten years later succeeded his father as Seventh Duke of Leeds.

Clara Jerome's concern was that her future son-in-law, although likewise the son of a Duke, would never succeed to the title, therefore her daughter would never be a Duchess. She was right. Lord Randolph Churchill, being the second son, would succeed to the dukedom only if his brother and his brother's son predeceased him. This did not happen.

---

15. Letter of 8 September 1873, Randolph S. Churchill, *Winston S. Churchill*, Vol-ume 1, Companion (document) Volume, Part 1, pages 8–11.

16. Letter of 31 August 1873, Randolph S. Churchill, *Winston S. Churchill*, Volume 1, Companion (document) Volume, Part 1, pages 12–13.

17. Letter of 11 September 1873, Randolph S. Churchill, *Winston S. Churchill*, Vol-ume 1, Companion (document) Volume, Part 1, pages 14–15.

18. Letter of 7 October 1873, Randolph S. Churchill, *Winston S. Churchill*, Volume 1, Companion (document) Volume, Part 1, pages 17–18.

The financial settlement proved a cause of conflict between the Duke of Marlborough and Leonard Jerome. The American wanted to settle an annuity on his daughter for her independent use. The Duke wanted his son to be the beneficiary. It was agreed to divide the annuity. "In the settlement as finally arranged," Leonard Jerome wrote to the Duke from Paris, "I have ignored American custom and waived all my American prejudices."[19] A week later Lord Randolph Churchill and Jennie Jerome were married in Paris, at the British Embassy. The Duke and Duchess were not present—the Duchess was not well—but sent their blessings. The Duke also sent his son a letter wishing him well, but pointing out that he had chosen his bride "with less than usual deliberation."[20]

In future years some were to call this union between the son of a British Duke and the daughter of a wealthy American a "snob-dollar" marriage. Churchill rejected this, writing to a friend shortly before the outbreak of the Second World War: "This was a love match if ever there was one, with very little money on either side. In fact, they could only live in the smallest way possible to people in London society."[21] Lady Randolph Churchill—as Jennie Jerome had become—was soon, however, a center of attention at the season's balls. The first she attended in London was in honor of Czar Alexander II. Later, at a costume ball given by the Prince of Wales, she came, at the Prince's request, dressed as the Queen of Clubs.

Toward the end of November 1874, when she was seven and a half months into her first pregnancy, Lady Randolph was at Blenheim Palace, staying there for several weeks. During her visit there were two mishaps. "She had a fall on Tuesday walking with the shooters," Lord Randolph explained in a letter to Mrs. Jerome, "& a rather imprudent & rough drive in a pony carriage brought on the pains on Saturday night. We tried to stop them, but it was no use. They went on all Sunday."[22]

---

19. Letter of 9 April 1874, Randolph S. Churchill, *Winston S. Churchill*, Volume 1, Companion (document) Volume, Part 1, page 20.
20. Letter of 14 April 1874, Randolph S. Churchill, *Winston S. Churchill*, Volume 1, Companion (document) Volume, Part 1, page 22.
21. Letter of 30 April 1973, Sir Edward Marsh papers.
22. Letter of 30 November 1874, Randolph S. Churchill, *Winston S. Churchill*, Volume 1, Companion (document) Volume, Part 1, pages 1–2.

On 30 November 1874 Lord and Lady Randolph Churchill's first child was born, a son. He was christened Winston Leonard Spencer Churchill. In absentia, his American grandfather, Leonard Jerome, was one of the godparents. In February 1880, when Churchill was five, his brother Jack was born.

The young Winston's American mother was to become his confidante and helper, furthering his plans and ambitions as best she could. She provided him with the books and contacts he craved, to replace the university education he never had. She entertained those whom he felt would advance his career, and put in strong commendations for him in high places. He once remarked: "She left no stone unturned and no cutlet uncooked"—as she sought to help him in his struggle toward his military advancement and political life. Their early relationship was not easy, however. Churchill later recalled, a decade after her death, "She shone for me like the Evening Star. I loved her dearly—but at a distance." [23]

An explanation of the words "at a distance" may be found in a letter Lady Randolph wrote to her husband, after mother and son—then aged eight—had spent a few days together: "It appears that he is afraid of me." [24] Nevertheless, it was from his British father that Churchill felt a deep gulf of distance and misunderstanding; from his American mother he was to receive support and encouragement on an impressive scale.

In 1882, when Winston was seven, he was looking through back issues of *Punch* magazine—then a staple in every British school library—when he came across several cartoons about the American Civil War. "First of all," Churchill later wrote, "Mr Punch was against the South, and we had a picture of a fierce young woman, Miss Carolina, about to whip a naked slave, a sort of Uncle Tom, with a kind of scourge which, not being yet myself removed out of the zone of such possibilities, I regarded as undoubtedly severe." Churchill added: "I was all for the slave."

Churchill remembered other aspects of the Civil War cartoons: a

---

23. Winston S. Churchill, *My Early Life,* page 19.
24. Letter of 26 December 1882, Randolph S. Churchill, *Winston S. Churchill,* Volume 1, Companion (document) Volume, Part 1, page 49.

whole regiment of Yankees "running away from a place called Bull Run"; a cartoon of the North and South as "two savage, haggard men in shirts and breeches, grappling and stabbing each other with knives as they reeled into an abyss called Bankruptcy"; and finally a drawing of Lincoln's tomb "and Britannia, very sad, laying a wreath upon the cold marble. . . ."[25]

In the summer of 1887, when Winston was twelve, the American soldier and showman, Colonel William "Buffalo Bill" Cody, came to London. He had earned his nickname at the age of twenty, supplying buffalo meat for the workers on the Kansas Pacific Railroad. His Wild West show, inaugurated in Omaha in 1885, spent ten of its thirty years in Europe. His advertisement in *The Times* trumpeted its attractions in capital letters: "Grandstand for 20,000 people. Bands of Sioux, Arapahoes, Shoshones, Cheyennes, and other Indians, Cowboys, Scouts and Mexican Vacqueros." There would be riding, shooting, lassoing and hunting, attacks on a stagecoach and on a settler's cabin, as well as "Frontier Girl Riders and Cowboy Bands."

Churchill, then at boarding school in Brighton, wrote several times to his mother, urging her to write to the two sisters who ran the school to let him go up to London. When his mother hesitated, he drafted the letter that he wanted her to send, insisting she make no mention of the real reason for his visit. Churchill was emphatic. "I want to see Buffalo Bill . . . ," he wrote. "Don't disappoint me."[26] His mother did as she was asked, and Churchill went to see Buffalo Bill. It was an early example of his powers of persuasion.

As his thirteenth birthday approached, Churchill wrote to his mother about his preferred present: "I would rather Gen Grant's History of the American war—Illustrated."[27] The young man was already conscious of, and intrigued by, his American heritage.

-----

25. Winston S. Churchill, "Cartoons and Cartoonists," *Strand Magazine*, June 1931. This article was reprinted in book form in Winston S. Churchill, *Amid These Storms* (New York: Charles Scribner's Sons, 1932; British edition, *Thoughts and Adventures*, London: Thornton Butterworth, 1932).

26. Letter postmarked 11 June 1887, Randolph S. Churchill, *Winston S. Churchill*, Volume 1, Companion (document) Volume, Part 1, pages 134–35.

27. Letter of 15 November 1887, Randolph S. Churchill, *Winston S. Churchill*, Volume 1, Companion (document) Volume, Part 1, page 147.

Chapter Two

🔁

THE "TALL YANKEE" AND
"A GREAT LUSTY YOUTH"

In February 1888, when Churchill was thirteen years old, he made his second written reference to the United States. It was while he was studying for an examination at Harrow School. "You will be pleased to hear that we are learning the Geography of the US," he wrote to his mother. "When I come home you must question me."[1] As to his character at this time, his American grandmother, Clara Jerome, described him to her husband as "a naughty, sandy-haired little bulldog."[2]

In November 1888 an American soldier-inventor came to Harrow: Colonel George E. Gouraud. A month later, as Thomas Edison's representative in Britain, he recorded Gladstone speaking, a recording that survives to this day.[3] For his demonstration to the boys at Harrow, Gouraud produced a wax-cylinder phonograph, sang into it—"John Brown's Body"—and then played back what he had sung. "He showed it us in private on Monday," Churchill wrote to his mother. "We went in 3 or 4 at a time." Churchill added that Gouraud's wife "was at school with you." The Colonel himself had fought at Gettysburg.[4] In a letter to his father, Churchill reported that Gouraud had asked him to ask "if

---

1. Letter of 28 February 1888, Randolph S. Churchill, *Winston S. Churchill*, Volume 1, Companion (document) Volume, Part 1, page 156.
2. Quoted in Ralph G. Martin, *Jennie: The Life of Lady Randolph Churchill, The Romantic Years, 1854–1895*, page 255.
3. Recording of 18 December 1888, National Park Service, catalog No. EDIS 39852. Gladstone had been Prime Minister 1868–74, 1880–85 and 1886.
4. Letter of 7 November 1888, Randolph S. Churchill, *Winston S. Churchill*, Volume 1, Companion (document) Volume, Part 1, page 174.

you remembered the 'tall Yankee' to whom you gave letters of recommendation, when you were Secretary of State for India."[5]

The United States again figured in Churchill's life at the end of 1890, when he took the preliminary examination for Sandhurst, the first step toward a career in the army. Three essay titles were offered: Rowing versus Riding, Advertisements their Uses and Abuses, and the American Civil War. "I did the last," he told his mother.[6] Churchill passed in all subjects, something achieved by only twelve of the twenty-nine candidates from Harrow.

Aged seventy-three, Leonard Jerome returned to Europe in 1890. "He was a magnificent looking man," Churchill later recalled, "with long flowing moustachios, a rather aquiline nose, and very bright eyes. All these I remember."[7] While in Britain, Leonard Jerome was taken ill. "Grandpapa is fairly well—but weak," Lady Randolph wrote to her son in early February.[8] Leonard Jerome died in Brighton later that year. Among those at his funeral was President Lincoln's son Robert T. Lincoln, then American Ambassador to Britain. Five years after Leonard Jerome's death, Lord Randolph Churchill died, almost certainly from a brain tumor.[9] He was only forty-five years old. Churchill, just nineteen, and about to embark on an army career, was devastated.

Another American family link was created for Churchill in the year of his father's death, when his cousin "Sunny," who three years earlier had succeeded his father to become Ninth Duke of Marlborough, married an American heiress, Consuelo Vanderbilt. The wedding took

---

5. Letter of 7 November 1888, Randolph S. Churchill. *Winston S. Churchill*, Volume 1, Companion (document) Volume, Part 1, page 175.

6. Letter of 18 December 1890, Randolph S. Churchill, *Winston S. Churchill*, Volume 1, Companion (document) Volume, Part 1, page 135.

7. Winston S. Churchill, draft essay on Leonard Jerome, April 1932, Martin Gilbert, *Winston S. Churchill*, Volume 5, Companion (document) Volume, Part 2, pages 422–23.

8. Letter of 7 February 1890, Randolph S. Churchill, *Winston S. Churchill*, Volume 1, Companion (document) Volume, Part 1, pages 197–98.

9. It has frequently been asserted, and Lord Randolph Churchill's doctor so informed the Prince of Wales's doctor at the time, that Churchill's father died of one of the advanced symptoms of syphilis. This has been authoritatively challenged by Dr. John H. Mather, in "Lord Randolph Churchill: Maladies et Mort," *Finest Hour*, Number 93, Winter 1996–1997, pages 23–28.

place in New York on 6 November 1895. Churchill was even then crossing the Atlantic for his first visit to the United States, on his way to Spanish-ruled Cuba. He reached New York three days after the wedding.

Churchill's aim in making this transatlantic journey, while he was not yet twenty-one, was to be an observer with the Spanish forces as they sought to crush a Cuban insurgency. The Spanish military authorities were pleased that Churchill and a fellow soldier, his friend Reginald Barnes, who accompanied him throughout this first American journey, wanted to witness the struggle of the Spanish forces. For its part, the British Army's Military Intelligence branch suggested that Churchill and Barnes report on the efficacy of the new Spanish rifle.

Churchill told his mother about his travel plans less than a month before setting off. She was not pleased. "I'm very much afraid it will cost a great deal more than you think," she wrote. "NY is fearfully expensive & you will be bored to death there—all men are."[10] Churchill and Barnes had intended to lodge at the Brunswick Hotel in Manhattan, but while they were crossing the Atlantic, Churchill's mother arranged for them to stay at the home of one of her closest American friends, Bourke Cockran, who had an apartment at 763 Fifth Avenue, at the Bolkenhayn Building, on the corner of Fifty-eighth Street. Cockran, an Irishman born in County Sligo in 1854, had emigrated to the United States at the age of seventeen, becoming a lawyer and a politician. In 1891 he had been elected to Congress as a Democrat. One of the noted American orators of his day, he was a man of powerful presence.

Reaching New York on 9 November 1895, Churchill went straight to Bourke Cockran's apartment. In his first letter from the city, written the day after his arrival, he told his mother: "Mr Cockran is one of the most charming hosts and interesting men I have met." His apartment was "beautifully furnished and fitted with every convenience." The two men were drawn to each other instantly. "I have had great discussions with Mr Cockran on every conceivable subject from Economics to yacht racing. He is a clever man and one from whose conversation much is to be learned."

---

10. Letter of 11 October 1895, Randolph S. Churchill, *Winston S. Churchill*, Volume 1, Companion (document) Volume, Part 1, page 590.

But Cockran was more than that. "When he entered a room," the Irish statesman Sir Horace Plunkett wrote of Bourke Cockran, "it was like someone turning on the electric light."[11] Churchill's father had just died; Cockran had no son. Only five years younger than Lord Randolph, he was to become Churchill's first political confidant.

Everybody whom Churchill met in New York, he told his mother, was "very civil"; he and Barnes had "engagements for every meal for the next few days about three deep." On their first night in New York, a Saturday, they were invited to dinner with a group of lawyers, including Judge Ingraham, a New York State Supreme Court judge who was trying a notorious murder case. The judge invited Churchill to hear his charge to the jury in three days' time. After this judicial dinner a Jerome relative took Churchill and Barnes to a nightclub, and then to supper at the Waldorf. "The Entertainment was good & supper excellent," Churchill told his mother, adding that Eva Purdy, a niece of Grandmother Jerome, had engaged "an excellent valet" and made "every sort of arrangement for us." On his second day in New York, Churchill lunched with Eva Purdy, called on one of his mother's friends at three o'clock, and went on to Consuelo Vanderbilt's uncle Cornelius Vanderbilt at five. At eight he dined with Eva Purdy's sister, Kitty Mott, another of his American cousins, "so you see," he wrote to his mother, "there is not much chance of time hanging heavily."[12]

On his third day in New York, Churchill went to the headquarters of the Atlantic Military District and was then shown around the forts of New York harbor in a tugboat, a visit arranged by Bourke Cockran. On the Tuesday, also thanks to Cockran, he went to West Point. In a letter to his brother, Churchill gave an account of the visit. "I am sure you will be horrified by some of the Regulations of the Military Academy, he wrote. The cadets enter from 19–22 and stay 4 years. This means that they are most of them 24 years of age. They are not allowed to smoke or have any money in their possession nor are they given any leave except 2 months after the 1st two years. In fact they have far less liberty than any private school boys in our country." Churchill added:

---

11. Quoted in Ralph G. Martin, *Jennie: The Life of Lady Randolph Churchill, The Dramatic Years, 1895–1921*, page 28.

12. Letter of 10 November 1895, Randolph S. Churchill, *Winston S. Churchill*, Volume 1, Companion (document) Volume, Part 1, pages 596–97.

"I think such a state of things is positively disgraceful and young men of 24 or 25 who would resign their personal liberty to such an extent can never make good citizens or fine soldiers. A child who rebels against that sort of control should be whipped—so should a man who does not rebel." [13]

Bourke Cockran also arranged a somewhat unusual entertainment for the visitors. "The other night," Churchill wrote to his brother before leaving New York, "Mr Cockran got the Fire Commissioner to come with us and we alarmed four or five fire stations. This would have interested you very much. On the alarm bell sounding the horses at once rushed into the shafts—the harness fell on to them—the men slid half dressed down a pole from their sleeping room and in 52 seconds the engine was galloping down the street to the scene of the fire. An interesting feat which seems incredible unless you have seen it." [14]

Churchill's cousin Kitty Mott had invited him and Barnes to the November 11 opening night of the annual Horse Show at Madison Square Garden, where she had a private box. The *New York Times* reported on the opening events: "New York's prettiest girls, best-dressed matrons, and most perfect-groomed beaus were on hand to watch the judging of the horses, and incidentally to show off the best bib and tucker. Boston, Philadelphia, Washington, and Baltimore were represented in the thousands of fashionable people who filled the 114 boxes and crowded the arena walk." [15]

"They really make rather a fuss over us here and extend the most lavish hospitality," Churchill wrote to his mother. "We are members of all the Clubs and one person seems to vie with another in trying to make our time pleasant." As to the journalists who had begun to pester him, he had been "very civil and vague" to them, "and so far I can only find one misstatement in the papers." The United States captivated him. "What an extraordinary people the Americans are!" he wrote to his mother. "Their hospitality is a revelation to me and they make you feel at home and at ease in a way that I have never before experi-

---

13. Letter of 15 November 1895: Randolph S. Churchill, *Winston S. Churchill,* Volume 1, Companion (document) Volume, Part 1, pages 599–600.

14. Letter of 15 November 1895, Randolph S. Churchill, *Winston S. Churchill,* Volume 1, Companion (document) Volume, Part 1, pages 599–600.

15. "Finest of Horse Shows," *New York Times,* 12 November 1895.

enced." On the other hand, he added, "their press and their currency impress me very unfavourably."[16]

During his visit to the harbor, Churchill and Barnes were shown over the armored cruiser *New York.* To his aunt Leonie he wrote: "I was much struck by the sailors: their intelligence, their good looks and civility and their general businesslike appearance." These had interested him more than the ship itself, "for while any nation can build a battleship—it is the monopoly of the Anglo-Saxon race to breed good seamen."[17]

Churchill reported to his aunt: "I have been industriously seeing American institutions of all kinds, and have been impressed by many things—but I feel I should like to think over and digest what I have seen for a few weeks before forming an opinion on it." Still, he already had formed some opinions, which he set down for her. So far, he wrote: "I think the means of communication in New York have struck me the most. The comfort and convenience of elevated railways—tramways—cable cars and ferries, harmoniously fitted into a perfect system accessible alike to the richest and the poorest—is extraordinary." When "one reflects," Churchill added, "that such benefits have been secured to the people not by confiscation of the property of the rich or by arbitrary taxation but simply by business enterprise—out of which the promoters themselves have made colossal fortunes, one cannot fail to be impressed with the excellence of the active system."

American capitalism had won his admiration, but, he commented to his aunt: "New York is full of contradictions and contrasts. I paid my fare across Brooklyn Bridge with a paper dollar. I should think the most disreputable 'coin' the world has ever seen." Churchill was used to the gold and silver coinage in use in Britain. The silver one-shilling piece would have been sufficient to cross Brooklyn Bridge. The lowest silver coin was the three-pence piece (then the equivalent of five cents). Churchill told his aunt, "I wondered how to reconcile the magnificent system of communication with the abominable currency—for

---

16. Letter of 10 November 1895, Randolph S. Churchill, *Winston S. Churchill,* Volume 1, Companion (document) Volume, Part 1, pages 596–97.

17. In May 1898, during the Spanish-American War, the *New York* participated in the bombardment of San Juan, Puerto Rico, and in July that year in the naval battle of Santiago, Cuba. She was finally scuttled in Subic Bay, the Philippines, in the 1970s: Patrick McSherry, "Cruiser *New York,*"www.spanamwar.com.

a considerable time and at length I have found what may be a solution. The communication of New York is due to private enterprise while the state is responsible for the currency: and hence I come to the conclusion that the first class men of America are in the counting houses and the less brilliant ones in the government."

As Churchill had written to his mother two days earlier, so also to his aunt he confided his dilemma: "My mind is full of irreconcilable and conflicting facts. The comfort of their cars and the disgraceful currency—the hospitality of American Society and the vulgarity of their Press—present to me a problem of great complexity. I am going to prolong my stay here a few more days on purpose to see more." [18]

That night Churchill went to the courthouse to hear Judge Ingraham instruct the jury. The judge invited him to sit next to him on the bench. "Quite a strange experience," Churchill wrote to his brother, "and one which would be impossible in England. The Judge discussing the evidence as it was given with me and generally making himself socially agreeable—and all the while a pale miserable man was fighting for his life." Churchill added: "This is a very great country my dear Jack. Not pretty or romantic but great and utilitarian. There seems to be no such thing as reverence or tradition. Everything is eminently practical and things are judged from a matter of fact standpoint." Churchill went on to explain: "Take for instance the Court house. No robes or wigs or uniformed ushers. Nothing but a lot of men in black coats and tweed suits. Judge prisoner jury counsel and warders all indiscriminately mixed. But they manage to hang a man all the same, and that after all is a great thing." In fact, in this particular case, the accused was acquitted on the grounds of insanity.

On the Thursday evening Churchill dined with his cousin Sunny, Duke of Marlborough. "He is very pleased with himself and seems very fit," Churchill wrote to his brother Jack, and he added: "The newspapers have abused him scurrilously." In its report on the Horse Show, the *New York Times* noted: "Marlborough and His Duchess Entirely Eclipse the Horses," and went on to write: "The Duke of Marlborough, who isn't much more than one-half as big as his titles, had his introduction to an American horse show and one of its crowds last evening.

---

18. Letter of 12 November 1895, Randolph S. Churchill, *Winston S. Churchill*, Volume 1, Companion (document) Volume, Part 1, pages 597–98.

The Garden was packed to its utmost capacity with a crowd that simply bubbled and fizzled and fumed with curiosity." [19]

The "essence of American journalism," Churchill wrote to Jack, "is vulgarity divested of truth. Their best papers write for a class of snotty housemaids and footmen, & even the nicest people here have so much vitiated their taste as to appreciate their style." Churchill added: "I think mind you that vulgarity is a sign of strength. A great, crude, strong, young people are the Americans—like a boisterous healthy boy among enervated but well bred ladies and gentlemen."

Churchill had one final reflection. "Picture to yourself the American people as a great lusty youth," he wrote to his brother, "who treads on all your sensibilities, perpetrates every possible horror of ill manners—whom neither age nor just tradition inspire with reverence—but who moves about his affairs with a good hearted freshness which may well be the envy of older nations of the earth. Of course there are here charming people who are just as refined and cultured as the best in any country in the world—but I believe my impressions of the nation are broadly speaking correct." [20]

On Sunday, 17 November 1895, Churchill and Barnes left New York by train for Tampa, Florida, from where they went by sea to Havana. Churchill's eight days in New York had made an indelible impression on him, and created a sense of intimacy with his mother's land. It had also introduced him to Bourke Cockran, whose influence was to be a lasting one. Fifty-eight years later the American Democratic contender for the presidency of the United States, Adlai Stevenson, asked Churchill who had most influenced his oratory. Churchill replied: "It was an American who inspired me when I was 19 & taught me how to use every note of the human voice like an organ." Churchill told Stevenson: "He was my model. I learned from him how to hold thousands in thrall." [21]

---

19. "The Duke at the Garden, Marlborough and his Duchess Entirely Eclipse the Horse," *New York Times*, 14 November 1895.

20. Letter of 15 November 1895: Radolph S. Churchill, *Winston S. Churchill*, Volume 1, Companion (document) Volume, Part 1, pages 599–600.

21. Anita Leslie, recolllections of a conversation with Adlai Stevenson (the day before his death), in a letter to Randolph Churchill, 20 July 1965, Randolph S. Churchill, *Winston S. Churchill*, Volume 1, pages 282–83.

⚎

CUBA AND BEYOND

The first reference to Winston Churchill to appear in the *New York Times*, of which his American grandfather had been a substantial shareholder several decades earlier, was made on 20 November 1895, ten days before his twenty-first birthday. The newspaper reported that the leader of the Spanish forces in Cuba, General Martínez Campos, had accepted Churchill's services "in the Spanish Army in Cuba." This seven-line item was headed, "Randolph Churchill's Son in Cuba." [1] Churchill was still best known as his late father's son.

On his twenty-first birthday, 30 November 1895, Churchill was under rebel fire in Cuba. As the battles continued, he repeatedly found himself in the thick of the action. On December 6 the *New York Times* reported that "especial mention" had been made in the battle reports of the "valorous conduct" of Churchill and Barnes.[2] Churchill also found time to report on the fighting in five long letters to the British *Daily Graphic:* his first sustained journalistic effort. In the first letter he noted that one of the aims of the rebels was "to obtain recognition as belligerents from the United States." [3] This was something they failed to do. Three months later, in an article in the *Saturday Review,* Churchill warned the Spaniards that if they perpetrated "senseless cruelties" in Cuba, it would "precipitate the intervention of the United States." [4]

On Churchill's departure from Cuba the Spanish authorities

---

1. *New York Times,* 20 November 1895.
2. *New York Times,* 6 December 1895.
3. "Letters from the Front," sent on 22 November 1895, printed on 13 December 1895, *Daily Graphic.*
4. "The Revolt in Cuba," *Saturday Review,* 15 February 1896.

awarded him his first military decoration, the Red Cross of the Spanish Order of Military Merit, First Class. The citation referred to "the distinguished comportment observed by you in military action."[5]

Churchill and Barnes returned from Cuba to New York as they had left, by sea and train. Some New York newspapers spread rumors that, in going to Cuba, they had done so as secret emissaries of the British government, thus breaking the rules of the Monroe Doctrine, which reserved to the United States all direct involvement in Latin American disputes. As the more responsible *New York World* explained, with a sneer at two imaginary provincial newspapers. "The *Bungtown Bird of Freedom* and the *Kalamazoo Daily Celery Stalk* printed many flaming editorials on the conduct of these gentlemen in going to Cuba, declaring that they were emissaries of the British Government sent to teach Campos how to whip the secessionists, and that England was throwing more bricks at the Monroe doctrine. Of course this was nonsense. Churchill is not yet twenty-one years old, and knows only the amount of strategy necessary for the duties of a second lieutenant. He and Barnes went on the trip actuated only by youthful enthusiasm."[6]

The two lieutenants reached the Cunard pier in New York on December 14, shortly before their ship was to sail for Britain. Churchill was at once surrounded by a crowd of American journalists eager to hear his opinion on the Spanish efforts to crush the Cuban insurgents. In the words of the *New York Herald:* "When Lieutenant Churchill and party reached the Cunard dock it was within five minutes of the *Etruria*'s sailing time, but the pleasant faced young officer submitted as gracefully to the requests of the waiting group of interviewers as though there were hours of leisure on his hands." The newspaper added that Churchill's answers were given "in straightforward fashion, with his beardless, boyish face flushed with eagerness." Churchill forecast that the Spanish struggle in Cuba might last several years, and that "the insurgents will be in a position to demand more favorable terms in the event of any attempt at settlement or arbitration."[7]

The reporter from the *New York World* recorded another of Chur-

---

5. Quoted in Douglas S. Russell, *The Orders, Decorations and Medals of Sir Winston Churchill*, pages 17–18.
6. *New York World*, 15 December 1895.
7. *New York Herald*, 19 December 1895.

chill's reflections. "Of course the war isn't like a European war," he said, "but there was a great deal that interested us. The most remarkable fact seems to be that two armies will shoot at each other for hours and no one will get hit. I believe that statisticians say that in a battle it takes 2,000 bullets to kill a man. When the calculations are arranged I think it will be found that in the Cuban war it took 2,000 bullets to miss each individual combatant."[8]

Another version of this comment was published in the *New York Herald*, which reported Churchill saying: "It has always been said, you know, that it takes 200 bullets to kill a soldier, but as applied to the Cuban war 200,000 shots would be closer to the mark."[9] As for the insurgent troops—well versed in the art of retreat—the secret of their strength "is the ability to harass the enemy and carry on a guerrilla warfare."

Churchill saw a role for the United States in Cuba. Because the war being fought between the Spaniards and the Cuban insurgents was "absolutely ruinous" to Cuba, "I think that the upshot of it will be that the United States will intervene as a peacemaker."

When asked by the journalists about the alleged political significance of his journey, he was not amused, exclaiming in one word, "Rot!" with, the *New York World* reported, "a look that showed how tired the question made him feel." He was then told "about the fulminations of the *Bungtown Bird of Freedom* and of the *Kalamazoo Daily Celery Stalk*, and he laughed impatiently, but he evidently thought the attitude of these great journals too silly to talk about."

The *Etruria* was ready to sail. The *New York World* told its readers that Churchill had in his pocket "a rough insurgent bullet that struck and killed a Spanish soldier . . . standing quite close to him."[10]

As Churchill returned to Britain on his first eastward crossing of the Atlantic, a potential Anglo-American conflict arose when the United States accused Britain of violating the Monroe Doctrine with regard to Venezuela. The issue centered on the boundary between British Guiana (now Guyana) and the Venezuelan Republic. In a unilateral

---

8. *New York World,* 15 December 1895.
9. *New York Herald,* 19 December 1895.
10. *New York World,* 15 December 1895.

move by the United States, President Grover Cleveland sent a message to Congress announcing that his government would fix the boundary line independently and would oblige both Britain and Venezuela to accept the American decision.

"For a few days," Churchill later wrote, "war with Britain seemed possible, and even imminent." He expected to be sent back across the Atlantic, to Canada, as part of a British force confronting the United States. Approaching home, he remembered "looking at ships off the English coast and wondering which one would be our transport to Canada." [11]

This was the last time that war between Britain and the United States was even a remote possibility. It would have been ironic had Churchill, on reaching port, been ordered to transfer to a troopship returning westward, to join his regiment at war stations on the Canadian-American border. To Bourke Cockran, Churchill wrote, "do please be pacific and don't go dragging the 4th Hussars over to Canada in an insane and criminal struggle."

Although Cockran had just been in London, their paths did not cross. "You must think me a very faithless and unreliable person," Churchill wrote him at the end of February, "for I never—as I promised, came to see you before your departure from these shores." Churchill went on to raise the question of American policy toward the continuing Cuban rebellion against Spain, telling Cockran: "I hope the United States will not force Spain to give up Cuba—unless you are prepared to accept responsibility for the results of such action. If the States care to take Cuba—though this would be very hard on Spain—it would be the best and most expedient course for both the island and the world in general." But he considered it "a monstrous thing if you are going to merely procure the establishment of another South American Republic—which however degraded and irresponsible is to be backed in its action by the American people—without their maintaining any sort of control over its behaviour."

A voracious reader, Churchill recommended to Cockran "rather a good book." It was the recently published novel *The Red Badge of Courage,* by Stephen Crane, a book that was to become a classic story of

---

11. Winston S. Churchill, *A History of the English-Speaking Peoples,* Volume 4, page 259, note 1.

the American Civil War. "Believe me," Churchill wrote, "it is worth reading." [12]

The correspondence between Churchill and Cockran continued. Cockran sent Churchill copies of his speeches, which gave Churchill ideas and inspiration. Twenty years Churchill's senior, Cockran provided the younger man with advice and encouragement in equal measure, as well as sharpening his powers of sustained argument. In a letter to Cockran on 12 April 1896, the twenty-one-year-old Churchill wrote of his considered conclusion "that the duty of governments is to be first of all practical. I am for makeshifts and expediency. I would like to make the people who live on this world at the same time as I do better fed and happier generally. If incidentally I benefit posterity—so much the better—but I would not sacrifice my own generation to a principle—however high or a truth however great."

Cockran had sent Churchill a speech he had just made, harshly critical of British rule in Ireland and advocating Home Rule. Churchill called the speech "one of the finest I have ever read," and he added: "You are indeed an orator. And of all the gifts there is none so rare or so precious as that." But while he was clear that no one had ever attempted "to deny that England has treated Ireland disgracefully in the past"—in the Cromwellian era "death was the punishment of every crime; and the treatment of the Irish by the stronger power was in harmony with the treatment of the French peasantry, the Russian serfs and the Huguenots. Mercy and economics were alike unknown"; it was unfair "to depict the English government of today as part and parcel of Mountjoy's ravages and Cromwell's massacres."

As for Cockran's advocacy of Home Rule, Churchill was pugnacious in defense of the integrity and goodwill of the United Kingdom: "There is no tyranny in Ireland now," he wrote, and went on to explain: "The Irish peasant is as free and as well represented as the English labourer. Everything that can be done to alleviate distress and heal the wounds of the past is done—and done in spite of rhetorical attempts to keep them open. Your contention that government from a 'foreign' city cannot produce prosperity—is not borne out by other in-

---

12. Letter of 29 February 1896, Cockran Papers.

stances." There was, "for example," Scotland, "whose population and wealth have increased manifold since the Act of Union."

Churchill argued in his letter that six years of "firm, generous government" in Ireland would create a material prosperity that "will counteract the efforts which able and brilliant men—like yourself—make to keep the country up to the proper standard of indignation." Not for twenty years could a Home Rule bill pass the English people, "so sick and tired are they of the subject," and by that time the necessity for such a bill would have passed away. Home Rule, Churchill told his friend and mentor, "may not be dead but only sleeping—but it will awake like Rip Van Winkle to a world of new ideas. The problems and the burning questions of today will be solved and Home Rule for Ireland as likely as not will be merged in a wider measure of Imperial Federation."

Twenty-five years after writing this letter, Churchill was to secure one of his finest parliamentary, diplomatic and legislative achievements, the Irish Free State Act, effectively separating the Catholic South from British rule and setting it on the road to full independence. Cockran lived to see his young friend bring to fruition the very cause he had rejected so strongly when Cockran urged it upon him.

Churchill's final argument in 1896 against Home Rule drew in the United States. Should the United States, he asked, "accede to the demand for Confederate independence?"[13] In his reply Cockran conceded that if Churchill's idea of "Imperial Federation" proved to be the solution of the Irish question "nobody will rejoice at it more than the men who have struggled for the same result under the name of Home Rule." It was not on Ireland, however, that Cockran wished to dwell. He had advice to give his young friend on a wider theme. Whatever might be the "ultimate outcome of the Irish agitation," he wrote, "I hope you will allow me to assume the privilege of my years and advise you strongly to take up the study of sociology and political economy. These two subjects are more closely interwoven than most people ever believe. They are considered dry and uninteresting by those who are not familiar with them, but they are the two branches of inquiry which in the future will bear the most important fruits to the human family."

---

13. Letter of 12 April 1896, Cockran Papers.

This advice was well meant. "Do not my dear Winston feel that I am troubling you with this long letter merely to air my views," Cockran explained. "I was so profoundly impressed with the vigor of your language, and the breadth of your views as I read your criticisms of my speech that I conceived a very high opinion of your future career. . . ." [14]

Churchill was to benefit from Cockran's advice enormously, to create, a decade later, a remarkable career as a social reformer. Among the books that were to influence him were Henry Fawcett's *Manual of Political Economy*, and Benjamin Seebohm Rowntree's *Poverty, A Study of Town Life*, a study of the life of the poor in the city of York.

In August 1896 Cockran's success in New York politics gave Churchill pleasure. "Fifteen thousand people forms a larger concourse than ever collects in England to hear political speeches," he wrote. "You know how keenly I regret that I was not there to see—still more to hear." Cockran was in the process of conducting his most ambitious political campaign, challenging his fellow Democrat, William Jennings Bryan, for the Democratic nomination for the Presidency of the United States. At a stormy Democratic convention, Bryan and his "free silver" movement advocated the predominance of silver coinage over gold. Cockran was opposed to "free silver" and argued in favor of maintaining the Gold Standard, as did the Republicans.

The silver question was one, Churchill told Cockran, "about which I know very little and hence my views are proportionately strong." Those views were also clear and articulate. "It seems to me however," Churchill wrote, "that no sweeping changes in currency are possible— far less expedient. Even if you prove to me that our present system is radically bad—my opinion is unaltered. A man suffering from dyspepsia might pray for fresh intestines but he would fare badly while the alteration was being effected. How much more does this apply to changes which affect the chief—the most delicate and sensitive—organs which produce and on which depends our wealth—Capital, Credit and Commerce."

It might be, Churchill added, "that some reform and readjustment are necessary in the currency of the world, but those who endeavour to deal with so complicated and vital a subject should approach it tenta-

---

14. Letter of 27 April 1896, Cockran Papers.

tively—feeling their way with caution. What Bryan has done is like an inebriate regulating a chronometer with a crowbar. It is monstrous that such subjects should be made the bagatelle of political parties and that issues so vast should be handed over to excited and flushed extremists. At least so it strikes me." Cockran failed to win the Democratic nomination and, determined to see the Gold Standard maintained, declared himself a supporter of the Republican challenger, William McKinley.

When Cockran's letter reached him, with the American election battle in full swing, Churchill was about to leave Britain for India with his regiment. It was their regular tour of duty on the subcontinent. He hoped that he and Cockran would meet again soon, "if possible within a year. I may return to England via Japan after a little of India so perhaps I shall once more eat oysters and hominy with you in New York."[15]

A month after he reached India, Churchill and his fellow officers learned of McKinley's victory in the American Presidential election. Churchill wrote the next day to congratulate Cockran, agreeing with him that McKinley's election "vindicates the common sense of an Anglo-Saxon democracy." Churchill then ventured a criticism of the American electoral system as compared with the British. "I wonder if you would care to calculate," he asked, "how much this year's Presidential election has cost you—in dollars—considering for the purpose not only the actual electoral expenses, but also the disturbance of business and the fluctuations of capital."

Churchill added: "Of course I know you maintain that the contest is of great value as an educating institution, & I am prepared to willingly admit that no price was too much to smash Bryan and display to the world on what firm foundation American credit and honour repose. But I am inclined to think if you consider one election with another—you will agree with me that your system of government costs you more than ours." Churchill added: "You may rejoice, that it is better to be free than wealthy. That is a question about which discussion is possible: but I assert that the English labourer enjoys an equal freedom with the American workman & in addition derives numerous advantages from the possession of those appurtenances of monar-

---

15. Letter of 31 August 1896, Cockran Papers.

chy—which make government dignified and easy—and the inter-course with foreign states more cordial."

Churchill asked Cockran to "look at the questions philosophi-cally—cynically if you like. Calculate the profit and the loss. Consider the respect human beings instinctively and involuntarily feel for that which is invested with pomp and circumstance. As a legislator, discard unbending principles and ethics and avail yourself of the weaknesses of humanity." Churchill's conclusion: "Yours may be the government for gods—ours at least is suitable to men."

Cockran's political struggle had caught Churchill's imagination. "Your tour of political meetings must indeed have been interesting and I regret so much that I had not the opportunity of accompanying you and listening to your speeches." From what he had already seen, as Lord Randolph's son, "I know that there are few more fascinating ex-periences than to watch a great mass of people under the wand of the magician. There is no gift—so rare or so precious as the gift of ora-tory—so difficult to define or impossible to acquire."[16]

Churchill had already sent Cockran one of the books he most ad-mired, whose contents he had learned by heart: the two-volume edi-tion of his father's speeches. Henceforth he was to be able to recite by heart not only Lord Randolph's great orations but Cockran's as well. Not politics, however, but the army was uppermost in Churchill's mind. In the course of the next three years he was to take part, both as a soldier and a war correspondent, in three wars. He was to be men-tioned in dispatches for his "courage and resolution."[17] He was to win four campaign medals, and on several occasions to be near death: on the North-West Frontier of India, in the Sudan, and in South Africa.

Even while he was soldiering, Churchill, a voracious reader, ac-quired and absorbed the books of the day. One of these was Henry De-marest Lloyd's *Wealth Against Commonwealth,* a fierce critique of the "Robber Barons," "Monopoly," and the Standard Oil Company. "Na-ture is rich," wrote Lloyd, "but everywhere man, the heir of nature, is poor. . . . What we call Monopoly is Business at the end of its journey. The concentration of wealth, the wiping out of the middle classes, are

---

16. Letter of 10 June 1897, Cockran Papers.
17. Dispatch dated 27 October 1897, Douglas S. Russell, *The Orders, Decorations and Medals of Sir Winston Churchill,* page 20.

other names for it." [18] Forty years after reading Lloyd's book, Churchill recalled: "It made a profound impression on me. It roused me to anger against the oil magnates and against great trusts. There was set out in scathing argument the methods by which the Standard Oil Company attained a monopoly position. . . . I read how the railroads were cajoled or browbeaten or blackmailed into playing the Standard's game of illegal rebates and drawbacks. . . . [19]

An American author had made his mark on the young subaltern's social philosophy and instinct for fair play. Churchill's own book, *The Malakand Field Force*, about the fighting a year earlier on the North-West Frontier of India, was published in the United States in 1898. The *New York Times* review noted that its author had "an especial" interest for the American reader because he had an American grandfather, and because "his education has been paid for in part from the rental of the house of the University Club in New York, which his mother owns." [20]

---

18. Henry Demarest Lloyd, *Wealth Against Commonwealth*, page 1.
19. Winston Churchill, "Oldest and Richest," *Collier's*, 11 July 1936.
20. *New York Times*, 20 April 1898.

Chapter Four

⌗

"HOW LITTLE TIME REMAINS!"

In July 1899, at the age of twenty-four, Churchill stood for Parliament, but after a vigorous election campaign he was narrowly defeated. When, three months later, war in South Africa seemed imminent, he decided to go out with the British forces as a war correspondent and conceived a remarkably innovative plan—to take a film camera and its operator with him, to make a film of the war. This plan was frustrated just as he was about to leave Britain, when he learned that an American film company was already on its way. But he set off nevertheless, to report on the war for the London *Morning Post*.

On November 15, while traveling as a war correspondent with a British armored train through Boer-held territory, Churchill was captured by the Boers. He was taken to a prisoner-of-war camp in the capital, Pretoria. While in captivity, he was surprised to receive a message from the American Consul in Pretoria, telling him that a telegram had arrived for him from Bourke Cockran. It was to wish him well on his imminent twenty-fifth birthday, November 30. It was a birthday full of anguish that he was not a free man. That day Churchill set down his thoughts in a long letter to Cockran.

"I am alive," Churchill wrote, "and have added another to the several vivid experiences which have crowded my last four years. I am also a prisoner, of which fact—as I am a correspondent and a noncombatant—I complain. But, that I am kept in it, is the only serious objection I have to make to this place."

Churchill said nothing to Cockran about the plan he was making, even then, to escape. He wrote instead: "I fear I shall be held until the end of the war, which I earnestly hope may come about March next. I want to come over to America afterwards and I rather contemplate some lectures." Although Churchill had never lectured before on the public circuit, he felt that he would be able to convey the excitement of his experiences to audiences in both Britain and the United States.

Churchill suspected that Cockran would share the general American criticism of Britain's war against the Boers, but made a spirited defense. "I wonder what view you will take of this war!" he wrote. "I expect that you—like too many Americans, forgetful of the moral assistance we rendered your country no longer ago than the war with Spain, will disapprove of the British policy. But as you probably know, our existence as an Imperial power is staked on the issue and I do not believe that the nation will shrink from any sacrifice however great, however prolonged, to remove the causes of unrest from South Africa."

Churchill also had strong views on the nature of the struggle with the Boers, but, as he explained to his friend, "I must not write more of local politics or perhaps this letter will not reach you. Enough to say that this great country is reaping a bitter harvest which is sprung from the mistakes and follies of former years." There was another conflict that Churchill believed was imminent, not in South Africa but in the United States, the conflict created by capitalism, to which his reading of Henry D. Lloyd's *Wealth Against Capitalism* had alerted him. As Churchill explained to Cockran: "You too have a big quarrel impending; and I take the very greatest interest in the struggle against vast combinations of capital, which I am told will be the feature of the next Presidential election. I think we are on opposite sides in this matter. The economics of former days are on your side. But capitalism in the form of Trusts has reached a pitch of power which the old economists never contemplated and which excites my most lively terror."

The way in which capitalism had developed was not to Churchill's liking. "Merchant-princes are all very well," he told Cockran, "but if I have anything to say to it, their kingdom shall not be of this world. The new century will witness the great war for the existence of the Individual."

In this argument, devised in captivity, Churchill conceded that "up to a certain point combination has brought us nothing but good: but we seem to have reached a period when it threatens nothing but evil. I do not want to see men buy cheaper food and better clothes at the price of their manhood. Poor but independent is worth something as a motto."

Churchill then posed the question that his argument invited: "'Then why' you will ask 'with such views, do you not sympathise with the Boers?'" He conceded that he did perhaps sympathize with the Boer "love of freedom and pride of race: but self preservation seems to involve a bigger principle." What, "for example," he asked Cockran, about the Philippines, which the United States had taken from Spain a year earlier, and he went on to exclaim sarcastically: "Oh champions of the cause of Freedom!"

In his prisoner-of-war camp in a Pretoria school building, Churchill felt the frustration of not being able to speak to his American friend face-to-face. "I suppose you have never been in prison," he wrote. "It is a dull occupation—even under the mildest circumstances, perhaps all the duller because the circumstances are mild. I could nurse a savage anger in a dungeon. This is damnably prosaic. My mind has become as stagnant as my body is penned up: and all the while great matters are being settled and history made—the history—mind you—I was to have recorded."

Churchill then reported that Reginald Barnes, his companion on his New York visit, had been badly wounded in the leg. "He hopes to be well enough to come back to his duty and participate in the final actions of the war—which—rest assured in spite of all difficulties we shall carry through to the bloody bitter end: bloody that is to say as small wars go."

More experience of war, Churchill confided to Cockran, "would make me religious." He had been in three wars, and had been nearly killed in each of them. "The powerlessness of the atom is terribly brought home to me," he confided, "and from the highest human court of appeals we feel a great desire to apply to yet a higher authority. Philosophy cannot convince the bullet." Churchill ended his letter: "I am 25 today—it is terrible to think how little time remains!"[1]

Eleven days after writing this letter Churchill escaped, making his way by train from Pretoria to Lourenço Marques in Portuguese Mozambique, from where he took a ship back to Durban, in South Africa. The war had been going badly for Britain. Churchill's escape made him a hero. On the day after her son's escape, Lady Randolph

---

1. Letter of 30 November 1899, Cockran Papers.

Churchill sailed from Britain to South Africa in a hospital ship, the *Maine,* named after the American warship sunk by the Spanish navy in Havana harbor two years earlier. She had equipped the vessel through the generosity of the "American Ladies in London," of whose committee she was the chairman. "My dearest Mamma," Churchill wrote to her in his first letter since his escape, from an army camp facing the Boer-held town of Colenso. "I am so glad & so proud to think of your enterprise & energy in coming out to manage the Maine. Your name will long be remembered by many poor broken creatures."[2]

Following his dramatic and widely publicized escape, Churchill had returned to the fighting, no longer as a war correspondent but as a lieutenant in the South African Light Horse. From the beginning of January to the third week of March he took part in all the regiment's actions and was often in danger. His brother, Jack, who had joined him in South Africa to fight, was one of the first to be taken aboard their mother's hospital ship after it reached Cape Town. He had been wounded in the foot.

In February 1900 Churchill learned from his London literary agent, A. P. Watt, that "one of the best" American magazines wanted him to write three articles dealing with the war.[3] The total payment was a remarkable £300.[4] He accepted. A month later, shortly after he had been among the first British troops to enter the besieged town of Ladysmith, he received a letter from an American lecture agent, Major James B. Pond of the Lyceum Lecture Bureau. It was an invitation to lecture in the United States about his Boer War experiences. His first reaction to Major Pond's request was to see the financial advantages, and to ask his mother to find out what the rewards would be. An American lecture tour, he wrote to her, "might be made into a really sound business." But he would not go to the United States, he warned his mother, "unless guaranteed at least a thousand pounds a month for three months and I should expect a great deal more. £5,000 is not too

---

2. Letter of 6 January 1900, Randolph S. Churchill, *Winston S. Churchill,* Volume 1, Companion (document) Volume, Part 2, pages 1142–43.
3. Letter of 16 February 1900, Randolph S. Churchill, *Winston S. Churchill,* Volume 1, Companion (document) Volume, Part 2, pages 1156–57.
4. The equivalent of £20,000/$40,000 in the monetary values of 2005.

much for such a labour and for making oneself so cheap. I beg you to take the best advice on these matters. I have so much need of the money and we cannot afford to throw away a single shilling."[5]

There was good publicity for Churchill that summer in the United States, when, on May 19, the ladies' magazine *Harper's Bazaar* published the first reference to him in an American periodical, together with a photograph of him in army uniform. "He loves danger," the magazine reported, "and welcomes adventure eagerly, but he has also found time to combine with his military occupations the duties of an enterprising war correspondent."[6] In July, after being in action several times, including at the Battle of Diamond Hill, where his bravery was noted by his commander, Churchill returned to Britain. Five days after his return he was adopted as a prospective Parliamentary candidate for Oldham, a predominantly working-class constituency. Three days after that, his mother married again, becoming Mrs. George Cornwallis-West. Her new husband, a soldier, author and playwright, was only thirteen days older than her elder son.

That July in New York, *Harper's Monthly Magazine* carried an article by Fred McKenzie about five English war correspondents in South Africa. Churchill was "the youngest," described by McKenzie as: "Somewhat heavy-looking, ambitious, hard-working, with a touch of mysticism that attracts the mob, a born orator, with the power to move people as he wills. . . ." For this reason he "must go far."[7]

While his mind was much on a lucrative American lecture tour, which would also include some speaking engagements in Canada, Churchill wrote to Major Pond, suggesting delaying the tour until early in 1901. One reason for the delay was the forthcoming American Presidential election in November, when "your country will be convulsed with political excitement to such an extent that I am advised by many I have talked to that lecturing would suffer—however, you are a better judge on that point than I." Another reason for waiting until the new year was, Churchill explained, "I have had in England a good many offers

---

5. Letter of 22 March 1900, Randolph S. Churchill, *Winston S. Churchill*, Volume 1, Companion (document) Volume, Part 2, page 1158.
6. *Harper's Bazar*, 19 May 1900.
7. Fred A. McKenzie, "English War-Correspondents in South Africa," *Harper's Monthly Magazine*, July 1900, pages 215–16.

of large sums to lecture at our leading towns and I propose to devote November to that purpose." There was also the financial aspect, for, as Churchill explained, his British offers "aggregate to over £2,000 for this single month's work, and, unless you can show me something very much better than that, I propose to carry out that arrangement."

Major Pond had been concerned that hostile criticism of Churchill's lectures in Britain might affect the American audiences. Churchill sought to put his mind at rest. "I don't think you need be afraid of unfriendly criticisms being telegraphed over. I have had some success in dealing with audiences without the aid of magic lanterns and I have dealt with facts of dry politics."

Churchill added that he would leave the whole arrangement of the lecture tour to Pond, "but at the same time, you must not drag me about too much and I don't want to wear myself out by talking to two penny-half-penny meetings in out of the way places." As for his social arrangements during the tour, "I shall exercise my entire discretion." He had "a certain number of friends in America of whose hospitality I shall avail myself. I don't want to be dragged about to any social functions of any kind nor shall I think of talking about my experiences to anybody except when I am paid for so doing."[8]

On 1 October 1900 Churchill was elected to Parliament, in which he was to serve, with only a two-year break, for more than sixty years. With great enthusiasm, he wrote to Bourke Cockran: "I daresay you will have learned from the newspapers that I have been returned to Parliament as representative of almost the greatest constituency in England, containing 30,000 thriving working men electors; and this victory happening to come at the outset of the general contest, was of great use and value to the Conservative Party, as it gave them a lead and started the movement."

At twenty-five Churchill was proud of his achievement. "I have suddenly become one of the two or three most popular speakers in this election," he told Cockran, "and am now engaged on a fighting tour, of the kind you know—great audiences (five and six thousand people) twice and even three times a day, bands, crowds and enthusiasm of all kinds." At the same time Churchill was looking forward to his next

---

8. Letter of 31 July 1900, Robert Hastings Papers.

American journey: "It will be very pleasant to meet you again and to see something of American quiet and seclusion after the clatter here."[9]

Major Pond was worried that Churchill by himself might not be such a draw. He therefore wrote to Churchill's mother, "Have you any idea how green your memory is here in New York City?" and he added: "I would suggest that you accompany your son on the voyage and witness his reception here. It seems to me it would be a very proud day for you, and your friends here would appreciate it, and I need not add that it would doubly enhance the value of the lecture."[10]

The newly married Mrs. Cornwallis-West was unable to accompany her son. He, meanwhile, was carrying out a strenuous—and stunningly successful—lecture tour throughout Britain, thirty lectures within forty days, the last on his twenty-sixth birthday. To Cockran he wrote: "I am looking forward very much to seeing you again, although I feel no small trepidation at embarking upon the stormy ocean of American thought and discussion."[11]

Churchill's mother was about to edit a literary magazine, the *Anglo-Saxon Review*. Her son devised a stirring advertisement for the first number, complete with crossed British and American flags.[12] Its twin themes were "Blood is thicker than water" and "Union is strength."

9. Letter of 7 October 1900, Randolph S. Churchill, *Winston S. Churchill*, Volume 1, Companion (document) Volume, Part 2, page 1206.

10. Letter of 2 November 1900, Randolph S. Churchill, *Winston S. Churchill*, Volume 1, Companion (document) Volume, Part 2, page 1215.

11. Letter of 25 November 1900, Cockran Papers.

12. Original drawing, Sir Shane Leslie Papers.

Chapter Five

辈

LECTURER IN THE UNITED STATES:
"THE STORMY OCEAN
OF AMERICAN THOUGHT
AND DISCUSSION"

On 1 December 1900, two months after his election to Parliament, Churchill sailed for the United States. It was almost five years since his first visit. His ship, the *Lucania*, reaching New York City on December 8, was met by a crowd of journalists. Focusing on sartorial details, the *Brooklyn Eagle* noted that Churchill wore a dark suit, a square-top Derby hat, and an Astrakhan-trimmed coat. The *New York Evening Journal* reported his response to a question about his marriage plans—with an American heiress: "I am not here to marry anybody. I am not going to get married, and I would like to have that stated positively."

Following the Press Conference, Churchill was driven from the quayside to his hotel, the Waldorf-Astoria, accompanied by his American cousin Kitty Mott. That evening he was the guest of the New York Press Club. "After seeing many nations, after traveling through Europe, and after having been a prisoner of the Boers," he told them, "I have come to see that, after all, the chief characteristic of the English-speaking people as compared with other 'white' people is that they wash, and wash at regular periods. England and America are divided by a great ocean of salt water, but united by an eternal bathtub of soap and water."[1]

---

1. *New York Tribune,* 9 December 1900.

After a quiet Sunday with Bourke Cockran in New York, Churchill traveled to Albany to meet the Vice President–elect, Governor Theodore Roosevelt. The two men had a lively conversation. "I saw the Englishman Winston Churchill here," Roosevelt wrote to a friend several months later, "and although he is not an attractive fellow, I was interested in some of the things he said." From Churchill's book *The Malakand Field Force,* Roosevelt had "very emphatically gained the idea that the Gurkha, Sikh, Punjabi-Moslem and Pathan regiments when led by English officers were better than the purely English regiments. He denied this."[2]

Even before his first lecture, Churchill was displeased with the exaggerations in Pond's advertisements, in which he was described as "the hero of five wars." He had fought only in four. He was called "the author of six books," whereas he had written five. He was called "the future Prime Minister of England," although he had not yet taken his seat in the House of Commons. Despite Churchill's vexation, the tour went ahead, with the first speech in Philadelphia. His theme was the Boer War through the eyes of one who had reported on it, fought in it, been taken prisoner, escaped and returned to the fighting. At this first presentation the pro-Boer sympathies of his audience erupted when he showed a magic-lantern picture of a Boer cavalryman. The audience cheered. "You are quite right to applaud him," Churchill replied. "He is the most formidable fighting man in the world."[3]

Churchill's Philadelphia speech was considered balanced and thoughtful. The reporter for the Massachusetts *Springfield Republican* characterized him thus: "His accent is pronounced, his mannerism ultra-British, and his stage presence rather awkward, owing, principally, to inexperience. But he spoke readily, without notes, and produced a decidedly favorable impression."[4]

From Philadelphia, Churchill returned to New York, where he spoke in the Grand Ballroom of the Waldorf-Astoria at a gathering organized for him by Bourke Cockran. It was a year to the day since he had escaped from the prisoner-of-war camp in Pretoria. He was intro-

---

2. Letter of 12 July 1901, to Hermann Speck von Sternberg, Elting E. Morison, editor, *The Letters of Theodore Roosevelt,* Volume 3, page 116.
3. *Springfield Republican,* 16 December 1900.
4. *Springfield Republican,* 16 December 1900.

duced by Mark Twain, who declared: "Mr. Churchill by his father is an Englishman, by his mother he is an American, no doubt a blend that makes the perfect man." Mark Twain stressed that he had approved neither of Britain's war in South Africa nor of America's conquest of the Philippines two years earlier. "England and America; we are kin," he said. "And now that we are also kin in sin, there is nothing more to be desired. The harmony is perfect—like Mr Churchill himself, whom I now have the honor to present to you."[5]

Churchill gave a spirited account both of his own adventures and of the British cause. An account in the British *Westminster Gazette* commented that the audience "left him nothing to desire in quantity, quality, or in cordiality of reception and attention." The journalist added that, according to one report from New York, "the lecture was so moderate in tone, so generous in its tribute to the beaten enemy, so loyal, so vivid in narrative, so effective in proportion and perspective, as to win the entire sympathy of a very brilliant and very critical audience."

The composition of that New York audience was the object of some controversy, as a result of Pond's advertising techniques. In the placards announcing the lecture it was stated that both the Mayor of New York and the President of Princeton University would be attending as Churchill's patrons. The *Westminster Gazette* noted that "these gentlemen have written to the Press repudiating any connexion with Mr Churchill. He is in turn indignant, and blames his lecture manager, Mr Pond, and, it is reported, threatens to abandon his tour."[6]

Immediately after his New York lecture at the Waldorf-Astoria, Churchill crossed the hall from the Grand Ballroom to a dining room where he was the guest of the Pennsylvania Society. There he gave a variant of his remarks in Philadelphia three days earlier, telling his New York hosts that there were two points that were not often mentioned in Britain or America, on which the two countries were similar. One was that both peoples had "a prejudice against attacking a man except in front." The other was that both peoples "like cold water; we want our daily plunge. I've not known that in any other nation, but though the salt ocean separates us, we are united by soap and fresh water."[7]

---

5. *New York Tribune*, 13 December 1900.
6. *Westminster Gazette*, 14 December 1900.
7. *New York Tribune*, 13 December 1900.

The *New York Times* took offense at Churchill's words. "Without the slightest apparent suspicion as to the good taste of his remarks," it wrote, "the amiable Lieutenant ran on at great length about the superior cleanliness of Englishmen and Americans as compared with all the rest of the world, and pictured them as advancing hand in hand from land to land, introducing the bath tub wherever they go and so elevating reluctant nations to unwonted heights of civilization. . . ." Such remarks, although "very funny," were, in the view of the *New York Times,* also "rather outrageous and just a little disgusting." There were, the newspaper pointed out, "probably twenty real bath tubs in America for every one on equal areas in England, and yet this fact is utterly ignored as a topic of polite conversation in this country. Why can't the Britishers be similarly reserved with respect to the intimate secrets of the toilet?"[8]

From New York, Churchill went by train to New Haven, Connecticut, where a group of Yale University students took him on an open-carriage tour of the campus, after which he gave his lecture in the Hyperion Theater. He was introduced by the Dean of the Yale Law School, who declared: "Mr. Churchill, descended as he is from the best blood of England and America, is at least one beneficial result of Anglo-American matrimony. I take pleasure in introducing our English cousin. . . ."

After giving the New Haven audience an account of his escape from the Boers, Churchill remarked, as any author will if he can: "This experience I have already embodied into a book which I have written, and while I ought not to advertise this book here, I hope everyone here will make it their business to procure it."[9] The book was *Ian Hamilton's March,* which had been published in the United States that October.

From New Haven, Churchill took the night train to Washington, his first visit to the American capital, where he stayed with a Republican Senator, Chauncey Depew, from New York. Depew was a congenial host: "He was very civil," Churchill wrote to his mother, "showed me the Capitol, introduced me to a great many Senators of note and also

---

8. *New York Times,* 16 December 1900.
9. *New Haven Morning Journal,* 14 December 1900.

presented me to the President, with whom I was considerably impressed." The President was William McKinley.

The Washington visit had its share of setbacks. "A certain amount of nervousness in starting my tour," Churchill confided to his mother, "and the hard work attendant on it, together with a chill I think I must have got travelling in these stuffy trains, alternately too drafty to sit in and too hot to live in, brought on an attack of fever and my temperature ran up to 102, in which condition I had to give my lecture in Washington," but "I found a good doctor who gave me some medicine which had the effect of driving my temperature down and since then I have had no recurrence of fever, although I have a good deal of cold hanging about me."[10] Churchill's illness had affected his delivery. "He appeared embarrassed when he began," the *Washington Post* noted, "and throughout his lecture his words came in a jerky and hesitating way."[11]

From Washington, Churchill went to Baltimore, where the size of the audience disappointed him: "only a few hundred assembled in a hall which would have held 5,000," he recalled thirty years later.[12] But his efforts were appreciated, the *Baltimore Sun* reporting that he "made a pleasant impression."[13]

Still not entirely well, Churchill returned to Washington, where once again he was the guest of Senator Depew. On December 16 he took the night train to Boston. From the station he went directly to the main post office to collect a package of letters that he had asked to be redirected to him from Baltimore. The letters had, however, been sent by the post office to the house of another Winston Churchill, a well-known and successful American novelist.

Having instructed Major Pond to retrieve his letters from his American namesake, Churchill was driven to the Hotel Tourraine. The package of letters sent on from Baltimore had not yet been delivered to his namesake's house, but Pond was able to bring back with him to the hotel the American Winston Churchill himself, whom he introduced with the words "Mr. Churchill—Mr. Churchill."[14] After lunching

----

10. Letter of 21 December 1900, quoted in Randolph S. Churchill, *Winston S. Churchill,* Volume 1, Companion (document) Volume, Part 2, pages 1222–23.
11. *Washington Post,* 15 December 1900.
12. Winston S. Churchill, *My Early Life,* page 362.
13. *Baltimore Sun,* 17 December 1900.
14. *Boston Herald,* 18 December 1900.

together at the hotel, the two Winston Churchills walked across Boston Common to the Charles River. An artist's sketch in the *Boston Herald* showed them strolling arm in arm. When they reached the river the British Winston Churchill was said to have told his American counterpart, who was just three years older than he, "Why don't you go into politics? I mean to be Prime Minister of England: it would be a great lark if you were President of the United States at the same time."[15]

The American Winston Churchill entered the New Hampshire legislature two years later, and in 1906 was a candidate for Governor of New Hampshire. By that time Churchill was Under-Secretary of State for the Colonies, his first step on the government ladder that was to take him to the top. That year the London *Sketch* had a headline WATCH THE WINSTONS. One had just "set the Empire ringing" with a speech setting out a new constitution for the Transvaal that returned political power to the defeated Boers. The other, "whose goal is the Presidency," was a political contender in New Hampshire.[16] Alas for the prospect of the two leaders of the Western world both being named Winston Churchill, the American failed in his New Hampshire bid and returned to his career as a writer.

On the evening of December 17, Churchill spoke at the Tremont Temple in Boston. On the platform were three hundred American members of the Anglo-American Society, resplendent in red uniforms. One Boston newspaper remarked that those three hundred constituted "one of the largest audiences ever seen within that edifice."[17] The impact of his remarks, and of his presence, was considerable. "He is very youthful in appearance, and, in complete harmony with this, has a quiet, modest manner which is most engaging," wrote the *Boston Herald* reporter. "In a quarter of an hour you find the address throbbing with the mingled humor and pathos of all battle experiences worthy of name; in half an hour he gives you the impression, boy as he seems, of a keen and resourceful intelligence, not only familiar with

---

15. Quoted in Robert H. Pilpel, *Churchill in America, 1895–1961: An Affectionate Portrait,* page 48.
16. Quoted in Robert H. Pilpel, *Churchill in America, 1895–1961: An Affectionate Portrait,* pages 61–62.
17. *Boston Herald,* 18 December 1900.

the ways of the world, but also able to hold his own in it, and then you want to hear him to the end."[18]

When the lecture was over, Churchill turned toward the Stars and Stripes that was on the stage and told his audience: "There is no one in this room who has a greater respect for that flag than the humble individual to whom you, of the city which gave birth to the idea of a "tea party," have so kindly listened. I am proud that I am the natural product of an Anglo-American alliance; not political, but stronger and more sacred, an alliance of heart to heart."[19]

Churchill had four more lectures to give before Christmas, the first in New Bedford, Massachusetts; the second in Hartford, Connecticut; the third in Springfield, Massachusetts; and the fourth in Fall River, Massachusetts. "His mannerisms are many," the local Springfield paper reported, "and he is thoroughly English, but his personality is pleasant and genial, and the sense of oddity inspired by his address is soon lost in the interest in his subject, which he treats in a fine literary as well as graphic style, and in the quaint humor with which his speech abounds."[20]

From Springfield, Churchill traveled to Fall River for his final American lecture before the holidays. Returning briefly to Boston, on December 21 he sent his mother his reflections on the tour thus far. "I encountered a great deal of difficulty in starting my tour properly," he confided. "First of all the interest is not what Major Pond made out and secondly there is a strong pro-Boer feeling, which has been fomented against me by the leaders of the Dutch, particularly in New York. However, all is now in train, but the profits are small compared to England and so far the result to me as follows." Churchill then totaled the receipts thus far, £581; he was disappointed.[21]

Reflecting on his first eleven lectures, Churchill told his mother: "I get on very well with the audiences over here, although on several occasions I have had almost one-half of them strongly pro-Boer, and of course I do not have the great crowds that always came in England."[22]

---

18. *Boston Herald,* 18 December 1900.
19. *Boston Globe,* 18 December 1900.
20. *Springfield Republican,* 21 December 1900.
21. In the monetary values of 2005, this was almost £40,000/$80,000.
22. Letter of 21 December 1900, Randolph S. Churchill, *Winston S. Churchill,* Volume 1, Companion (document) Volume, Part 2, pages 1222–23.

Churchill wrote this letter the day before taking a Christmas break in Canada, staying with the Governor-General, Lord Minto. It was Churchill's first visit to Canada. His lectures there had been contracted out by Major Pond to a sub-agent, William Lathan. Churchill was outraged to discover that as a result of this arrangement he would receive less than 20 percent of the receipts. On December 29 the *New York Times* reported in a headline: "Disagreement Leads to the Correspondent Refusing to Lecture at Brantford, Ontario, Last Night." Churchill was demanding a larger percentage of the receipts. Pond himself had traveled to Toronto, threatening Churchill with "the vengeance of the law" if his client did not fulfill his contract.[23] It looked for a few days as if the remaining lecture tour would be canceled, but Churchill was determined to get a fair return for his efforts, and on 1 January 1901 he was able to write to his mother: "Peace has been patched up on my terms, and I propose to go ahead with the tour." Of Pond he wrote: "He is a vulgar Yankee impresario and poured a lot of mendacious statements into the ears of the reporters and the whole business has been discussed in the columns of all the newspapers."[24]

While Churchill was in Canada, the *Saturday Evening Post* published his thoughts on the British officer class for American readers. In the article he gave his view that intelligence was not a prized quality for advancement in the British army. A person might then ask him, "Will you make generals of professors?" to which he commented: "But when I think of Lee and Jackson, I am not disinclined to reply 'Why not?'"[25] He was already a keen student of the American Civil War.

On 9 January 1901, after two weeks' lecturing in Canada, Churchill was back in the United States. His schedule was grueling, and there were difficult moments. At the University of Michigan at Ann Arbor, his declaration that "when we have won this war—as we surely shall" was loudly interrupted by pro-Boer sympathizers. Late that evening a law student asked Churchill for an interview. The topics ranged far beyond the Boer War. "I believe that as civilized nations become more powerful they will get more ruthless," Churchill told his in-

23. *New York Times*, 29 December 1900.

24. Letter of 1 January 1901, quoted in Randolph S. Churchill, *Winston S. Churchill*, Volume 1, Companion (document) Volume, Part 2, pages 1224–25.

25. Winston Spencer Churchill, MP, "Officers and Gentlemen," *Saturday Evening Post*, 29 December 1900.

terlocutor. He was concerned about what he saw as a growing sloppiness and divergence in language between Britain and the United States. "The tendency of language nowadays is to diverge into dialect," he said. "It is an enormous commercial advantage for the United States and Great Britain to speak the same language." [26]

On January 10 Churchill traveled by train to Chicago, where he found considerable pro-Boer sentiment and hostility, as he had in Ann Arbor, but he later recalled, "when I made a few jokes against myself, and paid a sincere tribute to the courage and humanity of the Boers, they were pleased." [27] Churchill's moment of winning over his audience came, as on at least one earlier occasion, when he was projecting one of his Boer War pictures on a screen. The picture was of a Boer soldier. As it was being shown, a man in the balcony stood up and called out, "Hurrah for the Boers!" Many in the audience joined in, while a few of Churchill's supporters began to hiss. Churchill at once called out: "Don't hiss. There is one of the heroes of history. The man in the gallery is right." [28]

That night at the University Club, on being asked to say a few words, Churchill gave yet another variant of his earlier Anglo-American comparison, telling his audience that "the greatest common trait by which I lay most store is the fact that Englishmen and Americans wash. It remains after all is said and done that the symbol of Anglo-Saxon unity is the bathtub and the toothbrush." [29]

Churchill spoke again in Chicago two days later, on January 12, at the Central Music Hall. There were many Irishmen in the audience, and he was loudly heckled. But somehow he drew from this hostility a means of turning the tables on his critics. Recounting an episode of the struggle, Churchill spoke of a fearful moment on the battlefield when all seemed lost. A British force was about to be wiped out. But help was at hand. "In this desperate situation the Dublin Fusiliers arrived! Trumpeters sounded the charge and the enemy was swept from the field." [30]

---

26. Quoted in *Michigan Quarterly Review* 5, No. 2 (1966), pages 75–78.
27. Winston S. Churchill, *My Early Life*, page 362.
28. *Chicago Tribune*, 11 January 1901.
29. *Chicago Tribune*, 11 January 1901.
30. Quoted in Kay Halle, editor, *Irrepressible Churchill*, page 42.

It was a magnificent moment, which the historian Robert Pilpel has described: "The audience sat stunned for a second, torn between blood loyalties and political convictions. Eventually the blood won, and cheers rang out for the immensely gratified Lieutenant Churchill."[31]

The lecture tour continued with a brief return across the Canadian border to Winnipeg, then back to the United States, where, still under the auspices of Pond's sub-agent, William Lathan, Churchill spoke in Milwaukee, Minneapolis and St. Louis. In Minneapolis there was much heckling. Thirty years later a friend of Lathan wrote to Churchill of how the sub-agent had recounted "the Minneapolis incident, stating that in all his experiences in touring with notables, that he never saw or heard anyone handle an antagonistic crowd, such as the Irishmen in your audience, as you managed that crowd."[32]

On January 31 Churchill was back in New York for his final lecture of the tour, at Carnegie Hall. During less than two months lecturing in the United States—following three months lecturing in Britain—he had earned an enormous amount of money by the standards of the day, more than $6,000 in all.[33] "I was exhausted," he recalled thirty years later. "For more than five months I had spoken for an hour or more every night except Sundays, and often twice a day, and had travelled without ceasing, usually by night, rarely sleeping twice in the same bed. And this had followed a year of marching and fighting with rarely a roof or a bed at all."[34]

Churchill's last day in New York was a Friday, February 1. He spent it with Bourke Cockran. The following day was Queen Victoria's funeral. At midday Cockran took Churchill to the docks, where he boarded the steamship *Etruria*, on which he had traveled to the United States on his first American journey five years earlier. It was to be twenty-eight years before he returned to the United States.

---

31. Robert H. Pilpel, *Churchill in America, 1895–1961*, pages 454–55.

32. Letter from D. E. Perry, Manager and Assessor, Sanitary District No. 1, Marin County, California, 3 October 1929, Churchill Papers, Churchill College, Cambridge (CHAR 1/207).

33. $160,000/£80,000 in the monetary values of 2005.

34. Winston S. Churchill, *My Early Life,* page 363.

Chapter Six

※

"DARK WOULD BE THE DAY"

Churchill reached Britain from the United States on 10 February 1901. Four days later he entered the House of Commons for the first time as a Member of Parliament. On February 18 he made his maiden speech. Henceforth the House of Commons was to be the main arena of his political battles, setbacks and achievements. In his third speech, three months after he had entered Parliament, he referred to Anglo-American relations, which had been so disturbed five years earlier on the British Guiana–Venezuela boundary—telling the House: "Evil would be the counsellors, dark would be the day when we embarked on that most foolish, futile, and fatal of all wars—a war with the United States." If such a "fit of madness" were to occur, he warned, "both nations, having long enjoyed a glorious immunity from the curse of militarism, would be similarly placed, and no decisive events could be looked for until the war had been in progress for a year or two and enormous armies had been raised on both sides."[1]

Amid his new Parliamentary duties, Churchill did not neglect his love of the theater. He was a frequent attendee, usually on first nights, at almost every show in the capital. One actress, the American Ethel Barrymore, five years younger than he, won more than his acting approval. Thirty years later his daughter Diana told one of Churchill's secretaries that her father, in those early days, had a "crush" on the brilliant actress. "Papa besieged her with notes and flowers, and every night he used to go to Claridges for supper where she always went after her performance. But I'm afraid he never got very far. You see Papa was rather shy in those days and Miss Barrymore always had heaps of

---

1. *Hansard,* Parliamentary debates, 13 May 1901.

admirers around her."[2] Many years later Ethel Barrymore confirmed to Churchill's son, Randolph, that his father had proposed to her, and that she had been "much attracted" to him but felt "that she would not be able to cope with the great world of politics."[3]

In 1903, in only his third year as a parliamentarian, Churchill emerged as a leading voice in the ruling Conservative Party for the maintenance of the policy of Free Trade. While the Conservative Party was committed to Free Trade, within its ranks a call for Tariffs and Protections was gaining strength. In Parliament and on public platforms throughout Britain, Churchill and a group of fellow Conservative Members of Parliament, mostly young like himself, were warning of the dangers of Tariff walls and barriers. Among Churchill's arguments was one that directly involved the United States. Even if it came to a European war, he wrote to a leading Conservative in the Midlands, "Do you not think it very much better that the United States should be vitally interested in keeping the English markets open, than that they should be utterly careless of what happens to their principal customer?"[4]

In a letter to a Liberal parliamentary candidate, Churchill stressed that Free Trade would eventually be United States policy: "At this present time in spite of monopolies and all kinds of corruption," he wrote, "millions of Free Traders in Germany & America are struggling forward to that liberty & justice we have so long enjoyed. We must not extinguish our beacon just when its light is most needed."[5]

Toward the end of December 1903, Churchill wrote an account of the Free-Trade-versus-Tariffs battle to Bourke Cockran. He had been pleased to read in the *Democratic Campaign Guide of Massachusetts* Cockran's "excellent Free Trade speech," and wanted more ammunition for his own speeches, telling Cockran: "I wish you would send me some good Free Trade speeches that have been made in America, and some facts about corruption, lobbying, and so forth."

Churchill also told Cockran that he wanted to return to the United

---

2. Phyllis Moir, *I Was Winston Churchill's Private Secretary,* page 68.

3. Randolph S. Churchill, *Winston S. Churchill,* Volume 2, page 252.

4. Letter of 20 May 1903, Randolph S. Churchill, *Winston S. Churchill,* Volume 2, Companion (document) Volume, Part 1, pages 182–83.

5. Letter of 19 December 1903, Randolph S. Churchill, *Winston S. Churchill,* Volume 2, Companion (document) Volume, Part 1, pages 266–67.

States "to see the Presidential Election next autumn," and he added: "It is rather an inspiring reflection to think that so many of us on both sides of the Atlantic are fighting in a common cause—you to attack protection, we to defend Free Trade. I think what the double victory would mean for the wealth and welfare of the world."[6]

On 31 May 1904, having failed to persuade the Conservative Party to adhere to Free Trade, Churchill "crossed the floor" of the House of Commons, joining the Liberal benches. In crossing the floor—in Churchill's case he literally walked across the floor of the House of Commons from the Conservative to the Liberal benches—Churchill made an unusual political move in the most visual manner possible, alienating the mass of Conservatives for many decades. One moment he was facing the Liberal opposition from the government benches, and the next moment he was looking at those who had hitherto regarded him as one of their own from the serried ranks of the critics of government policy. A new career was about to begin, suffused with radical energies that were anathema to most of his former Conservative colleagues.

In the House of Commons, Churchill became the scourge of the Conservative Government, and was so active in debate that he could see no way to leave his post to cross the Atlantic for the Democratic Convention. Cockran was disappointed. He had also been upset to read in the newspapers an account of Churchill collapsing in the House of Commons during the course of a speech. Churchill sought to set his friend's mind at rest by explaining that it was nothing more than strain and overwork, but that merely strengthened Cockran's resolve to invite Churchill to the United States, not only to the Convention but for a real rest in the country.

"While it is clear that the newspaper accounts were greatly exaggerated," Cockran wrote, "it is equally clear that the hard work of the last year must have told on you to some extent, and therefore it seems to me a rest is highly desirable, if not absolutely necessary now, as a precaution against graver trouble hereafter."[7] But Churchill would not set his political work—and passions—aside. In helping to secure the demise of the Conservative Government, he emerged as a leading con-

6. Letter of 21 December 1903, Cockran Papers.
7. Letter of 1 July 1904, Cockran Papers.

tender for high office should the Liberals come to power. His crossing the floor of the House of Commons, from the Conservative to the Liberal benches, at the age of thirty, with the expectation of joining his new colleagues in political office, was the object of intense interest and speculation.

Returning to the United States from a visit to Britain in the summer of 1905, Bourke Cockran wrote to Churchill that he had seen how "everyone has made up his mind that you are eagerly bent on being admitted to the Cabinet." Under "ordinary conditions" this would be an ambition "so natural that it would be praiseworthy. Indeed to acknowledge yourself without it would be to confess yourself unfitted for public life. But your circumstances now are not normal. They are unusual." Cockran had startling advice: "The thing above all others for you to do now," he wrote, "is exactly the opposite of that which your enemies expect and which your lukewarm associates rather anticipate. All these are agreed that you will insist on entering the Cabinet or fight. Why not confound the hostile and surprise the indifferent by declaring now that you won't seek or even accept membership in a Liberal Government if one is formed with the new parliament?"

Cockran believed that such a declaration by Churchill "would be in the nature of a bomb whose explosion would resound throughout the whole Empire but whose fragments would damage none but your critics." Cockran added: "It would stamp as absolutely unselfish you whom all the Tory leaders and organs have combined to brand as self-seeking, self-centered, and self-conscious. It would not have one rag left of the garment which they have been laboriously trying to fit on your shoulders for the last two years and all the world would realize how baseless this conspiracy of slander has been."

Cockran knew what arguments Churchill would give against such an act of political sacrifice: "First you will say that of course it involves renunciation of high office. That may be, but the renunciation would not be final. Indeed at the very worst it would be merely a brief adjournment. The man who has made your position in the House and in the Country can't keep out of office. If he refuse to seek it then office must in the nature of things seek him. Moreover the moment you cease to be a competitor all the men now watching you suspiciously on your own side of the House will at once turn their jealousies in other directions—and you, no longer an object of their distrust, will very likely acquire their friendship." If that were to be the result, as Cockran believed it must be, "then you would be the only man prominent in your party without personal animosities or rancor. Think what such a position would mean. Conceive to what it must inevitably lead. Beyond any doubt it must result in your becoming the unquestioned leader before the lapse of ten years."

It was a rosy picture that Cockran painted, if only Churchill would not rush to join the new Liberal Government. "Your word in the House would thus acquire a weight that no other could possibly possess. You would be the chief support of your Party but not its beneficiary." It would be a course of action "which would keep you free from jealousies and competitions while at the same time placing a whole Party under a steadily growing burden of obligation to you."

In a postscript Cockran hinted at the highest political future for his friend. "Personally I should prefer that you kept out of office altogether for the present," he explained. "A man who could support all Party measures effectively and yet keep free from the differences and jealousies inherent in the most homogeneous Cabinets would establish such a position,—in my judgment, that very soon he must be invited to join the government on his own terms—even though these embraced the Premiership."

Here, then, was the core of Cockran's argument: that Churchill should "renounce the small merely to make sure of the great," to be slow about looking for a minor post "in order to increase the chances of having the greatest placed at your feet. And this great result I would have you reach not by conduct that the most envious or hostile could criticize but by a course that the most scrupulous must praise."[8]

Churchill did not take his friend's advice. In December 1905, six months after Cockran's letter, the Conservative Government fell. Churchill having been a leading figure in the election battle, within a few days he was offered and accepted his first government office, as Under-Secretary of State for the Colonies in the new Liberal administration. It was a junior position, but with his political chief, Lord Elgin, in the House of Lords, it meant that, from the first days of the new government, Churchill was at the center of all House of Commons de-

---

8. Letter of 12 June 1905, Cockran Papers.

bates and controversies regarding a vast range of British territories across the globe.

Churchill also continued his literary work. Within a month of entering the Liberal Government he published a two-volume biography of his father, *Lord Randolph Churchill*. The new book, Churchill's sixth major work, was also published, as all its predecessors had been, in the United States. "I have been over Winston Churchill's life of his father," President Theodore "Teddy" Roosevelt wrote to Henry Cabot Lodge. "I dislike the father and dislike the son, so I may be prejudiced." Although "both the biographer and his subject possess some real farsightedness," yet, Roosevelt wrote, "they both possess or posset such levity, lack of sobriety, lack of permanent principle, and an inordinate thirst for that cheap form of admiration which is given to notoriety, as to make them poor public servants." [9]

Teddy Roosevelt also wrote to his son, Theodore Roosevelt Jr., who had liked Churchill's book. "Yes," he replied, "that is an interesting book of Winston Churchill's about his father, but I can't help feeling about both of them that the older one *was* a rather cheap character, and the younger one *is* a rather cheap character." [10] Two years later that "cheap character" was to go on a journey much after Theodore Roosevelt's heart, following the course of the River Nile from Lake Victoria to Cairo. On his return to Britain he published the stories of his adventures, first in serial form, both in Britain and the United States, and then as a book, *My African Journey*. The front cover of the book was a color engraving of Churchill standing, gun in hand, over a dead rhinoceros he had shot. The President was planning just such a journey as soon as his presidency came to an end. "I should consider my whole African trip a success," Roosevelt wrote to the American Ambassador in London, Whitelaw Reid, if he could "find the game as Churchill describes it." [11]

Learning of the President's impending journey, Churchill sent him a copy of the book. "I do not like Winston Churchill," Roosevelt wrote to the Ambassador, "but I suppose I ought to write to him." [12]

9. Letter of 12 September 1906, Elting E. Morison, editor, *The Letters of Theodore Roosevelt*, Volume 5, page 408.
10. Letter of 23 May 1908, Theodore Roosevelt Papers.
11. Letter of 28 November 1908, Theodore Roosevelt Papers.
12. Letter of 6 January 1909, Theodore Roosevelt Papers.

Roosevelt's letter was enclosed. It was Churchill's first letter from an American President:

> My dear Mr Churchill:
>
> Thru Mr Reid I have just received the beautiful copy of your book, and I wish to thank you for it. I had read all the chapters as they came out, and with a great deal of interest; not only the chapters upon the very difficult and important problems of the Government itself, but also the hunting chapters and especially the one describing how you got that rare and valuable trophy, a white rhinoceros head. Everyone has been most kind to me about my proposed trip to Africa. I trust I shall have as good luck as you had.
>
> > Again thanking you, believe me,
> > Sincerely yours,
> > Theodore Roosevelt [13]

No reply has been found to this letter, but later that year Churchill was told by the British Ambassador in Washington that Roosevelt had complained to him privately about the attempts of the Governor of Jamaica "deliberately and quite needlessly" to impede the efforts of the American authorities to procure labourers for the Panama Canal works.[14] Churchill did what he could to help the Americans; and not long afterward he again intervened, in order to force the Governor to apologize to an American admiral for his criticism of the admiral's help after an earthquake.[15]

In an essay Churchill wrote in 1930 on one of the "what ifs" of history—if the Confederate Army had won the Battle of Gettysburg—he fixed one of the subsequent historical events on Christmas Day 1905. On that day, he wrote, "was signed the Covenant of the English-speaking Association." The essence of this "extraordinary measure" was "common citizenship" for the peoples of the British Empire and

---

13. Letter of 6 January 1909, Elting E. Morison, editor, *The Letters of Theodore Roosevelt*, Volume 6, page 1467.
14. Letter of 13 December 1909, Randolph S. Churchill, *Winston S. Churchill*, Volume 2, Companion (document) Volume, Part 1, page 635.
15. Colonial Office Papers, Jamaica, 884/9, folios 14–16.

the United States. "Hundreds of millions of people suddenly adopted a new point of view. Without prejudice to their existing loyalties and sentiments, they gave birth in themselves to a new higher loyalty and a wider sentiment." And in 1914, according to Churchill's scenario, that English-speaking Association was able to prevent the coming of world war by putting forward a plan for a United States of Europe.[16]

Shortly after the 1905 election, at which he was elected as a Liberal, Churchill met a fellow Member of Parliament who sat on the Liberal benches, Sir Archibald Sinclair. Like Churchill, Sinclair had an American mother: Mabel Sands of New York (she had died within a month of her son's birth). The two men struck up an immediate friendship. Their first meeting took place in London at the home of the American actress Maxine Elliot, a friend of Churchill's mother. A decade later Sinclair wrote, "I remember sounding you out upon the possibility of drawing closer to the States on that first walk we took together at Maxine's. How delighted I was when you treated the idea seriously & not as an impracticable dream."[17]

Churchill was becoming noticed in the United States. In 1906 a book appeared in New York with a chapter on him. That he was "half an American," wrote Richard Harding Davis in *Real Soldiers of Fortune*, "gives all of us an excuse to pretend we share in his successes."[18] Davis, a well-known American writer, had been a war correspondent in South Africa. That same year Churchill was so struck by the power of Upton Sinclair's novel *The Jungle*, about the Chicago stockyards, that he wrote a sustained account of it in the first two issues of a British weekly newspaper, *PTO*, edited by the Irish radical T. P. O'Connor, praising Sinclair's "great skill and ingenuity" in his portrayal of the harshest of conditions in the meat-packing industry: "a human tragedy . . . a hundred pages of lively and elaborate art."[19]

• • •

---

16. Winston Churchill "If Lee Had Not Won the Battle of Gettysburg," *Scribner's Magazine*, December 1930, pages 587–97.

17. Letter of July 1918, Martin Gilbert, *Winston S. Churchill*, Volume 4, Companion (document) Volume 4, Part 1, pages 338–39.

18. Richard Harding Davis, *Real Soldiers of Fortune*, page 117.

19. Winston Spencer Churchill, "The Chicago Scandals: The Novel Which Is Making History," *PTO*, 16 and 23 June 1906.

On 12 September 1908, Churchill married Clementine Hozier. The *New York Times* devoted two columns to the event, describing Churchill as "one of the most-discussed men in the United Kingdom." In listing some of the wedding gifts, it noted: "Winston Churchill is an author, and the inkpot is therefore an appropriate present for him. But what author can make use of twenty-two inkpots. . . ."[20] A week later the paper published a "special cable" from London, reporting criticisms of the coat Churchill had worn at his wedding as a "shocking bad garment . . . too long and too heavy as a morning coat and too short and skimpy as a frock coat. It gave the wearer a sort of glorified coachman appearance." Of course, the paper added, "Churchill has never aspired to be considered a mirror of modes. In fact, he has always cultivated individuality, rather then slavishly followed fashion. . . ."[21]

Three decades before he became Prime Minister, Churchill's life had become a feature in American newspapers. Within three weeks of his wedding it was reported that "even in the midst of the final preparations" he had been working on his book *My African Journey,* and that during his honeymoon he was "writing the last chapters and selecting the illustrations."[22]

In his first full Cabinet post, as President of the Board of Trade, where he pioneered important social legislation, Churchill wrote a public letter advocating close Anglo-American naval cooperation. Although the letter was much criticized, Churchill saw clearly the interdependence of Britain and the United States in trade and commerce. In a Board of Trade memorandum at the end of 1909 he wrote that the improvement of conditions in the United States was "a favourable indication of the outlook for the near future" for all industrial nations.[23] For Churchill this was not mere theory. Six months earlier his brother, Jack, a stockbroker, had advised him not to sell his shares in American railways, even when railway shares had fallen. Both brothers had faith in the recovery of the American economy, and in this instance their faith was rewarded.

---

20. "Winston Churchill Weds Miss Hozier," *New York Times,* 13 September 1908.
21. "Churchill's Wedding Coat," *New York Times,* 20 September 1908.
22. "Literary London and Its Gossip," *New York Times,* 2 October 1908.
23. Memorandum of 15 November 1909, Randolph S. Churchill, *Winston S. Churchill,* Volume 2, Companion (document) Volume, Part 2, pages 921–23.

As a member of the Committee of Imperial Defence, Churchill was present in 1909 during a discussion of aerial navigation. One of the pioneers of aircraft design, C. S. Rolls, had asked to use government land to experiment with a Wright biplane. The secret record of the meeting reported Churchill's intervention: "Mr Churchill thought that there was a danger of these proposals being considered too amateurish. The problems of the use of aeroplanes was a most important one, and we should place ourselves in communication with Mr Wright and avail ourselves of his knowledge."[24] Churchill's sense was strong even then that the new science of flying would have a military use. It was through an American, Orville Wright, that he saw the way forward.

In March 1911, at the age of thirty-six, Churchill emerged as an advocate of efforts to resolve, without conflict, all future foreign policy confrontations between Britain and the United States. The method being explored, he explained to King George V, was a "Treaty of Unlimited Arbitration," to cover all such disputes between the two countries. Such a treaty, Churchill believed, "glittered with splendid hopes."[25]

In October 1911 Churchill became First Lord of the Admiralty, the Cabinet Minister responsible for the Royal Navy. Less than three years later, in the summer of 1914, Britain found itself in a secret rivalry with the United States. While studying a Foreign Office telegram, Churchill discovered that Greece was about to purchase two American battleships. He at once urged his senior naval advisers to do everything possible to secure the contract for Britain. "It is incredible," he wrote, "that our Naval Mission can have let the Greeks go to the United States without, at any rate, giving us the option."[26]

Two months after sending out this inquiry, Churchill was no longer the man responsible for preparing the Royal Navy for war. From August 1914 he was the one who had to use it to defend Britain's sea lifelines, and to use it to make war.

---

24. Report of Committee of Imperial Defence, Sub-Committee on Aerial Navigation, 25 February 1909, Asquith Papers.
25. Letter of 14 March 1911, Royal Archives.
26. Admiralty minute of 4 June 1914, Randolph S. Churchill, *Winston S. Churchill*, Volume 2, Companion (document) Volume, Part 3, page 982.

Chapter Seven

⚏

CHURCHILL AT WAR, AND A NEUTRAL AMERICA

On 4 August 1914, as the German army advanced through Belgium in its attack on France, Britain declared war on Germany. Churchill, as First Lord of the Admiralty, had mobilized the Royal Navy in the week leading up to war so that Germany could not make a surprise attack. With the coming of war he ensured the safe transit of the British Expeditionary Force (BEF) to France. Even those who had hitherto been Churchill's opponents and critics were impressed by his naval vigilance. "I have never liked Winston Churchill," former President Teddy Roosevelt wrote to a British friend eighteen days after the outbreak of war, "but in view of what you tell me about his admirable conduct and nerve in mobilizing the Fleet, I do wish if it comes your way you would extend to him my congratulations on his action."[1]

The United States was neutral and remained so for more than two and a half years. Two months after the outbreak of war, however, Churchill arranged to meet Charles Schwab, the Chairman of Bethlehem Steel. Coming to England on the ocean liner *Olympic*, Schwab witnessed the sinking of the British warship *Audacious* on October 27 off the north coast of Ireland. On reaching London, Schwab pledged the support of his factories to the Allied cause, agreeing to manufacture Royal Navy submarines in the United States. In order to avoid a breach of United States neutrality legislation, the submarines were transferred

---

1. Letter of 22 August 1914, to Arthur Lee (later Lord Lee of Fareham), quoted in Albert Bushnell Hart and Herbert Ronald Ferleger, editors, *Theodore Roosevelt Cyclopaedia*, page 78.

by train, in sections, to Canada and then assembled in Montreal, hence their name: "Montreal boats."

Twenty-five years later, Churchill recalled his work with Schwab. "We got on very well," he wrote to a friend, "and settled everything on the dead level quite easily in an hour or two. He risked his life to carry out his contract."[2] Schwab built the submarines in seven months instead of the usual two years. He also agreed with Churchill's proposal to transfer to Britain the four fourteen-inch gun turrets being built by Bethlehem Steel for a Greek battleship then under construction in Germany. These turrets subsequently formed part of the principal armament of the British Monitor Fleet. Each monitor was essentially a flat-bottomed barge, equipped with battleship-sized guns, but with no masts or superstructure.

As First Lord of the Admiralty, one of Churchill's tasks was the air defense of Britain. On October 31, having read a favorable report of the trial flight of the first flying boat in the United States, he instructed his officials: "Order a dozen as soon as possible." Eight days later the Admiralty ordered four of the new flying boats from the Curtiss Company of New York and Buffalo, and a further eight from the Aircraft Manufacturing Company of New York.[3]

In November, the General European Manager of the United Press Association of America protested to Gilbert Parker, the British Member of Parliament in charge of "American Publicity," at the "stupidity" of the Admiralty in trying to keep the sinking of the *Audacious* secret. Parker sent the protest to Churchill, adding his own warning that "the American public will put the worst construction on our silence, and no after-explanation will enable us to regain their confidence in our willingness to take our gruel." Churchill adopted a robust tone, telling Parker: "You alarm yourself unnecessarily about American opinion; & the value attached to reports in American newspapers."[4]

Churchill understood the importance of the United States not

2. Letter of 28 July 1929, Martin Gilbert, *Winston S. Churchill,* Volume 5, Companion (document) Volume, Part 2, page 29.

3. Admiralty Minute, Churchill Papers, 2/93, Martin Gilbert, *Winston S. Churchill,* Volume 3, page 66.

4. Letters of 10 and 11 November 1914, Martin Gilbert, *Winston S. Churchill,* Volume 3, Companion (document) Volume, Part 1, pages 262–63.

only as a provider of war materials, but as an ally and a belligerent. To Walter Runciman, his Cabinet colleague in charge of war shipping, he wrote in early 1915: "It is of the utmost importance to attract neutral shipping to our shores, in the hope especially of embroiling the US with Germany. The German formal announcement of indiscriminate submarining has been made to the United States to produce a deterrent effect on traffic. For our part, we want the traffic—the more the better; and if some of it gets into trouble, better still."

To encourage American shipping to cross the Atlantic, Churchill asked Runciman: "Therefore do please furbish up at once your insurance offer to neutrals trading with us after February 18th. The more that come, the greater our safety and the German embarrassment. Please act promptly so that the announcement may synchronize with our impending policy."[5]

Churchill's expectations were to be disappointed. The sinking of American merchant ships by German submarines, even the sinking of the British ocean liner *Lusitania,* with the loss of 128 Americans among the 1,198 dead, did not precipitate the entry of the United States into the war in the crucial year 1915. But it did, as Churchill later pointed out, arm "all friends of Britain and France in America with overwhelming arguments against interfering with the British blockade" of Germany. Henceforth the neutral United States "acquiesced," Churchill noted, "in all kinds of embarrassing restrictions upon ships and commerce, and thus that great process of encirclement and economic pressure ate into the life and strength of Germany".[6]

In March 1915, Churchill proposed shortening the war by an attack on Germany's weakest ally, Turkey. The method chosen was a naval assault on the Dardanelles, to break through into the Sea of Marmara and threaten Constantinople. Even the attack on the Dardanelles had an American dimension. From the moment that German control of the waterways between the Mediterranean and the Black Sea—the Bosphorus and the Dardanelles—had been secured in October 1914, Russia was unable to export wheat to those countries that

---

5. Letter of 15 February 1915, Runciman Papers.
6. Winston S. Churchill, "Tragedy of the Torpedoed Lusitania, Blunder Which Sealed the Fate of Germany," *News of the World,* 6 June 1937.

had become dependent on it. This forced Greece and Italy to draw their supplies from the United States, requiring a far longer sea voyage, a greater demand for shipping and the raising of freight charges, which raised the cost of wheat considerably. Even Britain suffered from this rise in the cost of wheat, the Cabinet Secretary later explained to the Dardanelles Commission of Enquiry.[7]

The naval attack failed. It was followed by a British military expedition, organized by Field Marshal Earl Kitchener, the Secretary of State for War, to seize the Gallipoli Peninsula and overrun the Dardanelles from the land. This too failed to achieve its object, although a precarious, bloody foothold was secured on the peninsula for nine months. While the battle was still being fought on the Gallipoli Peninsula, the Conservative opposition leaders, distressed at not having been given any part in war policy, demanded an all-Party government. One of their conditions for joining the coalition was that Churchill, the traitor to their Party a decade earlier and its outspoken opponent since then, should be removed from the Admiralty.

In July 1915 Churchill prepared to set off on an official mission to Gallipoli, approved by the Prime Minister. But the hostility of the senior Conservative politicians, who had already secured his removal from the Admiralty to a minor Cabinet office, forced him to cancel the mission the moment they learned of it. Before he was told that the mission was canceled he had written a letter to his wife, Clementine—whom he had married eight years earlier—to be opened in the case of his death on the peninsula. In the course of this letter he set out his financial worth. This included his two American stock holdings, each of which was substantial: $10,000 United States Steel Corporation 5 Percent Sinking Fund Bonds, and $10,000 Atchison, Topeka and Santa Fe Railway 4 Percent Convertible Bonds.[8]

In November 1915, shortly before his forty-first birthday, Churchill resigned from the government and crossed to France as a Lieutenant Colonel, commanding a Scottish battalion on the Western Front for the first six months of 1916. For his second-in-command he chose Sir Archibald Sinclair, the young Member of Parliament whom

---

7. Evidence given by Sir Maurice Hankey, Lord Hankey Papers.
8. Letter of 17 July 1915, Baroness Spencer-Churchill Papers. In the monetary values of 2005, these shares were worth approximately $363,000/£726,000.

he had befriended before the war, and who was then also serving on the Western Front.

While serving with his battalion, Churchill met Harvey Butters, a twenty-three-year-old American volunteer who was fighting with the British forces. Butters made a strong impression on him. As Churchill wrote to Clementine from the front: "I visited the high ground to our left a few days ago and found a jolly young artillery officer—a pure Yankee—unnaturalised, unsworn but as he explained—'just as faithful.' 'Yes Sir' he said 'I was at Loos. That was the first time I had the opportunity of studying the staff work of the British Army.' To which I replied 'Canada!' and he answered 'A little South of it, San Francisco.'"

The young American hoped to be commissioned in the Royal Artillery. Churchill promised to help him. As to how he had managed to get into the British army at all, he told Churchill: "I just lied to 'em and said I was British born." Churchill told Clementine: "His name is Butters. He is coming to dinner tonight. There were we three Archie, me and Butters—2 half-breeds and a total Yank all in one artillery dug out!"[9]

Butters was killed in action a year later. "Poor Harvey Butters," Churchill wrote to Sinclair when the news reached him.[10] For the *Observer* newspaper, Churchill wrote an obituary of Butters. Born in South Africa in 1892 of British ancestry, he had been educated in both the United States and Canada before taking up residence in San Francisco, where he became an American citizen. Churchill wrote of how he had first met Butters in his artillery observation post near Churchill's own front-line position, "and was charmed by his extraordinary fund of wit and gaiety. His conversation was delightful, full at once of fun and good sense."

"He was a great 'character,'" Churchill wrote, "and had he lived to enjoy his bright worldly prospects he could not have failed to make his mark." Churchill added: "He did not come all the way from San Francisco only out of affection for the ancient home of his forebears or in a spirit of new adventure. He was in sentiment a thorough American. . . . But he had a very clear and firm conception of the issues which are at stake in this struggle."[11]

---

9. Letter of 15 April 1916, Baroness Spencer-Churchill Papers.
10. Letter of 15 September 1916, Lord Thurso Papers.
11. "Mr Churchill's Tribute," *Observer,* 10 September 1916.

Churchill later discussed those "issues" in his book *The World Crisis*. Woodrow Wilson, he noted, "distrusted and repressed those sentiments of indignation which the scenes in Belgium or the sinking of the *Lusitania* aroused in his breast. He did not truly divine the instinct of the American people. He underestimated the volume and undervalued the quality of the American feeling in favour of the Allies."

It was the "desperate action" of Germany's war leaders, Churchill later reflected, that left Wilson "no loophole of escape." On 31 January 1917 the German government informed the United States of its intention to begin unrestricted submarine warfare. On February 3 the German Ambassador in Washington was told to leave the United States. At the same time the senior American diplomat in Berlin was recalled to Washington, and the President announced to Congress the severance of diplomatic relations with Germany.

Yet Wilson still "declined to believe"—as Churchill expressed it—that any "overt act" of aggression would follow the German declaration of unrestricted submarine warfare. On February 26 an American merchant ship was sunk and eight Americans drowned. On March 1 the American Government published a document received from the British Intelligence Service. It was a top-secret message from the German Foreign Secretary, Arthur Zimmermann, to the German Ambassador in the United States, Count von Bernstorff, who had not yet left Washington, instructing Bernstorff to negotiate a German alliance with Mexico in the event of war between Germany and the United States. According to this "Zimmermann telegram," in return for Mexico making war on the United States, Germany would give Mexico—when victory came—the whole of Texas, Arizona and New Mexico.

During March, four more American merchant ships were sunk, with the loss of twelve American lives. On April 1, when the *Aztec* was sunk, twenty-eight Americans drowned. On the following day Wilson asked the United States Congress for a declaration that a state of war existed between the United States and Germany. Churchill reflected in his war history: "Step by step the President had been pursued and brought to bay. By slow merciless degrees, against his dearest hopes, against his gravest doubts, against his deepest inclinations, in stultification of all he had said and done and left undone in thirty months of carnage, he was forced to give the signal he dreaded and abhorred."

Then came the declaration of war. "Amid the clink and clatter of a cavalry escort the President has reached the Senate. He is reading his message to Congress and to mankind. Out roll the famous periods in which the righteousness of the Allied cause was finally proclaimed."[12] Wilson's words to Congress were indeed memorable: "The world must be made safe for Democracy. . . . we shall fight for the things we have always carried nearest our hearts—for Democracy, for the rights of those who submit to authority to have a voice in their own governments, for the rights and liberties of small nations, for a universal dominion of right by such a concert of free people as shall bring peace and safety to all nations and make the world itself at last free."[13]

On April 6 the House of Representatives resolved that a state of war was formally declared. "From the Atlantic to the Pacific," Churchill later reflected, "the call was answered and obeyed. Iron laws of compulsory service, reinforced by social pressures of mutual discipline in which the great majority of the population took part, asserted an instantaneous unity of opinion." Churchill added: "No one stood against the torrent. Pacifism, indifference, dissent, were swept from the path and fiercely pursued to extermination; and with a roar of slowly gathered, pent-up wrath which overpowered in its din every discordant yell, the American nation sprang to arms."[14] Churchill also wrote of his sense of relief: "Suddenly a nation of one hundred and twenty millions unfurls her standard on what is already the stronger side; suddenly the most numerous democracy in the world, long posing as a judge, is hurled, nay, hurls itself into the conflict."[15]

Churchill looked back on that moment with an exhilaration that was to be reached only once more in his lifelong link with the United States: on the day of the Japanese attack on Pearl Harbor in 1941. He was convinced, however, that what Wilson did in April 1917 could have been done in May 1915. "And if done then what abridgment of the slaughter; what sparing of the agony; what ruin, what catastrophes would have been prevented; in how many million homes would an empty chair be occupied to-day; how different would be the shattered world in which victors and vanquished alike are condemned to live!"

----

12. Winston S. Churchill, *The World Crisis*, Volume 3, *1916–1918*, Part 1, pages 231–33.

13. Woodrow Wilson speech, *New York Times*, 3 April 1917.

14. Winston S. Churchill, *The World Crisis*, Volume 3, *1916–1918*, pages 233–34.

15. Winston S. Churchill, *The World Crisis*, Volume 3, *1916–1918*, pages 225–27.

Always understanding the American point of view, even when he was its opponent, Churchill wrote, ten years after the American entry into the war: "It was natural that the Allies, burning with indignation against Germany, breathless and bleeding in the struggle, face to face with mortal dangers, should stand amazed at the cool, critical, detached attitude of the great Power across the Atlantic." In England particularly, "where laws and language seemed to make a bridge of mutual comprehension between the two nations, the American abstention was hard to understand." But this was to do "less than justice," Churchill believed, to important factors: "The United States did not feel in any immediate danger. Time and distance interposed their minimizing perspectives. The mass of the people engaged in peaceful industry, grappling with the undeveloped resources of the continent which was their inheritance, absorbed in domestic life and politics, taught by long constitutional tradition to shun foreign entanglements, had an entirely different field of mental interest from that of Europe."

Churchill went on to ask: "Was it not a frightful responsibility to launch a vast, unarmed, remote community into the ranging centre of such a quarrel? That all this was overcome is the real wonder. All honour to those who never doubted, and who from the first discerned the inevitable path."[16]

Five days after the United States entered the war, Churchill wrote to Sir Archibald Sinclair setting out the adverse elements that faced Britain, France and Italy on the battlefield. The "tendencies" of the war, he feared, "are no longer so favourable as they used to be." But he added: "Still America, dear to your heart & mine, is please God a final makeweight."[17]

---

16. Winston S. Churchill, *The World Crisis*, Volume 3, *1916–1918,* page 228.
17. Letter of 11 April 1917, Thurso Papers.

Chapter Eight

✠

"THE FUTURE DESTINY OF THE ENGLISH-SPEAKING PEOPLES"

On 10 May 1917, a month after the entry of the United States into the war, the House of Commons went into Secret Session. This procedure enabled Cabinet Ministers and critics of government policy to discuss the war without any newspaper coverage. One of those present at the Secret Session, Leo Amery, noted in his diary: "Churchill opened with a very adroit but rather unsound speech, mainly in the direction of passive defence on the Western Front till America can come in."[1] Churchill, who had been out of the Cabinet since November 1915 but was still a Member of Parliament, argued that no renewed British offensive should be launched on the Western Front "before the American power begins to be felt on the battlefields."[2]

Churchill knew that American troops would not be ready to go into action until the summer of 1918. He was therefore, in the view of his British critics, "condemning" the British to a static defense on the Western Front for at least nine months. His fear was that any renewed British offensive could only meet with disaster. He was confident that the arrival of fresh American troops in 1918 would prove decisive in any attempted breakthrough. As he told the Secret Session: "We have not the numerical superiority necessary for such a successful offensive. We have no marked artillery preponderance over the enemy. We have

---

1. L. S. Amery, diary entry, 10 May 1917, Amery Papers.
2. Speech of 10 May 1917, Winston S. Churchill, *The World Crisis,* Volume 3, *1916–1918,* Part 1, pages 253–54.

not got the number of tanks which we need. We have not established superiority in the air."[3]

In a letter to the Commander-in-Chief of the British forces in France, Sir Douglas Haig, a friend, Lord Esher, wrote in typical Tory scorn of Churchill's "clever but unbalanced mind." Esher added: "At this moment he is captured by the picture of what 1918 may bring forth in the shape of accumulated reserves of men and material poured out from England in one great and final effort; while at the same time a million Americans sweep over Holland on to the German flank."[4] The distance from the coast of neutral Holland to the German industrial heartland of the Ruhr was one hundred miles, mostly across neutral soil. The distance from the Western Front to the Ruhr was 160 miles, all of it across German-occupied territory or Germany itself.

On June 4 the United States began the dispatch of regular transatlantic convoys with destroyer escorts. These, Churchill later wrote, were a "precious aid" for Allied merchant ships. Henceforth more than a quarter of the Atlantic escorts were provided by American destroyers: "the comradeship of this hard service," Churchill wrote, "forms an ineffaceable tradition for the two navies."[5]

At the beginning of July, Churchill wrote a memorandum for the Prime Minister, David Lloyd George, pointing out that at the beginning of the war the British margin of battleship superiority over the Germans had been seven; that it had risen by the summer of 1917 to twenty-two; but that with the addition of fourteen American battleships, there would be a numerical superiority over Germany of thirty-six.[6]

Lloyd George felt the need for Churchill's energies inside his Cabinet. On July 18, just over two months after the United States entered the war, he appointed him Minister of Munitions. Churchill's first concern was to improve communications between the Ministry of Munitions in London and the British War Purchasing Mission to the United States, headed by the newspaper magnate Lord Northcliffe. On August 2 Churchill explained the threefold structure he was putting in

3. Speech of 10 May 1917, Winston S. Churchill, *The World Crisis*, Volume 3, *1916–1918*, Part 1, pages 253–54.

4. Letter of 30 May 1917, Sir Philip Sassoon Papers.

5. Winston S. Churchill, *The World Crisis*, Volume 3, *1916–1918*, Part 2, page 367.

6. Memorandum of 7 July 1917, "Naval War Policy, 1917," Martin Gilbert, *Winston S. Churchill*, Volume 4, Companion (document) Volume, Part 1, page 97.

place to streamline the provision of Anglo-American war supplies. First was an Inter-Allied Council, as called for by the American Secretary of the Treasury, William G. McAdoo, "to settle," Churchill explained, "a united demand on America on the basis of shipping and credit, and to divide up the total agreed upon between the respective Allies."

The second organization was established within each department of his Ministry, to prepare "the detailed formulation of their needs and for the day to day conduct of their business with America." Churchill noted: "At present a variety of persons communicate through various channels with their Agents and opposite numbers in America. This cannot be a good way of carrying on business and must lead to gaps, contradictions and over-lapping." Churchill was arranging that all communications for the United States from the Ministry of Munitions "are collated and despatched by one man with a proper Staff."

The third element in the new structure that Churchill created, in the interests of efficiency, was an interdepartmental organization to supervise all "business communications" with America from the many different government departments that had hitherto dealt independently with their American opposite numbers. "It is undoubtedly necessary that such co-ordinating machinery should exist," he wrote to Lloyd George, "and it ought to be possible to create it and set it in motion without either interfering with the departmental responsibility and initiative, or introducing a new element of delay." With his threefold organization, Churchill explained, "all our business communications with the United States will pass through one transmission point on this side, and will be received at the same point for distribution to the various Departments."

On the American side of the ocean, Churchill wanted Lord Northcliffe's mission in Washington to be the focal point of all British departmental communications to and from the United States. To this end, he told Lloyd George, he would be quite prepared, as Minister of Munitions, "to place all our business agents in America directly under Lord Northcliffe in exactly the same way as departmental officers are under a Minister here."[7]

By August the Anglo-American aspect of Churchill's work as Minis-

---

7. Letter of 2 August 1917, Churchill Papers, Martin Gilbert, *Winston S. Churchill,* Volume 4, Companion (document) Volume, Part 1, pages 121–22.

ter of Munitions—central to Britain's ability to wage successful war—
was in operation. "My duties brought me into intimate and constant
contact with the leading representatives in Europe of the United States
Supply Services," Churchill later wrote, "as well as with General Bliss
and upon occasion with General Pershing. From the first we worked
together without a single misunderstanding or disagreement." Tasker
Howard Bliss was the United States Army Chief of Staff; John Joseph
Pershing was the Commander of the American Expeditionary Forces
in Europe.

The representative in Europe of the American War Department
was Edward Stettinius. To "business aptitudes of the highest order,"
Churchill recalled, Stettinius added "a delightful simplicity and direct-
ness of character. He was already experienced in the munitions
sphere, having handled the bulk of the great affairs which the British
Government transacted through Messrs. Morgan before the American
declaration of war." In August 1917 an agreement was signed under
which all Britain's requirements from the United States were to be undertaken by an official Purchasing Commission, consisting of three
members of the United States War Industries Board, Bernard M.
Baruch, Robert S. Lovett and Robert S. Bookings. Baruch was then
Commissioner in Charge of Raw Materials on the War Industries
Board, and soon to become head of the entire Board. A New Yorker, by
profession a banker, Baruch was of German-Jewish parentage, tall, imposing, efficient and effective.

Churchill was pleased with the system he had set up. "The arrangements worked excellently," he later wrote. "We 'carried on the war in
common' in every sense of the expression. We transferred masses of
every kind of material, in every stage of production, from one ledger to
the other in accordance with our very different needs as easily as two
friends might share a luncheon-basket. There was no rigmarole or for-
malism in our affairs. We ransacked our cupboards," Churchill added,
"to find anything the American troops in France required, and the
Americans on the other hand, once the case was clearly explained in
conversation, drew without hesitation from their own remoter programmes for our more urgent needs. We built common factories for
tanks and aviation material. The Americans offered us their earliest
supply of mustard gas."

Not until after the war did Churchill meet Baruch, his American opposite number, but, he later recalled, "the almost daily telegrams soon put us on excellent terms. I could feel at the other end of the cable a strong clear mind taking quick decisions and standing by them."[8]

From the United States, Churchill received an unexpected vote of confidence. It came in a letter from his cousin Shane Leslie, written from Vermont to Churchill's mother. Leslie wrote: "The appointment to office has pleased Americans, who look on Winston as ⅞ Yankee and ⅛ Blenheim. It is a pledge that senility has not the last way in everything."[9]

In mid-August 1917 Churchill dined with the head of the American Liaison Mission to Britain, Admiral William S. Sims, who gave him the set of binoculars that he would take on his journeys during the Second World War. At this dinner, with four other people "equally acquainted with State affairs of a secret character," Churchill explained to Lloyd George, Admiral Sims spoke about a number of "extremely confidential" Admiralty matters. He told his British guests "of the latest methods of dealing with submarines, of the projected naval programmes both of this country and the United States, and of the discussions and decisions of the recent Paris naval conference."[10]

Churchill's ability to have close and confidential conversations with leading Americans about top-secret matters was to be a significant part of his leadership in the Second World War.

Britain and France were working closely together to try to fulfill their munitions needs. But no formal mechanism existed whereby the Anglo-French needs, evolved over nearly three years of war, and America's new needs and capabilities could be coordinated. On September 17, during his first visit to Paris with his new ministerial responsibilities, Churchill agreed with his French opposite number, Louis Loucheur, to establish an Inter-Allied Munitions Council, with which

---

8. Winston S. Churchill, *The World Crisis, 1916–1918*, Part 2, pages 472–74.
9. Letter of 8 August 1917, Churchill Papers, Martin Gilbert, *Winston S. Churchill*, Volume 4, Companion (document) Volume, Part 1, page 127.
10. Letter of 19 August 1917, Churchill Papers, Martin Gilbert, *Winston S. Churchill*, Volume 4, Companion (document) Volume, Part 1, page 142.

the Americans would be associated. The main role, Churchill believed, was for Britain and France, the two long-established partners. "The matter is most urgent and should be pressed from day to day," Churchill wrote to Loucheur, "with the sole object of presenting to the US the agreed joint proposals of the Allies, in whose decision the accord of England & France should play the dominating part." [11]

That evening Churchill dined in Paris with several members of the United States War Industries Board. With him was his Private Secretary, Eddie Marsh, who wrote to a friend: "Winston very eloquent on the necessity of bringing every possible American over to France as soon as possible, and training them here or in England instead of in America—so as not to waste transport during the time of training." [12]

Back in London, Churchill was alerted to a serious shortage of howitzer ammunition on the Western Front. Hitherto adequate supplies had been purchased in the United States, but the Americans had recently decided to decrease production, as their own needs for howitzer shells had diminished. This decision, Churchill telegraphed to Lord Northcliffe in Washington, was causing "grave anxiety." It had been discussed in the War Cabinet, and they "urge that you will make every endeavour to induce United States Government to authorise placing of contracts asked for by the Ministry of Munitions." This supply of howitzer ammunition "is of vital importance for the Allied cause." [13]

Churchill's telegram was taken to Bernard Baruch by the deputy chairman of the Northcliffe mission, Robert Brand. Recognizing the urgency of Churchill's request, Baruch agreed that the United States would manufacture, as a priority, a million howitzer shells, followed, when America's urgent munitions needs allowed, by a second million.

This order was among the most effective, and also the most expensive, of the war. Of the total British expenditure on gun ammunition from the United States, more than a fifth was for these howitzer shells. Sir Ernest Moir, the Munitions Council representative in the United States, later told his niece, Churchill's future secretary Phyllis Moir,

---

11. Letter of 17 September 1917, Churchill Papers, Martin Gilbert, *Winston S. Churchill*, Volume 4, page 48.
12. Letter of 17 September 1917, Sir Edward Marsh Papers.
13. Telegram of 5 October 1917, Churchill Papers, Martin Gilbert, *Winston S. Churchill*, Volume 4, page 49.

"It's a joy to work for him. There's a lot of Yankee in Winston. He knows how to hustle and how to make others hustle too."[14]

Churchill's satisfaction at the close cooperation of the British War Purchasing Mission and the War Industries Board, whereby an immense volume of war supplies was being manufactured, was offset by the American failure to enter the battlefield. "I have witnessed with profound disappointment," he wrote to the War Cabinet in October, "the slow and frugal development of American fighting strength in France. From the day when America entered the war, the stream of American manhood, trained, half-trained, or untrained, to Europe should have been continuous, and all the available means of transportation should have been assembled and continually used to their utmost capacity— the men, of course, being properly trained either on one side of the Atlantic or the other."

There was another cause for the slow pace of American reinforcements to the battlefield. The "melancholy decision" to adopt different forms of armament, both for the infantry and artillery of the two armies, had "seriously retarded the development of American war power," Churchill warned. "This is now being realized by the American authorities, but too late. We cannot therefore count on any great superiority in numbers on the Western Front in 1918. Our calculations must proceed upon an assumption that there will be no decisive preponderance in the number of formed divisions or in the number of men in the line or in the reserves available within the year."[15]

Churchill was not content to purchase weapons from the United States, with the inevitable accumulation of financial indebtedness. Britain could also be a supplier. He therefore persuaded Bernard Baruch to take a historic step, whereby Britain would find, and purchase for the United States, all the munitions of war that the United States would need once its troops reached Europe. Churchill thus made himself a principal provider of the weapons with which the United States would contribute to the defeat of Germany.

---

14. Phyllis Moir, *I Was Winston Churchill's Private Secretary,* page 20.
15. Memorandum of October 1917, Winston S. Churchill, *The World Crisis, 1916–1918,* Part 2, pages 304–9.

One remarkable achievement of Churchill's exercise in Anglo-American cooperation was a contract for more than one hundred million pounds.[16] It was a sum that would enable Britain to supply the whole requirements of the United States Army in medium artillery—six-inch guns and howitzers—for the campaign of 1919. "The principles of this contract were simple," Churchill explained. "We guaranteed the United States we would make no profit, and they guaranteed us we should suffer no loss, however the event might turn."[17]

In public Churchill always gave the fullest praise to Britain's new ally. Addressing more than four thousand munition workers in London—in the presence of his mother—Churchill spoke of how "there had come from across the ocean the last of all the great Allies, perhaps the most powerful of all, certainly the most welcome to us here, our cousins, our brothers, the great Republic of the United States."[18]

To manufacture munitions for the United States, whose forces had yet to cross the Atlantic, Churchill negotiated with France, Spain and Canada to buy the raw materials needed. During the sixteen months that he was Minister of Munitions, Britain provided the United States with, among other items, 164 heavy guns, 1,800 trench mortars, 300,000 grenades, 15,000 rifles, 11 million rounds of ammunition, more than 4,500 trucks and ambulances, and 452 airplanes.

With regard to tanks, Churchill took another wide-ranging initiative on behalf of the United States. In negotiations in Paris at the end of 1917 he persuaded Louis Loucheur to let him set up on French soil, at Bordeaux, an Anglo-American tank factory, where Britain would be responsible for assembling tank parts sent over from both Britain and the United States. Churchill was planning for the moment when the United States would enter the battlefield in force in the summer of 1918. Churchill's target, noted the Chief of the Imperial General Staff, Sir Henry Wilson, was "to turn out 1,500 big tanks by about July-August."[19]

In questions of manpower Churchill also understood the crucial part to be played by the United States, telling the War Cabinet that the

---

16. In the monetary values of 2005, £3,500 million/$7 billion.
17. Winston S. Churchill, *The World Crisis, 1916–1918*, Part 2, page 473.
18. *The Times*, 10 October 1917.
19. General (later Field Marshal) Sir Henry Wilson, diary entry, 3 December 1917, Henry Wilson Papers.

Admiralty's demand for an extra 90,000 trained men—which could be met in Britain only by detracting from the military manpower needed on the Western Front—could, for small naval vessels, be fulfilled by "the 60,000 American sailors now available."[20]

Within two days Churchill saw another area in which Britain could benefit as a result of the adherence of the United States Navy to the Allied cause. The British Admiralty wanted money for an acceleration of warship construction. Churchill opposed this, writing to the First Sea Lord: "The accession of the American Fleet to our resources, already so much greater relatively than they were at the beginning of the war, ought to have put the final quietus on further construction for Grand Fleet purposes."[21] In the United States, the Director-General of the Emergency Fleet Corporation, Churchill's former naval collaborator Charles Schwab, was in charge of America's "Shipbuilding Crusade," which was responsible for building 495 ships in sixteen months, including the 12,000-ton *Defiance*, built in thirty-eight days, and the 12,000-ton *Invincible*, built in twenty-four days. Six months was the usual construction time.

The eventual participation of American troops on the battlefield was central to Churchill's confidence in ultimate victory. As he explained in a letter to Sir Archibald Sinclair at the end of 1917, "elastic defence," tanks, a good "army of manoeuvre" in reserve, and the "steady influx of Americans" ought to make in combination "a singularly cheerless outlook for the Hun general staff." Churchill added: "I do not think there will be any weakness here or in America."[22]

In a secret memorandum for the War Cabinet, Churchill stressed that Britain's "only role and only chance of escaping defeat is to bridge the long intervening months before the Americans can become a decisive factor."[23] In December 1917, as British and French forces battled on the Western Front against a determined, better-armed enemy, that moment was at least six months away.

---

20. War Cabinet meeting, 6 December 1917, Cabinet Papers, 23/4.
21. Letter of 8 December 1917, Churchill Papers, Martin Gilbert, *Winston S. Churchill*, Volume 4, Companion (document) Volume, Part 1, page 213.
22. Letter of 29 December 1917, Thurso Papers.
23. War Cabinet memorandum, "Man-Power and the Situation," 8 December 1917, Winston S. Churchill, *The World Crisis, 1916–1918*, Part 2, pages 378–84.

Chapter Nine

⚜

1918: "COME OVER AS QUICKLY AS POSSIBLE"

The year 1918 was to be decisive for Churchill's close working relationship with the United States, as both a skillful negotiator and a facilitator of victory. As the year began his predominant concern was when the American troops would be ready to be sent into action. It appeared that this would take at least eight months. The men had to be brought across the Atlantic and trained, and each division fully equipped with weapons and ammunition.

The British government urged the United States to allow each American battalion—a thousand men—as soon as it was ready for action, to become part of whatever French or British brigade or division was in need of reinforcements. Pershing, the Commander-in-Chief of the American Expeditionary Forces in Europe, rejected this. He wanted each American battalion to wait until it could join a fully equipped American division. At a Cabinet meeting on 4 January 1918, Churchill noted "that the United States Government had declared their willingness to intervene in the war. It should be pointed out to them that by their plan of forming complete Divisions under General Pershing in France, they would be intervening, but that they would intervene on a still larger scale if they would agree to the embodiment of American Battalions in British Brigades."[1]

Pershing would not agree to what he regarded as the piecemeal participation of his troops. In a memorandum to the War Cabinet on the munitions program for 1919, Churchill stressed that until the ar-

---

1. Cabinet meeting, 4 January 1918, Cabinet Papers, 23/5.

rival of the Americans in force, "that is to say during the whole of this year, we are not in a position, without running a desperate risk, to seek a general battle." In 1919, however, the Allies might be "unmistakably superior in strength."[2]

Starting on 12 March 1918, Churchill was made responsible for providing 384 Lewis guns and 168 Vickers guns, together with their ammunition and spare parts, for each American division training with the British troops in France, as well as their steel helmets and gas helmets.[3] Two days later, unaware that a major German breakthrough was imminent, Churchill wrote to the War Cabinet urging an immediate diversion of British naval resources for the transport of American troops to Europe. In his letter he emphasized the "immense political and military advantages of drawing American manhood into the war, and of thus partially filling the gap caused by the diminution of our own forces." This, Churchill insisted, "ought to outweigh all other considerations and make us ready to submit to the further reduction in food, civil imports and munitions rather than lose the benefit which should now be reached." Churchill added: "A true sense of relative values at the present time would assign supreme priority to the rapid augmentation by every conceivable means of the numbers of American soldiers in France."

Another aspect of Anglo-American relations was much on Churchill's mind. "Quite apart from the imperious military need," he explained to the War Cabinet, "the intermingling of British and American units on the field of battle and their endurance of losses and suffering together may exert an immeasurable effect upon the future destiny of the English-speaking peoples, and will afford us perhaps the only guarantee of safety if Germany emerges stronger from the War than she entered it."[4]

On 21 March 1918 the Germans launched a massive assault on the Western Front, driving the British and French troops back across ground that had been taken at enormous cost during the previous two

2. War Cabinet memorandum, "Munitions Programme, 1919," 5 March 1918, Winston S. Churchill, *The World Crisis, 1916–1918,* Part 2, pages 394–403.

3. "Training of American Divisions," 12 March 1918, *With the British and French,* Volume 3, Center of Military History, United States Army, page 65.

4. War Cabinet minute, "America and Shipping," 14 March 1918, Winston S. Churchill, *The World Crisis, 1916–1918,* Part 2, page 469.

years. General Ludendorff, the German master planner, was confident he could bring Britain and France to their knees before the Americans could make any significant contribution on the battlefield. Churchill, who had been visiting the Western Front at the time of the German breakthrough, prepared a letter to Lloyd George advising various emergency measures. One of them was that the American army, then slowly forming in France but not yet ready for concerted action as a unified all-American force, should be broken up and sent to the British and French divisions that were most in need.[5]

General Pershing remained adamant that American troops should not go into action except under their own divisional badges and commanders. Determined to challenge this, Lloyd George sent Churchill to Paris to obtain the support of the French Prime Minister, Georges Clemenceau, for the use of American troops, as they arrived in France, as integral parts of Anglo-American divisions.

While in Paris, Churchill had several meetings with Clemenceau, also conferring with Major General Charles John Sackville-West, senior British military representative with the French General Staff, and Major Edward Louis Spears, head of the British Military Mission in Paris, whom Churchill had befriended on the Western Front two years earlier—and whose wife was the American novelist Mary Borden. The pressure on Pershing was considerable. So too was the urgent logic of the German threat to the Allied forces on the Western Front. Finally recognizing the grave danger that faced the Anglo-French armies, Pershing told the Chief of the French General Staff, General Philippe Pétain, that all American troops in France "were at his disposal to do what he likes with."[6]

Churchill later reflected on the generosity of the Americans at this moment of "extreme crisis," writing of how General Pershing and General Bliss—newly appointed American representative on the Supreme War Council—"spontaneously, in the finest manner" placed all their resources in France at the Allied disposal. The American divisions, even battalions if needed, would, Churchill noted, "enter the

5. Draft letter of 24 March 1918, Churchill Papers, Martin Gilbert, *Winston S. Churchill*, Volume 4, Companion (document) Volume, Part 1, pages 276–77.
6. Letter of 29 March 1918 (Major Spears to General Sir Henry Wilson), Spears Papers.

line forthwith in spite of their training and organization being incomplete. This decision was at the true height of circumstances, and in itself went far to repair the injuries of Ludendorff's inroad."[7]

It would be another five months before the American troops would go into action as an exclusively American force.

On March 30 Churchill spent the day with Clemenceau at the front, meeting the French commanders. The two men also discussed, as Lloyd George had asked Churchill to do, a telegram from Lloyd George to President Wilson, asking for 120,000 American troops to be sent each month to France. Having returned to Paris with Clemenceau at one o'clock on the morning of March 31, Churchill managed to get a few hours' sleep, before writing to Clemenceau: "This is the moment to press Mr Wilson. It will be all the better if your telegram strikes a different note and comes from a different point of view, so long as it has the same object namely 120,000 Americans a month." Churchill added: "Let us strike while the iron is hot. I don't see how else we can get the life energy which the armies will need this summer."[8]

Churchill saw Clemenceau at noon that same day. Together they drafted a telegram, to be sent in Clemenceau's name, asking President Wilson, "to be so good as to give immediate instructions that 120,000 American infantry may be embarked monthly for Europe, from now onwards until the end of July."[9] Within twenty-four hours Wilson agreed to send 120,000 infantrymen a month, for four consecutive months. Churchill's mission had been a success.

As the German advance continued, it seemed that the Channel ports would be threatened, and a wedge driven between the British and French armies—as was to happen in 1940. "During these tremendous struggles," Churchill later wrote, "while the fate of the Channel ports and even of the union between the British and French armies hung in the balance, by far the greater part of my duties and thoughts lay in the future." Throughout the summer of 1918 the Munitions

---

7. Winston S. Churchill, *The World Crisis, 1916–1918,* Part 2, page 470.

8. Letter of 31 March 1918, Churchill Papers, Martin Gilbert, *Winston S. Churchill,* Volume 4, Companion (document) Volume, Part 1, page 293.

9. Letter of 31 March 1918, Churchill Papers, Martin Gilbert, *Winston S. Churchill,* Volume 4, page 100.

Council worked for the battles of 1919, a campaign, Churchill later wrote, "which, in God's mercy, was never fought."[10]

On April 30 Churchill received two telegrams from the War Industries Board. Both appealed to him to provide British artillery pieces for the American troops on whom so much depended, as they could not be provided with adequate artillery from American sources alone. Churchill wrote at once to his French opposite number, Louis Loucheur, asking for French help in providing the Americans with at least half the artillery for which they had asked. "In my view we must do everything in our power," Churchill wrote, "to encourage the United States to pour troops into France as rapidly as possible, by making them feel that there will be no lack of artillery from one source or another to sustain American infantry when they enter the line of battle."

Churchill would provide the United States with extra heavy guns, over and above the original orders of November 1917, and wanted France to make a similar extra effort, explaining to Loucheur: "The moral which we want to convey to the Americans is 'Come over as quickly as possible; we can provide you with plenty of artillery for all the men you send.'"[11]

On July 4, the 142nd anniversary of the American Declaration of Independence, Churchill was the principal speaker at the Central Hall, Westminster, at a meeting of the Anglo-Saxon Fellowship. "When I have seen during the past few weeks," he said, "the splendour of American manhood striding forward on all the roads of France and Flanders, I have experienced emotions which words cannot describe." The presence in Europe of a million American soldiers "is an event that seems to transcend the limits of purely mundane things and fills us with the deepest awe."

Britain's reward for answering the appeals of Belgium and France in 1914, Churchill asserted, was not territorial or commercial advantage, but the "supreme reconciliation" of Britain and the United States. "We seek no higher reward than this supreme reconciliation.

10. Winston S. Churchill, *The World Crisis, 1916–1918,* Part 2, page 468.
11. Letter of 1 May 1918, Churchill Papers, Martin Gilbert, *Winston S. Churchill,* Volume 4, Companion (document) Volume, Part 1, page 308–9.

That is the reward of Britain. That is the lion's share."[12] Churchill's speech was printed in pamphlet form and distributed throughout the United States.

After reading an account of his speech, Churchill's friend Sir Archibald Sinclair wrote from the Western Front that it was "certainly absolutely true of all Englishmen and Scotsmen with recent American connections and probably of the vast majority of thinking men in our country that they will be willing to regard the complete understanding and co-operation with America as our highest reward—'the lion's share.'"[13] "If all goes well," Churchill replied, "England and US may act permanently together. We are living 50 years in one at this rate."[14]

Three and a half weeks after his speech to the Anglo-Saxon Fellowship, Churchill was one of the guests at a banquet for the Allied Ministers of War at Gray's Inn Hall. The main speakers were Lord Curzon, a member of the War Cabinet; Sir Robert Borden, the Canadian Prime Minister; and Lieutenant-General Jan Christiaan Smuts, the South African representative on the Imperial War Cabinet. Churchill did not speak. As the evening drew to a close there was a call for a speaker from the United States. The most senior American present was the Assistant Secretary of the Navy, thirty-six-year-old Franklin D. Roosevelt, who was on a tour of inspection of the Western Front. Roosevelt told the gathering: "We are with you to the end."[15]

The Gray's Inn Hall banquet of July 29 was to become a cause of future controversy. Twenty years later Roosevelt told the American Ambassador in London, Joseph Kennedy, that Churchill had "acted like a stinker to him" at the banquet. Roosevelt also told Kennedy that Churchill was "one of the few men in public life who was rude to me."[16] Churchill later had no recollection either of Roosevelt's speech or of any conversation with him.

Throughout the summer of 1918 Churchill resisted pressure from the War Cabinet to take men from the munitions factories and throw them

---

12. Speech of 4 July 1918, *The Times*, 5 July 1918.
13. Letter of early July 1918, Churchill Papers, Martin Gilbert, *Winston S. Churchill*, Volume 4, pages 123–24.
14. Letter of 11 July 1918, Thurso Papers.
15. *The Times*, 30 July 1918.
16. Quoted in Conrad Black, *Franklin Delano Roosevelt*, page 91.

into a renewed offensive on the Western Front. Men taken into the army from their factory work in Britain, he wrote, "will not reach the battle-front in time to influence the decision." On the other hand the Americans, "who have ten million men between 20 and 30 on whom to draw, are now arriving in great numbers, more than 270,000 having disembarked in a single month. The main contribution to our manhood next year must be derived from them."

If the Allies were to obtain "any effective superiority in numbers" it could only be by means of American aid. "No contribution that we can make can substantially alter the situation in a numerical sense." The provision of "the largest possible number of infantry soldiers" would fall on the Americans, whose forces in Europe had risen by mid-July to a million men.

Churchill pointed out to the War Cabinet that, according to the figures released, "more than two million Americans had already enlisted, that three million would have been enlisted by September 1, and that the War Department was preparing clothing for four million as from 1 January 1919." The solution of the Allied manpower problem therefore lay, Churchill insisted, not in any British or French recruiting of men from their essential factory tasks but in the "speedy transportation" to France of the millions of Americans, followed by "their training and organisation on the battle-front, and, lastly, their equipment and supply."

The first million American soldiers who had reached Europe, Churchill noted, had been "almost entirely" equipped by Britain and France. Not without pride in his own work as Minister of Munitions, he pointed out that, but for the fact "that we were able to supply them with artillery, machine-guns, rifles, trench mortars, etc, and to feed them with munitions of all kinds, no use in the present crisis could have been made of this first million." The latest report from the War Industries Board stated that the American army in France "will be almost entirely dependent during the whole of 1918 on British and French artillery production." To provide this, and to meet the even greater needs of 1919, Churchill would not allow his munition workers to be sent to the front.

Until the middle of 1919, Churchill informed the War Cabinet, the American munitions program, particularly in guns and airplanes, would be "woefully behind their available resources in manpower."

Unless Britain and France were able "to supplement promptly every deficiency in the American munition programme, the despatch of very large numbers of their troops may be retarded from this cause."

The two sources of potential fighting men were very different, Churchill explained. In the United States there were "enormous numbers of men in the prime of life." In Britain, by contrast, "for the sake of getting comparatively small numbers of men of inferior physique who will not be much use, or of superior skill who cannot be spared, we run the risk of endangering production of munitions on which not only our own Armies, but the rapid importation of American troops, depend." Despite the tremendous pressure of British military requirements across the whole spectrum of munitions, the network of Churchill's munitions factories, in which by 1918 women formed the bulk of the labor force, had become the principal supplier of America's needs, and produced what was asked of them.[17]

Six days after Churchill's memorandum, President Wilson signed General Order Number 62, establishing the United States Chemical Warfare Service, to exploit the use of gas on the battlefield, thereby creating yet more American needs that Churchill's munition workers would have to meet in 1919.

On 15 July 1918 the Germans launched a renewed offensive, pressing to within fifty miles of Paris. "During these tremendous days," Churchill recalled, "the British, French, American and Italian Munitions authorities had been in continuous conference in Paris." Their main task was to settle the munitions needs of the Allies for 1919. But, Churchill wrote, "The distant rumble of the cannonade and the dull crash of the half-hourly Bertha shells reminded us that the campaign of 1918 was going on."[18]

On August 8 the British and French armies launched a major offensive against the German front. Churchill crossed over to France to witness the triumph, spending a day visiting the battle zone. In a letter to Clementine the next day he wrote with pride of the British achievement. He had read in the newspapers high praise also for the Ameri-

---

17. War Cabinet memorandum. "Munitions and the Limits of Recruiting," 12 July 1918, Winston S. Churchill, *The World Crisis, 1916–1918*. Part 2, pages 485–87.
18. Winston S. Churchill, *The World Crisis, 1916–1918*, Part 2, page 501.

can troops, one regiment of which had fought as an integral part of the British front (the scheme Churchill had pressed for five months earlier), while others had fought for the first time as independent American Divisions. Churchill was not impressed by the total American contribution. "Would you believe it," he wrote to his wife, "only three American Divisions were in the line at any one moment between Rheims and Soissons. They certainly had a good press."

The relatively small American contribution was "one reason," Churchill explained, "why I rejoice that we should have won a great success which no one can take from us."[19] But it was still to the United States troops on their way to Europe that he pinned his hopes of victory, writing to the War Cabinet: "Clearly the dominating factor is the enormous reserve of American manhood which may be made available by wise and energetic action from now on."

Watching the advances on the Western Front, Churchill felt that the existing focus on the battles of 1919 should be changed, and that the resources being set aside for then should be pressed into service at once. "We are justified in running great risks to win an early and complete victory," he informed the War Cabinet, "because, even if we fail, we shall be steadily up-borne by the growing military power of America."[20]

No such acceleration of the plans for victory was agreed upon. The main thrust of the Inter-Allied Munitions Council remained the battlefield needs of 1919. On August 14, in Paris, Churchill presided at a meeting of the Council to allocate the coming year's munitions and raw material requirements of eight warring nations. Two days later he went with Edward Stettinius, officially designated the "Senior United States War Supplies Purchaser in Europe," to see the battlefield at Château-Thierry, fifty miles from Paris, where the Germans had been halted and driven back a month earlier.

During his talks with Stettinius, both at the front and in Paris, Churchill outlined a "really big deal"—as he described it to his wife

---

19. Letter of 10 August 1918, Churchill Papers, Martin Gilbert, *Winston S. Churchill*, Volume 4, Companion (document) Volume, Part 7, pages 368–70.

20. War Cabinet memorandum, August 1918, Winston S. Churchill, *The World Crisis, 1916–1918*, Part 2, pages 487–88.

Clementine—for the needs of the American troops in the battles of 1919. This would encompass steel, airplane engines and guns, all to be manufactured by Britain. If done well, Churchill told his wife, it should be "profitable to all concerned," adding: "I have had a lot to do here, and as this is the only place where all the threads—American, French and Italian—come together it is possible to get things done." He had been seeing "a good deal" of Stettinius, with whom he had established "excellent relations." As to Britain's relationship with the United States: "We depend on them for so many things now and I think we are steadily winning their confidence."

Churchill experienced one setback with regard to the promises he had made to the Americans. This concerned the Anglo-American Tank factory at Châteauroux, for which, he told Clementine, "I cannot secure either the labour or the organisation necessary for its completion. Meanwhile the material for the Tanks is nearly ready, and the Tanks are badly wanted. It is causing me such embarrassment."[21] The factory at Châteauroux had failed to produce the tanks for which it was designed. With Churchill's scrutiny and reorganization of its management, however, it was quickly back on course to achieve the production of the tanks needed by both the British and Americans for the battles still expected to be fought in 1919.

The intricacy and intimacy of the relations Churchill had established with the United States reached a high point on September 7. That day he learned that the Chilean government, the major source of Allied supplies of nitrates—an essential component of all munitions—had accepted his request that all of Chile's nitrate production should be sold to the Allies. It was the culmination of a year of secret negotiations with Chile, which had been reluctant to commit itself so decisively to the Allied cause. Churchill had conducted these negotiations not only for Britain and France but also for the United States. As United States purchases of nitrates were more than five times as large as those of Britain, Churchill's conduct of the negotiations was of even greater value to the United States than to Britain.

The agreement with Chile enabled Churchill to give both the French and United States governments the quantities of nitrates they

---

21. Letter of 17 August 1918, Baroness Spencer-Churchill Papers.

required, while retaining sufficient for British needs. On the evening of the conclusion of the agreement he telegraphed to Bernard Baruch in Washington: "I am going to begin discussing the 1919 production quite shortly and I should be glad if you would let me know as soon as possible what your monthly requirements will be."[22]

"When we met in Paris during the Peace Conference," Churchill later recalled, "I found that Mr Baruch apparently considered me an authority upon the deeper technical aspects of the nitrate trade. He one day asked me my advice upon an urgent and complicated question concerning it. But reputations are easier lost than gained. I thought I would let well alone, and disengaged myself with suitable modesty."[23]

The program for 1919 had come to dominate Churchill's work and thought, not only with regard to the essential supplies of nitrates but across the board of munitions and armaments. In a telegram to Baruch, Churchill confided: "I am becoming embarrassed by the difficulty of getting a definite answer from the American War Department as to what help they want us to give them in their artillery programmes for next year. You will understand that it is very difficult to keep my programmes in suspense for so long. I do not know whether you can say a helpful word to accelerate decision one way or the other, but if so I should be very grateful."[24]

On September 12, the day of this telegram to Baruch, General Pershing launched America's first independent military offensive of the war. Churchill, who was again in Paris on munitions business— discussing the provision of steel for the production of tanks needed by the Americans for the battles of 1919—wrote to Clementine that day describing the American success on the battlefield. The Americans, he reported, had launched an attack toward Metz "in overwhelming strength."[25]

Three days later Churchill wrote to his wife again from Paris: "The US have now accepted my large artillery offer—more than 2,000

22. Telegram of 7 September 1918, Churchill Papers, Martin Gilbert, *Winston S. Churchill*, Volume 4, page 142.
23. Winston S. Churchill, *The World Crisis, 1916–1918*, Part 2, page 475.
24. Winston S. Churchill, *The World Crisis, 1916–1918*, Part 2, pages 474–75.
25. Letter of 12 September 1918, Baroness Spencer-Churchill Papers.

guns—out of which they will be able to arm perhaps fifteen additional divisions or nearly half a million men, in time for the crisis of next year."

Even as the Americans were taking their first forward steps, advancing several miles into the St. Mihiel Salient, Churchill was looking ahead to what he and all other Allied leaders were convinced would be the decisive trial of strength in the summer and autumn of 1919. "We must finish it then," Churchill told his wife. He also told her that, as part of the British effort in 1919, he was negotiating with the United States to purchase 3,000 aircraft engines for the British air force, "particularly for the bombing of Germany."[26]

He was optimistic, Churchill informed the War Cabinet, that the French and British munition workers could supply the needs of all the United States troops that could be brought "by our maximum carrying capacity" to Europe, and could supply them "with good weapons and ample ammunition, provided only that the necessary raw materials are sent by America to be made up in our factories." No undue strain would be imposed on the British munition factories. "The gun plants and the shell plants are running so smoothly now that, given raw material, they can easily meet their share of American needs."

Churchill also told the War Cabinet that he had agreed to supply the United States with more than 2,000 guns in 1919, and to make the ammunition "for all these guns if they will send the raw materials." By this deal alone, Churchill reported, "considerably more than one hundred millions of British indebtedness to America will be extinguished."[27]

The war needs of 1919 were about to become academic. At the end of September Germany's ally Bulgaria signed an armistice with the Allies. On October 14 President Wilson refused a German request for an armistice. "That stern and formidable answer," Churchill told a public meeting in Manchester on the following day, "will be wholeheartedly endorsed throughout all the countries and nations of the Allies."[28]

---

26. Letter of 15 September 1918, Baroness Spencer-Churchill Papers.
27. War Cabinet memorandum, "Supplies to the United States Armies," 25 September 1918, Churchill Papers, Martin Gilbert, *Winston S. Churchill*, Volume 4, Companion (document) Volume, Part I, pages 397–98.
28. Speech of 15 October 1918, Churchill Press Cutting Albums, Churchill College, Cambridge.

Within three weeks of Wilson's firm stance, three armies, the German, Austro-Hungarian and Turkish, were each in retreat. On October 30 Turkey surrendered, followed by Austria-Hungary four days later. On November 11 the German armistice was signed. The First World War was over.

Looking back, Churchill noted that although the war ended "long before the material power of the United States could be brought to bear as a decisive or even as a principal factor," it ended nevertheless with more than two million American soldiers on the soil of France. And there would have been many more to come. "A campaign in 1919 would have seen very large American armies continually engaged," he wrote, noting that it would have been as many as five million men by 1920, "had the Germans still been able to continue at war."[29]

The United States recognized Churchill's efforts on its behalf. On 16 July 1919, General Pershing presented him with the American Distinguished Service Medal. The citation referred to Churchill's "exceptionally meritorious and distinguished services" that had been of "inestimable value" to the Allied cause when, as Minister of Munitions, "he was confronted with a task of great magnitude." The citation noted: "With ability of high order, energy, and marked devotion to duty, he handled with great success the trying problems with which he was constantly confronted." The final sentence read: "In the performance of his great task he rendered valuable service to the American Expeditionary Forces."[30]

On 20 July 1919, in a committee room in the House of Commons, Churchill introduced Pershing to a group of Members of Parliament, all of whom had seen active service between 1914 and 1918. Since the end of the war, Churchill told them, "our feeling has grown stronger for these gallant men and their gallant commander."[31] On the following day Churchill was present in London's Hyde Park for a review of three thousand American troops by the Prince of Wales and General

---

29. Winston S. Churchill, *The World Crisis, 1916–1918*, Part 2, pages 225–26.
30. Quoted in Douglas S. Russell, *The Orders, Decorations and Medals of Sir Winston Churchill*, 2nd edition, pages 48–50.
31. *New York Times*, 21 July 1919.

Pershing. A few days later, at the victory parade in London, Pershing and Churchill rode in the same horse-drawn carriage.

Ten years after these celebrations of victory, Churchill reflected that, during the First World War, "for the first time after so many generations of severance, all the English-speaking peoples found themselves in a common line of battle." When, on 4 July 1918, at Villers-Bretonneux, British, Australian and American troops had "advanced together against the enemy," and when, later that year, American troops had played a "notable part" in Field Marshal Haig's forcing of the Hindenburg Line, "new martial episodes superimposed themselves upon the sombre records of the past, and for the first time in a hundred and fifty years the two nations had a history to write in common." Apart from association on the field of battle, "valuable new ties" had been established "between individuals throughout the wide spheres of munition supply, war finance and diplomacy."[32] In these ties, though Churchill did not say so, he himself had played a significant part.

---

32. Winston Churchill, "What I Saw and Heard in America," *Daily Telegraph*, 18 November 1929.

Chapter Ten

☗

"AMERICA DID NOT MAKE GOOD"

With the ending of the First World War, Churchill left the Ministry of Munitions to become Secretary of State for War. The German war had ended, but from the moment of the Bolshevik seizure of power in Russia in November 1917, the Allies had launched a military intervention against the Bolsheviks. Throughout 1918, British, American, French, Italian, Czech, Japanese and other troops fought alongside the anti-Bolshevik Russian forces on six separate fronts. Whether those Allied forces were to stay in Russia and continue to fight the Bolsheviks or be withdrawn, leaving the Russian anti-Bolshevik armies to seek the destruction of Bolshevism unaided, was to be decided in Paris by the highest Allied body there, the Council of Ten, consisting of senior representatives of all the Allied Powers. The discussion, which was to begin on 14 February 1919, had added urgency because President Wilson was returning from Paris to the United States on the following day.

Lloyd George sent Churchill to Paris to represent the British War Cabinet. One possible outcome of the Paris meeting, Churchill told the Cabinet before he set off, was "a united declaration" by the Allies to make war on the Bolsheviks. If this were done, the British troops already in Russia—sent there by his predecessors—would have a part to play in North Russia, Ukraine, Estonia and the Caucasus.[1]

Churchill's task in Paris was to reach a decision with an American President and two of his senior officials, the Secretary of State, Robert Lansing, and the United States Peace Commissioner in Paris, Colonel Edward House. Traveling by train to Newhaven in the early morning of February 14, and then by destroyer to Dieppe, Churchill and the Chief

---

1. War Cabinet of 13 February 1919, Cabinet Papers, 23/9.

of the Imperial General Staff, Field Marshal Sir Henry Wilson, drove on to Paris. During the journey their car was in an accident that smashed the windshield and broke half the steering wheel. Cold and wet, the two men reached Paris at three in the afternoon. Three days of intense negotiation lay ahead, starting at seven that evening.

Asked by the senior British representative on the Council of Ten, Arthur Balfour—a former Prime Minister—to explain to the Council "the present views of the British Cabinet," Churchill pointed out the Cabinet's "great anxiety" about the Russian situation. He went on to explain that in view of the imminent departure of President Wilson, the Cabinet had asked him "to go over and obtain some decision as to the policy on this matter."

Churchill asked the Council to decide on the military aspects of the intervention. Britain had soldiers in Russia who were being killed in action, he explained. "Their families wished to know what purpose these men were serving. Were they just marking time until the Allies had decided on a policy, or were they fighting in a campaign representing some common aim?" The longer the delay continued, the worse would be the situation of the Allied troops on all the Russian fronts. "The Russian elements in these forces were deteriorating rapidly because of the uncertainty of the support they might expect from the victorious Allies. The Allied troops were intermingled with these Russian troops, which were weakening and quavering, and they were themselves becoming affected."

President Wilson told the meeting that he was opposed to any further Allied intervention in Russia, stating that the Allied troops "were doing no sort of good in Russia. They did not know for whom or for what they were fighting. They were not assisting any promising common effort to establish order throughout Russia. They were assisting local movements, like, for instance, that of the Cossacks, who could not be induced to move outside their own sphere." Wilson concluded that the Allies ought to withdraw their troops "from all parts of Russian territory."

Churchill spoke once more. It was essential, he believed, to institute a clear-cut policy. The complete withdrawal of all Allied troops was, at least, "a logical and clear policy," but he feared that its consequences "would be the destruction of all non-Bolshevik armies in Russia," a total of half a million men, whose numbers were increasing.

Such a policy, he warned, "would be equivalent to pulling out the linch-pin from the whole machine. There would be no further armed resistance to the Bolsheviks in Russia, and an interminable vista of violence and misery was all that remained for the whole of Russia."

Wilson was not impressed by Churchill's argument. "The existing Allied forces," he said, "could not stop the Bolsheviks," nor were any of the Allies "prepared to reinforce its troops." When the Italian representative, Baron Sonnino, asked whether the Allies might not at least continue to supply arms to the "non-Bolshevik elements," Wilson observed that the non-Bolshevik Russians "had made very little use of them when they had them."

Churchill made one further attempt to gain support for a more active Allied policy. He accepted that "none of the Allies could send conscript troops to Russia," but he thought that they might agree to send "volunteers, technical experts, arms, munitions, tanks, aeroplanes, etc." Wilson was skeptical of Churchill's suggestion and said so unequivocally. The minutes of the meeting recorded that the President "understood the problem was to know what use would be made of these forces and supplies. In some areas they would certainly be assisting reactionaries. Consequently, if the Allies were asked what they were supporting in Russia they would be compelled to reply that they did not know."

Wilson went on to say that conscripts could not be sent and that volunteers probably could not be obtained. He himself "felt guilty" that the United States had in Russia insufficient forces, "but it was not possible to increase them." Wilson added, according to the official notes of the meeting: "It was certainly a cruel dilemma. At present our soldiers were being killed in Russia, if they were removed many Russians might lose their lives. But some day or other the Allied troops would be withdrawn; they could not be maintained there for ever and the consequences to the Russians would only be deferred."

Churchill then asked, as Sonnino had done, whether the Council would approve of arming the anti-Bolshevik forces in Russia? President Wilson replied, somewhat offhandedly, "that he hesitated to express any definite opinion," but that whatever the Council of Ten decided, he would "cast in his lot with the rest."[2] The meeting then adjourned

---

2. Meeting of the Council of Ten, 14 February 1919, Lloyd George Papers.

until the following afternoon. A few hours later President Wilson left Paris by train for Cherbourg, and the United States. Churchill had failed to get a Presidential commitment, but he still hoped to influence the men Wilson had left behind—the Secretary of State, Lansing, and the Peace Commissioner, Colonel House—in proposing that the Council of Ten should immediately set up an Inter-Allied Commission to decide what military and economic action the Allies should take, in conjunction with Russia's neighbors, "to bring the Bolshevik regime to an end." This was agreed: a commission but not a decision.

When the Council of Ten met on the afternoon of February 17, Churchill proposed that the military aspects of intervention should be studied by a special committee of Allied military representatives. Colonel House was opposed to this, Henry Wilson noting in his diary: "House said neither American men nor material would be allowed to go to Russia."[3] All Churchill had asked for was an inquiry, but House wrote in his diary: "Although Churchill had received his instructions from Lloyd George, he was persistent in pushing his plan for a military committee to examine the question as to how Russia could best be invaded in the event it was necessary to do so." House added: "I opposed this plan with some vehemence."[4]

Disappointed and frustrated not to have obtained American support, Churchill took the night train to Boulogne and returned to London. From then on, as the Allied intervention came to an end, his main task was to evacuate the British troops in Russia, and to provide arms and ammunition for the anti-Bolshevik forces as they pressed in on St. Petersburg and Moscow but failed to capture either.

At the beginning of March a special envoy from President Wilson embarked on five days of negotiations in Moscow with the leading Bolsheviks, including Lenin. Churchill was indignant. "I do trust President Wilson will not be allowed to weaken our policy against them in any way," he wrote to Lloyd George. "His negotiations have become widely known and are much resented."[5] Churchill need not have upset himself. In early April the envoy brought back a peace offer from Moscow that was rejected by both Woodrow Wilson and Lloyd George.

---

3. Diary entry, 17 February 1919, Sir Henry Wilson Papers.
4. Diary entry, 17 February 1919, Colonel House Papers.
5. Letter of 10 April 1919, Lloyd George Papers.

Churchill never allowed the vexations of one item of policy to eclipse the wider reality of Anglo-American closeness. "As you say," he wrote to Admiral William S. Sims, commander of the United States naval forces in Europe, "the harmony & success of this co-operation form a clear precedent, & one which is of the highest value to the future in which such vast issues hang on unity between our two countries in ideals & in action."[6]

The evacuation of foreign troops from Russia continued. The last seven hundred American troops left North Russia on July 28. The British troops followed not long afterward. Despite Churchill's efforts in Paris, no coordinated Anglo-American or multinational policy had been created, whether for intervention, negotiation or withdrawal. Churchill still hoped that the Allied armies that had remained in the Russian Far East, helping the anti-Bolshevik Russian forces in eastern Siberia, would not withdraw. "It is more than likely," he wrote to the British Foreign Secretary in August, "that both America and Japan will make exertions to save the situation in this part of the world."[7] But Churchill was wrong, and a Soviet Far Eastern Republic was soon established.

The anti-Bolshevik forces in South Russia continued to fight, with British military aid. But early in 1920 Churchill urged them to make their peace with the Bolsheviks. As he told his senior military representative in South Russia: "America does nothing. France is completely indifferent. The British Government will not do any more."[8]

The Treaty of Versailles was signed on 28 June 1919, and with that signing the League of Nations was established. Then, on 19 November 1919 the United States Senate, in a decisive show of isolationist sentiment, voted by 56 votes to 37 against President Wilson's request for "unconditional acceptance" of the Versailles Treaty. With that vote, the United States turned its back on the League of Nations, which Wilson regarded as the essential forum for future world peace, a forum in

---

6. Letter of 31 March 1919, Admiral Sims Papers.
7. Letter of 14 August 1919, Churchill Papers, Martin Gilbert, *Winston S. Churchill*, Volume 4, page 319.
8. Telegram of 11 January 1920, Churchill Papers, Martin Gilbert, *Winston S. Churchill*, Volume 4, page 368.

which the United States would take a leading part. Wilson, who had suffered a stroke at the beginning of October, spoke bitterly of the "sullen and selfish isolation" of the Senators who voted to turn America's back on Europe, but President Warren G. Harding, his successor in the White House, spoke in support of the Senate and national majority when he declared: "We seek no part in directing the destinies of the world."

For the rest of his life Churchill saw America's failure to become part of the League of Nations as a turning point in the prospects not only for European but for global peace. This was not a retrospective stance. Between the Senate vote and Wilson's reluctant ratification of it, Churchill wrote one of his most powerful journalistic pieces, in the mass-circulation *Illustrated Sunday Herald,* entitled "Will America Fail Us?" The article was published on his forty-fifth birthday. "A more melancholy page in human history," he wrote, "could hardly be conceived" than the non-ratification of the Treaty of Versailles by the United States. "We cannot believe that it will be written by American hands."

Looking optimistically at the course of Anglo-American relations thus far, he pointed out to his readers that after all the "melancholy series of blunders and calamities, of hopeless misunderstandings" embodied in the history of Britain and the United States—"these two formidable kinsmen"—the fact that the two nations "have at last advanced in battle side by side" stood out as "a supreme event in the story of civilisation." The two "great branches of the English-speaking family" were at last able "to write their history in common." Instead of "the old and thank God, now obsolete chronicles of past antagonisms, we have the gleaming memory that together we saved Europe from the hands of the spoiler, and the sure conviction that by acting together we can safeguard ourselves from every peril which the future may have in store."[9]

There was no way that Churchill's article could influence events. When, on 10 January 1920—less than six weeks later—the victorious nations ratified the Treaty of Versailles, and the League of Nations came formally into existence, the United States cast no vote and took

---

9. Winston S. Churchill, "Will America Fail Us?" *Illustrated Sunday Herald,* 30 November 1919.

no subsequent part in the League's deliberations. A month later Churchill set out his confidence that all would be well in the end when he wrote, in a short but succinct message, in his own hand: "The consciousness of a common purpose—in great matters between Britain & the United States is the only sure guarantee of the future peace of the world."[10] But the American withdrawal from Europe rankled with Churchill for the rest of his life. When, in 1920, the French Government opposed an accommodation with Germany, Churchill pointed out that France was "unreasonable because she is terrified. . . . She sees herself abandoned by the United States."[11] Several decades later, after the Second World War, Churchill wrote to an American friend of his distress at "the lack of a world instrument of government for the prevention of war" between 1919 and 1939. This, he believed, "was largely because the United States abandoned the League of Nations at its birth."[12]

Yet whatever the vexations with the United States, Churchill was reluctant to make his distress public. Shortly before his appointment as Secretary of State for the Colonies in January 1921 he had been elected President of the English-Speaking Union and presided at their annual banquet. Anglo-American unity, he declared, "would be a barrier—an insurmountable barrier—against tyranny in every form, whether it was organized on the old Prussian model or according to the new Russian dispensation." As to the differences that had arisen between the two countries, he emphasized: "Far beneath the froth and scum of daily life and business moved the mysterious tides of national and human dignity," from which those "who believed in the moral governance of the universe" could take strength.[13]

In the United States there were outspoken criticisms of Britain's alleged reluctance to pay its considerable First World War debt to the United States, which stood at more than four billion dollars.[14] The

_____

10. Message of 16 February 1920, signed "Winston S. Churchill, War Office, 16.2.20," reproduced in facsimile, *Finest Hour,* Number 125, page 42.

11. Memorandum of 29 August 1920, Churchill Papers, Martin Gilbert, *Winston S. Churchill,* Volume 4, pages 426–27.

12. Letter to Henry Luce, 22 November 1947, Martin Gilbert, *Winston S. Churchill,* Volume 8, pages 357–58.

13. *The Times,* 14 February 1921.

14. In the monetary values of 2005, the equivalent of $100 billion (£50 billion).

United States Treasury was insisting that all the war debts of its Allies
be paid promptly and in full. "It was uphill work to make an enthusiastic speech about the United States at a time when so many hard things
are said about us over there and when they are wringing the last penny
out of their unfortunate allies," Churchill wrote to Clementine three
days later. "All the same there is only one road for us to tread, and that
is to keep as friendly with them as possible, to be overwhelmingly patient and to wait for the growth of better feelings which will certainly
come when the Irish question ceases to be in its present terrible condition."[15]

The American demand for rapid repayment of the war debt was
creating considerable anti-American feeling. "The United States has a
will of its own," Churchill wrote for the Cabinet, "very clearly expressed, namely, to exact payment from Great Britain."[16] But Churchill saw no virtue in alienating American opinion. One point of
confrontation was Ireland. During 1921 Churchill emerged as a
strong supporter of a truce with Sinn Fein and the IRA.[17] Lloyd George
was skeptical, but Churchill was convinced that conciliation was the
right path, and that it had a chance of ending the violence. One of his
arguments for giving the truce a try was that the confrontation in Ireland was "poisoning our relations with the United States."[18]

During the next two years Churchill took the lead in the discussions with Sinn Fein, and in the negotiations that led to the establishment of the Irish Free State, which held Dominion Status within the
British Empire, but from which the nine predominantly Protestant
counties of Ulster were excluded. This was accepted by the Sinn Fein
leaders headed by Michael Collins, but not by the extremists, who
wanted to continue the armed struggle for an Irish Republic, a repub-

---

15. Letter of 16 February 1921, Baroness Spencer-Churchill Papers.
16. Cabinet memorandum, 2 August 1922, Churchill Papers, Martin Gilbert, *Winston S. Churchill,* Volume 4, Companion (document) Volume, Part 1, pages 284–85.
17. Sinn Fein ("ourselves alone") was the British political party established in
1905, whose Members of Parliament refused, in 1919, to sit any longer at Westminster, and formed their own separate assembly in Dublin. The IRA (Irish Republican Army) was an anti-British paramilitary group set up in 1919 to end
British rule in Ireland. It opposed Churchill's 1921 Irish Treaty, and was later (in
1936) banned by De Valera's Government of Eire.
18. Cabinet minutes, 12 May 1919, Cabinet Papers, 24/91.

lic that would include Ulster. Three months before the treaty was signed Churchill warned that the extremists would be preparing war "at no distant date," a war in which Britain would be called to the aid of Ulster, "and in which the new republic would do their best to embroil their kith and kin in the United States."[19]

As well as Ireland, the Middle East also came within Churchill's sphere of ministerial responsibility at the Colonial Office. So shocked was he by the hostile reaction to British rule in both Palestine and Mesopotamia (now Iraq), where Arab protests had turned to violence, that he seized on a suggestion by Lloyd George that Britain's League of Nations' Mandates for both these countries should be transferred to the United States. He would announce this, Churchill told the Prime Minister, during the forthcoming Middle East debate in the House of Commons; but three days before the debate Lloyd George backed off. "Whatever may be the merits of offering either Mandate or both to the USA," he wrote to Churchill, "I am certain that a statement in this House of Commons, without previous reference to the American Government, is not the manner in which the subject should be broached."

The American Government, Lloyd George pointed out, "might very reasonably resent our making a proposal of such importance through the public Press." And if the United States were to refuse, Lloyd George warned, "a formidable agitation" might arise in Britain "to abandon such burdensome possessions."[20] Churchill could not go against the Prime Minister, and the United States lost the opportunity of taking charge of the administration and controlling the conflicts both in Jerusalem and Baghdad.

In the summer of 1921 Churchill's mother died, at the age of sixty-seven. She had fallen downstairs, breaking the bones above her left ankle. Gangrene set in, and the leg had to be amputated above the knee. Two weeks later, while recovering from the operation, she suffered a sudden hemorrhage. Summoned to his mother's bedside, Churchill found her unconscious and stayed with her until, without recovering consciousness, she died.

---

19. Speech of 24 September 1921, *The Times,* 26 September 1921.
20. Letter of 19 June 1921, Churchill Papers, Martin Gilbert, *Winston S. Churchill,* Volume 4, page 592.

Five days after his mother's death, Churchill had to attend a conference in London for the Dominion Prime Ministers. In a memorandum sent to them that day, he argued that there was a new potential enemy facing the world: Japan, whose naval and military strength was continually increasing. To forestall that danger he proposed an alliance "between the British Empire and the United States." Such an alliance, he was convinced, would be "overwhelmingly effective" in deterring Japan from making war on either British or American possessions.[21] A quarter of a century later he reflected: "as we had to choose between Japanese and American friendship I had no doubts what our course should be."[22] But his proposal for an alliance was rejected.

At a meeting of the Imperial Conference on 4 July 1921—the day of his memorandum on the danger from Japan—it was not Japan but Europe that was on the agenda, dominated by France's search for security. Churchill reminded the conference that France had given up its desire to build a strategic frontier along the Rhine in return for an Anglo-American guarantee of its existing frontier with Germany. "We said to her, if you give up the strategical position, England and America will be with you in the hour of need. Well, America did not make good."[23] The American renunciation of the League of Nations had been the cause.

Twenty-four years later, in November 1945, Churchill told a joint meeting of the Belgian Senate and Chamber of Deputies in Brussels that during the Second World War President Roosevelt had asked him what that war should be called. Churchill had replied, "The Unnecessary War," and went on to explain: "If the United States had taken an active part in the League of Nations, and if the League of Nations had been prepared to use concerted force, even had it only been European force, to prevent the re-armament of Germany, there was no need for further serious bloodshed."[24]

America's attitude to Britain's war debts also rankled with Churchill. He told an audience of five thousand in the Scottish city of

---

21. Memorandum of 4 July 1921, Churchill Papers, Martin Gilbert, *Winston S. Churchill*, Volume 4, pages 606–7.
22. Winston S. Churchill, *The Second World War*, Volume 3, page 516.
23. Meeting of 4 July 1921, Cabinet Papers.
24. Speech of 16 November 1945, Brussels, BBC Written Archives Centre.

Dundee that there were "mountains of gold" in the American vaults: "many of those bright sovereigns we used to see in by-gone days all safely packed away; piles of securities of all kinds gathered from Europe; ledgers showing the world her debtor." Yet there were as many unemployed in America as there were "in this poor old Britain of ours." Even in the United States there was "enormous and widespread" unemployment, often greater in degree and intensity than in Britain, and, Churchill noted, "provision for it was far less, and in many cases perfectly non-existent." And that, he said, was in the United States, "which had its vaults overflowing with the gold of Europe."[25]

---

25. Speech of 24 September 1921, *The Times,* 26 September 1921.

Chapter Eleven

"WE DO NOT WISH TO PUT OURSELVES IN THE POWER OF THE UNITED STATES"

In September 1922 Lloyd George's Government was defeated in the General Election. Churchill was out of the Cabinet and lost his seat in Parliament. While seeking a new parliamentary seat, and the return to active politics at the center, he wrote an article for *Nash's Pall Mall* magazine that, because of its remarkable prescience, was reprinted two weeks later in *The Nation* in the United States, and then printed in pamphlet form in New York and widely circulated. Entitled "Shall We All Commit Suicide?" it warned of a future world in which weapons would be far more devastating even than those of the recent war.

"Might not a bomb no bigger than an orange," Churchill asked, "be found to possess a secret power to destroy a whole block of buildings—nay to concentrate the force of a thousand tons of cordite and blast a township at a stroke?" Could not explosives, "even of the existing type be guided automatically in flying machines by wireless or other rays, without a human pilot, in ceaseless procession upon a hostile city, arsenal, campo or dockyard?" Nor was the world since November 1918 really at peace, but rather in a "period of Exhaustion which has been described as Peace."[1]

With the Conservative victory at the end of 1924, and his own re-election to Parliament, Churchill joined Stanley Baldwin's Conserva-

---

1. Winston S. Churchill, "Shall We All Commit Suicide?" *Nash's Pall Mall*, September 1924; *Nation*, 3 December 1924.

tive administration, accepting office as Chancellor of the Exchequer, responsible for Britain's finances. He also rejoined the Conservative Party, which he had left twenty years earlier. His first challenge came three weeks after entering the Treasury, when the United States put forward a claim for a share in German reparations payments.

The American claim was based on the cost incurred by the American army of occupation in Germany during 1919, and the material losses suffered by American nationals in Europe. One of Churchill's first decisions at the Treasury was to reject it. Although the amount of the American claim was unknown, if allowed, Churchill told his officials, it would reduce the sum available to those countries that had signed the Treaty of Versailles, including Britain.

Churchill had been advised by the Treasury lawyers that because the United States had not signed the Treaty of Versailles, legally it had no claim. "She cannot benefit under a Treaty whose obligations she has not assumed," Churchill wrote. "Moreover, the Treaty of Versailles gives the Reparation Commission a first charge on all the assets and revenues of Germany, and any subsequent agreement by Germany with America could only give a claim ranking after that first charge."

It was not on legal arguments alone that Churchill based his rejection of the American claim. All other countries that signed the Treaty of Versailles, he noted, had their claims to reparation valued by the Reparation Commission "and, in most cases, very considerably cut down." The United States had never put in a claim and had indeed disavowed any intention of claiming reparations. America had not had its new claim valued by the Reparation Commission "but by a private American-German Tribunal." Churchill wished to emphasize one more point. The Reparation Commission admitted claims only for damage done during the period when the claimant was a belligerent. The American claim was known to include claims for damage before the United States entered the war.

Churchill set out further causes of complaint against the United States on the reparations issue. The signatories of the Treaty of Versailles had been obliged to account to the Reparation Pool for the German assets they held. America was believed to have held about 300 million dollars of German private property, of which she had returned only some 20 to 30 million dollars to the owners. "In so far as she does not use this asset for prewar claims," Churchill wrote, "then she ought to make it available for the general Reparation Pool." Furthermore, when in 1920 the Allied countries received compensation for the tonnage lost in the war, the United States had retained the whole of the German tonnage seized in American ports: "about 164 per cent of her actual tonnage lost."

It could be argued, Churchill commented, that Britain should consider the American claim for reparations and recompense on the grounds of "international courtesy." If so, he commented wrily, Britain "must first be told to what figure it amounts in order that we may consider the price of our courtesy." But the United States could not make gains without undertaking responsibilities. "If Americans wish now to share in the benefits of the Treaty of Versailles," he concluded, "they ought, if not to undertake all the obligations of the Treaty, to at least have their claim valued in the same way as the Allies, setting off their assets against the claim, allowing the Reparation Commission to consider the basis of the claim, and accepting a method of payment that would ensure their ranking equally with the Allies both in benefits and responsibilities. None of this the American government was prepared to do."[2]

The conflict with the United States about reparations involved another issue with which Churchill had to deal from his first days at the Treasury: Britain's massive indebtedness to America for war purchases. Churchill proposed paying this debt to America in the same amount, and at the same time, as the money owed to Britain by the other Allies was repaid. Both debts were in the hundreds of millions of dollars. It would clearly be in Britain's interests, he wrote for the War Cabinet, as in the interests of all the other Allied countries, "to scale down these debts, reduce the interest, and if necessary defer the immediate annual instalments in order to strike a bargain." In making such a bargain, Britain should be bound to consider "what the United States have never considered, namely, shot and shell expended in the common cause."[3] The British burdens in the war, Churchill told the House

---

2. "American Claim to Reparation," Cabinet memorandum, 1 December 1924, Churchill Papers, Martin Gilbert, *Winston S. Churchill*, Volume 5, Companion (document) Volume, Part 1, pages 280–82.

3. Draft memorandum for the Cabinet, Churchill Papers, Martin Gilbert, *Winston S. Churchill*, Volume 5, Companion (document) Volume, Part 1, pages 282–84.

of Commons, "were not inferior to those borne by any other Allied nation."[4]

Churchill, who before the First World War had introduced the principle of independent arbitration into industrial disputes in Britain, sought a compromise. He would be willing to go to the forthcoming European Finance Ministers' conference in Paris, he told the Foreign Secretary, Austen Chamberlain, "on the basis that we do not accept the American view either in law or in equity but are willing to arbitrate." He went on to tell Chamberlain: "I do not contemplate a quarrel with the United States on this issue. I expect if we hold firm to receive some favourable definite proposition."

A central figure was Colonel James A. Logan, the American representative at the European Finance Ministers' conference. "Logan has made private approaches to me," Churchill explained to the Foreign Secretary, "through a relative of mine who was a friend of his in Washington." Since then Logan had adopted "a much more conciliatory tone" than the official American stance. As to Logan's motives, Churchill wrote: "My information is that he is disquieted at having drawn his Government into a position of some embarrassment on ground which is at least questionable and uncertain."

As the date of the conference approached, Churchill felt some trepidation, telling the Foreign Secretary he expected two or three days of disagreement "before things begin to clear and we begin to see where the possibilities of agreement lie." Meanwhile he did not despair, assuring Chamberlain that "we shall be in a very strong position, being quite independent and committed to no proposition which is not backed with massive arguments."[5]

In the first week of January 1925, as he prepared to leave for the Paris negotiations, Churchill was under pressure from both the Bank of England and the Prime Minister to return Britain to the Gold Standard. Uneasy about this, he argued persistently with his advisers. To one of them he set out an American-oriented argument. The United States,

---

4. *Hansard,* Parliamentary Debates, 11 December 1924.
5. Letter of 30 December 1924, Churchill Papers, Martin Gilbert, *Winston S. Churchill,* Volume 5, Companion (document) Volume, Part 1, pages 323–25.

he wrote, "has accumulated the greater part of the gold in the world and is suffering from a serious plethora. Are we sure that in trying to establish the gold standard we shall not be favouring American interests. Shall we not be making their hoard of gold more valuable than it is at present? Shall we not be relieving them from the consequences of their selfish and extortionate policy?"[6]

Churchill was overruled by both the Prime Minister and the Governor of the Bank of England, and the return to the Gold Standard went ahead. At the same time, in the negotiations with America over war debts, the same Prime Minister and Governor, as well as his Cabinet colleagues, looked to Churchill to obtain a beneficial agreement. He would try, he wrote in a private memorandum, to handle the matter so as "to avoid a painful or sharp dispute between the English-speaking representatives to the delectation of the European spectators." He expected Colonel Logan to make proposals for reducing the American claim "to much more moderate limits." As to the money owed to Britain by France, Britain's claim ought not to be affected by what the United States demanded from France, but, he warned, the Americans "are scarcely likely to err on the side of generosity."[7]

The Paris talks opened on 7 January 1925. Six wartime Allied Powers were present: France, Britain, Belgium, Italy, Japan and the United States. Churchill told his fellow Finance Ministers: "Hope flies on wings and international conferences plod afterwards along dusty roads."[8] After four days of continuous discussions he reported to Clementine: "I had a tremendous battle with the Yanks, & have beaten them down inch by inch to a reasonable figure. In the end we were fighting over tripe like £100,000! However, there was never any ill will, & I have now made quite a good arrangement with them."[9] The essence of that arrangement, he explained to the Cabinet after his return to London, "would probably enable us to secure from Europe a

---

6. Letter of 2 January 1925, Churchill Papers, Martin Gilbert, *Winston S. Churchill,* Volume 5, Companion (document) Volume, Part 1, page 329.
7. "Notes on the Paris Talks," 4 January 1925, Martin Gilbert, *Winston S. Churchill,* Volume 5, Companion (document) Volume, Part 1, pages 331–32.
8. Remarks, 7 January 1925, Treasury Papers, Treasury 188/6.
9. Letter of 10 January 1925, Baroness Spencer-Churchill Papers. In the monetary values of 2005, £100,000 was the equivalent of £3,500,000 ($7 million).

complete equivalent for our American payments."[10] Britain would actually reduce its claim against its Allies "to an amount necessary to cover their own payments in respect of the British war debt to the United States Government."[11]

Since the failure of the United States to join the League of Nations, Churchill had resented the extra burdens thrown on Britain for the defense of Europe. The League of Nations had asked all members to maintain "in all circumstances" the territorial integrity of all fellow members. "We do not feel justified," Churchill told the Committee of Imperial Defence, "in taking these great burdens upon the country in the absence of the United States." That was "at the bottom of everybody's mind and at the back of the arguments of every department."[12]

Amid these weighty issues, Churchill, a keen theatergoer, took time off to see an American play, *Lightnin'*, set in Nevada. "What a good play," he wrote to Clementine, "and what a life these Yankees lead! I have no doubt it is a very true picture."[13]

Those "Yankees" soon upset the British Foreign Office when they objected to Churchill's debt settlement with France, which, as he had anticipated, was more generous than the Americans intended their repayment plan for France to be. "I never had the slightest doubt of what the reception of the Anglo-French debt arrangement would be in the United States," he wrote to the Foreign Secretary, and went on to explain what he saw as the American state of mind. "Although sunk in selfishness in the present period," he wrote, "the American people have an extremely uncomfortable conscience, and when this conscience is being stirred, as it is now, they are naturally very resentful. I think you will find everything will calm down in a short time, and I am pretty sure that the secondary reaction will not be unfavourable."[14]

Churchill was right. In the first week of September, after speaking to Benjamin Strong, the Governor of the United States Federal Re-

10. "Inter-Allied Debts," Cabinet memorandum, 30 January 1925, Cabinet Paper No. 46, 1925.
11. "Inter-Allied Debts," Cabinet memorandum, 4 February 1925, Cabinet Paper No. 46 of 1925, Cabinet Papers, 24/171.
12. Committee of Imperial Defence Paper No. 559B, Cabinet Papers, 24/171.
13. Letter of 8 March 1925, Baroness Spencer-Churchill Papers.
14. Letter of 1 September 1925, Austen Chamberlain Papers.

serve Bank, he reported to Austen Chamberlain that he and Strong "had a long and very pleasant talk. He thinks we have acted very wisely in making a moderate settlement with France and he will use all his influence in America to procure a similarly reasonable solution." Nine days later, in a speech at Birmingham discussing "the general interests of the whole world," Churchill noted that "the United States, its fortunes and its policy, have become a dominant, and indeed, in some respects, a dominating influence" in the world.[15]

In preparing his budget for 1926, Churchill studied a possible increase in government revenue by taxing the profits of American films shown in Britain. It had been suggested to him, he wrote to one of his officials, that American films could be taxed much more effectively "if the tax was in proportion to the amount of money spent on the preparation of the film instead of on the length of the roll, etc." Churchill had read in a British newspaper that 25 million pounds a year were taken out of Britain as profit by American film producers. "It would naturally give great pleasure in this country," he wrote, "if any revenue could be derived from the profits of the American Film Producers and I should like to hear from you soon on both these matters."[16]

The taxation of American films became part of Churchill's second Budget. In his third Budget he imposed a tax on the importation of American tires. To avoid an influx of duty-free tires in the interval between the announcement of the tax and its imposition, he made the tax operative from the day of its announcement. The American Ambassador protested. Such a protest, Churchill wrote to Austen Chamberlain, "would appear merely to emphasise the rightness of the decision to make the duty immediately operative." Churchill added: "I am not surprised to learn that the American interests have been hit, as I heard just before the Budget that enormous consignments of American tyres were on their way to this country in the hope of escaping a possible duty."[17]

A more serious conflict arose between Churchill and the Americans in the spring of 1927 over the two countries' respective naval

---

15. Speech of 16 September 1925, *The Times*, 17 September 1925.
16. Letter of 16 February 1926, Churchill Papers, Martin Gilbert, *Winston S. Churchill*, Volume 5, Companion (document) Volume, Part 1, page 656.
17. Letter of 16 May 1927, Austen Chamberlain Papers.

strength. One Cabinet colleague noted in his diary that Churchill was "all out for defying the Yanks and saying that we will not allow anyone to build up a parity with us."[18] At a tripartite naval conference in Geneva, at which Britain, the United States and Japan were the participants, the American Government sought to extend the 1922 Washington Naval Treaty's limits on American, British, French, Italian and Japanese naval construction beyond the battleship class, to include cruisers. Churchill insisted, in a note for the Cabinet circulated on July 20 that Britain was "gravely endangering the foundation of British sea power and our security by entering into entangling engagements."

Churchill also warned his colleagues that "the Americans and their press will mar the workings of any such agreement by continued friction, together with reproaches that we are not acting fairly, that we are 'stealing a march,' 'pulling the wool over their eyes' &c—all of which, translated into endless technical complications, enables a fine case to be made out for local consumption."

Britain had seventy cruisers, America forty-seven. America sought parity—the right to build up to the British number. America already "indulges," Churchill pointed out to his Cabinet colleagues, "in a sensational cruiser programme." Numerical parity, he warned, "means British inferiority and potential subjugation." At the Geneva negotiations, Britain was becoming "deeply committed to the principle of absolute parity by treaty, although such a principle is fatal to British naval security."

Churchill's concerns about American naval expansion went beyond the naval aspect. "No doubt it is quite right in the interests of peace," he wrote, "to go on talking about war with the United States being 'unthinkable.' Everyone knows that this is not true. However foolish and disastrous such a war would be, it is in fact, the only basis upon which the Naval discussions at Geneva are proceeding." The truth of the matter, as Churchill saw it, was this: "We do not wish to put ourselves in the power of the United States. We cannot tell what they might do if at some future date they were in a position to give us orders about our policy, say, in India, or Egypt, or Canada, or on any other great matter behind which their electioneering forces were marshalled."

---

18. L. S. Amery diary, Amery Papers.

Parity in naval tonnage would mean that Britain could be "starved into obedience to any American decree." He neither trusted "America to command, nor England to submit." On the basis of American naval superiority, "speciously disguised as parity, immense dangers overhang the future of the world." Britain's "right to live" was at stake. Churchill saw a direct link between the American demands for naval parity with Britain and the forthcoming American presidential election, asking his Cabinet colleagues: "Who is most interested in producing something that can be hawked about the American platforms in 1928 as an English submission to American parity, i.e., supremacy? That is surely not our affair. Let us stick to the truth and to our needs." It might well be that the American Government "in their anxiety for some sort of an agreement will gradually conform to our view. We have certainly not lost anything by not immediately casting ourselves at their feet."

The only chance of a good naval agreement, Churchill told his Cabinet colleagues, was that the United States would accept "our considered and sober view." If they wanted an agreement, "let them pay the price for it in fair accommodation. They risk nothing, we risk everything. They are trying to buy the sovereignty of the seas by mere money power, and this has never been done in the history of the world. They do not even expect to have to cash the cheque."

It would be wrong, Churchill argued, for Britain to submit to superior force. The Americans were the world's steel master. "Therefore it is argued we had better give in now and come along quietly. But this takes altogether too narrow a view of the resources of the British Empire and of the sacrifices which an island people is prepared to make for vital objects. A poor man may pay for dear life what a rich man will not pay for mere prestige." Churchill then had harsh words for his mother's fellow countrymen. "They do not know much about shipbuilding," he wrote. "They do not know much about the sea. They do not like it. Naval competition would be a great evil, but it does not at all follow that over a long period of years we should emerge from it with inferior means of self-defence."

Churchill had raised the specter of American naval power, but he did not take it tragically. "I believe they would blow off steam in a few programmes of aggressive cruisers," he told his colleagues, "and that if we lay quiet and calm and studied scientific improvements we should find in a few years a strong reaction in the United States against unnecessary expenditure and a strong revival of Anglo-Japanese association. Anyhow, it is a very long business. Supreme Navies cannot be made with a stroke of a wand or the signing of a cheque. All sorts of intermediate processes come into operation, and at every stage there is room for negotiation and goodwill." He went on to insist that Britain not part with the essentials of its security to enable the United States "to gratify their prestige, or to protect them from the consequences of a wrong and imprudent policy." [19]

The American cruiser program was no immediate threat to Britain. As Churchill pointed out to his colleagues five days after his July 20 Cabinet memorandum: "There never has been any question of cruiser competition with the United States. They are hopelessly behind, having only twelve cruisers under sixteen years old." In addition the American navy had twenty-two prewar cruisers, some of which were thirty-four years old.[20] The Cabinet met on the following day. Supported by the Foreign Secretary, Churchill proposed a compromise whereby Britain and the United States could build a total cruiser and destroyer force of 590,000 tons each, and Japan 385,000. This proposal was rejected by the senior United States delegate and negotiations broke down.

The American cruiser-building program went ahead at an accelerated rate. But in a conciliatory response, Churchill proposed a halt to Britain's cruiser-building program, writing to the First Lord of the Admiralty: "We should give every opportunity for the Navy party in the United States to cool down; and if for a couple of programmes they build, say, six cruisers a year while we stand still, we shall perhaps have taken the most practical step to prevent a naval race developing. They will have put themselves in the worst position and us in a fairly good one." [21]

British cruiser construction continued, however, and by the end of 1927 Britain had sixteen warships with eight-inch guns, while the United States had only two, with a maximum of six more in prospect. Churchill noted for the Cabinet: "One can understand the irritation of the American Navalists at seeing what they consider to be the fruits of the Washington Conference in establishing parity in battlefleets, being entirely swept

19. "Cruisers and Parity," Cabinet memorandum, 20 July 1927, Cabinet Papers.
20. Cabinet memorandum, 25 July 1927, Cabinet Papers.
21. Letter of 18 August 1927, Baldwin Papers.

away by the large British new construction of the most powerful cruisers intended to be continued indefinitely year after year." [22]

An American Presidential election was in the offing. In a letter to the First Lord of the Admiralty, Churchill noted that President Calvin Coolidge and his administration were "evidently trying their best to go for a moderate programme in making up their large leeway." The renewed cutting back on Britain's part would give Coolidge "the best possible chance of deflecting American opinion from naval expansion to a sober and economical policy." [23]

Coolidge, whose health was failing, decided not to run for reelection. His replacement, fellow Republican Herbert Hoover, was successful. To Churchill's relief Hoover promised to follow the same "sober and economical" policy of his predecessor both in Britain's naval and economic interests.

While examining the details of his third Budget, Churchill discovered that it included the taxation of Americans who were temporarily resident in the United Kingdom. He was puzzled to find that this measure had been enacted, as he had earlier opposed it. "Two years ago," he wrote to his officials—on his fifty-third birthday—"I examined the question of the extension of taxation, i.e. Americans temporarily resident in this country. I expressed very strongly the view that it was to our interest to facilitate the use of this country for the temporary residence of wealthy Americans as it brought very substantial sums of money into the rural areas, especially in the sporting counties."

Churchill was worried that the new tax would induce "a considerable number of wealthy Americans, who used to spend very large sums of money at Melton Mowbray and elsewhere, to sell their horses and quit the country, while no doubt others again are being deterred from coming." [24] The tax was repealed. Foxhunting Americans could once more join the hunt for which Melton Mowbray was renowned, and spend without danger.

------

22. "Cruiser Programmes, 1927–1928," Cabinet memorandum, 6 November 1927, Cabinet Papers.

23. Letter of 28 November 1927, Baldwin Papers.

24. Departmental memorandum of 30 November 1927, Churchill Papers, Martin Gilbert, *Winston S. Churchill*, Volume 5, Companion (document) Volume, Part 1, pages 1119–20.

As the American Presidential campaign began in earnest, Churchill's wartime colleague Bernard Baruch sought his help on behalf of one of the Democratic challengers, Al Smith, the Governor of New York. Churchill reported to Clementine that when Baruch lunched with him, Churchill suggested his slogan for the Democratic Party: "Al for all, and all for Al." Baruch was so struck with this slogan, Churchill told Clementine, "that as he proceeded (very confidential) he told me that the Democratic Party believed that there was in existence a letter by Hoover, when in business in Burma many years ago, offering to take up British citizenship if he could get a certain important contract. This letter if produced at the right moment would of course be fatal to Hoover. Baruch seemed to want me to ferret this out for him, but I became unconscionably vague." Churchill would have nothing to do with what later became known as "dirty tricks."

"These American Presidential Elections," Churchill wrote to his wife, "are extraordinary games in which with the greatest zest and party bitterness the whole nation takes part, although there is no real difference between the parties except that of 'ins and outs.'"[25]

War debts were the cause of Churchill's ongoing distress in the autumn of 1928. The crisis came when the United States Agent General for Reparation, S. Parker Gilbert, a former Undersecretary of the Treasury, indicated that the United States would be willing to accept a change in the French system of payment of its war debt that went against the spirit of Churchill's negotiations of almost four years earlier. "We have suffered unequalled ill-usage," Churchill wrote to his senior officials, "having been committed to paying the American debt irrespective of reparations, having had to scale down to a fourth or a fifth of their values the debts due to us from France and Italy, and being now confronted with the repudiation by the French of the foundation of this scaling down." Parker Gilbert, he wrote, "is anxious to make a success of his work, and generally to show American generosity at British expense."[26]

A week after this angry reflection, Churchill was at Chartwell, his country home in Kent, twenty miles south of London. One of his week-

---

25. Letter of 10 August 1928, Baroness Spencer-Churchill Papers.
26. Letter of 14 September 1928, Churchill Papers, Martin Gilbert, *Winston S. Churchill,* Volume 5, Companion (document) Volume, Part 1, pages 1337–39.

end guests, James Scrymgeour-Wedderburn, who was soon to enter Parliament as a Conservative, wrote in his diary: "This evening Winston talked very freely about the USA. He thinks they are arrogant, fundamentally hostile to us, and that they wish to dominate world politics." Churchill talked to his young guest about the American war debt. "What I did not realise," he added, "was that we had actually paid £100,000,000 to America before we began to receive anything from Europe, and what Winston has secured is that we shall now be credited with these payments so that the future annual balance will be in our favour. This is good news and it was very interesting to hear it from the Chancellor of the Exchequer himself."[27]

The American intentions to ensure naval disarmament, while essentially allowing the American navy to build warships up to the British limit, continued to anger Churchill. "There is no doubt," he wrote to his advisers, "that the United States will seek at Washington in 1931 so to limit the British Navy as to make it quite certain that the Americans will be strategically superior." Once that condition had been established, "the centre of the British Empire will have been undermined." The disarmament discussions, Churchill warned, "have markedly impaired our relations with the United States."[28]

To lessen the conflict over naval construction, Churchill advocated "a period of silence and goodwill" rather than "a process of active and detailed negotiations." A discussion on the details of ships and guns, on the hypothesis "that such instrumentalities will be again invoked," he argued, "would be entirely out of harmony with the increasing confidence and intimacy now existing between the Great Powers, and particularly between Great Britain and the United States." In naval matters Britain's aim was "identical with that of the United States, namely that the two nations who have so much in common may be represented upon the waters of the world by what is truly and actually an equal naval strength and status."[29]

Churchill had harsh words, however, toward his mother's land. "Of

27. Diary entry, 21 September 1928, Earl of Dundee Papers.
28. Letter of 28 September 1928, Churchill Papers, Martin Gilbert, *Winston S. Churchill*, Volume 5, Companion (document) Volume, Part 1, pages 1348–49.
29. Cabinet memorandum, 30 September 1928, Churchill Papers, Martin Gilbert, *Winston S. Churchill*, Volume 5, Companion (document) Volume, Part 1, pages 1353–55.

course," he wrote to the Prime Minister, "it would be so much easier to 'give in' and follow along meekly in the wake of the new English-speaking authority. But I hope we shall try to keep the flag flying."[30]

At least some calm was in prospect in the reparations sphere. When Parker Gilbert visited London to discuss with Churchill the Anglo-American dispute over payments, he offered a conciliatory and satisfactory compromise. "Gilbert as usual was helpful and hopeful," Churchill told the Cabinet.[31]

In the American Presidential elections the Republicans retained their leadership. "So Hoover has swept the board," Churchill wrote to Clementine. "I feel this is not good for us," and he added, sadly, "Poor old England—she is being slowly but surely forced into the shade."[32]

As 1928 came to an end, Churchill worked at Chartwell on the volume of his war memoirs that included America's repudiation of the League of Nations eight years earlier. Before sending the chapters to the manager of *The Times,* who was arranging for extracts to be published in advance of publication, Churchill wrote: "There are some passages about the United States which are rather critical. If your selection should fall on these, I should have to ask that the counterbalancing passages of a complimentary and soothing nature should have publicity at the same time."[33] Churchill understood that Britain must not be separated from the country that had turned the tide of war in Britain's favor in 1918 and might well do so again.

---

30. Letter of 30 September 1928, Baldwin Papers.
31. Cabinet memorandum, 19 October 1928, Churchill Papers, Martin Gilbert, *Winston S. Churchill,* Volume 5, Companion (document) Volume, Part 1, pages 1360–63.
32. Letter of 7 November 1928, Baroness Spencer-Churchill Papers.
33. Letter of 27 December 1928, Archives of *The Times.*

Chapter Twelve

✠

"UNITED TO US BY THE CRIMSON THREAD OF FRIENDSHIP"

In May 1929 the Conservatives were defeated in the General Election and Churchill, while still a Member of Parliament, was out of political office. That summer he made plans to return to the United States, his first visit in almost three decades. His travel companions would be his son, Randolph, then aged eighteen; his brother, Jack; and Jack's son Johnny. "I want to see the country and to meet the leaders of its fortunes," he explained to Bernard Baruch. "I have no political mission and no axe to grind."[1] He did not want "too close an itinerary," he told Baruch. "One must have time to feel a country and nibble some of the grass."[2] To William Crocker, a leading California banker who had offered to be his host in San Francisco, Churchill wrote: "I am also most anxious to see the sea lions, of which I have heard for so many years. But please, no earthquakes!"[3]

The "Churchill Troupe," as Churchill called it, left England on 3 August 1929, on board the Canadian Pacific liner *Empress of Australia.* Reaching Quebec six days later, Churchill wrote to Charles Schwab, who had offered him the use of his private railway car from the Grand Canyon to Chicago: "It is twenty-nine years since I crossed the Atlantic so I daresay that there are a great many changes. Moreover, I have

---

1. Letter of 28 June 1929, Baruch Papers.
2. Letter of 7 July 1929, Baruch Papers.
3. Letter of 29 July 1929, Churchill Papers, Martin Gilbert, *Winston S. Churchill,* Volume 5, Companion (document) Volume, Part 2, page 31.

never been West of Winnipeg or Milwaukee, but have heard wonders of the Canadian and American Pacific shores."[4]

From Quebec the Churchills proceeded across Canada in a private railway car provided by Canadian Pacific. After traveling for a month across Canada they entered the United States, crossing by ferry from Vancouver to Seattle. Forewarned about the rigors of Prohibition, Randolph had hidden several flasks of whiskey and brandy in his luggage. At American customs, Churchill produced the troupe's collective diplomatic visa and a letter of introduction from the American Ambassador in London. This did not deter the customs officials, led by George D. Hubbard, the Collector of Customs, from making a thorough examination.[5]

"What are you looking for?" Churchill asked. "I have already told you that we have nothing to declare. The point of this letter from the Ambassador is to assure you of my integrity." The customs officials replied that they were looking for guns and ammunition. "Monstrous! Absolutely monstrous!" was Churchill's riposte. After their suitcases had been shut and locked, Johnny Churchill recalled that an "extraordinary change" came over the customs chief. "Mr Churchill," he said, "I apologize for this inconvenience. May I invite you and your party into my office for a drink?"[6] The Collector of Customs then drove the troupe to a hotel where, Churchill wrote to Clementine, "the local hotel proprietor entertained the whole party with delicious iced beer."[7]

At the quayside a young woman reporter had pressed for an interview. Asked to comment on Prohibition, Churchill, who had so recently been Chancellor of the Exchequer, replied by contrasting the British and American economies with regard to drink. "We realize one hundred million pounds a year from our liquor taxes," he said, "which amount, I understand, you give to your bootleggers."[8]

On the night of September 6 the Churchills set off southward. "We caught the night train," he wrote to Clementine, "travelling on this oc-

---

4. Letter of 10 August 1929 (from Quebec), Martin Gilbert, *Winston S. Churchill,* Volume 5, Companion (document) Volume, Part 2, pages 41–42.
5. George Hubbard's calling card is in the Churchill Papers at Churchill College, Cambridge (CHAR 1/209).
6. John Spencer Churchill, *A Churchill Canvas,* page 85.
7. Letter of 18 September 1929, Baroness Spencer-Churchill Papers.
8. *New York Times,* 8 September 1929.

casion like the ordinary public but quite comfortably and at 5 o'clock on Saturday got out at Grant's Pass." There, in the south of Oregon, the troupe was met by Gerald Campbell, the British Consul-General in San Francisco, with his large car, in which he was to take the troupe the rest of the journey by road. Churchill told Clementine: "We packed our light luggage into the motor car and set off on our six hundred mile journey."[9] During the first day the British Vice-Consul in San Francisco, Martin Watson, a twenty-four-year-old Oxford graduate, was contacted, and told that the Churchills were "complaining that there was not enough room in Campbell's enormous American car for five." To relieve the pressure on people and luggage, Watson borrowed a two-seater and drove north.

The Churchills' first night on that journey was spent at the Northern California oceanside town of Crescent City. On the second day Watson intercepted the Consul General's car at Eureka, a small port and naval base. "And so it came about," he recalled, "that I spent the greater part of two days with WSC sitting beside me and Randolph in the "rumble seat."[10]

From Eureka the Churchills continued their southward drive through the redwoods. "The greater part of it lay through the woods with these enormous trees," Churchill wrote to Clementine. "They are really astonishing. One we saw, the biggest, 380 foot high, three thousand or four thousand or even five thousand years old and it took fourteen of us to join our arms around its stem." The next night was spent at a small country hotel in Willits. "Everything very simple, very clean, gushing water and hot baths, no servants and no liquor," Churchill reported to Clementine. Fortunately Randolph's prudent supply of whiskey, acquired in Canada, had not run out.[11]

During this journey the Churchills encountered a new feature of travel in the United States. "Every dozen miles or so," Churchill wrote after his return, "rest camps—'motels' as they are called—have been built for the motorist population. Here simple and cheap accommodation is provided in clusters of detached cabins, and the carefree wan-

---

9. Letter of 18 September 1929, Martin Gilbert, *Winston S. Churchill*, Volume 5, Companion (document) Volume, Part 2, page 82.
10. Martin Watson, letter to the author, 30 September 1977.
11. Letter of 18 September 1929, Baroness Spencer-Churchill Papers.

derers on wheels gather round great fires, singing or listening to the ubiquitous wireless music."[12]

Late on the afternoon of September 9, having visited Georges de Latour's sacramental winery at Rutherford, the Churchills reached San Francisco. There they were the guests of the banker William Crocker, who lived in the southern suburb of Burlingame: "a rich man's suburb," Churchill called it in a letter to Clementine. Crocker had received them "most cordially in a lovely house and garden equipped with a splendid swimming pool" and given them "a considerable dinner party" on the night of their arrival. There was "a larger affair" at the Pacific Union Club in San Francisco the next evening.[13]

On September 11 Churchill was the guest of honor at a lunch in San Francisco given by Consul-General Campbell. Going after lunch to the headquarters of the Pacific Telephone and Telegraph Company, he was able to make a telephone call to Clementine, who was at Chartwell. "I take up the instrument," he later told readers of his American travel articles. "My wife speaks to me across one ocean and one continent—one of each. We hear each other as easily as if we were in the same room, or, not to exaggerate, say about half as well again as on an ordinary London telephone." Churchill added: "I picture a well-known scene far off in Kent, 7,000 miles away. The children come to the telephone. I talk to them through New York and Rugby. They reply through Scotland and Canada. Why say the age of miracles is past? It is just beginning."[14]

On their third evening at Burlingame, September 12, the Churchills drove sixty miles to the Lick Observatory, where they were entranced by views of Saturn, the Moon and the stars, returning late that night to Burlingame. The next morning they drove south again, to Pebble Beach on the Monterey Peninsula, where Richard M. Tobin, the American Minister to The Hague, had placed his sister Helen Russell's villa at their disposal. This was where Churchill hoped to see the famous seals, but none were in evidence that day. "The rocks were oc-

---

12. Winston Churchill, "Peter Pan Township of the Films," *Daily Telegraph*, 30 December 1929.

13. Letter of 25 September 1929, Martin Gilbert, *Winston S. Churchill*, Volume 5, Companion (document) Volume, Part 2, pages 93–96.

14. Winston Churchill, "Nature's Panorama in California," *Daily Telegraph*, 23 December 1929.

cupied only by large and dreary birds," he later wrote.[15] What Churchill did not write in his article was that he set up his easel at Pebble Beach and painted, a brief respite from the hectic pace of travel.[16]

On September 14, after another long day's motoring, the Churchills arrived late in the evening at William Randolph Hearst's ranch, San Simeon, which overlooked the Pacific. Hearst's life fascinated Churchill. "A vast income always overspent," he wrote to Clementine, "ceaseless building and collecting not very discriminatingly works of art: two magnificent establishments, two charming wives; complete indifference to public opinion, a strong liberal and democratic outlook, a 15 million daily circulation, oriental hospitalities, extreme personal courtesy (to us at any rate) and the appearance of a Quaker elder—or perhaps better Mormon elder."

The phrase "two charming wives" was a reference to Hearst's wife, Millicent, and his mistress, the film actress Marion Davies. "As the result of a week's intimacy," Churchill wrote to Clementine, "I like Hearst. He is a very serious sure spoken man and a trained politician of broad democratic and pacifist convictions. . . . His house is rudely described as Monte Carlo Casino on the top of the rock of Gibraltar—but it is better than this."[17] After the Churchills had been at San Simeon for four days, Hearst drove them to Los Angeles. "I thought five days of Hollywood would be a little too much," Churchill explained to Clementine, so he accepted William G. McAdoo's invitation to stay at Santa Barbara for two days.

McAdoo had been Woodrow Wilson's Secretary of the Treasury, and the Democratic candidate for the Presidency against Coolidge in 1924. McAdoo's wife was Wilson's daughter. "They have a delightful house here in the mountains overlooking the sea," Churchill wrote to Clementine. "They are in modest circumstances, but have extremely good taste. They opened up their country house especially for us for

---

15. Winston Churchill, "Peter Pan Township of the Films," *Daily Telegraph*, 30 December 1929.

16. A photograph of Churchill painting at Pebble Beach appears in Randolph S. Churchill and Helmut Gernsheim, *Churchill in Photographs*, Weidenfeld and Nicolson, plate 132.

17. Letter of 19 September 1929, Martin Gilbert, *Winston S. Churchill*, Volume 5, Companion (document) Volume, Part 2, pages 85–88.

two days or two weeks if we had the time—and then disappeared. So we are all alone. Tomorrow we return to Los Angeles."[18]

On September 18 the troupe drove from Santa Barbara to Hollywood, for a lunch in the Metro-Goldwyn-Mayer studios hosted by Louis B. Mayer and Hearst. As Churchill explained to Mrs. McAdoo: "The allurements of Hollywood have drawn us away."[19] The two hundred people at the lunch were mostly film stars and producers. They were entertained first by a chorus and then by a singer, after which there were speeches. At the end of his father's speech, Randolph noted in his diary, "A man proposing a vote of thanks said, 'I can only say that I would like to hear it again, and I dare say Mr Churchill could bear a little of it!' Whereupon through a hole in the roof came the speech again—absolutely perfect in tone and volume, and as clear as when he spoke himself!" The speech had been secretly recorded.

After Churchill's speech had been replayed, Randolph noted, "Papa, Hearst and Mayer had a talking film made of them. We then visited various studios and watched them "shoot the scenes."[20] That night Churchill returned to Santa Barbara, writing to William Van Antwerp, his American stockbroker, with his impressions of Hearst: "He seems very much set upon the idea of closer and more intimate relations between the English speaking peoples,—a cause, which, as you know, is very near my heart."[21]

On September 20 the Churchills were again entertained in Hollywood, lunching at the Montmartre Club with Hearst and Marion Davies. After lunch they visited several film studios before driving to Marion Davies's house. Writing to Clementine, Churchill gave an account of the two Hearst women: "I told you about Mrs Hearst (the official) and how agreeable she made herself. She is going to give me a dinner in New York and look after the boys on their way through." Mrs Hearst had been at San Simeon. At Los Angeles "we passed into the domain of Marion Davies; and were all charmed by her. She is not

18. Letter of 19 September 1929, Martin Gilbert, *Winston S. Churchill,* Volume 5, Companion (document) Volume, Part 2, pages 85–88.
19. Letter of 20 September 1929, William McAdoo Papers.
20. Randolph Churchill diary, 18 September 1929, Randolph Churchill, *Twenty-One Years,* pages 81–82.
21. Letter of 19 September 1929: Martin Gilbert, *Winston S. Churchill,* Volume 5, Companion (document) Volume, Part 2, pages 85–88.

strikingly beautiful nor impressive in any way. But her personality is most attractive; naive childlike, bon enfant. She works all day at her films and retires to her palace on the ocean to bathe and entertain in the evenings."

In his letter to Clementine, Churchill reported that Marion Davies had asked the troupe to use her house as if it were their own. "But we tasted its comforts and luxuries only sparingly," he explained, "spending two nights there after enormous dinner parties in our honour. We lunched frequently at her bungalow in the film works—a little Italian chapel sort of building very elegant where Hearst spends the day directing his newspapers on the telephone, and wrestling with his private Chancellor of the Exchequer—a harassed functionary who is constantly compelled to find money and threatens resignation daily."

After using Santa Barbara as their base, the Churchills moved to Los Angeles. Their hotel, the Biltmore, was "the last word in hotels," Churchill informed Clementine, but it cost them nothing. The suite, the services of a valet-waiter, the use of a motorcar, and "every kind of liquor" had been paid for by James R. Page, a "hearty banker." Los Angeles was a revelation to Churchill.[22] "The distances are enormous," he wrote in a newspaper article after his return. "You motor ten miles to luncheon in one direction and ten miles to dinner in another. The streets by night are ablaze with electric lights and moving signs of every colour. A carnival in fairyland."[23]

While in Los Angeles, Churchill wrote to Clementine, "I gave a dinner and a lunch to the leading men I like the best, mostly British born, and all keenly pro-England." These "Californian swells," he added, "do not of course know Hearst. He dwells apart. The first time they had ever come in contact with him or the film world was at the luncheon he gave to me. They regard him as the Devil. But when they heard him speak in friendly terms about England, they all said how right I had been to stay with him and praised the good work." The visit to Hearst, Consul-General Campbell wrote to Churchill, had pro-

---

22. Letter of 25 September 1929, Martin Gilbert, *Winston S. Churchill,* Volume 5, Companion (document) Volume, Part 2, pages 93–96.
23. Winston Churchill, "Peter Pan Township of the Films," *Daily Telegraph,* 30 December 1929.

duced "wonderful and immediate results amongst those who, up to recent times, have been antagonistic towards us and our interests."[24]

On September 22 the Churchills went on Hearst's yacht to Catalina Island, twenty-five miles off the coast. "We had only one hour there," Churchill wrote to Clementine. "People go for weeks and months without catching a swordfish—so they all said it was quite useless my going out in the fishing boat which had been provided—However I went out and of course I caught a monster in twenty minutes!"

Churchill also sent Clementine good news about his American stocks. "Since my last letter from Santa Barbara," he wrote, "I have made another £1,000 by speculating in a stock called Simmons."[25] Churchill explained: "It is a domestic furniture business. They say 'You can't go wrong on a Simmons mattress.' There is a stock exchange in every big hotel. You go and sit and watch the figures being marked up on slates every few minutes. Mr Van Antwerp advises me. He is a stockbroker in one of the leading firms. I think he is a very good man. This powerful firm watch my small interests like a cat and mouse."[26]

Van Antwerp was the head of a "far-reaching" stockbroking firm, Churchill wrote to Clementine, "a great friend of England and a reader of all my books—quite an old fashioned figure. He is going to look after some of my money for me. His firm has the best information about the American Market and I have opened an account with them in which I have placed £3,000. He will manipulate it with the best possible chances of success."[27]

On September 24 the Churchills lunched with Charlie Chaplin at the studio where he was making *City Lights*. Their three weeks in California were almost at an end. On the evening of September 26 they left Los Angeles by car, their first sightseeing stop being the Mariposa County Courthouse, the oldest functioning courthouse in California. Continuing on the three-hundred-mile journey from Los Angeles to

---

24. Letter of 30 September 1929, Martin Gilbert, *Winston S. Churchill*, Volume 5, page 349.

25. In the monetary values of 2005, Churchill had made a profit of £40,000/$80,000.

26. Letter of 25 September 1929, Martin Gilbert, *Winston S. Churchill*, Volume 5, Companion (document) Volume, Part 2, pages 93–96.

27. Letter of 29 September 1929, Baroness Spencer-Churchill Papers. In the monetary values of 2005, Churchill had invested £120,000/$240,000.

Yosemite, they were met by William Van Antwerp and his wife, who acted as their guides. From Yosemite they drove back south through California to a point on the railway line where Charles Schwab's private railway car awaited them.

"We are travelling across the Californian desert in Mr Schwab's car," Churchill wrote to Clementine on September 29, from Barstow, "and we have stopped for two hours at this oasis. We have left the train for a bath in the hotel." The hotel was a well-known haven, Fred Harvey's Casa de Desierto. From Barstow the train made its way to the South Rim of the Grand Canyon, where the Churchills spent twenty-four hours. "This is a mile deep," Churchill wrote to Clementine on a postcard of the Grand Canyon, "& the colours scarcely exaggerated."[28]

From the Grand Canyon the train embarked on its 1,800-mile journey to Chicago. During the journey, as Churchill wrote to his Los Angeles host, William McAdoo, "I enjoyed enormously 'Meet General Grant' which I read in the train."[29] The troupe reached Chicago on the morning of October 2. Bernard Baruch was at the station to meet them and take them to the Drake Hotel. Two days later Churchill spoke at the Commercial Club, stressing the need for a final naval agreement between Britain and the United States. If both fleets were ever used, he said, it would be together, "for the preservation of peace." But Americans must appreciate that Britain, "whose life and daily bread have always depended on the sea," would have to be cautious about binding itself "to limits of naval strength."[30]

While in Chicago, Churchill visited the stockyards. Twenty years later, having just seen photographs of Belsen concentration camp, he commented, in an imaginary conversation with his father about the Nazis: "They made human slaughter-pens like the Chicago stockyards."[31] He had not forgotten his visit to that grim scene.

Leaving Chicago on October 5 by overnight train for New York, the Churchills traveled with Bernard Baruch in his private railway car.

---

28. Undated postcard, unsent, Churchill Papers, Churchill College, Cambridge (CHAR 1/209).

29. Letter of 23 October 1929 (from New York), William McAdoo Papers. W. E. Woodward's *Meet General Grant* had been published in New York in 1928.

30. Speech of 4 October 1929, *Chicago Tribune*, 5 October 1929.

31. Winston S. Churchill, "The Dream," November 1947, first published in the *Sunday Telegraph*, 31 January 1966.

In New York they stayed at the Savoy-Plaza Hotel (now the Plaza) on Fifth Avenue and Fifty-ninth Street, as Baruch's guests. On October 8 the British Consul-General in New York, Godfrey Haggard, reported to the British Foreign Office about a speech Churchill gave at the Bond Club that evening, that those passages "which referred to the naval question, the United States of Europe etc, though delivered with weight and emphasis, were carefully limited and were read out to his audience. He gained his hearers' interest by describing himself as 'pro-British' and his remarks were listened to as a statement of the British point of view."[32]

One of the Americans present wrote to Churchill of the "profound impression" the Bond Club speech had made on him, adding: "I have been told by many members of the Club that they considered it the most interesting meeting we have ever held."[33] For his talk at the Bond Club, Churchill was paid an astonishing $12,500 by the sponsor of the dinner, the British industrialist Sir Harry McGowan.[34] Such a talk, wrote McGowan's American partner, in sending him the check, "can only further a great relationship between your Country and ours."[35]

On October 9 Randolph and Johnny sailed from New York for Britain. Churchill stayed on with his brother, Jack, working in Baruch's downtown office on the many articles he was committed to write for newspapers and magazines in both Britain and the United States. He had contracted to write twenty-two magazine articles, "all involving heavy work on return," he telegraphed to Clementine.[36] The work was indeed to be heavy, but the remuneration made him the highest-paid journalist of the day in either Britain or the United States, for these twenty-two articles were to earn him an astonishing £40,000.[37]

On the evening of October 18 Churchill was the guest of honor at

---

32. Letter of 8 October 1929, Foreign Office Papers.
33. Letter, undated, from Pierpont V. Davis, President of the National City Company, Churchill Papers, Churchill College, Cambridge (CHAR 1/208).
34. In the monetary values of 2005, $12,500 was the equivalent of $130,000/£65,000.
35. Letter from Norman K. Toerge, of 15 Broad Street, Churchill Papers, Churchill College, Cambridge (CHAR 1/208).
36. Telegram of 18 October 1929, Baroness Spencer-Churchill Papers.
37. The equivalent in the monetary values of 2005 of £1,500,000/$3 million. For each article Churchill was paid almost £80,000/$160,000.

a dinner and dance given by Millicent Hearst at her mansion on River-side Drive. During the evening, reported the *New York Times,* "a specially arranged motion picture was shown, its various flashes depicting some of the guests at important events in the past."[38] Those guests included William H. Hays, who, two years earlier, as head of the American motion picture industry's trade association, had been the leading public opponent of the taxes imposed by Churchill on imported American films.

That night, just after midnight, Churchill boarded a private Pennsylvania Railroad car attached to the night train from New York to Washington, which he reached on the morning of October 19. He then went to the White House to meet President Hoover before continuing in his private railway car to Richmond, Virginia. From there he visited some of the Civil War battlefields in Virginia. He was "astonished," he wrote in an article on his return for the *Daily Telegraph,* "by the many traces of the fighting which still remained, more than seventy years after the Civil War." At Spotsylvania his guide was an old man who, as a child, had passed over the battlefield strewn with dead.

Churchill recalled having traveled "from noon till night, with guides excelling in every detail of military history," in a semicircle around Richmond, from Beaver Dam Creek to Gaines' Mill, to Chickahominy, to Savage Station to White Oak Swamp to Malvern Hill to Harrison's Landing on the James River. "The farm-houses and the churches still show the scars of shot and shell," he wrote, "the woods are full of trenches and rifle pits; the larger trees are full of bullets. Before the War Museum in Richmond still flies a tattered rebel flag. If you could read men's hearts, you would find that they, too, bear the marks." No one could understand what happened in the Civil War, he believed, "merely through reading books and studying maps. You must see the ground; you must cover the distances in person; you must measure the rivers and see what the swamps were really like."[39]

From Richmond, Churchill drove sixty miles to Fredericksburg, where he again spent a whole day visiting the battlefields. "Admirable

---

38. *New York Times,* 19 October 1929.
39. Winston Churchill. "Old Battlefields of Virginia," *Daily Telegraph,* 16 December 1929.

descriptive plates," he wrote, "erected at the cost of Virginia, and in-scribed by deeply instructed hands, fix almost every historical point." He saw the stone wall and sunken road at Fredericksburg, the Union and Confederate cemeteries, and "the trench lines trailing away through deserted forests," all of which, he added, "revive the past with a strange potency."

Crossing the Rappahannock River, Churchill visited a battlefield "on which, perhaps, more soldiers have perished in an equal space than anywhere, excepting round Ypres and Verdun."

Churchill had hoped to meet the Governor of New York State, Franklin Roosevelt, when he returned to New York. But Henry Mor-genthau Jr., whom Roosevelt had just appointed Chairman of the New York State Agricultural Advisory Commission, wrote to Churchill en-closing a letter from Roosevelt, "which shows that unfortunately he will not be in New York on October 28th or 29th." [40]

Churchill's return to New York coincided with Black Thursday, the sudden collapse of the New York stock market. That night Churchill dined with Bernard Baruch on Fifth Avenue. "He had gathered around his table," Churchill later wrote, "forty or more of the leading bankers and financiers of New York, and I remember that when one of them proposed my health he addressed the company as 'Friends and former millionaires.'"

Churchill himself was deeply involved in the American stock mar-ket and suffered severe financial loss. But the payments he received for the articles he had contracted to write for such a high remuneration more than covered his losses.

On the day after the Crash, Churchill witnessed its consequences at first hand. "Under my window," he later wrote, "a gentleman cast himself down fifteen storeys and was dashed to pieces, causing a wild commotion and the arrival of the fire brigade." Churchill also told his readers: "I happened to be walking down Wall Street at the worst mo-ment of the panic, and a perfect stranger who recognised me invited me to enter the gallery of the Stock Exchange. I expected to see pan-

---

40. Letter of 23 October 1929, Martin Gilbert, *Winston S. Churchill*, Volume 5, Companion (document) Volume, Part 2, page 106.

demonium; but the spectacle that met my eyes was one of surprising calm and orderliness."

The 1,200 members of the New York Stock Exchange were precluded, Churchill wrote, "by the strongest rules from running or raising their voices unduly. So there they were, walking to and fro like a slow-motion picture of a disturbed ant heap, offering each other enormous blocks of securities at a third of their old prices and half their present value, and for many minutes together finding no one strong enough to pick up the sure fortunes they were compelled to offer."

From a window high up in the Stock Exchange building, Churchill looked out over the city. "Below lay the Hudson and the North Rivers," he wrote, "dotted with numerous tugs and shipping of all kinds, and traversed by the ocean steamers from all over the world moving in and out of the endless rows of docks. Beyond lay all the cities and workshops of the New Jersey shore, pouring out their clouds of smoke and steam. Around towered the mighty buildings of New York, with here and there glimpses far below of streets swarming with human life." No one who "gazed on such a scene," Churchill reflected, "could doubt that this financial disaster, huge as it is, cruel as it is to thousands, is only a passing episode in the march of a valiant and serviceable people who by fierce experiment are hewing new paths for man, and showing to all nations much that they should attempt and much that they should avoid."[41]

On October 30 Churchill sailed for Britain. He had seen the United States at its most magnificent and its most tormented.

---

41. Winston Churchill, "Fever of Speculation in America," *Daily Telegraph,* 9 December 1929. The rivers were in fact the Hudson and the *East* rivers. It was the Hudson that was also known as the North River.

Chapter Thirteen

⌖

BETWEEN TWO VISITS

Shortly after his return to Britain from the United States, Churchill celebrated his fifty-fifth birthday. Even on board ship he had worked on the articles he had agreed to write. Having lost almost all his substantial American investments during the Crash, he needed urgently to recoup his losses. Within two weeks of his return in November 1929, the *Daily Telegraph* began publication of twelve weekly articles on his Canadian and American experiences.

In each article Churchill revealed his sense of wonderment at America's achievements, and confidence in its powers of growth and prosperity. He also noted that with the creation of the Irish Free State in 1922, the "slow virulent poison distilled against Great Britain for more than a century has suddenly exhausted itself." Ireland was no longer an obstacle to Anglo-American friendship. During King George V's recent illness, "Genuine sympathy and anxiety were felt. Churches and chapels sent up their prayers."[1]

Churchill had also come to an arrangement to write six articles each for two American weekly magazines, six for *Collier's* and six for the *Saturday Evening Post*. In a telegram to his American literary agent, Edwin G. Rich, he outlined in telegraphese the contents of his first article. It would include "harmonies of American industry," focusing on the "mass production of standardised articles of, by and for the people under capitalist guidance spurred by speculative enhancement values not far off success," The Wall Street Crash would be portrayed as "an intense, audacious effort" to stimulate consuming power "and reach

---

1. Winston Churchill, "What I Saw and Heard in America," *Daily Telegraph*, 18 November 1929.

higher plane economic organisation now perhaps not far beyond fingertips."[2]

On reaching Britain from the United States, Churchill had learned of a Conservative Party leadership agreement—concluded the day after his ship left New York—to support the Labour Government's policy of self-government for India. Churchill, who despite his senior status in the Party had not been consulted, was convinced that the plan for self-government would create serious divisions within India, including—as came to pass—intense violence between Hindus and Muslims.

Challenging the Conservative Party leaders whose Cabinet colleague he had so recently been, Churchill gathered more than fifty supporters from the Conservative ranks in the House of Commons. During one of the India debates he clashed with the American-born Nancy Astor, who had been elected to the British Parliament as a Conservative just after the First World War. Churchill often bore the brunt of her sharp tongue, although he could have a sharp tongue of his own. It was Nancy Astor who was said to have told Churchill: "If you were my husband I would put poison in your coffee," to which he replied, "If you were my wife I would drink it."

During a debate on India, while the Conservative leader Stanley Baldwin was telling the House of Commons "I have been told that I have surrendered to my right hon. Friend the member for Epping . . ."—Churchill was the Member of Parliament for Epping—Nancy Astor called out: "God forbid! Never!" After the debate Churchill spoke angrily to her in the lobby of the House of Commons. She was spurred to protest. "As a personal friend of yours and Clemms," she wrote, "however much I may differ from you on certain political questions, I do feel that you break the ordinary decencies and relationships of public life when you drag in personalities. You hardly ever have a difference with me without calling me a Yankee (your mother was a Yankee—I am a Virginian) or asking me to get back to Virginia and leave British politics—or refer to our owning a paper."

Nancy Astor added: "No one is prouder of their Virginian birth than I am. As for my political life—dim tho it is—I would not change it for yours. But what I feel is, you would not dare use this kind of abuse

---

2. Telegram of 12 March 1930, Churchill Papers, Martin Gilbert, _Winston S. Churchill_, Volume 5, Companion (document) Volume, Part 2, pages 143–44.

(or what you mean for abuse) either to John or Waldorf. I don't think it cricket that because I am a woman you should use it to me." She hated having to fight back on grounds of Churchill's choosing, "so if our friendship is to continue could you treat me as fairly as you would a man?"[3]

"John" was John Jacob Astor, the Chief Proprietor of *The Times*. "Waldorf" was John Jacob's brother, proprietor of the weekly *Observer*, who had married Nancy Astor in 1906. Churchill replied to her rebuke: "I am sorry if I offended your Virginian sentiments. You provoked me dreadfully and I had a very bad sore throat. We really must not have these altercations in the lobby, and I shall take particular care to avoid them in the future." Churchill added: "I don't think you realise how keenly some of us who cannot take your detached views feel about our affairs, nor how wounded some of us are by the things you say. However, I certainly ought not to have lost my temper. I will not run the risk again."[4]

In the summer of 1930 Churchill found himself in a serious political disagreement with the United States. The issue was the treaty, signed after a naval conference in London, whereby Britain, the United States and Japan agreed on a maximum tonnage for cruisers, submarines and destroyers, and a ratio of 15:15:9 in capital ships. Under this ratio Britain would not be able to replace its older battleships when they fell below the required standard of efficiency and power.

In the House of Commons, Churchill criticized the treaty as "a formal acceptance by Great Britain of definite inferior sea power." Under it, he warned, "We are no longer to have a Navy equal even for purposes of battle—I say nothing of trade protection—to the other leading Navy in the world." Two days after making his parliamentary protest at Britain having accepted what was in effect a position of inferiority to the United States, Churchill wrote to Baldwin that the treaty "means that we accept in a solemn international instrument the position of second Power at sea." Even that, Churchill believed, would not

---

3. Letter of 13 March 1931, Churchill Papers, Martin Gilbert, *Winston S. Churchill*, Volume 5, Companion (document) Volume, Part 2, pages 300–301.

4. Letter of March 1931, Churchill Papers, Martin Gilbert, *Winston S. Churchill*, Volume 5, Companion (document) Volume, Part 2, page 301.

"end the naval controversies between Great Britain and the United States; it merely gives the United States an almost limitless right to criticise and interfere in our vital affairs."

Churchill had always been concerned about Britain losing naval superiority to the United States. "In my view the right course to adopt now is to reject the Treaty," he told Baldwin, "to revert to a state of complete freedom between Great Britain and the United States in naval building, to declare that we wish not to be influenced at all by what they do." The standard to be adopted must be related "to our own needs and actual dangers, which we are entirely free to build up to in any form of craft as we may think fit."[5]

Churchill was wary of the undue influence of the United States. In criticism of his friend Lord Beaverbrook's attempt to create a system of Empire tariffs, he told a fellow Member of Parliament that among its dangers was that "it will hand over South America to the Yanks."[6] Churchill also still resented the United States attitude to the Inter-Allied debt settlement he had negotiated five years earlier, but which had subsequently been renegotiated to Britain's detriment. In a talk at the German Embassy with the diplomat Prince Bismarck—a grandson of the "Iron Chancellor"—he was outspoken in his criticism, as reported by the Prince to Berlin. In the course of conversation, the Prince told his superiors, "Churchill turned to the reparations question and greatly regretted that no one had adopted his suggestion, made after the war, that the debtor and creditor nations, including Germany, should unite to form a common front against America." This opportunity, Churchill told the Prince, "had now gone for ever and he did not believe that America, in her present state, would ever grant Britain any remission."[7]

Among the topics on which Churchill asked the BBC to let him broadcast during 1930 was the need for "American rationalisation of British industry."[8] He was confident that the United States would recover

---

5. Letter of 17 May 1930, Lord Baldwin Papers.
6. Harold Nicolson diary, 6 July 1930, Sir Harold Nicolson Papers.
7. Report of 20 October 1930, German Foreign Office Documents.
8. Letter of 14 January 1930, Martin Gilbert, *Winston S. Churchill*, Volume 5, Companion (document) Volume, Part 2, page 134.

from the economic Depression. As he wrote to Bernard Baruch that summer: "There is not much "oh! Boy" about the markets lately, but my faith in the progress of the United States is unshakeable."[9]

That summer, Churchill entertained Baruch at Chartwell: "Never have I had such a week," Baruch wrote in thanks.[10] Phyllis Moir, who was shortly to become Churchill's secretary, later wrote: "There is in Mr Churchill just as much of Jerome, the American, as of the Churchill. Unlike most Englishmen, he is naturally at ease among Americans, who seem to understand him better than his own countrymen. Americans who have spent the weekend at Churchill's country home at Westerham are always astonished and touched by the warmth of his welcome and by the pains he takes to make their visit a memorable one."[11]

In Germany, Hitler and his Nazi Party were making considerable gains in the national and local elections. Fear of a dramatic rise in German extremism created international hostility to a proposed Customs Union between Germany and Austria. Churchill took a different view, writing in the *New York American* of the importance of a success in German foreign policy to bolster the democratic Weimar Government in Germany: "An assertion of reviving power," he wrote, "will bring to the constitutional, and at present peaceful German forces, a prestige which will rob the much more dangerous Hitler movement of its mainspring." Churchill went on to ask: "Will not the mastery of Hitlerism by constitutional forces in Germany be a real factor in the immediate peace of Europe?"[12]

From the beginning of 1931, Churchill made plans to return to the United States, not for pleasure as in 1929, but for profit. To this end, he contacted the American lecture agent Louis J. Alber, head of the Affiliated Lecture and Concert Association, of Cleveland, Ohio, who had been organizing lecture tours for three decades, most recently for Randolph, who, while still a university student at Oxford, was in the

---

9. Letter of 27 June 1930, Martin Gilbert, *Winston S. Churchill*, Volume 5, Companion (document) Volume, Part 2, pages 167–68.

10. Letter of 13 August 1930, Martin Gilbert, *Winston S. Churchill*, Volume 5, Companion (document) Volume, Part 2, pages 176–77.

11. Phyllis Moir, *I Was Winston Churchill's Private Secretary*, page 70.

12. *New York American*, 5 April 1931.

United States speaking from coast to coast about world affairs and an Englishman's impressions of the United States.

While Randolph was still lecturing in America, his father broke finally with the Conservative Party over India and was excluded from the Shadow Cabinet. "I am so thrilled at your stand on India," Randolph wrote from California, adding that the *New York Herald Tribune* had "a good two-column account of your departure from the Shadow Cabinet."[13]

Planning for his own forthcoming visit, Churchill contracted to give forty lectures, on the state of the world, and Anglo-American relations, for a total guaranteed minimum fee of £10,000.[14] In addition, as a result of an arrangement negotiated by his friend Brendan Bracken, the *Daily Mail* was paying almost as much money for a series of articles whose further sale in the United States he was free to negotiate. As Churchill made plans for a journey dictated by money rather than sentiment, Bracken wrote to him: "As you are going on this hateful American journey you will have time to dictate a number of articles on American and other topics which will give you but little labour and will swell your income."[15]

"I have practically closed with Alber for lectures in October and November," Churchill reported to Randolph at the beginning of 1931. "He wrote very nicely about you and seemed pleased with your work."[16] Father would follow in son's footsteps.

---

13. Letter of 3 February 1931, Randolph Churchill Papers.
14. Just under £400,000/$800,000 in the monetary values of 2005.
15. Letter of 22 August 1931, Churchill Papers, Martin Gilbert, *Winston S. Churchill*, Volume 5, Companion (document) Volume, Part 2, page 350.
16. Letter of 8 January 1931, Randolph Churchill Papers.

Chapter Fourteen

✠

"THERE'S NO BALONEY
ABOUT HIM AT ALL"

Churchill, his wife, Clementine—on her first visit to the United States—their twenty-two-year-old daughter, Diana, and Detective Sergeant Walter Thompson, Churchill's bodyguard, sailed from Britain on 5 December 1931. Thompson, who had first guarded Churchill during the "troubles" in Ireland in 1922, was there to protect him from a San Francisco–based terrorist group, consisting mostly of Sikhs who favored an independent Sikh nation in India. This group had been founded in California twenty years earlier. In 1917 the American government had imprisoned many of its leaders, who were then in contact with German officials in the United States.

Reaching New York on December 11, Churchill was besieged by journalists and photographers who had gone on board with the pilot and quarantine officials, determined to intercept him. The *New York Times* reported that "his eyes twinkled" as he sat smoking a cigar and talking to the journalists.[1] From the customs and immigration shed the three Churchills and the detective were driven to the Waldorf-Astoria Hotel, where they left their luggage before being driven straight to Grand Central Station for the five-hour train journey to Worcester, Massachusetts.

That evening, at Worcester, Churchill delivered his first lecture, in which he urged the closest possible Anglo-American cooperation, later writing to his son: "It certainly went extremely well. The people were

----

1. *New York Times,* 12 December 1931.

almost reverential in their attitude."[2] On December 13 he was back in New York, staying in Suite 39A in the Tower of the Waldorf-Astoria. That evening, after dining in the hotel with his wife and daughter, he received a telephone call from Bernard Baruch, inviting him to meet, that same evening, a few mutual friends who had gathered at Baruch's house on Fifth Avenue. Churchill, despite having finished dinner and being, he later recalled, "inclined to go to bed," agreed.[3] Descending by elevator the thirty-five stories from his apartment to the ground floor, he took a taxi from the Waldorf-Astoria, asking the driver to take him up Fifth Avenue.

Churchill had forgotten to take his address book with him, neither did he take his bodyguard, despite the latter's protestations. He had been to Baruch's apartment two years earlier, and although he could not remember the number, he felt certain he would recognize the house. He was unable to do so. There followed a prolonged, frustrating search, and Churchill grew increasingly impatient at the repeated stops for traffic lights. He had not traveled on streets with traffic lights before; they were not introduced in London until later that year.

After riding up and down Fifth Avenue for nearly an hour, after what should have been a ten- or fifteen-minute journey, Churchill asked the driver to stop on the Central Park side of the avenue and to wait for him while he crossed the street to the building opposite, which he hoped was Baruch's building. Getting out of the taxi in the middle of the street, he looked left instead of right, forgetting that American cars drove on the opposite side to British. Looking left, he saw the headlights of an approaching car more than two hundred yards away, and, feeling quite safe, made for the sidewalk. Suddenly, from the right, he was struck by an oncoming car and thrown to the ground.

The thought flashed through Churchill's mind: "Perhaps it is the end."

A passerby cried out: "A man has been killed!"[4]

The blow was a serious one, to Churchill's forehead and his thighs. The car had been traveling at between thirty and thirty-five miles an

---

2. Letter of 7 February 1932, Randolph Churchill Papers.
3. Winston S. Churchill, "My New York Misadventure," *Daily Mail,* 4 January 1932.
4. Winston S. Churchill, "I Was Conscious Through It All," *Daily Mail,* 5 January 1932.

hour. "I do not understand," Churchill wrote while still in the hospital, "why I was not broken like an egg-shell or squashed like a gooseberry."[5] A crowd gathered at the scene. Although in great pain, Churchill remained conscious. When a policeman pressed him for details of the accident, he insisted that it was entirely his own fault, not that of the driver.

An ambulance was seen hurrying along the street and was stopped by the crowd, who urged its crew to take Churchill to the nearest hospital. The ambulance, which already had a serious case on board, drove on. A passing taxi was hailed and took Churchill to Lenox Hill Hospital. As his wounds were being dressed, Clementine and Baruch arrived. His first question was to ask Baruch his address. It emerged that Churchill had crossed Fifth Avenue and been struck down ten blocks from where he should have been.

Clementine remained at her husband's bedside, telegraphing to Randolph on the morning of December 15 with a summary of his father's condition: "Temperature 100.6. Pulse normal. Head scalp wound severe. Two cracked ribs. Simple slight pleural irritation of right side. Generally much bruised. Progress satisfactory." Within twenty-four hours Churchill received several hundred telegrams and letters of sympathy from friends and strangers.

Among the visitors to the hospital was Mario Contasino, the driver of the car that had laid Churchill low. A mechanic and truck driver by profession, Contasino had been driving for more than eight years without an accident. At the time of the accident he had been out of work for two months. His mother having died, he needed to support his father and two sisters. Told that Contasino had been coming daily to the hospital, Churchill asked to see him. According to the *New York Times*, he was "deeply concerned lest the driver's part in the accident might hinder him in getting work."

For more than half an hour Churchill and Clementine questioned Mario Contasino about his life. Clementine offered to help financially, but when a check was produced he declined to take it. Churchill then asked for a copy of his most recent First World War volume, *The Unknown War,* signed it, and gave it to Contasino as a gift.[6]

---

5. Winston S. Churchill, "My New York Misadventure," *Daily Mail,* 4 January 1932.
6. "Churchill Greets Driver Who Hit Him," *New York Times,* 21 December 1931.

While Churchill was in the hospital, James S. McCulloh, President of the New York Telephone Company, provided him with what Churchill described in his thank-you letter as "very large facilities" to telegraph inside the United States and to Britain: "the princely courtesy which I have greatly valued and trust have not used in excess."[7]

On December 21, eight days after his admission to hospital, Churchill was well enough to return to the hotel, but he had to remain in bed for two more weeks. He was determined to get back on the lecture circuit; he needed the money badly if he were to begin to restore his finances, but he was in no condition to start soon.

Two days after leaving hospital, Churchill felt strong enough to dictate replies to some of the telegrams he had received. On the third day, having been offered a handsome fee, he telegraphed an account of the accident to the *Daily Mail:* "I certainly suffered every pang, mental and physical, that a street accident or, I suppose, a shell wound can produce," he wrote. "None is unendurable. There is neither the time nor the strength for self-pity. There is no room for remorse or fears. If at any moment in this long series of sensations a grey veil deepening into blackness had descended upon the sanctum I should have felt or feared nothing additional." Churchill added: "Nature is merciful and does not try her children, man or beast, beyond their compass. It is only where the cruelty of man intervenes that hellish torments appear. For the rest—live dangerously; take things as they come; dread naught, all will be well."[8]

Before resuming the lecture tour, Churchill decided to recuperate in the Bahamas with Clementine and Diana. Proudly he informed Randolph that all the lectures for January, February, and March were sold out. On his last full day in New York, December 30, he wrote to an American economist friend, the Egyptian-born securities and exchange expert René Leon, that he hoped to take up his lecturing again on January 12, "and shall certainly go forward with them as long as I have life and strength."[9] Also on December 30 Churchill gave a

7. Letter of 23 December 1931, Churchill Papers, Churchill College, Cambridge (CHAR 1/399B).
8. Winston S. Churchill, "I Was Conscious Through It All," *Daily Mail,* 5 January 1932.
9. Letter of 30 December 1931, Churchill Papers, Churchill College, Cambridge (CHAR 1/399B).

Press Conference in his hotel suite. The *New York Times* found him "pale, nervous and shaky after his ordeal." Churchill told the journalist he was convinced that the United States "had it in its power today to enter a period of prosperity for itself first, and for the rest of the world later."[10]

On December 31 Churchill, Clementine and Diana sailed from New York to the Bahamas. They were to have returned to New York in mid-January, but as Churchill was still weak from his accident, he prolonged his stay in the Caribbean and postponed his American lectures accordingly. On 15 January 1932 the *New York Times* reported "that he is still unable to raise his hands above the level of his elbows."[11] He remained in the Bahamas for three weeks. "I think the sunshine and the bathing are doing him good, but of course what is really needed is 3 or 4 months complete relaxation," Clementine wrote to Randolph, and she added: "Papa is worried about the Lectures and thinks he will not be able to stay the course. . . . I hope however that they may actually help his recovery, especially if he starts off with a big success in New York. As for staying the course after he has done, say, six or ten, if he is feeling the strain I shall persuade him to cancel the rest and I shall bring him home."[12]

On January 20 Churchill was feeling better. "The neuritis in my arms has diminished and I can move much more freely and sleep in any position," he wrote to Randolph. He wished he could have another two weeks in the Bahamas, but the lectures could be postponed no longer. "However," he told his son, "I expect that the electric atmosphere of New York will act as a tonic itself after this soothing and somewhat enervating climate."[13]

On January 22 Churchill, Clementine and Diana left the Bahamas by sea for New York, a three-day voyage. For the next three days Churchill worked on his lectures. Then, on January 28, he spoke at the Brooklyn Academy of Music, to an audience of two thousand. Mario Contasino, the driver who had knocked him down, was present. The

---

10. "Churchill Expects Revival Somehow," *New York Times*, 31 December 1931.

11. "Churchill's Recovery Slow; He Extends Stay in Bahamas," *New York Times*, 15 January 1932.

12. Letter of 12 January 1932, Randolph Churchill Papers.

13. Letter of 20 January 1932, Randolph Churchill Papers.

"great opposing forces in the future," Churchill forecast, would be the English-speaking peoples on the one side and Communism on the other. It would be the duty of Britain and the United States to stand together to protect "the distracted peoples of Europe" from Communist tyranny. Soviet Russia was the "new tyranny."

Churchill told his audience: "England and America are going in the same direction. They have the same outlook and no common discords. Why, then do we not act together more effectively? Why do we stand gaping at each other in this helpless way, ashamed that it be said that America and England are working together, as if that were a crime? We must be the strong nucleus at the council board of the nations." Churchill also spoke about Prohibition. Britain had been more successful than the United States at tackling the "frightful social evils" of drunkenness. "Like you," he said, "we attacked those evils by State interference with the liberty of the citizen, but we used the two sharp weapons of taxation and regulation. We treated the problem as a disease rather than a moral issue." [14]

After leaving New York by train on January 31, Churchill lectured almost every day in a different city. The pace of the tour was extraordinary by any standards, let alone for a man of fifty-seven who had been struck by a car six weeks earlier. Phyllis Moir, who had just joined him as his secretary, recalled the realities of the tour: "It means revising speeches in taxicabs and dressing out of suitcases. It means always being the social lion for the lion hunters, however tired and out-of-sorts one may feel. It means eating caterers' meals. It means living by a train schedule." All these hardships, she wrote, "Mr Churchill accepted almost cheerfully," and she went on to explain: "From the start of his tour he regarded himself as his lecture manager's employee, and being a man who expects complete satisfaction from those he employs, he was bent on giving complete satisfaction himself. However early or however late he had to catch a train to make his next engagement he acquiesced as a matter of course."

Phyllis Moir thought that Churchill "generally talked above the heads of his audience." It was however "characteristic," she added, "that he never made the same speech twice. After each engagement he would think of a number of improvements and would set to work the

---

14. "Anglo-American Tie Urged by Churchill," *New York Times,* 29 January 1932.

next morning on the text of his address. He polished and re-polished his speeches endlessly so that they seemed to grow considerably in scope and depth."[15]

The first stop in the renewed lecture tour was Hartford, Connecticut, where Churchill again spoke to as many as two thousand people. Then he went by car to Springfield, Massachusetts, to catch the overnight train to St. Louis. After speaking there, he traveled by train to Chicago, where he spoke on the world economic crisis to what the *Chicago Tribune* called "an extraordinarily distinguished gathering of solid men of Chicago." Churchill's theme was the "everlasting fundamentals" of the English-speaking peoples, and he quoted from a speech by Bourke Cockran, who had died in 1923: "The earth is a generous mother. She will produce food for all her children if they will but cultivate her soil in justice and peace."[16] Looking back almost two years later, Churchill wrote: "I well remember the cheers with which I was greeted in Chicago . . . when I pointed out that the Illinois farmer had at that time to plough a mile furrow to pay off the same amount of mortgage that a thousand yards would have done less than three years before."[17]

Churchill's remarks were well received. "I hear encomiums of you on all sides," wrote the publisher of the *Chicago Tribune,* Robert McCormick, "not the least of them being that of my driver who remarked, 'There's no baloney about him at all.'"[18] On February 6, while still in Chicago, Churchill wrote to his former Parliamentary Private Secretary, Robert Boothby. "I have had a most strenuous week," he explained, "travelling every night, lecturing every day, with much weakness caused by my accident and a bad sore throat, but with very fine meetings and very large profits. I am now back in Chicago for a second meeting." The American police, Churchill told Boothby, "have played up wonderfully, and I have been guarded every moment, night and day, by groups of armed plain-clothes men. Detroit and Chicago are both places where Indian trouble was expected, but as they had about two police gunmen alongside every Indian seen no trouble arose."

---

15. Phyllis Moir, *I Was Winston Churchill's Private Secretary,* pages 135–37.

16. *Chicago Tribune,* 3 February 1932.

17. "The Bond Between Us," *Collier's,* 4 November 1933.

18. Letter of 19 February 1932, Churchill Papers, Churchill College, Cambridge (CHAR 1/399B).

1. Churchill (in straw hat, back row) next to his mother (with feather hat). In front of her is Grandmother Jerome. Far left, Churchill's Aunt Leonie, and far right, Churchill's Aunt Clara, with their children.

2. Leonard Jerome, Churchill's grandfather. The photograph is signed "To Winnie from Grandpapa."

3. "Buffalo Bill" Cody. Churchill saw his Wild West show in London in 1887.

4. Colonel George Edward Gouraud, in a photograph taken around the time he spoke at Harrow School in 1888. He is wearing his American Civil War uniform.

5. Henry Demarest Lloyd, whose book *Wealth Against Commonwealth* much influenced Churchill.

6. Bourke Cockran, Churchill's American friend and mentor.

7. J. B. Pond, Churchill's first American literary agent.

8. Churchill during his first American lecture tour, a photograph taken in Boston on 17 December 1900.

9. Consuelo, Duchess of Marlborough (Consuelo Vanderbilt) with Churchill, a photograph taken at Blenheim Palace in 1904.

10. Ethel Barrymore.

11. Charles Schwab, Churchill's First World War colleague and interwar host

12. Harvey Butters, Churchill's First World War soldier friend. He was killed in action in 1916.

13. The Prince of Wales, General Pershing, Churchill and the American Ambassador in London, John W. Davis, at an investiture in Hyde Park, 19 July 1919.

14. Watched by his hostess, Mrs. Helen Russell, Churchill paints at
Pebble Beach, Monterey, California, 13 September 1929.

15. William Randolph Hearst, Churchill, Louis B. Mayer, unidentified and (far right)
Churchill's brother Jack, Los Angeles, 18 September 1929.

16. Churchill with his swordfish catch,
Santa Catalina Island, 22 September 1929.

17. Churchill and Charlie Chaplin,
in Chaplin's film studio, Hollywood,
where he was making *City Lights,* 24
September 1929.

18. Churchill outside the White House, after
calling on President Hoover, 9 October 1929.

19. Churchill at Chartwell with Governor Alfred "Al" Smith of New York, 1930, two years after Smith's failed Presidential race against Hoover. Churchill had suggested Smith's slogan, "Al for all and all for Al."

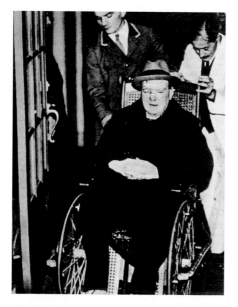

20. Churchill leaves Lenox Hill Hospital, New York, 31 December 1931, three weeks after being hit by a car while crossing Fifth Avenue.

21. Churchill as one of the lecture agent Harold Peat's "attractions" for the American lecture circuit, 1938–1939.

22. Harry Hopkins, Brendan Bracken (Churchill's Parliamentary Private Secretary) and Churchill outside 10 Downing Street, 10 January 1941. It was Churchill's first meeting with Roosevelt's envoy.

23. Churchill, his Naval ADC "Tommy" Thompson and Harry Hopkins on board a destroyer off the north coast of Scotland, 15 January 1941, after saying good-bye to Lord Halifax, who was on his way to Washington as Ambassador.

24. Averell Harriman with Churchill at a naval dockyard establishment in Plymouth, 2 May 1941, shortly after a severe German air raid (hence the steel helmet worn by the dockyard worker).

25. Churchill watches the arrival of a Boeing B-17 Flying Fortress at a Royal Air Force bomber station, 6 June 1941.

26. On board the United States battleship *Augusta* on 9 August 1941, Churchill hands President Roosevelt a letter from King George VI. Roosevelt is holding the arm of his son Elliott.

27. On board the British battleship *Prince of Wales* at Divine Service, Sunday 10 August 1941, Roosevelt and Churchill join in the hymn singing, with their staffs behind them. Harry Hopkins is in the second row, behind Churchill.

28. Churchill salutes the United States Marine Flag and the Stars and Stripes, Iceland, 16 August 1941. Just behind him are his Naval ADC Commander, "Tommy" Thompson, and (below the Marine Flag) Roosevelt's son Franklin, Jr. a naval ensign. Detective Sergeant Walter Thompson is on the far left, in civilian clothes, holding his hat.

29. Immediately after Pearl Harbor, Churchill returns to 10 Downing Street from
Chequers, entering Downing Steet by the backdoor entrance on Horse Guards
Parade. The headline of the evening newspaper he is holding says: "Japan makes
surprise attack."

30. Churchill in his "siren suit"—a comfortable one-piece coverall or boiler suit—on the White House lawn, 22 December 1941. Behind him is Harry Hopkins, whose daughter is leading Roosevelt's dog Fala, and walking with her is Churchill's Naval ADC Commander, "Tommy" Thompson.

31. Churchill addresses a joint session of the United States Congress, 26 December 1941, less than three weeks after Pearl Harbor. Behind Churchill, on the Senate rostrum, is Representative William Cole, Jr., the temporary Speaker of the House of Representatives, and to his left, Vice-President Henry A. Wallace. On Churchill's right is Senator Alben Barkley of Kentucky (later Truman's vice-president, 1948–53).

32. General George C. Marshall, Churchill and Secretary of War Henry L. Stimson (in pith helmet) watch an American parachute drop, Fort Jackson, South Carolina, 26 June 1942. Behind Stimson is Field Marshal Sir John Dill, Head of the British Joint Staff Mission in Washington.

33. Churchill meets Roosevelt at Quebec before the start of the first Quebec conference, 16 August 1943.

34. Churchill addresses United States Army and Navy cadets in Harvard Yard, 6 September 1943.

Churchill suggested to Boothby that they should go together to the Republican and Democratic Conventions that summer. "We should, of course, see all the politicians of both great Parties," he wrote, "and be in the very centre of their affairs." Churchill would write articles on the Conventions, and Boothby could pay his way either by writing articles of his own, "or failing that, by helping me with mine."[19] But just as he had been unable because of British politics to attend the American conventions before the First World War, so he was unable to attend these. Had he done so, he would have seen Franklin Roosevelt nominated for the Presidency.

In the meantime, Churchill's lecture tour continued without respite. From Chicago, he went by train to Cleveland, Ohio. While there he attended an informal discussion with the leading businessmen. Finding them inhibited in their questions, he encouraged them to speak their minds. "Now come now, this isn't the free American speech I've heard so much about—or that my mother always boasted about." The businessmen opened up, and Churchill was plied with questions about some of the thorniest issues, including war debts and naval armaments. He also warned them: "We are not through with wars. We will have another one."[20]

From Cleveland, Churchill went by train to Toledo, Ohio. Because his life "has been threatened repeatedly during his visit to this country," the *New York Times* reported, Federal Government special agents and Toledo police were working together to protect him from any Indians who might try to assassinate him. To reduce the risk, no Indians were allowed into the auditorium. When Churchill's train reached Toledo on February 4, a special guard of detectives and policemen met him at the station.[21]

That afternoon Churchill was taken ill: "stricken down with acute laryngitis," Phyllis Moir recalled. But he insisted on going through with his lecture "in defiance of doctors' orders, spraying his throat, sucking lozenges, taking large doses of medicine, waging a savage blitzkrieg against the affliction that might stop him from doing his

---

19. Letter of 6 February 1932: Boothby Papers.
20. Quoted in Kay Halle, editor, *Winston Churchill on America and Britain*, pages 86–87.
21. "Will Guard Churchill," *New York Times*, 4 February 1932.

duty by his lecture manager. And, of course, he made a splendid speech. He is always at his best when fighting something."[22]

From Toledo, Churchill went by train to Detroit, escorted by several detectives. He made "no objection to being guarded on the journey" or during his stay in Detroit, the *New York Times* reported. At his lecture there on the evening of February 5, "He was closely guarded by a dozen detectives from a special squad," as well as by half a dozen plainclothes men and several uniformed patrolmen.[23] It was in Detroit that the feared Indian hostility emerged, though not as an assassination attempt. As Sergeant Thompson recalled, Churchill's car was stoned twice, and a bag of human excrement was thrown into the lobby of his hotel.[24]

On February 6 Churchill took the morning train from Detroit back to Chicago. His host was the publisher of the *Chicago Tribune,* Colonel McCormick, who put his specially and sturdily built armored car at Churchill's disposal. On the following afternoon Churchill lectured at Orchestra Hall on the need for a closer union of the English-speaking peoples against "communism and the disintegrating forces of a disunited Europe." When people said, "Ah, look! The English and Americans are working together!" no one need be ashamed, he said, and went on to ask: "Why should we not frankly recognize that there must be some source of doctrine and authority to rescue nations from confusion?"[25]

The lecture was well received. "The handclapping was so prolonged," reported the *Chicago Tribune,* "and the attitude of the audience so manifestly intimate and affectionate, that the English statesman felt impelled to rise again and utter a few words expressive of his gratitude for the cordial and understanding reception which Chicago has given him in recent days."[26] On February 8 Churchill took the night train from Chicago back to New York, where he enthused a gathering of industrialists, bankers and economists with the words:

---

22. Phyllis Moir, *I Was Winston Churchill's Private Secretary,* page 136.
23. "Detroit Guards Churchill," *New York Times,* 6 February 1932.
24. Walter H. Thompson, *Assignment Churchill,* page 114.
25. "Chicago Audience Applauds Churchill," *New York Times,* 8 February 1932.
26. *Chicago Tribune,* 8 February 1932.

"Let us have good courage. Do not add to monetary deflation the hideous deflation of panic and despair."[27]

On the following day Churchill went to the top of the recently completed Empire State Building, the tallest building then in existence. His host was Al Smith, the former Governor of New York, who had just announced that he would again seek the Presidency. The two men went to the observation tower on the 102nd floor, and then descended to the more spacious observation platform on the 86th. That evening, February 10, Churchill spoke at Carnegie Hall. Fifteen hundred people were there to hear him, among them Bernard Baruch, Charles Schwab, Henry Morgenthau Jr., and the seventy-four-year-old oil magnate and philanthropist John D. Rockefeller.

Once again Churchill encouraged questions, which continued for more than an hour. The final question was: "Would you become an American citizen if we could make you President of the United States? I know our Constitution disqualifies you, but we can amend that." To which Churchill answered: "There are various little difficulties in the way. However, I have been treated so splendidly in the United States that I shall be disposed, if you can amend the Constitution, seriously to consider the matter."[28]

As Churchill's lectures continued, the *Daily Telegraph* reported that the tour had developed "into a triumphal progress"; at each lecture he was received with a "tumultuous welcome, the entire audience rising to their feet to cheer him." From New York he went to Rochester, where his grandfather Jerome had lived before moving to New York, and from Rochester he traveled to Washington, where he stayed at the British Embassy. Phyllis Moir described the sessions when the Ambassador, Sir Ronald Lindsay, came into Churchill's room to discuss each day's events. "These two made the oddest contrast," she wrote. "The immensely dignified diplomat standing extremely ill at ease at the foot of the old-fashioned four poster and the Peter Pan of British politics sitting up in bed, a cigar in his mouth, his tufts of red hair as yet uncombed, scanning the morning newspapers."[29]

---

27. *New York Times*, 10 February 1932.
28. Quoted in Jack Fishman, *My Darling Clementine*, page 78.
29. Phyllis Moir, *I Was Winston Churchill's Private Secretary*, pages 82–83.

While in Washington, Churchill discovered that Ethel Barrymore was performing in the city. With the box of flowers that he sent her, Phyllis Moir recalled, he included a note "reminding her of a young admirer who used to sup alone in Claridges in the glittering days of Edward VII's London."[30] On February 12 Churchill spoke to a large gathering of Washington's political elite at Constitution Hall. His lecture, on the economic crisis, was met with what the *Washington Post* called "prolonged and deafening" applause.[31] On the following day he called on President Hoover at the White House, their second meeting in just over two years, after which he visited the House of Representatives, where the session was briefly suspended so that the Congressmen present could greet him.

That evening Churchill was the guest of honor at a private home. "After the dinner was over," he later wrote, "the whole company formed a half-circle around me, and then began one of the frankest and most direct political interrogations to which I have ever been subjected." For two hours he and interlocutors "wrestled strenuously, unsparingly, but in the best of tempers with one another." Nowhere else in the world, he felt, "only between our two peoples, could such a discussion have proceeded."[32]

Churchill was encouraged by the enthusiastic reception of his central theme, that there was a special link between the British and American people, but on February 14 the *Washington Post* wrote sourly that the former Chancellor of the Exchequer was in the United States "for the general purpose of trying to hitch the British wagon to the American star." As for Churchill's call for "a working agreement between Great Britain and the United States," the *Washington Post* was hostile. "Not many years ago," it declared, "political and economic unity with the Yankees would have been repulsive to British statesmen." Things had changed in America's favor since then. "Now the tables are turned and Mr. Churchill is trying to flatter the United States into taking over some of Great Britain's liabilities." It was "rather strange," the newspaper added, "for a debtor to offer a partnership to his creditor," and it went

30. Phyllis Moir, *I Was Winston Churchill's Private Secretary*, page 68.
31. *Washington Post*, 13 February 1932.
32. Quoted in Kay Halle, editor, *Winston Churchill on America and Britain*, pages 266–67.

on to ask, scathingly: "What contribution has Britain to make to the co-operative bond that Mr. Churchill suggests for the two countries?"[33]

After a Washington Press Club lunch in his honor, Churchill went to Gettysburg, where he walked over the Civil War battlefield. Phyllis Moir, who accompanied him, later wrote that he "astonished us all with his knowledge of these campaigns. From his reading he was familiar with every foot of the terrain. At Gettysburg he startled the guide by correcting him as to the disposition of troops and guns. When a check-up was later made Mr Churchill was proved to have been completely right."[34]

Traveling to Richmond, Virginia, Churchill visited several more Civil War battlefields in the area. One of those with him was the American historian Douglas Southall Freeman. Two years later, sending Churchill the first two volumes of his four-volume biography of Robert E. Lee, Freeman wrote: "I hope the books reached you and if you have the opportunity to glance through them, I hope they may recall the day when some of your Richmond admirers had the privilege of carrying you over the battlefields around this city."[35] "I well remember that delightful tour of the Richmond battlefields in your company," Churchill replied, "and our memorable dinner that evening."[36]

After Richmond, Churchill lectured in Nashville, Chattanooga and Atlanta. When he spoke in Atlanta on February 23, he was introduced by the Governor of Georgia. The *Atlanta Constitution* reported his speech, which lasted more than an hour. "Whatever the pathway of the future may bring," he said, "we can face it more safely, more comfortably, and more happily if we travel it together, like good companions. We have quarrelled in the past, but even in our quarrels great leaders on both sides were agreed on principle. Let our common tongue, our common basic law, our joint heritage of literature and ideals, the red tie of kinship, become the sponge of obliteration of all the unpleasantness of the past."[37]

---

33. *Washington Post,* 14 February 1932.
34. Moir, *I Was Winston Churchill's Private Secretary,* page 87.
35. Letter of 23 October 1934, Martin Gilbert, *Winston S. Churchill,* Volume 5, Companion (document) Volume, Part 2, page 886.
36. Letter of 3 November 1934, Martin Gilbert, *Winston S. Churchill,* Volume 5, Companion (document) Volume, Part 2, page 908.
37. *Atlanta Constitution,* 24 February 1932.

Churchill then had a short respite from lecturing. Bernard Baruch had invited him to spend a weekend at his plantation at Myrtle Beach, South Carolina, by the water's edge. "It was a haven of peace," Phyllis Moir recalled, "the sort of place where work of any sort seemed a sacrilege. But we had no sooner arrived when Mr Churchill called for me to take a letter. He was already bursting to tell his wife who was in New York his first impressions of the plantation." Churchill did find time to relax, however. "He went crabbing with his host, spent part of the mornings discussing world affairs on the sunny terrace, painted several landscapes and played more backgammon than usual. But in the three days we were there he drafted his series of articles for *Collier's,* dashed off another article for a British newspaper and dictated a score of letters." [38]

The pace of lecturing was phenomenal. From Myrtle Beach, Churchill went by train to Maine, then to Toronto, then to Pittsburgh. In thanking Howard Heinz, of the ketchup manufacturers, for the offer to stay at his home in Pittsburgh and to be given a tour of one of the industrial heartlands of America, Churchill explained that he would be "the veriest bird of passage, as I arrive from Toronto at 7.45 a.m. and must leave towards midnight that same day for my next engagement"—having given two lectures, one at Sewickley at three in the afternoon and the other in Pittsburgh the same evening. "I must reserve my strength for these," Churchill added, "and it will not be possible for me, on this occasion, to see the great industries for which Pittsburgh is famous and which would have interested me so much." He would, however, accept Heinz's offer of a place "to rest during the morning"—after his long overnight train journey from Toronto—"and lunch and dine quietly with you and your family." [39]

There were yet more lectures to come: New Orleans, Minneapolis—his most westerly lecture—Grand Rapids, Cincinnati and Indianapolis. Clementine having returned to England, Churchill's daughter Diana traveled with him. On February 28 he telegraphed to Randolph from Indianapolis that his "lecture pilgrimage" was "drawing wearily" to its close. On the following day, on his way to the University of Michigan at Ann Arbor, he wrote to the British newspaper

---

38. Phyllis Moir, *I Was Winston Churchill's Private Secretary,* pages 94–96.
39. Letter of 14 February 1932, Churchill Papers, Churchill College, Cambridge (CHAR 1/399/60).

proprietor Esmond Harmsworth that he had found in the United States a different attitude to Britain than hitherto. "I have never seen anything like the friendliness of sentiment towards us in any of my former visits," he wrote. "All classes and both Parties are in an entirely favourable mood."[40]

During a final week in New York, Churchill discussed his future books with his American publisher Charles Scribner, reviewed his investments with Bernard Baruch and planned new articles with the editorial staff of *Collier's* magazine. On March 8 he went to Westchester County, just north of New York City, where, the *New York Times* reported, 1,500 people came to hear him. "Let us have no fear of the United States of Europe," he told them. "As long as the United States and England grow closer together. Any sinister result could then be properly dealt with."[41]

On the following day, March 9, Churchill lunched at the Waldorf-Astoria with his American kinsman William Travers Jerome. That night he left New York by sleeper to Boston, for his last lecture commitment. From the train station he went to the Copley Plaza Hotel for a morning sleep. At noon there was a Press Conference, followed by a live broadcast from the Boston office of the Columbia Broadcasting System. Asked about the possibility of a future war, Churchill warned: "The old pomp and circumstances are gone. There is nothing now but toil, blood, death, squalour and lying propaganda."[42] If France kept a strong army, and Britain and the United States "have good Navies," he believed, "no great war is likely to occur." His confidence in the British Empire, Churchill ended, "is equalled only by my confidence in the United States."[43]

That evening Churchill spoke at Boston's Symphony Hall, the final presentation of his English-speaking Peoples lecture. He then returned by night train to New York, reaching the city on the morning of March 11, and lunching with an American lawyer friend, Louis S. Levy,

---

40. Letter of 29 February 1932, Martin Gilbert, *Winston S. Churchill,* Volume 5, Companion (document) Volume, Part 2, pages 406–7.

41. "Churchill Warns of United Europe," *New York Times,* 9 March 1932.

42. On 13 May 1940, Churchill told the House of Commons, "I have nothing to offer but blood, toil, tears and sweat."

43. "Radio Interview," transcript, Churchill Papers, Churchill College, Cambridge (CHAR 1/399/folios 70–79).

to whom he had written about having a talk "before I leave your hospitable and friendly shores."[44] Churchill and his daughter Diana were then driven to the quayside to board the White Star liner *Majestic.* The ship sailed that night for Cherbourg and Southampton.

The aspect of American life that seemed most to have changed since Churchill's visit two years earlier was Prohibition. In 1929 most people he met had defended it. In 1932 they were against it. "In the audiences which I addressed," he wrote in a magazine article after his return to Britain, "comprising scores of thousands of American citizens from New York to Indiana and from Georgia to Maine, every critical or slighting allusion to Prohibition which I ventured to make—with all the reserves of courtesy due from a foreigner—was received with immediate, spontaneous appreciation." At the New York Economic Club, when he had asked, "Why don't you tax alcoholic liquor and strike a three-fold blow at drunkenness, Prohibition and crime?" he was met with "resounding applause." In his own final Budget as Chancellor of the Exchequer, he pointed out, he had raised "upward of six hundred million dollars from severe taxation of this indulgence."

Churchill ended his article with a question: "From this shattered cause of temperance," he asked, "from these plundered American revenues, from these hideous cephalopods of crime springing at so many points into dominant life, from this misguided and irritated new generation, from these insulted laws of a great people—is there then no escape?"[45]

Prohibition had come into effect by Constitutional amendment fourteen years earlier. Within a year of Churchill's article it had been voted out of existence, never to return.

---

44. Letter of 11 March 1932, Churchill Papers, Churchill College, Cambridge (CHAR 1/399/B).

45. Winston Churchill, "The Shattered Cause of Temperance," *Collier's,* 13 August 1932.

Chapter Fifteen

"WHY DO OUR TWO COUNTRIES NOT TAKE COUNSEL TOGETHER?"

Seven weeks after his return from his American lecture tour, Churchill made his first transatlantic radio broadcast to the United States. "They tell me I may be speaking to thirty millions of Americans," he said. "I am not at all alarmed. On the contrary I feel quite at home. I have often spoken to American audiences before. I know the goodwill and attention with which they will listen to fair and plain statements." It was the height of the Depression. The United States was in near-despair. Churchill wanted to convey his confidence that there was a way through to recovery, and prosperity. When men were "passing through rough and dangerous times," Churchill told his listeners, "the great thing is to have a good and trustworthy friend. Someone you can rely on in a crisis. Someone who will do his share of the work, and stand upright in the crowd," and he went on to ask, "as I have asked on so many American and British platforms, why do our two countries not take counsel together? Why do they not try to reach a common understanding about the money policy of the world?" Whatever course was decided to end the deflation that had followed the Great Crash, "Believe me, no one country however powerful can stop this evil alone."

What two nations should take the first steps, Churchill asked, "if it be not the two great English-speaking nations—the two great world creditor nations, the two great Anti-Communist nations, Britain and the United States?" Together, Britain and the United States should "set an example to the world in fortitude and fidelity, and let us also try to find a practical way out of this present ghastly world muddle, and set our feet firmly upon the upward road." It was essential to reach the end "of these absurd nightmare years when the plenty which springs from enterprise and science seems only to lead to privation; when generous harvests are dreaded like the plague; when all that Man has done, and has yet to do, is limited by the chance discoveries or releases of a single metal." The Gold Standard had to be abandoned: "All other questions fade into the background compared with this money question."[1] Churchill's suggestion was for a high-level monetary conference, and in a public statement eight weeks after his broadcast, he noted that both the British and American Governments had adopted his proposal.[2]

Churchill's confidence in the recovery of the American economy was reflected in his purchase of American stocks. In a single month between the end of May and the end of June 1931, he purchased through his stockbrokers, Vickers, da Costa, of which his brother, Jack, was a partner, a total of almost £8,000 worth of shares.[3] A year later he wrote to Horace Vickers, the chairman of Vickers, da Costa: "I want to put before you my view about the Americans. The more I study the stocks I know about, the more sure I am that the only way to recover the losses is to acquire some low priced solid securities without any reference to immediate dividends, and put them away for two, three or four years."

The stake would not be large, Churchill noted, "even if America founders, which I repudiate. Of course I am drawn to my old favourites now so down at heel. I have about 12,000 dollars in America free to invest." He was drawn to a range of shares, all languishing far below their pre-Crash prices, and he told his stockbroker: "Remember I only care about ultimate recovery and do not worry about any dividends now, therefore real value and expansive power is the only test." The market might easily go a little lower, but "a rise sooner or later is on the programme now."[4]

Churchill's confidence in America's economic recovery was re-

---

1. Broadcast of 8 May 1932, Martin Gilbert, *Winston S. Churchill*, Volume 5, Companion (document) Volume, Part 2, pages 426–30.
2. Statement of 29 June 1932, Martin Gilbert, *Winston S. Churchill*, Volume 5, Companion (document) Volume, Part 2, pages 445–46.
3. £340,000/$640,000 in the monetary values of 2005.
4. Draft letter of 4 June 1932, Martin Gilbert, *Winston S. Churchill*, Volume 5, Companion (document) Volume, Part 2, pages 438–39.

flected in a letter he wrote to his American lecture agent, Louis J. Alber, in the summer of 1932, after Alber invited him to lecture in the United States that winter. "I am sure it would be a great mistake," Churchill replied, "for me to come to lecture in the United States while conditions are so bleak." But he would come back before long: "In two or three years—perhaps sooner—everything will be booming again. Of this I have no doubt. And then the same number of lectures will be produced with no more effort for at least double what could be secured now." Churchill added: "The only thing that matters now is to survive. Those who have come through this pinch will reap the future." [5]

Five days after his letter to Alber, Churchill purchased yet more American shares, including Otis Elevator. Not only was he confident in the American recovery but he remained determined to arouse American opinion in favor of a common Anglo-American economic policy. In an article in *Collier's* in August 1932 he suggested that the British and American governments, through the Federal Reserve Bank and the Bank of England, "come to the definite conclusion that commodities must be revalued up to the 1927 or 1928 level, and that thereafter sufficient currency must be available to provide a stable measure for prices." If Britain and America were agreed, "it would not be long before the Bank of France would wish to be included in our consortium." Even without France, if Britain and the United States were in accord they would be "quite powerful enough to restore to human society the enormous benefits of which it is now deprived." [6]

On 6 November 1932, in Germany, Adolf Hitler's Nazi Party won the largest number of seats in the Reichstag elections. Two days later, in the United States, the Democratic candidate, Franklin D. Roosevelt, won the American Presidential election in a landslide victory. Hitler became Chancellor of Germany on 30 January 1933. Roosevelt was inaugurated President on March 4.

Churchill remained in the political wilderness. His opposition to Indian self-government had alienated him from almost all his former Conservative colleagues. When a campaign began in the Philippines

---

5. Letter of 25 July 1932, Alber Papers.
6. Winston Churchill, "Are We Too Clever?" *Collier's*, 27 August 1932.

for independence from the United States, Churchill explained to his American readers why he opposed any such course. "If so-called independence were granted today to the Philippines," he wrote, "the result would be even worse than the return to the corruption and incompetence of the old Spanish regime. A rich and important population raised by immense exertions and at great cost in American treasure, intellect and blood, would speedily sink into the primitive welter of Asiatic anarchy or misgovernment."

Churchill's scenario was highly colored: "The hungry jungle would soon invade the reclaimed spaces," he wrote. "The inhabitants would be rapidly diminished by warfare and disease. The roads would melt into forest trails. The schools and hospitals would become unlovely ruins and after a brief interlude of very eloquent speeches by the Filipino politicians, Chaos and Cold Night would resume their sway over this part of Asia."[7]

President-elect Roosevelt had no intention of granting independence to the Philippines, even if he did not share Churchill's apocalyptic vision. But Churchill's articles published in the United States won him lucrative contracts and a wide audience, as he sought both to educate and entertain his American readers.

In one of his articles, Churchill praised *Uncle Tom's Cabin* as the book "that shook the shackles from the slaves" and commended its author, Harriet Beecher Stowe, as a woman who "knew no fear."[8] In a lighter article he recalled his experiences of eating in the United States. "A dangerous yet almost universal habit of the American people is the drinking of immense quantities of iced water," he wrote. "This has become a ritual. If you go into a cafeteria or drugstore and order a cup of coffee, a tumbler of iced water is immediately set before you. This bleak beverage is provided on every possible occasion; whatever you order, the man behind the counter will supply this apparently indispensable concomitant. American meals nearly always start with a large slice of melon or grapefruit accompanied by iced water. This, Churchill reflected, "is surely a somewhat austere welcome for a hun-

7. Winston Churchill, "Defense in the Pacific," *Collier's,* 17 December 1932.
8. Winston S. Churchill, "The World's Great Stories Re-told," *News of the World,* 8 January 1933.

gry man at his midday or evening meal. Dessert, in my view, should be eaten at the end of the meal, not at the beginning."[9]

From the start of Roosevelt's presidency, Churchill gave an enthusiastic welcome to the New Deal. Five months after Roosevelt's inauguration he wrote to his lecture agent, Louis J. Alber, who had been given a post in the New Deal administration: "I am very glad to hear that you have been called to Washington to take part in the tremendous and noble effort your President is making to set North America to work again."

Alber still hoped to persuade Churchill to return to the United States for a second lecture tour under his auspices. Churchill told Alber that he already had a plan "in the next two or three years" to visit Japan, that such a visit would "fit in very well" with visiting the western United States, "and I could certainly revisit some of the most fertile centres in the East." Churchill added: "I have no doubt you could mark down a plan of some twenty-five or even thirty lectures on the kind of terms which you know I should expect." All this depended, however, Churchill wrote, "on the economic recovery of the United States, in which I have the fullest confidence. It is only a question of time, and I should look to you and your colleagues to advise me in good time when the prospects seem favourable."[10]

As the stock market began to recover, Churchill monitored his American shares with vigilance. A visitor to Chartwell noted in his diary: "He was receiving frequent reports of Stock Exchange prices in London and New York—his secretary brought one in while we were at tea."[11]

In October 1933 Churchill sent President Roosevelt a copy of the first volume of his four-volume life of his ancestor John Churchill, Duke of Marlborough, inscribing it: "With earnest best wishes for the success of the greatest crusade of modern times."[12] That October, Roosevelt's

---

9. Winston S. Churchill, "Land of Corn and Lobsters," *Collier's*, 5 August 1933.
10. Letter of 11 August 1933, Alber Papers.
11. Colin Thornton-Kemsley, diary entry, 20 September 1935, Sir Colin Thornton-Kemsley Papers.
12. Franklin D. Roosevelt Library, Hyde Park, New York.

eldest son, James, was among Churchill's dinner guests at Chart-well. After dinner Churchill initiated a guessing game, asking each of those present to describe their greatest wish. One of those present, Randolph's friend Kay Halle, recalled how, when Churchill's turn came to answer, he said, without hesitation: "I wish to be Prime Minister and in close and daily communication by telephone with the President of the United States. There is nothing that we could not do if we were together." Churchill then asked for a piece of paper, on which he drew the insignia of a pound sign and a dollar sign intertwined. Handing this to James Roosevelt, Churchill said to him: "Pray, bear this to your father from me. Tell him this must be the currency of the future."

"What will you call the new currency?" James Roosevelt inquired. "The sterling dollar," Churchill replied. "What, Sir, if my father should wish to call it the dollar sterling?" the young Roosevelt asked with a grin. "It's all the same," Churchill beamed. "We are together." [13]

Seven months into Roosevelt's Presidency, Churchill published an article in the United States in which he argued that no world economic conference, including one that had just ended, could succeed unless Britain and the United States, "who once in accord are masters of world finance," had been able to reach a common understanding "to settle between themselves the goal for which they were making." Churchill's solution was "a stable unit of value and exchange" between the leading trading nations. The danger was "economic nationalism." A race between the leading commercial powers "to see who can make his currency valueless in the international market first ought only to be held in some really large lunatic asylum." The only alternative to uniting the "joint strength and population" of a common Anglo-American economic policy was, Churchill warned, "that we wall ourselves up in our respective pens like the old robber barons in their feudal castles."

Churchill then commented, for the first time in public, on the new President. "It is evident from all that I have written and said in the past upon this subject," he wrote, "that I am, though a foreigner, an ardent admirer of the main drift and impulse which President Roosevelt has given to the economic and financial policy of the United States. I be-

---

13. Kay Halle recollections, Kay Halle, editor, *Winston Churchill on America and Britain*, pages 48–49.

lieve not only that it is for the good of the United States and consequently for the good of the World, but that it is independently for the good of the world besides." Churchill added: "The attempt already largely successful to wipe out the injustice caused to debtors of all kinds by the enhancement of the dollar compared to commodities is a resolve of noble and heroic sanity."[14]

Roosevelt had just announced that a conference would begin at the White House on 5 October 1933, to seek to settle all outstanding war debt questions between Britain and the United States. The question of debts, Churchill wrote to the editor of *Collier's*, who wanted an article on the subject, was one on which he "might easily offend." But, he added, "Happily the wise action of the President seems to me to make the matter capable of discussion in the form in which I have couched it."[15]

The new President and his New Deal were much in Churchill's thoughts in the first year of Roosevelt's presidency, and beyond. He studied with close attention Roosevelt's efforts to lift the curse of economic collapse, including the massive public works projects being built throughout the United States. In a broadcast over the BBC in January 1934 he remarked: "I don't say President Roosevelt is right in all his experiments; but one does admire the spirit in which he grapples with difficulties, especially in contrast with the timidity and wooliness and the mental imprecision which we see in some other places."[16] In a visit to Oxford, for a question-and-answer session with the Oxford University Conservative Association, Churchill was asked a hostile question about Roosevelt: whether he approved "of President Roosevelt's policy of neglecting the affairs of the rest of the world for the especial benefit of the United States, and whether he thinks it can ultimately succeed." To this Churchill replied that the President was a "bold fellow," adding, "I like his spirit."[17]

At the end of 1934 Churchill wrote an article in *Collier's* on Roosevelt. It was reprinted three years later in the second edition of his

---

14. Winston S. Churchill, "The Bond Between Us," *Collier's*, 4 November 1933.

15. Letter of 15 September 1933, Martin Gilbert, *Winston S. Churchill*, Volume 5, Companion (document) Volume, Part 2, pages 653–54.

16. Notes for a broadcast, 16 January 1934, Martin Gilbert, *Winston S. Churchill*, Volume 5, Companion (document) Volume, Part 2, pages 702–13.

17. Notes taken by Richard Storry, an undergraduate. Richard Storry Papers.

book *Great Contemporaries* as "Roosevelt from Afar." The article was widely circulated in the United States. "Many doubt if he will succeed," Churchill wrote. "Some hope he will fail. Although the policies of President Roosevelt are conceived in many respects from a narrow veil of American self-interest, the courage, the power and the scale of his efforts must enlist the ardent sympathy of every country, and his success could not fail to lift the whole world forward into the sunlight of an easier and more genial age."[18]

This was a strong endorsement of Roosevelt's vision. Churchill had taken special care that this should be so, writing the editor at *Collier's* that "if there are any phrases which you think would cause offence . . . you are quite at liberty to soften or excise them without reference to me. I have tried to strike a note of warning while at the same time expressing my sincere sympathy with the great effort the President is making."[19] Five months later, in February 1934, Churchill wrote in the *Sunday Chronicle* that Roosevelt's "impulse is one which makes towards the fuller life of the masses of the people in every land, and which as it grows the brighter may well eclipse both the lurid flames of German Nordic national self-assertion and the baleful unnatural lights which are diffused from Soviet Russia."[20] A month later Churchill wrote in the *Daily Mail* that the many measures that made up the New Deal "constitute a movement of thought and action which not only compels attention but stirs enthusiasms in the Old Country."[21] He had also warned the American people against being attracted to dictatorship, telling them it was "important that every Englishman and American should realize what he owes to free institutions, and how bitterly he would regret the loss of them."[22]

Churchill had found a new holiday destination in which to escape the British winters and also relax in summer. It was the Château de l'Hori-

---

18. Winston S. Churchill, "While the World Watches," *Collier's*, 29 December 1934.
19. Letter of 13 September 1934, Martin Gilbert, *Winston S. Churchill*, Volume 5, Companion (document) Volume, Part 2, pages 870–71.
20. Winston S. Churchill, "Every Working Man Will Be Affected If Roosevelt Fails," *Sunday Chronicle*, 10 February 1935.
21. Winston S. Churchill, "Roosevelt and the Future of the New Deal," *Daily Mail*, 24 April 1935.
22. Winston S. Churchill, "Why Not Dictatorship?" *Collier's*, 16 February 1935.

zon, at Golfe Juan in the South of France. His host there was Maxine Elliot, the American actress who had been a friend of his mother. It was from her villa that Churchill wrote to Clementine in September 1935 of his "general optimism & contentment engendered by old Brandy after a luncheon here alone with Maxine in her conservatory." There was other good news to report: "The Yankee market continues to improve & I have a good profit now on all my shares."

Churchill had just learned of the assassination of Huey Long, the populist governor of Louisiana, shot in the State House in Baton Rouge. Governor of Louisiana from 1928 to 1931, and a Democratic Senator from 1931, Long had been a ruthless manipulator of the Louisiana legislature and judiciary. Feared and reviled as a potential dictator, he had announced that he would stand against Roosevelt in the 1936 Presidential Elections. "The Louisiana Dictator," Churchill told Clementine, "has met his fate. 'Sic semper tyrannis,' which means so perish all who do the like again." He added: "This was the most clownish of the Dictator tribe. Let us hope that more serious tyrants will also lose their sway."[23]

In November 1935 a British General Election confirmed the Conservative predominance in the all-Party National Government that had been set up in 1931, during the economic crisis. Churchill hoped that the Prime Minister, Stanley Baldwin, would bring him into the Cabinet, with responsibility for some aspect of national defense. Baldwin declined, and Churchill, while still a Member of Parliament, remained in the political wilderness, without Cabinet office.

Among those who had urged Baldwin not to give Churchill a place was his old "Virginian" adversary, Nancy Astor. "Don't put Winston in the Government," she wrote. "It will mean war at home and abroad. I know the depths of Winston's disloyalty—and you can't think how he is distrusted by all the electors of the country."[24] Churchill did not know of this letter. It would have hurt him. His determination to preserve peace in Europe was total.

One American family gave Churchill pleasure that November, however—his own. His cousin Shane Leslie, another of Leonard

---

23. Letter of 11 September 1935, Baroness Spencer-Churchill Papers.
24. Letter of 17 November 1935, Lord Baldwin Papers.

Jerome's grandsons, had sent him the American family pedigree. "It certainly is inspiring," Churchill wrote, "to see so great a name as George Washington upon the list. I understand however that if you go back far enough everyone is related to everyone else, and we end up in Adam."[25]

A potentially lucrative literary offer reached Churchill from the United States, to write the biography of John D. Rockefeller, whom he had met in New York during his lecture tour. The idea came from Rockefeller's friends, among them the public relations consultant, Ivy L. Lee, who hoped Churchill would see Rockefeller as "a gigantic figure moving across the stage of modern life."

Churchill wanted a substantial sum for the book, but, Lee explained, there had been so much criticism of Rockefeller that if the definitive biography should give a favorable impression of him, "and the public should at some time find out (as they would inevitably find out) that so large a guaranty of royalties had been made, the larger part of the value of the favorable impression would be lost."[26]

Churchill did not have the financial resilience to take on the Rockefeller biography without a large advance payment. Four years later, however, he published an essay on Rockefeller in *Collier's* entitled "Oldest and Richest." It was reprinted in Britain under the title "Moneygrabber—but Money-giver too."[27]

Rockefeller's friends had been influenced in approaching Churchill by his First World War history, *The World Crisis*. When the Cleveland department store heiress Kay Halle, whom Randolph had met and fallen in love with during his American lecture tour, visited fifteen-year-old John F. Kennedy in hospital, at his bedside was a volume of *The World Crisis*.[28]

25. Letter of 18 November 1935, Martin Gilbert, *Winston S. Churchill*, Volume 5, Companion (document) Volume, Part 2, page 1327.

26. Letter of 1 April 1932, Martin Gilbert, *Winston S. Churchill*, Volume 5, Companion (document) Volume, Part 2, page 411.

27. Article of 11 July 1936, *Collier's;* 12 July 1936, *Sunday Pictorial*.

28. Sally Bedell Smith, *Grace and Power: The Kennedy White House*, page 34.

Chapter Sixteen

✠

"A UNION OF SPIRIT"

A t the beginning of 1936, as both Japan and Germany were accelerating their rearmament, an attempt was made to secure naval parity in the Pacific. But the attempt failed. "The Naval Conference has of course collapsed," Churchill wrote to Clementine. "Japan has ruptured it. The good thing is that we and the United States are working hand in glove and will encourage each other to strengthen the navies."[1]

In Britain Churchill had helped set up an Anti-Nazi League, where opponents of Nazism could meet, whatever their political affiliation or background. A similar organization was being created in the United States. Churchill was invited to present his anti-Nazi arguments there, and to address meetings in New York, Philadelphia and Chicago. To Randolph, who was in the United States, Churchill wrote that, subject to a "satisfactory" fee, "I am prepared to sail after Christmas for New York and would make a programme for the lectures and speeches as indicated."[2] He was offered a total of £5,000 for the three lectures.[3] It was not a moment too soon. Three days before his sixty-second birthday, Churchill learned that he would have to pay at least £6,000 in income tax and additional "super" tax in the coming year, a massive sum. "This being so," he wrote to Clementine, "I feel it necessary to take this US offer, & I am satisfied that it is quite proper for me to do so."

––––––

1. Letter of 17 January 1936, Baroness Spencer-Churchill Papers.
2. Letter of 13 November 1936, Martin Gilbert, *Winston S. Churchill*, Volume 5, Companion (document) Volume, Part 3, pages 401–2.
3. In the monetary values of 2005, £5,000 is the equivalent of just over £200,000/ $400,000.

Churchill made his plans. He would sail on December 18, meet the American Anti-Nazi Committee in New York to finalize the arrangements for the meetings, and go to Consuelo Balsan's villa at Palm Beach in Florida until January 10. Consuelo, having divorced Churchill's cousin the Ninth Duke of Marlborough in 1921, had married the pioneer French aviator Colonel Jacques Balsan. While staying with Consuelo, Churchill would prepare the speeches required of him and return to Britain from New York on January 20, in time for the reopening of Parliament six days later. As well as the importance of the Anti-Nazi platform, Churchill felt he must make the journey for the sake of his finances. "I am disappointed not to be with you all at Christmas," he wrote to Clementine, "and I don't know how I shall spend my poor Christmas Day. But everything is so uncertain (except taxation) that it would be wise to have this large sum safely banked in US. I have always hitherto managed to provide the necessaries, and I feel that this particular toil is a measure of prudence."[4]

It was Randolph who brought an end to the lecture plan, telegraphing to his father from New York that those who had invited him were not quite what they had seemed. No contract had been drawn up, no committee formed "nor cash raised."[5] Deferring to his son's advice, Churchill decided to make the transatlantic journey nevertheless, solely for a holiday, to spend three weeks with Consuelo Balsan in Palm Beach, and then see friends in New York and Washington. Six days before sailing he wrote to an English friend: "I am going to Palm Beach for a little sunshine, sailing on Tuesday."[6]

While preparing for his American journey, Churchill was invited to a meeting of senior Conservative politicians and the Prime Minister, Stanley Baldwin. The record of the meeting noted that Churchill "begged the Government not to hesitate to make contracts with the United States and elsewhere for the largest possible quantities of aviation material and equipment of all kinds." At this meeting Churchill asked the Minister for Coordination of Defence: "Are you adopting at

---

4. Letter of 27 November 1936, Baroness Spencer-Churchill Papers.
5. Telegram of 28 November 1936, Martin Gilbert, *Winston S. Churchill*, Volume 5, Companion (document) Volume, Part 3, page 445.
6. Letter of 16 December 1936, Martin Gilbert, *Winston S. Churchill*, Volume 5, Companion (document) Volume, Part 3, pages 491–92.

all the method of making a contract with an American aeroplane firm to start a branch establishment over here?" He had been advised "by people high up in American affairs" that that was Britain's "most safe method of getting round neutrality laws." There was nothing in those laws to prevent American engineers and skilled workmen "coming over to keep the thing running over here." A branch of that kind in Britain, Churchill urged, "would give you an additional element of production in connection with your War expansion scheme."[7]

As Churchill worked on his revised travel plans for the United States, the Prime Minister, Stanley Baldwin, insisted that King Edward VIII, who had succeeded his father as King in January 1935, must either give up all idea of marrying the American divorcée Wallis Simpson or abdicate the throne. It was widely believed that Churchill wanted, by rousing public opinion, to force Baldwin to allow the King to marry Mrs. Simpson. This was not so. Churchill's advice was quite different: that Mrs Simpson, in order to enable the King to remain on the throne, should renounce all idea of marriage.

When the King refused to give up marriage to Mrs. Simpson, Churchill asked in Parliament for a little more time to enable the King to decide. Baldwin, however, refused any further delay. On December 11 the King abdicated, taking the title Duke of Windsor. Churchill's support for Edward led to harsh words. One author published a book criticizing "the King's champions," among them "an unstable ambitious politician, flitting from Party to Party, extreme reactionary, himself the first-fruit of the first famous snob-dollar marriage: 'half an alien and wholly undesirable,' as long ago was said."[8]

Churchill still intended to cross the Atlantic. But on the day before he was to sail he learned that Parliament was to be recalled a week early. It had to decide the payments to be made by the Treasury— known as the Civil List—for both the new and the former King. As a senior parliamentarian, Churchill would be expected to take part in the debate. He also wanted, he explained to Bernard Baruch, "to

---

7. Record of a Discussion, 23 November 1936, Premier Papers 1/193.
8. Geoffrey Dennis, *Coronation Commentary,* quoted in Churchill's letter to H. Osborne, 26 April 1937, Martin Gilbert, *Winston S. Churchill,* Volume 5, Companion (document) Volume 3, pages 653–54.

watch over the interests about which I have an enduring sentiment."[9] That is, he would speak up for the interests of the former King, already in exile, whom he had known for more than a quarter of a century.

As soon as he learned of the early recall of Parliament, Churchill realized that he would be unable to get back to Britain from the United States in time for the session. From the Duke of Windsor, who was in France, about to marry Mrs. Simpson, Churchill received a telegram on the day he had been due to sail: "Hope you have a nice trip."[10]

Unable to recoup his finances from the planned American lectures, Churchill had to obtain a massive bank overdraft and two substantial loans. A major lecture tour in America remained an economic necessity. "I have every hope that I shall be able to come over to the States in April and hope to inaugurate the Defence of Freedom and Peace movement," he told Baruch. This movement was already active in Britain, with Churchill as the focal point of a growing national determination to defend the way of life of the democracies, if necessary by force, against any external threat. But that trip, like the one so recently abandoned, was not to be.

In his letter to Baruch, Churchill also reflected on the impact on Europe of America's repudiation of the League of Nations. "How you must regret," he wrote, "how we all regret, that Wilson's dream was not carried through, for I have no doubt it would have made the difference between a safe, happy and prosperous world and the present hideous panorama."[11] Churchill also feared the strength of current American isolationist sentiment, and the legal restrictions imposed by the 1935 and 1936 Neutrality Acts, preventing the sale of American arms and munitions overseas. Hence his delight when Roosevelt introduced a new Neutrality Act, to allow American arms and munitions to be delivered to other countries, with the sole proviso that consignments should be paid for in cash and should be collected in the United States by their purchasers: the "cash and carry" provision.

---

9. Letter of 1 January 1937, Martin Gilbert, *Winston S. Churchill*, Volume 5, Companion (document) Volume, Part 3, pages 520–22.

10. Telegram of 22 December 1936, Martin Gilbert, *Winston S. Churchill*, Volume 5, Companion (document) Volume, Part 3, page 515.

11. Letter of 1 January 1937, Martin Gilbert, *Winston S. Churchill*, Volume 5, Companion (document) Volume, Part 3, pages 520–22.

"Deepest gratitude for your wonderful neutrality Bill," Churchill telegraphed to Baruch, and went on to ask: "Would it do harm if we showed ourselves pleased about it over here."[12] The new American Neutrality Bill became law on 1 May 1937. "Am greatly pleased at trend American opinion," Churchill telegraphed Baruch again.[13] The doctrine of "cash and carry," Churchill explained in the *Evening Standard*, "means that no American ships will carry supplies to the warring countries, but if these countries choose to present themselves in ships at the American doorstep with ready money in their hands they will be allowed to buy non-military supplies." This arrangement, Churchill added, "certainly has the merit of rendering to superior sea power its full deserts. It avoids for Great Britain, if engaged in war, the danger of any dispute with the United States such as caused so much anxiety in 1914 and 1915. It may be rather chilling comfort, but it is comfort none the less."

Churchill struck a warning, realistic note, however, in this same article, when he warned his readers that the "main movement" of American opinion was "more set on avoiding foreign entanglements and keeping out of another world war than ever before." No European statesman "should be so foolish as to count upon the armed assistance of the United States even if his country were the victim of unprovoked aggression."[14]

Among Roosevelt's advisers with whom Churchill was in contact during the New Deal era was the securities and exchange expert René Leon. A month after visiting Churchill at Chartwell in 1937, Leon reported back to Churchill how "particularly pleased" Roosevelt was to hear of those Britons who were, like Churchill, "so definitely in favour of closer Anglo-American cooperation in the monetary field." In the Oval Office, Leon saw the drawing of the intertwined pound-dollar that Churchill had sent the President four years earlier. "Mr. Roosevelt

---

12. Telegram of 5 March 1937, Martin Gilbert, *Winston S. Churchill*, Volume 5, Companion (document) Volume, Part 3, page 592.
13. Telegram of 17 March 1937, Martin Gilbert, *Winston S. Churchill*, Volume 5, Companion (document) Volume, Part 3, page 625.
14. Winston Churchill, "America Looks at Europe," *Evening Standard*, 31 May 1937.

had it on his desk," Leon reported, "and was gazing at it with considerable interest." [15]

Churchill's planned return to the United States did not come to pass. With the accelerating German rearmament, he did not feel able to absent himself from Parliament for so long a journey. He was deep into his biography of his ancestor John Churchill, 1st Duke of Marlborough, determined to fulfill the publisher's contract, which would enable him to pay his bills. Even a visit to Maxine Elliot in the South of France proved impossible. "Thinking much of you all and the pool," he telegraphed to her at the end of the summer. "Alas I am tied here by work on Marlborough." [16] To Nicholas Murray Butler, the President of Columbia University, who had hoped to see Churchill when he was next in New York, Churchill wrote: "I fear I shall not be able to leave England this autumn. Everything is so uncertain, and the powers of evil are so strong." [17]

In the autumn of 1937 a second economic crisis struck Wall Street. Churchill was again hard hit. His losses made him consider another American lecture tour, provided the money was right. His New York lawyer friend, Louis Levy, who was chairman of the Board of Art Associates Inc., was eager to set up a tour. "Most grateful for your cable and invitation," Churchill replied, and he added: "Have so much work over here that I could not undertake visit US unless assured minimum twenty-five thousand dollars." [18] Churchill was tempted. "Do not anticipate difficulty about topics," he telegraphed to Levy. [19]

"If all could be arranged," Churchill explained to Levy, he would travel to the United States in December "and do some work both before and after Christmas." He would spend Christmas in Jamaica. If the

---

15. Letter of 23 July 1937, Martin Gilbert, *Winston S. Churchill,* Volume 5, Companion (document) Volume, Part 3, pages 732–33.

16. Telegram of 4 September 1937, Martin Gilbert, *Winston S. Churchill,* Volume 5, Companion (document) Volume, Part 3, page 760.

17. Letter of 8 September 1937, Martin Gilbert, *Winston S. Churchill,* Volume 5, Companion (document) Volume, Part 3, page 762.

18. The equivalent in the monetary values of 2005 of more than $325,000/ £162,500.

19. Telegram of 26 October 1937, Martin Gilbert, *Winston S. Churchill,* Volume 5, Companion (document) Volume, Part 3, page 816.

American fee was unacceptable, he would winter in the South of France, "where I can do my literary work." [20]

As in the previous year, the plans for another American lecture came to nothing, but Churchill still wanted to return, to earn the large sums of money that his lectures could command. "I am now contemplating another tour this autumn," he wrote to the Permanent Under-Secretary of State at the Home Office at the beginning of 1938, "in the course of which I shall certainly visit the Pacific Coast." The reason for Churchill's letter was to find out if he would still need to be protected from the Sikh secret society that had been responsible at the time of his 1931 visit "for several political murders." [21]

Churchill had no illusions about the attitude of the Americans toward Europe. In an article in the American magazine *Collier's,* he wrote with understanding of America's desire to keep clear of European entanglements, as a result of having in recent years "become more closely acquainted with the thought and feeling of the American people." He understood "something" of the American point of view: "If I had had an American father instead of an American mother, I have little doubt I should share it," nor could he "conceive any argument" that could be addressed to the Americans "if the European war suddenly began again, which should lead them to seek to take part in it." If the power of the United States could be joined to that of the League of Nations, "perhaps we could say with confidence that the world we live in would not suffer the supreme misfortune." [22]

Churchill continued to tell his British readers not to place their hopes in an American entry into any future European war. In an article in the *Evening Standard,* the theme of which was the dangers of Roosevelt's "ruthless war" against private enterprise, he also warned that although United States sentiment was "far more favourable to Britain" than it had been in 1914, this must not "mislead the Parliamentary nations into supposing that the United States is coming over again to fight their battles. On the contrary, the first resolve of the great major-

---

20. Telegram of 27 October 1937, Martin Gilbert, *Winston S. Churchill,* Volume 5, Companion (document) Volume, Part 3, pages 816–17.

21. Letter of 22 January 1938, Martin Gilbert, *Winston S. Churchill,* Volume 5, Companion (document) Volume, Part 3, page 896.

22. Winston Churchill, "Can America Keep Out of War?" *Collier's,* 2 October 1937.

ity is to avoid European, or even Far Eastern entanglements, and at all costs keep out of war."[23]

At the end of 1937 Churchill agreed to see an American lecture agent, Harold Peat, head of Management of Distinguished Personalities. H. G. Wells was one of his clients. Churchill wrote to Wells to report that his visitor had made him "serious proposals for a tour next autumn."[24] In reply Wells recommended Peat, and Churchill decided to go ahead. From his winter holiday in the South of France with Maxine Elliot, he wrote to his American lawyer, Louis Levy: "I have decided to make another lecture tour next October in the United States. A provisional agreement has been drafted over here, but I wish the contract to be made in New York. I should be very much obliged to you if you would sign the contract on my behalf, and I am sending you by the next mail the necessary Power of Attorney."[25]

In January 1938 Roosevelt put forward a plan to bring Britain, France, Germany and Italy to a conference in Washington. The new British Prime Minister, Neville Chamberlain, wanted this conference postponed until his own efforts with Germany and Italy had made further progress, and it never took place. "Thus it was," Churchill wrote in his war memoirs, "that President Roosevelt's proposal to use American influence for the purpose of bringing together the leading European Powers to discuss the chances of a general settlement, this of course involving the mighty power of the United States, were rebuffed by Mr. Chamberlain."[26]

As Hitler intensified his military, naval and air expansion, and spoke both of union with Austria and of German territorial claims against Czechoslovakia, Churchill challenged those who, like his cousin Lord Londonderry, insisted that Britain had no quarrel with Nazi Germany. In his rebuttals he always linked Britain and America. "It would be contrary to the whole tide of British and United States

---

23. Winston Churchill, "Europe's Plea to Roosevelt," *Evening Standard*, 10 December 1937.

24. Letter of 30 December 1937, Martin Gilbert, *Winston S. Churchill*, Volume 5, Companion (document) Volume, Part 3, pages 870–71.

25. Letter of 28 January 1938, Martin Gilbert, *Winston S. Churchill*, Volume 5, Companion (document) Volume, Part 3, page 899.

26. Winston S. Churchill, *The Second World War*, Volume 1, page 198.

opinion," he wrote to Londonderry, "for us to facilitate the spread of Nazi tyranny over countries which now have a considerable measure of democratic freedom."[27]

Churchill also believed that Britain and the United States, if they acted together, would be able to confront Japan, whose troops were even then wreaking destruction throughout eastern China. In an article in the *Evening Standard* he noted that Japan was believed already to have embarked on the construction of several battleships "which exceed in tonnage and size of cannon those that are being built in Britain and America." Roosevelt's recent declarations, he wrote, "seem to show that the Government of the United States would not be willing to see their naval power seriously rivalled in the Pacific Ocean at the present time." Churchill looked with confidence at the outcome of any conflict with Japan. "It is quite certain," he wrote, "that Japan cannot possibly compete with the productive energies of either branch of the English-speaking peoples."[28]

In mid-March 1938, in the very week that Hitler annexed Austria, Churchill learned that his American share losses were considerable—more than £250,000 ($500,000) in the monetary values of 2005—forcing him to put his beloved Chartwell on the market. He was only able to save Chartwell because a wealthy friend, Sir Henry Strakosh, offered to take over his shares at their original price. He was also much relieved when a potential new source of income emerged that spring: the American lecture agent Harold Peat had done his work well, and in mid-April the contracts were signed for Churchill to speak in twelve cities. Starting at Northwestern University, in Chicago, on October 25, he would speak in Kansas City, Cincinnati, Philadelphia, Dallas, Fort Worth, Los Angeles, Pasadena, San Francisco and Washington, before ending on December 14 in New York.[29]

Peat told Churchill that "other engagements" would be fitted in "as consecutively as possible with a view to making your traveling as

---

27. Letter of 23 October 1937, Martin Gilbert, *Winston S. Churchill*, Volume 5, Companion (document) Volume, Part 3, pages 812–13.
28. Winston Churchill, "What Japan Thinks Of Us," *Evening Standard*, 21 January 1938.
29. See Map 6, page 457.

easy as possible."[30] The expected total fees would be in excess of $30,000.[31] "Unless the unexpected happens," Churchill wrote to the editor of *Collier's*, "I shall be in New York in the third week of October, as my lecture tour has taken definite shape."[32] From the moment the lecture contracts had been signed, however, the European crisis intensified, and Churchill cancelled his lecture tour, watching in distress as Hitler's demands on Czechoslovakia intensified, and as the British Government, led since the previous October by Neville Chamberlain, sought a closer accommodation with Germany, at the expense of Czechoslovakia's territorial integrity. "I feel sure that what has happened has done no end of harm in the United States," Churchill confided to a friend that April.[33]

In mid-May, in an article in the *News of the World*, Churchill discussed the risk to Britain of war, and the American dimension. "If Britain and the United States were agreed to act together," he wrote, "the risk would be slight. These two great kindred powers, in collaboration, could prevent—or at least localize and limit—almost any quarrel that might break out among men." This was not a call for war. Britain and America could, he wrote, "almost certainly, without any resort to force themselves, by moral, economic and financial power, provided that in reserve there were armaments of sufficient strength to ensure that moral, economic and financial powers were not violently ruptured and suspended."

Anglo-American collaboration of the sort Churchill advocated so strongly did not, he wrote, "imply any formal union of the English-speaking peoples. It is a union of spirit, not of forms, that we seek." There need not even be an alliance. "All that is necessary is a willingness to consult together, an understanding that Britain and America shall pursue, side by side, their mutual good and the good of the whole world." There would be nothing in such an understanding that need

30. Letter of 18 April 1938, Martin Gilbert, *Winston S. Churchill*, Volume 5, Companion (document) Volume, Part 3, pages 997–98.

31. The equivalent in the monetary values of 2005 of $390,000/£195,000.

32. Letter of 21 April 1938, Martin Gilbert, *Winston S. Churchill*, Volume 5, Companion (document) Volume, Part 3, pages 1001–2.

33. Letter of 22 April 1938 (to Philip Guedalla), Martin Gilbert, *Winston S. Churchill*, Volume 5, Companion (document) Volume, Part 3, page 1004.

arouse fears elsewhere. "Collaboration of the English-speaking peoples threatens no one. It might safeguard all."

Seeking close links with the United States, Churchill urged his readers, if they had American business visitors, to invite them into their homes: "The friendliness of Americans to the traveller from Britain, their unfailing kindness, their generous hospitality, are something to marvel at," he wrote. "I am afraid that we do not always extend the same welcome to American visitors to our shores." It was "in the homes, not the hotels of a nation that we each can learn the truth about our people." By personal contacts and by more British visitors to the United States, he believed, "the two great divisions of the English-speaking race may be drawn closer together."[34]

---

34. Winston Churchill, "The Union of the English-Speaking Peoples," *News of the World*, 15 May 1938.

Chapter Seventeen

⌖

ROAD TO WAR

In the summer of 1938, when Bernard Baruch visited Chartwell, he brought encouraging news with regard to the European crisis. Churchill passed this on to Clementine: "The President is breast-high on our side and will do everything in his power to help," he wrote. In addition, "Baruch admitted opinion in the States had never yet been so friendly to us." There was, however, a limit to what the United States would do. "It is a great pity matters cannot be carried further now." Churchill added: "Apparently, you always have to have a disaster before anything sensible can be done which would prevent it."[1]

In his talks with Baruch, Churchill was pessimistic about his own prospects but confident about those of his American friend. "War is coming very soon," he told Baruch. "We will be in it and you will be in it. You will be running the show over there, but I will be on the sidelines over here."[2] In fact, when Roosevelt set up a War Resources Board nine months later, Baruch was neither consulted nor appointed.

There was a new "riddle of a Sphinx" in the world, Churchill wrote in the *Daily Telegraph and Morning Post* on 4 August 1938—the twenty-fourth anniversary of Britain's declaration of war in 1914: "Will the United States throw their weight into the scales of peace and law and

---

1. Letter of 8 July 1938, Martin Gilbert, *Winston S. Churchill,* Volume 5, Companion (document) Volume, Part 3, pages 1092–95.
2. Quoted in a letter from Baruch to Margaret L. Coit, published in Margaret L. Coit, *Mr. Baruch: The Man, the Myth, the Eighty Years,* page 467.

freedom while time remains. Or will they remain spectators until the disaster has occurred; and then, with infinite cost and labour, build up what need not have been cast down?"[3]

Churchill still hoped that his cancelled October–December lecture tour might go ahead. "It may be," he wrote to the law firm that had handled the cancellation, "that everything will blow over and that after Parliament has met and the situation is clear I could come for a portion of the tour." Churchill had in mind crossing the Atlantic in early November. "The series of lectures beginning at Fort Worth and Dallas, Texas, on November 21 and comprising the Pacific Coast finishing in New York December 14," he pointed out to the lawyers, "is a fairly compact block. This would entail my leaving England about November 11."

Churchill accepted that everything that had been planned before November 21 "would have to be definitely cancelled or indefinitely postponed." If, however, his lecture agent, Harold Peat, "likes to take a chance upon this he might at his own risk let these engagements stand for a few weeks, but I can give no guarantee beyond my natural desire to undertake the tour."[4] Peat was indignant, writing to Churchill from New York to remind him that, as he had informed him at Chartwell and again in the South of France, "and in which you concurred," the only basis of cancellation that the local sponsors would permit was the coming of war or Churchill's entry into the Cabinet. Twenty-five lectures had been scheduled, including at seven major universities, in the presence of "the most influential groups in the USA." The local sponsors "have all heralded your appearance as the event of the year, season tickets have been sold and programs printed."[5]

Churchill still hesitated to break off the tour altogether. If "matters clear up," he wrote to his lawyers, "I might be able to go later and do the Californian part of the tour before Christmas, ending December 14." But he realized that it was no use encouraging Peat "with vain

---

3. Winston S. Churchill, "Influence the US May Wield on Europe's Destiny," *Daily Telegraph and Morning Post,* 4 August 1938.
4. Letter of 17 August 1938, Martin Gilbert, *Winston S. Churchill,* Volume 5, Companion (document) Volume, Part 3, pages 1118–19.
5. Letter of 23 August 1938, Martin Gilbert, *Winston S. Churchill,* Volume 5, Companion (document) Volume, Part 3, pages 1124–25.

hopes."[6] The lecture tour was therefore abandoned altogether, which cost Churchill a substantial four-thousand-dollar forfeit.[7]

As German demands on Czechoslovakia to cede the Sudetenland region intensified, threatening a second "Great War," Churchill wrote an article about the American dimension. "It would be foolish of the European democracies, in their military arrangements, to count on any direct aid from the United States," he warned. "It would be still more foolish for war-making forces in the Dictator Governments of Europe to ignore or treat with contempt this slow but ceaseless marshalling of United States opinion around the standards of freedom and tolerance. The more weightily the personality of the United States is accounted in Europe in these years, perhaps even in these months, the better are our chances of escaping another lurch into the pit."[8]

Seeking to persuade Hitler not to use force against Czechoslovakia, Chamberlain flew to see Hitler at Berchtesgaden, the German Chancellor's mountain retreat overlooking German-annexed Austria. Seven days later he flew again to see Hitler at Bad Godesberg, on the Rhine. Chamberlain's journeys were a low point for Churchill, excluded as he was from government, and fearful that Chamberlain's policy of appeasement would only encourage Hitler. At Bad Godesberg, however, Chamberlain appeared to be toughening the British stance, so much so that war over Czechoslovakia seemed imminent.

At that moment, an exchange of telegrams between Baruch and Churchill revealed a gulf between their understanding of the situation. "In case war," Baruch telegraphed, "send children and expectant mother to me."[9] The expectant mother was Churchill's eldest daughter, Diana. Churchill replied: "Many thanks, but Diana is air-raid warden in London. Now is the time for your man to speak."[10] "Your man" was Roosevelt.

Roosevelt did not speak but watched, powerless, like Churchill, as

6. Letter of 31 August 1938, Martin Gilbert, *Winston S. Churchill*, Volume 5, Companion (document) Volume, Part 3, page 1129.

7. In the monetary values of 2005, $50,000/£25,000.

8. Winston S. Churchill, "Can Europe Stave Off War?" *Daily Telegraph and Morning Post*, 15 September 1938.

9. Telegram of 26 September 1938, Martin Gilbert, *Winston S. Churchill*, Volume 5, Companion (document) Volume, Part 3, page 1182.

10. Telegram of 27 September 1938, Baruch Papers.

Chamberlain made a third journey by air to Germany, where, at Munich, Britain and France, in conference with Germany and Italy, put pressure on Czechoslovakia to cede its mineral-rich, strongly defended Sudeten border regions to Germany. The British pressure was the most severe and effective. Czechoslovakia gave way. Chamberlain returned from Munich brandishing a piece of paper on which he and Hitler pledged "never to go to war with one another again." [11]

Churchill was appalled at the way in which Czechoslovakia's territorial integrity had been sacrificed. Two weeks after the Munich agreement, in an attempt to influence American opinion, he broadcast to the United States. "I avail myself with relief of the opportunity of speaking to the people of the United States," he said. "I do not know how long such liberties will be allowed. The stations of uncensored expression are closing down; the lights are going out; but there is still time for those to whom freedom and parliamentary government mean something, to consult together." Churchill went on: "Let me then speak in truth and earnestness while time remains. The American people have, it seems to me, formed a true judgement upon the disaster which has befallen Europe. They realise, perhaps more clearly than the French and British publics have yet done, the far-reaching consequences of the abandonment and ruin of the Czechoslovak Republic."

Churchill's broadcast continued: "If ever there was a time when men and women who cherish the ideals of the founders of the British and American Constitutions should take earnest counsel with one another, that time is now." China was being "torn to pieces" by Japan. Italy had overrun Ethiopia. "Far away, happily protected by the Atlantic and Pacific Oceans, you, the people of the United States, to whom I now have the chance to speak, are the spectators, and may I add the increasingly involved spectators of these tragedies and crimes."

There was, Churchill declared, "no doubt where American conviction and sympathies lie: but will you wait until British freedom and independence have succumbed, and then take up the cause, when it is three-quarters ruined, yourselves alone?" People said that "we ought not to allow ourselves to be drawn into a theoretical antagonism between Nazidom and democracy; but the antagonism is here now. It is

---

11. Statement signed on 30 September 1938 by Hitler and Chamberlain (having been drafted by Chamberlain), *The Times*, 1 October 1938.

this very conflict of spiritual and moral ideas which gives the free countries a great part of their strength." The threatened nations had to be united in their opposition to dictatorship and tyranny: "Is this a call to war? Does anyone pretend that preparation for resistance to aggression is unleashing war? I declare it to be the sole guarantee of peace."

Churchill's final words were a powerful statement of his faith in what close Anglo-American unity could achieve. "The swift and organized gathering of forces to confront not only military but moral aggression," he asserted, "the resolute and sober acceptance of their duty by the English-speaking peoples and by all the nations, great and small, who wish to walk with them; their faithful and zealous comradeship, would almost between night and morning clear the path of progress and banish from all our lives the fear which already darkens the sunlight to hundreds of millions of men." [12]

On 4 January 1939, echoing Churchill's call, Roosevelt called for defense against aggression, while stressing the need for "methods short of war." [13] On 15 March 1939 Hitler's forces occupied Prague and annexed the Czech provinces of Bohemia and Moravia. Within a few weeks his propaganda machine was pouring out venom against Poland. As Hitler's threats against Poland intensified, Bernard Baruch once again offered to take in members of Churchill's family, telegraphing: "My home open to all Grandchildren if trouble comes." [14] Churchill replied at once: "Grateful your offer. Consider countryside fairly safe for children. Hope you are bringing your end along." [15] "Your end" was public opinion in the United States, wedded to neutrality.

Still not invited to join the Cabinet, Churchill absorbed himself in trying to finish his history of the English-speaking peoples. "In the main," he wrote to a historian friend, "the theme is emerging of the growth of freedom and law, of the rights of the individual, of the subordination of the State to the fundamental and moral conceptions of an ever-comprehending community. Of these ideas the English-

---

12. Broadcast, 16 October 1938, notes, Martin Gilbert, *Winston S. Churchill*, Volume 5, Companion (document) Volume, Part 3, pages 1216–27.

13. Franklin D. Roosevelt, Annual Message to Congress, 4 January 1939, *The Times*, 5 January 1939.

14. Telegram of 6 April 1939, Martin Gilbert, *Winston S. Churchill*, Volume 5, Companion (document) Volume, Part 3, page 1431.

15. Telegram of 6 April 1939, Baruch Papers.

speaking peoples were the authors, then the trustees, and must now become the armed champions."[16]

On 14 April 1939 Roosevelt sent both Hitler and Mussolini a "Peace Appeal" in which he asked for assurances that the German armed forces would not invade a wide range of countries. Roosevelt listed these countries by name. There were twenty-five in all, including Britain and Poland. Two weeks after Roosevelt's appeal, Hitler summoned the Reichstag to give his answer. When he read out the list of countries, there was much derisive laughter. That evening Churchill again broadcast to the United States. President Roosevelt, he said, "is the object of a good many jibes and taunts from the German Führer. The President's high purpose and great station will enable him to rise superior to these. The American democracy is likewise subjected to ridicule. They will get over that." By Roosevelt's intervention, Churchill told his American listeners, the President had rendered a service to the cause of peace: "It may well be also that designs we do not know of were prevented, or at least suspended, by a message which has earned the gratitude of almost the whole world."

Hitler's speech had included the denunciation of the German-Polish Non-Aggression Pact of 1934, a solemn agreement that was stipulated to remain in force until 1944. The end of that pledge not to make war must be regarded, Churchill told his listeners, "as the most serious feature of the speech and as a new cause for anxiety. The Hitler method has always been to take one step at a time and, while reassuring others, to get one country shut up with him alone. For all these reasons it is of the highest consequence that there should be no slackening of the vigilance and preparation of the peace-seeking Powers of Europe and no diminution of the influence which the United States is exercising for the common good."[17]

American isolationism was however, still strong, and there was much skepticism about Britain's ability to fight. On June 14 Churchill was the guest at a dinner party at which the American journalist Walter Lippmann was present. Another guest, Harold Nicolson, noted in

16. Letter of 12 April 1939, Martin Gilbert, *Winston S. Churchill*, Volume 5, Companion (document) Volume, Part 3, page 1445.

17. Broadcast of 28 April 1939, transcript, Martin Gilbert, *Winston S. Churchill*, Volume 5, Companion (document) Volume, Part 3, pages 1478–80.

his diary: "Winston is horrified by Lippmann saying that the Ambassador Joe Kennedy had informed him that war was inevitable and we should be licked." Kennedy's forecast of a British defeat was anathema to Churchill. "Winston is stirred by this defeatism into a magnificent oration," Nicolson wrote. "He sits hunched there, waving his whiskey and soda to mark his periods, stubbing his cigar with the other hand."

Nicolson recorded Churchill's words: "It may be true, it may well be true," he told Lippmann, "that this country will at the outset of this coming and to my mind almost inevitable war be exposed to dire peril and fierce ordeals. It may be true that steel and fire will rain down upon us day and night scattering death and destruction far and wide. It may be true that our sea communications will be imperilled and our food supplies placed in jeopardy. Yet these trials and disasters, I ask you to believe me Mr Lippmann, will but serve to steel the resolution of the British people and to enhance our will for victory."

The American Ambassador should not have spoken about defeat, Churchill went on to tell Walter Lippmann. But supposing, he continued, "as I do not for one moment suppose, that Mr Kennedy were correct in his tragic utterance, then I for one would willingly lay down my life in combat rather than, in fear of defeat, surrender to the menaces of these most sinister men. It will then be for you, for the Americans, to preserve and to maintain the great heritage of the English-speaking peoples." It would be for the American people "to think Imperially, which means to think always of something higher and more vast than one's own national interests. Nor should I die happy in the great struggle which I see before me, were I not convinced that if we in this dear, dear island succumb to the ferocity and might of our enemies, over there in your distant and immense continent the torch of liberty will burn untarnished and (I should trust and hope) undismayed."[18]

Lippmann also made a note of Churchill's words in which he insisted that the Royal Air Force could inflict harsh casualties on an attacking air force, that German raids against British shipping were no threat for convoyed ships, and that the submarine had been mastered "and can be hunted successfully." This was a remarkably optimistic ac-

18. Diary entry, 14 June 1939, Harold Nicolson Papers.

count of Britain's strength, but Churchill feared that any American lack of confidence would strengthen isolationist sentiment and even affect adversely the Neutrality Acts. Churchill's account was emphatic in its confidence. "Great Britain has nearly one million soldiers already," Lippmann recorded. "German army can't pierce French carapace." Poland was "a new force," and behind it the "pad" of the Russian bear. As for a negotiated peace, Churchill told Lippmann, "there never can be peace in Europe while eight million Czechs are in bondage." [19]

On June 28 Churchill spoke in London to the City Carlton Club of the "intimate comprehension of the cause of freedom now at stake in Europe which was shown by the United States. We asked favours from nobody. Every country must judge its own interest and its own duty for itself, but the understanding, goodwill and sympathy, of the Great Republic and its eminent President were a very great encouragement to us in months and weeks of increasing anxiety." [20]

Most British newspapers were demanding Churchill's inclusion in the government. A poster in the Strand asked provocatively: "What Price Churchill?" But Chamberlain refused to bring him in, and he was still without any government position when Germany attacked Poland on September 1. Only then did Chamberlain invite him to join his administration. When Britain declared war on Germany two days later, Churchill was First Lord of the Admiralty and a member of the War Cabinet.

Among the messages of congratulation that Churchill received was one from Roosevelt's friend Justice Felix Frankfurter, who had been appointed to the United States Supreme Court nine months earlier. "Since you are sponsoring the cause of free men everywhere," Frankfurter wrote, "perhaps you will not decree it the act of an impertinent outsider for me to express satisfaction that you now are where you ought to be." Frankfurter added: "In thought, this country is certainly not neutral. There is a unanimity of opinion for the democracies unlike the confusion of feeling in 1914."

----

19. Notes, 14 June 1939, Walter Lippmann Papers.
20. Speech of 28 June 1939, *The Times*, 29 June 1939.

Churchill could take heart from Frankfurter's final words: "And since there is this clear conviction that Hitler has challenged our way of life and that you and the French are defending it, I have high hopes that we shall not be wanting in giving effective expression to our convictions."[21]

21. Letter of 4 September 1939, Martin Gilbert, *Winston S. Churchill,* Volume 5, Companion (document) Volume, Part 3, page 1620.

Chapter Eighteen

⬚

"HOPE BURDEN WILL NOT BE MADE TOO HEAVY FOR US TO BEAR"

On 3 September 1939, the day Britain declared war on Germany, Churchill entered the War Cabinet as First Lord of the Admiralty. Twenty-four hours later he learned that the steamship *Athenia*, with many British and American passengers on board, had been sunk by a German submarine in the Atlantic. He told the War Cabinet: "The occurrence should have a helpful effect as regards public opinion in the United States."[1] It was later learned that more than a hundred passengers were drowned, including twenty-eight Americans. German radio announced that Churchill was responsible; that he had placed a bomb on board. "This falsehood," he later recalled, "received some credence in unfriendly quarters."[2]

Two weeks after the outbreak of war, contemplating the long, hard course of the previous war, Churchill asked himself: "Would America ever come in again?"[3] At a meeting of the War Cabinet on September 18, after the sinking of the aircraft carrier *Courageous* with the death of more than five hundred of its crew, he suggested, at the request of his Admiralty advisers, that Britain do everything in its power "to purchase destroyers from the United States."[4] Churchill knew the limitations of such a course, however, telling his advisers: "The dollar contingency

---

1. War Cabinet No. 2 of 1939, 4 September 1939, 11.30 a.m., Cabinet Papers, 4/95.

2. Winston S. Churchill, *The Second World War*, volume 1, page 331.

3. Winston's Churchill, *The Second World War*, volume 1, pages 339–40.

4. War Cabinet No. 19 of 1939, 18 September 1939, Cabinet Papers, 65/1.

will be very great, and nothing should be bought abroad which we can make at home."[5]

The American dimension was constantly on Churchill's mind. In advocating the mining of Norwegian territorial waters to prevent the transit of Swedish iron ore to Germany, he noted that it had been done in the First World War "with the approval and co-operation of the United States," but only after America's entry into the war.[6]

In the second week of October, two weeks after it had been sent, Churchill received a letter from the White House. "My dear Churchill," the President began, "It is because you and I occupied similar positions in the World War that I want you to know how glad I am that you are back again in the Admiralty. Your problems are, I realize, complicated by new factors, but the essential is not very different. What I want you and the Prime Minister to know is that I shall at all times welcome it if you will keep me in touch personally with anything you want me to know about. You can always send sealed letters through your pouch or my pouch." Roosevelt added: "I am glad you did the Marlboro volumes before this thing started—and I much enjoyed reading them. With my sincere regards, Faithfully yours, Franklin D. Roosevelt."[7]

Churchill circulated a copy of this letter to his War Cabinet colleagues, to whom he proposed that his "exchange of correspondence" with Roosevelt should take place "in sealed envelopes conveyed by diplomatic bag." He also told his colleagues that on the previous day Roosevelt had given an order "forbidding any publicity" for the moves of American warships, an order, Churchill commented, "which in normal circumstances was only given when a country was on the point of declaring war."

Churchill proposed that in his reply to Roosevelt he would use as his theme the Pan-American Conference being held that week in Panama City, to discuss a "safety belt" area to be declared around the Americas, extending three hundred miles out to sea, within which all "belligerent activities" would be outlawed and all passenger and merchant ships of whatever nationality, moving from one American port to

------

5. "First Lord's Comments," 18 September 1939, Admiralty Papers, 205/2.
6. War Cabinet No. 20 of 1939, 19 September 1939, Cabinet Papers, 65/1.
7. Letter dated 11 September 1939, Admiralty Papers, 199/1928.

another, would be "immune from attack." This proposal, Churchill explained to the War Cabinet, would "relieve the Royal Navy of a great load of responsibility." It would set more British ships free to take part in the Atlantic convoys, and mean that the German Navy could not attack a British ship "approaching, say, Jamaica or Trinidad without risking hostilities with the United States."[8]

This telegram to Roosevelt was headed, "The following from Naval person," a reference to Churchill being First Lord of the Admiralty. In his first draft, Churchill began on a personal note. "Your letter," he wrote, "takes me back to 1914 and it is certainly a most unusual experience to occupy the same post fighting the same enemy 25 years later." This opening sentence was lost when the full reply, concerned entirely with the Panama proposals, was redrafted within the Admiralty. "We like the idea of a wide limit of say 300 miles within which no submarines of any belligerent country should act," the final draft declared. But it went on to warn of the difficulties that would be created if a German warship raider were to operate from, or take refuge in, the American zone. In such an event, Churchill told the President, "we should have to be protected or allowed to protect ourselves." There would also be "great difficulty" in Britain accepting a zone "which was only policed by some weak neutral. But of course if the American Navy takes care of it, that is all right."

Churchill's first wartime telegram to Roosevelt ended: "We wish to help you in every way in keeping the war out of American waters."[9] That night Churchill dined at his London flat with Rear-Admiral Bruce Fraser and Sir Stanley Goodall, in order to discuss the shipbuilding program. Fifteen years later Fraser recalled how, toward the end of dinner, the telephone rang and the butler came in. Churchill, "who rather disliked telephones," asked the butler:

> "Who is it?"
> "I don't know, sir," said the butler.
> "Well, say I can't attend to it now."
> "I think you ought to come, sir," said the butler, and Chur-

---

8. War Cabinet No. 38 of 1939, 5 October 1939, Cabinet Papers, 65/1.

9. Telegram of 5 October 1939, Cabinet Papers, 65/3.

chill got up rather testily. Then we heard his replies, "Yes, sir . . . No, sir."

Churchill told Fraser: "Admiral, I think you must now excuse me. This is very important and I must go and see the Prime Minister at once." [10] It was Roosevelt who had telephoned, passing on a warning given on German radio, that the United States steamship *Iroquois,* which had left Ireland on September 3 bound for the United States, would be sunk "in similar circumstances" to the sinking of the *Athenia,* the implication being that it would be the work of the Royal Navy and indeed of Churchill himself.

Churchill understood the danger of these accusations and appreciated Roosevelt's tip-off. Not only the sinking of the *Athenia* in 1939 but also of the *Lusitania* in 1915 had been laid at his door by German propaganda. The following morning he told the War Cabinet that the Germans might have secreted a bomb on board the *Iroquois,* "timed to explode when she was in mid-Atlantic." Should this happen, he commented, "the Germans no doubt hoped to claim credit for the friendly gesture of having warned the Americans and so enabled them to save the crew." [11] In fact the *Iroquois* reached port safely.

On October 14 a German submarine torpedoed the battleship *Royal Oak.* More than eight hundred officers and men were killed. Knowing Roosevelt's interest in naval matters, Churchill prepared an account of the sinking for him. "I think we ought to send something more to our American friend," he explained to the First Sea Lord, Admiral Sir Dudley Pound, "in order to keep him interested in our affairs." Churchill also told the Admiral: "If you think of anything else which could be added with advantage, please pencil it in. We must not let the liaison lapse." [12]

A few days later, in a gesture intended to bring war-making Britain and neutral America closer together, Churchill offered Roosevelt access to Britain's ASDIC anti-submarine location devices "whenever you

---

10. Admiral Fraser (Lord Fraser of North Cape) in Sir James Marchant, editor, *Winston Spencer Churchill: Servant of Crown and Commonwealth,* pages 80–81.
11. War Cabinet No. 39 of 1939, 6 October 1939, Cabinet Papers.
12. Minute of 16 October 1939, Admiralty Papers, 199/1928.

feel they would be of use to the United States Navy."[13] But when Roosevelt followed up on this offer, the British Air Ministry insisted that it be in exchange for the secrets of an American invention, the Norden bombsight, which Britain was eager to acquire. Advised by his officials, Roosevelt was unwilling to proceed on the basis of an exchange.

Churchill's initiative had failed. But his faith in the closer involvement of the United States was unshaken. The American willingness to create a three-hundred-mile submarine-free zone in the western Atlantic was an important first fruit. In a radio broadcast in November he told his British listeners: "The great English-speaking Republic across the Atlantic Ocean makes no secret of its sympathies or of its self-questioning, and translates these sentiments into actions of a character which anyone may judge for himself."[14]

Churchill did his utmost not to fall foul of American interests. Eager to move in Norwegian territorial waters against the ships carrying Swedish iron ore to Germany, he asked Joseph Kennedy, the American Ambassador, to find out what Roosevelt's reaction would be "to the suggestion that we should mine Norwegian territorial waters." On December 11 Churchill was able to report to the War Cabinet that he had received a reply from Washington "which indicated that the President's reactions were more favourable than he had hoped."[15]

To maintain his link with Roosevelt, unprecedented between a British War Cabinet Minister and an American President, at Christmas 1939 Churchill sent Roosevelt details of the Admiralty's success in mastering the German magnetic mine, which had caused grave havoc to British merchant ships. "Magnetic mines were deadly weapons," Churchill told the President, "on account of possibility of varying sensitiveness of discharge, but we think we have got hold of its tail, though we do not want them to know this."[16]

That winter trouble arose with the United States in the South Atlantic. After the Battle of the River Plate and the scuttling of the Ger-

---

13. Telegram of 16 October 1939, "Naval Person to President Roosevelt," copy in Churchill Papers, 20/15, Martin Gilbert, *The Churchill War Papers*, Volume 1, pages 246–47.
14. Broadcast of 12 November 1939, BBC Written Archives.
15. War Cabinet No. 111 of 1939, 11 December 1939, Cabinet Papers.
16. Message of 24 December 1939, Admiralty Papers, 199/1928.

man pocket battleship *Graf Spee* off the Uruguayan port of Montevideo, the United States supported protests from several South American governments that the British warships involved had entered the three-hundred-mile noncombatant zone. There were also complaints, in which the United States joined, of British warships seizing German supply ships within the noncombatant zone. Britain was, however, at war, and with a ruthless adversary. Churchill could not allow the Royal Navy to be unduly restricted in challenging German naval depredations.

Anxious to avoid friction with the United States, Churchill drafted a telegram for Roosevelt apologizing for "recent incidents" in which the seizures had taken place. "We cannot always refrain," he explained, "from stopping enemy ships outside International three-mile limit when these may well be supply ships for U-Boats or surface raiders." Nevertheless, Churchill told the President, instructions had been given "only to arrest or fire upon them out of sight of United States shore." He went on to defend the British warships, pointing out that as a result of the scuttling of the *Graf Spee* the whole of the South Atlantic "is now clear and may perhaps continue clear of warlike operations." This fact, Churchill commented, "must be a blessing to South American Republics whose trade was hampered by activities of raiders and whose ports were used for his supply ships and information centres." German use of these ports had, thanks to the British action, come to an end.

Churchill explained to Roosevelt that the laws of war had given the *Graf Spee* the right to "capture, or sink" all ships trading with Britain in the South Atlantic. "No protest was made about this," Churchill stressed, "although it injured Argentine commercial interests," and he went on to ask: "Why then should complaints be made of our action in ridding seas of this raider in strict accordance with same International Laws from which we had been suffering." Even a single German raider "loose in the North Atlantic," Churchill pointed out, required the use of half of Britain's battle fleet "to give sure protection" to the merchant ships. If Britain "should break under load," he warned, the South American republics "would soon have many worse enemies than the sound of one day's distant seaward cannonade. And you also, Sir"— Churchill added—"in quite a short time would have more direct cares."

Churchill went on to ask Roosevelt that "full consideration" should be given to Britain "at this crucial period," and that the United States should put the "best construction" on British action "indispensable to end war shortly in right way." On a personal note, Churchill told Roosevelt that he was sending him various reports of the Battle of the River Plate.[17] "Of course," Churchill wrote to Chamberlain on Christmas Day, "the President is our best friend, but I expect he wants to be re-elected and I fear that isolationism is the winning ticket."[18]

At the end of January 1940 Churchill renewed his correspondence with Roosevelt. "I gave orders last night," he telegraphed on January 29, "that no American ship should in any circumstances be diverted into the combat zone round the British Islands declared by you. I trust this will be satisfactory."[19] On the following day, when complications arose, Churchill telegraphed again: "It has been pointed out to me that my signal to Fleet can only be maintained if measures are taken in advance of their departure that US ships carry no objectionable cargo." Moreover, Churchill explained, "in exceptional cases it may be necessary to divert United States ships if we have definite ground for suspicion against them."[20]

In his reply Roosevelt thanked Churchill for the "tremendously interesting account" of the *Graf Spee* action. As for the "search and detention of American ships," the conversations on this were, he believed, "working out satisfactorily." Roosevelt added, however: "I would not be frank unless I told you that there has been much public criticism here. The general feeling is that the net benefit to your people and to France is hardly worth the definite annoyance caused to us." That, Roosevelt added with a verbal twinkle, "is always found to be so, in a nation which is 3,000 miles away from the fact of war." Roosevelt ended: "I wish much that I could talk things over with you in person—but I am grateful to you for keeping me in touch, as you do."[21]

In April, the first full-scale British battle of the war began for control of the Norwegian coast. But at the very moment when Britain

---

17. Message of 25 December 1939, Admiralty Papers, 199/1928.

18. Letter of 25 December 1939, Neville Chamberlain Papers.

19. Telegram of 29 January 1940, Churchill Papers, 20/15, Martin Gilbert, *The Churchill War Papers*, Volume 1, page 703.

20. Telegram of 30 January 1940, Admiralty Papers, 199/1928.

21. Letter of 1 February 1940, Admiralty Papers, 199/1928.

sought to prevent the movement of iron ore essential for the German war effort through the Norwegian port of Narvik, German troops landed in Oslo and moved rapidly northward. At the height of the battle Churchill wrote to Roosevelt about an earlier naval engagement: "My dear Mr President, In view of the interest you displayed in the Battle of the River Plate, I thought you would like to see an advance copy of the official account of the Battle which we shall shortly be publishing." [22]

Denmark was overrun by Germany by the end of April. By the beginning of the second week of May, the British forces that had landed in Norway were being beaten back. Confidence in Neville Chamberlain's leadership was waning. On the morning of May 10, without warning or declaration of war, German forces attacked westward, against Britain's ally France and two neutral countries, Holland and Belgium. Later that day Chamberlain resigned, and Churchill became Prime Minister.

---

22. Letter of 7 May 1940, Admiralty Papers, 199/1928.

Chapter Nineteen

⌘

"I SHALL DRAG
THE UNITED STATES IN"

On 10 May 1940, Prime Minister at last, Churchill formed what he called the "Grand Coalition" from across the political spectrum. In his War Cabinet, the Labour Party and its leader Clement Attlee held major positions. Sir Archibald Sinclair, then Leader of the Liberal Party, became Secretary of State for Air. That day, as German troops advanced through Belgium, Holland and France, and with Britain facing a strong adversary in the air, Churchill asked Roosevelt, through the head of the British Purchasing Mission in Washington, D.C., Arthur Purvis, to allow a British aircraft carrier to sail at once to a United States East Coast port. This was to enable the American aircraft that Britain had already bought to be shipped to Britain uncrated and ready to fly. Roosevelt told Purvis that because of the Neutrality Act this could not be done.

This was a blow to Churchill's hopes for the swift arrival of these essential aircraft. It was Roosevelt himself, however, who then suggested, as Purvis telegraphed to London, that the British aircraft carrier sail instead to Botwood, Newfoundland, "which incidentally would be the shorter trip. We could then arrange to have the aircraft flown to the Canadian border, pushed across that border and flown on to Botwood."

Roosevelt had hit upon a device to circumvent his own Neutrality Act. "We already know," Purvis added, "that this method is feasible and legal." Churchill also asked Roosevelt to increase the rate of warplane production for Britain. In response Roosevelt suggested using American reserve civil transport planes "and private-owner planes" for trans-

port and light-bombing purposes. Thirty-five such aircraft were immediately switched from American to British purchasers. Three days later,
however, Purvis warned that stocks of military aircraft in the United
States "which our technical people feel would have value" were limited
to 150 pursuit planes and 144 bombers. Roosevelt had been advised
that the pursuit planes "represent the only planes available for training
purposes" and that their release to Britain would delay the American
pilot-training program for four to six months. Nor, Purvis warned, was
United States public opinion "yet considered ripe" to allow the release
of the naval equipment Britain had requested, although opinion was
"moving rapidly in that direction."[1]

In a telegram to Roosevelt on May 15, the first direct message since
he had become Prime Minister—and no longer sent from "Naval Person" but from "Former Naval Person," as he was no longer at the Admiralty—Churchill began with a personal note. "Although I have
changed my office," he wrote, "I am sure you would not wish me to dis-
continue our intimate, private correspondence." Churchill then gave a
survey of the first five days of his premiership. "As you are no doubt
aware," he wrote, "the scene has darkened swiftly. The enemy have a
marked preponderance in the air, and their new technique is making a
deep impression upon the French. I think myself the battle on land
has only just begun, and I should like to see the masses engage. Up to
the present, Hitler is working with specialized units in tanks and air."

The small countries, Churchill told Roosevelt, "are simply
smashed up, one by one, like matchwood." "We expect to be attacked
here ourselves," Churchill added, "both from the air and by parachute
and air-borne troops in the near future, and are getting ready for
them."

Churchill then turned in his telegram to what would be, in the
weeks and months ahead, his steady refrain. "If necessary," he told
Roosevelt, "we shall continue the war alone, and we are not afraid of
that. But I trust you realise, Mr. President, that the voice and force of
the United States may count for nothing if they are withheld too long.
You may have a completely subjugated Nazified Europe established

---

1. Telegram of 15 May 1940, Cabinet Papers, 85/14.

with astonishing swiftness, and the weight may be more than we can bear."

Britain's "immediate needs," Churchill told the President, were six in all, starting with "the loan of forty or so of your older destroyers to bridge gap between what we have now and the large new construction we put in hand at the beginning of the war." In a year's time Britain would have "plenty," but if in the interval "Italy comes in against us with another 100 submarines, we may be strained to breaking-point."

The second need was for "several hundred of the latest types of aircraft, of which you are now getting delivery." These could be repaid "by those now being constructed in the United States for us." A third need was for anti-aircraft equipment and ammunition, "of which again there will be plenty next year, if we are alive to see it." Fourth, because Britain's iron ore supply was "being compromised from Sweden, from North Africa, and perhaps from Northern Spain," Britain must purchase steel in the United States. "We shall go on paying dollars for as long as we can," Churchill assured the President, "but I should like to feel reasonably sure that when we can pay no more, you will give us the stuff all the same."

Having received many reports of possible German parachute or airborne descents in Ireland, Churchill also asked for the visit of a United States naval squadron to Southern Irish ports. Sixth, Churchill wrote, "I am looking to you to keep that Japanese dog quiet in the Pacific, using Singapore in any way convenient."[2]

Most of Churchill's requests could not be met. Replying two days later, Roosevelt stated that the loan or gift of forty or fifty older destroyers would require the authorization of Congress, "and I am not certain that it would be wise for that suggestion to be made to the Congress at this moment." Furthermore, Roosevelt added, it seemed doubtful "from the standpoint of our own defense requirements," including American obligations in the Pacific, "whether we could dispose even temporarily of these destroyers." He was, however, doing all in his power to make it possible for the Allied governments "to obtain the latest types of aircraft in the United States," and to discuss the question of possible purchases of anti-aircraft equipment, ammunition and

---

2. Telegram of 15 May 1940, Premier Papers, 3/468.

steel. As for Japan, the American fleet "is now concentrated at Hawaii," where it would remain "at least for the time being."[3]

Disappointed, Churchill replied on May 18 that if American assistance was to play any part, "it must be available soon."[4] His distress at Roosevelt's inability to provide the destroyers was reflected on the following day when he told his son, Randolph—"with great intensity," Randolph later recalled—"I shall drag the United States in."[5]

On May 19 Churchill prepared another telegram to Roosevelt: "Considering the soothing words he always uses to Americans, and particularly to the President," his Junior Private Secretary, John "Jock" Colville, noted in his diary, "I was somewhat taken aback when he said to me: 'Here's a telegram for those bloody Yankees. Send it off tonight.'"[6]

The reason for this telegram was a message from the British Ambassador in Washington, Lord Lothian, informing Churchill that the President could not yet provide even the minimum of destroyers. Lothian added that there was little faith in Washington about Britain's ability to withstand a German attack; even Roosevelt had expressed his concern. "Lothian has reported his conversation with you," Churchill telegraphed to the President. "I understand your difficulties, but I am very sorry about the destroyers. If they were here in six weeks they would play an invaluable part."

The battle in France, Churchill told Roosevelt, "is full of danger to both sides. Though we have taken heavy toll of enemy in the air and are clawing down two or three to one of their planes, they have still a formidable numerical superiority. Our most vital need is, therefore, the delivery at the earliest possible date of the largest possible number of Curtiss P. 40 fighters now in course of delivery to your Army."

Churchill then referred to Roosevelt's concern at Britain's ability to withstand a German invasion. "With regard to the closing part of your talk with Lothian," Churchill wrote, "our intention is, whatever happens, to fight on to the end in this Island, and, provided we can get

---

3. Telegram of 17 May 1940, Premier Papers, 3/468.
4. Telegram of 18 May 1940, Premier Papers, 3/468.
5. Randolph S. Churchill, recollections, dictated on 13 February 1963, Martin Gilbert Papers.
6. Diary entry, 19 May 1940, Colville Papers.

the help for which we ask, we hope to run them very close in the air battles in view of individual superiority." Members of his administration "would likely go down during this process should it result adversely, but in no conceivable circumstances will we consent to surrender."

If his own Cabinet Ministers "were finished," Churchill warned the President, "and others came in to parley amid the ruins, you must not be blind to the fact that the sole remaining bargaining counter with Germany would be the Fleet, and, if this country was left by the United States to its fate, no one would have the right to blame those then responsible if they made the best terms they could for the surviving inhabitants."

These were stern, fearful words. For several hours Churchill hesitated to send them. But they were the reality as he saw it. "Excuse me, Mr President, putting this nightmare bluntly," he ended. "Evidently I could not answer for my successors, who in utter despair and helplessness might well have to accommodate themselves to the German will. However, there is happily no need at present to dwell upon such ideas. Once more thanking you for your goodwill."[7]

Britain could not afford to quarrel with the United States if the supplies already on their way were to continue to flow. Churchill's task was to accelerate and increase the lifeline. From Washington, Lothian sent an American proposal that Britain lease to the United States the British airfields in Trinidad, Bermuda and Newfoundland. Churchill opposed this, unless Britain received something in return. The United States had "given us practically no help in the war," he told the War Cabinet, "and now they saw how great was the danger, their attitude was that they wanted to keep everything that would help us for their own defence."[8]

Not all the news reaching Churchill from America was unpalatable. On May 30, following an appeal for the urgent purchase of 12,700 tons of steel bars, Purvis was able to report that he had purchased 4,300 tons for shipment to Britain in June, July and August, with a further 8,400 tons to come by the end of August, some of it diverted from orders then being carried out in America for dispatch to Chile.

---

7. Telegram of 20 May 1940, Premier Papers, 3/468.
8. War Cabinet No. 141 of 1940, 27 May 1940, Cabinet Papers, 65/7.

•   •   •

France was facing a sustained German onslaught. Flying to Paris on May 31, Churchill told the French leaders that the United States had been "roused" by recent events. Even if they did not enter the war they "would soon be prepared to give us powerful aid." The French should order steel and other essentials "in vast quantities." Should Britain and France become unable to pay, "America would nevertheless continue to deliver."

The French were skeptical, but Churchill knew what America was already doing for Britain behind a cloak of deepest secrecy. He had just learned from Purvis that the American Chief of Staff, General George C. Marshall, was prepared to bypass the Neutrality Act by declaring substantial quantities of army munitions "as surplus" and therefore available for purchase. There was also a prospect of Britain being given priority to buy 15,000 tons of the new trinitrotoluol explosive, TNT.[9] In addition, at Churchill's request the Americans agreed to hold up delivery of raw materials requested by Germany, and available from United States stocks, which Britain judged essential to German war-making capacity.

On June 1, following General Marshall's suggestion, Roosevelt authorized the dispatch to Britain of a substantial quantity of American "surplus" war supplies, including nine hundred field guns with a million rounds of ammunition, 80,000 machine guns, and half a million rifles manufactured in the First World War. With these rifles came 125 million rounds of ammunition. Churchill later wrote: "All this reads easily now, but at that time it was a supreme act of faith and leadership for the United States to deprive themselves of this very considerable mass of arms for the sake of a country which many deemed already beaten." [10]

A continuing cause of friction was the much-needed destroyers. On June 4 Churchill learned from Purvis that Roosevelt had decided "to his regret" that as far as the destroyers were concerned "the United States could not spare any." [11] When the Canadian Prime Minister, William Mackenzie King, suggested to Churchill that in the event of a

---

9. Message of 31 May 1940, Cabinet Papers, 85/14.
10. Winston S. Churchill, *The Second World War,* Volume 2, page 116.
11. Note of 4 June 1940, Premier Papers, 3/468.

British defeat the Royal Navy should be transferred to Canada, Churchill replied caustically: "We must be careful not to let Americans view too complacently prospect of a British collapse, out of which they would get the British Fleet and the guardianship of the British Empire, minus Great Britain."

Churchill then revealed his innermost anguish. "Although President is our best friend," he told the Canadian Prime Minister, "no practical help has been forthcoming from the United States as yet. We have not expected them to send military aid, but they have not even sent any worthy contribution in destroyers or planes, or by a visit of a squadron of their Fleet to Southern Irish ports." [12]

In the second week of June, Lord Lothian raised the question of what Churchill had meant two weeks earlier, at the time of the evacuation of 300,000 British and French troops from imminent German captivity at Dunkirk, when he spoke about the New World eventually stepping forth "to the rescue and liberation of the Old." Churchill explained that his words were addressed primarily as a warning to Germany and Italy, "to whom the idea of a war of Continents and a long war are at present obnoxious," but he went on to warn that if Britain "broke under invasion" a pro-German Government might obtain far easier terms from Germany by surrendering the Fleet, "thus making Germany and Japan masters of the New World." This would not be done by his government, but if a Quisling Government were set up "it is exactly what they would do, and perhaps the only thing they could do, and the President should bear this very clearly in mind."

Churchill told Lothian that he should see the President and "discourage any complacent assumption on United States' part that they will pick up the débris of the British Empire by their present policy. On the contrary, they run the terrible risk that their sea-power will be completely over-matched. Moreover, islands and naval bases to hold the United States in awe should certainly be claimed by the Nazis." A final warning to Roosevelt reflected a real terror in Churchill's mind. "If we go down," he wrote, "Hitler has a very good chance of conquering the world." [13]

---

12. Telegram of 5 June 1940, Premier Papers, 4/43B/1.
13. Telegram of 9 June 1940, Martin Gilbert, *The Churchill War Papers*, Volume 2, pages 270–71.

Toward midnight on June 10, Churchill listened to a broadcast of a speech by Roosevelt at the University of Virginia. "We will extend to the opponents of force," said Roosevelt, "the material resources of this nation. We will not slow down or detour. Signs and signals call for speed: full speed ahead." Roosevelt added: "I call for effort, courage, sacrifice, devotion, and the love of freedom. All these are possible."[14]

It was, Churchill later wrote, "a magnificent speech, instinct with passion, and carrying to us a message of hope."[15] He at once dictated a message to the President, telling him that all who listened "were fortified by the grand scope of your declaration." The statement that the material aid of the United States would be given to the Allies in their struggle was, Churchill believed, "a strong encouragement in a dark but not unhopeful hour." Churchill then put before Roosevelt once again Britain's immediate needs, telling him that airplanes and flying boats were essential "in the impending struggle for the life of Great Britain." But even more pressing, he reiterated, was the need for destroyers.

Italy had just declared war on France and Britain. "The Italian outrage," Churchill told the President, "makes it necessary for us to cope with a much larger number of submarines, which may come out into the Atlantic and perhaps be based on Spanish ports. To this the only counter is destroyers. Nothing is so important as for us to have the thirty or forty old destroyers you have already had reconditioned." They would "bridge the gap of six months before our wartime new construction comes into play. We will return them or their equivalents to you, without fail, at six months' notice if at any time you need them."

Churchill had expended all his arguments and offers. "The next six months are vital," he warned the President. "If while we have to guard the East Coast against invasion a new heavy German-Italian submarine attack is launched against our commerce the strain may be beyond our resources." Reading this telegram before it was sent off, Churchill added at this point, in his own handwriting: ". . . and the

14. Speech of 10 June 1940, Samuel I. Rosenman, editor, *The Public Papers and Addresses of Franklin D. Roosevelt*, Volume 9, number 58.

15. Winston S. Churchill, *The Second World War*, Volume 2, page 116.

ocean's traffic by which we live may be strangled. Not a day should be lost."

Feeling that he should not end on too critical a note, Churchill dictated a final sentence: "I send you my heartfelt thanks and those of my colleagues for all you are doing and seeking to do for what we may now indeed call the Common Cause."[16]

Churchill's appeal for destroyers crossed with a telegram from Lothian that raised serious questions of how Roosevelt might respond. "Have just learned from authoritative source," the Ambassador wrote, "that the President is not convinced that our need for destroyers is serious, and is therefore concentrating on the Allies' other needs." It was "imperative," Lothian advised, for Churchill to inform Roosevelt "as soon as possible" of the numbers, types and tonnages of destroyers lost, of the numbers damaged, of the time taken to repair these, "and any other information necessary to convince him of our case." Lothian added ominously that the American newspapers had been carrying a statement "that we have already made good all destroyers lost."[17]

Churchill did as Lothian advised, but the situation remained frustrating and vexatious. On June 11, as the French leaders fled south from Paris to the Loire, Churchill had set off by air at the request of the Prime Minister, Paul Reynaud, to offer what help he could, but he was convinced that effective help could only come in some form of American commitment. Before leaving London he had telegraphed to Roosevelt: "Anything you can say or do to help them now may make the difference."[18]

Roosevelt did not reply. When Churchill returned from France he telegraphed again, desperate for some American initiative that could stiffen the resolve of the French Ministers, some of whom were already talking of making peace with the German invader. "It seems to me," Churchill told the President, "that there must be many elements in France who will wish to continue the struggle either in France or in the French Colonies, or in both. This therefore is the moment for you to strengthen Reynaud the utmost you can, and try to tip the balance in favour of the best and longest possible French resistance. . . . If there is

---

16. Telegram of 11 June 1940, Premier Papers, 3/468.
17. Telegram of 12 June 1940, Premier Papers, 3/468.
18. Telegram of 11 June 1940, Premier Papers, 3/468.

anything you can say publicly or privately to the French, now is the time."[19]

When Churchill returned to France five days later, he assured the French leaders that Roosevelt would act. Back in England again, he was excited to read a message from Roosevelt to Reynaud, stating that the American government was doing "everything in its power to make available to the Allied Governments the material they so urgently require, and our efforts to do still more are being redoubled."[20] This message, Churchill told the War Cabinet, "came as near as possible to a declaration of war and probably as much as the President could do without Congress." The President, Churchill told his colleagues, "could hardly urge the French to continue the struggle, and to undergo further torture, if he did not intend to enter the war to support them." The French Army was even then being beaten back on the battlefield, and French civilians subjected to vicious German air attack as they fled their towns and villages.

If Roosevelt was not "disavowed" by his own country, Churchill believed, it was "clear" that he would bring the Americans into the war "on our side" in the near future. The fact that Roosevelt's reply had come in advance of Reynaud's final appeal made the effect of that reply "even more striking." Leaving the War Cabinet meeting for a few moments to see Joseph Kennedy, Churchill returned with the information, vouchsafed by the American Ambassador, that Roosevelt "must have authorized" the publication of his message to Reynaud, even if no such authorization had been formally received.

The War Cabinet's discussion of Roosevelt's intentions centered on the virtual certainty of an American declaration of war. No Head of State could send such a message to France, it was argued, "urging her to continue her agony, unless he was certain that his country was coming to her aid." It was therefore agreed, at Churchill's suggestion, to tell Reynaud that Roosevelt's message, even though it had not yet been made public, "fulfilled every hope and could only mean that the United States intended to enter the war on our side."

This was a grave misconception on Churchill's part—his most serious error of judgment with regard to the United States in his whole

19. Telegram of 12 June 1940, Premier Papers, 3/468.
20. Message of 13 June 1940, Cabinet Papers, 65/7.

career—yet it seemed fully justified. After Churchill left the War Cabinet a second time to speak to the American Ambassador, Kennedy told him that he had just spoken to the President on the telephone and—as Churchill reported back to the War Cabinet—Roosevelt had been "agreeable" to the publication of his message to France. Kennedy did, however, add some dispiriting news, that Secretary of State Cordell Hull "was opposed" to making the message public, and that even Roosevelt "did not realise how critical the situation was."[21]

Churchill sought to remedy this situation at once. The only possibility of continuing French resistance, he telegraphed to Roosevelt that night, was if Reynaud could give his people the hope of ultimate victory. Such a hope "could only be kindled by American intervention up to the extreme limit open to you." The publication of Roosevelt's reply to Reynaud would be the decisive factor. The British Cabinet, Churchill assured Roosevelt, had been "profoundly impressed" by the message, "but Mr President, I must tell you that it seems to me absolutely vital that this message should be published tomorrow 14th June in order that it may play the decisive part in turning the course of world history."

Publication of the Roosevelt message, Churchill added, "will I am sure decide the French to deny Hitler a patched-up peace with France. He needs this peace in order to destroy us and take a long step forward to world mastery. All the far-reaching plans, strategic, economic, political and moral which your message expounds, may be still-born if the French cut out now. Therefore I urge that the message should be published now." The moment "Hitler finds he cannot dictate a Nazi peace in Paris he will turn his fury on to us."[22]

Immediately after the War Cabinet meeting on the night of June 13, Churchill also sent a telegram to Reynaud, assuring him that if France were to remain in the war "we feel that the United States is committed beyond recall to take the only remaining step, namely, becoming a belligerent in form as she has already constituted herself in fact." If France continued to resist, Churchill added, an American declaration of war "must inevitably follow."[23]

------

21. War Cabinet No. 165 of 1940, Cabinet Papers, 65/7.
22. Telegram of 14 June 1940, Cabinet Papers, 65/13.
23. Telegram of 13 June 1940, Cabinet Papers, 65/7.

This was Churchill's ultimate hope, his ultimate delusion, and within a few days his ultimate disappointment. At dawn on June 14 Joseph Kennedy telephoned to tell him that Roosevelt refused to make his message public, and that it "was in no sense intended to commit and did not commit the Government to military participation in support of Allied governments." Only Congress could make any such commitment.[24] Churchill was bitterly disappointed. "If we go down," he telegraphed Roosevelt on the night of June 14, "you may have a United States of Europe under the Nazi command, far stronger, far better armed than the New World."[25]

Churchill made one last effort—as the French Government, forced to do so by the continuing German advance, fell back to Bordeaux—to persuade Roosevelt to change his mind. In a telegram on June 15 he warned the President that there was "no getting away from the fact" that France would not be prepared to continue the war, even from its territory in North Africa, if America declined to enter the war. "Indeed," Churchill told Roosevelt, "the British Ambassador in Bordeaux tells me that if your reply does not contain the assurance asked for, the French will very quickly ask for an armistice, and I much doubt whether it will be possible in that event for us to keep the French Fleet out of German hands."

Churchill set out what he wanted Roosevelt to do. "When I speak of the United States entering the war," he explained, "I am, of course, not thinking in terms of an expeditionary force, which I know is out of the question. What I have in mind is the tremendous moral effect that such an American decision would produce, not merely in France but also in all the democratic countries of the world, and, in the opposite sense, on the German and Italian peoples."[26]

Roosevelt remained unbending. His refusal to contemplate "entering the war" to try to maintain France at war was a low point for Churchill. Yet at the same time, Roosevelt's material help to Britain, while falling far short of what Churchill had asked for, was impressive and welcome. Starting on June 15 Churchill was given a daily secret report of the loading and departure from various American East Coast ports

---

24. Telegram of 14 June 1940, Premier Papers, 3/468.
25. Telegram of 15 June 1940, Cabinet Papers, 65/13.
26. Telegram of 15 June 1940, Premier Papers, 3/468.

of the guns, rifles and ammunition that had been authorized by Roosevelt two weeks earlier.

On June 16 France asked the Germans for an armistice. At that desperate moment for Britain, Roosevelt rejected yet another appeal by Churchill for the immediate dispatch of thirty-five American destroyers.

The imminent fall of France confronted Churchill with what he saw as a grave danger from the United States itself. If Roosevelt were asked to mediate, Churchill warned the War Cabinet, he might give advice "that was of application to the United Kingdom as well as France." Churchill feared above all that Roosevelt might "issue an appeal to all belligerent Governments to call the war off." Such an appeal "might to some extent shake some sections of British public opinion, the whole of which was at present united and inflexible. At the present juncture all thoughts of coming to terms with the enemy must be dismissed so far as Britain was concerned. We were fighting for our lives and it was vital that we should allow no chink to appear in our armour."[27]

Churchill had been Prime Minister for thirty-six days. In that short time, Germany had conquered Denmark, Norway, Belgium, Holland, Luxembourg and France. And the United States, his mother's land, had given him both aid and anguish.

---

27. War Cabinet No. 168 of 16 June 1940, Cabinet Papers, 65/13.

Chapter Twenty

✠

"UNTIL THE OLD WORLD—
AND THE NEW—CAN JOIN HANDS"

Following the fall of France in June 1940, the German air force began a sustained attack on British airfields, submitting the Royal Air Force to a ferocious assault. If this "Battle of Britain" failed, Churchill warned Parliament, "then the whole world, including the United States, and all that we have known and cared for, will sink into the abyss of a new dark age made more sinister, and perhaps more protracted, by the lights of a perverted science."[1]

As the Battle of Britain began, Churchill received encouraging news from the United States: Britain's tank production targets for the following year would be met due to the production of crucial tank parts in the United States. On June 20, at a Secret Session of the House of Commons, he spoke with remarkable optimism about the eventual participation of the United States: "Nothing will stir them like fighting in England," he said. It was "no good" suggesting to them that Britain was down and out. It was Britain's "heroic struggle" that offered the "best chance of bringing them in."

If Britain could hold out until after the American elections that November, Churchill told the House, "I cannot doubt the whole English-speaking world will be in line together." Hitler would then have against him "the Oceans and the Air" and all the continents except Europe. Meanwhile America was providing "the fullest aid."[2] The phrase

---

1. Speech of 18 June 1940, *Hansard*, Parliamentary debates.
2. Speech notes, 20 June 1940, Charles Eade, editor, *Secret Session Speeches by the Right Hon. Winston S. Churchill, OM, CH, MP,* pages 8–16.

"fullest aid" was an optimistic gloss on what Churchill knew. When he asked General Hastings Ismay, the Chief of his Defense Staff, for a list of American aircraft and munitions "which have actually arrived in this country," Ismay answered with one word: "Nil." Nor was anything expected for another two weeks.[3] In another setback the Americans turned down a request for an additional quarter of a million rifles.

In Washington on June 26, the head of the British Purchasing Mission, Arthur Purvis, spoke to Henry Morgenthau about the urgent transfer to Britain of twenty American motor torpedo boats. As a result of criticism in Congress, Purvis reported to London, the United States administration had "backwatered" on granting Britain priority aid. At the same time Roosevelt had issued a statement that the transfer of the much-needed torpedo boats was "no longer valid." The United States Navy had invoked an Act of Congress of 1917, which the United States Attorney General had confirmed, "that the sale to a belligerent of an armed vessel is illegal." Purvis warned that this law "also prevents the sale of destroyers."[4]

In answer to a suggestion from Lord Lothian, that American public opinion needed the spur of a Churchill broadcast, Churchill replied on June 28: "No doubt I will make some broadcast presently, but I don't think words count for much now," and he told the Ambassador: "Too much attention should not be paid to eddies of United States opinion. Only force of events can govern them. Up till April they were so sure the Allies would win that they did not think help necessary. Now they are so sure we shall lose that they do not think it possible." Churchill added that if Britain were invaded, feeling against the United States "would be similar to French bitterness against us now," and he added: "We have really not had any help worth speaking of from the United States so far."

"We know President is our best friend," Churchill told Lothian, "but it is no use trying to dance attendance upon Republican and Democratic Conventions. What really matters is whether Hitler is master of Britain in three months or not. I think not. But this is a matter which cannot be argued beforehand."[5]

---

3. Minute of 21 June 1940 and reply, Premier Papers, 3/479.
4. Telegram of 26 June 1940, Cabinet Papers, 84/14.
5. Telegram of 28 June 1940, Churchill Papers, 20/14, Martin Gilbert, *The Churchill War Papers*, Volume 2, page 436.

In a dramatic turn of fortune, at the end of June, Churchill learned that General Marshall, without informing Congress, had arranged for the release from United States Army and Navy stocks of sufficient war material to equip ten British Divisions. This included 521 operational aircraft.[6] The first sixteen, all Northrop biplanes, were put on board ship in New York on June 30 for the transatlantic crossing.

As part of the Franco-German Armistice, France had agreed to transfer its warships to German control. Part of that fleet was at Oran, in French North Africa. When Lothian asked Roosevelt if he would support Britain's "forcible seizure" of the ships, Roosevelt replied, "certainly." He would expect the French ships to be seized rather than "fall into German hands."[7]

Before taking action against the French warships at Oran, Churchill instructed the British admiral outside the port to open negotiations with his French counterpart. One offer was that the French ships sail to the United States for the duration of the war, their crews being repatriated to France if they wished. When negotiations failed, the British warships opened fire. It was one of the hardest, and harshest, of Churchill's wartime decisions. More than 1,250 French sailors, Britain's allies of two-and-a-half weeks earlier, were killed, and most of the ships disabled. Seven months later Roosevelt's personal emissary to Churchill, Harry Hopkins, told a member of Churchill's Private Office that it was Britain's action at Oran that convinced Roosevelt, in spite of Ambassador Kennedy's "defeatist opinions," that Britain would continue to fight.[8]

After Oran, Churchill drafted a strong telegram to Roosevelt, asking yet again for destroyers, and telling him the United States would bear "a grievous responsibility if she failed Britain now." The Foreign Secretary, Lord Halifax, persuaded him not to send it.[9] That day more than a quarter of a million American rifles, seventy-seven million rounds of ammunition, more than three hundred field guns and nearly half a million rounds of high-explosive shells were on board

---

6. Note of 23 June 1940, Premier Papers, 3/479/1.
7. Telegram of 3 July 1940, Cabinet Papers, 65/14.
8. Sir John Colville recollection in Warren Tute, *The Deadly Stroke,* page 17.
9. Colville diary, 5 July 1940, Colville Papers.

ship crossing the Atlantic to Britain. Churchill was informed of their safe arrival five days later.

That week Roosevelt sent Colonel "Wild Bill" Donovan, head of the Office of Strategic Services (OSS), to Britain, to suggest an exchange of secrets between the two countries. But when Donovan proposed that Britain share its ASDIC anti-submarine and radar secrets with the United States, Churchill wrote to General Ismay: "Are we going to throw all our secrets into the American lap, and see what they give us in exchange? If so, I am against it." It would be "very much better to go slow," Churchill advised, "as we have far more to give than they."

He was not "in a hurry," Churchill told Ismay, "to give our secrets until the United States is much nearer to the war than she is now." He also had a security reason for hesitation, telling Ismay that he expected "that anything given to the United States Services, in which there are necessarily so many Germans, goes pretty quickly to Berlin in time of peace." Once in a state of war, Churchill added, "very much better controls are operative."[10]

With Roosevelt's authority behind him, Donovan was insistent. Given Britain's dependence on American supplies, Churchill acquiesced. The exchange of secrets would go ahead. Each country would gain something valuable. There was an added benefit for Britain: The research on the secret devices it shared with America could be carried out in the United States, and these devices could then be manufactured for Britain there.

Encouraging news reached Churchill on July 25. An agreement had been signed in Washington whereby the United States would manufacture war materials for Britain according to a ratio of their respective needs of 19 to 14, putting British and American requirements almost on parity. This ratio meant that 14,375 aircraft would be manufactured for Britain during the coming twenty-one months. A similar agreement was being negotiated for arms and ammunition.

Pressed to do so by the Admiralty, Churchill asked Lord Lothian to reactivate the request for American destroyers. "Need of American destroyers is more urgent than ever," he wrote, "in view of losses and the need of coping with invasion threat as well as keeping Atlantic approaches open and dealing with Italy." And he went on to explain:

---

10. Minute of 17 July 1940, Premier Papers, 3/475/1.

"There is nothing that America can do at this moment that would be of greater help than to send fifty destroyers, except sending a hundred. The flying-boats also are of the greatest importance now in the next two months. As I have repeatedly explained, the difficulty is to bridge the gap until our new war-time production arrives in a flood."[11]

Churchill had been persuaded by Lord Halifax to hold back his previous telegram to Roosevelt about the destroyers. But according to Lothian, "This is the moment to press the President about destroyers."[12] Churchill did so, setting out the scale of British merchant shipping losses and warning the President: "We could not sustain the present rate of casualties for long, and if we cannot get a substantial reinforcement the whole fate of the war may be decided by this minor and easily-remediable factor."

Churchill continued: "Mr President, with great respect I must tell you that in the long history of the world this is a thing to do now. Large construction is coming to me in 1941, but the crisis will be reached long before 1941. I know you will do all in your power, but I feel entitled and bound to put the gravity and urgency of the position before you." He was sure, Churchill ended, "that, with your comprehension of the sea affair, you will not let this crux of the battle go wrong for want of these destroyers."[13]

Even while Churchill pressed for destroyers, Arthur Purvis telegraphed from Washington with disappointing news about some of Britain's other needs. Roosevelt's Defense Advisory Board, he reported, "appear to be unwilling to consider adoption of our types of tanks and field guns and may make it difficult to secure them in America."[14] Churchill decided to hold back on the exchange of secrets. A week later, when the Board relented, he let the exchange proceed.

In Washington a debate was taking place about Britain's prospects and needs. On August 2, Joseph Kennedy reported from London that if the Germans possessed the air power they claimed, they could put the Royal Air Force "out of commission," after which a British surren-

---

11. Minute of 26 July 1940, Churchill Papers, 20/14, Martin Gilbert, *The Churchill War Papers,* Volume 2, page 576.
12. Minute of 30 July 1940, Premier Papers, 3/462/2, 3.
13. Telegram of 31 July 1940, Premier Papers, 3/462/2, 3.
14. Telegram of 27 July 1940, Premier Papers, 3/457.

der "would be inevitable."[15] That same day the Secretary of the Interior, Harold L. Ickes, appealed to the President to send the much-debated destroyers. If Britain went down, he wrote, the American people would want to know why American destroyers had not been sent to help prevent an invasion. "It seems to me," Ickes added, "that we Americans are like the householder who refuses to lend or sell his fire extinguisher to help put out the fire in the house that is next door, although that house is all ablaze and the wind is blowing from that direction."[16]

Roosevelt would not authorize the dispatch of the destroyers, even as a loan, fearing that if Britain were defeated they would fall into German hands. On August 6 Churchill was perturbed by a telegram from the President asking for reassurance that if Britain were overrun, the Royal Navy would neither be surrendered nor sunk. Nor was Churchill pleased by an American suggestion that Britain transfer British ships to Canada in the event of defeat. The only situation in which Churchill would give an undertaking to transfer British ships, Jock Colville noted, was "in return for an Anglo-US alliance."[17]

This low point did not last long: There was an important improvement in Anglo-American relations when Roosevelt decided to send to Britain a three-man military mission. The "cover" for this mission was a technical discussion on the standardization of arms, and the title "Standardization of Arms Committee" was to be used on all documents relating to it. But the reality of the mission was the holding of the first Staff Conversations between senior military personnel on both sides. Roosevelt chose three senior emissaries: Admiral Robert L. Ghormley, Assistant to the Chief of Naval Operations; Brigadier-General George V. Strong, Deputy Chief of the General Staff; and General Delos C. Emmons, Commanding General, General Headquarters, Air Force.

The British Chiefs of Staff suggested to Churchill that "complete frankness" should be the basis for the discussion of strategy with "the American trio."[18] Churchill agreed. He also sought to encourage the

---

15. Telegram of 2 August 1940, William L. Langer and S. Everett Gleason, *The World Crisis and American Foreign Policy: The Challenge to Isolation, 1937–1940*, page 744.
16. Letter of 2 August 1940, Roosevelt Papers.
17. Diary entry, 6 August 1940, Colville Papers.
18. Minute of 9 August 1940, Premier Papers, 3/457.

mission personally, asking on August 10, on the eve of their arrival: "I should see them almost as soon as they come, and I could give them a dinner at No. 10. Pray let me know in good time."[19] The American delegation dined with Churchill on the following day.

In the second week of August, Churchill received encouraging news. The first 26 of a total order of 238 Glenn Martin reconnaissance aircraft had reached Britain in July; the next 50 were due in the following two weeks. The first eight of 50 Hudson reconnaissance aircraft to be flown over would also come in August. The first two flying boats, of 90 already ordered, were expected in October; the first of 150 four-engine bombers were due to be delivered in February 1941.

Desperate for the American destroyers to help protect Britain's sea lifelines, Churchill was prepared to give the United States the benefit of one of Britain's recent technological advances, the ASDIC submarine sonar detection device: "Now is the time when we want the destroyers." He telegraphed to Lord Lothian on August 3: "We can fit them with ASDICs in about ten days from the time they are in our hands, all preparation having been made. We should also be prepared to give a number of ASDIC sets to the United States Navy and assist in their installation and explain their working. Go ahead on these lines full steam."[20]

The Americans were not interested. Churchill then offered Roosevelt the use of British bases in Newfoundland and the Caribbean, in return for the destroyers. Roosevelt agreed. Belatedly the long drawn out destroyer crisis was resolved, and the Destroyers-for-Bases agreement came into effect. The sovereignty of the British bases was not to be transferred. Instead a ninety-nine-year lease would be granted to the United States. "Undoubtedly," Churchill told the House of Commons, "this process means that these two great organisations of the English-speaking democracies, the British Empire and the United States, will have to be somewhat mixed up together in some of their affairs for mutual and general advantage." He did not view that process "with any misgivings. I could not stop it if I wished; no one can stop it. Like the Mississippi, it just keeps rolling along. Let it roll. Let it roll on full

---

19. Minute of 10 August 1940, Premier Papers, 3/457.
20. Telegram to Lord Lothian, 3 August 1940, Premier Papers.

flood, inexorable, irresistible, benignant, to broader lands and better days."[21]

His speech over, Churchill returned to Downing Street with Jock Colville, who noted: "he sang Ole Man River in the car all the way back."[22] That same week Churchill balked at a proposal to allow American newspaper correspondents to check Britain's figures of German aircraft shot down. "I must say," he wrote to the Secretary of State for Air, Sir Archibald Sinclair, "I am a little impatient about the American scepticism. The event is what will decide all." As he explained to Sinclair: "The important thing is to bring the German aircraft down and to win the battle, and the rate at which American correspondents and the American public are convinced that we are winning, and that our figures are true, stands in a much lower plane. They will find out quite soon enough when the German air attack is plainly shown to be repulsed." There was "something rather obnoxious," Churchill added, "in bringing correspondents down to air squadrons in order that they may assure the American public that the fighter pilots are not bragging and lying about their figures."[23]

In six weeks, as the productive resources of the United States were increasingly geared to British military, naval and air needs, Britain's gold reserves fell from £380 million to £290 million.[24] The Chancellor of the Exchequer suggested requisitioning wedding rings and gold ornaments, a measure expected to raise more than £20 million.[25] Churchill told the War Cabinet that such a measure should only be adopted at a later stage, "if we wished to make some striking gesture for the purpose of shaming the Americans."[26]

To Roosevelt, who was to face reelection that November, Churchill sent various proposals to enable British purchases to continue. "I am

---

21. Speech of 20 August 1940, *Hansard*, Parliamentary debates.
22. Diary entry, 20 August 1940, Colville Papers.
23. Minute of 21 August 1940, Churchill Papers, 20/13, Martin Gilbert, *The Churchill War Papers*, Volume 2, pages 700–701.
24. A fall, in the monetary values of 2005, from £12 billion ($24 billion) to £9 billion ($18 billion).
25. The wedding rings would have raised the equivalent of £667 million ($1,334 million) in the monetary values of 2005.
26. War Cabinet No. 232 of 1940, 22 August 1940, Cabinet Papers, 65/14.

so grateful for all the trouble you have been taking," Churchill told the President, "and I am so sorry to add to your burdens, knowing what a good friend you have been to us."[27]

To his British guests at Chequers, the Prime Minister's official country residence northwest of London, Churchill expressed his frustration and disappointment with the United States. The Americans, he told them, were "very good in applauding the valiant deeds done by others."[28]

Starting on September 7, German bombers attacked London in force. In a radio broadcast Churchill spoke of how Hitler had "lighted a fire which will burn with a steady and consuming flame until the last vestiges of Nazi tyranny have been burned out of Europe, and until the Old World—and the New—can join hands to rebuild the temples of man's freedom and man's honour, upon foundations which will not soon or easily be overthrown."[29]

Roosevelt's reaction to the German bombing of London was firm; he told Sir Walter Layton, the British Treasury representative in Washington, that he "had always urged that we should bomb Germany everywhere, not merely at a few major points."[30] A German invasion of Britain was expected at any moment. At that critical juncture Roosevelt authorized the release of the second batch of 250,000 American rifles, which had been withheld since June. The rifles were already under way to New York for shipment, the President informed Churchill on September 24. "We will use them well," Churchill replied.[31]

Even as the Presidential election date drew near, Roosevelt authorized a new American commitment. It was signed in Washington on October 24 by General Marshall and Sir Walter Layton, who explained to Churchill that the United States would "equip fully and maintain" ten additional Divisions of British and British Empire troops, over and above the substantial June commitment, using American weapons, and equipping these Divisions in time for the "campaign of 1942."

---

27. Telegram of 25 August 1940, Premier Papers, 3/462/2, 3.
28. John Colville diary, 1 September 1940, Colville Papers.
29. Broadcast of 11 September 1940, His Master's Voice gramophone record, ALP 1436.
30. Note of a conversation, 27 September 1940, Cabinet Papers, 115/32.
31. Telegram of 25 September 1940, Premier Papers, 3/276.

The United States would "ensure priority" in the allocation of American rifles, guns and ammunition to maintain the Divisions. This would be "in supplement to and not in substitution" of Britain's existing orders. Layton also told Churchill that the United States Treasury would finance the capital costs necessary to prepare the special factory plant needed to manufacture the equipment for the ten Divisions.[32]

Following a meeting of his Cabinet on October 26, Roosevelt told Arthur Purvis that he had decided to intervene personally "to achieve rapid progress" on supplies for Britain. Roosevelt wanted Churchill to telegraph a full account of the materials needed, "stressing their urgency," which the President would then use "as a means of sweeping away opposition to swift action."[33] Even before Churchill could respond to the request for a comprehensive list of what Britain needed, Roosevelt broadcast to the American people that he had directed the British request for more aircraft "to be given most sympathetic consideration." Roosevelt added that "large additional orders are being negotiated for artillery, machine guns, rifles and tanks, with equipment and ammunition." The plant capacity necessary to produce this military equipment, Roosevelt assured his listeners, "will be available to serve the needs of the United States in any emergency."[34]

Churchill prepared the telegram Roosevelt wanted. He began by setting out Britain's weaknesses in both the eastern Mediterranean and the Atlantic. "You will see, therefore, Mr President, how very great are our problems and dangers. We feel, however, confident of our ability, if we are given the necessary supplies, to carry the war to a successful conclusion, and anyhow we are going to try our best." Four days earlier Roosevelt had been asked for a substantial quantity of new supplies, including 156 million rounds of rifle and machine-gun ammunition, and two and a half million gallons of explosives. Churchill assumed, rightly, that he would agree to this. "You will, however," Churchill wrote, "allow me to impress upon you the extreme urgency of accelerating the delivery of the programme of aircraft and other munitions which has already been laid before you by Layton and Purvis."

Churchill then asked Roosevelt two questions: "So far as aircraft is

---

32. Telegram of 25 October 1940, Premier Papers, 3/483/2.
33. Telegram of 26 October 1940, Premier Papers, 3/483/2.
34. Report of 26 October 1940, Cabinet Papers, 92/27.

concerned, would it be possible to speed up the deliveries of the existing orders so that the numbers coming to our support next year will be considerably increased? Furthermore, can the new orders for the expanded programme also be placed so promptly that deliveries may come out in the middle of 1941?" Churchill added: "The equipment of our Armies, both for Home Defence and Overseas, is progressing, but we depend upon American deliveries to complete our existing programme, which will certainly be delayed and impeded by the bombing of factories and the disturbance of work."

Churchill explained that a memorandum on technical details was being sent to Roosevelt through Purvis and Layton, and he ended his telegram: "Having placed all the facts before you, I feel confident that everything humanly possible will be done. The World Cause is in your hands." [35]

On 2 November 1940 Roosevelt was elected to a third term as President of the United States. "I did not think it right," Churchill telegraphed four days later, "for me as a foreigner to express my opinion upon American politics while the election was on, but now I feel you will not mind my saying that I prayed for your success and that I am truly thankful for it." Churchill added: "Things are afoot which will be remembered as long as the English language is spoken in any quarter of the globe, and in expressing the comfort I feel that the people of the United States have once again cast these great burdens upon you I must avow my sure faith that the lights by which we steer will bring us all safely to anchor." [36]

Sometimes the American contribution was immediately effective, as when a squadron of Glenn Martin reconnaissance aircraft, on reaching Malta from the United States, contributed to the British naval victory over the Italians at Taranto in mid-November. Sometimes Roosevelt's personal intervention secured a breakthrough, as when he agreed, in discussion with Purvis, that whenever British and American military needs were in conflict, "his rule of thumb" was to make arms and munitions available to Britain "on a fifty-fifty basis." [37]

---

35. Telegram of 27 October 1940, Premier Papers, 3/483/2.
36. Telegram of 6 November 1940, Premier Papers, 3/468.
37. British Purchasing Commission (PURCO) telegrams for week ended 26 October 1940, Cabinet Papers, 92/27.

During his discussion with Purvis, Roosevelt raised the issue of how Britain might pay for this swelling stream of production. The problem of Britain's "dollar resources," he told Purvis, was "some six months off". Roosevelt proposed building ships and renting them to the United Kingdom. Purvis noted that the President "indicated that this system might be extended to cover certain other similar items."[38]

To build and to rent. This concept became the eventual solution, Lend-Lease. But both the House of Representatives and the Senate had to approve it, which would take time. The crisis in payment came far sooner than Roosevelt had anticipated, as Britain's needs grew with every week.

Churchill was at Chequers on November 30, his sixty-sixth birthday, working on the comprehensive list of requirements to submit to Roosevelt. Purvis had come to Britain to help. The letter would include a schedule of Britain's munition production, to show the urgency of American help. Churchill warned the War Cabinet, however, "that if the picture was painted too darkly, elements in the United States would say that it was useless to help us, for such help would be wasted and thrown away. If too bright a picture was painted, then there might be a tendency to withhold assistance."

Churchill then told his colleagues that he had been "rather chilled by the attitude of the United States since the Election." It might well be, however, that Roosevelt was waiting for the election atmosphere to disperse before taking any "striking action."[39]

On December 8 Churchill sent Roosevelt the letter on which he had worked for so many days. The previous five months, he told the President, had witnessed "a strong and perhaps unexpected recovery" by Great Britain, fighting alone except for "the invaluable aid in munitions and in destroyers placed at our disposal by the great Republic of which you are for the third time the chosen Chief."

Churchill asked Roosevelt for a reassertion by the United States of the doctrine of the freedom of the seas, backed up by United States destroyer protection for all lawful trading on the high seas, and the use by the United States, for convoy protection purposes, of bases in Eire

---

38. Telegram of 10 November 1940, Cabinet Papers, 115/83.
39. War Cabinet minutes, 2 December 1940, Cabinet Papers, 65/10.

for the duration of the war. Failing this, he wanted Roosevelt to agree to "the gift, loan, or supply of a large number of American vessels of war," particularly destroyers, to enable Britain to maintain the Atlantic route.

To help secure the convoy routes, Churchill wanted the United States to extend its naval control on the American side of the Atlantic "so as to prevent molestation by enemy vessels" of the approaches to the American bases being established in the British West Indies. To ensure "final victory," Churchill told Roosevelt, not less than three million tons of additional merchant-shipping capacity would have to be built. "Only the United States can supply this need." In the military sphere, manufacture of machine tools and the release of equipment from American army stock remained essential if Britain were to equip fifty Divisions in 1941.

As for finance, Churchill wrote: "The moment approaches when we shall no longer be able to pay cash for shipping and other supplies." This was the danger point for Britain. "While we will do our utmost, and shrink from no proper sacrifice to make payments across the Exchange, I believe you will agree that it would be wrong in principle and mutually disadvantageous in effect if at the height of this struggle Great Britain were to be divested of all saleable assets, so that after the victory was won with our blood, civilisation saved, and the time gained for the United States to be fully armed against all eventualities, we should stand stripped to the bone."

These were stern words, but sterner ones were to come. Churchill told the President he did not believe that the Government and people of the United States "would find it in accordance with the principles which guide them to confine the help which they have so generously promised only to such munitions of war and commodities as could be immediately paid for." Roosevelt should not regard his letter, Churchill ended, "as an appeal for aid, but as a statement of the minimum action necessary to achieve our common purpose."[40]

That common purpose suddenly seemed endangered. At that very moment Churchill was confronted by American demands for payment in gold for all purchases. To offset the projected British expenditure of

---

40. Letter of 8 December 1940, circulated to the War Cabinet as War Cabinet Paper 466 of 1940, Cabinet Papers, 65/10.

$1 billion for December, January and February, Britain had only just over half that—$574 million—in gold and United States dollar balances.[41] Churchill drafted a harsh telegram to Roosevelt. "If you were to 'wash your hands of us' i.e. give us nothing we cannot pay for with suitable advances," he wrote, "we should certainly not give in, and I believe we could save ourselves and our own National interests for the time being. But we should certainly not be able to beat the Nazi tyranny and gain you the time you require for your re-armament."

Churchill added: "You may be absolutely sure that whatever you do or do not feel able to do, we shall go on to the utmost limits of our resources and strength, but that strength unaided will not be sufficient to produce a world-result of a satisfactory and lasting character."[42]

In anticipation of a public statement by Roosevelt that same day, Churchill held back his telegram. As soon as he read Roosevelt's statement he cancelled the telegram. Roosevelt announced that, to resolve the payment crisis, the United States would take over the munitions orders Britain had placed in the United States, and "enter into some kind of arrangement for their use by the British on the grounds that it was the best thing for American defence, with the understanding that when the show was over, we would get repaid sometime in kind, thereby leaving out the dollar mark" and "substituting it for a gentleman's obligation to repay in kind."

Roosevelt added, by way of explanation of this plan—drawing on the analogy put forward earlier by Harold Ickes—that if his neighbor wanted to borrow his garden hose to put out a fire, he would not say "Neighbor, my garden hose cost me $15; you have to pay me $15 for it." It was not the $15 he wanted, but "my garden hose back after the fire is over."[43]

This was the Lend-Lease concept, whose origins Arthur Purvis had reported to Churchill five weeks earlier. It would take several months before it could be perfected and passed through Congress, but it would enable Britain to remain at war.

---

41. In the monetary values of 2005, Britain had almost $8 billion (£4 billion) in gold and United States dollar balances, but a projected expenditure of almost $13 billion (£6.5 billion).

42. Draft telegram of 17 December 1940, Premier Papers, 4/17/1.

43. Statement of 17 December 1940, *The Times,* 18 December 1940.

• • •

An air raid on London on the night of December 29–30 brought the number of civilian deaths from bombing that month to 3,793. On the night of the raid, Roosevelt told the American people, in one of his "Fireside Chats," that if Britain were defeated, "all of us, in all the Americas, would be living at the point of a gun—a gun loaded with explosive bullets economic as well as military." Roosevelt added: "Frankly and definitely there is danger ahead—danger against which we must prepare. But we well know that we cannot escape danger, or the fear of danger, by crawling into bed and pulling the covers over our heads."

In a phrase that gave the British people, and Churchill, enormous encouragement, Roosevelt declared: "We must be the great arsenal of democracy."[44] Churchill had drafted a strong rebuke to Roosevelt about the poor quality of the destroyers that had, at last, arrived. Following Roosevelt's speech, Churchill withheld the telegram. But even as Roosevelt spoke his words of encouragement, an American warship was on its way to Cape Town, to collect the British gold reserves that had been sent there for safekeeping. Britain would be bankrupted long before Lend-Lease could become law. Churchill "obviously fears," Jock Colville noted when the news reached Downing Street, "that the Americans' love of doing good business may lead them to denude us of all our realisable resources before they show any inclination to be the Good Samaritan."[45]

In a telegram to Roosevelt, Churchill told of his anxiety with regard to Lend-Lease "because we do not know how long Congress will debate your proposals and how we should be enabled to place orders for armaments and pay our way if this time became protracted." Forcefully he declared: "Remember, Mr President, we do not know what you have in mind, or exactly what the United States is going to do, and we are fighting for our lives," and he went on to ask: "What would be the effect upon the world situation if we had to default in payments to your contractors, who have their workmen to pay? Would not this be exploited by the enemy as a complete breakdown in Anglo-American co-operation? Yet, a few weeks' delay might well bring this upon us."

What was to be done, Churchill asked Roosevelt, about "the im-

---

44. Speech of 29 December 1940, *The Times,* 30 December 1940.
45. Diary entry, 1 January 1941, Colville Papers.

mense heavy payments still due to be made under existing orders before delivery is completed? Substantial advance payments on these same orders have already denuded our resources." Britain had a "continued need" for various American commodities, including raw materials and oil. In addition, "Canada and other Dominions, Greece and refugee Allies have clamant dollar needs to keep their war effort alive."

Churchill added, in reference to Roosevelt's Fireside Chat: "I thank you for testifying before all the world that the future safety and greatness of the American Union are intimately concerned with the upholding and the effective arming of that indomitable spirit." This telegram was sent to Roosevelt on the last day of 1940. "All my heartiest good wishes to you," Churchill ended, "in the New Year of storm that is opening upon us."[46]

46. Telegram of 31 December 1940, Premier Papers, 4/17/1.

Chapter Twenty-One

✠

"WE ARE NO LONGER ALONE"

On 8 January 1941 Roosevelt's personal emissary, Harry Hopkins, arrived in Britain. His mission was to find out whether Churchill really could lead his country through the perilous times and make it possible for American aid to be used effectively. Hopkins and Churchill met for the first time at Downing Street on January 10, spending three hours alone. In a message to Roosevelt, Hopkins reported that Churchill had assured him that he would make "every detail of information and opinion available to me," and hoped that Hopkins would not leave England until he was fully satisfied "of the exact state of England's need and the urgent necessity of the exact material assistance Britain requires to win the war." [1]

That afternoon Hopkins drove to Ditchley, in Oxfordshire, the house where Churchill stayed on weekends when the full moon made Chequers vulnerable to German air attack. While he and Churchill talked, the text of the Lend-Lease Bill was published in Washington. In addition to providing all the war material Britain needed on a rental basis, the Bill proposed allowing British warships to use United States ports, despite the American neutrality legislation. Churchill, "delighted," told Jock Colville that this was "tantamount to a declaration of war by the United States." [2]

That weekend Colville noted the almost immediate rapport between the President's emissary and the Prime Minister. He also reported a comment by Hopkins that Roosevelt "was resolved" that

---

1. Report for 10 January 1941, Robert E. Sherwood, *The White House Papers of Harry L. Hopkins,* Volume 1, pages 239–40.
2. Diary entry of 11 January 1941, Colville Papers.

Britain should have "the means of survival and of victory." After dinner on January 11 Colville noted that Hopkins "paid a graceful tribute to the PM's speeches which had, he said, produced the most stirring and revolutionary effect on all classes and districts in America." Hopkins also reported that at an American Cabinet meeting "the President had had a wireless-set brought in so that all might listen to the Prime Minister." Churchill was "touched and gratified" by this. Churchill also told Hopkins that the text of the Lend-Lease Bill, which he had read that morning, "made him feel that a new world had come into being."[3]

After forty-eight hours in Britain, Hopkins wrote to Roosevelt that "people here are amazing from Churchill down, and if courage alone can win—the result will be inevitable." But, Hopkins added, "they need our help desperately, and I am sure you will permit nothing to stand in the way." Hopkins also sought to reassure Roosevelt about Churchill's attitude to him. "I cannot believe that it is true that Churchill dislikes either you or America—it just doesn't make sense," Hopkins wrote. "This island needs our help now, Mr President, with everything we can give them."[4]

Churchill asked Hopkins to accompany him to Scotland for a tour of Royal Navy bases. "I am most grateful to you," he telegraphed to Roosevelt before they set off, "for sending so remarkable an envoy, who enjoys so high a measure of your intimacy and confidence."[5] On January 15 Churchill and Hopkins were given dinner in Glasgow by the Regional Commissioner for Scotland, Tom Johnston. Churchill's doctor, Sir Charles Wilson (later Lord Moran), who was among those present, recorded in his diary how, after a time, Hopkins got up and, turning to Churchill, said: "I suppose you wish to know what I am going to say to President Roosevelt on my return. Well, I'm going to quote you one verse from that Book of Books in the truth of which Mr Johnston's mother and my own Scottish mother were brought up."

Hopkins then quoted: "Whither thou goest, I will go; and where thou lodgest, I will lodge: thy people shall be my people, and thy God

---

3. Diary entry, 12 January 1941, Colville Papers.
4. Report for 12 January 1941, Robert E. Sherwood, *The White House Papers of Harry L. Hopkins,* Volume 1, pages 239–40.
5. Telegram of 13 January 1941, Martin Gilbert, *The Churchill War Papers,* Volume 3, page 78.

my God." Then he added, very quietly, "Even to the end." "I was sur-prised," the doctor wrote, "to find the PM in tears. He knew what it meant. Even to us the words seemed like a rope thrown to a drown-ing man."[6]

On January 24 Churchill took Hopkins to Dover to see the gun batteries and to look across the Channel to German-occupied France. That evening they returned to Chequers for the weekend. During their talks Hopkins told Churchill—as Colville recorded—that Roo-sevelt "was convinced that if England lost, America, too, would be en-circled and beaten. He would use his powers if necessary; he would not scruple to interpret existing laws for the furtherance of his aim; he would make people gape with surprise, as the British Foreign Office must have gaped when it saw the terms of the Lease and Lend Bill."

Hopkins also told Churchill: "The boldness of the President was a striking factor in the situation. He did not want war, indeed he looked upon America as an Arsenal which should provide the weapons for the conflict and not count the cost, but he would not shrink from war."[7]

In a telegram to Roosevelt, Hopkins told Roosevelt that Churchill "is not only the Prime Minister, he is the directing force behind the strategy and the conduct of the war in all its essentials. He has an amaz-ing hold on the British people of all classes and groups." He was partic-ularly strong "both with the military establishments and the working people."[8]

On January 27, while Hopkins was still in Britain, *Life* magazine published a profile of Churchill by one of America's leading journal-ists, Dorothy Thompson, illustrated with photographs from every stage of Churchill's career. The cover showed Churchill's five-week-old grandson, "Winston II" as *Life* called him, and his mother, Pamela, Randolph's wife. In introducing the article, the magazine wrote of how Churchill's "stooped figure, treading the ruins of London, Birming-ham, Coventry, rouses the British to unsuspected martial heights." The article itself was the text of a speech Dorothy Thompson had given in the summer of 1940 over the Canadian Broadcasting Corporation. "In

---

6. Diary entry, 17 January 1941, Lord Moran (Sir Charles Wilson), *Winston Chur-chill: The Struggle for Survival, 1940–1965,* page 6.
7. Diary entries, 25–27 January 1941, Colville Papers.
8. Diary entry, 25 January 1941, Colville Papers.

it she declared: "The master of the dyke against world chaos is you, Churchill, you gallant, portly little warrior."[9]

Also on January 27, in strictest secrecy, Staff Conversations opened in Washington, to determine "the best methods by which the armed forces of the United States and British Commonwealth, with its present Allies, could defeat Germany and the Powers allied with her, should the United States be compelled to resort to war." The participants were also instructed to seek agreement on the methods and nature of Anglo-American military cooperation, strategy, strength of forces, and eventual "unity of field command in cases of strategic or tactical joint operations."[10]

On the day these Staff Conversations began in Washington, Churchill lunched in London with Roosevelt's recent opponent for the Presidency, Wendell Willkie, who brought him a letter from the President. In it Roosevelt had written out a verse from a Longfellow poem. "I think," Roosevelt noted, "this verse applies to your people as it does to us."[11] It read:

> *Sail on, O Ship of State!*
> *Sail on, O Union, strong and great!*
> *Humanity with all its fears,*
> *With all the hope of future years*
> *Is hanging breathless on thy fate*

"I received Willkie yesterday," Churchill telegraphed to Roosevelt on January 28, "and was deeply moved by the verse of Longfellow's which you had quoted. I shall have it framed as a souvenir of these tremendous days, and as a mark of our friendly relations, which have been built up telegraphically but also telepathically under all the stresses."[12]

Hopkins remained one more week in Britain. Two of the items he discussed with Churchill's Ministers were using American aircraft carri-

---

9. Dorothy Thompson, "Winston Churchill: He Inspires an Empire in Its Hour of Need," *Life*, 27 January 1941, pages 59–70.

10. Report of 27 March 1941, Premier Papers, 3/489/2.

11. Letter of 20 January 1941, delivered 27 January 1941, reproduced in facsimile in Winston S. Churchill, *The Second World War*, Volume 3, page 24.

12. Letter of 28 January 1941, Churchill Papers, 20/49, Martin Gilbert, *The Churchill War Papers*, Volume 3, pages 145–46.

ers to transport aircraft to Britain "in case of urgent need," and the pooling of material gathered by the British and American Intelligence Services in "enemy-occupied countries."[13] On January 31 Churchill took Hopkins to Southampton and Portsmouth, where recent German bombing raids had led to several hundred civilian deaths. "One cannot help feeling enormously encouraged," Churchill told the citizens of Portsmouth, "by the spirit of the ever-growing movement to aid Britain which we see laying hold of the mighty mass of the United States."[14]

Churchill and Hopkins returned to Chequers. "After dinner," Churchill's Principal Private Secretary, Eric Seal, wrote to his wife, "Hopkins produced a big box of gramophone records, all American tunes or ones with an Anglo-American significance. We had these until well after midnight, the PM walking about, sometimes dancing a *pas-seul*, in time with the music. We all got a bit sentimental and Anglo-American under the influence of the good dinner & the music."

Seal noted that Churchill "kept stopping on his walk, & commenting on the situation—what a remarkable thing that the two nations should be drawing so much together at this critical time, how much we had in common etc. He feels a great bond of sympathy for America, and in particular for Roosevelt." Seal added: "I feel sure that great things may come of this extraordinary feeling of close relationship."[15]

On February 8 Hopkins arrived at Chequers for a farewell visit. Churchill was working on a broadcast for the following evening: his first in five months. After discussing it with Churchill, Hopkins left for the first stage of his journey back to the United States. On the evening of February 9, Hopkins, who had reached Bournemouth and was about to take the flying boat from Poole to Lisbon, listened to the broadcast in his hotel. What he heard was Churchill quoting the verse from the Longfellow poem Roosevelt had sent him two weeks earlier, after which he asked his millions of listeners throughout Britain: "What is the answer that I shall give, in your name, to this great man, the thrice-chosen head of a nation of a hundred and thirty millions?"

Churchill told his listeners: "Here is the answer which I will give to President Roosevelt. Put your confidence in us. Give us your faith and

13. Notes of a discussion, Admiralty Papers, 1/11168.
14. Speech of 31 January 1941, *The Times*, 1 February 1941.
15. Letter of 2 February 1941, Sir Eric Seal Papers.

your blessing and, under Providence, all will be well. We shall not fail or falter; we shall not weaken or tire. Neither the sudden shock of battle, nor the long-drawn trials of vigilance and exertion will wear us down. Give us the tools, and we will finish the job." [16]

Those tools were on their way. At the end of February a quarter of a million rifles and fifty million rounds of ammunition reached Britain by sea, far ahead of schedule. It was, Churchill telegraphed to Hopkins, "a great addition to our security." But Churchill warned of the increased German submarine sinkings of British merchant ships. "This has darkened since I saw you. Let me know when the Bill will be through. The strain is growing here." [17]

The Lend-Lease Bill was making its way through Congress, a slow process. As it did so, Roosevelt followed the Hopkins mission with two appointments intended to bridge the gulfs of distance and misunderstanding. The first was a new American Ambassador, John G. Winant—known as "Gil"—who was immediately struck by Churchill's "appreciation of the defence needs of the United States." [18] Winant was to become a regular attendee at Chequers. "He was the quiet man sitting in the corner taking it all in," Churchill's daughter Mary later recalled. [19]

The second American appointment, suggested by Hopkins, was that of a forty-nine-year-old banker and businessman, Averell Harriman, to whom Roosevelt wrote in the third week of February: "I want you to go over to London and recommend everything that we can do, short of war, to keep the British Isles afloat." [20] Harriman's daughter, Kathleen, later told the writer Jon Meacham that Churchill soon discovered that her father could play bezique, Churchill's favorite card game, and that "the conversation while shuffling the several decks at the end of the game took time and helped them resolve all kinds of issues." [21]

---

16. Broadcast of 9 February 1941, His Master's Voice, Gramophone record, ALP 1554.

17. Telegram of 28 February 1941, Foreign Office Papers, 954/29.

18. John G. Winant, *A Letter from Grosvenor Square*, pages 24–25.

19. Lady Soames, in conversation with the author, 6 December 2005.

20. W. Averell Harriman and Elie Abel, *Special Envoy to Churchill and Stalin, 1941–1946*, pages 18–19.

21. Quoted in Jon Meacham, *Franklin and Winston: A Portrait of a Friendship*, page 129.

With the arrival in Britain of Winant and Harriman, hardly a day passed without these two Americans ensuring that Britain's needs were understood in Washington, and acted upon. Those needs were many. As the German submarine sinking of merchant ships in the Atlantic wreaked havoc on Britain's food and war supplies lifeline, Churchill telegraphed to Lord Halifax, who had become Ambassador in Washington after Lord Lothian's death three months earlier: "We cannot get through 1942 without several million tons of United States' new construction of merchant ships."[22]

On the night of March 7, Hopkins telephoned Chequers to say that the Lend-Lease Bill had passed the Senate by 60 votes to 31. "Thank God for your news," Churchill telegraphed in reply.[23] To Roosevelt, who gave his formal assent to the Bill two days later, Churchill telegraphed on March 9: "Our blessings from the whole British Empire go out to you and the American nation for this very present help in time of trouble."[24]

Lend-Lease made enormous purchases possible. The first appropriation, for British orders placed up to the end of August 1941, enabled Britain to draw $4,736 million.[25] When, however, the Americans raised questions about the eventual repayment of the Lend-Lease money, Churchill wanted Britain to take a strong stance. This was no time, he telegraphed to Halifax, "for us to be driven from pillar to post," and he was angered by the American attitude, telling the Ambassador: "Remember that although they may not all realise it their lives are now in this business too. We cannot always be playing up to minor political exigencies of Congress politics." The American Secretary of the Treasury might be having "a bad time" before a congressional committee, "but Liverpool and Glasgow are having a bad time now."[26] German bombers were at that very moment attacking docks, factories and railway marshaling yards on Liverpool's Merseyside and Glasgow's the Clyde. That month 4,259 British civilians were killed in German air raids.

----

22. Telegram of 9 March 1941, Premier Papers, 3/487/1.
23. Telegram of 9 March 1941, Premier Papers, 3/224/1.
24. Telegram of 9 March 1941, Churchill Papers, 20/49, Martin Gilbert, *The Churchill War Papers*, Volume 3, page 332.
25. In the monetary values of 2005, this was $60 billion/£30 billion.
26. Telegram of 15 March 1941, Premier Papers, 4/17/2.

Churchill took Winant and Harriman with him to visit the bombed cities and repeatedly invited them to Chequers for weekend discussions. The fruits of these discussions were quickly apparent. As Churchill told the War Cabinet on March 20: "These two gentlemen were apparently longing for Germany to commit some overt act that would relieve the President of his election and pre-election declaration regarding keeping out of the war." Churchill added that Averell Harriman "had said that the United States might be prepared to escort their own ships outside the prohibited area. He was working out a scheme whereby United States ships would take over the long hauls, leaving us with the short hauls. They were also planning a very big merchant shipbuilding programme, which would mature in 1942."

Churchill did not hide from Winant or Harriman the extent of Britain's weakness. In a speech on March 18, formally welcoming Winant to Britain, he described Britain's shipping losses as "this potentially mortal challenge." It would be met, however, by a naval and air strength that was growing "every week," and with that strength came the "words and acts" of the President and people of the United States, "like a draught of life, and they tell us by an ocean-borne trumpet call that we are no longer alone."[27]

The good and the bad marched side by side. On the continuing Lend-Lease repayment dispute Churchill wrote to his Chancellor of the Exchequer: "As far as I can make out we are not only to be skinned, but flayed to the bone" (Churchill underlined the word "I"). His hope was that the "power of the debtor" would be in the ascendant, "especially when he is doing all the fighting."[28] That week Roosevelt agreed to repair a damaged British warship in an American navy yard, and ten days later put ten United States revenue cutters at Britain's disposal for convoy duties. "The ten cutters will be a Godsend," Churchill telegraphed in appreciation.[29]

On April 11 Churchill took Harriman and Winant with him to Bristol. While they slept in the train that had brought them overnight from London, Bristol was heavily bombed. "A grim determined peo-

---

27. Speech of 18 March 1941, *The Times,* 19 March 1941.
28. Minute of 20 March 1941, Premier Papers, 4/17/2.
29. Telegram of 30 March 1941, Premier Papers, 3/324/10.

ple," Harriman wrote in a draft telegram to Roosevelt, "but he was met everywhere with cheers and smiles." Churchill said to Harriman, as they toured the bombed areas: "They have such faith. It is a grave responsibility."[30]

As the Battle of the Atlantic intensified, Harriman wrote to Roosevelt: "England's strength is bleeding. In our own interest, I trust that our Navy can be directly employed before our partner is too weak."[31] At Chequers on April 12, Winant received a telegram from Roosevelt announcing that the United States would extend its security zone and patrol areas in the Atlantic as far to the east as the twenty-fifth meridian. America would immediately inform Britain of the location of "aggressor ships or planes."[32]

In reply Churchill expressed his deep gratitude "for your momentous cable." United States patrols to the twenty-fifth meridian were "a long step towards salvation."[33] At midnight on April 24, the United States Atlantic Fleet took up its new positions in the western Atlantic, to establish this extended Security Zone two thousand miles out from the East Coast of the United States. "We are deeply impressed," Churchill telegraphed to Roosevelt, "by the rapidity with which it is being brought into play." The "action you have taken may well decide the battle of the Atlantic in a favourable sense."[34]

Traveling with Harriman, Churchill went to Merseyside to study the shipping and convoy situation. In a broadcast on his return to Chequers, he declared that the war had entered "a grim but at the same time a far more favourable phase." The United States was "very closely bound up with us now." Churchill then quoted from "Say Not the Struggle Naught Availeth," a poem by Arthur Hugh Clough, which he had first heard and learned by heart before the First World War. They were lines, he told his listeners, "apt and appropriate to our fortunes

30. Draft telegram of 12 April 1941, Averell Harriman Papers.

31. W. Averell Harriman and Elie Abel, *Special Envoy to Churchill and Stalin, 1941–1946,* page 31.

32. Message of 11 April 1941, Premier Papers, 3/460/2.

33. Winston S. Churchill, *The Second World War,* Volume 3, page 116.

34. Telegram of 25 April 1941, Premier Papers, 3/460/1. For the extent of the extended Security Zone (also known as the Neutrality Zone), see Map 8, page 459.

tonight," and would be so judged "wherever the English language is spoken or the flag of freedom flies."[35] The lines Churchill spoke were:

For while the tired waves, vainly breaking,
Seem here no painful inch to gain,
Far back, through creeks and inlets making,
Comes silent, flooding in, the main.

And not by eastern windows only
When daylight comes, comes in the light;
In front the sun climbs slow, how slowly!
But westward, look, the land is bright!

---

35. Broadcast of 27 April 1941, BBC Written Archives Centre.

Chapter Twenty-Two

⚜

FIVE MONTHS OF ANGUISH

Following the German invasion of Greece in April 1941, British forces hastened to assist their ally, but after hard fighting and heavy losses, were forced to evacuate to Crete. In North Africa, German troops were driving the British and Commonwealth troops back across the Libyan border into Egypt. In anguish Churchill telegraphed to Roosevelt, appealing for the entry of the United States into the war. "We must not be too sure that the consequences of the loss of Egypt and the Middle East would not be grave," he wrote. "It would seriously increase the hazards of the Atlantic and the Pacific, and could hardly fail to prolong the war, with all the suffering and military dangers that this would entail."

Britain would fight on "whatever happens," Churchill wrote, "but please remember that the attitude of Spain, Vichy, Turkey, and Japan may be finally determined by the outcome of the struggle in this theatre of war." If all Europe and the greater part of Asia and Africa became "either by conquest or agreement under duress, a part of the Axis system, a war maintained by the British Isles, United States, Canada, and Australasia against this mighty agglomeration would be a hard, long, and bleak proposition. Therefore, if you cannot take more advanced positions now, or very soon, the vast balances may be tilted heavily to our disadvantage."

Churchill then came to his point: "Mr President, I am sure that you will not misunderstand me if I speak to you exactly what is in my mind. The one decisive counterweight I can see to balance the growing pessimism in Turkey, the Near East, and in Spain would be if United States were immediately to range herself with us as a belligerent Power." If this were possible, Churchill had "little doubt" that

Britain "could hold the situation in the Mediterranean until the weight of your munitions gained the day."

Britain was determined to fight, Churchill assured Roosevelt, "to the last inch and ounce" for Egypt, "But I adjure you, Mr President, not to underrate the gravity of the consequences which may follow from a Middle Eastern collapse. In this war every post is a winning-post, and how many more are we going to lose?"[1]

Having sent his telegram, Churchill told Averell Harriman, General Ismay and Jock Colville, who were with him: "With Hitler in control of Iraq oil and Ukrainian wheat, not all the staunchness of 'our Plymouth Brethren' will shorten the ordeal."[2]

No American declaration of war was forthcoming; indeed, Roosevelt made no reply to this anguished appeal. Other appeals soon followed. On May 10—a year after Churchill had become Prime Minister—during a devastating German air raid on London, 1,400 civilians were killed. That night Churchill telegraphed to Roosevelt that he had just learned of a hitch in the "splendid offer" of United States Army Air Force General Henry H. "Hap" Arnold, whom he had seen earlier in London. Arnold, who had been taught to fly by the Wright brothers, offered to make one-third of the United States pilot-training capacity available to British pilots. "We have made active preparations," Churchill told Roosevelt, "and the first 550 of our young men are now ready to leave," but legal difficulties had arisen. Churchill appealed to Roosevelt to overcome the remaining obstacles.[3]

Roosevelt took the matter up personally. Ten days later he reported that no legal impediment remained and that the training could begin "promptly." In addition, Roosevelt told Churchill, "We are rushing six additional small aircraft carriers for you. First three should be available in three or four months."[4] "All this will be most helpful," Churchill replied.[5]

---

1. Telegram of 4 May 1941, Churchill Papers, 20/38, Martin Gilbert, *The Churchill War Papers*, Volume 3, pages 599–600.

2. Diary entry, 2 May 1941, Colville Papers.

3. Telegram of 10 May 1941, Churchill Papers, 20/38, Martin Gilbert, *The Churchill War Papers*, Volume 3, page 654, note 4.

4. Telegram of 21 May 1941, Churchill Papers, 20/49, Martin Gilbert, *The Churchill War Papers*, Volume 3, page 693.

5. Telegram of 27 May 1941, Foreign Office Papers, 954/29.

On May 21, when the battle for Crete was at its height, Churchill twice expressed his fears about American intentions. In a telegram to Wendell Willkie, which he held back from Willkie, but did send to Roosevelt, Churchill was emphatic. "I have never said that the British Empire cannot make its way out of this war without American belligerence," he had written, "but no peace that is any use to you or which will liberate Europe can be obtained without American belligerence."

Every day's delay, Churchill was convinced, "adds to the length of the war and the difficulties to be encountered. West Africa, Spain, Vichy, Turkey, the Arab world, all hang in the balance. Japan hangs in the balance. Wait three months and all this may be piled up against us in adverse sense, thus lengthening the war to periods no man can pretend to know about, and increasing immensely the danger and burden to be borne by everyone before Hitler is beat. How easy now—how hard a year hence will be the task."

Churchill calculated that in the coming twelve months "we shall lose four and a half million tons of shipping. The United States, by a prodigy of generous constructive effort, will build perhaps three and a half and we build the other million. Where have we got to then? Just marking time and swimming level with the bank against the stream. Whereas co-operation of even a third of the American Navy would save at least one-half of the tonnage beforehand and give that mastery which alone can abridge the torments of mankind."[6]

To Roosevelt, to whom he had sent a copy of his unsent telegram to Willkie, Churchill telegraphed that same day: "I hope you will forgive me if I say there is anxiety here. We are at a climacteric of the war, when enormous crystallisations are in suspense but imminent." As for the war at sea, Churchill told the President, "At heavy cost in other waters we have been doing better in Battle of the Atlantic lately, but as I send this message Admiralty tell me that eight ships have been sunk in a convoy as far out as the fortieth meridian west longitude. You will see from my cancelled message to Willkie how grievous I feel it that the United States should build 3 or 4 million tons of shipping and watch their equivalent being sunk beforehand."

As he had done before when asking for help, Churchill ended with

---

6. Telegram No. 2721 to Washington, 21 May 1941, Foreign Office Papers, 954/29.

words of thanks for so much American help already given. "Let me once again express my gratitude," he wrote, "and that of the British Empire, for all you have done for us."[7]

In May 1941, after a North Sea encounter between the German battleships *Bismarck* and *Prinz Eugen* and several British ships, the British battleship *Hood* was sunk and more than fifteen hundred sailors killed. That same month a pro-German revolt broke out in Baghdad. Also in May, following German paratroop landings in Crete, and fierce, often hand-to-hand fighting, more than 13,000 British and Commonwealth troops were killed, wounded or taken prisoner. In North Africa the German Army regained the initiative. In German air raids on Britain during May, 5,394 civilians were killed. The one light in the gloom came from the United States: Roosevelt's willingness to take over the British military and air bases in Iceland. This, Churchill told Roosevelt, "will liberate a British division for defence against invasion or the Middle East" and would enable the British flying boats already in Iceland "to concentrate on the North Western Approaches."[8]

In a further telegram to Roosevelt a day later, Churchill pointed out that the capture of Crete would be exploited "to the full" by German propaganda, and that any public move Roosevelt could make, "like sending even a Brigade to Iceland," could not come at a more "timely" moment. Churchill added: "See also second epistle to the Corinthians, chapter 6, verse 2."[9] The verse read: "For he saith, I have heard thee in a time accepted, and in the day of salvation I have succoured thee; behold, *now* is the accepted time; behold *now* is the day of salvation."

Roosevelt had begun to respond with increasing alacrity to Churchill's detailed requests, encouraged to do so by Harriman and Winant in London and Hopkins in Washington. On June 4 Churchill was able to inform the Commander-in-Chief Middle East, General Sir Archibald Wavell, that in addition to the thirty ships under the American

---

7. Telegram No. 2723 to Washington, 21 May 1941, Foreign Office Papers, 954/29.

8. Telegram of 30 May 1940, Churchill Papers, 20/39, Martin Gilbert, *The Churchill War Papers*, Volume 3, pages 739–40.

9. Telegram of 31 May 1941, Roosevelt Papers.

flag, another forty-four vessels, "which carry among other things, two hundred additional Light Tanks from the United States Army Production," were on their way to him.[10]

Roosevelt also agreed that "large numbers" of American engineers and mechanics could go to Egypt to service and repair the American aircraft, tanks and motor vehicles reaching the British forces in the Middle East. Harriman was on his way to Cairo to help arrange these armament needs. Churchill told Wavell: "Mr Harriman enjoys my complete confidence and is in the most intimate relations with the President and Mr Harry Hopkins. No one can do more for you."[11]

On June 11 Roosevelt finally agreed to send American troops to Iceland to help the Britain garrison there. On the following day, in a speech to Dominion and Allied representatives, Churchill referred to "our American friends and helpers drawing ever closer in their might across the ocean."[12] Two days later Roosevelt announced publicly that he was freezing all German and Italian assets in the United States. In thanking Roosevelt, Churchill reflected: "People must have hope, to face the long haul that lies ahead."[13] That same day Churchill broadcast to the United States, speaking of the "sense of kinship and unity" that existed between the two peoples. For more than a year, he said, "we British have stood alone, uplifted by your sympathy and respect and sustained by our own unconquerable will-power and by the increasing growth and hopes of your massive aid."

Churchill ended his broadcast on a rousing note of confidence:

And now, the old lion with her lion cubs at her side stands alone against hunters who are armed with deadly weapons and impelled by desperate and destructive rage. Is the tragedy to repeat itself once more? Ah no! This is not the end of the tale. The stars in their courses proclaim the deliverance of mankind. Not so easily shall the onward progress of the peoples be barred. Not so easily shall the lights of freedom die. But time is short. Every month that passes adds to the length and to the perils of the journey that

---

10. Telegram of 4 June 1941, Premier Papers, 3/298/2.
11. Telegram of 3 June 1941, Cabinet Papers, 120/10.
12. Speech of 12 June 1941, BBC Written Archives Centre.
13. Telegram of 14 June 1941, Premier Papers, 3/230/1.

will have to be made. United we stand. Divided we fall. Divided, the dark age returns. United, we can save and guide the world.[14]

The war was about to take a dramatic turn. On 22 June 1941 Hitler ordered the invasion of the Soviet Union, his ally for almost two years. As Soviet forces were pushed back, Churchill feared that a German victory would leave Hitler free to attack Britain, making use of the raw materials and oil reserves of Russia. Desperate to avert a German victory in Russia, he not only gave the Soviet Union large quantities of military equipment but also persuaded Roosevelt to do likewise.

Churchill was greatly angered that summer to read in a Foreign Office telegram from Washington of a British Admiralty proposal, about which he had not been told by the Admiralty. It was that American destroyers should, for strategic reasons, operate "on their side of the Atlantic rather than upon ours." Whoever had "put this about," Churchill wrote to his senior colleagues, "has done great disservice, and should be immediately removed from all American contacts." Churchill added: "No question of Naval strategy in the Atlantic is comparable with the importance of drawing the Americans to this side. May I ask that this should be accepted at once as a decision of policy."[15]

Churchill remained vigilant about American help; his fears intensified of a Soviet defeat within two months, followed by a German invasion of Britain. In asking Roosevelt to accelerate still further the American merchant shipbuilding program, and to increase the number of American escort vessels on the transatlantic convoy routes, he informed the President: "I am asking that everything here shall be at concert pitch for invasion from September 1."[16]

Two days after sending this telegram, as Churchill scrutinized the charts, graphs, statistics and reports that were put before him daily, he was struck by the lack of sufficient American escort vessels. At the next meeting of the Defence Committee he said he would draw American

---

14. Broadcast of 16 June 1941, text printed in full in *The Times*, 17 June 1941.

15. Minute of 28 June 1941, Churchill Papers, 20/36, Martin Gilbert, *The Churchill War Papers*, Volume 3, pages 864–65.

16. Telegram of 1 July 1941, Churchill Papers, 20/40, Martin Gilbert, *The Churchill War Papers*, Volume 3, pages 880–81.

attention to "the futility of a policy which, through lack of effective help, permitted sinkings to continue at a high rate and relied on making them good by future building."[17]

This situation, detrimental to Britain, was about to change. On July 4 a new United States Defense Plan was ready for Presidential approval. That day the Chief of the United States Navy Staff, Admiral Robert Ghormley, informed the British Chiefs of Staff Committee: "It is the policy of the United States to ensure the safe arrival at destination of all of the material being furnished by the United States to nations whose security is essential to the defense of the United States." In order to carry out this policy, United States naval forces would conduct operations for the protection of all shipping used in the transportation of this material within the Western Hemisphere. "Axis naval and air forces within the Western Hemisphere will be deemed potential threats to this shipping and will be attacked where ever found."

Ghormley cautioned: "It is intended that this action should be taken as a measure short of war and one that may not necessarily lead to existence of formal war between the United States and Axis powers."[18] But for Churchill this caveat was unimportant. "I was encouraged," he telegraphed to Roosevelt on July 7, "to read the documents on Defence Plan No. 3." Putting such a plan "into immediate operation would give timely and needed aid. At present the strain upon our resources is far too great."[19] The new United States ocean escort would consist of six battleships, five heavy cruisers, fifty-six destroyers and forty-eight patrol aircraft. There would also be a United States Striking Force of three aircraft carriers, four light cruisers, twelve destroyers and twelve patrol aircraft. This impressive force, a major American contribution to Britain's survival, had instructions to operate under war conditions, including darkening ships at sea, something usually done only by ships of nations at war.

On July 12 Churchill received welcome news directly from Roosevelt: a planned increase in United States tank production from six hundred to a thousand tanks a month. "Assuming these schedules are maintained," Roosevelt wrote, "and I believe they will be, it means that

---

17. Defence Committee minutes, 3 July 1941, Cabinet Papers, 69/2.
18. Notes of 4 July 1941, Cabinet Papers, 127/16.
19. Telegram of 7 July 1941, Premier Papers, 3/460/2.

we can give you eight hundred to a thousand light tanks and eight hundred to a thousand medium tanks prior to January 1." As of August 1, Roosevelt added, the United States could also start training five hundred British Tank Corps soldiers "in this country, if you think that would be helpful."[20]

Churchill no longer had any doubt about the American determination to help in every way possible short of an actual declaration of war. But there were formidable tasks ahead. Britain had begun to consider its war plans, Churchill informed Roosevelt on July 25, "not only for the fighting of 1942, but also for 1943." It had become urgent to frame "an agreed estimate of our joint requirements of the primary weapons of war," and to consider how those requirements were to be met "by our joint production."[21] This was a prodigious undertaking. The time had come for Churchill and Roosevelt to meet.

---

20. Telegram of 12 July 1941, Premier Papers, 3/469, folio 176.
21. Telegram of 25 July 1941, Cabinet Papers, 65/23.

Chapter Twenty-Three

⚜

"A MEANS OF WAGING
MORE EFFECTIVE WAR"

O n 4 August 1941 Churchill left Britain on the battleship *Prince of Wales*. Reaching Placentia Bay, off Newfoundland, near the small port of Argentia, on August 9, he crossed by barge to the American battle cruiser *Augusta*. Awaiting him on the upper deck was President Roosevelt, supported—because polio contracted twenty years earlier had weakened his legs—on the arm of his son Elliott. Churchill handed Roosevelt a letter from King George VI. "This is just a note," the King had written, "to bring you my best wishes, and to say how glad I am that you have an opportunity at last of getting to know my Prime Minister. I am sure that you will agree that he is a very remarkable man, and I have no doubt that your meeting will prove of great benefit to our two countries in the pursuit of our common goal."[1]

Roosevelt invited Churchill to a tour of *Augusta* and to lunch. "The PM has been in his best form," Averell Harriman wrote to his daughter Kathleen. Roosevelt, he added, "is intrigued and likes him enormously."[2] On Sunday August 10 Roosevelt and Churchill attended Divine Service on the *Prince of Wales*. Churchill's new Principal Private Secretary, John Martin, wrote in his diary: "The PM had given much thought to the preparations for his Service (which he said should be fully choral and fully photographic), choosing the hymns (O God Our Help in Ages Past, Onward Christian Soldiers, and Eternal Father

---

1. Letter dated 3 August 1941, Franklin D. Roosevelt Papers.
2. Undated letter, W. Averell Harriman and Elie Abel, *Special Envoy to Churchill and Stalin, 1941–1946,* page 76.

Strong to Save), and vetting the prayers (which I had to read to him while he dried after his bath)."

Martin commented: "You would have had to be pretty hard-boiled not to be moved by it all—hundreds of men from both fleets all mingled together, one rough British sailor sharing his hymn sheet with one American ditto. It seemed a sort of marriage service between the two navies, already in spirit allies, though the bright peace-time paint and spit and polish of the American ships contrasted with the dull camouflage of the *Prince of Wales,* so recently in action against the *Bismarck.* "[3]

Formal talks between Churchill and Roosevelt began on August 11. After Hopkins told them of his recent meetings with the Soviet leader, Joseph Stalin, Roosevelt agreed to give immediate aid to the Soviet Union "on a gigantic scale." He also agreed to Churchill's suggestion to send an Anglo-American mission to Moscow to settle the nature and scale of munitions and other supplies to the Soviet Union by Britain and the United States "conjointly."[4]

Churchill and Roosevelt agreed on a new American naval commitment, Defense Plan No. 4, whereby the United States Navy would take over all Atlantic patrols between America and Iceland. Agreement was also reached to make every effort to restrain Japan from further aggression in the Far East, "to make no encroachment upon Siam" and to remove its military forces from Indochina. Churchill told the British Deputy Prime Minister, Clement Attlee, that Roosevelt had agreed to end his message to Japan "with a very severe warning, which I drafted."[5] Churchill's draft read: "Any further encroachment by Japan in the South-West Pacific would produce a situation in which the United States Government would be compelled to take counter-measures, even though these might lead to war between the United States and Japan."[6] Once back in Washington, however, Roosevelt modified the warning, losing its reference to war.

Churchill's hope remained that Roosevelt would see the way forward to an American declaration of war against Germany. "At the At-

---

3. Diary entry, 10 August 1941, Sir John Martin Papers.
4. *The Memoirs of General the Lord Ismay,* page 228.
5. Telegram of 11 August 1941, Premier Papers, 3/485/1.
6. Draft announcement, 11 August 1941, Premier Papers, 3/485/1.

lantic Meeting," he later told Field Marshal Smuts, "I told his circle that I would rather have an American declaration of war now and no supplies for six months than double the supplies and no declaration. When this was repeated to him he thought it a hard saying."[7]

At his first talk with Churchill on August 9, Roosevelt had raised the question of what was to become known as the Atlantic Charter: a joint Anglo-American declaration of principles that, despite continuing American neutrality, would link Britain's war aims with the aspirations of the United States. Churchill had handed Roosevelt a draft declaration on August 10, immediately after Divine Service. The discussions of Churchill's draft and Roosevelt's additions continued during August 11. In a telegram to Attlee that day, Churchill commented on a paragraph drafted by Roosevelt pledging an "effective international organization" that would afford all nations security "within their own boundaries . . . without fear of lawless assault or the need to maintain burdensome armaments." Churchill told Attlee: "The President undoubtedly contemplates the disarmament of the guilty nations, coupled with the maintenance of strong united British and American armament both by sea and air for a long indefinite period."[8]

The British War Cabinet asked for the inclusion of a point on the need to secure after the war "improved labour standards, economic advancement and social security" for all. Churchill and Roosevelt approved this. Also in the final draft was a sentence, written by Churchill, envisaging in the name of both Britain and the United States "a world at peace" after "the final destruction of the Nazi tyranny." This was a remarkable commitment by the United States while still a neutral power.

In the Atlantic Charter, Britain and the United States pledged themselves, first, to "no aggrandisement, territorial or other" as a result of the war; second, to no territorial changes "that do not accord with the freely expressed wishes of the peoples concerned"; and third—this point became the central attraction of the Atlantic Charter for millions of captive peoples—to "respect the right of all peoples to choose the form of government under which they will live; and they wish to see sovereign rights and self-government restored to those who have been forcibly deprived of them."

---

7. Telegram of 8 November 1941, Premier Papers, 3/476/3.
8. Telegram of 11 August 1941, Premier Papers, 3/485/1.

One final decision remained: the setting up of a joint Anglo-American mission to Moscow, to be headed by Lord Beaverbrook and Averell Harriman. Intending to discuss Soviet supply needs in relation to British needs and American production, Beaverbrook and Arthur Purvis set off from Scotland by air for Newfoundland, to join the conference. They flew in separate planes. Beaverbrook reached Newfoundland safely. Purvis and those with him were killed when their plane flew into a hillside within minutes of takeoff. The death of Purvis, Churchill later recalled, was "a grievous loss, as he held so many British, American and Canadian threads in his hands, and had hitherto been the directing mind in their harmonious combination." Churchill had been convinced that Beaverbrook and Purvis together would give Britain the best chance "of coping with the painful splitting" of American supplies between Britain and the Soviet Union.[9]

In a telegram to Attlee, Churchill explained that the presence of the Soviet Union "as a welcome guest at hungry table," and the need for a large supplementary program both for British and American forces, "makes review and expansion of US production imperative." As for American aid to Britain, Churchill informed Attlee, the Americans were sending immediately a further 150,000 rifles, and had promised improved allocations of merchant shipping to carry bombers and tanks across the Atlantic as well as delivering bombers both to Britain and West Africa "by American pilots," many of whom would then "stay for war training purposes with us."

On August 16, on his way back from Newfoundland, Churchill stopped in Iceland. There he addressed the sailors of the destroyer *Churchill,* one of the fifty American destroyers of the Destroyers-for-Bases agreement. The *Churchill* was then on convoy escort duty out of Halifax. Churchill also went ashore for a few hours, and, accompanied by Roosevelt's son Franklin, Jr., a naval ensign, inspected a unit of American Marines based in Iceland. Both the Marine Flag and the Stars and Stripes were paraded before him.

Churchill was pleased with more than the practical decisions reached between him and Roosevelt, telling Attlee: "I am sure I have estab-

---

9. Winston S. Churchill, *The Second World War,* Volume 3, pages 396–97.

lished warm and deep personal relations with our great friend."[10] As for Roosevelt's attitude toward the entry of the United States into the war, Churchill told the War Cabinet that the President "was obviously determined that they should come in." On the other hand, Churchill pointed out, he had been "extremely anxious about the Bill for further appropriations for Lease-Lend, which had only passed with a very narrow majority. Clearly he was skating on pretty thin ice in his relations with Congress, which, however, he did not regard as truly representative of the country. If he were to put the issue of peace and war to Congress, they would debate it for three months." Roosevelt had told Churchill "that he would wage war, but not declare it, and that he would become more and more provocative." If the Germans "did not like it they could attack American forces!"

Churchill then told the War Cabinet that as a result of his discussion with Roosevelt, each British North Atlantic convoy would be escorted by five American destroyers, together with a capital ship or cruiser. The President's orders to these escorts were "to attack any U-boat which showed itself, even if these were 200 or 300 miles away from the convoy." But Churchill had warned Roosevelt, as he told the War Cabinet, "that he would not answer for the consequences if Russia was compelled to sue for peace and, say, by the Spring of next year, hope died in Britain that the United States were coming into the war."

The President "had taken this very well," Churchill reported, "and had made it clear that he would look for an "incident" which would justify him in opening hostilities."[11]

Churchill was enthusiastic about what had been achieved, telling the crew of the *Prince of Wales* when he said good-bye to them at Scapa Flow on August 18, "We have brought back a means of waging more effective war and surer hope of final and speedy victory."[12]

---

10. Telegram No. 23 of 12 August 1941, Premier Papers, 3/485/1.

11. War Cabinet No. 84 of 1941, 19 August 1941, Cabinet Papers, 65/19.

12. Speech of 18 August 1941, Premier Papers, 4/71/1.

Chapter Twenty-Four

"AMERICAN BLOOD FLOWED
IN MY VEINS"

On his return to the United States from Newfoundland, Roosevelt made a series of statements assuring the American people that the United States had made no commitments and was no nearer to war than before the shipboard meeting. Churchill was profoundly disappointed, telegraphing to Harry Hopkins: "I ought to tell you that there has been a wave of depression through Cabinet and other informed circles here about President's many assurances about no commitments and no closer to war, etc. I fear this will be reflected in Parliament."

If the year 1942 were to open "with Russia knocked out and Britain left again alone," Churchill warned Hopkins, "all kinds of dangers may arise. . . . You will know best whether anything more can be done. Should be grateful if you could give me any sort of hope."[1] Churchill understood that an American declaration of war would not easily come to pass. On August 25 he had told his War Cabinet colleagues that he "sometimes wondered whether the President realised the risk which the United States were running by keeping out of the war." If Germany beat Russia "to a standstill," and the United States "had made no further advance towards entry into the war, there was a great danger that the war might take a turn against us. While no doubt we could hope to keep going, this was a very different matter from imposing our will on Nazi Germany."[2]

---

1. Telegram of 28 August 1941, Churchill Papers, 20/42, Martin Gilbert, *The Churchill War Papers*, Volume 3, page 1125.
2. Cabinet Papers, 65/19.

Five days later Churchill wrote to his son, Randolph, then serving in Cairo as a Major on press liaison duties, of how, in the three days when he and Roosevelt "were continually together I feel we made a deep and intimate contact of friendship. At the same time one is deeply perplexed to know how the deadlock is to be broken and the United States brought boldly and honourably into the war. There is a very dangerous feeling in America that they need not worry now as all will be well." As to Roosevelt, Churchill wrote: "The President, for all his warm heart and good intentions, is thought by many of his admirers to move with public opinion rather than to lead and form it. I thank God however that he is where he is."[3]

On August 30, in the presence of Ambassador Winant, Churchill insisted—as Jock Colville noted—that if the United States entered the war "the conviction of an Allied victory would be founded in a dozen countries." Churchill was emphatic, telling Winant: "We must have an American declaration of war, or else, though we cannot now be defeated, the war might drag on for another four or five years, and civilisation and culture would be wiped out. If America came in, she could stop this. She alone could bring the war to an end—her belligerency might mean victory in 1943."[4]

Welcome news reached Churchill from Roosevelt on September 6. United States Navy transports, manned by American crews, would transport up to 20,000 British troops to the Middle East. The United States would also lend Britain ten or twelve cargo ships for the North Atlantic run, to release British cargo ships for the Middle East supply routes. The American ships, Roosevelt assured Churchill, would be "our best."[5]

Five days later, on September 11, following an unsuccessful German torpedo attack on the American destroyer *Greer*, Roosevelt declared, in a radio broadcast, that henceforth any German or Italian vessels of war that entered the American-protected Atlantic zone did so "at their own peril." When you see a rattlesnake "poised to strike,"

---

3. Letter of 29 August 1941, Churchill Papers, 1/362, Martin Gilbert, *The Churchill War Papers*, Volume 3, pages 1132–33.
4. Diary entry, 30 August 1941, Colville Papers.
5. Telegram of 6 September 1941, Churchill Papers, 20/42, Martin Gilbert, *The Churchill War Papers*, Volume 3, page 1177, note 1.

Roosevelt explained, "you do not wait until he has struck before you crush him."[6] Churchill, who had listened to Roosevelt's broadcast, wrote that day to a former fellow army cadet: "Roosevelt this morning excellent. As we used to sing at Sandhurst 'Now we *shan't* be long!' "[7]

At the beginning of October, Roosevelt authorized Naval Defense Plan No. 5. The United States Navy would undertake escort duties from Canada to the mid-Atlantic for all Canadian troop convoys, as well as for merchant-shipping convoys. By this decision, Admiral Pound explained to Churchill, British naval forces would be released in mid-Atlantic instead of having to make the passage the whole way across.[8]

One burden for Churchill throughout the autumn of 1941 was that British and American aid to the Soviet Union, judged essential by both Churchill and Roosevelt to prevent a German victory in the East, ate into the whole range of British supplies from America for which Churchill had fought so hard. "The offers which we are both making to Russia," Churchill telegraphed Hopkins on October 2, "are necessary and worthwhile," but there was "no disguising the fact" that these offers made "grievous inroads into what is required by you for expanding your forces and by us for intensifying our war effort."[9]

Among the commitments to the Soviet Union was one that intensified the dire shortage of Anglo-American merchant shipping. Because the Soviet Union had almost no merchant shipping capability, Churchill and Roosevelt were providing shipping from their respective merchant navies on a substantial scale. This enabled the transport to the Soviet Union of half a million tons a month of cargo: food, oil and war material imports, medical supplies on a vast scale, including more than ten million surgical needles, half a million pairs of surgical gloves, four thousand kilograms of local anesthetics, and more than a million doses of antibiotics.[10] These had only just become available in clinical form. Soviet troops were to be their first beneficiaries.

6. Broadcast of 11 September 1941, B. D. Zevin, editor, *Nothing to Fear: The Selected Addresses of Franklin Delano Roosevelt, 1932–1945,* pages 287–89.
7. Letter of 12 September 1941, Churchill Papers, 20/22, Martin Gilbert, *The Churchill War Papers,* Volume 3, pages 1204–5.
8. Notes on Defence Plan No. 5, Premier Papers, 3/460/4.
9. Telegram of 2 October 1941, Foreign Office Papers, 954/24.
10. Moscow Conference, 1941, Cabinet Papers, 99/7.

On October 4, Churchill telegraphed to Roosevelt: "How I wish we could have another talk." [11] Meanwhile, he lost no opportunity to draw Roosevelt into the business of war. On the eve of a renewed British offensive in the Western Desert he telegraphed to the Commander-in-Chief, Middle East: "It is necessary for me to take the President into our confidence, and thus stimulate his friendly action." [12]

An attempted German invasion of Britain was much on Churchill's mind in the late autumn of 1941, particularly if the Soviet Union had been defeated by the end of the year. In a letter to Roosevelt, marked "For yourself alone," he confided that Britain must be prepared "to meet a supreme onslaught from March onward." [13] Churchill was also concerned about a Japanese threat to Britain's possessions in the Far East. To draw in Roosevelt as an ally in the Far East, on October 20 Churchill gave the President a formal assurance that should the United States find itself at war with Japan, "you may be sure that a British declaration of war upon Japan will follow within the hour." [14]

Eleven days later the focus switched back to Europe when, on October 31, an American destroyer on convoy duty for Britain, the *Reuben James,* was torpedoed in the North Atlantic: 115 of her crew, including all the officers, were drowned. As with the sinking of the *Lusitania* in the First World War, however, and the *Athenia* in 1939, this act of German aggression did not lead to an American declaration of war. Churchill telegraphed to Roosevelt: "I am grieved at loss of life you have suffered with *Reuben James.* I salute the land of unending challenge." [15]

The failure of the United States to enter the war as a belligerent led to growing anger in British Government circles. Despite his own frustrations, Churchill did not share this anger. He understood the workings of the American Constitution and American public opinion.

---

11. Telegram of 4 October 1941, Churchill Papers, 20/43, Martin Gilbert, *The Churchill War Papers,* Volume 3, page 1301.
12. Telegram of 18 October 1941, Churchill Papers, 20/44, Martin Gilbert, *The Churchill War Papers,* Volume 3, page 1348.
13. Letter of 20 October 1941, Churchill Papers, 20/20, Martin Gilbert, *The Churchill War Papers,* Volume 3, pages 1351–52.
14. Telegram of 20 October 1941, Premier Papers, 3/486/2.
15. Telegram of 1 November 1941, Churchill Papers, 20/40, Martin Gilbert, *The Churchill War Papers,* Volume 3, pages 1398–99.

On November 12 he spoke to the War Cabinet about the difficulties facing Roosevelt as a result of "the slow development of American opinion and the peculiarities of the American Constitution." Nobody but Congress could declare war, Churchill explained. "It was, however, in the President's power to make war without declaring it."

In the previous twelve months, Churchill told his War Cabinet, American opinion had moved under Roosevelt's leadership to an extent that nobody could have anticipated. "They had made immense credits available to us; they had made immense resources available to us under the Lease Lend Act; their Navy was escorting the Atlantic convoys; and finally they were taking a firm line with the Japanese." It would, however, Churchill warned, "be a great error" for him to press President Roosevelt to act "in advance of American opinion." [16]

One of Churchill's Private Secretaries, John Peck, later recalled a remark by Churchill at this time. "The American Constitution," Churchill remarked, "was designed by the Founding Fathers to keep the United States clear of European entanglements—and by God it has stood the test of time." [17] To Field Marshal Smuts, who had written to Churchill criticizing Roosevelt's failure to declare war on Germany, Churchill replied: "Naturally if I saw any way of helping to lift this situation on to a higher plane I would do so. In the meanwhile we must have patience and trust to the tide which is flowing our way, and to events." [18]

That tide saw a small but significant flow in favor of Britain in mid-November, when Roosevelt secured an amendment of the Neutrality Act, making it lawful for American merchant ships to be armed. "The American decision," Lord Beaverbrook wrote to Churchill, "is worth more than many million tons of shipping. It is a victory for you in the battle of the Atlantic where you fought so long & such a lonely struggle." [19] After dining with Churchill on the night that the Neutrality Act was amended, Churchill's friend Lord Camrose wrote to his elder son: "Winston was highly delighted. He said he did not care a damn about the smallness of the Majority. The thing was that the President now

---

16. War Cabinet of 12 November 1941, Cabinet Papers, 65/24.

17. Sir John Peck recollection, in conversation with the author, 18 August 1982.

18. Telegram of 8 November 1941, Premier Papers, 3/476/3.

19. Letter of 14 November 1941, Beaverbrook Papers.

had power to act and the size of the majority would soon be forgotten. He anticipated great things from this new decision and I could see he feels that it cannot now be many days before America is finally in the war." [20]

On November 21, two British-based American entertainers, Bebe Daniels and her husband, Ben Lyon, went to Downing Street to give Churchill five special "thumbs up" badges that were being sold in New York by the Mayor, Fiorello La Guardia, on behalf of the British War Relief Society in the United States. That winter an American author, Stanley Nott, published *The Young Churchill*. "In Mr Nott's book," wrote Lord Halifax, "young Americans will be able to perceive the courage, the energy, and the enterprise of the young Churchill and understand better the qualities which have given the British people such faith in their Prime Minister." [21]

Unknown to Washington or to London, on November 26, even as Japan's disputes with the United States were the subject of prolonged diplomatic exchanges between Tokyo and Washington, a Japanese naval force set sail from the Kurile Islands, north of Japan, through fogs and gales, toward the Pearl Harbor naval base in Hawaii. Churchill still believed that a firm warning to Japan might avert war. He had often reflected on the effect such a warning might have had on Germany during the Rhineland crisis of 1936, when Hitler's move in remilitarizing the area, unopposed by Britain and France, seemed to have set a pattern for unchallenged aggression.

Britain's continuing shortage of rifle ammunition was also much on Churchill's mind. On November 27 he asked Harriman for help. "I realise that the Russian requirements must be heavy," he wrote, "but if there is anything you can do to obtain increased supplies for us from the United States during the coming months I should be very grateful." [22]

On November 30, his sixty-seventh birthday, Churchill sent Roosevelt his thoughts on what might still be done to prevent a resurgent, over-

---

20. Letter of 14 November 1941, Lord Camrose Papers.
21. Lord Halifax, Foreword to Stanley Nott, *The Young Churchill*.
22. Letter of 27 November 1941, Averell Harriman Papers.

confident Japan from deciding to go to war. "It seems to me," he wrote, "that one important method remains unused in averting war between Japan and our two countries, namely, a plain declaration, secret or public, as may be thought best, that any further act of aggression by Japan will lead immediately to the gravest consequences." Churchill explained to Roosevelt that he realized his constitutional difficulties, "but it would be tragic if Japan drifted into war by encroachment without having before her fairly and squarely the dire character of a further aggressive step."

Churchill told the President: "I beg you to consider whether, at the moment which you judge right, which may be very near, you should not say that 'any further Japanese aggression would compel you to place the gravest issues before Congress,' or words to that effect. We would of course make a similar declaration or share in a joint declaration, and in any case arrangements are being made to synchronise our action with yours."

"Forgive me, my dear friend," Churchill ended, "for presuming to press such a course upon you, but I am convinced that it might make all the difference and prevent a melancholy extension of the war."[23] No such declaration was made; even the discussion of it was overtaken by events.

On 7 December 1941 Churchill was spending the weekend at Chequers. By one o'clock all but one of his luncheon guests had arrived. The missing guest was the American Ambassador, Gil Winant. "When I reached Chequers," Winant later recalled, "the Prime Minister was walking up and down outside the entrance door—the others had gone in to lunch twenty minutes before. He asked me if I thought there was going to be war with Japan. I answered 'Yes.' With unusual vehemence he turned to me and said: 'If they declare war on you, we shall declare war on them within the hour.'"

Churchill then asked Winant whether, if Japan declared war on Britain, the United States would declare war on Japan. "I can't answer that, Prime Minister," Winant replied. "Only the Congress has the right to declare war under the United States Constitution." Winant's account continued: "He did not say anything for a minute, but I knew

---

23. Telegram of 30 November 1941, Premier Papers, 3/156/6.

what was in his mind. He must have realized that if Japan attacked Siam or British territory it would force Great Britain into an Asiatic war, and leave us out of the war. He knew in that moment that his country might be 'hanging on one turn of pitch and toss.' Nevertheless he turned to me with the charm of manner that I saw so often in difficult moments, and said, 'We are late, you know. You get washed and we will go in to lunch together.'" [24]

Churchill's nightmare was that Britain would be at war with Japan and the United States would not. A Japanese attack on the principal British possessions in the Far East—Hong Kong, Malaya or Burma—would not automatically bring the United States into war against Japan. If prudent, Japan would avoid attacking the United States and overrun the British territories without American intervention. Britain would be without a war-making American ally in either the Far East or Europe.

Then, on the morning of December 7 in London—late evening of December 6 in Washington—Churchill learned that Roosevelt was finally prepared to announce publicly what Churchill had so desperately wanted: that the United States would regard it as a hostile act against the United States if Japan were to invade British possessions in the Far East. This new American commitment was to be announced publicly by Roosevelt on Wednesday, December 10. "This is an immense relief," Churchill telegraphed to the Commander-in-Chief, Middle East, "as I had long dreaded being at war with Japan without or before the United States." Churchill added: "Now I think it is all right." [25]

Early on the morning of December 7, Hawaii time, Japanese carrier-borne aircraft attacked the United States Fleet at Pearl Harbor. Four American battleships were destroyed. Two thousand American servicemen were killed. It was early evening on December 8 in Britain. Churchill was dining at Chequers with Harriman and Winant. "I turned on my small wireless set shortly after the nine o'clock news had started," Churchill later wrote. "There were a number of items about the fighting on the Russian front and on the British front in Libya, at

24. John G. Winant, *A Letter from Grosvenor Square*, pages 196–97.
25. Telegram of 7 December 1941, Churchill Papers, 20/46, Martin Gilbert, *The Churchill War Papers*, Volume 3, pages 1574–75.

the end of which some few sentences were spoken regarding an attack by the Japanese on American shipping at Hawaii, and also Japanese attacks on British vessels in the Dutch East Indies."

There then followed, Churchill remembered, "a statement that after the news Mr Somebody would make a commentary, and that the Brains Trust programme would then begin, or something like this. I did not personally sustain any direct impression, but Averell said there was something about the Japanese attacking the Americans, and, in spite of being tired and resting, we all sat up."

At that moment Churchill's valet, Sawyers, who had likewise been listening to the news, came into the room. "It's quite true," he said, "we heard it ourselves outside. The Japanese have attacked the Americans."[26] Winant later recalled the ensuing scene: "We looked at one another incredulously. Then Churchill jumped to his feet and started for the door with the announcement, 'We shall declare war on Japan.'"

Winant added: "There is nothing half-hearted or un-positive about Churchill—certainly not when he is on the move. Without ceremony I too left the table and followed him out of the room. 'Good God,' I said, 'you can't declare war on a radio announcement.' He stopped and looked at me half-seriously, half-quizzically, and then said quietly, 'What shall I do?' The question was asked not because he needed me to tell him what to do, but as a courtesy to the representative of the country attacked. I said, 'I will call up the President by telephone and ask him what the facts are.' And he added, 'And I shall talk with him too.'"

A telephone call was put through to the White House. Winant told the President that he had "a friend" with him who wanted to speak to the President. Winant added: "You will know who it is, as soon as you hear his voice."[27] Churchill then asked: "Mr President, what's this about Japan?" "It's quite true," Roosevelt replied. "They have attacked us at Pearl Harbor. We are all in the same boat now."[28]

Roosevelt told Churchill that he was going to ask Congress the next day, Monday, "to declare a state of open hostility." Churchill asked

---

26. Winston S. Churchill, *The Second World War*, Volume 3, page 538.
27. John G. Winant, *A Letter from Grosvenor Square*, pages 198–99.
28. Winston S. Churchill, *The Second World War*, Volume 3, page 538.

what the President wanted him to do about Britain's declaration of war on Japan. This, Churchill said, would follow the President's "within the hour." [29] It was not the United States alone whose territory had been attacked by Japan. "Soon after the first excitement," Churchill's Principal Private Secretary, John Martin, later recalled, "I was able to obtain on the telephone from the Admiralty news of the Japanese attack on Malaya." [30] Britain and the United States had been attacked simultaneously by the same enemy.

Churchill went to bed that night knowing it could only be a matter of a few hours before America was at war with Japan. This was indeed so. "The Senate passed the all-out declaration of war 82 to nothing," Roosevelt telegraphed him on December 8, "and the House has passed it 382 to 1." Roosevelt added: "Today all of us are in the same boat with you and the people of the Empire, and it is a ship which will not and cannot be sunk." [31]

Immediately after learning of the Japanese attack on Pearl Harbor, Churchill had telegraphed to Harry Hopkins, signing the telegram jointly with Averell Harriman. Their message read: "Thinking of you much at this historic moment." [32] Reflecting on that historic moment a decade later, Churchill wrote: "No American will think it wrong of me if I proclaim that to have the United States at our side was to me the greatest joy. I could not foretell the course of events. I do not pretend to have measured accurately the martial might of Japan, but now at this very moment I knew the United States was in the war, up to the neck and in to the death. So we had won after all! Yes, after Dunkirk, after the fall of France; after the horrible episode of Oran; after the threat of invasion, when, apart from the Air and the Navy, we were an almost unarmed people; after the deadly struggle of the U-boat war—the first Battle of the Atlantic, gained by a hand's-breadth; after seventeen months of lonely fighting and nineteen months of my responsibility in dire stress. We had won the war. England would live;

---

29. Sir John Martin, letter to the author, 3 September 1982.
30. Message of 8 December (Malayan Time), 7 December (Pacific Time) 1941, Sir John Martin Papers.
31. Telegram of 8 December 1941, Premier Papers, 3/469.
32. Telegram of 8 December 1941, Winston S. Churchill, *The Second World War,* Volume 3, page 539.

Britain would live; the Commonwealth of Nations and the Empire would live."

"How long the war would last," Churchill added, "or in what fashion it would end no man could tell, nor did I at this moment care. Once again in our long Island history we should emerge, however mauled or mutilated, safe and victorious. We should not be wiped out. Our history would not come to an end. We might not even have to die as individuals. Hitler's fate was sealed. Mussolini's fate was sealed. As for the Japanese, they would be ground to powder. All the rest was merely the proper application of overwhelming force."

Of the ability of that force to prevail in the end, Churchill had no doubt: "The British Empire, the Soviet Union, and now the United States, bound together with every scrap of their life and strength, were, according to my lights, twice or even thrice the force of their antagonists. No doubt it would take a long time. I expected terrible forfeits in the East; but all this would be merely a passing phase. United we could subdue everybody else in the world. Many disasters, immeasurable cost and tribulation lay ahead, but there was no more doubt about the end."

Churchill then reflected on the attitude of those who did not share his understanding—derived from more than four decades of personal experience—of American opinion. "Silly people," he wrote, "and there were many, not only in enemy countries, might discount the force of the United States. Some said they were soft, others that they would never be united. They would fool around at a distance. They would never come to grips. They would never stand bloodletting. Their democracy and system of recurrent elections would paralyse their war effort. They would be just a vague blur on the horizon to friend or foe. Now we should see the weakness of this numerous but remote, wealthy, and talkative people." Such was one view. "But I had studied the American Civil War, fought out to the last desperate inch. American blood flowed in my veins. I thought of a remark which Edward Grey had made to me more than thirty years before—that the United States is like 'a gigantic boiler. Once the fire is lighted under it there is no limit to the power it can generate.' Being saturated and satiated with emotion and sensation, I went to bed and slept the sleep of the saved and thankful." [33]

---

33. Winston S. Churchill, *The Second World War,* Volume 3, pages 539–40.

Chapter Twenty-Five

✠

THE WASHINGTON
WAR CONFERENCE:
"ALL IN IT TOGETHER"

On 8 December 1941, within a few hours of learning of the Japanese attack on Pearl Harbor, Churchill prepared to go to the United States. "The whole plan of Anglo-American defence and attack," he explained to King George VI, had to be coordinated in the light of the new war. "We have also to be careful that our share of munitions and other aid which we are receiving from the United States does not suffer more than is, I fear, inevitable."[1]

A strange situation had arisen: The United States was at war with Japan, but not with Germany. Churchill had Roosevelt as a full ally in the war against Japan, but not in the war against Germany. Roosevelt had no plans to ask Congress to declare war on Germany. Then, on December 11, Hitler and Mussolini declared war on the United States. On the following day Churchill wrote to Clement Attlee: "We have no longer any need to strike attitudes to win United States' sympathy, we are all in it together."[2]

One worry remained, Churchill told Field Marshal Smuts—that the Americans "may be too much preoccupied with the war with Japan."[3] To avert this, on December 12 Churchill left by sea for the

---

1. Letter of 8 December 1941, Royal Archives.
2. Minute of 12 December 1941, Churchill Papers, 20/36, Martin Gilbert, *The Churchill War Papers,* Volume 3, page 1612.
3. Telegram of 12 December 1941, Churchill Papers, 20/46, Martin Gilbert, *The Churchill War Papers,* Volume 3, page 1613.

United States, his first wartime visit, on board the battleship *Duke of York*. During one of his shipboard conversations with Averell Harriman he pointed out that it was "in the hands" of the United States "to make this a long or short war." If America defended "each town on the Pacific with fighter aircraft etc, it will be long—five years. If you let the raider come—what does it matter—then it can be finished in two years."[4]

Reaching Hampton Roads, Virginia, on December 22, Churchill flew immediately to Washington. There, he recalled, "the President was waiting in his car. I clasped his strong hand with comfort and pleasure."[5] That same evening, at the first meeting of the British and American Chiefs of Staff, it was agreed "that it was vital to forestall the Germans in North West Africa and in the Atlantic islands," and that plans should be made for a joint Anglo-American landing in French North Africa. Churchill's fears of an American "Asia-first" strategy were quickly dispelled, as the two senior Americans present, General Marshall and Admiral Harold R. Stark, reiterated the American-British Staff Conversations conclusion of February 1941, that the Atlantic and European theater of war was the "decisive one." Notwithstanding Japan's entry into the war, they confirmed: "Our view remains that Germany is still the key to victory. Once Germany is defeated, the collapse of Italy and the defeat of Japan must follow."[6]

That day Japanese troops landed in the Philippines. The British garrison in Hong Kong was under siege. Speaking to the British Dominion representatives at the White House on the morning of December 23, Churchill reflected that the United Kingdom had avoided "the worst possible situation," whereby Japan would have made war on Britain alone, and America remained out of the war. "On balance we could not be dissatisfied with the turn of events." The "powerful assistance" of the United States was assured; "we could therefore look to the future with hope and confidence."[7] That afternoon Roosevelt introduced Churchill to a Press Conference of American journalists and

---

4. Notes of a conversation, 20 December 1941, Averell Harriman Papers.
5. Winston S. Churchill, *The Second World War*, Volume 3, page 588.
6. "Summation" of 22 December 1941, quoted in W. Averell Harriman and Elie Abel, *Special Envoy to Churchill and Stalin, 1941–1946*, page 117.
7. Meeting of 23 December 1941, Premier Papers, 3/458/4.

broadcasters. In answer to a question about Singapore—was it not "key to the whole situation" in the Far East?—Churchill replied: "The key to the whole situation is the resolute manner in which the British and American Democracies are going to throw themselves into the conflict."[8]

It was Christmas Eve. Churchill and Roosevelt stood together on the White House portico as the lights of the White House Christmas tree were turned on. Churchill then spoke to a crowd of many thousands, telling them that although he was far from his family "yet I cannot truthfully say that I feel far from home." His remarks continued: "Whether it be the ties of blood on my mother's side, or the friendships I have developed here over many years of active life, or the commanding sentiment of comradeship in the common cause of great peoples who speak the same language, who kneel at the same altars, and, to a very large extent, pursue the same ideals, I cannot feel myself a stranger here in the centre and at the summit of the United States. I feel a sense of unity and fraternal association which, added to the kindliness of your welcome, convinces me that I have a right to sit at your fireside and share your Christmas joys."[9]

On Christmas Day, Hong Kong surrendered. That morning Churchill went to church with the President. They then continued their talks, Roosevelt agreeing, as Churchill reported to his Commander-in-Chief, Middle East, that in French North Africa either the Vichy authorities there would bow to American pressure or "some highly trained American divisions" would be sent into action. They also agreed that American bombing squadrons "could come over to attack Germany from the British Isles."[10]

Churchill's shorthand writer, Patrick Kinna, was with him throughout his stay at the White House. "One morning the Prime Minister wanted to dictate while he was in his bath—not a minute could be wasted," Kinna later recalled. "He kept submerging in the bath and when he 'surfaced' he would dictate a few more words or sentences. Eventually he got out of the bath when his devoted valet, Sawyers,

---

8. Press Conference, 23 December 1941, Premier Papers, 4/71/2.
9. Broadcast of 24 December 1941, BBC Written Archives Centre.
10. Telegram of 25 December 1941, Churchill Papers, 20/49, Martin Gilbert, *The Churchill War Papers*, Volume 3, pages 1681–82.

draped an enormous bath-towel around him. He walked into his adjoining bedroom, followed by me, notebook in hand, and continued to dictate while pacing up and down the enormous room. Eventually the towel fell to the ground but, quite unconcerned, he continued pacing the room dictating all the time." A typical Churchillian scene, but with a difference: "Suddenly President Roosevelt entered the bedroom and saw the British Prime Minister completely naked walking around the room dictating to me. WSC never being lost for words said, 'You see, Mr President, I have nothing to conceal from you.'"[11]

On December 26 Churchill addressed a joint session of the Senate and House of Representatives. "I cannot help reflecting," he said, "that if my father had been American and my mother British, instead of the other way round, I might have got here on my own. In that case, this would not have been the first time you would have heard my voice." At this there was much laughter, and later a great shout of approval when he said of the Japanese, "What sort of a people do they think we are?" There was less applause when Churchill declared: "If we had kept together after the last war, if we had taken common measures for our safety, this renewal of the curse need never have fallen upon us." And there was silence when he told Congress: "Five or six years ago it would have been easy, without shedding a drop of blood, for the United States and Great Britain to have insisted on the fulfilment of the disarmament clauses of the treaties which Germany signed after the Great War."

In 1935 or 1936, Churchill told the legislators, "there would have been the opportunity for assuring to Germany those raw materials which we declared in the Atlantic Charter should not be denied to any nation, victor or vanquished. That chance has passed. It is gone. Prodigious hammer-strokes have been needed to bring us together again."

Churchill ended as he always did after stern remarks to the Americans, on a note of optimism and encouragement, expressing his hope and faith, "sure and inviolate, that in days to come the British and American peoples will for their own safety and for the good of all walk together side by side in majesty, in justice, and in peace."[12] Churchill

---

11. Patrick Kinna, recollections, letter to the author, 10 October 1984.
12. Speech of 26 December 1941, BBC Written Archives Centre.

received many congratulations on his speech. To Felix Frankfurter's praises he replied: "I rejoice we are all together at last." [13]

On the afternoon of December 26, Churchill and Roosevelt discussed the transport of American troops to the North African theater of operations, to Northern Ireland and to Iceland. That night, as Churchill lay in bed at the White House, it was so hot from the central heating that he went to open the bedroom window. As he did so he felt short of breath, followed by a dull pain over his heart that went down his left arm. It had never happened to him before.

Sir Charles Wilson, the doctor who had traveled with Churchill to the United States, believed that it was an attack of angina, noting in his diary that "the textbook treatment for this is at least six weeks in bed. That would mean publishing to the world—and the American newspapers would see to this—that the PM was an invalid with a crippled heart and a doubtful future. And this at a moment when America has just come into the war, and there is no one but Winston to take her by the hand." The doctor told neither Churchill nor the President what he believed had occurred. Nor did he tell Churchill's wife. All he told Churchill himself was that his "circulation was a bit sluggish" and that he must not "do more than you can help in the way of exertion for a little while." [14]

The doctor's diagnosis of angina may well have been at fault. After a careful scrutiny of Churchill's subsequent medical history, Dr. John Mather writes that an alternative, "and reasonable, medical conclusion is that the pain was no more than a muscle strain, or a strain of the body and cartilaginous chest wall. This may actually be more likely, since there were no apparent adverse effects on Churchill. . . ." [15]

Churchill made no change to his schedule. On the following morning he had a meeting with General Marshall at the White House to discuss the question of a Supreme Commander for the Allied forces in the Far East. In what Churchill described to Attlee as "this broad-

---

13. Letter of 26 December 1941, Felix Frankfurter Papers.
14. Diary notes, 26 December 1941, Lord Moran (See Charles Wilson), *Winston Churchill: The Struggle for Survival, 1940–1965*, pages 15–18.
15. John H. Mather, "Sir Winston Churchill: His Hardiness and Resilience," *Finest Hour*, Churchill Proceedings, 1996–1997, pages 83–97.

minded and selfless American proposal," an English general was to be chosen.[16] The overall naval command of the Australian and New Zealand area of the Pacific would be given to an American admiral. As well as these specific decisions, Churchill and Marshall established the principle, which was to be effective for the rest of the war, that wherever British and American armies were fighting in the same war theater, they would share a Supreme Commander.

That evening Churchill held a conference with the British Chiefs of Staff. The next morning, December 28, he and Roosevelt spent five hours together meeting representatives of the other Allied powers, friendly neutrals and the British dominions. He and Roosevelt were also, Churchill reported to Attlee, "making great exertions to find shipping necessary for the various troop movements required."[17] In the afternoon Churchill left Washington by train for Canada, Roosevelt having given him the use of the Presidential train for the journey. On December 30 he spoke to the Canadian Parliament and on the morning of December 31 gave a Press Conference. That night he returned by train to Washington. While he was on the train, the year 1941 came to an end.

Back at the White House on 1 January 1942, Churchill approved Roosevelt's draft declaration establishing a "United Nations" of Allied Powers and nations under Nazi rule. Twenty-six nations pledged themselves "not to make a separate armistice or peace with the enemies" in order to defend "life, liberty, independence and religious freedom, and to preserve human rights and justice in their own lands as well as in other lands." Churchill later commented: "The Declaration could not by itself win battles, but it set forth who we were and what we were fighting for."[18]

On January 2 Churchill and Roosevelt presided jointly over a meeting on supply, to work out the scale of United States war production for 1942 and the increased scales for 1943. As a result of these discussions the 1942 program was massively increased: up to 70 percent

---

16. Telegram of 27 December 1941, Churchill Papers, 20/50, Martin Gilbert, *The Churchill War Papers*, Volume 3, page 1694.
17. Telegram of 27 December 1941, Churchill Papers, 20/47, Martin Gilbert, *The Churchill War Papers*, Volume 3, page 1696.
18. Winston S. Churchill, *The Second World War*, Volume 3, page 605.

more than the figures agreed upon before the United States had entered the war. Most important for Britain, the planned 12,750 aircraft and 15,450 tanks were each increased to 45,000. The 1943 production of aircraft was fixed at 100,000 and of tanks at 75,000: unprecedently high figures. Britain's needs were secured.

On January 3 Churchill sent Attlee an account of life at the White House. "We live here as a big family in the greatest intimacy and informality," he wrote, "and I have formed the very highest regard and admiration for the President. His breadth of view, resolution and his loyalty to the common cause are beyond all praise." There was not "the slightest sign here of excitement or worry about the opening misfortunes," Churchill added. These "are taken as a matter of course and to be retrieved by the marshalling of overwhelming forces of every kind." [19]

On January 5 Churchill left Washington by air for Florida, together with his doctor, Sir Charles Wilson, and his Principal Private Secretary, John Martin. In a secluded bungalow at Pompano, north of Miami, he worked, rested and swam. The ocean was so warm, the doctor noted, "that Winston basks half-submerged in the water like a hippopotamus in a swamp." [20] In a letter home John Martin wrote of how the story had been put about "that a Mr Lobb, an invalid requiring quiet, was staying in the house and, to explain my untransatlantic accents when answering the phone, I was his English butler." [21] John Lobb, of London, were Churchill's shoemakers.

During Churchill's five days in Florida, a daily courier, and on one occasion two couriers in a single day, flew from Washington with official papers and telegrams. In a letter to the Foreign Secretary, Anthony Eden, on January 8, Churchill cast his mind to the future. "No one can foresee how the balance of power will lie or where the winning armies will stand at the end of the war," he wrote. "It seems probable however that the United States and the British Empire, far from being exhausted, will be the most powerful armed and economic bloc the

---

19. Undated telegram, Cabinet Papers, 120/29.
20. Diary notes, 5 January 1942, Lord Moran (Sir Charles Wilson), *Winston Churchill, The Struggle for Survival, 1940–1965*, pages 20–21.
21. Letter of 11 January 1942, Sir John Martin Papers.

world has ever seen, and that the Soviet Union will need our aid for re-construction far more than we shall then need theirs." [22]

On January 10 Churchill felt rested enough to return to Washington. In telling Roosevelt about his plans—having been warned to be careful talking on the telephone—he informed the President: "I mustn't tell you on the open line how we shall be travelling," he said, "but we shall be coming by puff puff." [23] Two days later, at the White House, Churchill and Roosevelt presided jointly over their joint Chiefs of Staff for the final meeting of the Washington War Conference. There would be a combined Anglo-American landing in North Africa, for which Britain and the United States would each contribute 90,000 troops. The conference also created a unified structure for the British and American Chiefs of Staff—the central war-policy-making bodies in each country—they would be known as the Combined Chiefs of Staff.

As a unified body the Combined Chiefs of Staff would determine the military, naval and air requirements of Anglo-American strategy; establish a Combined Raw Materials Board to allocate the raw materials needed for the prosecution of the war; and form a common pool of the munitions resources of Britain and the United States. The note on their munitions responsibilities ended: "Any differences arising, which it is expected will be rare, will be resolved by the President and the Prime Minister in agreement."

Two decisions made at the Washington War Conference were of the greatest importance for Britain, and a culmination of Churchill's persuasive powers. One was the creation of an Anglo-American Shipping Adjustment Board, whereby the shipping resources of Britain and America "will be deemed to be pooled." The other was the agreement that "only the minimum of forces necessary for safeguarding of vital interests in other theatres should be diverted from operations against Germany." [24]

On January 14 Churchill left Washington for London, by Boeing flying boat from Norfolk, Virginia, and on to Bermuda, where he went on board the battleship *Duke of York*. On his return to Britain he told

---

22. Telegram of 8 January 1942, Cabinet Papers, 120/9.
23. Notes by John Martin, Sir John Martin Papers.
24. Washington War Conference, Memorandum of 14 January 1942, Cabinet Papers, 99/17.

the War Cabinet that Roosevelt's last words to him, on leaving, had been: "Trust me to the bitter end."[25] Churchill also gave an account of the Washington War Conference to King George VI, who recorded in his diary that his Prime Minister "was now confident of ultimate victory, as the United States of America were starting on a full output of men and material." During their conversation Churchill told the King that Britain and the United States "were now 'married' after many months of 'walking out.'"[26]

25. War Cabinet of 17 January 1942, Cabinet Papers, 65/25.

26. Diary entry, 19 January 1942, John W. Wheeler-Bennett, *King George VI: His Life and Reign,* page 535.

Chapter Twenty-Six

器

"OKAY FULL BLAST"

The Washington War Conference was a culmination of Churchill's
efforts to create an Anglo-American war instrument, and to ensure that the defeat of Hitler in Europe was given priority over the defeat of Japan. Henceforth he saw his main Anglo-American role as
maintaining his personal link with Roosevelt and activating it when
conflicts arose between the two sets of Chiefs of Staff, or between the
British and American strategic plans.

On 30 January 1942 Roosevelt was sixty. "Many happy returns of
the day," Churchill telegraphed, "and may your next birthday see us a
long lap forward on our road." [1] Roosevelt replied that same day: "It is
fun to be in the same decade with you." [2] "The Americans are very
broadminded," Churchill telegraphed to his Commander-in-Chief,
Middle East, a week later, "but if they think they are being squeezed
out by what they call 'Britishers' you will get the contrary reactions in a
vehement form." [3]

Within three weeks Churchill made the decision to reveal to Roosevelt that, before Pearl Harbor, British Signals Intelligence had been
able to read some of the American diplomatic telegrams. "From the
moment we became allies," Churchill assured the President, "I gave instructions that this work should cease." Churchill also warned Roo-

---

1. Telegram of 30 January 1942, Churchill Papers, 20/59, Martin Gilbert, *Winston
S. Churchill*, Volume 7, page 52.
2. Telegram of 7 February 1942, Churchill Papers, 20/69, Martin Gilbert, *Winston
S. Churchill*, Volume 7, page 53.
3. Telegram of 14 February 1942, War Office Papers.

sevelt of the danger of "our enemies" being able to read these same messages.[4]

On February 15 the British and Dominion forces in Singapore surrendered to the Japanese: 85,000 men were taken into captivity. In a somber broadcast, Churchill tried to put the best possible gloss on such a major defeat. "Are we up or down?" he asked, and went on to tell his listeners that with the United States and its "vast resources" as an ally, America and the British Commonwealth were in the war "all together, however long it may last, till death or victory." He could not believe that there was "any other fact in the whole world which can compare with that. That is what I have dreamed of, aimed at, worked for, and now it has come to pass."[5]

When the fall of Singapore led to criticism in Britain of Churchill's war leadership, his confidence was boosted by a telegram from Roosevelt, who wrote sympathetically that the fall of Singapore "gives the well-known back seat driver a field day but no matter how serious our setbacks have been, and I do not for a moment underrate them, we must constantly look forward to the next moves that need to be made to hit the enemy." Roosevelt added: "I hope you will be of good heart in these trying weeks because I am very sure that you have the great confidence of the masses of the British people. I want you to know that I think of you often and I know you will not hesitate to ask me if there is anything you think I can do."[6]

"I am most deeply grateful to you for your warm-hearted telegram," Churchill replied. "I do not like these days of personal stress and I have found it difficult to keep my eye on the ball. We are however in the fullest accord in all main things."[7] Every aspect of war policy was thrashed out in the long, often daily telegrams between Churchill and Roosevelt, and in the telegrams Churchill exchanged with Harry Hopkins. In one message to Hopkins, after appealing for "drastic action" to provide additional American escort warships in the

---

4. Letter of 25 February 1942, Roosevelt Papers.
5. Broadcast of 15 February 1942, BBC Written Archives Centre.
6. Telegram of 19 February 1942, President to Prime Minister, No. 106 (at Churchill's suggestion, he and Roosevelt had begun to number their telegrams, beginning with No. 100), Martin Gilbert, *Winston S. Churchill*, Volume 7, page 64.
7. Telegram of 20 February 1942, Prime Minister to President, No. 130, Franklin D. Roosevelt Papers.

Atlantic, Churchill wrote: "I am enormously relieved by the splendid telegrams I have had from the President on the largest issues. It is most comforting to feel we are in such complete agreement on war outlook."[8]

Roosevelt could be supportive in charming, personal ways. "Here is a thought from this amateur strategist," he wrote to Churchill on March 18. "There is no use giving a single further thought to Singapore or the Dutch Indies. They are gone."[9]

The day-to-day burden of war policy fell on the Combined Chiefs of Staff. In writing to Roosevelt on one occasion about what he regarded as Japan's future moves, Churchill began his telegram in a Rooseveltian mode: "Speaking as one amateur to another . . ."

Churchill had confidence that when crises arose, he and Roosevelt could settle them. Perhaps when the weather got better, he wrote at the beginning of April, "I may propose myself for the weekend with you and flip over. We have so much to settle that would go easily in talk."[10]

Each month, Churchill put a series of small but important British needs directly to Roosevelt. When he asked if the American aircraft carrier *Wasp* could transport fifty British Spitfires to Malta, because Britain had no carrier available, Roosevelt agreed within forty-eight hours.[11] Two weeks later, after another direct appeal from Churchill, Roosevelt agreed that the *Wasp* could make a second run.

In early April 1942 General Marshall and Harry Hopkins traveled to Britain to present to Churchill the plan, favored by Roosevelt, for an Anglo-American amphibious landing in Europe as soon as practicable. Churchill and his Chiefs of Staff spent many hours with the two Americans discussing the logistics and timing. In a speech to a Secret Session of the House of Commons on April 23, Churchill told the House that the war would not be ended by defeating Japan, but "only through the

---

8. Telegram of 12 March 1942, Churchill Papers, 20/71, Martin Gilbert, *Winston S. Churchill*, Volume 7, page 74.

9. Letter of 18 March 1942, Averell Harriman Papers.

10. Telegram of 1 April 1942, Prime Minister to President, No. 162, Franklin D. Roosevelt Papers.

11. Telegram of 1 April 1942, Churchill Papers, 20/73, Martin Gilbert, *Winston S. Churchill*, Volume 7, page 83.

defeat in Europe of the German armies" or a German internal collapse, which could not be counted on. "We have, therefore, to prepare
for the liberation of the captive countries of western and southern Europe by the landing at suitable points, successively or simultaneously,
of British and American armies strong enough to enable the conquered populations to revolt."

Churchill told the House of Commons "that these simple but clas-
sical conceptions of war" were shared "earnestly and spontaneously" by
the United States Government and its "dominant forces." The visit of
Hopkins and Marshall was "to concert with us the largest and swiftest
measures of this offensive character." The liberation of the continent
of Europe by equal numbers of British and American troops "is the
main war plan of our two nations." Since the evacuation of more than
335,000 British and French troops from Dunkirk in 1940, Churchill
had always regarded the liberation of the German-occupied countries
of Europe as the principal Allied aim. "The timing, the scale, the
method, the direction of this supreme undertaking," he told the
House, "must remain unknown and unknowable till the hour strikes
and the blow falls."[12]

Encouraged to do so by Stalin, the Americans were pressing for a
major cross-Channel operation later in 1942. Churchill and his Chiefs
of Staff, while fully aware of the urgent needs of the Russian front,
were convinced that the resources then available to put ashore a permanent force in northern Europe were insufficient. To try to resolve
this point of disagreement, Churchill decided to return to Washington. "I feel it my duty," he telegraphed to Roosevelt on June 12, "to
come and see you."[13] Five days later he flew by Boeing flying boat from
Stranraer in Scotland to the Anacostia Naval Air Station on the Potomac. General Marshall was there to meet him. After a night at the
British Embassy he flew the next morning by United States Navy plane
to New Hackensack airfield, near Roosevelt's home at Hyde Park. Roosevelt met him at the airfield.

It was Churchill's third meeting with Roosevelt in ten months. "He

---

12. Speech of 23 April 1942, Winston S. Churchill, *Secret Session Speeches,* pages
46–75.
13. Telegram of 13 June 1942, Churchill Papers, 20/76, Martin Gilbert, *Winston S.
Churchill,* Volume 7, page 122.

welcomed me with great cordiality," Churchill later recalled, "and, driving the car himself, took me to the majestic bluffs over the Hudson River on which Hyde Park, his family home, stands." The President drove him "all over the estate, showing me its splendid views." Churchill's account continued: "In this drive I had some thoughtful moments. Mr Roosevelt's infirmity prevented him from using his feet on the brake, clutch, or accelerator. An ingenious arrangement enabled him to do everything with his arms, which were amazingly strong and muscular. He invited me to feel his biceps, saying that a famous prize-fighter had envied them. This was reassuring; but I confess that when on several occasions the car poised and backed on the grass verges of the precipices over the Hudson I hoped the mechanical devices and brakes would show no defects." Churchill added: "All the time we talked business, and though I was careful not to take his attention off the driving we made more progress than we might have done in formal conference."[14]

Later that day Churchill gave Roosevelt a note to say that "No responsible authority" had been able to make a case for a cross-Channel landing in September 1942—the "Second Front" for which Stalin had been asking with considerable persistance. To help take the pressure off the Soviet Union, Churchill suggested a study should be made of the operation against French North Africa.[15] That night Churchill and Roosevelt traveled by Presidential Train to Washington, reaching the White House on the morning of Sunday, June 21. After breakfast in his room, Churchill went to the Oval Office with the head of his Defence Office, General Ismay.

As Churchill and Roosevelt talked, news was brought in that the 33,000 British and Commonwealth troops in the Libyan coastal town of Tobruk had surrendered to the Germans. For a moment, recalled General Ismay, "no one spoke." The silence was then broken by Roosevelt, whose only words were: "What can we do to help?"[16] To help the British forces in the Western Desert, where General Erwin Rommel's army was almost at the border of Egypt, General Marshall suggested

---

14. Winston S. Churchill, *The Second World War,* Volume 4, pages 338–39.
15. Note of 20 June 1942, Cabinet Papers, 99/20.
16. *The Memoirs of General The Lord Ismay,* page 255.

sending out an American armored division that had been trained in desert warfare in California.[17]

On June 23 Churchill rested. On the following afternoon agreement was reached on the dispatch of further American assistance to the British in the Western Desert. American bomber squadrons then in Florida and California, the former about to leave for China, would be rushed to Cairo. All ten American heavy bombers in India would be sent to join them there.[18]

That evening Churchill took the night train to South Carolina, where, in the presence of the Secretary of War, Henry Stimson, and the Chief of Staff, General Marshall, he saw a battalion of American troops make a parachute drop. "I had never seen a thousand men leap into the air at once," he later recalled. That afternoon, after lunching with Stimson and Marshall in the train, Churchill watched a brigade of young soldiers at a field-firing exercise using live ammunition. Churchill warned his hosts that in his experience "it takes two years or more to make a soldier."[19] Two years later, many of those whom he saw in training were to be among the American forces in the Normandy landings.

In his letter of thanks to Stimson and Marshall, Churchill wrote of the "instructive day" they had allowed him to spend with their troops. "I have had considerable experience of such inspections," he wrote, "and I can say that I have never been more impressed than I was with the bearing of the men whom I saw. The undemonstrative, therefore grim, determination which was everywhere manifest not only in the seasoned troops but in the newly-drafted, bodes ill for our enemies."[20] In reply Stimson telegraphed to Churchill on his and Marshall's behalf: "We are delighted that you are pleased. My regret is that all of our troops could not have had the great inspiration of your presence and interest in their efforts in our common cause."[21]

On June 24 Churchill flew back to Washington. On the following day it became clear that the armored division offered by Marshall

17. Meeting of 21 June 1942, Cabinet Papers, 99/20.
18. Meeting of 24 June 1942, Cabinet Papers, 99/20.
19. Winston S. Churchill, *The Second World War,* volume 4, page 347.
20. Letter of 25 June 1942, Churchill Papers, 20/53, Martin Gilbert, *Winston S. Churchill,* Volume 7, page 133.
21. Telegram of 25 June 1942, Premier Papers, 4/71/3.

would not be able to go to the Middle East. To transport it round the Cape of Good Hope would involve "serious interference" with the next two Cape of Good Hope convoys. Marshall therefore proposed sending in its place three hundred Sherman tanks and a hundred howitzers. To accelerate the dispatch of this important reinforcement, two merchant ships would be used, taken from the Havana–United States sugar traffic, and routed across the Southern Atlantic, around the Cape of Good Hope, and through the Indian Ocean to the Red Sea and the Suez Canal. Churchill was relieved. That night he left the United States by flying boat from Baltimore, seen off by Harry Hopkins.

On his return to London, Churchill told the War Cabinet that the attitude of the American administration to Britain's setbacks in the Western Desert had been "very staunch."[22] Even while he was flying home, Rommel's troops advanced fifty miles inside the Egyptian border. In a telegram to Churchill on June 28, General Marshall reported from Washington that not only would the promised howitzers and tanks be ready for shipping in two weeks' time, but that the tanks would include "British-type radio and compass," as well as tools, spare parts and water cans.[23] The tanks had not yet been fitted with engines; these were being sent out on a separate ship, to be installed on arrival at Suez. When that ship was sunk by a German submarine off Bermuda, Roosevelt and Marshall, without even troubling Churchill, ordered a further supply of tank engines to be sent in a fast ship to overtake the Suez-bound convoy. These Sherman tanks were to play an important part in the eventual desert victories, starting with General Sir Bernard Montgomery's turn of the tide at Alamein.

As a result of his two visits to Washington, Churchill had secured a series of Anglo-American joint ventures. On June 27 the first Russia-bound convoy with a joint Anglo-American escort—two British and two American cruisers—sailed from Iceland. Three weeks later Hopkins, Marshall and Admiral Ernest J. King—Chief of Naval Operations—reached London to determine Anglo-American strategy

---

22. War Cabinet, 27 June 1942, Cabinet Papers, 65/26.
23. Telegram of 28 June 1942, Churchill Papers, 20/77, Martin Gilbert, *Winston S. Churchill*, Volume 7, page 136.

for the end of 1942. Churchill, his War Cabinet and military advisers opposed the American preference—a landing at Cherbourg—as it lay at the limit of fighter cover from air bases in Britain. The Americans deferred to this, agreeing that an attack on French North Africa would be that year's joint Anglo-American effort to help the Soviet Union, then facing a renewed German offensive in the direction of Stalingrad and the Caucasus.

After five days' intense discussion, agreement had been reached. When the talks ended, Churchill took Hopkins, Marshall and King to a magnificent dinner and sing-along at the Royal Naval College at Greenwich, ending with the singing of the two National Anthems. The next day he entertained them at Chequers. "Besides reaching complete agreement on action," Churchill telegraphed to Roosevelt, "relations of cordial intimacy and comradeship have been cemented between our high officers."[24] In reply Roosevelt expressed his own happiness at the "successful meeting of minds," and he added: "I cannot help feeling that the past week represented a turning-point in the whole war and that now we are on our way shoulder to shoulder."[25]

Stalin was angered by the abandonment of the Cherbourg plan. Churchill decided to fly to Moscow and explain the new strategy to him, and asked Roosevelt if Averell Harriman could travel with him. Churchill explained: "I feel it would be easier if we all seemed to be together. I have a somewhat raw job."[26] During the journey Churchill agreed to Harriman's suggestion, which emanated from Roosevelt, that the United States should have full responsibility for the newly completed Trans-Persia Railway, on which Allied supplies would travel from the Persian Gulf ports to the Caspian Sea and on to the Soviet Union.

The Moscow visit lasted five days. After Churchill had explained the North African landings to Stalin in detail, Stalin understood their potential, telling Churchill: "May God help this enterprise to succeed."[27]

---

24. Telegram of 27 July 1942, Churchill Papers, 20/78, Prime Minister to President, No. 123.
25. Telegram of 28 July 1942, Churchill Papers, 20/78, Martin Gilbert, *Winston S. Churchill*, Volume 7, page 153.
26. Telegram of 5 August 1942, Premier Papers, 3/76A/3.
27. Meeting of 12 August 1942, Premier Papers, 3/76A/12.

Churchill flew back to Britain. He had been away, both in Russia and Italy, for more than three weeks. "If disposal of all the Allied decorations were today placed by providence in my hands," General Douglas MacArthur told the senior British Intelligence officer at his headquarters in the Far East, "my first act would be to award the Victoria Cross to Winston Churchill. Not one of those who wear it deserves it more than he. A flight of 10,000 miles through hostile and foreign skies may be the duty of young pilots, but for a Statesman burdened with the world's cares, it is an act of inspiring gallantry and valour."[28]

For his part Churchill was never slow to recognize the achievements of his American colleagues. On learning of the efforts being made in the United States by Averell Harriman to increase the number of merchant ships for both their countries, he wrote to him: "You have undertaken an enormous task, but I am sure that it will not prove beyond your capacity."[29] In the strictest secrecy, another aspect of Churchill's Anglo-American efforts came to fruition in September 1942, the sharing of Signals Intelligence derived from the German "Enigma" and Japanese "Purple" top-secret communications systems, that were being decrypted, with increasing frequency and success, at Bletchley Park, fifty miles north of London. That month Edward Travis, the Director of Bletchley Park, traveled to Washington to conclude this sharing arrangement. The historian David Stafford, who has studied this aspect of Anglo-American relations in detail, writes: "No such intimate an intelligence alliance between two sovereign powers had been seen in history before."[30]

In Washington efforts were being made to reduce the scale of the North African landings. Churchill appealed directly to Roosevelt to intervene. "I feel that a note must be struck now," he telegraphed on August 27, "of irrevocable decision and the superhuman energy to execute it."[31] Roosevelt still sought a much-reduced North African assault. Churchill was so distressed that he prepared to fly once more to

---

28. Reported to Churchill by the head of the Secret Intelligence Services, 25 August 1942, Churchill Papers, 20/58, Martin Gilbert, *Winston S. Churchill,* Volume 7, page 217.

29. Letter of 11 July 1942, Averell Harriman Papers.

30. David Stafford, *Roosevelt & Churchill: Men of Secrets,* page 142.

31. Telegram of 27 August 1942, Prime Minister to President, No. 136, Martin Gilbert, *Winston S. Churchill,* Volume 7, page 219.

Washington, but his doctor warned him that it would be unwise for him to go. He might not survive the journey. Instead Churchill appealed to Roosevelt by telegram. "We have accepted an American command and your leadership," he wrote, "and we will do our utmost to make a success of any plan you decide." Roosevelt agreed to retain the wider plan. Churchill's perseverance had proved effective. When he expressed his appreciation, Roosevelt answered with a single word, "Hurrah!"[32] To this Churchill replied: "Okay full blast."[33]

The North African landings were ready to go ahead. "We British will come in only as and when you judge expedient," Churchill telegraphed to Roosevelt on September 14. "This is an American enterprise in which we are your helpmeets."[34] Britain had its own part to play both in North Africa and in the Western Desert, where the British Eighth Army under Montgomery was on the verge of driving Rommel westward. Churchill told Roosevelt of the "great satisfaction" felt in the Eighth Army for the Sherman tanks Roosevelt had sent after the fall of Tobruk.[35] As for the imminent North African landings: "I pray that this great American enterprise, in which I am your Lieutenant and in which we have the honour to play an important part, may be crowned by the success it deserves."[36]

Driven out of Egypt, Rommel was in retreat. In the first week of November, nine thousand German soldiers were taken prisoner. "Having been privileged to witness your courage and resolution on the day of the fall of Tobruk," wrote General Marshall, "I am unable to express my full delight over the news from the Middle East and my admiration for the British Army."[37] "I am most grateful to you for your message,"

---

32. Telegram of 5 September 1942, Churchill Papers, 20/79, Martin Gilbert, *Winston S. Churchill*, Volume 7, page 226.

33. Telegram of 6 September 1942, Prime Minister to President, No. 145, Franklin D. Roosevelt Papers.

34. Telegram of 14 September 1942, Prime Minister to President, No. 148, Franklin D. Roosevelt Papers.

35. Telegram of 31 October 1942, Prime Minister to President, No. 179, Franklin D. Roosevelt Papers.

36. Letter of 31 October 1942, Churchill Papers, 20/54, Martin Gilbert, *Winston S. Churchill*, Volume 7, page 246.

37. Telegram of 7 November 1942, Churchill Papers, 20/82, Martin Gilbert, *Winston S. Churchill*, Volume 7, page 250.

Churchill replied. "I was indeed touched at the time of Tobruk by the kindness and delicacy you all showed." [38]

In the early hours of November 8, while Churchill's telegram was on its way to Marshall, American troops landed in French North Africa, capturing Casablanca, Oran and Algiers, and overthrowing the French Vichy regime there. Randolph Churchill was among the British troops who landed at Algiers. That morning he reported to his father: "All goes well between us and the Americans." [39] By nightfall it was clear that the landings had succeeded. "Let me congratulate you," Churchill telegraphed to Marshall, "on all the news so far received of the great events taking place in French North Africa," and he added, with foresight: "We shall find the problems of success not less puzzling though more agreeable than those we have hitherto surmounted together." [40] Speaking in London two days later, Churchill declared that Britain's victory in the Western Desert and the American victory in North Africa constituted "a new bond between the English-speaking peoples and a new hope for the whole world." [41]

---

38. Telegram of 8 November 1942, Churchill Papers, 20/82, Martin Gilbert, *Winston S. Churchill,* Volume 7, page 250.

39. Telegram of 8 November 1942, Churchill Papers, 1/369, Martin Gilbert, *Winston S. Churchill,* Volume 7, page 251–52.

40. Telegram of 8 November 1942, Churchill Papers, 20/82, Martin Gilbert, *Winston S. Churchill,* Volume 7, page 252.

41. Speech of 10 November 1942 (broadcast), BBC Written Archives Centre.

Chapter Twenty-Seven

"THE TACT AND CONSIDERATION WHICH THE HARMONY OF THE COMMON CAUSE REQUIRES"

At a meeting of the Chiefs of Staff Committee on the evening of 30 November 1942—his sixty-eighth birthday—Churchill spoke of the intense pressure that was certain to come from the Russians for the launching of "a Continental operation" in the summer of 1943. Assuming that North Africa was in Anglo-American hands by the end of 1942, the Allies would be in a position to launch a cross-Channel landing in August or September 1943. The Germans, "already extended at so many points," would not know "where the next main thrust would come."[1] To try to ensure a cross-Channel landing within nine months, Churchill pressed for a Three-Power conference for himself, Roosevelt and Stalin, "the sooner the better."[2] All prospect of launching the liberation of Europe in 1943 depended on an early decision.

In a telegram to General Dwight D. Eisenhower, Commander-in-Chief of the American forces who were then pushing the Germans eastward into Tunisia, Churchill said how much he admired the way "you had pressed forward so vehemently." By December 12, however, two German counterattacks brought Eisenhower's forces to a halt. Two weeks later a renewed attack against the strongly defended German lines failed after bitter fighting, and Eisenhower postponed the at-

---

1. Chiefs of Staff Committee, 30 November 1942, Cabinet Papers, 79/58.
2. Telegram of 3 December 1942, Premier Papers, 3/420/1.

tempt to take Tunis. The cross-Channel timetable Churchill envisaged for 1943 was being impeded.

Stalin was unwilling to leave his fighting forces. Churchill and Roosevelt therefore made plans to meet in North Africa without him. The city they decided on was Casablanca. "I am greatly relieved," Churchill telegraphed to Roosevelt on December 21. "It is the only thing to do."[3] On Christmas Day they exchanged telegraphic greetings. "Last year I passed a happy Christmas in your home," Churchill told the President, "and now I send my heartfelt wishes to you and all around you on this brighter day than we have yet seen."[4] Roosevelt's message came back that evening: "The old team-work is grand."[5]

Churchill continued to monitor Eisenhower's battle in Tunisia, and wanted to help. At six o'clock on New Year's Eve he summoned three senior advisers to discuss sending a brigade of tanks to Eisenhower as reinforcements. "A strenuous effort must be made," Churchill instructed, "with full battle urgency, to have this brigade embarked complete in the convoy which leaves about the 17th January."[6]

Flying through the night, Churchill reached Casablanca on the morning of 13 January 1943. Roosevelt arrived the next day. "It gave me intense pleasure," Churchill later wrote, "to see my great colleague here on conquered or liberated territory which he and I had secured in spite of the advice given him by all his military experts."[7] The two men spent eleven days together, as did the Combined Chiefs of Staff, devising a series of war plans for the leaders to approve. As the discussions proceeded, it became clear that Roosevelt wanted the next Allied move to be against Sicily. Churchill supported him. The night of July 9 was set for the landings. With regard to the Far East, Churchill told Roosevelt that he wished to make it clear "that if and when Hitler

---

3. Telegram of 21 December 1942, Prime Minister to President, No. 238, Franklin D. Roosevelt Papers.
4. Telegram of 25 December 1942, Prime Minister to President, No. 241, Franklin D. Roosevelt Papers.
5. Telegram of 25 December 1942, Churchill Papers, 20/59, Martin Gilbert, *Winston S. Churchill*, Volume 7, page 283.
6. Minute of 31 December 1942, Churchill Papers, 20/67, Martin Gilbert, *Winston S. Churchill*, Volume 7, page 287.
7. Winston S. Churchill, *The Second World War*, Volume 4, page 605.

breaks down, all of the British resources and effort will be turned towards the defeat of Japan."[8]

The buildup of British, American and Canadian troops in Britain for a cross-Channel assault would continue: "a return to the Continent with all available resources," Churchill described it to Attlee. If the Germans were to show "definite signs of collapse," it too could take place in 1943, as Churchill had earlier suggested.[9] To prepare a definite plan for the cross-Channel assault, Churchill and Roosevelt set up an Inter-Allied Service Staff, predominantly British and American, to begin work at once in London.

One American who met Churchill at Casablanca was General George S. Patton. "He strikes me as cunning rather than brilliant," Patton wrote in his diary, "but with great tenacity and an absolute extrovert. He is easily flattered—all of them are."[10]

At Casablanca, Churchill had successfully maintained the British point of view. The priority of "Hitler's extinction" over the defeat of Japan had been reestablished. Priority had also been secured for action in the Mediterranean as against the cross-Channel assault that summer, but without prejudice to the "maximum" development of the buildup in Britain of the forces needed for a cross-Channel assault when it came in 1944. In the Far East, Britain had secured American naval and landing craft help for the assault on the Japanese in Burma. Changes in command had been agreed upon "with the greatest cordiality"—Churchill informed the War Cabinet—whereby one of Britain's most senior generals, Sir Harold Alexander, would be Eisenhower's deputy, charged with the "plans and execution" of the capture of Sicily. A British airman, Air Marshal Sir Arthur Tedder, would command the Anglo-American air forces in the whole Mediterranean theater. "It now remains," Churchill concluded, "to add speed and weight to all our actions."[11]

On January 23 the Eighth Army entered Tripoli. On the following day, the last day of the Casablanca conference, Churchill and Roo-

---

8. Meeting of 18 January 1943, Cabinet Papers, 99/24.
9. Telegram of 19 January 1943, Premier Papers, 4/72/1.
10. Diary entry, 18 January 1943, General George S. Patton Papers.
11. Telegram of 23 January 1943, Cabinet Papers, 120/76.

sevelt gave a joint Press Conference. Churchill told the fifty journalists what they should be conveying to their readers: "Give them the picture of unity, thoroughness, and integrity of the political chiefs. Give them that picture, and make them feel that there is some reason behind all that is being done."[12] Immediately after the Press Conference the journalists were given the text of a new Allied declaration, agreed by Churchill and Roosevelt, for the "unconditional surrender" of Germany, Italy and Japan. It was "false," Churchill wrote to Harry Hopkins two years later, to suggest that the demand for unconditional surrender had prolonged the war: "Negotiation with Hitler was impossible. He was a maniac with supreme power to play his hand out to the end, which he did; and so did we."[13]

The Casablanca conference was over. Churchill then indulged in a moment of pure delight, driving with Roosevelt to Marrakech to show the President something Roosevelt had never seen: a sight that had delighted and moved him while on holiday there six years earlier, the sunset tinting the snow a vivid red on the distant Atlas mountains. The two men spent the night in Marrakech at the Villa Taylor. So beautiful was the place that the two leaders named it Flower Villa. At dinner, Churchill's doctor noted, they made "affectionate little speeches to each other, and Winston sang."[14] During dinner Hopkins and Harriman brought in various documents to sign, setting out what had been agreed at Casablanca. For the eventual cross-Channel landing, a substantial force of trained and equipped American soldiers would be assembled in Britain, almost a million men, by the last day of 1943.

In a joint note for the Combined Chiefs of Staff, Churchill and Roosevelt set out four central points that had been agreed upon at Casablanca: the importance of achieving a June landing in Sicily, the desirability of running convoys to northern Russia even through the period of the Sicily landings, the urgency of air reinforcements to the American forces in China, and the need to build up the American

---

12. Press Conference, 24 January 1943, Premier Papers, 4/72/1.

13. Robert E. Sherwood, *The White House Papers of Harry L. Hopkins,* Volume 2, pages 692–93.

14. Diary notes and recollections, 24 January 1943, Lord Moran (Sir Charles Wilson), *Winston Churchill: The Struggle for Survival, 1940–1965,* page 191.

forces in Britain more quickly than planned, in order to carry out a limited cross-Channel attack in August 1943 if circumstances allowed.[15]

On the morning of January 25 Roosevelt left Marrakech to return to the United States. Churchill stayed for the rest of the day to paint: the only painting he did during the Second World War. Two days later, while he was in Cairo, American bombers based in Britain made their first major air raid on Germany. Having reached Britain on February 7, Churchill told the House of Commons four days later that the "dominating aim" of Anglo-American policy was "to make the enemy burn and bleed in every way that is physically and reasonably possible, in the same way as he is being made to bleed and burn along the vast Russian front." It was to make the necessary plans for action that he had gone to Casablanca.[16]

Following his return to Britain, Churchill expressed his concern about criticism of General Eisenhower in a British newspaper, for the setback to the American forces in Tunisia, at the Kasserine Pass, and the harm that criticism was doing. "I appeal to all patriotic men on both sides of the Atlantic Ocean," he told the House of Commons, "to stamp their feet on mischief-makers and sowers of tares, wherever they may be found, and let the great machines roll into battle under the best possible conditions for our success."[17] Defending Eisenhower publicly did not deter Churchill from criticizing him in private. Two days after these stern words he was distressed by a message from Eisenhower that the Sicily invasion would have to be postponed from June to July. A month's delay, Churchill warned Eisenhower, would be a "disastrous hiatus."[18] To Hopkins he telegraphed: "I think it is an awful thing that in April, May and June, not a single American or British soldier will be killing a single German or Italian soldier while the Russians are chasing 185 divisions around."

Britain and America would be "very much open to grievous reproach at the hands of Russia," Churchill told Hopkins, "if, consider-

---

15. Note of 25 January 1943, Premier Papers, 3/420/5.
16. Speech of 11 February 1943, *Hansard,* Parliamentary debates.
17. Speech of 11 February 1943, *Hansard,* Parliamentary debates.
18. Telegram (T. 155) of 13 February 1943, Churchill Papers, 20/106, Martin Gilbert, *Winston S. Churchill,* Volume 7, page 338.

ing how very small is the sphere on which we are acting, we impose these enormous delays." There would not have been a North African landing at all, he recalled, "if we had yielded to the fears of the professionals."[19]

"We shall become a laughing stock," Churchill repeated that day to the Chiefs of Staff Committee, "if, during the spring and early summer, no British and American soldiers are firing at any German and Italian soldiers." Every effort should be made to try to reinstate the June date, "so that if at the worst it fails, it does not fail through us or our side."[20]

Eisenhower pointed out to Churchill that in clearing Rommel from Tunis "we must be prepared for hard and bitter fighting and the end may not come as soon as we hope."[21] Eisenhower was right. Churchill decided that Britain should plan to go ahead in Sicily without American participation. "In view of the delaying attitude adopted by General Eisenhower" he wrote on February 19, "I wish a final Joint Planners Sub-Committee and the Chief of Combined Operations Department to work out a study of our doing it all alone by ourselves in June, and taking nothing from the United States except landing craft, escorts etc."

In pursuing his theme of an all-British invasion of Sicily, Churchill told his Chiefs of Staff that there would be "great advantages in having it all done by British troops, with the Americans giving us a hand at the landings, with the air force, etc." The Americans could then come in to the ports Britain had taken "and go into action without having to go through the training for assault landings."[22] Churchill's plan was set aside when, at his own request, Harry Hopkins intervened. The Combined Chiefs of Staff then ordered Eisenhower to prepare for the invasion of Sicily in June. "Tell Marshall I am deeply grateful," Churchill

---

19. Telegram (T. 156) of 13 February 1943, Churchill Papers, 20/106, Martin Gilbert, *Winston S. Churchill*, Volume 7, page 338.

20. Minute of 13 February 1943, Churchill Papers, 4/397A, Martin Gilbert, *Winston S. Churchill*, Volume 7, pages 338–39.

21. Telegram of 17 February 1943, Churchill Papers, 20/106, Martin Gilbert, *Winston S. Churchill*, Volume 7, page 341.

22. Minute of 19 February 1943, Churchill Papers, 4/397A, Martin Gilbert, *Winston S. Churchill*, Volume 7, page 342.

telegraphed to the head of the British Military Mission in Washington when this was confirmed.[23]

Churchill had already spoken out publicly against criticism of Eisenhower and the American battle in Tunisia. Of the American troops who had been worsted in battle there, he assured King George VI, "I need scarcely say that no word of mine is intended in disparagement of the Americans. They are brave but not seasoned troops, who will not hesitate to learn from defeat, and who will improve themselves by suffering until all their strongest martial qualities have come to the front." Churchill added: "What a providential thing it was that I perpetually pressed for General Eisenhower to take the Command, as the defeat of the American Corps, if it had been under a British general, would have given our enemies in the United States a good chance to blaspheme."[24]

This letter was sent on February 22. Two days later the Americans fighting in Tunisia regained control of the Kasserine Pass, redeeming their earlier setback. Churchill was pleased at this hard-fought reversal of American battlefield ill fortune, telegraphing to Eisenhower two days later: "I was sure the Kasserine battle would turn out all right in the end."[25]

On March 5, the tenth anniversary of Roosevelt's first inauguration, the Americans won a major naval battle against Japan. "Accept my warmest congratulations on your brilliant victory in the Pacific," Churchill telegraphed to Roosevelt, "which fitly salutes the end of your first ten years."[26] That same day Churchill sent Roosevelt, by air, a new film, *Desert Victory,* "which I saw last night and thought very good. It gives a vivid and realistic picture of the battles, and I know that you will be interested in the photographs of your Sherman tanks in action."[27] On the following day, in Tunisia, Rommel's last-gasp counterattack was de-

---

23. Telegram of 7 March 1943, Churchill Papers, 20/107, Martin Gilbert, *Winston S. Churchill,* Volume 7, page 356.

24. Letter of 22 February 1943, Royal Archives.

25. Telegram of 25 February 1943, Churchill Papers, 4/397A, Martin Gilbert, *Winston S. Churchill,* Volume 7, page 353.

26. Telegram of 5 March 1943, Prime Minister to President, No. 272, Franklin D. Roosevelt Papers.

27. Telegram of 5 March 1943, Franklin D. Roosevelt Papers.

feated. He was betrayed by his own top-secret signals, as a result of Britain's ability to read them, through Enigma, the German coded communications system, believed by the Germans to be unbreakable, that was being decrypted on a regular basis at Bletchley Park, north of London. That month a breakthrough at Bletchley in decrypting the German naval Enigma finally enabled the British to master the German submarine attacks in the Atlantic, after many setbacks and severe losses.

During the final battle for Tunis, Eisenhower was upset when a message from King George VI to the British troops was not sent through him, as Supreme Commander, but through General Alexander. Churchill urged Alexander to take every opportunity "to remove any soreness that may exist in Eisenhower's mind," and to give Eisenhower the assurance "that I and all at home wish to work wholeheartedly with him and that we recognize what a vital part he plays in keeping the whole show together." Given that the British troops had become the largest single force in Tunis, Churchill told Alexander, "All the more I and others at home must not fail at any time in the tact and consideration which the harmony of the common cause requires."[28]

At the end of April, Churchill learned that the United States Chiefs of Staff had invited the senior British generals in the Far East to a conference on Washington. He was worried that the Pacific war would supersede Europe as the main focus of America's war effort. He therefore decided to return to Washington, leaving the Clyde on board the *Queen Mary* on May 5. After four days sailing westward, the *Queen Mary* reached the waters patrolled by American warships. "Since yesterday," Churchill telegraphed to Roosevelt on May 10—the third anniversary of his becoming Prime Minister—"we have been surrounded by US Navy and we all greatly appreciate high value you evidently set upon our continued survival. I look forward to being at White House with you tomorrow afternoon and also to going to Hyde Park with you at weekend. The voyage has been so far most agreeable and staff have done vast amount of work."[29]

At noon on May 12 the *Queen Mary* reached the United States.

---

28. Telegram of 31 March 1943, Churchill Papers, 20/109, Martin Gilbert, *Winston S. Churchill*, Volume 7, pages 371–72.

29. Telegram of 10 May 1943, Premier Papers, 4/72/2.

That night Churchill slept in the White House. On the following day he was warned by Lord Halifax, the British Ambassador, that there might be questions during his visit about the repayment of Britain's Lend-Lease debt. Churchill retorted: "Oh, I shall like that one. I shall say, yes by all means let us have an account if we can get it reasonably accurate, but I shall have my account to put in too, and my account is for holding the baby alone for eighteen months, and it was a very rough brutal baby I had to hold. I don't quite know what I shall have to charge for it." [30]

The conference began on the afternoon of May 13 in the Oval Office. The battle in North Africa was over. The invasion of Sicily was near. "What should come next?" Churchill asked Roosevelt. The "great prize," he believed, was to get Italy out of the war "by whatever means might be the best." The British alone had thirteen divisions in northwest Africa. If Sicily were conquered by the end of August, "what should these troops do between that time and the date, seven or eight months later, when the cross-Channel operation might first be mounted?" They could not possibly "stand idle," Churchill told the President, "and so long a period of apparent inaction would have a serious effect on Russia, which was bearing such a disproportionate weight." Soviet forces were in daily and bloody conflict with the Germans along the whole length of the Eastern Front.

Churchill then spoke about the proposed smaller-scale cross-Channel landing, Operation Roundup—to secure a bridgehead but not a launching pad—tentatively envisaged for August or September 1943. Churchill did not feel it should go ahead, telling Roosevelt that "he could not pretend that the problem of landing on the Channel coast had been solved. The difficult beaches, with the great rise and fall of tide, the strength of the enemy's defences, the number of his reserves and the ease of his communications, all made the task one which must not be underrated." He wished to make it "absolutely clear," however, that Britain "earnestly desired to undertake a full-scale invasion of the Continent from the United Kingdom as soon as a plan offering reasonable prospects of success could be made."

Roosevelt did not dissent: "Everyone was agreed," he said, that

---

30. Private letter of May 1943, Lord Birkenhead, *Halifax: The Life of Lord Halifax*, page 537.

there was "no possibility" of a cross-Channel enterprise in 1943. He also shared Churchill's view that the operation must be carried out "on the largest scale" in the spring of 1944. He was worried, however, that this date might be set back by a campaign in Italy. Churchill, in reply, was emphatic that the armies that would have been victorious on Sicily must do something after August 1943, rather than "sit idle" for six months, and that it was not necessary to try to occupy all Italy.[31]

That day news reached Washington that the German forces in Tunisia had surrendered, and more than 150,000 German soldiers taken prisoner. As the Combined Chiefs of Staff began their detailed discussions in Washington, Roosevelt took Churchill to his weekend retreat at Shangri-La—now Camp David—in the Allegheny Mountains. Back in Washington, on May 19 Churchill addressed both Houses of Congress. He had spent nine and a half hours dictating and polishing his speech, which was broadcast throughout the United States and transmitted to Britain. It was in the "dragging-out of the war at enormous expense," Churchill warned, "until the democracies are tired or bored or split, that the main hopes of Germany and Japan must now reside. We must destroy this hope."[32]

That evening, at their third meeting with the Combined Chiefs, Churchill and Roosevelt learned that agreement had been reached for the buildup in England "of a sufficient force to secure a bridgehead on the Continent from which further offensive operations could be carried out." Churchill, the notes of the meeting recorded, "indicated his pleasure" that a cross-Channel operation "had finally been agreed upon."[33] On May 21 Churchill sent Attlee and Eden an account of the progress of the meetings. "The fact that the President and I have been living side by side seeing each other at all hours," he reported, "that we are known to be in close agreement, and that the President intends to decide himself on the ultimate issues—all this together with the priceless work of Hopkins, had exercised throughout a mollifying and also a dominating influence on the course of Staff discussions."

The essence of those discussions, Churchill explained to Attlee, was that Britain would have "a free hand" in the Mediterranean until

---

31. Meeting of 12 May 1943, Cabinet Papers, 99/22.
32. Speech of 19 May 1943, BBC Written Archives Centre.
33. Minutes of Third Meeting, 19 May 1943, Cabinet Papers, 99/2.

November, and after that the Allies would concentrate on the cross-Channel landing, to take place by 1 May 1944. No delay would be incurred even if the Italian campaign led to an opening up of possibilities in the Balkans.[34] The Normandy landings were only a year away. Sicily would be the next objective of the Allied armies, followed by the prize—Italy.

Henry A. Wallace, Roosevelt's third Vice-President, lunched with Churchill at the White House on May 22. It was their second meeting within a few days. They discussed the proposed postwar United Nations. "He made it more clear than he had at the luncheon on Saturday," Wallace wrote in his diary, "that he expected England and the United States to run the world and he expected the staff organizations which had been set up for winning the war to continue when the peace came, that these staff organizations would by mutual understanding really run the world even though there was a supreme council and three regional councils."

Wallace replied that he "thought the notion of Anglo-Saxon superiority, inherent in Churchill's approach, would be offensive to many of the nations of the world as well as to a number of people in the United States." Churchill was quick to challenge this. Wallace noted: "Churchill had had quite a bit of whiskey, which, however, did not affect the clarity of his thinking process but did perhaps increase his frankness." Churchill asked Wallace: "Why be apologetic about Anglo-Saxon superiority, that we were superior, that we had the common heritage which had been worked out over the centuries in England and had been perfected by our Constitution. He himself was half American, he felt that he was called on as a result to serve the function of uniting the two great Anglo-Saxon civilizations in order to confer the benefit of freedom on the rest of the world."[35]

While still in Washington, Churchill persuaded Roosevelt to let him go direct from the United States to North Africa, and to take General Marshall with him. Churchill wanted to make sure that Eisenhower realized the importance of the Italian campaign, explaining to

---

34. Telegram of 21 May 1943, Churchill papers, 20/128, Martin Gilbert, *Winston S. Churchill*, Volume 7, page 410.
35. Henry Wallace, diary entry, 22 May 1943, Library of Congress Manuscript Division, MsC177.

Field Marshal Smuts two months later that the aim of his new journey was "there upon the spot to convince Eisenhower and others that nothing less than Rome could satisfy the requirements of this year's campaign." [36]

Churchill set off once more on his travels, flying on May 26 from Washington to Newfoundland, for refueling, and then to Gibraltar. He was seventeen hours in the air. From Gibraltar he made the three-hour flight to Algiers. After his third meeting with Eisenhower, Churchill telegraphed to Roosevelt: "We have had long, most agreeable and fruitful discussion and I am not aware of the slightest difference existing between the British and American outlooks." [37]

---

36. Telegram of 16 July 1943, Churchill Papers, 20/131, Martin Gilbert, *Winston S. Churchill*, Volume 7, page 443.

37. Telegram of 4 June 1943, Prime Minister to President, No. 290, Franklin D. Roosevelt Papers.

Chapter Twenty-Eight

꒰꒱

"IF WE ARE TOGETHER
NOTHING IS IMPOSSIBLE"

Despite their friendship and frequent meetings, there were many moments of disagreement and tension between Churchill and Roosevelt. Late in 1942 Roosevelt had reneged on an agreement he had reached with Churchill that summer for a full exchange of information about the atomic bomb program on which both countries had been working in tandem for almost two years. Many months of confrontation and disagreement followed the American breach of the agreement, until, in May 1943, Roosevelt accepted that the exchange of information should be resumed, and, as Churchill explained to his own advisers, "that the enterprise should be considered a joint one, to which both countries would contribute their best endeavours."[1]

Britain and the United States resumed partnership in a deadly race. "I am very grateful," Churchill telegraphed to Harry Hopkins, "for all your help in getting this question settled so satisfactorily. I am sure that the President's decision will be to the best advantage of both our countries." Churchill added: "We must now lose no time in implementing it."[2] In utmost secrecy a severely damaged plank of Anglo-American cooperation had been repaired.

Hardly had agreement been reached on the atomic dispute than Churchill learned from Averell Harriman that Roosevelt had suggested, rather than a tripartite Churchill-Stalin-Roosevelt meeting, that Roosevelt and Stalin should meet alone. The location had been

---

1. Telegram of 26 May 1943, Premier Papers, 3/139/8A.
2. Telegram of 10 June 1943, Premier Papers, 3/139/8A.

chosen: Alaska. Churchill telegraphed in anguish to Roosevelt: "You must excuse me expressing myself with all the frankness that our friendship and the gravity of the issue warrant." He was concerned about the use German propaganda would make "of a meeting between the heads of Soviet Russia and the United States at this juncture with the British Commonwealth and Empire excluded. It would be serious and vexatious, and many would be bewildered and alarmed thereby."

Churchill wanted a meeting of the Big Three. Such a meeting, he told the President, either at Scapa Flow in Scotland, "or anywhere else on the globe that can be agreed," of the three leaders and their Staffs, coming together for the first time, would be "one of the milestones of history." Not wanting an open breach with the United States, however, he ended his telegram, "whatever you decide I shall sustain to the best of my ability here."[3]

On 9 July 1943 Anglo-American forces landed in Sicily. "I am thinking a great deal about our partnership and friendship now that our second great venture is launched," Churchill telegraphed to Roosevelt.[4] Twenty-four hours later Churchill telegraphed to Eisenhower: "It is a tremendous feat to leap on shore with nearly 200,000 men."[5] Amid fierce fighting, the Anglo-American forces made rapid progress. As to the follow-up campaign in Italy, Churchill told General Smuts: "I believe the President is with me: Eisenhower in his heart is naturally for it. I will in no circumstances allow the powerful British and British-controlled armies in the Mediterranean to stand idle."[6]

These were strong words. To put his concept of a full-scale Italian campaign yet again to the President and Combined Chiefs of Staff, Churchill proposed another visit to the New World, his fourth since the Washington War Conference in December 1941. Anthony Eden's Private Secretary, Oliver Harvey, noted in his diary on July 16: "I must say, the PM doesn't let the grass grow under his feet." The meeting was

---

3. Telegram of 25 June 1943, Prime Minister to President, No. 328, Franklin D. Roosevelt Papers.

4. Telegram of 9 July 1943, Prime Minister to President, No. 355, Franklin D. Roosevelt Papers.

5. Telegram of 10 July 1943, Churchill Papers, 20/115, Martin Gilbert, *Winston S. Churchill*, Volume 7, page 441.

6. Telegram of 16 July 1943, Churchill Papers, 20/131, Martin Gilbert, *Winston S. Churchill*, Volume 7, page 443.

to be held at Quebec. Its aim, wrote Harvey, was to discuss the next stage of military operations in view of "the unexpected feebleness of Axis resistance on Sicily." Churchill, he added, was "anxious to pin the Americans down before their well-known dislike of European operations except cross-Channel gets the better of them again, and they pull out their landing craft and send off their ships to the Pacific."[7]

On July 25, before Churchill had set off for Quebec, Mussolini resigned and his Fascist government fell. Churchill and Roosevelt at once exchanged views by telegram of how to proceed. Roosevelt wished to insist in the coming armistice negotiations on the use "of all Italian territory and transportation against the Germans in the north and against the whole Balkan peninsula."[8] Roosevelt was putting forward the Balkan "soft under belly" scheme usually attributed to Churchill, for an attack against German-held Yugoslavia, Albania and Greece, but Churchill had a different set of suggestions: first the surrender of the Italian fleet, then the withdrawal of all Italian forces from southern France, Corsica, Yugoslavia, Albania and Greece, and finally the use by the Allies of air bases in Italy "on which we can base the whole forward air attack on South and Central Germany."[9]

On August 5 Churchill sailed from the Clyde, once again on the *Queen Mary*, accompanied by the Chiefs of Staff as well as by Clementine and their daughter Mary. Reaching the Canadian port of Halifax on August 9, he went by train to Quebec, a twenty-four-hour journey. From Quebec he took the night train south across the American border for another twenty-four-hour journey to Roosevelt's home at Hyde Park. There, on the evening of August 12, he dined with Roosevelt. Harry Hopkins was among the guests. On August 13 and 14 there were hot-dog and hamburger picnics. It was so hot, Churchill recalled, "that I got up one night because I was unable to sleep and hardly able to breathe, and went outside to sit on a bluff overlooking the Hudson. Here I watched the dawn."[10]

---

7. Diary entry, 16 July 1943, John Harvey, editor, *The Diplomatic Diaries of Oliver Harvey, 1937–1940*, page 276.
8. Telegram of 26 July 1943, Churchill Papers, 20/116, Martin Gilbert, *Winston S. Churchill*, Volume 7, page 453.
9. Telegram of 26 July 1943, Prime Minister to President, No. 383, Franklin D. Roosevelt Papers.
10. Winston S. Churchill, *The Second World War*, Volume 5, page 73.

The most secret agreement reached at Hyde Park concerned the atomic bomb. Signed by Churchill and Roosevelt, it stated that Britain and the United States "will never use this agency against each other," nor would they use it "against third parties without each other's consent," nor communicate any information about it to a third party "except by mutual consent." As for postwar industrial and commercial atomic research and development, Churchill agreed that Britain "expressly disclaims any interest" in these "beyond what may be considered by the President of the United States to be fair and in just harmony with the economic welfare of the world."[11]

Before his talks with Roosevelt, Churchill had offered the cross-Channel supreme command to a British general. At Hyde Park he agreed to Roosevelt's proposal that the supreme commands would go to a national of the army providing the largest number of troops. This meant that an American would command the cross-Channel landings and a Briton would lead South-East Asia Command. In due course these were to go to Eisenhower and Mountbatten, respectively.

At dinner at Hyde Park on August 14, Churchill expressed his hope that the "fraternal relationship" of Britain and the United States would be perpetuated in peacetime. Harriman, who was present, noted that Churchill liked the idea of a "loose association" better than a formal treaty. It would be an association "flexible enough to adjust itself to historical developments." One of those at the dinner table was apprehensive. As Harriman noted: "Mrs. Roosevelt seemed fearful this might be misunderstood by other nations and weaken the UN concept." This was the hope of a post-war United Nations organization to which all nations would belong, and work together in harmony against potential aggressors. Churchill did not agree, insisting that "any hope of the UN would be in the leadership given by the intimacy of the US and Britain in working out misunderstandings with the Russians—and the Chinese too—if they become a nation."[12]

That night Churchill took the Presidential Train back to Quebec. Roosevelt joined him there two days later. During the Quebec meetings Churchill emphasized the need to give fullest priority to the cross-

---

11. "Articles of Agreement," 19 August 1943, Premier Papers, 3/139/8A.

12. Harriman notes, W. Averell Harriman and Elie Abel, *Special Envoy to Churchill and Stalin, 1941–1946*, page 222.

Channel landings. He also expressed his confidence that the surrender of Italy would, once the Allies reached Naples, allow the release of landing craft for the cross-Channel landings. In a joint telegram, Churchill and Roosevelt informed Stalin: "We shall begin our invasion of Italy before the end of the month."[13]

On September 2 Churchill went by overnight train from Quebec to Washington. He was in Washington on the following day, the fourth anniversary of Britain's declaration of war on Germany. That morning he learned that British and Canadian troops had landed on the Italian mainland. He remained in Washington for five days. "I deliberately prolonged my stay in the United States," he later recalled, "in order to be in close contact with our American friends at this critical moment in Italian affairs."[14]

"Winston will, I think, settle down in US!" a senior British official, Sir Alexander Cadogan, noted in his diary.[15] On the evening of September 4, with Cadogan as adviser, Churchill and Roosevelt worked on their respective messages to Stalin, inviting him to a conference of the three leaders. "I was there till 8," Cadogan wrote home, "running between the PM in bed and the President in his study." The Prime Minister's sleeping arrangements, Cadogan added, "have now become quite promiscuous. He talks with the President till 2 a.m., and consequently spends a large part of the day hurling himself violently in and out of bed, bathing at unsuitable moments and rushing up and down corridors in his dressing gown."[16]

On the night of September 5, the indefatigable sixty-eight-year-old British Prime Minister left Washington by overnight train to Boston. He was then driven straight to Harvard, where he was robed for an honorary degree. In his acceptance speech, before an audience of 1,400 people, he spoke of how "the long arm of destiny" had twice in his lifetime reached out to the United States, and twice the United States had responded. The price of greatness was responsibility. One

---

13. Telegram of 18 August 1943, Churchill Papers, 20/117, Martin Gilbert, *Winston S. Churchill*, Volume 7, page 476.

14. Winston S. Churchill, *The Second World War*, Volume 5, page 110.

15. Diary entry, 3 September 1943, David Dilks, editor, *The Diaries of Sir Alexander Cadogan, OM, 1938–1945*, page 558.

16. Letter of 3 September 1943, David Dilks, editor, *The Diaries of Sir Alexander Cadogan, OM, 1938–1945*, page 559.

could not rise to be "in many ways the leading community in the civilized world" without being involved in its problems, "convulsed by its agonies and inspired by its causes."

During his speech Churchill emphasized the need for the closest possible Anglo-American intimacy, both during the war and after it. Both countries shared common conceptions of what was "right and decent." Both had "a marked regard for fair play," especially to the weak and poor. Both shared "a stern sentiment of impartial justice, and above all the love of personal freedom." As for the "gift of a common tongue," it was, he urged, "a priceless inheritance" that might some day become the foundation of a common citizenship. "I like to think," Churchill said, "of British and Americans moving about freely over each other's wide estates with hardly a sense of being foreigners to one another." He did not see why the two countries should not try "to spread our common language even more widely throughout the globe."

For both the British and Americans the war was entering "upon its most severe and costly phase," Churchill warned, but his message was one of faith in the Anglo-American partnership. "If we are together nothing is impossible," he said. "If we are divided all will fail." This was his firm belief. "I therefore preach continually the doctrine of the fraternal association of our two peoples, not for any purpose of gaining invidious material advantages for either of them, not for territorial aggrandisement or the vain pomp of earthly domination, but for the sake of service to mankind and for the honour that comes to those who faithfully serve great causes." [17]

The *New York Times* noted that Churchill's speech "has opened up a vast and hopeful field of discussion. Down the grim corridors of war light begins to show." [18] Immediately after his speech, he was driven the short distance to the Memorial Church of Harvard University where, from the South Portico, he addressed some six thousand men and women of the Reserve Officers' Training Corps (ROTC). In a brief talk he urged the future officers to make the best of their time of study "so that the troops they would one day command would be able to accomplish their tasks without unnecessary sacrifices." The *New York Times* de-

17. Speech of 6 September 1943, *New York Times,* 7 September 1943.
18. *New York Times,* 7 September 1943.

scribed his message as "inspirational." [19] One young officer present later recalled Churchill "punctuating many points with the tapping of his cane." [20]

That evening Churchill put to Roosevelt a proposal he had broached during his Harvard speech, to maintain the Combined Anglo-American Chiefs of Staff after the war. As he explained in a telegram to Attlee, Eden and King George VI, Roosevelt had "liked the idea at first sight. It involves no treaty and can be represented simply as a war-time measure." Once the Combined Chiefs structure had been maintained for even ten years in peacetime it would have "such great advantages to both sides that it might well become permanent." There would be a "complete interchange" of officers in the colleges, "continued sharing of research and inventions," joint training and weaponry, mutual accommodation at bases, all "springing up under the guise of military needs but in fact weaving the two countries together as the one ultimate bulwark against another war." [21]

Three days later, to the British Embassy staff in Washington, Churchill stressed that Britain would "do much better with the Russians if we first got on to intimate terms with the US." It was important, he added, "not to allow the Russians to try to play the US and the UK off against each other." [22]

On 8 September 1943 the Italian government surrendered unconditionally to the Allies. That night German troops occupied Rome. On the following day Allied troops landed at Salerno, south of Naples. Roosevelt left Washington for Hyde Park. Churchill stayed in Washington, the President telling him: "Winston, please treat the White House as your home. Invite anyone you like to any meals, and do not hesitate to summon any of my advisers with whom you wish to confer at any time you wish. Please break your journey to Halifax at Hyde Park and tell me all about it." [23]

---

19. *New York Times,* 7 September 1943.

20. John T. Hay, "Harvard: Fifty Years Ago," *Finest Hour,* No. 80, Third Quarter, 1993.

21. Telegram of 7 September 1943, Churchill Papers, 20/129, Martin Gilbert, *Winston S. Churchill,* Volume 7, page 496.

22. Record of a meeting, 10 September 1943, Cabinet Papers, 120/89.

23. Lord Ismay, *The Memoirs of General the Lord Ismay,* page 319.

Churchill did as Roosevelt suggested; at a meeting at the White House on September 11 he pressed the American Chiefs of Staff for swifter reinforcement of the Allied troops already on the Italian mainland. The existing pace of reinforcement, he said, was "unacceptable." General Marshall agreed to accelerate the current plans.[24] That same day, half an hour before midnight, Churchill, Clementine and their daughter Mary left Washington by train for the overnight journey to Hyde Park. On the morning of September 12 they were greeted by Roosevelt, with whom they spent the rest of the day. It was Winston and Clementine's thirty-fifth wedding anniversary. At dinner that night Roosevelt proposed their health. Afterward, Mary Churchill recalled, the President "drove us all down to the little railway station near Hyde Park, where we took our leave of him."[25]

That night the Churchills' train left for Halifax, Nova Scotia, a journey of more than thirty-seven hours. From the train Churchill wrote to Roosevelt—his letter beginning "Dear Franklin"—of how much he had enjoyed Roosevelt's hospitality at the White House and Hyde Park. His letter ended: "You know how I treasure the friendship with which you have honoured me and how profoundly I feel that we might together do something really fine and lasting for our two countries and, through them, for the future of all."[26]

Three hours after reaching Halifax on September 14, the Churchills sailed for home. On September 19, more than six weeks after leaving, they were back in Britain. On October 1 British troops entered Naples. That week Sardinia and Corsica came under Allied control with almost no fighting. But all was not smooth in Anglo-American relations. As October progressed, Churchill and the British Chiefs of Staff found themselves in acrimonious discussions with the Americans over the Italian campaign versus the cross-Channel landings. At the very moment when landing craft needed to be transferred from the Mediterranean to Britain for the cross-Channel landings, the British wanted the campaign in Italy to have priority, even at the cost of postponing those landings.

---

24. Minutes of a meeting, 11 September 1943, Martin Gilbert, *Winston S. Churchill*, Volume 7, page 502.

25. Mary Churchill diary and recollections, Mary Soames, *Clementine Churchill*, page 340.

26. Letter of 13 September 1943, Franklin D. Roosevelt Papers.

Churchill saw danger in this dispute over strategy, telegraphing to Roosevelt: "Hitherto we have prospered wonderfully, but I now feel that the year 1944 is loaded with danger. Great differences may develop between us and we may take the wrong turning. Or again we may make compromises and fall between two stools. The only hope is the intimacy and friendship which has been established between us and between our High Staffs. If that were broken I should despair of the immediate future."[27]

In a gesture of support for Churchill's wishes, Roosevelt agreed to keep back for an extra six weeks some of the landing craft in the Mediterranean that were to have been transferred to Britain. But Churchill was angered when it was suggested that the American Chief of Staff, General Marshall, be made Supreme Commander of both the cross-Channel and Mediterranean operations. Such an appointment, Churchill informed Admiral William D. Leahy, Roosevelt's senior staff officer, "would not be conformable to the principle of equal status which must be maintained among the great Allies," and went on to point out that Britain had fourteen to fifteen Divisions under its command in Italy as against seven to eight American Divisions. For the cross-Channel landings the number of Divisions would be about equal, and indeed more tilted toward the British if the Canadian Divisions were included in their count, as they were in the British command.

Churchill then raised a sensitive point he had not raised before. "Hitherto," he told Leahy, "we have successfully prevented any carping here at the fact that we have been fighting and sustaining casualties in Tunis, Sicily and Italy on something like a two-and-a-half to one basis, although we are serving loyally under a United States general." If he were to attempt to propose an American commander over the predominantly British operation in Italy "there would be an explosion."[28]

Churchill was told in confidence that the proposal had come from the White House and had "never received any proper consideration by the US Chiefs of Staff."[29] Following his protest the proposal for a single American commander in both Northern Europe and the Mediterranean was dropped.

---

27. Telegram of 27 October 1943, Franklin D. Roosevelt Papers.
28. Telegram (IZ 4258) of 8 November 1943, War Office Papers.
29. Telegram (IZ 4242) of 8 November 1943, War Office Papers.

• • •

On November 12 Churchill once more left Britain, by ship from Plymouth, reaching Alexandria nine days later and then flying the short distance to Cairo. On November 22 he was at Cairo airport to greet Roosevelt. At the first plenary session of the Cairo Conference, held in Roosevelt's villa on the following day, Churchill agreed to a major British offensive against the Japanese forces in Burma, something Roosevelt was eager for in order to help the Chinese. "All contacts with the President are favourable," Churchill telegraphed to Eden that night, "and I feel much easier in my mind about the larger issues of the war."[30]

Churchill was surprised to learn that Roosevelt had never seen the Sphinx or the Pyramids, which Churchill first visited in 1921. As soon as the first plenary ended he went with his daughter Sarah to see if it would be possible for Roosevelt to drive up to them in a car. "Finding we could drive right round them," Sarah Churchill wrote to her mother that evening, "we went back and got the President and all three of us bumbled along for a second tour. It was a lovely drive, and the President was charming—simple and enthusiastic. I think he enjoyed himself—I think he appreciated the trouble Papa took. Papa loved showing them to him. It really is wonderful how they both get on—they really like and understand each other."[31]

The second plenary session was held on November 24. Two amphibious landings were agreed upon. The main one would be a cross-Channel assault, to be followed by an Allied landing in the South of France. "I am making good progress with the President and his high officers," Churchill told King George VI, "and I am pretty sure all will end up harmoniously."[32] The next night was Thanksgiving. Roosevelt gave Churchill a traditional dinner and carved the turkey. Eden, who reached Cairo in time for the dinner, recorded in his diary Churchill's view of Roosevelt: "FDR was 'a charming country gentleman,' but business methods were almost non-existent, so Winston had to play the

---

30. Telegram of 23 November 1943, Churchill Papers, 20/130, Martin Gilbert, *Winston S. Churchill*, Volume 7, page 560.
31. Letter of 23 November 1943, Sarah Churchill, *Keep on Dancing: An Autobiography*, page 69.
32. Telegram of 24 November 1943, Royal Archives.

role of courtier and seize opportunities as and when they arose. I am amazed at patience with which he does this. Winston admits that our war progress in the last two months has been below level of events."[33]

On the morning of November 27 Churchill flew from Cairo to Teheran for the first meeting of the Big Three. Churchill stayed at the British Embassy, but at Stalin's urging, to avert an assassination plot the Soviets claimed to have uncovered, Roosevelt agreed to stay in a villa on the grounds of the Soviet Legation. That evening, having lost his voice, Churchill was unable to dine as planned with Stalin and Roosevelt. The next morning he hoped to have a private meeting with Roosevelt before the first plenary session, but, to Churchill's alarm, Roosevelt met privately with Stalin instead. Hopkins, who was at that meeting, told Churchill's doctor that Roosevelt had "made it clear that he was anxious to relieve pressure on the Russian front" as if to distance himself from Churchill's hope of a more vigorous Mediterranean strategy.[34]

The first plenary session of the Teheran Conference took place that afternoon. Stalin, briefed by Roosevelt, spoke in accordance with the American strategy. Important though the Italian campaign was, he said, it "was not a suitable jumping-off ground for the invasion of Germany." Churchill then explained to Stalin that the cross-Channel plans were in fact absorbing most of the "preparation and resources" of Britain and the United States, and that both "were resolved to do it in 1944." In answer to a question from Stalin as to whether he and the British Chiefs of Staff really believed in the cross-Channel landing, Churchill assured him that if the conditions of German relative strength were met "it will be our stern duty to hurl across the Channel against the Germans every sinew of our strength."[35] The immediate issue, Churchill explained to Stalin, was what the Allies could do in Italy in the six months before the cross-Channel assault "that would best take the weight off Russia."

At dinner that evening Roosevelt was not feeling well and left early.

---

33. Diary entry, 25 November 1943, Earl of Avon (Anthony Eden), *The Reckoning: Eden Memoirs*, page 424.

34. Notes for 28 November 1943, Lord Moran (Sir Charles Wilson), *Winston Churchill: The Struggle for Survival, 1940–1965*, pages 134–35.

35. Minutes of a meeting, 29 November 1943, Cabinet Papers, 80/77.

Churchill stayed on and discussed the postwar world with Stalin. The next day, November 29, Churchill invited Roosevelt to lunch but the President declined, sending Harriman to explain "that he did not want Stalin to know that he and I were meeting privately." [36] That afternoon it was Stalin and Roosevelt who met privately, with Churchill excluded.

On the evening of November 30—his sixty-ninth birthday—Churchill hosted a dinner for Roosevelt and Stalin. During the toasts Churchill raised his glass to Roosevelt for having by his courage and foresight prevented "a revolutionary upheaval in the United States in 1933." [37]

Churchill and the British Chiefs of Staff left Teheran on December 2, flying to Cairo for further talks with Roosevelt and his Chiefs. Final agreement was reached that the cross-Channel landing would take place in five months' time. That was the task, Churchill said, "transcending all others." [38] During another drive together to the Pyramids, Roosevelt told Churchill that, as he could not spare Marshall for the task, he had nominated Eisenhower as Supreme Commander of the Allied Expeditionary Forces that would go ashore in France. Asked his opinion, Churchill responded: "I said it was for him to decide, but that we also had the warmest regard for General Eisenhower, and would trust our fortunes to his direction with hearty goodwill." [39]

In the early hours of December 11, Churchill flew to Tunisia, intending to fly on to Italy to visit British troops. When he reached Eisenhower's seaside villa near Carthage, however, he fell ill. He was suffering from pneumonia. As his condition worsened he suffered a heart attack. Clementine flew out from London to be with him. "I feel relieved," Roosevelt telegraphed, "that she is with you as your superior officer." [40]

---

36. Harriman recollections, W. Averell Harriman and Elie Abel, *Special Envoy to Churchill and Stalin, 1941–1946*, page 276.

37. Harriman recollections, W. Averell Harriman and Elie Abel, *Special Envoy to Churchill and Stalin, 1941–1946*, page 276.

38. Meeting of 4 December 1943, Cabinet Papers, 80/77.

39. Winston S. Churchill, *The Second World War,* Volume 5, page 370.

40. Telegram of 20 December 1943, Churchill Papers, 20/125, Martin Gilbert, *Winston S. Churchill,* Volume 7, page 611.

Churchill's recovery was such that, by December 21, he was holding daily meetings with his commanders and communicating at length by telegram to London and Washington. On Christmas Day all five commanders-in-chief in the Mediterranean, including Eisenhower, the Supreme Commander who was shortly to fly to England to take up his cross-Channel responsibilities, came to Churchill's bedside to coordinate plans for an amphibious landing at Anzio, with a view to the rapid capture of Rome.

On December 27 Churchill made a five-hour flight from Carthage to Marrakech, using an oxygen regulator as the plane rose to 12,000 feet to cross the mountains. From the airport he was driven to the Villa Taylor—"Flower Villa," he and Roosevelt had called it during their one-day visit almost a year earlier. From there he telegraphed to Roosevelt on the following day that he was living "in the lap of luxury, thanks to overflowing American hospitality." He was also delighted that the Americans had agreed to the Anzio landings. "I thank God for this fine decision," he told Roosevelt, "which engages us once again in whole-hearted unity upon a great enterprise." The Chiefs of Staff would be telegraphing that day "in full" to their American opposite numbers. "Meanwhile here the word is 'Full Steam Ahead.'"[41]

---

41. Telegram of 28 December 1943, Churchill Papers, 20/125, Martin Gilbert, *Winston S. Churchill*, Volume 7, page 628.

Chapter Twenty-Nine

※

TOWARD OVERLORD:
"OUR BAND OF BROTHERS"

O n New Year's Day 1944, Churchill was in Marrakech, recovering from pneumonia and a heart attack. That day he telegraphed to Roosevelt: "Last night Eisenhower was with us on his way to you, and I had long talks with him. Montgomery is here now on his way to England. I think we have a fine team, and they certainly mean to pull together." Churchill sent the President his best wishes "for a New Year which will not only be marked by triumph but will open wider doors to our future work together."[1] At dinner that night, with his friend Lord Beaverbrook, while going over the whole course of both the First World War and the current war, Churchill turned to his Naval ADC with the words: "But, Tommy, you must bear witness that I do not repeat my stories so often as our dear President of the United States."[2]

Feeling that he should be at his command post in London when the Anzio landings took place, Churchill left Marrakech on January 14 and flew to Gibraltar. He then went on board the battleship *King George V* for the three-day voyage home. One aspect of Anzio was worrying him: the possibility, he telegraphed to the overall commander, General Sir Henry Maitland Wilson, that it might, when successful, be represented as a "purely American victory." Churchill added: "No one is keener than I am in working with the Americans in the closest comradeship," but in General Mark Clark's Fifth Army—"which is at least

---

1. Telegram of 1 January 1944, Prime Minister to President, No. 430, Franklin D. Roosevelt Papers.
2. Colville diary, 2 January 1944, Colville Papers.

one-half British," Churchill noted—it was an American, Clark, who conducted the operations. Two other Americans were in charge of the Tactical Air and Strategical Air Forces, while an American admiral was to command the Naval Squadron, and an American general had been designated Military Commander of Rome.

Churchill did not want the British forces to be wrongly overshadowed by the Americans. This would "only lead to a feeling of bitterness in Great Britain," he told General Wilson, "when the claim is stridently put forward, as it surely will be, that 'the Americans have taken Rome.'" It was "most desirable," Churchill believed, "that an even balance should be maintained and the credit, of which there will be enough for all, fairly shared."[3]

On the evening of January 17 Churchill reached Plymouth. Traveling by night train, he was in London the next morning. Two hours later he was in the House of Commons for Prime Minister's Questions. "I have now got home safely again," he telegraphed to Roosevelt, "and am all right except for being rather shaky on my pins."[4] On January 22, five days after Churchill's return to Britain, an Anglo-American force went ashore at Anzio. The landings were virtually unopposed, and by midnight 36,000 troops and 3,000 vehicles were safely ashore. "The Americans are fighting very bravely," Churchill told a journalist friend, Colin Coote, five days after the landings, "and their Third Division in particular are first-class troops. General Clark is first-class." The casualties, however, were beginning to be heavy: "British and American blood is flowing in great volumes."[5]

Poor leadership at the bridgehead led to a failure to push inland in the early days. Within a week what was to have been the gateway to Rome was a siege. Churchill was despondent, telling Sir Alexander Cadogan that "this had now become an American operation, with no punch in it."[6] With the problems at Anzio in his mind, Churchill asked Roosevelt if the American Chiefs of Staff could come to London to

---

3. Telegram of 16 January 1944, Churchill Papers, 20/154, Martin Gilbert, *Winston S. Churchill*, Volume 7, page 653.

4. Telegram of 18 January 1944, Prime Minister to President, No. 547, Franklin D. Roosevelt Papers.

5. Memorandum of 27 January 1944, Lord Camrose Papers.

6. Diary entry, 31 January 1944, David Dilks, editor, *The Diaries of Sir Alexander Cadogan, OM, 1938–1945*, pages 601–2.

discuss the details of both the cross-Channel landing—code-named Overlord—and the planned landings in the South of France, Anvil, that were to follow it. At a meeting with the British Chiefs of Staff, Churchill reported on the "negative character" of Roosevelt's reply.[7]

As the Anzio bridgehead saw increasing German bombardment from outside the narrow perimeter, Churchill wanted a senior British commander, General Sir Harold Alexander, who was Mark Clark's immediate superior, to exercise his authority. "I have a feeling that you may have hesitated to assert your authority," he telegraphed to Alexander on February 10, "because you were dealing so largely with Americans and therefore urged an advance instead of ordering it. You are however quite entitled to give them orders, and I have it from the highest American authorities that it is their wish that their troops should receive direct orders."

Churchill reported to Alexander on his own talks with American generals. "They say their Army has been framed more on Prussian lines than on the more smooth British lines," Churchill wrote, "and that American Commanders expect to receive positive orders which they will immediately obey. Do not hesitate, therefore, to give orders just as you would to our own men. The Americans are very good to work with and quite prepared to take the rough with the smooth."[8] On learning the following day of the death of eighteen-year-old Private Stephen Hopkins— one of the three sons of Harry Hopkins—during the United States Marine assault on Kwajalein Atoll in the Pacific, Churchill telegraphed his condolences to Hopkins and told Roosevelt: "He is an indomitable spirit. I cannot help feeling anxious about his frail body and another operation. I shall always be grateful for news about him, for I rate him high among the Paladins."[9]

Churchill remained concerned that the fighting in Italy, both at the Anzio beachhead and farther south at Cassino, was seen by the British public as a predominantly American effort. When the Germans launched a fierce but unsuccessful counterattack at Anzio on February

---

7. Meeting of 8 February 1944, Cabinet Papers, 79/70.

8. Telegram received on 12 February 1944, Churchill Papers, 20/156, Martin Gilbert, *Winston S. Churchill*, Volume 7, page 679.

9. Telegram of 13 February 1944, Prime Minister to President, No. 577, Franklin D. Roosevelt Papers.

16, Churchill answered what one of his Private Secretaries called an "inspired" question in the House of Commons about British casualties in Italy, "so as to give some ammunition for countering the American view that American troops are doing all the fighting." [10]

A week later, on learning that the Anzio army, in which there were more than 60,000 British troops, was called the "6th United States Corps," Churchill wrote to the Chief of the Imperial General Staff, General Sir Alan Brooke: "This really is a shame, and greatly increases the need for calling it either 'The Sixth Allied Army' or 'The Bridge-head Army.' I cannot agree that this term 'The 6th United States Corps' should continue, as it is most unfair to our troops who have lost three men to four American in the fighting." [11]

Churchill was not averse to learning from the Americans. After Admiral Cooke of the United States Navy visited him at Chequers and described the role of naval guns in one of the actions in the Pacific, the Kwajalein Atoll landing, when the guns had fired from 2,000 yards off-shore at Japanese fortified positions, Churchill raised this on the following day with the British Admiralty, suggesting that naval guns be used during the cross-Channel assault, and put the issue on the agenda of the Defence Committee on February 28. In the cross-Channel landings three months later, long-range naval guns, including those of six battleships and twenty-two cruisers, were to be in action against German shore positions.

At the beginning of March, Churchill received two telegrams from Roosevelt about the postwar international economic cooperation that—from the complexity of their detail—were clearly not from the President's dictation or pen. When he refused to reply to them, Lord Halifax pressed him, through Eden, to reply. Churchill would not do so, telling Eden: "I cannot believe any of these telegrams come from the President. They are merely put before him when he is fatigued and pushed upon us by those who are pulling him about." Churchill added: "All this frantic dancing to the American tune is silly. They are only busy about their own affairs and the more immobile we remain the better." [12]

---

10. Diary entry, 16 February 1944, Sir John Colville Papers.

11. Minute of 23 February 1944, Martin Gilbert, *Winston S. Churchill*, Volume 7, page 681.

12. Minute of 4 March 1944, Foreign Office Papers (Eden Papers).

The focus of Anglo-American efforts had turned from Anzio to the cross-Channel landings. Once a week Churchill met Eisenhower and his Chief of Staff, General Walter Bedell Smith, to discuss progress and problems. In addition, he informed General Marshall on March 11, "I have presided at a series of meetings at which either Ike or Bedell has been present, and I am satisfied that everything is going on well."[13] When Bedell Smith raised the question of the "very high and extortionate" prices being charged to American officers in Britain for apartments and small houses, Churchill took the matter up at once with the Chancellor of the Exchequer and the Minister of Works and Buildings.[14]

The focus on the needs of the cross-Channel assault against the Normandy beaches did not mean that other matters of Anglo-American concern could be neglected. Churchill wanted to cross the Atlantic to see Roosevelt, to discuss every aspect of the war, but his doctor warned him yet again that if he attempted the journey he might become a permanent invalid, get another bout of pneumonia or have another heart attack. Churchill was determined to meet the President, however, telegraphing to him on March 18: "I wonder whether you would care to spend Easter with me at Bermuda?"

Churchill proposed reaching the island on April 5 and staying for six days. "I would not suggest bringing the great Staffs," Churchill wrote, "but only the principals on the scale with which we went to Teheran. It is not so much that there are new departures in policy to be taken but there is a need after more than ninety days of separation for checking up and shaking together."[15]

Roosevelt declined a Bermuda meeting, telling Churchill that his doctors had ordered "a complete rest of about two or three weeks." A meeting of their Staffs, however, would be "most useful," Roosevelt suggested.[16] Churchill disagreed. Such a meeting would not be worthwhile "without your being there," he replied. No Bermuda meeting took place, but in mid-March, Roosevelt agreed to an urgent appeal

---

13. Telegram of 11 March 1944, Martin Gilbert, *Winston S. Churchill*, Volume 7, pages 705–6.
14. Minute of 14 March 1944, Martin Gilbert, *Winston S. Churchill*, Volume 7, pages 707–8.
15. Telegram of 18 March 1944, Premier Papers, 4/75/2.
16. Telegram of 21 March 1944, Premier Papers, 4/75/2.

from Churchill to divert thirty United States transport aircraft from the China run to Lord Mountbatten's forces on the Indian-Burmese border.

On March 23, after a particularly intense German air raid, Churchill left London by train with Eisenhower on a two-day inspection of American troops preparing for the Normandy landings. "I thank God you are here," he told the men of one airborne unit, "and from the bottom of my heart I wish you good fortune and success."[17] On April 3 Churchill gave one of his regular Downing Street lunches to Eisenhower and Bedell Smith. There were no other guests. The problem to be resolved was the imminent destruction of the French railway network in northern France, to prevent German reinforcements from reaching the Normandy beaches.

Churchill was concerned by the high civilian losses that were expected. At the War Cabinet later that day the Chief of the Air Staff advised that between 20,000 and 40,000 French civilians might be killed if the plan went ahead. Churchill told his colleagues that he "felt some doubts as to the wisdom of this policy."[18] That evening he wrote to Eisenhower: "The Cabinet to-day took rather a grave and on the whole an adverse view of the proposal to bomb so many French railway centres, in view of the fact that scores of thousands of French civilians, men, women, and children, would lose their lives or be injured. Considering that they are all our friends, this might be held to be an act of very great severity, bringing much hatred on the Allied Air Forces." Churchill added: "The advantage to enemy propaganda seems to me very great, especially as this would not be in the heat of battle but a long time before."[19]

As Supreme Commander, Eisenhower was the ultimate arbiter of the scale of these bombing raids. Churchill put the matter to Roosevelt. These "slaughters," he told the President, "may easily bring about a great revulsion in French feeling towards their approaching

---

17. Speech of 23 March 1944, Churchill Papers, 9/166, Martin Gilbert, *Winston S. Churchill*, Volume 7, page 717.

18. War Cabinet, 4 April 1944, Cabinet Papers, 65/46.

19. Letter of 3 April 1944, Churchill Papers, 20/137, Martin Gilbert, *Winston S. Churchill*, Volume 7, page 727.

United States and British liberators. They may leave a legacy of hate behind them."[20] The President, however, supported the Supreme Commander, telling Churchill: "I am not prepared to impose from this distance any restriction on military action by the responsible commanders that in their opinion might militate against the success of 'Overlord' or cause additional loss of life to our Allied forces of invasion."[21] The bombing went ahead. The casualties were high, more than four thousand civilian dead, but less than feared, and the railway disruptions were effective.

On April 7, Good Friday, Churchill was present when the senior officers involved in the Normandy landings gathered at Montgomery's headquarters in London, at St. Paul's School. "On Good Friday I gave a good talk," Churchill telegraphed to Roosevelt five days later, "to all the Generals, British and American, who were gathered at General Montgomery's Headquarters, expressing my strong confidence in the result of this extraordinary but magnificent operation." He did not agree, Churchill told the President, "with the loose talk which has been going on on both sides of the Atlantic about the unduly heavy casualties which we shall sustain. In my view it is the Germans who will suffer very heavy casualties when our band of brothers gets among them."[22]

In the third week of April, with the cross-Channel landings less than two months away and the question of landing craft becoming acute, General Marshall declined to transfer even spare landing craft from the Pacific to the Mediterranean. Learning that same day that the American Chiefs of Staff had also rejected a British appeal to increase the number of landing craft being manufactured in the United States—the source of more than 90 percent of the total—Churchill warned Roosevelt that the American decision would limit Britain's power to help, in due course, in the war against Japan. "I hope you will bear this in mind," Churchill told Roosevelt, "if there are any com-

---

20. Telegram of 7 May 1944, Winston S. Churchill, _The Second World War_, Volume 5, pages 529–30.
21. Telegram of 11 May 1944, Winston S. Churchill, _The Second World War_, Volume 5, page 530.
22. Telegram of 12 April 1944, Prime Minister to President, No. 643, Franklin D. Roosevelt Papers.

plaints hereafter."[23] On receiving this telegram, Roosevelt instructed his Staff neither to acknowledge it, nor to reply to it.[24]

When Churchill asked his representative in Washington, Field Marshal Sir John Dill, to see the President and put the problem of the American cutback in landing-craft manufacture direct to him, Dill was doubtful. "The President, as you know, is not militarily minded," he told Churchill, "and you will, in my view, gain little by referring purely military questions to him."[25] Churchill took Dill's advice, but the landing craft issue continued to rankle. The Americans "had not been very forthcoming in providing craft for the European theatre," Churchill told the Dominion Prime Ministers at the beginning of May.[26]

Roosevelt, unsure how seriously Churchill favored the Normandy landings over the Italian campaign, sent two Americans to Britain to see him: John J. McCloy, the Assistant Secretary for War, and Lieutenant General Joseph T. McNarney, the Deputy Chief of Staff. Churchill invited them to lunch, and was able to convince them that he was completely behind the cross-Channel assault and the preparations being made for it throughout Britain by British, Canadian and American forces in their final month of intensive training. "We were greatly reassured by all we saw in England," McNarney wrote in early May, "and by your courage and confidence."[27]

One of Churchill's strengths was his ability to convey confidence; that had been his achievement in the dark days of 1940. He also knew his own limitations, as well as knowing those of the President. "He said Roosevelt was not well and that he was no longer the man he had been," General Brooke noted in his diary on May 7; "this, he said, also applied to himself. He said he could still always sleep well, eat well and especially drink well, but that he no longer jumped out of bed the way

---

23. Telegram of 14 April 1944, Prime Minister to President, No. 645, Franklin D. Roosevelt Papers.

24. Warren F. Kimball, *Churchill & Roosevelt: The Complete Correspondence,* Volume 3, page 91.

25. Telegram of 24 April 1944, Churchill Papers, 20/163, Martin Gilbert, *Winston S. Churchill,* Volume 7, page 745.

26. Meeting of 1 May 1944, Cabinet Papers, 99/28.

27. Letter of 27 April 1944, Premier Papers, 4/69/2.

he used to, and felt as if he would be quite content to spend the whole day in bed." [28]

All day in bed was not an option. To impart his fears to John J. McCloy, Churchill took him one evening to the bombed-out House of Commons. "Suddenly," McCloy later recalled, "he referred to the number of his early contemporaries who had been killed during what he called the hecatombs of World War I." Churchill then described himself "as a sort of 'sport' in nature's sense as he said most of his generation lay dead at Passchendaele and the Somme. An entire British generation of potential leaders had been cut off and Britain could not afford the loss of another generation."

Churchill then told McCloy that if the Americans felt that he was "using all his efforts to avoid such another slaughter as had taken place in World War I due to inadequately equipped men," it was not a false accusation. "The Americans should understand this as it was extremely important that in the coming post-war period both Britain and the United States should have vigorous and competent leaders at hand to ensure the peace and democratic governments." Churchill spoke, McCloy recalled, "with great conviction and vigor." [29]

Churchill hoped that Roosevelt would come to Britain in time for the Normandy landings: The President had not visited Britain once since America's entry into the war two and a half years earlier. Adopting what the historian David Stafford calls the "jocular" tone he used "when faced with Roosevelt's resistance," [30] Churchill telegraphed: "Doctor Churchill informs you that a sea voyage in one of your great new battleships will do you no end of good." [31] Roosevelt declined.

On May 14 the Allied troops on the Cassino front began to move forward. Nine days later those at Anzio began their breakout. The race to enter Rome was on. "How lucky it was," Churchill telegraphed to Alexander, "that we stood up to our United States Chiefs of Staff

---

28. Diary entry, 7 May 1944, Arthur Bryant, *The Turn of the Tide, 1939–1943*, Volume 2, pages 187–88.

29. John J. McCloy, recollections, letter to the author, 26 April 1982.

30. David Stafford, *Ten Days to D-Day*, page 18.

31. Telegram of 28 May 1944, Prime Minister to President, No. 685, Franklin D. Roosevelt Papers.

friends and refused to allow you full exploitation of this battle!" Churchill added: "I hope that British as well as Americans will enter the city simultaneously."[32] Mark Clark had other ideas. On June 4 it was his troops who entered the Italian capital.

Churchill did not allow his disappointment at the American capture of Rome to lure him from his principal object, the maintenance of Anglo-American harmony. "I hear that relations are admirable between our armies in every rank there," he telegraphed to Roosevelt on June 4, and in Britain "certainly it is an absolute brotherhood."[33] Two days later the cross-Channel assault was launched against the Normandy beaches.

---

32. Telegram of 31 May 1944, Churchill Papers, 20/165, Martin Gilbert, *Winston S. Churchill*, Volume 7, page 785.

33. Telegram of 4 June 1944, Churchill Papers, 20/165, Prime Minister to President, No. 692, Franklin D. Roosevelt Papers.

Chapter Thirty

⌖

FROM NORMANDY TO QUEBEC

The Normandy landings on the morning of 6 June 1944 were the culmination of intensive Anglo-American planning and preparation. By dawn, 18,000 American, British and Canadian paratroopers were ashore. By midnight 73,000 American, 61,715 British and 14,000 Canadian troops had landed. The numbers killed that day included 2,500 Americans, 1,641 Britons and 359 Canadians. During the afternoon Churchill went to Eisenhower's headquarters in London, where on large maps he was shown "the latest position."[1] Speaking that evening in the House of Commons, he declared that Eisenhower's courage "is equal to all the necessary decisions that have to be taken in these extremely difficult and uncontrollable matters."[2] Roosevelt also sent Churchill a gift that day, two electric typewriters he hoped Churchill would accept "as a gift from me and as a symbol of the strong bond between the people of America and Great Britain."[3] Unfortunately the machines were of the "noisy" variety and thus unsuitable for dictation, for which Churchill's secretaries used a silent typewriter.[4]

On the fifth day of the Normandy battle a dispute arose between Churchill and Roosevelt about how to deal with Soviet penetration in the Balkans. Churchill's plan, which he had put forward ten days earlier with Roosevelt's apparent approval, was to grant the Soviets a predominant role in Romania in return for their not supporting the local

---

1. Letter of 8 June 1944, Sir John Martin Papers.
2. Speech of 6 June 1944, *Hansard*, Parliamentary debates.
3. Letter of 6 June 1944, Premier Papers, 4/69/2.
4. Note of 12 June 1944, Premier Papers, 4/69/2.

Communist insurgents in Greece. But, Roosevelt telegraphed on June 11, that arrangement would result in the division of the Balkan region "into spheres of influence despite the declared intention to limit the arrangement to military matters."

Roosevelt told Churchill that the United States preferred to set up a "consultative machinery" to dispel misunderstandings and "restrain the tendency towards the development of exclusive spheres."[5] Churchill disagreed vehemently: "I am much concerned to receive your message," he replied that same day. "Action is paralysed if everybody is to consult everybody else about everything before it is taken. Events will always outstrip the changing situations in these Balkan regions. Somebody must have the power to plan and act." A "Consultative Committee" such as the United States favored would, Churchill insisted, be "a mere obstruction, always overridden in any case of emergency by direct interchanges between you and me, or either of us and Stalin."

Churchill pointed out that the Soviet Union had been "ready to let us take the lead" in the recent Greek crisis, which had been dealt with effectively and without bloodshed. "I always reported to you, and I always will report to you," he assured the President. "You shall see every telegram I send. I think you might trust me in this." The agreement with Russia had meant that the Communist movement in Greece and "all its malice" could be controlled by the "national forces" of Greece. Otherwise, Churchill warned, what beckoned was "civil war and ruin to the land you care about so much."

Seeking to maintain the policy that he favored, Churchill reminded Roosevelt of his previous help in supporting Britain in Greece. "Your telegrams to me in the recent crisis worked wonders," Churchill wrote. "We were entirely agreed, and the result is entirely satisfactory." Why, then, he asked, "is all this effective direction to be broken up into a committee of mediocre officials such as we are littering about the world? Why can you and I not keep this in our own hands, considering how we see eye to eye about so much of it?" If it became necessary to consult other Allied Powers, and a "set of triangular or quadrangular telegrams got started," the only result would be "chaos or impotence."[6]

---

5. Telegram of 11 June 1944, Churchill Papers, 20/166, Martin Gilbert, *Winston S. Churchill,* Volume 7, page 804.

6. Telegram of 11 June 1944, Churchill Papers, 20/166, Prime Minister to President, No. 700, Franklin D. Roosevelt Papers.

Roosevelt deferred to Churchill's argument, but warned: "We must be careful to make it clear that we are not establishing any post-war spheres of influence."[7] It was to be Stalin who would ensure that the countries his armies liberated came under Soviet political control.

On June 11 Churchill was upset to learn that the American newspapers, "with their human interest stories" about American units and individuals in the Normandy battle, were leaving an impression "in the mind of the average American" that the major part in these operations was being played by the United States forces."[8] The next day he crossed to France to visit the British troops, whose work he did not want to see eclipsed.

With the battle in Normandy testing the Allied forces to their uttermost, Churchill's relations with Roosevelt were under strain, both in the strategic sphere and on wider political issues, including Greece and Yugoslavia. When Churchill tried to build a bridge between Marshal Tito's Communist movement inside Yugoslavia—and its anti-German partisans—and the Royal Yugoslav Government-in-Exile, Roosevelt was so hostile that Churchill was stung to telegraph in rebuke. "I am struggling to bring order out of chaos in both cases," he wrote, "and concentrate all efforts against the common foe. I am keeping you constantly informed, and I hope to have your confidence and help within the sphere of action in which initiative is assigned to us."

Churchill was angry that what for him were essential "spheres of action" were regarded by Roosevelt as malignant "spheres of influence." After words of congratulation for the "brilliant fighting" by the American troops in both the Cherbourg Peninsula and Italy, Churchill told the President: "We have immense tasks before us. Indeed I cannot think of any moment when the burden of the war has laid more heavily upon me or when I have felt so unequal to its ever-more entangled problems."[9]

In the last week of June a further Anglo-American dispute arose over strategy in the Mediterranean and Adriatic. Churchill put his au-

---

7. Telegram of 13 June 1944, Churchill Papers, 20/166, Martin Gilbert, *Winston S. Churchill*, Volume 7, page 805.
8. Report of 11 June 1944, Cabinet Papers, 105/46.
9. Telegram of 23 June 1944, Prime Minister to President, No. 712, Franklin D. Roosevelt Papers.

thority behind an appeal from his Chiefs of Staff to the American Chiefs of Staff not to take forces away from the Italian campaign for the amphibious landing planned for the South of France in mid-August. On June 28 an Enigma decrypt of a top-secret Hitler directive revealed that the battle in Italy would draw in more and more German divisions. These divisions would therefore be unavailable to be sent against the Allied forces in Normandy.

Churchill put his Chiefs of Staffs' points to Roosevelt. "For my own part," he wrote, "while eager to do everything in human power which will give effective and timely help to 'Overlord,' I should greatly regret to see General Alexander's army deprived of much of its offensive power in northern Italy for the sake of a march up the Rhône valley, which the Combined Chiefs of Staff have themselves described as unprofitable." This was a reference to the planned South of France landing.

Churchill wondered whether Roosevelt would really involve himself in the intricacies of the decision. "I most earnestly beg you to examine this matter in detail for yourself," he wrote. "Please also take into consideration the very important information which General Menzies is sending you separately on my instructions." This information, from the head of the British Secret Service, was a summary of the Enigma decrypt of June 28: Hitler's order to reinforce the Italian front.[10]

Roosevelt rejected Churchill's appeal. "My interests and hopes," the President repled, "centre on defeating the Germans in front of Eisenhower and driving on into Germany, rather than on limiting this action for the purpose of staging a full major effort in Italy." Even with five divisions withdrawn from Italy for the South of France operation, Roosevelt asserted, there would be sufficient Allied forces in Italy "to chase" the Germans northward and "maintain heavy pressure" against the German Army.[11] Roosevelt made no reference to the Hitler directive that seemed to Churchill and his Chiefs of Staff to be the decisive factor. He also told Churchill that for "purely political considerations" in the United States "I should never survive even a slight setback in

---

10. Telegram of 28 June 1944, Cabinet Papers, 122/1246.

11. Telegram of 29 June 1944, Churchill Papers, 20/167, Martin Gilbert, *Winston S. Churchill*, Volume 7, page 827.

'Overlord' if it were known that fairly large forces had been diverted to the Balkans."

This was a misconception. Neither Churchill nor the British Chiefs of Staff had suggested advancing into the Balkans, but rather, by landing at the northern end of the Adriatic—far from the Balkans—they would then move northeast through the Ljubljana Gap toward Vienna.[12] At a meeting with his Chiefs of Staff on the evening of June 30, Churchill reminded them that when future operations in the Mediterranean had been discussed at both Cairo and Teheran, "it had been the President who had suggested the possibility of our striking North-East from the head of the Adriatic." Churchill also referred to a recent report from Alexander that American troops in Italy, some of whom "were actually in contact with the enemy, were already being withdrawn" in preparation for the South of France landing, "and that the present uncertainty regarding future operations in the Mediterranean was causing his army to 'look over their shoulder.' "[13]

At ten o'clock that evening the Chiefs of Staff went to see Churchill to discuss how to proceed. Churchill told them he had ordered a flying boat and a Lancaster bomber to stand by, "so we may be flying off to Washington before we are very much older." General Brooke noted in his diary that he doubted they would go. "Winston will realize there is nothing more to be gained by argument."[14]

Churchill made one last effort to influence Roosevelt. His reply was first discussed by the Chiefs of Staff. "We are deeply grieved by your telegram," it began. It continued with a strong protest against the South of France landings and the abandonment of a major Italian offensive. The splitting up of the Italian campaign into two operations, Italy and the South of France, "neither of which can do anything decisive," Churchill told the President, "is in my humble and respectful opinion, the first major strategic and political error for which we two have to be responsible."

At Teheran, Churchill reminded the President, "you emphasized to me the possibilities of a move eastward when Italy was conquered,

---

12. For this strategic plan, see Map 10, page 461.
13. Meeting of 30 June 1944, Cabinet Papers, 79/77.
14. Diary entry, 30 June 1944, Arthur Bryant, *The Turn of the Tide, 1939–1943*, pages 225–26.

and mentioned particularly Istria." No one involved in those discussions "has ever thought of moving armies into the Balkans; but Istria and Trieste in Italy are strategic and political positions, which as you saw yourself very clearly might exercise profound and widespread reactions, especially now after the Russian advances."

After Teheran, Churchill added, he had been made doubtful about the South of France landing by Eisenhower's "dislike of it." Eisenhower had then argued—and Churchill quoted for Roosevelt from the records of the meeting—that it was of "vital importance" to continue "the maximum possible operations in an established theatre, since much time was invariably lost when the scene of action was changed, necessitating, as it did, the arduous task of building up a fresh base." Those had been Eisenhower's words. The American decision to proceed with the landings in the South of France, Churchill added, meant that "little account" was to be taken of Alexander's operations in Italy. The "air effort" was also about to be curtailed.

Roosevelt had proposed that he and Churchill "should lay our respective cases before Stalin." Churchill rejected this, pointing out that Stalin, on a "long-term political view," might prefer that the British and Americans "should do their share in France in this very hard fighting that is to come, and that East, Middle and Southern Europe should fall naturally into his control." Churchill then referred to his dashed hope of a face-to-face meeting: "It is with the greatest sorrow that I write to you in this sense. But I am sure that if we could have met, as I so frequently proposed, we should have reached a happy agreement."

At the end of his telegram Churchill reverted, as he always did when beset by anger and frustration, to the wider friendship: "However we may differ on the conduct of the war," he told the President, "my personal gratitude to you for your kindness to me and for all you have done for the cause of freedom will never be diminished."[15] Neither Churchill's arguments nor his Chiefs of Staffs' unanimity were to any avail. Roosevelt and the American Chiefs of Staff insisted on the landing in the South of France. To ensure its success, Alexander's army in Italy bore the brunt of troop and landing-craft withdrawals.

---

15. Telegram of 1 July 1944, Churchill Papers, 20/167, Martin Gilbert, *Winston S. Churchill*, Volume 7, pages 828–30.

• • •

The question of Britain's eventual war debts to the United States was another cause of concern for Churchill. Again and again in his relations with America, starting with the First World War, it was the money owed by Britain to the United States that created unease and confrontation. He felt strongly, he told the War Cabinet on July 18, that in any settlement of her war debts, Britain must press "that the fullest weight should be given to the contribution we had made to the victory of the Allies and to the preservation of those who were fighting with us." The survival of the Allies would be "very largely due" to the fact that Britain had held Germany at bay for a year and a half "single-handed," and to the assistance it had given "in men, money and materials." Those considerations could not be ignored. Britain should be entitled, Churchill argued, "to present the other side of the account in terms of these imponderables when the question of settlement was under consideration."[16]

Churchill again felt the need for another meeting with Roosevelt. "Our affairs are getting into a most tangled condition," he telegraphed to Hopkins on July 19. "We have to deal with the affairs of a dozen States," he explained, "some of which have several civil wars brewing and anyhow are split from top to bottom, by means of the concerted action of three great Powers or four if you still include China, every one of which approaches the topic from a different angle and in a different mood." Because he and Roosevelt and their Staffs could only meet "at intervals of six months," it was "very hard for anyone to have a policy." There were economic, financial and political issues "of the utmost stress and consequence advancing in a steady parade." However, Churchill added, "the war news makes amends for much. We look like getting a fine Anglo-American victory in the next few days."[17]

Hardly had he sent this telegram than Churchill was disturbed by an announcement from Eisenhower's headquarters that the British had sustained "quite a serious set-back" in Normandy. "I am not aware," he telegraphed to Montgomery, "of any facts that justify such a statement." Nor did it have any justification. At one point British com-

---

16. War Cabinet, 18 July 1944, Cabinet Papers, 65/43.
17. Telegram of 19 July 1944, Churchill Papers, 20/142, Martin Gilbert, *Winston S. Churchill*, Volume 7, pages 858–59.

mandos had been forced back a thousand yards, that was all. But the word "set-back" had created, Churchill wrote, "a good deal of talk here. I should like to know exactly what the position is, in order to maintain confidence among wobblers or critics in high places."[18]

The next set of telegrams concerned Churchill's emphatic support for his Chiefs of Staffs' new proposal that instead of the South of France landing, the Allies could put a force ashore in Brittany, on the French Atlantic coast, possibly at St Nazaire, the more easily to help the battle in Normandy. When Eisenhower expressed his opposition, Churchill asked Hopkins to put the plan to the President. Hopkins replied: "I am sure his answer will be in the negative."[19] Rebuffed with regard to a Brittany landing, Churchill telegraphed to Roosevelt: "It is impossible to resolve these thorny matters by correspondence and I am sure if we and the Staff were together, good working agreements could be reached."[20]

Having lost his battle against the South of France landing, Churchill made his peace with the Americans by witnessing that landing from offshore. "Have just returned from watching the assault from a considerable distance," he telegraphed to Roosevelt. "Everything seems to be working like clockwork here, and there have been few casualties so far and none that I know of amongst the mass of shipping deployed."[21] If he had had his way, Churchill wrote to Clementine, "the armies now cast on shore 400 miles from Paris would have come in at St Nazaire in about a week and greatly widened the front of our advance with corresponding security against German movement east of Paris. This will all become blatantly apparent to the instructed." One of his reasons for making his visit to the South of France landing public, he explained to Clementine, "was to associate myself with this well-conducted but irrelevant and unrelated operation."[22]

Churchill had witnessed the South of France landings while on an

---

18. Telegram of 27 July 1944, Churchill Papers, 20/169, Martin Gilbert, *Winston S. Churchill*, Volume 7, page 865.

19. Telegram of 7 August 1944, Churchill papers, 20/169, Martin Gilbert, *Winston S. Churchill*, Volume 7, page 879.

20. Telegram of 10 August 1944, Premier Papers, 4/75/2.

21. Telegram of 16 August 1944, Churchill Papers, 20/170, Martin Gilbert, *Winston S. Churchill*, Volume 7, page 899.

22. Letter of 17 August 1944, Baroness Spencer-Churchill Papers.

extended tour of inspection of Allied troops in Italy. A telegram that he sent to the President of Brazil, congratulating him on the "quality and bearing" of the Brazilian troops in Alexander's army, was sent in error not to the President of Brazil but to the President of the United States. "The cipher people," Churchill explained to Roosevelt, "had apparently not realized there was any other President in the World."[23]

While still in Italy, Churchill made strenuous efforts to help the Polish insurgents who had raised the flag of revolt in Warsaw, hoping to drive the Germans out, and establish a provisional government before the Soviet forces arrived. From their bases in southern Italy, Allied planes flew the 785 miles to drop supplies to the Poles, a perilously long journey, and aircraft losses were high. Churchill pressed Stalin to allow the planes to refuel at Soviet-controlled air bases less than 150 miles east of Warsaw, before beginning their equally long and dangerous return journey. When Stalin refused, Churchill sought Roosevelt's help in pressing the Soviet leader. If Stalin resented the Anglo-American support for Poland, Churchill telegraphed to Roosevelt: "We are Nations serving high causes and must give true counsels towards world peace."[24]

Churchill drafted a telegram to be sent to Stalin under his signature and that of Roosevelt: a joint appeal to allow American planes flying from their bases in England, a distance of 878 miles, to drop supplies on Warsaw and then land behind the Russian lines and refuel. Roosevelt rejected Churchill's plan. One reason, he explained, was Stalin's "definite refusal" to allow Soviet airfields to be used by Allied planes seeking to drop supplies in Warsaw. The other was the "current American conversations" with the Soviet Union about the future use of Soviet air bases in Siberia, for use by American bombers on their way to bomb Japan. "I do not consider it advantageous to the long range general war prospect," Roosevelt explained, "for me to join with you in the proposed message to Uncle J."[25] As a result of Roosevelt's refusal to make a joint approach to Stalin (the "Uncle Joe" of their telegraphic

---

23. Telegram of 24 August 1944, Churchill Papers, 20/170, Prime Minister to President, No. 768, Franklin D. Roosevelt Papers.

24. Telegram of 18 August 1944, Churchill Papers, 20/170, Prime Minister to President, No. 760, Franklin D. Roosevelt Papers.

25. Telegram of 26 August 1944, Churchill Papers, 20/170, Martin Gilbert, *Winston S. Churchill*, Volume 7, page 927.

exchanges), the help sent to Warsaw remained inadequate and ineffective, and the loss of Allied aircrew—all volunteers—was high.

As disagreement over aid to Warsaw intensified, Churchill determined to hold another conference with Roosevelt. At that very moment, however, having already made his travel plans, he was taken ill. Recovery took several days. "Tonight his temperature is back to normal," Ambassador Winant reported to Hopkins on September 1, "and he seems on the way to a quick recovery. But each journey has taken its toll and the interval between illnesses has been constantly shortened." There was no one in Britain, Winant added, "who cares so much about friendly relations between Great Britain and the United States, and few people anywhere who have been more loyal in their friendship with the President." [26]

Churchill persevered with his travel plans. "This visit of mine to the President," he wrote to Clementine, "is the most necessary one that I have ever made since the very beginning, as it is there that various differences that exist between the Staffs, and also between me and the American Chiefs of Staff, must be brought to a decision." While visiting the war zone in Italy he had reflected on the military and strategic disagreements between Britain and the United States, and on the imbalance of effort and reward.

Britain, Churchill told Clementine, had three armies in the field. The first, in France, was fighting "under American command." The second, in Italy under General Alexander, was relegated to "a secondary and frustrated condition" by American "insistence" upon the South of France landings. The third, on the Burmese frontier, was fighting "in the most unhealthy country in the world under the worst possible conditions" in order to guard the American air route over the Himalayas "into their very over-rated China."

Thus, Churchill pointed out, "two-thirds of Britain's forces," those in Italy and Burma, were being "mis-employed" on behalf of the American command, and the remaining third, in France, were directly under American command. Churchill ended his letter: "These are delicate and serious matters to be handled between friends in careful

---

26. Letter of 1 September 1944, Robert E. Sherwood, *The White House Papers of Harry L. Hopkins,* Volume 2, page 806.

and patient personal discussion. I have no doubt we shall reach a good conclusion, but you will see that life is not very easy."[27]

Paris was liberated on August 25. On September 5 Churchill left London by train for Greenock, on the Clyde. That evening he boarded the *Queen Mary*. It would be his sixth meeting with Roosevelt since the summer of 1941. During the voyage he discovered that there were a large number of American servicemen on board, returning home, whose period of leave was counted from the beginning of their date of embarkation. As some had been waiting on board as long as a week, because the *Queen Mary* had been kept waiting for him, they were going to lose those days at home. "May I indicate through your good offices," he telegraphed to Roosevelt, "this will be made up to them? It would be a pleasure to me if this could be announced before end of voyage and their anxiety relieved."[28] Roosevelt replied that same day, agreeing to Churchill's request, and thanking him for his "thoughtfulness."[29]

On September 10 Churchill disembarked at Halifax and boarded the train for Quebec, arriving the following morning. Roosevelt, whose train had arrived in Quebec City ten minutes earlier on the adjoining track, was waiting for him in his car. Much was agreed by the two men and their Staffs at this second Quebec Conference. To Churchill's relief, Roosevelt accepted the two main British requests. If the Italian campaign prospered, there could be an amphibious landing at the top of the Adriatic, for which the Americans would provide the landing craft required, followed by a thrust through the Ljubljana Gap into Austria and toward Vienna. And in the Far East, British forces could make their own thrust against Rangoon, rather than serve as an adjunct to American efforts in support of China. In return Roosevelt accepted Churchill's offer of a substantial British battle fleet to take part in operations against Japan under United States Supreme Command.

As the conference continued, Roosevelt agreed to Churchill's request that, after the European war, but while the war against Japan was

---

27. Letter of 17 August 1944, Baroness Spencer-Churchill Papers.

28. Telegram of 7 September 1944, Prime Minister to President, No. 783, Franklin D. Roosevelt Papers.

29. Telegram of 7 September 1944, Churchill Papers, 20/171, Martin Gilbert, *Winston S. Churchill,* Volume 7, page 940.

still being fought, Britain would continue to get food and other supplies to cover its "reasonable needs" at home, and that the United States would not attach any conditions to supplies delivered under Lend-Lease that would "jeopardize the recovery" of Britain's export trade.[30] Roosevelt also agreed that British forces could be used to support the "ultimate entry" of the Greek Government into Athens "as soon as the strength of the German forces in that area had been sufficiently reduced to make that operation practicable."[31]

On the last afternoon of the conference, senior officials and faculty of McGill University traveled from Montreal to confer honorary degrees on the two leaders. During his acceptance speech, Churchill described how his friendship with Roosevelt had grown "under the hammer blows of war." After the degree ceremony, at a conference for newspaper and radio reporters, Churchill spoke of his wish to meet Roosevelt as often as possible. When he had "the rare and fortunate chance to meet the President of the United States," he said, "we are not limited in our discussions by any sphere. We talk over the whole position in every aspect—the military, economic, diplomatic, financial. All—all is examined. And obviously that should be so." The fact that they had worked so long together, "and the fact that we have got to know each other so well under the hard stresses of war, makes the solution of problems so much simpler, so swift and so easy it is."[32]

While in Quebec, Churchill gave Roosevelt a signed copy of the most recent volume of his war speeches, *Onward to Victory,* covering the year 1943. It was inscribed: "To FDR from WSC, 'A fresh egg from the faithful hen!' Quebec 1944."[33] From Quebec, Churchill went by train overnight to Hyde Park, where he stayed with Roosevelt for two days. Observing Roosevelt at both Quebec and Hyde Park, Clementine Churchill wrote to her daughter Mary that the President, "with all his genius, does not—indeed cannot (partly because of his health and partly because of his make-up)—function round the clock, like your Father. I should not think that his mind was pinpointed on the war for

30. Telegram of 15 September, Cabinet Papers, 120/153.
31. Meeting of 15 September 1944, Cabinet Papers, 120/144.
32. Press and Radio Conference, 16 September 1944, Premier Papers, 4/75/2.
33. Franklin D. Roosevelt Library, Hyde Park, Facsimile in Richard Harrity and Ralph G. Martin, *Man of the Century: Churchill,* page 222.

more than four hours a day, which is not really enough when one is supreme war lord."[34]

In the seclusion of Hyde Park, Churchill and Roosevelt discussed the atomic bomb. During their talk they rejected the suggestion that the world should be informed about it "with a view to an international agreement regarding its control and use." They also felt that when a bomb was finally available, "it might perhaps, after mature consideration, be used against the Japanese, who should be warned that this bombardment will be repeated until they surrender." Churchill and Roosevelt also agreed that full collaboration between Britain and the United States in developing atomic power "for military and commercial purposes" should continue after the defeat of Japan "unless and until terminated by joint agreement."[35]

On the evening of September 19 Churchill left Hyde Park for the railroad station at nearby Poughkeepsie. "Leaving Hyde Park was an experience," his secretary Marian Holmes noted in her diary. "The PM sat with the President in his car which was surrounded by Cadillac autos full of bodyguards and G-men. When we drove through Poughkeepsie, they jumped on the running boards and made a terrific show. All traffic on the roads was brought to a standstill by order of the State Police."[36] At Poughkeepsie the Presidential train was waiting to take Churchill overnight to New York, where, on the morning of September 20, he embarked on the *Queen Mary* for the voyage home.

---

34. Letter of 18 September 1944, Spencer-Churchill Papers.

35. Agreement of 19 September 1944, Premier Papers, 3/139/8A.

36. Diary entry, 19 September 1944, Spicer Papers.

Chapter Thirty-One

✠

"IT GRIEVES ME VERY MUCH
TO SEE SIGNS OF OUR
DRIFTING APART"

O n his return to London at the end of September 1944, Churchill
gave the House of Commons an account of the Quebec Conference. He also told Members of Parliament that he had been "somewhat concerned" to observe, during the reading of the American
newspapers in which he had "indulged" while in the United States,
"that widespread misconception exists in the public mind, so far as
that is reflected by the newspapers, about the scale of our effort in
Burma and the results to date of Admiral Mountbatten's campaign."

Many important American newspapers had seemed to give the impression, Churchill pointed out, "that the British campaign of 1944 in
Burma had been a failure, or at least a stalemate, that nothing much
had been done." Such was not the case. The Fourteenth British Imperial Army, "of more than a quarter of a million men," under Mountbatten's command, had "by its aggressive operation guarded the base of
the American air link to China and protected India against the horrors
of a Japanese invasion."[1]

Churchill planned another journey, this time eastward. As he explained to Roosevelt on the day after his House of Commons speech,
he would go to the Soviet Union and meet Stalin, to "clinch his coming in against Japan" as soon as Hitler had been defeated, as agreed at
the Teheran Conference, and "to try to effect an amicable settlement

---

1. Speech of 28 September 1944, *Hansard*, Parliamentary debates.

with Poland." He would also discuss the political future of Yugoslavia and Greece. "I feel certain," Churchill told the President, "that personal contact is essential."[2]

Five days later Churchill explained to Roosevelt that Averell Harriman would "sit in" on all the principal conferences, except "tête-a-têtes" between Churchill and Stalin. Churchill added: "You can rely on me to keep you constantly informed of everything that affects our joint interest, apart from the reports that Averell will send."[3] Jock Colville noted in his diary: "The PM's visit to Moscow, which is really very dangerous to his health, is, he assured me yesterday, entirely because he wants to discourage any idea that the UK and the USA are very close (as exemplified by the Quebec Conference) to the exclusion of Russia." The visit would make it quite clear "that our counsels with Russia are close too, and that there is no tendency to leave her in the cold."[4]

On the evening of October 7, Churchill flew from London to Naples. From there he asked Roosevelt for American reinforcements to be sent to Mark Clark's forces in Italy, to enable Alexander to continue the advance. Roosevelt declined. "I appreciate the hard and difficult task which our armies in Italy have faced and will face," he replied, "but we cannot withhold from the main effort forces which are needed in the Battle of Germany."[5] There was to be no return to Churchill's hopes for the Italian campaign.

On October 8 Churchill flew from Naples to Cairo and on to Moscow, which he reached shortly after midday on October 9. The encouraging news from northern Europe, he telegraphed to Field Marshal Smuts, was that "enormous American reinforcements are pouring in."[6] That day, during his talks with Stalin on the postwar future of Germany, Churchill told the Soviet leader that he was "all for hard terms,"

---

2. Telegram of 29 September 1944, 20/172, Prime Minister to President, No. 789, Franklin D. Roosevelt Papers.

3. Telegram of 4 October 1944, Prime Minister to President, No. 790, Franklin D. Roosevelt Papers.

4. Diary entry, 8 October 1944, Colville Papers.

5. Telegram of 16 October 1944, Churchill Papers, 20/173, Martin Gilbert, *Winston S. Churchill*, Volume 7, page 988.

6. Telegram of 9 October 1944, Churchill Papers, 20/173, Martin Gilbert, *Winston S. Churchill*, Volume 7, page 983.

but in the United States opinions were divided: "The President was for hard terms, others were for soft." In Churchill's view the problem was "how to prevent Germany getting on her feet in the lifetime of our grandchildren." Churchill also wanted Stalin to know that the British had "as many divisions fighting against Germany in Italy and France as the United States," and "nearly as many" fighting Japan.[7]

On Churchill's second day in Moscow, he and Stalin telegraphed jointly to Roosevelt that Harriman would sit in as an observer at all meetings "where business of importance is transacted," and that the head of the United States Military Mission in Moscow, Major-General John R. Deane, would be present "whenever military topics are raised."[8] But when Churchill showed Harriman a sheet of paper he had presented to Stalin, together with a letter to Stalin setting out numerical spheres of influence, set out in percentages, in Romania, Bulgaria, Hungary and Yugoslavia, Harriman told him that Roosevelt and Cordell Hull would certainly "repudiate" it.[9]

The letter which conceded postwar Soviet predominance in Hungary, Romania, Bulgaria and Yugoslavia, but not in Greece, was never sent. Instead Churchill telegraphed to Roosevelt: "It is absolutely necessary we should try to get a common mind about the Balkans, so that we may prevent civil war breaking out in several countries, when probably you and I would be in sympathy with one side and Uncle Joe with the other." He would keep the President informed "of all this," and nothing would be settled "except preliminary agreements between Britain and Russia, subject to further discussion and melting down with you."[10]

Churchill confided to Clementine: "I have to keep the President in constant touch & this is the delicate side."[11] On the previous day he had telegraphed to Hopkins with details of the percentages agreement. As to Romania, Churchill told Hopkins, the Soviets "claim fullest responsibility," but they were "prepared largely to disinterest

7. Meeting of 9 October 1944, Premier Papers, 3/434/4.
8. Telegram of 10 October 1944, Cabinet Papers, 120/158.
9. Recollection, W. Averell Harriman and Elie Abel, *Special Envoy to Churchill and Stalin, 1941–1946*, page 358.
10. Telegram of 11 October 1944, Cabinet Papers, 120/158.
11. Letter of 13 October 1944, Baroness Spencer-Churchill Papers.

themselves in Greece."[12] During the discussions about the future frontiers of Poland, Churchill pressed the delegates of the Polish Government in London, who had flown specially to Moscow, to accept the 1919 Curzon Line, which involved the loss of the eastern third of Poland, including the city of Lvov, to the Soviet Union, in return for Polish independence. "If you accept the frontier," he told the Poles in Harriman's presence, "the USA will take a great interest in the rehabilitation of Poland and may grant you a big loan after this war possibly without interest."[13] Unknown to Churchill, Roosevelt had already told Stalin at one of his private meetings at Teheran that he accepted the Curzon Line frontier. Churchill only learned this during the Moscow talks.

On October 19 Churchill flew from Moscow to Cairo. There he was told that the United States Chiefs of Staff had decided on the "impossibility" of any amphibious operation in the northern Adriatic that year, and would begin withdrawing landing craft from the Mediterranean within two weeks.[14] Speaking in the House of Commons on October 27 about the "different views" of Britain, the United States and the Soviet Union, Churchill declared: "The marvel is that all has hitherto been kept so solid, sure and sound between us." His own travels had been an attempt to give this process "constant care and attention." He had not hesitated "to travel from court to court like a wandering minstrel, always with the same song to sing, or the same set of songs." His aim was the unity of the Allied powers. "Let all hope die in German breasts that there will be the slightest division or weakening among the forces which are closing in upon them, and will crush the life out of their resistance."[15]

On November 7 Roosevelt was elected to a unique fourth term as President. "I always said that a great people could be trusted to stand by the pilot who weathered the storm," Churchill telegraphed. "It is an indescribable relief to me that our comradeship will continue and will

---

12. Telegram of 12 October 1944, Churchill Papers, 20/173, Martin Gilbert, *Winston S. Churchill*, Volume 7, page 1005.

13. Conversation of 14 October 1944, *Documents on Polish-Soviet Relations, 1939–1945*, Volume 2, document 239, pages 416–22.

14. Memorandum of 20 October 1944, Cabinet Papers, 105/47.

15. Speech of 27 October 1944, *Hansard*, Parliamentary debates.

help to bring the world out of misery." [16] Four days later Churchill was in Paris, celebrating Armistice Day. "I certainly had a wonderful reception from about half a million French in the Champs-Elysées," he telegraphed to Roosevelt, adding that while in Paris he had felt "a considerable feeling of stability in spite of communist threats, and that we could safely take them more into our confidence. I hope you will not consider that I am putting on French clothes when I say this." [17]

From Paris, Churchill went to Eisenhower's Advanced Headquarters, where he offered Eisenhower the use of the British heavy-gun batteries from Dover, with their greater range than the American artillery, for Eisenhower's bombardment of the Ruhr. As Secretary of State for War in 1919, it was Churchill who had prevented those guns from being scrapped.

Three days later Churchill was upset when Roosevelt telegraphed that he did not want the French to have a zone of occupation in Germany, and that he "must bring American troops home as rapidly as transportation permits." Quoting this phrase, Churchill asked the President that if the French could not have a zone of occupation, "how will it be possible to hold down Western Germany beyond the present Russian occupation line?" Britain could not undertake the task without American aid and that of the French. "All would therefore rapidly disintegrate as it did last time." Churchill added: "I hope however that my fears are groundless. I put my faith in you." [18]

Churchill dreaded the withdrawal of the United States from Europe, as had happened after the First World War. To his relief Roosevelt eventually agreed to French participation in the postwar occupation of Germany. But the disputes between Britain and the United States seemed endless. On November 25 Ambassador Winant was at Chequers with a telegram from the President about civil aviation. "It was pure blackmail," Colville wrote, "threatening that if we did not give way to certain unreasonable American demands, their attitude about Lease-Lend supplies would change." Colville noted that

---

16. Telegram of 8 November 1944, Prime Minister to President, No. 816, Franklin D. Roosevelt Papers.

17. Telegram of 15 November 1944, Prime Minister to President, No. 822, Cabinet Papers, 120/170.

18. Telegram of 19 November 1944, Prime Minister to President, No. 825, Franklin D. Roosevelt Papers.

Winant was "shame-faced about presenting it and didn't want to stay to lunch, but the PM said that even a declaration of war should not prevent them having a good lunch." Colville added: "The Americans are also being tough, and even threatening, about a number of other things and the PM is disturbed at having to oppose them over so many issues." One was "a sharp wrangle" about British imports of Argentine meat, "the Americans being anxious to bring economic pressure on the Argentine."[19]

The civil aviation dispute concerned the future American role in worldwide civil air traffic routes. Churchill feared an American attempt to dominate these, and telegraphed Roosevelt, setting out in detail the British fears. His telegram ended with a strong assertion of Britain's hopes of fair dealing. He had "never advocated competitive 'bigness' in any sphere between our two countries in their present state of development," he wrote, and went on to explain to the President that, after the war, the United States "will have the greatest navy in the world. You will have, I hope, the greatest air force. You will have the greatest trade. You have all the gold. But these things do not oppress my mind with fear because I am sure the American people under your re-acclaimed leadership will not give themselves over to vainglorious ambitions, and that justice and fair-play will be the lights that guide them."[20]

On November 30 Churchill celebrated his seventieth birthday. "Ever so many happy returns of the day," Roosevelt telegraphed. "I shall never forget the party with you and Uncle Joe a year ago and we must have more of them that are even better."[21] For Churchill, the many disputes with the United States were distressing. He wanted another meeting, at least of the Staffs, before the next Big Three meeting at

---

19. Diary entry, 25 November 1944, Colville Papers. Following a military coup in Argentina in July 1944, and the persistent refusal of the Argentine government to enter the war on the Allied side, the United States was seeking every possible means of pressure. It was not until March 1945 that Argentina declared war on the Axis Powers, the last American country to do so.

20. Telegram of 28 November 1944, Prime Minister to President, No. 836, Franklin D. Roosevelt Papers.

21. Telegram of 30 November 1944, Churchill Papers, 20/139, Martin Gilbert, *Winston S. Churchill*, Volume 7, page 1079.

Yalta, in the Crimea, which Stalin had set for February. "My anxiety is increased," Churchill telegraphed to Roosevelt, "by the destruction of all hopes of an early meeting between the three of us and the indefinite postponement of another meeting of you and me with our Staffs."

Churchill went on to explain to the President: "Our British plans are dependent on yours, our Anglo-American problems at least must be surveyed as a whole, and the telegraph and the telephone more often than not only darken counsel." If Roosevelt did not feel able to come to Britain, as Churchill wished, before the Big Three conference at Yalta in February, "I am bound to ask you whether you could not send your Chiefs of Staff over here as soon as possible, where they would be close to your main armies and to General Eisenhower and where the whole stormy scene can be calmly and patiently studied with a view to action as closely concerted as that which signalised our campaign of 1944."[22]

Churchill felt it was essential for him and Roosevelt to meet before the Crimean Conference examined the final phase of the war and came to decisions about the postwar world, in particular about the future of Poland, for which Britain had gone to war, but which Stalin was determined to incorporate into the Soviet sphere. But Roosevelt declined either to come to Britain or to send his Chiefs of Staff. A week later another crisis arose in Anglo-American relations as British troops moved into Greece—earlier agreed to by Roosevelt—to try to maintain law and order on behalf of the Greek Government, then battling a Greek Communist insurgency. In Washington the new Secretary of State, Edward Stettinius Jr., the son of Churchill's First World War colleague, sharply criticized Britain's intervention in Greece. Churchill appealed to Hopkins, in a telegram on December 9, hoping through him to influence Roosevelt. "I hope you will tell our great friend," Churchill wrote, "that the establishment of law and order in and around Athens is essential to all future measures of magnanimity and consolation towards Greece. After this has been established will be the time for talking."

It had been "a great disappointment" to him, Churchill told Hopkins, to have been confronted by the challenge of the Greek Commu-

22. Telegram of 6 December 1944, Prime Minister to President, No. 844, Franklin D. Roosevelt Papers.

nist Party's military wing (ELAS) when Britain's only aim was to form "a united Greece which could establish its own destiny." Britain had been "set upon, and we intend to defend ourselves." His attitude was clear: "I consider we have a right to the President's support in the policy we are following. If it can be said in the streets of Athens that the United States are against us, then more British blood will be shed and much more Greek."

The dispute over Greece had wide implications. "It grieves me very much," Churchill told Hopkins in his telegram of December 9, "to see signs of our drifting apart at a time when unity becomes ever more important, as danger recedes and faction arises."[23] That same day, those signs of "drifting apart" intensified, when Admiral King cancelled the order whereby American landing craft were helping British troops in Greece, at Britain's request. Two of these landing craft were due to sail for Athens on the following day, and seven were already engaged in their essential task when the American cancellation was issued.

Churchill learned that same morning, December 9, that the orders to the landing craft commanders were "to cease forthwith conveying troops, stores and supplies to Greece." This, General Maitland Wilson warned, "would gravely endanger the security of the forces now in Greece, and delay the introduction of relief vehicles and supplies."[24] Churchill at once drafted a strong telegram of protest to Roosevelt, but decided not to send it. Admiral King's orders, he wrote in the draft, "might produce a disaster of the first magnitude, which might endanger all the relations between Great Britain and the United States and by so doing affect the progress of the main war against Germany and thereafter against Japan." Churchill's final draft paragraph read: "I am sure that you have never seen these orders and that you will have them stamped upon at the earliest moment. If this were not so, I am sure you would have let me know in good time. I shall be forced when the House of Commons meets on Tuesday to make full explanation and I would like to be able to assure them that there is no fundamental breach between Britain and the United States."[25]

---

23. Telegram of 9 December 1944, Churchill papers, 20/177, Martin Gilbert, *Winston S. Churchill,* Volume 7, page 1096.
24. Telegram of 9 December 1944, Premier Papers, 3/212/5.
25. Draft telegram of 10 December 1944, Premier Papers, 3/212/5.

Instead of sending this telegram, Churchill telephoned Hopkins to tell him in person "of the dangerous character of the alleged American orders to withdraw all American ships and to cut our communications from Italy to Greece." Hopkins promised Churchill he would bring the matter to the President's notice the next morning.[26] In fact Hopkins saw Admiral King, who agreed to cancel his order. Hopkins also let Churchill know, through Lord Halifax, that King "had apparently issued the order on his own." As to the cancellation of the order, Halifax told Churchill, "the President has not been in on it, though Harry will probably tell him what had passed."

Halifax added that Hopkins was "anxious to avoid further trouble."[27] But further trouble was soon to come. It arose from the error by Churchill's Private Secretary Jock Colville in dispatching a telegram from Churchill to General Scobie, instructing him to act in Athens as though he were in "a conquered city."

Because the Combined Headquarters of the Mediterranean Command at Caserta, in Italy, contained both British and American officers, there was "a convention," Colville later explained, "that any telegrams which we did not wish the Americans to read, because they were concerned with purely British matters, should be headed 'Guard.'" Because they were all very tired at Downing Street, Colville wrote, and because, at five in the morning, Churchill "insisted that the telegram should be sent off straightaway," Colville had sent it across to the Foreign Office for dispatch but omitted to put the word "Guard" on top.[28] As a result of this simple error, Churchill's telegram passed to the American officers at Combined Headquarters, who leaked it. On December 11 it was published in the *Washington Post*.

The Americans were outraged that a British general had been ordered to act as though he were in "a conquered city." In Britain's defense, Churchill drafted a telegram to Roosevelt setting out the various occasions on which the United States had earlier expressed its support for British action in Greece. He decided to send this telegram not to Roosevelt but to Hopkins. "I must frankly confess," he told Hopkins in a covering note, that he never knew that the Greek Communist parti-

---

26. Note of 10 December 1944, Premier Papers, 3/212/5.
27. Telegram of 10 December 1944, Premier Papers, 3/212/5.
28. Note attached to diary entry of 4 December 1944, Colville Papers.

sans would prove so powerful. "I only wish they had fought one tenth as well against the Germans. We have got many troops coming in now but I certainly do not want to fight another war." Churchill went on to tell Hopkins that if he could get "any word of approval spoken by the United States" in favor of the Allied intervention in Athens by British troops, "you may save many British and Greek lives and set free soldiers who are needed elsewhere."[29]

The Americans could not accept the British justification for intervention in Greece. Yet three and a half months earlier, when Churchill had asked Roosevelt to approve the dispatch of a force not exceeding ten thousand men to Athens to forestall the establishment of "a tyrannical Communist government," Roosevelt had replied: "I have no objection to your making preparations to have in readiness a sufficient British force to preserve order in Greece when German forces evacuate the country." Nor was there any objection, Roosevelt had added, "to the use by General Wilson of American transport airplanes that are available to him at the time and can be spared from other operations."[30]

Recalling this exchange, Churchill finally appealed directly to Roosevelt on December 17. "I am sure you would not wish to cast down our painful and thankless task at this time," he wrote. "We desire nothing from Greece but to do our duty by the common cause. In the midst of our task of bringing food and relief and maintaining the rudiments of order for a Government which has no armed forces, we have become involved in a furious, though not as yet very bloody, struggle. I have felt it much that you were unable to give a word of explanation for our action but I understand your difficulties."[31]

The dispute over Greece marked a low point in Churchill's relations with the President. Particularly upsetting to Churchill was that Roosevelt no longer seemed to be taking an active interest in the daily demands, and disputes, of war making. There could be little immediate comfort for Churchill in a most encouraging remark, made to him by Eisenhower in the middle of the Greek dispute, that after the war

---

29. Telegram of 11 December 1944, Premier Papers, 3/212/5.
30. Telegram of 26 August 1944, Churchill Papers, 20/170, Martin Gilbert, *Winston S. Churchill,* Volume 7, page 906, footnote 2.
31. Telegram of 17 December 1944, Prime Minister to President, No. 855, Franklin D. Roosevelt Papers.

he was going to resign from the army "and devote himself to the promoting of good US-British relations."[32] In urging a renewed British offensive in support of the Americans, at the time of the fierce German attack against American forces in the Ardennes, Churchill told his Chiefs of Staff that one reason was to show that British forces were "still capable of vigorous action," and that it would "stimulate feeling in America" in favor of Britain.[33]

On December 24, intent on creating a broad-based government in Greece, in which the Communist insurgents would agree to participate, Churchill abandoned his Christmas Eve festivities at Chequers for yet another mission. Half an hour before midnight he left Chequers for Northolt airport, from where he flew overnight to Naples and then on to Athens. During the flight he dictated a telegram to Roosevelt. He was going to Greece, he informed the President, to see what could be done "to square this Greek entanglement," and he assured his apparent adversary: "It must always be understood that we seek nothing from Greece, in territory or advantage. We have given much and will give much more if it is in our power." Churchill ended with a hope and a plea: "I count on you to help us in this time of unusual difficulty."[34]

Reaching Athens on Christmas Day, Churchill began talks with the Greek leaders at once, first on board the British warship *Ajax,* and then, on December 26 and 27, at the British Embassy. During a break in talks on December 27, he saw the American Ambassador, Lincoln MacVeagh, and, as Jock Colville noted, "gave him a piece of his mind about the very inadequate support the USA have given us in this affair."[35] By December 28 it was clear that the Communist leaders would not participate in the government. That afternoon Churchill flew back to Naples, and then on to London, arriving on the afternoon of December 29. Neither during his Greek mission nor when it ended did he receive one word of support or comment from Roosevelt or the White House.

---

32. Admiral Sir Andrew Cunningham, diary entry, 12 December 1944, Cunningham Papers.

33. Meeting of 19 December 1944, Cabinet Papers, 79/84.

34. Telegram of 25 December 1944, Prime Minister to President, No. 858, Franklin D. Roosevelt Papers.

35. Diary entry, 27 December 1944, Colville diary.

• • •

Over the New Year, Churchill worked on the plans for the forthcoming Crimean Conference. On New Year's Day 1945 he invited Roosevelt to have a preliminary meeting with their respective Chiefs of Staff in Malta, on the way to the Crimea. "I shall be waiting on the quay," Churchill wrote, and added a short jingle: "No more let us falter! From Malta to Yalta! Let nobody alter!"[36]

As Roosevelt hesitated to commit himself to a meeting in Malta, Churchill wrote to him despondently: "At the present time I think the end of this war may well prove to be more disappointing than was the last."[37] The failure of the United States to take any part in the League of Nations between the wars still seemed to Churchill a main cause of the failure of European peace. One of the topics to be discussed at Yalta was the nature of the future World Organization—the United Nations. Churchill wanted to use the Malta meeting to work out a common Anglo-American policy. "I do not see any other way of realizing our hopes about World Organization in five or six days," he told Roosevelt. "Even the Almighty took seven." Realizing that Roosevelt might be vexed by his persistent requests for a meeting at Malta, Churchill added: "Pray forgive my tenacity."[38] Roosevelt deferred to Churchill's urgings, and agreed to meet at Malta on his way to Yalta.

On January 12 a truce was signed in Greece between the British and Communist forces. Churchill was relieved at this development, for which he had made such an arduous journey three weeks earlier. But he had not forgotten American opposition to his Greek policy. "Naturally," he telegraphed to his American friend Bernard Baruch, "I felt the sudden way in which very large sections of the American press, which has hitherto appreciated my ceaseless efforts to keep our two countries in harmony, turned upon me over the Greek affair." Churchill added: "How stultified they must feel today when, after infinite toils and many hazards, every ideal in the Atlantic Charter is being secured for Greece, and when the gratitude of her people for their deliv-

36. Telegram of 1 January 1945, Prime Minister to President, No. 871, Franklin D. Roosevelt Papers.

37. Telegram of 8 January 1945, Prime Minister to President, No. 880, Franklin D. Roosevelt Papers.

38. Telegram of 10 January 1945, Prime Minister to President, No. 884, Franklin D. Roosevelt Papers.

erance from a dictatorship of a Communist gang is expressed on every side."

American criticism of his Greek policy—to support the Greek Government against the Communist insurgency—led Churchill to draw a wider lesson. As he told Baruch: "We have only to stand together and fight down harsh, premature judgements of each other's solutions of war problems, to bring the whole world out of its miseries and secure our children from a renewal of these torments."[39]

On 22 January 1945 units of the Red Army reached the Oder River. All Poland and much of eastern Germany were under Soviet control. Five days later the last German forces were driven out of Lithuania.

The Malta and Yalta meetings were imminent. On January 24 Harry Hopkins, who was then in London, sent Roosevelt a comment by Churchill on the location of Yalta: "If we had spent ten years on research we could not have found a worse place in the world."[40] Yalta involved both Churchill and Roosevelt taking a long and complicated journey to a region that had been ravaged by war. Stalin, the youngest and healthiest of the three, had refused to leave Soviet soil, even though Churchill had offered either Scotland or Jerusalem, sending Stalin a note of the continuous rail connection between Moscow and Palestine.

On January 29, Churchill left London by air for the Mediterranean and the Black Sea.

---

39. Telegram of 12 January 1945, Baruch Papers.

40. Robert E. Sherwood, *The White House Papers of Harry L. Hopkins*, Volume 2, page 839.

Chapter Thirty-Two

⌗

MALTA, YALTA AND BEYOND

Churchill reached Malta in the early hours of 30 January 1945. He was to spend three days there before flying to Yalta. He had a high fever and, after transferring to HMS *Orion*, spent the day in bed. That evening Averell Harriman was among his guests at dinner; after the other guests had left, the two played bezique together. For two more days Churchill rested. On the morning of February 2 President Roosevelt arrived on the cruiser *Quincy*. As the ship steamed slowly past HMS *Orion*, the two leaders waved to each other across the water. Two hours later Churchill went aboard the *Quincy* to lunch with Roosevelt. "What a change in the President since we saw him in Hyde Park last October," Churchill's secretary Marian Holmes noted in her diary. "He seems to have lost so much weight, has dark circles under his eyes, looks altogether frail and as if he is hardly in this world at all."[1]

At 6 o'clock that evening Churchill returned to the *Quincy*, where he and Roosevelt attended a meeting of the Combined Chiefs of Staff and listened to the results of their three days of discussion. General Ismay, who was present, later recalled: "Roosevelt looked a very sick man."[2] There was no Anglo-American dissent at the meeting. Churchill agreed to the withdrawal of three British Divisions from Alexander's army in Italy, on whose behalf he had earlier fought so hard, being anxious "that the British contribution to the heavy fighting which would be taking place in North-West Europe should be as great as possible."[3] That night, at 3.30 A.M., Churchill flew eastward to the

---

1. Diary entry, 2 February 1945, Marian Walker Spicer Papers.
2. Lord Ismay, *The Memoirs of General the Lord Ismay*, page 385.
3. Meeting of 2 February 1945, Cabinet Papers, 120/170.

Crimea, a journey of 1,400 miles, and a flight of seven hours. Reaching Simferopol, Churchill walked across the tarmac to Roosevelt's aircraft, which had arrived before his. He stood there while Roosevelt was helped out by his bodyguard and lifted into a jeep. "He could not get out of the open motor car," Churchill later wrote, "and I walked at his side while he inspected the guard."[4]

Sir Alexander Cadogan recorded the scene in his diary. "The PM walked by the side of the President, as in her old age an Indian attendant accompanied Queen Victoria's phaeton," he wrote. "They were preceded by a crowd of cameramen, walking backwards as they took snapshots. The President looked old and thin and drawn; he had a cape or shawl over his shoulders and appeared shrunken; he sat looking straight ahead with his mouth open, as if he were not taking things in. Everyone was shocked by his appearance and gabbled about it afterwards."[5]

From the airfield Churchill was driven to Yalta, where the Crimean Conference began on February 4. At the first plenary meeting, Eden noted in his diary: "President vague and loose and ineffective. W, understanding that business was flagging, made desperate efforts and two long speeches to get things going again."[6] Lord Halifax told Churchill two months later that Harry Hopkins had doubted if, at Yalta, the President "had heard more than half of what went on round the table."[7]

The first discord between Churchill and Roosevelt came when Roosevelt told him and Stalin that, while the United States would take "all reasonable steps" to preserve peace after the war, it would not be "at the expense of keeping a large army indefinitely in Europe 3,000 miles away from home." That was why the American occupation would be "limited to two years." For Churchill this statement rang loud alarm bells. What would happen, he asked, "if the Germans were to rise again." Without French help, the British "might be in difficulties."

Roosevelt and Stalin, while agreeing to a French zone of occupa-

---

4. Notes dictated by Churchill in 1950, Churchill Papers, 4/362, Martin Gilbert, *Winston S. Churchill*, Volume 7, page 1171.

5. Diary entry, 4 February 1945, David Dilks, editor, *The Diaries of Sir Alexander Cadogan, OM, 1938–1945.* page 703.

6. Diary entry, 4 February 1945, *The Reckoning: Eden Memoirs*, page 512.

7. Telegram of 15 April 1945, Churchill Papers, 20/214, Martin Gilbert, *Winston S. Churchill*, Volume 7, page 1282.

tion in Germany, opposed Churchill's desire for French participation in the proposed Allied Control Commission that would administer Germany. Britain would need "a strong French army to contain Germany in the West," Churchill told them, and went on to warn his fellow leaders that "the prolonged control of Germany without French participation would be very difficult." The Americans were "free to go away from Europe but the French would always remain next door to Germany; and the security of Great Britain demanded that France should have a strong army and should be in a position to prevent rocket sites etc., being built on the French coast."[8]

Churchill was outnumbered. Reporting five days later to the War Cabinet, he noted that the Russians were "as determined as the Americans to keep France, and especially the leader of the Free French, General Charles de Gaulle, out of the so-called Big Three."[9] For more than three years, both Churchill and Roosevelt had been vexed by de Gaulle's insistence on being the sole arbiter of the future of France.

During the second plenary session on February 6, the discussion turned to the future World Organization, and the voting on the Security Council. Churchill told Stalin and Roosevelt that while the "achievement of world peace on a lasting foundation" depended in the last resort "on the friendship and collaboration of the three Great Powers," the British government would not be doing justice to their true intentions if no provision was made "for a full statement of grievances by the many smaller nations of the world."[10] When Roosevelt agreed with Stalin that peace should be made by the Great Powers and not by the small powers, one of the Americans present, the interpreter Charles Bohlen, recalled Churchill's comment: "The eagle should permit the small birds to sing and care not wherefore they sang."[11]

One of those "small birds" was the next issue on the agenda: Poland. "Coming from America," Roosevelt remarked, and speaking as one of "the inhabitants of another hemisphere," he took "a distant view of the Polish question." The five or six million Poles in the United States, he added, were "mostly of the second generation." This

---

8. Meeting of 5 February 1945, Cabinet Papers, 120/170.

9. Telegram of 10 February 1945, Cabinet Papers, 120/180.

10. Meeting of 6 February 1945, Cabinet Papers, 120/170.

11. Charles E. Bohlen, *Witness of History*, page 181.

dismissive—indeed callous—attitude toward the future government and independence of Poland did not help Churchill when he insisted that he was "more interested to see a strong, free, independent Poland than he was in a particular national boundary."[12]

At the third plenary session on February 7 Churchill again asked that France should have a place on the Control Commission for Germany in addition to a zone of occupation, asking Stalin and Roosevelt: "Why not therefore settle the question here before parting?" Roosevelt replied, however, that they should "let it rest for several weeks." Churchill was not satisfied. Once they separated, he said, "he did not know what would happen, as correspondence on a matter such as this might drag on for months." His argument was in vain. Stalin supported Roosevelt, pointing out that they had "settled many questions by correspondence."[13] Before the conference ended, however, Churchill's persistence was rewarded: Roosevelt and Stalin agreed that France should be a member of the Allied Control Commission for Germany.

In the bilateral Anglo-American sphere, Churchill was pleased to report to Attlee and the War Cabinet on February 8 that, in the discussions that were talking place at Yalta about postwar American help for Britain, the Americans "tell us repeatedly that they are resolved to see us through after the war till we can get into a normal position." He then quoted the new American Secretary of State, Edward Stettinius, saying that "they will pile ships to us beyond any tonnage we have ever possessed in our history," and commented: "This shows the good spirit prevailing."[14]

At a meeting of the British and American delegations at noon on February 9, Churchill put forward a proposal to shorten the war against Japan: a Four-Power ultimatum, in which China would be the fourth power, calling on Japan "to surrender unconditionally, or else be subjected to the overwhelming weight of all the forces of the Four Powers." If Japan accepted this ultimatum, he said, some "mitigation" might be extended to it; there was "no doubt that some mitigation would be worthwhile if it led to the saving of a year or a year and a half

---

12. Meeting of 6 February 1945, Cabinet Papers, 120/170.
13. Meeting of 7 February 1945, Cabinet Papers, 120/170.
14. Telegram of 8 February 1945, Churchill Papers, 20/223, Martin Gilbert, *Winston S. Churchill*, Volume 7, page 1195.

of a war in which so much blood and treasure would be poured out." Roosevelt disagreed. The Japanese, he said, "would be unlikely to wake up to the true state of affairs until all of their islands had felt the full weight of air attack."[15] No ultimatum was sent. The bombing of the mainland islands went on.

Following the plenary session on the afternoon of February 9, there was a serious disagreement between Churchill and Roosevelt over Poland. At the plenary meeting the Big Three had agreed a formula pledging "free and unfettered elections as soon as practical" in Poland, "on the basis of universal suffrage and secret ballot." The next morning Churchill learned from Anthony Eden that Roosevelt, at a private meeting with Stalin, had offered the Soviet leader a modification of the pledge, withdrawing the universal suffrage and secret ballot "tail piece" from the formal document, in return for saying "something of the kind" publicly. Eden told Churchill: "The Americans gave us no warning and I don't propose to agree to their action." Churchill replied: "Certainly do not agree."[16] He wanted no modification or amendment to the promise of free elections in Poland. But it was too late to change what had been agreed.

Roosevelt's compromise with Stalin was to distress Churchill for many years. Eight years after Yalta, as part of Eisenhower's campaign for election as President, the Republicans denounced the "immorality" of the Yalta agreements in abandoning Poland to Communism Jock Colville pointed out to Churchill that by implication "these charges might have been extended to you and the Coalition Government in this country."[17] Churchill wrote to Eden—who was again his Foreign Secretary: "I do not think that you and I should be compelled to linger under this vague but implied censure of having made agreements involving enslavement etc. The facts of what happened at Yalta should be disclosed, namely that arrangements were made between the President and Stalin direct. We were only informed of them at our parting luncheon, when all had been already agreed, and we had no part in making them."[18]

15. Meeting of 9 February 1945, Cabinet Papers, 120/170.
16. Note of 10 February 1945, Foreign Office Papers, 954/20.
17. Note of 27 February 1953, Premier Papers, 11/432.
18. Minute of 22 February 1953, Premier Papers, 11/432.

• • •

On the afternoon of February 10 Roosevelt announced that he would
be leaving Yalta on the following day, thus ending the Crimean Conference. "The President is behaving very badly," Churchill remarked to
his doctor at breakfast on February 11. "He won't take any interest in
what we are trying to do."[19] That afternoon the President left Yalta, followed an hour later by Churchill. While both men were on board their
respective warships, Roosevelt on the *Quincy* and Churchill on the
Franconia, another Anglo-American operation of war took place, the
bombing of Dresden. On the night of February 13–14, 774 British
bombers drooped 2,646 tons of high-explosive and incendiary bombs,
followed on the morning of February 14 by 450 American bombers,
which dropped 689 tons of bombs.

This massive and devastating raid was carried out as a result of an
urgent Soviet request to interrupt the movement of large numbers of
German troops through Dresden toward the embattled Eastern Front.
Enigma had revealed these troop movements: The Soviet High Command saw no other way of preventing them than by appealing for help
to Britain and the United States.[20] At Yalta the British, American and
Soviet Chiefs of Staff had jointly approved the raid. When Churchill
learned of the extent of the devastation he was horrified, calling the
destruction of Dresden "a serious query against the conduct of Allied
bombing."[21] Roosevelt's reaction—he was commander-in-Chief of the
United States Army Air Forces—is not known.

Four days after leaving Yalta, Churchill and Roosevelt met again,
off the coast of Egypt, on board the *Quincy.* Churchill later recalled
Roosevelt's "placid, frail, aspect."[22] Alone for a while with Roosevelt
and Hopkins, Churchill read them a proposal for the development of
atomic bomb research in Britain after the war. The President "made
no objection of any kind," Churchill noted.[23]

The President left Egyptian waters that afternoon. "This was the

---

19. Notes for 11 February 1945, Lord Moran (Sir Charles Wilson), *Winston Churchill: The Struggle for Survival, 1940–1965,* page 231.
20. Martin Gilbert, *Second World War,* pages 636, 638 and 640.
21. Minute of 28 March 1945, Premier Papers, 3/12, folio 25.
22. Notes written in December 1950, Churchill Papers, 4/362, Martin Gilbert,
Winston S. Churchill, Volume 7, page 1222.
23. Minute of 16 February 1945, Premier Papers, 3/139/11A.

last time I saw Roosevelt," Churchill later wrote. "We parted affectionately. I felt he had a slender contact with life."[24]

Returning to Britain, Churchill reflected on the workings of the Big Three, telling his visitors at Chequers on February 24, "a small lion was walking between a huge Russian bear and a great American elephant, but perhaps it would prove to be the lion who knew the way."[25]

On March 3 Churchill flew to Holland, from where he went to the sector of the front held by the American Ninth Army. Escorted by the Ninth Army Commander, Lieutenant-General William H. Simpson, he was taken to the Siegfried Line, the German anti-tank barrier the Americans had recently overrun.

While standing in the anti-tank "dragon teeth" defenses, Churchill asked the journalists present to put down their cameras, whereupon he and Simpson, and two recently promoted Field Marshals, Brooke and Montgomery, relieved themselves on the once much-feared Siegfried Line.[26]

Within days of leaving Yalta, Stalin reneged on the Yalta pledge of free elections in Poland. In challenging this, Churchill was in regular contact with Averell Harriman, who had been appointed American Ambassador in Moscow, and who worked closely with his British opposite number. Their efforts were in vain. Stalin's troops and secret police, already in control of Poland, had no intention of sharing that control with the Polish democrats. When the United States wavered with regard to the inclusion in the new Polish Government of Stanislaw Mikolajczyk, the leader of the Polish Government in London, Churchill told the War Cabinet that, in making it clear to the Russians that Mikolajczyk must be included, Britain was "entitled to expect the full support of the USA in doing so, and must carry them with us; for we could do no more to help the Poles than the United States would help us to."[27]

---

24. Notes dictated by Churchill while writing his war memoirs, Churchill Papers, 4/361, Martin Gilbert, *Winston S. Churchill,* Volume 7, page 1223.
25. Diary entry, 24 February 1945, Colville Papers.
26. Recollection of Ralph G. Martin, then a writer with the United States forces newspaper *Stars and Stripes,* in conversation with the author, 18 April 2005.
27. War Cabinet of 6 March 1945, Cabinet Papers, 65/51.

Churchill appealed directly to the ailing Roosevelt. "I think you will agree with me," he telegraphed, "that far more than the case of Poland is involved." Poland was "the test case between us and the Russians of the meaning which is to be attached to such terms as democracy, sovereignty, independence, representative Government and free and unfettered elections."[28] Roosevelt was not well enough to respond. On the following day Churchill learned that the Americans were proposing a political truce in Poland. Fearing that this would give total control to the Communist forces, whose deportations and killings of opponents had become widely known, he decided to telegraph to Roosevelt again. One sentence, which Churchill deleted before the telegram was sent, read: "If we two get out of step the doom of Poland is sealed."[29] The telegram as sent urged Roosevelt to press Stalin to carry out the "spirit and intent" of the Yalta pledge.

The reply, sent from "President to Prime Minister," was written in its entirety by Admiral Leahy and the State Department. Even the Yalta decision that high-level observers should monitor the Polish elections was to be watered down. The American view—and Churchill believed that the telegram came from Roosevelt—was that "more would be accomplished by pressing for low-level observers at this point," who would "certainly see as much if not more than some spectacular body."[30]

Churchill received a second telegram that day, also entirely the work of Leahy and the State Department, but again written in the first person, as if by the President. The telegram asked Churchill to wait to see how their respective diplomats managed the matter "before either you or I intervene personally with Stalin. . . . I very much hope, therefore, that you will not send any message to Uncle Joe at this juncture—especially as I feel certain that parts of your proposed text might produce a reaction quite contrary to your intent."[31] Not one "I" in this telegram had been written or even seen by Roosevelt.

---

28. Telegram of 8 March 1945, Prime Minister to President, No. 905, Franklin D. Roosevelt Papers.

29. Draft telegram, 10 March 1945, Premier Papers, 3/356/9.

30. Telegram of 11 March 1945, Churchill Papers, 20/212, Martin Gilbert, *Winston S. Churchill,* Volume 7, page 1249.

31. Telegram of 11 March 1945, Churchill Papers, 20/212, Martin Gilbert, *Winston S. Churchill,* Volume 7, pages 1249–50.

Unaware that Roosevelt was not a party to this exchange, ostensibly in his name, Churchill made one last effort. "At Yalta also," he wrote, "we agreed to take the Russian view of the frontier line. Poland has lost her frontier. Is she now to lose her freedom?" That question "will undoubtedly have to be fought out in Parliament and in public here." Three members of his government had already resigned in protest at what they saw as the betrayal of Poland. Churchill went on to warn Roosevelt: "I do not wish to reveal a divergence between the British and the United States Governments, but it would certainly be necessary for me to make it clear that we are in the presence of a great failure and an utter breakdown of what was settled at Yalta, but that we British have not the necessary strength to carry the matter further and that the limits of our capacity to act have been reached." Churchill believed, he told Roosevelt, that "combined dogged pressure and persistence along the lines on which we have been working and of my proposed draft message to Stalin, would very likely succeed."[32]

Roosevelt was too ill to apply that "dogged pressure." Yet without American concurrence and common action, the limits of Britain's "capacity to act" had indeed been reached, not only toward Poland but throughout Eastern Europe and the Balkans. In a note to Eden on March 13, Churchill commented on "the weakness of the United States diplomacy."[33] Not only American diplomacy, but American economic policy, was causing him distress. At the War Cabinet on March 14, it was announced that during the second quarter of 1945, for economic reasons, in view of Britain's growing indebtedness, the United States proposed a halt to all meat exports to Britain.[34]

Churchill received one more telegram from Roosevelt about Poland that had been written in the President's name by his staff. It rebuked Churchill for claiming that there was a "divergence" between the two Governments on the Polish question. It again set out, however—the third telegram in three days to do so—American reluctance to challenge the Soviet Union over the question of the diplomatic ob-

---

32. Telegram of 13 March 1945, Prime Minister to President, No. 910, Franklin D. Roosevelt Papers.

33. Minute of 13 March 1945, Churchill Papers, 20/209, Martin Gilbert, *Winston S. Churchill*, Volume 7, page 1251.

34. War Cabinet of 14 March 1945, Cabinet Papers, 85/44.

servers. The "demand for freedom of movement and communications," the telegram stated, "would arouse needless discussion at this stage in the negotiations."[35] Churchill's wish for plain speaking and a sterner stance had been dismissed.

On March 13 Churchill had a long talk with Roosevelt's friend and emissary Judge Samuel Rosenman about postwar American food supplies to Britain. During their talk Rosenman told him that Roosevelt was gravely ill. Pondering the crucial nature of their communications, and their obvious breakdown, on March 18 Churchill sent Roosevelt words of encouragement, family news and reflections. "I hope that the rather numerous telegrams I have to send you on so many of our difficult and intertwined affairs are not becoming a bore to you," he wrote. "Our friendship is the rock on which I build for the future of the world so long as I am one of the builders."

Churchill continued on a personal note of encouragement and warmth, listing the high points of their relationship: "I always think of those tremendous days when you devised Lend-Lease, when we met at Argentia, when you decided with my heartfelt agreement to launch the invasion of Africa, and when you comforted me for the loss of Tobruk by giving me the 300 Shermans of subsequent Alamein fame. I remember the part our personal relations have played in the advance of the World Cause now nearing its final military goal." As for the future, peace with Germany and Japan "on our terms will not bring much rest to you and me (if I am still responsible). As I observed last time, when the war of the giants is over, the wars of the pygmies will begin. There will be a torn, ragged and hungry world to help to its feet; and what will Uncle Joe or his successor say to the way we should both like to do it?"

Churchill wanted to put Roosevelt's mind at rest that he was not raising any policy issue. "The advantage of this telegram," he wrote, "is that it has nothing to do with shop except that I had a good talk with Rosenman about our daily bread," and he signed off as he would have ended had it been a letter: "All good wishes, Winston."[36]

That day American forces entered Bingen, on the west bank of the Rhine. British troops were in Holland. In Moscow the Soviets were still

---

35. Telegram of 16 March 1945, Premier Papers, 3/359/9.
36. Telegram of 18 March 1945, Prime Minister to President, No. 914, Franklin D. Roosevelt Papers.

refusing to allow Western diplomats to act as observers in the Polish elections. On March 24 Eden told Churchill that the British Ambassador in Moscow was being hampered in his advocacy "by lack of support from Harriman."[37]

Another area that caused Churchill distress was the misrepresentation in the United States of Britain's food reserves. Publicity had been given in American newspapers to the figure of 700 million tons of food in Britain. This figure was a figment of an anti-British imagination. On March 22 Churchill authorized the War Cabinet "to state the actual figure at which these reserves now stood, viz., only about 6 million tons."[38]

On March 25 Churchill was on German soil, where he spent time with Eisenhower at his headquarters. Six days later, after his return to London, he and Eisenhower were in serious dispute. The Soviets had persuaded Eisenhower to direct his final offensive not against Berlin but farther south, through Leipzig to Dresden. Eisenhower defended this change of plan on the grounds that the German Government departments had left or were leaving Berlin for the south. "General Eisenhower may be wrong in supposing Berlin to be largely devoid of military and political importance," Churchill wrote to the British Chiefs of Staff. Although the German Government departments had "to a great extent moved to the south," he added, "the dominating fact on German minds of the fall of Berlin should not be overlooked. The idea of neglecting Berlin and leaving it to the Russians to take at a later stage does not appear to me correct."

Churchill told the Chiefs of Staff: "As long as Berlin holds out and withstands a siege in the ruins, as it may easily do, German resistance will be stimulated. The fall of Berlin might cause nearly all Germans to despair." Under Eisenhower's plan, Churchill noted, British forces "might be condemned to an almost static role in the North and virtually prevented from crossing the Elbe until an altogether later stage in the operations has been reached. All prospect also of the British entering Berlin with the Americans is ruled out."[39]

In reply, Eisenhower explained to Churchill that the aim of the

---

37. Minute of 24 March 1945, Premier Papers, 3/339/11.
38. War Cabinet of 21 March 1945, Cabinet Papers, 65/9.
39. Minute of 31 March 1945, Premier Papers, 3/398/5.

more southerly thrust was to "join hands with the Russians or to attain the general line of the River Elbe."[40] To this Churchill replied: "If the enemy's resistance should weaken, as you evidently expect and which may well be fulfilled, why should we not cross the Elbe and advance as far eastward as possible?" This had an "important political bearing," Churchill explained, "as the Russian armies of the South seem certain to enter Vienna and overrun Austria. If we deliberately leave Berlin to them, even if it should be in our grasp, the double event may strengthen their conviction, already apparent, that they have done everything."[41]

Churchill still could not accept that Berlin should be bypassed. "The fall of Berlin would have a profound psychological effect on German resistance in every part of the Reich," he told Eisenhower. While Berlin held out, "great masses of Germans will feel it their duty to go down fighting." While Berlin remained "under the German flag it cannot, in my opinion, fail to be the most decisive point in Germany." Churchill went on to urge Eisenhower to persist in the earlier plan "that the 9th US Army should march with the 21st Army Group to the Elbe and beyond Berlin." Churchill added: "This would not be in any way inconsistent with the great central thrust which you are now so rightly developing as the result of the brilliant operations of your Armies south of the Ruhr. It only shifts the weight of one army to the northern flank and this avoids the relegation of His Majesty's forces to an unexpectedly restricted sphere."[42]

This last sentence spurred Eisenhower to a strong response. "I am disturbed, if not hurt," he wrote, "that you should suggest any thought on my part to 'relegate His Majesty's forces to an unexpectedly restricted sphere.' Nothing is further from my mind and I think my record of over two and a half years conduct commanding the Allied forces should eliminate any such idea."[43] On the following day Churchill replied to Eisenhower, seeking to mollify him. "It would be a grief to me if anything in my last disturbed or still more pained you," he wrote. "I only meant that the effect of the 21st Army Group arriving on

---

40. Telegram of 30 March 1945, Premier Papers, 3/398/5.
41. Telegram (IZ 3172) of 31 March 1945, Premier Papers, 3/398/5.
42. Telegram (T. 374/5) of 31 March 1945, Premier Papers, 3/398/5.
43. Telegram of 1 April 1945, Premier Papers, 3/398/5.

the Elbe so spread out that it would be condemned to a static role would be a good deal less than what we hoped for, namely, to enter Berlin side by side with our American comrades."

In Churchill's mind the possibility of the Anglo-American forces reaching Berlin had an even more significant objective: Poland itself. As he told Eisenhower, he was "all the more impressed with the importance of entering Poland, which may well be open to us." This was especially so, he pointed out, in the light of a recent Soviet message to Eisenhower that stated: "Berlin has lost its former strategic importance." This sentence, Churchill added, "should be read in the light of what I mentioned of the political aspects. I deem it highly important that we should shake hands with the Russians as far to the East as possible."[44] The Soviet message to Eisenhower was clearly designed, and successfully so, to lull Eisenhower into continuing with the southern thrust, leaving the Red Army to take Berlin.

Churchill did not want Roosevelt to feel that the Berlin dispute had created a breach with Eisenhower. "My personal relations with General Eisenhower are of the most friendly character," he wrote to assure the President, who was then at Warm Springs, Georgia. "I regard the matter as closed, and to prove my sincerity I will use one of my very few Latin quotations: *Amantium irae amoris integratio est.*"[45] When Churchill's secretary Marian Holmes said she did not know the meaning of this quotation, Churchill told her: "It means the wrath of lovers hots up their love."[46] Roosevelt's staff translated the quotation for him somewhat more prosaically as "Lovers' quarrels always go with true love."[47]

On the following day Churchill wrote to his wife, who was in the Soviet Union for her Red Cross Aid to Russia Fund, describing the dispute with Eisenhower. "The only times I ever quarrel with the Americans," he wrote, "are when they fail to give us a fair share of opportunity to win glory."[48]

44. Telegram of 2 April 1945, Premier Papers, 3/398/5.
45. Telegram of 5 April 1945, Prime Minister to President, No. 933, Premier Papers, 3/398/5.
46. Marian Walker Spicer (Marian Holmes) Papers.
47. Quoted in Warren F. Kimball, *Churchill & Roosevelt: The Complete Correspondence,* Volume 3, page 612. Literally: "The quarrels of lovers are the renewal of love."
48. Letter of 6 April 1945, Baroness Spencer-Churchill Papers.

• • •

Churchill understood that, for all his efforts to advance the British point of view, henceforth the United States would always be the dominant partner. On April 3, at a meeting of the War Cabinet attended by Dominion and Indian representatives, he explained that the American resources in men and war material were "vastly superior to our own; and they had acquired during this war a new capacity and experience in marshalling these resources in war."[49] Four days later Churchill told his guests at Chequers, including Judge Rosenman, that "there was no greater exhibition of power in history than the American army fighting the battle of the Ardennes with its left hand and advancing from island to island towards Japan with its right."[50]

Britain and the British Commonwealth could only "hold their own," Churchill had told the War Cabinet, "by our superior statecraft and experience, and above all, by the unity of the British Commonwealth of Nations."[51] That statecraft included Churchill's own blunt speaking. At Chequers he told Judge Rosenman: "Britain shall not starve or lower her exiguous rations still further to feed Axis satellites, while the American army and civil population live on their present gigantic diet."[52]

On April 9 came a telegram from Roosevelt rejecting Churchill's wish to raise once more with Stalin the suppression of democratic procedures in Poland. This telegram, the historian Warren Kimball has noted, was "one of the very few messages the President drafted personally during his stay in Warm Springs."[53] It was not as supportive as Churchill wished. "I would minimize the general Soviet problem as much as possible," Roosevelt wrote, "because these problems, in one form or another, seem to arise every day and most of them straighten out." The telegram ended, in a somewhat different tone: "We must be firm, however, and our course thus far is correct."[54]

This telegram apart, Roosevelt was relying almost entirely on oth-

---

49. War Cabinet of 3 April 1945, Cabinet Papers, 65/50.
50. Diary entry, 7 April 1945, Colville Papers.
51. War Cabinet of 3 April 1945, Cabinet Papers, 65/50.
52. Diary entry, 7 April 1945, Colville Papers.
53. Warren F. Kimball, *Churchill & Roosevelt: The Complete Correspondence*, Volume 3, page 630.
54. Telegram of 9 April 1945, Premier Papers, 3/356/6.

ers to write his messages to Churchill. Harry Hopkins later told Lord Halifax—who telegraphed to Churchill from Washington—that Roosevelt was so ill that "hardly anything" of his recent telegrams to Churchill "had been his own."[55] One such telegram had quite deceived Churchill by its skillful drafting, ending, he told Clementine, "with a flash of his old fire, and is about the hottest thing I have seen so far in diplomatic intercourse."[56]

On the night of April 12, shortly after midnight, Churchill went to bed. "It was three o'clock in the morning," his detective later recalled, "when the Prime Minister's bell rang in my room. I went at once to his bedroom and through the half-open door heard his voice saying: 'Terrible, terrible.' When I entered he was walking across the floor with his head bowed. When he turned to look at me, I saw there were tears running down his cheeks. 'Have you heard the awful news, Thompson?' he said. I replied, 'No, sir.' 'President Roosevelt has passed away.'"[57]

55. Telegram of 15 April 1945, Churchill Papers, 20/214, Martin Gilbert, *Winston S. Churchill*, Volume 7, page 1282.
56. Letter of 6 April 1945, Baroness Spencer-Churchill Papers.
57. W. H. Thompson, *I Was Churchill's Shadow*, page 153.

Chapter Thirty-Three

⚙

"WE MUST MAKE SURE THAT THE UNITED STATES ARE WITH US"

In the early hours of 13 April 1945, within minutes of learning that Roosevelt was dead, Churchill telegraphed to Lord Halifax in Washington to ask if it would be all right if he came to the funeral. "Have spoken to Harry Hopkins and Stettinius, who are both much moved by your thought of possibly coming over," Halifax replied that same night, "and who both warmly agree with my judgment of the immense effect for good that would be produced. Nor do I overlook the value if you came of your seeing Truman." As Vice-President, Truman had automatically succeeded Roosevelt as President. The funeral at Hyde Park would be private except for Roosevelt's Cabinet, Halifax added, "and of course you if you came."[1]

Halifax's telegram arrived at dawn on April 13. That morning Churchill made plans to fly to New York in time for Roosevelt's funeral at Hyde Park, telling the head of his map room, Captain Pim: "I am much weakened in every way by his loss."[2] Churchill's first message of condolence was to Eleanor Roosevelt. "Accept my most profound sympathy in your grievous loss," he wrote, "which is also the loss of the British nation and of the cause of freedom in every land. I feel so deeply for you all. As for myself, I have lost a dear and cherished friendship which was forged in the fire of war. I trust you may find consolation in the magnitude of his work and the glory of his

---

1. Telegram of 12 April 1945, Churchill Papers, 20/214, Martin Gilbert, *Winston S. Churchill*, Volume 7, page 1291.
2. Sir Richard Pim, recollections, Pim Papers.

name."[3] To Harry Hopkins, Churchill also wrote that morning: "I understand how deep your feelings of grief must be. I feel with you that we have lost one of our greatest friends and one of the most valiant champions of the causes for which we fight. I feel a very painful personal loss quite apart from the ties of public action which bound us so closely together." Churchill added: "I had a true affection for Franklin."[4]

Churchill's third message was to the new President, Harry S. Truman, with whom from that moment he would have to be in the closest touch on a daily basis. "Pray accept from me the expression of my personal sympathy in the loss which you and the American nation have sustained in the death of our illustrious friend," Churchill wrote. "I hope that I may be privileged to renew with you the intimate comradeship in the great cause we all serve that I enjoyed through these terrible years with him. I offer you my respectful good wishes as you step into the breach in the victorious lines of the United Nations."[5]

The new President was anxious to see Churchill, the two men never having met. "Truman's idea," Halifax telegraphed, "was that after the funeral you might have two or three days' talk with him.[6]

That afternoon Churchill went to the House of Commons, where he moved the adjournment of the House as a tribute to Roosevelt, "whose friendship for the cause of freedom and for the causes of the weak and poor have won his immortal renown."[7] One of those present wrote in a private letter: "I feel deeply for Winston, and this afternoon it was evident from his manner that it was a real body-blow."[8] That same afternoon Churchill made plans to fly to the United States. The airplane would leave at 8:30 that night. By 7:45 P.M., however, no deci-

---

3. Telegram (T.450/5) of 13 April 1945, Churchill Papers, 20/214, Martin Gilbert, *Winston S. Churchill*, Volume 7, page 1292.

4. Telegram (T.454/5) of 13 April 1945, Churchill Papers, 20/199, Martin Gilbert, *Winston S. Churchill*, Volume 7, page 1292.

5. Telegram (T.455/5) of 13 April 1945, Truman Papers.

6. Telegram (No. 2487) of 13 April 1945, Churchill Papers, 20/199, Martin Gilbert, *Winston S. Churchill*, Volume 7, page 1294.

7. Speech of 13 April 1945, *Hansard*, Parliamentary debates.

8. Harold Nicolson, letter of 13 April 1945, Nigel Nicolson, editor, *Harold Nicolson: Diaries and Letters, 1939–1945*, page 447.

sion had been reached whether to go or not to go. Alexander Cadogan noted in his diary, "PM said he would decide at aerodrome."[9]

Churchill decided not to go. "It would have been a solace to me to be present at Franklin's funeral," he telegraphed to Hopkins that night, "but everyone here thought my duty next week lay at home, at a time when so many Ministers are out of the country."[10] Ironically, Churchill had already intimated this to Roosevelt, to whom he had telegraphed a month earlier: "I am sending to Washington and San Francisco most of my Ministerial colleagues on one Mission or another, and I shall on this occasion stay at home to mind the shop."[11]

Clement Attlee, Anthony Eden and another senior Cabinet Minister were in the United States for the San Francisco Conference, for the establishment of the United Nations. "I was tempted during the day to go over for the funeral and begin relations with the new man," Churchill wrote to King George VI. "However so many of Your Majesty's Ministers are out of the country, and the Foreign Secretary had arranged to go anyhow, and I felt the business next week in Parliament and also the ceremonies connected with the death of Mr Roosevelt are so important that I should be failing in my duty if I left the House of Commons without my close personal attention." Churchill explained to the King that he had also to consider "the tribute which should be paid to the late President, which clearly it is my business to deliver. The press of work was also very heavy. Therefore I thought it better that I should remain here in charge at this juncture."[12]

Truman was sorry to lose the chance of an immediate meeting with Churchill. His Secretary of State made it clear to him in a memorandum on April 13 that "Mr Churchill's policy is based fundamentally upon cooperation with the United States."[13] "At no time in our respec-

---

9. Diary entry, 13 April 1945, David Dilks, editor, *The Diaries of Sir Alexander Cadogan, OM, 1938–1945*, page 727.

10. Telegram (T.459/5) of 13 April 1945, Churchill Papers, 20/199, Martin Gilbert, *Winston S. Churchill*, Volume 7, page 1294.

11. Telegram of 18 March 1945, Prime Minister to President, No. 624, Franklin D. Roosevelt Papers.

12. Letter of 13 April 1945, Royal Archives.

13. Edward Stettinius to President Truman, "Special Information for the President," 13 April 1945, Warren F. Kimball, editor, *Churchill and Roosevelt: The Complete Correspondence*, Volume 3, pages 633–37.

tive histories," Truman telegraphed to Churchill that day, "has it been more important that the intimate, solid relations which you and the late President had forged between our countries be preserved and developed. It is my earnest hope that before too long, in the furtherance of this, we can arrange a personal meeting."

In the meantime, Truman continued, there were urgent problems requiring their immediate and joint consideration. "I have in mind the pressing and dangerous problem of Poland and the Soviet attitude towards the Moscow negotiations. I am, of course, familiar with the exchanges which you and President Roosevelt have had between yourselves and with Marshal Stalin. I also know in general what President Roosevelt had in mind as the next step." [14]

The reference Truman made to the "dangerous problem of Poland," and to the Moscow negotiations on the composition of a Polish Provisional Government of National Unity—in which both Communist and non-Communist Polish leaders would participate—was the first of a series of almost daily exchanges between Churchill and the new President on the questions of Poland and the emerging conflicts with the Soviet Union. Theirs was to prove a far closer meeting of minds on the Soviet Union than had existed between Churchill and Roosevelt. "I have had a very nice telegram from President Truman," Churchill wrote to Clementine, "opening our relations on the best conditions." [15] On April 15 Churchill and Truman sent a joint telegram to Stalin, urging that the leading London Poles should be invited to Moscow "to participate in the discussions about the composition of a Polish Government of National Unity." [16]

On the morning of April 17 Churchill was in St. Paul's Cathedral at Roosevelt's memorial service. Henry Channon, a Conservative Member of Parliament, noted in his diary how, after the service, Ambassador Winant "escorted Winston, who was in tears, to the door." A few minutes later Channon and his son left the cathedral, and "turning back towards St Paul's we saw Winston standing bare-headed,

---

14. Telegram of 13 April 1945, Churchill Papers, 20/214, President to Prime Minister, No. 1, Martin Gilbert, *Winston S. Churchill*, Volume 7, page 1295.

15. Telegram of 14 April 1945, Baroness Spencer-Churchill Papers.

16. Telegram of 15 April 1945, Churchill Papers, 20/214, Martin Gilbert, *Winston S. Churchill*, Volume 7, page 1298.

framed between two columns of the portico, and he was sobbing as the shaft of sunlight fell on his face and the cameras clicked."[17]

After lunching alone, Churchill went to the House of Commons to make his tribute to Roosevelt. Of their exchange of more than 1,700 messages, and their nine wartime meetings, he declared: "I conceived an admiration for him as a statesman, a man of affairs, and a war leader. I felt the utmost confidence in his upright, inspiring character and outlook, and a personal regard—affection I must say—for him beyond my power to express today."

Churchill then spoke of Roosevelt's qualities. "His love of his own country, his respect for its Constitution, his power of gauging the tides and currents of its mobile public opinion were always evident," he said, "but added to these were the beatings of that generous heart which was always stirred to anger and to action by spectacles of aggression and oppression by the strong against the weak. It is, indeed, a loss, a bitter loss to humanity that those heart-beats are stilled for ever."

It was Roosevelt who had devised Lend-Lease, "which will stand forth as the most unselfish and unsordid financial act of any country in all history." Even in his last months he faced his innumerable tasks unflinchingly: "When death came suddenly upon him 'he had finished his mail.' That portion of his day's work was done. As the saying goes, he died in harness, and we may well say in battle harness, like his soldiers, sailors, and airmen, who side by side with ours are carrying on their task to the end all over the world. What an enviable death was his. He had brought his country through the worst of its perils and the heaviest of its toils. Victory had cast its sure and steady beam upon him." In President Roosevelt, Churchill ended, "there died the greatest American friend we have ever known, and the greatest champion of freedom who has ever brought help and comfort from the new world to the old."[18]

After a week of Truman's presidency, Churchill had formed a clear opinion of his new Washington partner. "My appreciation is," he telegraphed to Eden on April 20, "that the new man is not to be bul-

---

17. Diary entry, 17 April 1945, Robert Rhodes James, editor, *Chips: The Diaries of Sir Henry Channon*, page 402.
18. Tribute of 17 April 1945, *Hansard*, Parliamentary debates.

lied by the Soviets. Seeking as I do a lasting friendship with the Russian people, I am sure this can only be founded on the recognition of Anglo-American strength."[19] In Washington, Eden was discussing Poland with Stettinius and Molotov. "I am in full accord with all you are doing to stiffen the Americans and back them up to the hilt," Churchill telegraphed to Eden. "Especially should they not be sensitive to a charge of 'ganging up' with us. Of course we shall work together and assist each other when we are in close agreement on large moral issues like this."[20]

Churchill's new transatlantic partner was an ally in firmness, under no illusions about the harshness of Soviet intentions. On April 23 in Washington, Truman told the Soviet Foreign Minister, Vyacheslav Molotov, that the American Government "cannot agree to be a party to the formation of a Polish Government which is not representative of all Polish democratic elements." Truman added that the American Government was "deeply disappointed that the Soviet Government had not found it possible to carry out consultations with a representative group of Polish leaders, other than those new officials of the Warsaw regime." Truman at once telegraphed an account of this conversation to Churchill.[21]

As Germany's defeat drew ever closer, with American and Soviet forces having linked up on the Elbe, cutting Germany in half, the political divisions of postwar Europe emerged as an imminent source of Anglo-American conflict. Speaking by telephone to General Eisenhower on the morning of April 24, Churchill expressed his hope for an American military drive to Prague, which, with American troops already inside Czechoslovakia, was entirely within the realm of possibility. "I asked him," Churchill wrote to the Chiefs of Staff, "whether he had deflected his troops from Prague to the south-east, to which he replied that he had never meant to go to Prague as there were two or three good [German] divisions in the very west of Czechoslovakia, and it

---

19. Telegram of 20 April 1945, Foreign Office Papers (Eden Papers).
20. Telegram of 24 April 1945, Foreign Office papers (Eden Papers).
21. Telegram of 23 April 1945, Churchill Papers, 20/216, Martin Gilbert, *Winston S. Churchill*, Volume 7, page 1309.

would mean a serious alteration in the long-laid-down plans." Resigned to watch a Soviet occupation of Prague, Churchill added: "I thought it was too late now to bring the political aspect before him."[22]

On the following day, Stalin's suspicions were aroused when he was told, by telegram from Churchill, that the head of the SS, Heinrich Himmler, had offered to surrender all the German forces fighting in northern, western and southern Germany to Britain and the United States. Half an hour after informing Stalin of this offer, Churchill telephoned Truman, who took the call at the communications center in the Pentagon. It was the first time they had spoken to each other. The conversation, recorded by the Americans, began as follows:

Churchill: "Is that you, Mr. President?"

Truman: "This is the President, Mr. Prime Minister."

Churchill: "How glad I am to hear your voice."

Truman: "Thank you very much, I am glad to hear yours."

Churchill: "I have several times talked to Franklin, but. . . . Have you received the report from Stockholm by your Ambassador?"

Truman: "Yes, I have."

Churchill: "On that proposal?"

Truman: "Yes. I have just a short message saying that there was such a proposal in existence."

It was obvious to both Churchill and Truman that Himmler's aim was to turn Britain and America into allies of Germany against the Soviet Union. Britain had already made it clear, Churchill told Truman, "that there could be no question as far as His Majesty's Government is concerned of anything less than unconditional surrender simultaneously to the three major powers." "All right," Truman replied. "I agree to that."

Churchill and Truman then spoke about the possibility of a conference between them in little more than a month's time. He would be sending "some telegrams about that quite soon," Churchill told Truman, and he added: "I entirely agree with all that you've done on the Polish situation. We are walking hand in hand together."

Truman: "Well, I want to continue just that."

_____

22. Minute of 24 April 1945, Premier Papers, 3/139/11A.

Churchill: "In fact, I am following your lead, backing up whatever you do on the matter."

Truman: "Thank you. Good night."[23]

On April 30 Churchill proposed to Truman that they issue a joint protest to Stalin about the way the Soviet military authorities were exploiting their arrival in Austria to establish political control before the arrival of the British and American troops, who were even then approaching its borders. Truman agreed. Churchill also saw danger in the rapid imposition of Soviet control in Czechoslovakia, and in a second telegram to Truman on April 30 suggested that Eisenhower's forces take advantage of "any suitable opportunity that may arise" to advance into Czechoslovakia.

"There can be little doubt," Churchill informed Truman, that the liberation of Prague and as much as possible of the territory of western Czechoslovakia by American forces "might make the whole difference to the post-war situation in Czechoslovakia and might well influence that in nearby countries." On the other hand, Churchill warned, "if the Western Allies play no significant part in Czechoslovakia's liberation, that country will go the way of Yugoslavia."[24] At that moment, Marshal Tito and the Yugoslav Communists were in control of Slovenia, Croatia, Serbia, Bosnia-Herzegovina and Macedonia, the component parts of the prewar Yugoslav kingdom.

Even as Churchill's telegram was on its way to Truman, any chance of an American thrust to Prague was lost. On the following day, May 1, Eisenhower telegraphed that he would not advance beyond Austria. On the previous evening he had informed the Deputy Chief of the Soviet General Staff, General Antonov, of this self-denying ordinance. "From the political point of view," the Permanent Under-Secretary of State at the Foreign Office, Sir Orme Sargent, wrote to Churchill on May 1, "it would have been better if he had said nothing and advanced as far as he could until he met the Russian forces to the East of Vienna." Churchill commented: "I agree."[25]

---

23. Transcript of a telephone conversation, 25 April 1945, Harry S. Truman, *Memoirs*, Volume 1, pages 88–94.
24. Telegram of 30 April 1945, Truman Papers.
25. Minute of 1 May 1945 and Note of 2 May 1945, Premier Papers, 3/398/5.

In northern Europe, where the zones of occupation of Germany had been agreed, the American armies had already advanced farther eastward than the most easterly portion of their zone. Eisenhower told the Russians that after a short time the line of the original zones would be restored. "There will be a great shock to public opinion in many countries," Churchill warned Truman, "when the American Armies of the North withdraw, as they have to do under the occupational zone scheme, on a front of several hundred miles to a distance of upwards of 120 miles to the West, and when the Soviet advance overflows all those vast areas of central Germany which the Americans had conquered." If at the same time, Churchill added, "the whole of the Northern Adriatic is occupied by Yugoslavs, who are the Russian tools and beneficiaries, this shock will be emphasized in a most intense degree." [26]

On April 30 Hitler committed suicide in his bunker in Berlin. Berlin surrendered to the Red Army on May 2. In Italy almost a million German soldiers laid down their arms. On May 3 British troops reached Lübeck on the Baltic Sea. The aim of this move was to forestall a Soviet advance into Denmark. In this region Anglo-American strategy was in harmony. Churchill told Eden he was grateful to Eisenhower, who "threw in an American corps with great dexterity to help Montgomery in his advance on Lübeck." [27]

Churchill was still worried about the American intention to pull back to the zonal boundaries in Germany that had been agreed a year earlier. "I fear terrible things have happened during the Russian advance through Germany to the Elbe," he telegraphed to Eden on May 4. Details of the execution, rape and mass expulsion of Germans were being widely reported. "The proposed withdrawal of the United States Army to the occupational lines which were arranged with the Russians and Americans in Quebec and which were marked in yellow on the maps we studied there, would mean the tide of Russian domination sweeping forward 120 miles on a front of 300 or 400 miles." That would be an event "which, if it occurred, would be one of the

---

26. Telegram of 30 April 1945, Prime Minister to President, No. 22, Truman Papers.
27. Telegram of 5 May 1945, Foreign Office Papers (Eden Papers).

most melancholy in history." When the withdrawal was completed, and the territory occupied by the Red Army, "Poland would be completely engulfed and buried deep in Russian-occupied lands." [28]

Although a German surrender was imminent, it was the fate of fifteen Poles whom the Soviets had arrested outside Warsaw, and who had been imprisoned in the Lubyanka Prison in Moscow, that was Churchill's main concern on May 5. These Poles had earlier been nominated by the British and American governments to become members of the new Polish government. "We must make sure our Russian allies understand what is at stake," Churchill telegraphed to Eden, "but also we must make sure that the United States are with us." [29]

"I am most concerned about the fate of the fifteen Polish representatives," Churchill telegraphed that day to Truman, "in view of the statement made by Molotov to Stettinius at San Francisco that they had been arrested by the Red Army, and I think you and I should consult together very carefully upon this matter. If these Poles were enticed into Russian hands and are now no longer alive, one cannot quite tell how far such a crime would influence the future." [30]

On May 6 Churchill received a telegram from Stalin justifying the arrest of the Polish negotiators, who were, he said, "undergoing investigation in Moscow" as "diversionists and disturbers of order" in the rear of the Red Army. Churchill telegraphed at once to Truman: "It seems to me that matters can hardly be carried farther by correspondence and that, as soon as possible, there should be a meeting of the three heads of Governments." Meanwhile Britain and America "should hold firmly to the existing position obtained or being obtained by our armies in Yugoslavia, in Austria, in Czechoslovakia, on the main central United States front and on the British front reaching up to Lübeck including Denmark." Churchill was as anxious as Truman, he said, "to avoid giving the impression of 'ganging up' against Stalin." At the same time it was necessary to maintain the Anglo-American "essential unity of action on matters affecting good faith and international morality." [31]

---

28. Telegram of 4 May 1945, Foreign Office Papers (Eden Papers).
29. Telegram of 5 May 1945, Foreign Office Papers (Eden Papers).
30. Telegram of 5 May 1945, Foreign Office Papers (Eden Papers).
31. Telegram of 6 May 1945, Foreign Office Papers (Eden Papers).

In the early hours of May 7 the principal German instrument of surrender in the West was signed at Eisenhower's headquarters in Rheims. The following day was celebrated in Britain and the United States as Victory-in-Europe Day: VE-Day. Despite a spate of telephone calls and telegrams between Churchill and Truman, and telegrams from both of them to Moscow, Stalin chose May 9 for the Soviet Union to celebrate. Even in victory, divisions existed at every level of policy and practice.

The war in Europe was over. In a broadcast on the afternoon of May 8, Churchill spoke of how Britain had fought "single-handed" for a year, until joined by "the military might" of the Soviet Union, "and later by the overwhelming power and resources of the United States of America." [32] This was a compliment, but one that Churchill had set in the historical perspective he never forgot, and was to refer to unambiguously in the years ahead. For all its massive help before Pearl Harbor, the full weight of the United States as an ally had come twenty-seven months after Britain had declared war on Germany, and had faced, without the full participation of the United States, the brunt of German land, sea and air supremacy.

Churchill did not hesitate, however, in a telegram to Truman, to give the fullest praise to the "valiant and magnanimous deeds" of the United States. Those deeds, he told the President, "will forever stir the hearts of Britons in all quarters of the world in which they dwell, and will I am certain lead to even closer affections and ties than those that have been fanned into flame by the two world wars through which we have passed with harmony and elevation of mind." [33] Those "even closer affections and ties" were Churchill's hope. He was to work hard in the final decade of his political life to secure them.

---

32. Broadcast of 8 May 1945, BBC Written Archives Centre.
33. Telegram of 9 May 1945, Prime Minister to President, No. 39, Truman Papers.

Chapter Thirty-Four

⌖

"BRITAIN, THOUGH A SMALLER POWER THAN THE UNITED STATES, HAD MUCH TO GIVE"

For the ten years between 1935 and 1945, Churchill's relations with America were focused on Germany. For the ten years after 1945, they were dominated by the Soviet Union. Four days after the end of the war in Europe, Churchill set out his anxieties about Soviet policy and the future of Europe in a telegram to Truman. "I have always worked for friendship with Russia," he wrote, "but, like you, I feel deep anxiety because of their misinterpretation of the Yalta decisions, their attitude towards Poland, their overwhelming influence in the Balkans, excepting Greece, the difficulties they make about Vienna, the combination of Russian power and the territories under their control or occupied, coupled with the Communist technique in so many other countries, and above all their power to maintain very large armies in the field for a long time."

This was a strong indictment, strongly expressed. What would be the position, "after one or two years," Churchill asked, "when the British and American Armies have melted and the French has not yet been formed on any major scale, when we may have a handful of divisions, mostly French, and when Russia may choose to keep two or three hundred on active service?"

Churchill then expressed his deepest fears for the years ahead. "An iron curtain is drawn down upon their front," he told Truman. "We do not know what is going on behind." Following "this enormous Muscovite advance into the centre of Europe," Churchill warned, a

353

broad band of many hundreds of miles of Russian-occupied territory, the Russian-occupied regions of eastern Germany, "will isolate us from Poland," making it impossible to have any direct overland contact with the country for whose independence Britain had gone to war. "Surely it is vital now," Churchill wrote, "to come to an understanding with Russia, or see where we are with her, before we weaken our armies mortally or retire to the zones of occupation." This could only be done by a personal meeting between himself, Truman and Stalin. Whatever Stalin's intention, "the issue of a settlement with Russia before our strength has gone seems to me to dwarf all others."[1]

Churchill felt that he had an ally in firmness. Truman was proving as strong as Churchill in resisting the pressure of the Yugoslav Communists to annex the Italian port of Trieste and its hinterland. Truman also suggested that Stalin be informed of the Anglo-American position, telegraphing to Churchill: "If we stand firm on this issue, as we are doing on Poland, we can hope to avoid a host of other similar encroachments."[2] Churchill was impressed, telling Lord Halifax. "I must regard this as one of the most far-sighted, sure-footed and resolute telegrams which it has ever been my fortune to read."[3] If the situation was "handled firmly before our strength is dispersed," Churchill replied to Truman, "Europe may be saved another bloodbath. Otherwise the whole fruits of our victory may be cast away and none of the purposes of World Organization to prevent territorial aggression and future wars will be attained."[4]

In a broadcast on May 13, Churchill spoke of the Anglo-American relationship. It would be "an ill day for all the world," he said, if Britain and the United States "did not go on working together and marching together and sailing together and flying together, whenever something has to be done for the sake of freedom and fair play all over the world. That is the great hope of the future."[5] To this end Churchill was vigi-

---

1. Telegram of 12 May 1945, Prime Minister to President, No. 44, Cabinet Papers, 120/186.
2. Telegram of 12 May 1945, Churchill Papers, 20/218, Martin Gilbert, *Winston S. Churchill*, Volume 8, page 8.
3. Telegram of 12 May 1945, Churchill Papers, 20/218, Martin Gilbert, *Winston S. Churchill*, Volume 8, page 8.
4. Telegram of 12 May 1945, Prime Minister to President, No. 45, Truman Papers.
5. Broadcast of 13 May 1945, BBC Written Archives Centre.

lant with regard to any weakening of the Anglo-American link. At Chequers on May 26 and 27 his principal guest was Joseph Davies, a former American Ambassador in Moscow. Davies favored an initial meeting between Stalin and Truman, with Churchill excluded.[6]

Churchill protested, reminding Davies that Britain and the United States "are united at this time upon the same ideologies, namely, freedom, and the principles set out in the American Constitution and humbly reproduced with modern variations in the Atlantic Charter." The Soviets, Churchill pointed out to Washington's former man in Moscow, "have a different philosophy, namely Communism, and use to the full the methods of police government, which they are applying in every State which had fallen a victim to their liberating arms."

He could not readily bring himself, Churchill told Davies, to accept the idea that the American position "is that Britain and Soviet Russia are just two foreign Powers, six of one and half a dozen of the other, with whom the troubles of the late war have to be adjusted." Except in so far as force was concerned, "there is no equality between right and wrong. The great causes and principles for which Britain and the United States have suffered and triumphed are not mere matters of the balance of power. They in fact involve the salvation of the world."[7]

These were to be among Churchill's last words as wartime Prime Minister. On the day he set them down, May 28, the all-Party "Grand Coalition" Government was dissolved, at the insistence of the Labour Party, and Britain, although still at war with Japan, returned to prewar Party politics and a General Election. While waiting for the election to be held, a Conservative "Caretaker Government" was set up, headed by Churchill. His worry in the first week of the new government was not the coming election but the intended withdrawal of United States troops from those areas of Czechoslovakia and eastern Germany that would then fall within the Soviet sphere of military occupation. "I view with profound misgivings," he telegraphed to Truman on June 4, "the retreat of the American army to our line of occupation in the central sector, thus bringing Soviet power into the heart of Western Europe

---

6. Winston S. Churchill, *The Second World War,* Volume 6, page 502.
7. "Note by the Prime Minister," 28 May 1945, Churchill Papers, 20/209, Martin Gilbert, *Winston S. Churchill,* Volume 8, page 26.

and the descent of an iron curtain between us and everything to the Eastward." His one hope was that "this retreat, if it has to be made, would be accompanied by the settlement of many great things which would be the true foundation of world peace."[8]

A week later Churchill gave a dinner for Eisenhower. "A cheerful party," wrote Admiral Sir Andrew Cunningham in his diary, "but the PM rather gloomy about Russia. He has always wanted to use the Anglo-American retirement to their own Zones as a lever to extract similar treatment for us in Berlin and Vienna from the Russians; but the Americans will not go along with him."[9] The American troop withdrawals began nine days later. Simultaneously, at Churchill's insistence, Soviet troops withdrew from the agreed area of the British zone in Austria.

In a note written to help Eden with an election broadcast, Churchill commented that while "the gulf between Britain and Russia is unbridgeable except by friendly diplomatic relations, the similarity and unity which we have with the United States will grow and it is indispensable to our safety."[10]

On 15 July 1945, Churchill arrived in Berlin for the Potsdam Conference. Clement Attlee, his wartime Deputy Prime Minister, and Leader of the Labour Party, was with him as part of the British delegation. The British General Election results would become known while the conference was still in session, and there was always the chance that Attlee might become Prime Minister.

On July 16 Churchill and Truman met for the first time. They were together for two hours. "When Papa at length emerged," Mary Churchill wrote to her mother, "we decided to walk home. He told me he liked the President immensely—they talk the same language. He says he is sure he can work with him. I nearly wept for joy and thankfulness, it seemed like divine providence. Perhaps it is FDR's legacy. I can see Papa is relieved and confident."[11] Churchill later wrote in his memoirs

---

8. Telegram of 4 June 1945, Prime Minister to President, No. 72, Cabinet Papers, 120/186.

9. Diary entry, 11 June 1945, Cunningham Papers.

10. Minute of 23 June 1945, Churchill Papers, 2/548. Martin Gilbert, *Winston S. Churchill*, Volume 8, page 45.

11. Letter of 16 July 1945, Mary Soames, *Clementine Churchill*, page 384.

how he had been impressed with Truman's "gay, precise, sparkling manner and obvious power of decision."[12]

Truman's reaction to Churchill was mixed. "We had a most pleasant conversation," he wrote in his diary. "He is a most charming and a very clever person—meaning clever in the English and not the Kentucky sense. He gave me a lot of hooey about how great my country is and how he loved Roosevelt and how he intended to love me etc etc." Truman added that he was sure he and Churchill could get along "if he doesn't try to give me too much soft soap."[13]

The first plenary meeting at Potsdam took place on July 17. At this first meeting Churchill stated that he attached great importance to the early holding of free elections in Poland, "which would truly reflect the wishes of the Polish people."[14] Truman supported Churchill, but Stalin refused to honor the pledge he had signed to that effect at Yalta, five months earlier.

On July 18 Truman lunched alone with Churchill for almost two hours. Churchill's main concern was the future of the countries of Eastern Europe that were behind what he had named the Iron Curtain. Were all the countries that had passed into Soviet control "to be free and independent, or not?" he asked Truman. To this, Churchill noted, Truman "attached great importance . . . he evidently intends to press with severity the need of their true independence in accordance with free, full and unfettered elections."

The next topic was Britain's indebtedness. "I spoke," Churchill wrote, "of the melancholy position of Great Britain, who had spent more than one-half of her foreign investments since the time when we were all alone for the common cause, and now emerged from the War the only nation with a great external debt of £3,000 millions."[15] Churchill then explained to Truman the way in which this debt "had grown up for war purposes through buying supplies from India, Egypt, etc. with no Lease-Lend arrangement," and the economic burden it would impose on Britain. Truman followed his remarks "attentively and with sympathy," Churchill noted. Truman also spoke of "immense debt"

---

12. Winston S. Churchill, *The Second World War*, volume 6, page 545.
13. Diary entry, 16 July 1945, quoted in David McCullough, *Truman*, page 412.
14. Meeting of 17 July 1945, Cabinet Papers, 99/38.
15. In the monetary values of 2005 this was £80 billion/$160 billion.

owed by the United States to Great Britain "for having held the fort at the beginning." In Truman's words: "If you had gone down like France, we might well be fighting the Germans on the American coast at the present time." It was this, Truman said, that "justified the United States in regarding these matters as above the purely financial plane."

Churchill then raised his concerns about the continuing war against Japan, speaking about "the tremendous cost in American life and, to a smaller extent, in British life which would be involved in enforcing 'unconditional surrender' upon the Japanese." It was for Truman to consider, he said, whether "unconditional surrender" might not be expressed in some other way, "so that we got all the essentials for future peace and security, and yet left the Japanese some show of saving their military honour and some assurance of their national existence, after they had complied with all safeguards necessary for the conqueror."

Truman countered "that he did not think the Japanese had any military honour after Pearl Harbor," but went on to speak of the "terrible responsibilities that rested upon him in regard to unlimited effusion of American blood." This gave Churchill the impression that there was "no question of a rigid insistence upon the phrase 'unconditional surrender,' apart from the essentials necessary for world peace and future security, and for the punishment of a guilty and treacherous nation."

The next question raised by Truman was that of the British airfields and bases, particularly in West and North Africa, which had been built by the Americans "at enormous cost." Churchill told Truman: "We must come to the best arrangements in our common interest," but President Roosevelt "knew well that I wished to go much further." What Churchill wished was a reciprocal arrangement, including naval and air bases, between Britain and America "all over the world." Although Britain was "a smaller Power" than the United States, Churchill told Truman, it had much to give. "Why should an American battleship calling at Gibraltar not find the torpedoes to fit her tubes, and the shells to fit her guns deposited there? Why should we not share facilities for defence all over the world? We could add 50 per cent to the mobility of the American Fleet."

Churchill's language, Truman replied, "was very near to his own heart." But any such plans would have to be put in place as part of the policy of the United Nations. Churchill did not disagree, "so long as the facilities were shared between Britain and the United States. There was nothing in it if they were made common to everybody." A man might make a proposal of marriage to a young lady, Churchill explained, but "it was not much use if he were told that she would always be a sister to him. I wanted, under whatever form or cloak, a continuation of the present war-time system of reciprocal facilities between Britain and the United States in regard to bases and fuelling points in their possession."

The President, Churchill noted, "seemed in full accord with this, if it could be presented in a suitable fashion, and did not appear to take crudely the form of a military alliance à deux. These last were not his words, but are my impression of his mind." Encouraged by this, Churchill put to Truman his "long-cherished idea of keeping the organization of the Combined Chiefs of Staff in place, at any rate until the world calmed down after the great storm and until there was a world structure of such proved strength and capacity that we could safely confide ourselves to it." Truman was replying to him "in an encouraging way," Churchill noted, "when we were interrupted by his officers reminding him that he must now start off to see Marshal Stalin."

As he left, Truman told Churchill "that this had been the most enjoyable luncheon he had had for many years." Churchill was impressed by Truman. "He invited personal friendship and comradeship," he wrote, "and used many expressions at intervals in our discussion which I could not easily hear unmoved. He seems a man of exceptional character and ability, with an outlook exactly along the lines of Anglo-American relations as they have developed, simple and direct methods of speech, and a great deal of self-confidence and resolution."[16]

Two days later Churchill sent Truman a letter thanking him for two gifts he had received from the President on the previous day. "My dear Truman (If you will allow me to address you thus)," he wrote, "I am delighted with your charming and invaluable present of the three suitcases. They are indeed a practical souvenir of our meeting. The clock also stood on my bed-table, and I consulted it when I woke during the night. It speaks in darkness. What a pleasure it is to me to find so splendid a comrade and colleague, and now I hope that our work

---

16. Conversation of 18 July 1945, Premier Papers, 3/408/8.

will continue together till the dark days of world tragedy have passed away." [17]

On the morning of July 22, Churchill was given a detailed account of the first atomic bomb test in New Mexico. Inside a one-mile circle the devastation had been absolute. Churchill then went to see Truman. "Up to this moment," Churchill later recalled, "we had shaped our ideas towards an assault upon the homeland of Japan by terrific air bombing and by the invasion of very large armies. We had contemplated the desperate resistance of the Japanese fighting to the death with Samurai devotion, not only in pitched battles, but in every cave and dug-out." Recalling "the spectacle" of Okinawa, "where many thousands of Japanese, rather than surrender, had drawn up in line and destroyed themselves by hand-grenades after their leaders had solemnly performed the rite of hara-kiri," Churchill realized that to overcome Japanese resistance "man by man" and conquer Japan "yard by yard" might require the loss of a million American soldiers and half a million British—or more if we could get them there: for we were resolved to share the agony." With the news that the atomic bomb was a reality, "all this nightmare picture had vanished. In its place was the vision—fair and bright indeed it seemed—of the end of the whole war in one or two violent shocks." [18]

On the morning of July 24 Churchill raised with Truman the question of the future of Lend-Lease. As a result of agreements reached early in the war, he explained, many British military units had been furnished with American equipment "and no provision had been made to replace this equipment from British sources." To make such provision would take time. He hoped "very much" that Truman would make it possible for Britain "to pass smoothly from this position of dependence on the United States to one in which British forces could be independent." Churchill trusted that the rules that applied to the supply of Lend-Lease equipment would not be held to limit British sovereign rights over it. He must be free, he told Truman, "to give British equipment, for example, to the Belgians if His Majesty's Government felt that this was desirable, and he hoped that this would not result in the drying up of equivalent supplies from the United States."

-----

17. Letter of 20 July 1945, Truman Papers.
18. Winston S. Churchill, *The Second World War*, volume 6, pages 552–53.

35. Roosevelt, Churchill, Stalin and Churchill's interpreter Major Birse at Churchill's sixty-ninth birthday party, during the Teheran Conference, Teheran, 30 November 1943. Roosevelt had traveled 7,000 miles, Churchill 4,000 and Stalin 1,500 to discuss war policy.

36. General Dwight D. Eisenhower and Churchill at Carthage, 25 December 1943. Churchill, in his dragon dressing gown and siren suit, was recuperating from pneumonia and a heart attack. Behind Eisenhower is General Sir Harold Alexander. Eisenhower had just been appointed Supreme Commander, Allied Expeditionary Forces, Northern Europe; and Alexander, Commander-in-Chief of the Allied Armies in Italy (Fifteenth Army Group).

37. Churchill demonstrates the zipper of his siren suit to General Eisenhower, 15 May 1944, during a break in a tour of inspection of Allied troops who would be taking part in the Normandy landings.

38. Churchill and General Eisenhower visit American troops in Britain, 15 May 1944, three weeks before the Normandy landings.

39. General Eisenhower and Churchill in France, 12 June 1944, six days after the Normandy landings.

40. Roosevelt and Churchill on board the American cruiser *Quincy,* at Malta, 2 February 1945, for preliminary talks while on their way to the Yalta Conference.

41. Churchill, Roosevelt and Stalin, the "Big Three," at the Livadia Palace, Yalta, 11 February 1945. Immediately behind Roosevelt is Admiral Harold R. Stark, Commander of the United States Naval Forces in Europe. Next to him, behind Churchill, is Air Chief Marshal Sir Charles Portal, Chief of the British Air Staff.

42. Roosevelt and Churchill at the conference table, Yalta.

43. Field Marshal Sir Alan Brooke, Field Marshal Sir Bernard Montgomery, Churchill and United States Ninth Army Commander, Lieutenant-General William H. Simpson, stand in the antitank "dragon's teeth" of the Siegfried Line, just outside the German city of Aachen, 3 March 1945.

44. Churchill goes on board an American landing craft to cross the river Rhine, 25 March 1945. General Simpson is already on the ramp.

45. Churchill leaves St. Paul's Cathedral after the memorial service to President Roosevelt, 17 April 1945. Behind him is his daughter Sarah, a Royal Air Force officer working in Photo Reconnaissance. Five weeks earlier, she had accompanied her father to Yalta.

46. President Harry S. Truman and Churchill at Potsdam, 15 July 1945.

47. Churchill on board the bridge of the *Queen Elizabeth*, reaching New York, 14 January 1946.

48. President Truman and Churchill ride through Fulton, Missouri, on their way to Westminster College, 5 March 1946.

49. While President Truman watches, Churchill speaks in the gymnasium, Westminster College, Fulton, Missouri, 5 March 1946, delivering the "Iron Curtain" speech.

50. Three days after his "Iron Curtain" speech, Churchill reaches Richmond, Virginia, by train, 8 March 1946. Behind him, General Eisenhower; behind Eisenhower, Clementine Churchill; behind Clementine Churchill, Mamie Eisenhower.

51. Eleanor Roosevelt and Churchill at Franklin Roosevelt's grave, Hyde Park, New York, 16 March 1946.

52. Churchill at the grave of General Patton, American Military Cemetery, Luxembourg, 15 July 1946. With him are his daughter Mary, next to him, and his son Randolph, holding his father's top hat and cane.

53. President Truman and Churchill on the Presidential yacht, 4 January 1952.

54. Anthony Eden, Churchill, Secretary of State Dean Acheson and President Truman with a photograph taken at the Potsdam Conference.

55. Churchill arrives for the Bermuda Conference, 7 January 1953, in Eisenhower's Presidential plane. Behind Churchill is his son-in-law, Christopher Soames, and behind him Churchill's Joint Principal Private Secretary, Jock Colville.

56. Churchill's fourteenth visit to the United States, June 1954. With him at the White House are Vice-President Richard Nixon and President Eisenhower.

57. Churchill with his American friend Bernard Baruch.

58. On board the yacht *Christina*, off Palm Beach, Florida, 8 April 1961. Churchill reads the *New York Times*. The front page shows President John F. Kennedy and the British Prime Minister, Harold Macmillan, on board the Presidential yacht.

Truman replied that he was "striving" to give the Lend-Lease Act "the broadest interpretation possible." He had, however, to ask Churchill "to be patient as he wished to avoid any embarrassment with Congress over the interpretation of the Act and it might be necessary for him to ask for additional legislation in order to clear the matter up."[19]

For eight days, at the plenary sessions in Potsdam, Churchill and Truman made strenuous efforts to persuade Stalin to allow free elections in Poland. Stalin, with his troops and secret police in place in Poland, ignored them. On July 25, in midconference, Churchill returned to Britain to learn the election results. The Conservative Party had been defeated, and Clement Attlee, the leader of the victorious Labour Party, succeeded Churchill as Prime Minister and returned to Potsdam without him.

On the evening after his resignation, Churchill held a farewell dinner at Chequers. Among his guests was the American Ambassador, Gil Winant, his tenacious ally of the previous four years. Mary Churchill recalled that among the songs they sang was "We're Off to See the Wizard" from the *Wizard of Oz,* which, after much gloom earlier in the evening, had "a cheering effect."[20]

At Potsdam, Attlee and his Foreign Secretary Ernest Bevin took over from Churchill and Eden. On July 29 Truman wrote to his daughter that Churchill was "a likable person, and these two are sourpusses."[21] Four days after his resignation, Churchill received a letter from Truman, written in Berlin on White House notepaper. "My dear Mr. Churchill," the President began, "I could hardly refrain from saying as my predecessor used to say, 'Winston.' In the short time we were associated here I became a very great admirer of yours. . . . We miss you very much here, the Secretary of State, Admiral Leahy and I, but we wish you the happiest possible existence from now to the last call and we shall always remember that you held the barbarians until we could prepare."[22]

---

19. Meeting of 24 July 1945, Cabinet Papers, 99/39.
20. Mary Soames, *Clementine Churchill,* page 388.
21. Monte Poen, editor, *Letters Home by Harry Truman,* pages 194–95.
22. Letter of 30 July 1945, Churchill Papers, 2/142, Martin Gilbert, *Winston S. Churchill,* Volume 8, page 123.

"I am sorry indeed that our work together has been nipped in the bud," Churchill replied, "but I cherish the hope that our friendship will continue to ripen, and that there may be occasions when it may be of service to both our countries and to the common causes they pursue."[23]

On August 6 the atomic bomb was dropped on Hiroshima. Churchill had taken no part in the decision to bomb, which was an entirely American one, or in the choice of target. On the following day he visited his friend Lord Camrose. If Churchill had continued in office, Camrose wrote in his notes on their conversation, "he is of the opinion that he could have persuaded the American Government to use this power to restrain the Russians." He would have had "a show-down with Stalin and told him he had got to behave reasonably and decently in Europe, and would have gone so far as to be brusque and angry with him if needs be."

If Truman and his advisers had shown weakness in this policy of confronting the Soviet Union with the threat of atomic power, Churchill added, "he would have declared his position openly and feels certain that the American people would have backed the policy on the grounds that it would have been carrying out the Atlantic Charter."[24]

On August 15 Japan surrendered unconditionally to the Allied powers. "With the termination of hostilities," General Marshall wrote to Churchill, "my thoughts turn to you and the long hard pull up the heights to final triumph of your labor."[25]

As Leader of the Opposition, Churchill used whatever contacts he could to further his aim of the closest possible Anglo-American unity. The Canadian Prime Minister, William Mackenzie King, who saw him at the end of October 1945, noted Churchill's strong advocacy of "a continued alliance between the US and Britain." Churchill told King about this alliance: "It must not be written, it must be understood. But if you can get them to preserve the Joint Chiefs of Staff arrangement

---

23. Letter of 30 July 1945, Truman Papers.
24. Notes of a conversation, 7 August 1945, Camrose Papers.
25. Telegram of 16 August 1945, Cabinet Papers, 127/50.

and have plans made to keep the two together you will be doing the greatest service that can be done to the world."[26]

To the new British Foreign Secretary, Ernest Bevin, Churchill wrote that the long-term advantage to Britain and the Commonwealth "is to have our affairs so interwoven with those of the United States in external and strategic matters, that any idea of war between the two countries is utterly impossible," and that "however the matter may be worded, we stand or fall together." Churchill added: "It does not seem likely that we should have to fall. In a world of measureless perils and anxieties, here is the rock of safety."

Were the British Commonwealth and the United States to be "one organism" for strategic purposes, Churchill told Bevin, "we should be able to achieve more friendly and trustful relations with Soviet Russia" and could "build up the United Nations organisation around us and above us with greater speed and success." Churchill then quoted for Bevin: "Whom God hath joined together, let no man put asunder," and he added: "Our duties to mankind and all States and nations remain paramount, and we shall discharge them all the better hand in hand."

Churchill also hoped that a joint Anglo-American structure for postwar Japan would make it indispensable to preserve "indefinitely" the wartime Combined Chiefs of Staff Committee. From this, Churchill believed, "should flow the continued interchange of military and scientific information and Intelligence, and also, I hope, similarity and interchangeability of weapons, common manuals of instruction for the Armed Forces, inter-related plans for the war mobilization of civil industry, and finally, interchange of officers at schools and colleges."

Such was Churchill's vision for the future of the Anglo-American relationship. "What we may now be able to achieve," Churchill ended his letter to Bevin, "is, in fact, Salvation for ourselves, and the means of procuring Salvation for the world."[27]

---

26. Mackenzie King diary, 26 October 1945, J. W. Pickersgill and D. F. Forster, *The Mackenzie King Record*, Volume 3, *1945–1946*, pages 83–87.
27. Letter of 13 November 1945, Churchill Papers, 2/2, Martin Gilbert, *Winston S. Churchill*, Volume 8, pages 166–67.

Chapter Thirty-Five

✠

FULTON AND ITS AFTERMATH

In November 1945 President Truman invited Churchill to lecture at Westminster College, Fulton, Missouri, his home State, and to receive an honorary degree there. In a preview of what he would say at Fulton, Churchill told Truman in his acceptance letter that the United States had reached "a pinnacle of glory and power not exceeded by any nation in the whole history of the world, and with that come not only opportunities literally for saving misguided humanity but also terrible responsibilities if these opportunities cannot be seized." Churchill added: "Often and often I think of you and your problems as I did of those of our dear friend FDR. I am most thankful you are there to fill his place."[1]

Churchill and Clementine prepared to leave for the United States, on board the *Queen Elizabeth*. "I shall rejoice," his daughter Mary wrote to him, "to imagine you both tossed by star-spangled waves and petted by your friends and kinsmen—Americans."[2] Disembarking at New York on 14 January 1946, on what for Churchill was his tenth visit to the United States, he and Clementine went by train directly to Miami Beach, where they were the guests of the Canadian Colonel Frank W. Clarke, who had been Churchill's host in 1943 in the Laurentian Mountains, after the Quebec Conference. On January 15, his first day at Miami Beach, Churchill gave a Press Conference on the patio of the Colonel's house.

Asked if any resentment existed in Britain toward the American ninety-year lease of British bases under the wartime Destroyers-for-

---

1. Letter of 29 November 1945, Truman Papers.
2. Letter of 1 January 1946, Lady Soames Papers.

Bases agreement, Churchill replied: "No, we didn't trade those islands for fifty old destroyers. We did it for strategic use by the United States and for your safety and ours."

The main question at the Press Conference concerned the four-billion-dollar loan Britain was seeking from the United States. Churchill told the journalists: "We suffered far more than any other country during the war. Some other countries were overrun, but they were not fighting. We were fighting and using up our credit. We borrowed all we could." But, he assured his questioners, Britain was "most anxious" to earn its own living and to be independent. "If we are not given the opportunity to get back on our feet again we may never be able to take our place among other nations."[3]

One of the journalists present, Walter Locke, gave his readers a pen portrait of Churchill in Miami. "A round-faced, round-headed, benevolent, almost jolly gentleman. . . . A soft hat with brim upturned in front gives him a look of genial impishness not incompatible with a brownie or kewpie doll. His hat removed, one wisp of hair serves as a cover to his crown." Locke noted: "The humor which has lubricated his life flashes in his face and sparkles in his tongue. Lubricated his life? Who that has fought as he has fought could live at all except a saving humor balanced him? As to pose, he sits slumped, looking never an inch the statesman, this atomic bomb of an Englishman."[4]

While Churchill was in Miami, he read a series of articles by Eisenhower's Naval Aide, Captain Harry C. Butcher. These articles contained diary extracts of conversations between Eisenhower and Churchill. Butcher had not been present at most of their conversations, so he had relied, as many memoir writers were to do after him, upon trivia, stressing, for example, Churchill's late hours of work, eating soup with a slurping sound, and calling for a change of socks in the middle of the evening.[5] "I have skimmed over the Butcher articles," Churchill wrote to Eisenhower on January 26, "and I must say I think you have been ill-used by your confidential aide."

Butcher's articles, Churchill told Eisenhower, "are, in my opinion, altogether below the level upon which such matters should be treated.

---

3. *Miami Daily News,* 16 January 1946.
4. Walter Locke, "Churchill in Miami," collection of press clippings, Bonar Papers.
5. *Saturday Evening Post,* December 1945–February 1946 (ten issues).

Great events and personalities are all made small when passed through the medium of the small mind. Few people have played about with so much dynamite and made so little of it. I am not vexed myself at anything he has said, though I really do feel very sorry to have kept you up so late on various occasions. It is a fault I have and my host here, Colonel Clarke, has already felt the weight of it. It is rather late at my age to reform, but I will try my best."[6] In reply Eisenhower assured Churchill: "I never complained about staying up late. I didn't do it often and certainly I always came away from one of those conferences with a feeling that all of us had gotten some measure of rededication to our common task."[7]

While in Miami, Churchill set up his easel at the Miami Surf Club and painted, his favorite relaxation.[8] From Miami, Churchill went briefly to Cuba, which he had last visited fifty years earlier. While there, painting and swimming, he pondered the speech he was to make at Fulton. "I am worried about the way things are going," he wrote to Eisenhower on February 6. "There is only one safe anchor; which both you & I know."[9] Returning to Miami, Churchill made a considerable effort, encouraged to do so by Lord Halifax, to seek to moderate the conditions being imposed by the Americans on the new loan to Britain. This new loan, essential for Britain's economic recovery after the privations of the war, was not to have any of the favorable terms that had earlier applied to Lend-Lease.

At Churchill's request Bernard Baruch and the new Secretary of State, James F. Byrnes, flew from Washington to see him. Baruch had "repeated continually," Churchill reported to Attlee, that the United States would supply Britain with all the food it needed in the transition period, but that he considered no case had been made out "for so large an amount as four billion dollars, and commented adversely upon our heavy dollar credits. I explained to him that these were more

---

6. Letter of 26 January 1946, Eisenhower Papers.

7. Letter of 30 January 1946, Churchill Papers, 2/226, Martin Gilbert, *Winston S. Churchill*, Volume 8, page 187.

8. Two of these paintings (the waves at the shore, and the view from a bathing hut) are reproduced in color in David Coombs with Minnie Churchill, *Sir Winston Churchill's Life Through his Paintings*, page 190. Both paintings are now at the Studio, Chartwell.

9. Letter of 6 February 1946, Eisenhower Papers.

than balanced by the indebtedness we had incurred in India, Egypt, etc., for the war effort." Churchill asked Attlee to send him particulars "of exactly what we wanted the Loan for," as he would have a further opportunity of showing them to Baruch when he was in New York.

Churchill ended his letter to Attlee with a reference to his forthcoming speech in Missouri. It would be "in the same direction as the one I made at Harvard two years ago, namely fraternal association in the build-up and maintenance of UNO"—the United Nations Organization—"and inter-mingling of necessary arrangements for mutual safety in case of danger, in full loyalty to the Charter." Churchill told Attlee that while in Washington he had "tried this" on both the President and the Secretary of State, Byrnes, "who seemed to like it very well." Churchill added: "There is much fear of Russia here as a cause of future trouble." In his reply Attlee thanked Churchill for his talk with Baruch: "I am sure that you will have done much good." Attlee added: "I am sure your Fulton speech will do good."[10]

In his first speech since reaching the United States more than a month earlier, at the University of Miami on February 26, Churchill addressed a crowd of 17,500 in Burdine Stadium. He spoke of the help the university had given, before the United States "became a belligerent," in training cadets for the Royal Air Force. Some 1,200 British cadets, he recalled, "received here a very high quality of technical, navigational and meteorological training." They flew five and a half million miles over Florida on instructional courses, he told his audience, and "the majority, indeed a very large majority, gave their lives shortly afterwards for their country and our common cause."[11]

From Miami, Churchill traveled by train to Washington where, as Halifax's guest at the British Embassy, he worked on his speech for Westminster College. While Churchill was in Washington, Truman learned that the Soviet government, contrary to its earlier assurances, would withdraw only a portion of its troops from northern Persia. News of the Soviet decision not to abide by the agreed date, March 2, came shortly after the Soviet government had made it clear in Ankara

---

10. Letters of 17 and 25 February 1946, Churchill Papers, 2/210, Martin Gilbert, *Winston S. Churchill*, Volume 8, pages 191–93.

11. Speech of 26 February 1946, Randolph S. Churchill, editor, *The Sinews of Peace: Post-War Speeches by Winston S. Churchill*, pages 89–92.

that it would like to see the Turkish government replaced by one more amenable to Soviet wishes. The mood Churchill found at the White House was therefore one of alertness and uncertainty. Admiral Leahy, to whom Churchill showed the draft of his speech, was, Churchill informed Attlee and Bevin, "enthusiastic." Secretary of State Byrnes, to whom he also showed it, "was excited about it and did not suggest any alterations." [12]

On March 4 Churchill went to the White House, where both President Truman and Leahy drove with him to Washington's Union Station. The three men then boarded a special train for the twenty-four-hour journey to Jefferson City, Missouri. That night, as the train steamed westward, Churchill and Truman played poker. According to another of the players, at about 2:30 A.M. Churchill put down his cards and said: "If I were to be born again, there is one country in which I would want to be a citizen. There is one country where a man knows he has an unbounded future." When his companions asked Churchill to name the country he replied: "The USA, even though I deplore some of your customs." "Which customs," he was asked. "You stop drinking with your meals," Churchill replied. [13]

On the train during the morning of March 5, Churchill completed his Fulton speech. It was then mimeographed on the train and a copy shown to Truman. "He told me he thought it was admirable," Churchill told Attlee and Bevin, "and would do nothing but good, though it would make a stir." [14] Reaching Jefferson City shortly before noon on March 5, Churchill and Truman drove to Fulton, a distance of twenty miles, where Dr. Frank L. McCluer, the President of Westminster College, was waiting for them and hosted them at lunch. Immediately after the lunch Churchill and Truman headed an academic procession to the college gymnasium. There, to the assembled dignitaries, professors and students, Churchill made his speech.

In words that were broadcast throughout the United States, Churchill told those assembled in the gymnasium: "I am glad to come to

12. Letter of 7 March 1946, Churchill Papers, 2/4, Martin Gilbert, *Winston S. Churchill*, Volume 8, pages 195–96.
13. Clark Clifford recollections, Kay Halle, editor, *Irrepressible Churchill*, page 223.
14. Letter of 7 March 1946, Churchill Papers, 2/4, Martin Gilbert, *Winston S. Churchill*, Volume 8, page 197.

Westminster College this afternoon, and am complimented that you should give me a degree. The name 'Westminster' is somehow familiar to me. I seem to have heard of it before. Indeed, it was at Westminster that I received a very large part of my education in politics, dialectic, rhetoric, and one or two other things. In fact we have both been educated at the same, or similar, or, at any rate, kindred establishments."

It was an honor, Churchill said, "perhaps almost unique," for a private visitor to be introduced to an academic audience by the President of the United States. "Amid his heavy burdens, duties, and responsibilities, unsought but not recoiled from," the President had traveled a thousand miles "to dignify and magnify our meeting here to-day and to give me an opportunity of addressing this kindred nation, as well as my own countrymen across the ocean, and perhaps some other countries too."

Churchill went on to point out that the United States stood "at the pinnacle of world power." That was a solemn moment for American democracy, for "with primacy in power is also joined an awe-inspiring accountability to the future. If you look around you, you must feel not only the sense of duty done but also you must feel anxiety lest you fall below the level of achievement." The "supreme task and duty" of both the British and Americans was "to guard the homes of the common people from the horrors and miseries of another war."

For the threatened world the method of protection was the United Nations. "We must make sure," Churchill emphasized, "that its work is fruitful, that it is a reality and not a sham, that it is a force for action, and not merely a frothing of words, that it is a true temple of peace in which the shields of many nations can some day be hung up, and not merely a cockpit in a Tower of Babel." Before the victorious powers "cast away the solid assurances of national armaments for self-preservation," they must make sure that the temple of the United Nations was built "not upon shifting sands or quagmires, but upon the rock." Churchill proposed, as a first step to strengthen the United Nations, the creation of an international air force. Each country should provide a number of air squadrons, which would be "directed" by the United Nations. "I wished to see this done after the First World War," he explained, "and I devoutly trust it may be done forthwith."

If the dangers of war and tyranny were removed, Churchill was convinced, then there was no doubt that science and cooperation could bring the world, "in the next few decades," an expansion of material well-being beyond anything that had yet occurred in human experience. There was, however, a shadow that had fallen "upon the scenes so lately lighted by the allied victory." Nobody knew "what Soviet Russia and its Communist international organisation intends to do in the immediate future, or what are the limits, if any, to their expansive and proselytising tendencies."

Churchill then spoke of his strong admiration and regard "for the valiant Russian people and for my wartime comrade, Marshal Stalin." There was deep sympathy and goodwill in Britain, "and I doubt not, here also," toward the peoples of all the Russias, "and a resolve to persevere through many differences and rebuffs in establishing lasting friendships. We understand the Russian need to be secure on her western frontiers by the removal of all possibility of German aggression. We welcome Russia to her rightful place among the leading nations of the world. We welcome her flag upon the seas." But it was his duty, Churchill said, "to state the facts as I see them to you, to place before you certain facts about the present position in Europe."

Churchill then used a phrase he had first used almost a year earlier in a telegram to Truman, in the last weeks of the war: "From Stettin in the Baltic to Trieste in the Adriatic," he told his listeners throughout the United States, "an iron curtain has descended across the Continent." Behind that line "lie all the capitals of the ancient states of Central and Eastern Europe—Warsaw, Berlin, Prague, Vienna, Budapest, Belgrade, Bucharest and Sofia. All these famous cities and the populations around them," Churchill pointed out, "lie in what I must call the Soviet sphere, and all are subject in one form or another, not only to Soviet influence but to a very high and, in many cases, increasing measure of control from Moscow." Athens alone—"Greece, with its immortal glories"—was free to decide its future, at an election under British, American and French observation.

Turning to the secret information that had reached Truman in Washington while Churchill was there—though he made no reference to the source—Churchill told his listeners: "Turkey and Persia are both profoundly alarmed and disturbed at the claims which are being made upon them and at the pressure being exerted by the Moscow Government." In addition an attempt was being made "by the Russians in Berlin to build up a quasi-Communist party in their zone of Occupied Germany by showing special favours to groups of left-wing German leaders." Whatever conclusions might be drawn from these facts "—and facts they are—this is certainly not the Liberated Europe we fought to build up. Nor is it one which contains the essentials of permanent peace."

Churchill then set out his view of Soviet intentions, and how to contain them. "I do not believe that Soviet Russia desires war," he told his audience. "What they desire is the fruits of war and the indefinite expansion of their power and doctrines. But what we have to consider here today, while time remains, is the permanent prevention of war and the establishment of conditions of freedom and democracy as rapidly as possible in all countries." The present difficulties and dangers would not be removed "by closing our eyes to them. They will not be removed by mere waiting to see what happens; nor will they be removed by a policy of appeasement. What is needed is a settlement, and the longer this is delayed, the more difficult it will be and the greater our dangers will become."

This was Churchill's underlying theme: the need to reach an agreement with the Soviet Union. "From what I have seen of our Russian friends and Allies during the war," he said, "I am convinced that there is nothing they admire so much as strength, and there is nothing for which they have less respect than weakness, especially military weakness." If the Western democracies were to "stand together in strict adherence to the principles of the United Nations Charter, their influence for furthering those principles will be immense and no one is likely to molest them. If however they become divided or falter in their duty and if these all-important years are allowed to slip away then indeed catastrophe may overwhelm us all."

The unity of the Western democracies, above all of Britain and the United States, was Churchill's clarion call. But he could not end his appeal without a reference to his personal position in the prewar years. "Last time," he said, "I saw it all coming and cried aloud to my own fellow-countrymen and to the world, but no one paid any attention," and he went on to explain one of his deepest beliefs—that up until 1933 or even 1935:

Germany might have been saved from the awful fate which had overtaken her and we might all have been spared the miseries Hitler let loose upon mankind. There never was a war in all history easier to prevent by timely action than the one which has just desolated such great areas of the globe. It could have been prevented in my belief without the firing of a single shot, and Germany might be powerful, prosperous and honoured to-day; but no one would listen and one by one we were all sucked into the awful whirlpool.

A similar catastrophe in the postwar world could only be prevented by reaching "now" a good understanding on all points with Russia under the general authority of the United Nations Organization, "and by the maintenance of that good understanding through many peaceful years, by the world instrument, supported by the whole strength of the English-speaking world and all its connections." There was the solution "which I respectfully offer to you"—in a speech, he pointed out, to which he had given the title "The Sinews of Peace." If all Britain's "moral and material forces and convictions" were joined with those of the United States "in fraternal association, the high-roads of the future will be clear, not only for us but for all, not only for our time, but for a century to come."[15]

Such was Churchill's vision, pacific and pragmatic. Returning to Washington, he stayed once more at the British Embassy. From there he sent Attlee and Bevin an account of White House opinion. "Having spent nearly three days in the most intimate, friendly contact with the President and his immediate circle," he wrote, "and also having had a long talk with Mr Byrnes, I have no doubt that the Executive forces here are deeply distressed at the way they are being treated by Russia and that they do not intend to put up with treaty breaches in Persia or encroachments in Manchuria and Korea, or pressure for the Russian expansion at the expense of Turkey or in the Mediterranean." Churchill added: "I am convinced that some show of strength and resisting power is necessary to a good settlement with Russia. I predict

---

15. Speech of 5 March 1946, recording, BBC Written Archives Centre, Library No. T18184. The speech was subsequently printed in Randolph S. Churchill, editor, *The Sinews of Peace: Post-War Speeches by Winston S. Churchill*, pages 93–105.

that this will be the prevailing opinion in the United States in the near future."[16]

There were fierce protests in America at Churchill's Fulton speech. His object, the *Chicago Sun* declared, "is world domination, through arms, by the United States and the British Empire."[17] "The United States wants no alliance," declared the *Wall Street Journal*, "or anything that resembles an alliance, with any other nation."[18] According to *The Nation*, Churchill had "added a sizeable measure of poison to the already deteriorating relations between Russia and the Western powers," and Truman had been "remarkably inept" in associating himself with the speech by his presence."[19]

At a Press Conference on March 8, Truman not only denied that his presence indicated endorsement of Churchill's ideas but stated that he had not known in advance what Churchill was going to say. To distance the United States even further from Churchill's warnings, Truman instructed Dean Acheson, the Under-Secretary of State, not to attend a reception for Churchill in New York. Ironically Churchill had spoken at Fulton more than a week after the arrival in Washington of a telegram—then highly secret—from the American diplomat George F. Kennan in Moscow, which, by pointing out the extent of Soviet ambitions, and the need to contain them, was to change the concerns and direction of United States foreign policy exactly as Churchill had envisaged in his speech. Soviet success, Kennan noted in his telegram, "will really depend on the degree of cohesion, firmness and vigor which Western World can muster."[20]

Despite the adverse reaction to his speech, Churchill had no intention of falling silent. From Missouri he returned by train to Washington, then continued on to Richmond, Virginia, where on March 8, in the presence of General Eisenhower, he told the General Assembly of

---

16. Letter of 7 March 1946, Churchill Papers, 2/4, Martin Gilbert, *Winston S. Churchill*, Volume 8, page 205.

17. "Churchill's Call for World Domination," *Chicago Sun*, 6 March 1946.

18. *Wall Street Journal*, quoted in John P. Rossi, "Winston Churchill's Iron Curtain Speech: Forty Years After," *Modern Age* (Spring 1986), Bryn Mawr, Pennsylvania.

19. *The Nation*, quoted in John P. Rossi, "Winston Churchill's Iron Curtain Speech: Forty Years After," *Modern Age* (Spring 1986), Bryn Mawr, Pennsylvania.

20. Telegram of 22 February 1946, *Foreign Relations of the United States, 1946*, Volume 6, pages 696–707.

Virginia: "Peace will not be preserved by pious sentiments expressed in terms of platitudes or by official grimaces and diplomatic correctitude, however desirable this may be from time to time. It will not be preserved by casting aside in dangerous years the panoply of warlike strength. There must be earnest thought. There must also be faithful perseverance and foresight." Churchill continued: "Greatheart must have his sword and armour to guard the pilgrims on their way. Above all, among the English-speaking peoples, there must be the union of hearts based upon conviction and common ideals. That is what I offer. That is what I seek."[21]

Returning once more to Washington, Churchill spoke, at Eisenhower's suggestion, in the office of the Secretary of War, to an informal meeting of senior officers, telling them that during the war "the prevailing feature of our work together was the intimacy of association." As well as a common language and "many, many ideas" in common and also in practice, "there was a spirit of loyalty, of good will, of comradeship which never has been seen in all the history of war between Allied Armies, Navies and Air Forces fighting together side by side."[22]

While Churchill was in Washington, the Soviet Communist Party newspaper *Pravda* warned of the dangers in Churchill's call for "a special relationship" between Britain and the United States. "What are Churchill's proposals leading to?" *Pravda* asked, and it went on to give the Stalinist answer: "To create an Anglo-American military alliance that will liquidate the coalition of the three powers and at the same time destroy the United Nations Organization, by a policy of force." Having lost politically in England, Churchill had decided "to try his luck in the United States."[23] From Truman, on the following day, came private words of encouragement, at variance with his earlier public utterance. "The people in Missouri were highly pleased with your visit," he wrote, "and enjoyed what you had to say."[24]

During his last week in Washington, Churchill continued to sup-

---

21. Speech of 8 March 1946, Randolph S. Churchill, editor, *The Sinews of Peace: Post-War Speeches by Winston S. Churchill*, pages 106–10.
22. Speech of 9 March 1946, Churchill Papers, 2/226, Martin Gilbert, *Winston S. Churchill*, Volume 8, pages 207–8.
23. "Churchill rattles the saber" *Pravda*, Moscow, 11 March 1946.
24. Letter of 12 March 1946, Churchill Papers, 2/158, Martin Gilbert, *Winston S. Churchill*, Volume 8, pages 209–10.

port the British government's search for a fairer American loan. The British Minister of Health, Sir Ben Smith—who had been Minister Resident for Supply in Washington for the last two years of Churchill's premiership—informed Attlee of the "very helpful remarks" Churchill had made about the American loan at a National Press Club luncheon. Attlee wrote to Churchill: "I should like to send my warm thanks and appreciation for the friendly line you took."[25]

In the hope of obtaining the most favorable terms possible for Britain, Churchill went by train to New York, where he held further talks with Bernard Baruch. As a result of their discussions, Churchill was able to telegraph to Attlee on March 19: "I do not think he will take any action against the Loan." This did not mean, Churchill explained, that Baruch's opposition to it had changed, "but he considers that the Russian situation makes it essential that our countries should stand together. He is of course in full agreement with me on that." Indeed, Churchill added, "he spoke last night to me in the sense that he might urge that the Loan should be interest-free as a gesture of unity."[26]

Churchill was proud of his intervention in this crucial area of Anglo-American relations. In the House of Commons a year later, he explained, in defense of his claim that the Conservative opposition wished to work with Labour in the economic sphere to the national advantage: "I used such personal influence as I had in the United States, as the Chancellor of the Exchequer knows, to clear away American misunderstandings, so far as it is in the power of any private citizen to do any such thing."[27]

Churchill's efforts on behalf of Britain's financial indebtedness to the United States concerned the money owed by Britain for war purchases during two world wars. These sums were massive: In 1946 they totalled 860 million pounds outstanding for the First World War and 930 million pounds for the Second World War.[28] Following Churchill's

---

25. Telegram of 14 March 1946, Churchill Papers, 2/4, Martin Gilbert, *Winston S. Churchill*, Volume 8, page 210.

26. Telegram of 19 March 1946, Churchill Papers, 2/4, Martin Gilbert, *Winston S. Churchill*, Volume 8, page 210.

27. Speech of 12 March 1947, *Hansard*, Parliamentary debates.

28. The total sum, in the monetary values of 2005, is £45 billion/$90 billion.

efforts in 1946, the United States extended Britain a line of credit and Lend-Lease loan facility to cover the outstanding debt, to be paid in annual instalments.[29] The final repayment will have been completed on 31 December 2005, sixty years after Churchill's intervention.

While still in New York, Churchill was the guest of the Mayor and civic authorities of New York at a reception at the Waldorf-Astoria. Referring to the criticism of his having advocated a military alliance between Britain and the United States, Churchill told his distinguished audience: "I have never asked for an Anglo-American military alliance or a treaty. I asked for something different and in a sense I asked for something more. I asked for fraternal association, free, voluntary, fraternal association. I have no doubt that it will come to pass, as surely as the sun will rise to-morrow." One did not need a treaty "to express the natural affinities and friendships which arise in a fraternal association." Nothing could prevent Britain and the United States "drawing ever closer to one another and nothing can obscure the fact that, in their harmonious companionship, lies the main hope of a world instrument for maintaining peace on earth and goodwill to all men."

The United States stood, Churchill pointed out, "at the highest point of majesty and power ever attained by any community since the fall of the Roman Empire." This imposed upon the American people a duty that should not be rejected. "With opportunities come responsibility." If Britain and the United States were together, he was sure that "we shall succeed in lifting from the face of man the curse of war and the darker curse of tyranny. Thus will be opened ever more broadly to the anxious toiling millions, the gateways of happiness and freedom."[30]

On March 20 Churchill's tenth visit to the United States came to an end. His last published interview in New York was with his own son. In answer to a question from Randolph, "Have you any message to give the United States on your departure?" he replied: "The United States must realize its power and its virtue. It must pursue consistently the great themes and principles which have made it the land of the free. All the world is looking to the American democracy for resolute guid-

---

29. Letter to the author, 27 January 2005, from Shanez Cheytan, Debt and Reserves Management Team, H.M. Treasury, London.

30. Speech of 15 March 1946, Churchill Papers, 5/4, Martin Gilbert, *Winston S. Churchill*, Volume 8, pages 215–17.

ance. If I could sum it up in a phrase I would say, 'Dread nought, America.'"[31]

Two days after Churchill sailed from New York, the Soviet Union announced that all Soviet troops would be evacuated from Persia. Randolph telegraphed to his father from New York that the *New York Times* "attributes changed Russian tactics to your two speeches," as well as to a firmer attitude in Washington. Randolph added: "This view widespread here."[32] James W. Gerard, who had been United States Ambassador to Germany from 1913 to 1917, wrote to Churchill that his "winged words" had contributed "in no small degree to the settlement of the affairs of the world and the supremacy of the United Nations."[33]

For Churchill the American visit had been a success. On April 16 he asked the diplomat Pierson Dixon to see him in the House of Commons. He told Dixon that he had seen a film showing the President "applauding my Fulton speech in all the most controversial places." Churchill added: "The great American eagle stood immobile, poised, with sharp beak and ready talons; the Russians put a dart in under a wing, another under the tail, & still the bird remained immobile, but there is movement in the breast of the bird."[34]

31. Press Release, 20 March 1946, Churchill Papers, 2/225, Martin Gilbert, *Winston S. Churchill*, Volume 8, pages 217–19.

32. Radiogram of 24 March 1946, Churchill Papers, 2/8, Martin Gilbert, *Winston S. Churchill*, Volume 8, page 219.

33. Letter of 4 April 1946, Churchill Papers, 2/226, Martin Gilbert, *Winston S. Churchill*, Volume 8, page 219.

34. Pierson Dixon diary, 16 April 1946, Sir Pierson Dixon Papers.

Chapter Thirty-Six

✠

"I HAVE ALWAYS WORKED
FOR FRIENDSHIP WITH THE
UNITED STATES"

Three months after his return from the United States, Churchill traveled to Europe, flying to Metz where he was feted as a liberator, and then to Luxembourg. After luncheon in Luxembourg on July 15, he visited the American military cemetery, and laid a wreath on General Patton's grave.

Following his return from Europe, and having assembled a mass of hitherto secret wartime documentation, Churchill settled down to write his war memoirs. "I am by no means certain that I should wish to publish these documents in my lifetime," he wrote to Attlee, "but I think they would certainly win sympathy for our country, particularly in the United States, and make them understand the awful character of the trials through which we passed especially when we were fighting alone, and the moral debt owed to us by other countries."

Two recent American books, the one by Eisenhower's Naval Aide, Captain Butcher, another by the prewar publisher of *Time* magazine, Ralph Ingersoll, were both "very offensive and disparaging" to Britain, Churchill told Attlee, as well as to Churchill's own conduct of the war. Many statements were made "which are quite untrue and in some cases malicious."[1] Ingersoll's book was particularly offensive, his theme being that Churchill had worked systematically and deviously to en-

---

1. Letter of 29 May 1946, Churchill Papers, 2/4, Martin Gilbert, *Winston S. Churchill*, Volume 8, page 235.

sure that the Normandy landings were to be "under all-British management."[2] Ingersoll also alleged that the Anzio landings had been "Winston Churchill's own personal undertaking. He had thought of it while recovering from pneumonia in Marrakech."[3] As for the first months of peace, Ingersoll wrote, "We had agreed at Yalta to turn over the Russian sphere in Germany as soon as hostilities were over. Instead, on Churchill's personal persuasion, we rattled a sabre at the Russians across the Elbe for months before we went back to our territory with all the grace of a grudging giver."[4]

During the Second World War, Ingersoll had been awarded seven campaign stars and had been decorated for his part in the Normandy landings. He had later served on Montgomery's Staff in northern Europe. Churchill worked hard, helped by a team of researchers, to rebut Ingersoll's charges in his own war memoirs narrative. As he did so, one of Roosevelt's sons added to his distress. "Elliott Roosevelt has been writing a foolish book; he attacks me," he told his doctor. "I don't care what he says. He's not much of a fellow." Elliott Roosevelt had written that Churchill delayed the cross-Channel landings for two years. Churchill told his doctor: "A short time ago I asked Monty whether we could have invaded France before we did. Monty answered: It would have been madness. We could not have done it without the landing craft."[5]

Current events continually intruded on historical research. Even as he worked to tell the story of his wartime administration, Churchill wrote to George Bernard Shaw: "Do you think that the atomic bomb means that the architect of the universe has got tired of writing his non-stop scenario? There was a lot to be said for his stopping with the Panda. The release of the bomb seems to be his next turning-point."[6]

Churchill wrote this letter seventeen days after the signing into law by Truman of the McMahon Act, under which the United States could no longer share its atomic secrets with other countries. This act abrogated the agreement Churchill and Roosevelt had signed in Quebec

------

2. Ralph Ingersoll, *Top Secret*, page 11.
3. Ralph Ingersoll, *Top Secret*, page 50.
4. Ralph Ingersoll, *Top Secret*, page 270.
5. Diary entry, 8 August 1946, Lord Moran (Sir Charles Wilson), *Winston Churchill: The Struggle for Survival, 1940–1965*, pages 313–15.
6. Letter of 18 August 1946, Churchill Papers, 2/165, Martin Gilbert, *Winston S. Churchill*, Volume 8, page 254.

on 19 September 1944, which stated that the "full collaboration" between Britain and the United States in developing atomic power "for military and commercial purposes" should continue "after the defeat of Japan until and unless terminated by joint agreement."[7]

The Quebec Agreement on atomic power had never been made public. Under the new American legislation it was abandoned, to Britain's immediate and subsequent disadvantage. "I cannot but regret," Churchill wrote to Eisenhower nine years later, "that you had not the power at the time the McMahon Act was under discussion. If the agreement signed by me and FDR had not been shelved we should probably already have been able to add a substantial reinforcement to your vast and formidable deterrent power."[8] Learning that Bernard Baruch had been appointed head of the United States Atomic Energy Commission, Churchill wrote in congratulation: "We British have our solemn rights but the prime responsibility rests with the United States." It was for his friend, he added, "to raise this fearful agency above the level of national or material conflict and make it the servant and not the destroyer or the enslaver of the human race."[9]

Churchill sought, while Leader of the Opposition, a means of ending the centuries-old animosities in Europe. Speaking in Zurich in September 1946, he argued that France and Germany should take the lead, together, in the "urgent work" of creating a United States of Europe. At the same time Britain and the British Commonwealth—as well as "mighty America, and I trust Soviet Russia, for then indeed all would be well"—must be "friends and sponsors of the new Europe, and must champion its right to live and shine."[10]

Churchill's Zurich speech had one unexpected result. Nine months later, when introducing the Marshall Plan at a news conference, General Marshall revealed that it was Churchill's call for a United States of Europe in his Zurich speech that had influenced his own belief that the countries of Europe could work out their own economic recovery, with financial help from the United States.[11] Churchill

---

7. Premier Papers, 3/139/8A.
8. Letter of 12 January 1955, Eisenhower Papers.
9. Telegram of 6 October 1946, Baruch Papers.
10. Speech of 19 September 1946, recording, BBC Written Archives Centre.
11. News conference, 12 June 1947, *New York Times*, 13 June 1947.

was proud of this endorsement. "I feel greatly honoured," he wrote to the French leader Léon Blum, "to have been the link in setting in train the Marshall Plan upon which all our Governments are united and all our hopes depend."[12] Through the Marshall Plan, every war-devastated country in Europe, including Britain, was invited to set up a "self-help" program for its reconstruction, with substantial American economic assistance.[13]

The American dimension of a United Europe, ever-present in Churchill's thoughts, led to a warning. In a speech in London, at the Albert Hall, on the theme "Let Europe Arise," he stressed that it should be made "absolutely clear that we shall allow no wedge to be driven between Great Britain and the United States of America."[14]

Churchill's sense of the importance of the Anglo-American link was heightened in February 1947, when Attlee's government informed the United States of its intention to withdraw from its role as protector of Greece and Turkey within thirty-eight days. The dangers of which Churchill had spoken at Fulton a year earlier led Truman to take over the role Churchill had urged on him then, by introducing a bill to Congress that gave legal form to what became known as the Truman Doctrine. The Bill declared that the United States would not realize its objectives unless it was "willing to help free people to maintain their institutions and their national integrity against aggressive movements that seek to impose upon them totalitarian regimes." This was "no more than a frank recognition that totalitarian regimes imposed on free peoples, by direct or indirect aggression, undermine the foundation of international peace and hence the security of the United States."[15]

"I cannot resist," Churchill wrote to Truman, "after the year that has passed and all that has happened, writing to tell you how much I admire what you have done for the peace and freedom of the world,

---

12. Letter of 7 April 1948, Churchill Papers, 2/18, Martin Gilbert, *Winston S. Churchill,* Volume 8, pages 399–400.

13. "Marshall Sees Europe in Need of Vast New U.S. Aid; Urges Self-Help in Reconstruction," *Washington Post,* 6 June 1947.

14. Speech of 18 April 1947, Randolph S. Churchill, editor, *Europe Unite: Speeches 1947 and 1948 by Winston S. Churchill,* pages 60–67.

15. "An Act to Provide for Assistance to Greece and Turkey," Public Law 75, 80th Congress, 1st Session, 22 May 1947.

since we were together." [16] On May 22 the Bill passed into law, and the Truman Doctrine came into effect. It was the impressive outcome of Churchill's Fulton speech.

Wartime controversies were ever present in the immediate postwar years. In January 1947, it was alleged in the United States that Churchill had opposed appointing General Marshall as Supreme Commander of the Allied forces before the Normandy landings. From Washington the new British Ambassador, Lord Inverchapel, reported, as Churchill was told by the Foreign Office on January 23, "that this rumour, which could easily have an exacerbating effect on day to day Anglo-American relations, is so widely believed that he considers that no unilateral repudiation by His Majesty's Government, any more than a mere undocumented statement by General Marshall at a Press Conference, would kill it successfully." [17]

Churchill drafted a letter to be used by the Foreign Office if the occasion arose. During the crucial Staff discussions, he wrote—using the third person—"Mr Churchill still remained under the impression that General Marshall would command 'Overlord' and that Eisenhower would take his place at Washington; and that a British Commander would be nominated by him (Mr Churchill) for the Mediterranean. However, a few days before they left Cairo the President told him that he could not spare Marshall for 'Overlord' and proposed Eisenhower. Mr Churchill immediately accepted this suggestion, having complete confidence in the military attainments of both these great officers." [18]

Churchill's recollection of events was borne out by Averell Harriman—then Truman's Secretary of Commerce—who told the Associated Press in New York that at the Teheran Conference "Mr. Churchill urged President Roosevelt" to appoint Marshall as Supreme Commander but that, "after weighing all the factors," Roosevelt decided that Marshall "could not be spared from his post in Washington." [19]

---

16. Letter of 12 May 1947, Truman Papers.
17. Letter of 23 January 1947, Churchill Papers, 2/144, Martin Gilbert, *Winston S. Churchill*, Volume 8, page 310.
18. Letter dated 24 January 1947, Churchill papers, 2/144, Martin Gilbert, *Winston S. Churchill*, Volume 8, page 311.
19. "Harriman Tells How Marshall Won the Praise of Churchill," *New York Herald Tribune*, 25 January 1947.

Churchill's war memoirs were to give him a chance to put the record straight. They were also an important source of income. Three days before his seventy-second birthday, he learned that Henry Luce, owner of *Life* magazine, had offered $1,150,000 for the serialization of the war memoirs in the United States.[20] In addition the Boston publishers Houghton Mifflin would pay $250,000 to publish the memoirs in book form.[21] "I am devoting all my leisure, such as it is, upon the book," Churchill wrote to Luce on February 19, "and I have already more than 600,000 words in print." Churchill continued: "I am much amused to see all the rubbish that has been published so far in the United States about our affairs. How easily the documents will blow it all away."[22]

Churchill's literary work prospered. His war memoirs were to be serialized not only in *Life* but also in the *New York Times* and the *Daily Telegraph*. On April 14 *Life* and the *New York Times* published jointly a long article by Churchill entitled "If I Were an American." The article was a sustained defense of his previous year's Fulton speech, of Britain's intervention in Greece in 1944, and an appeal for the United States "to take a leading part, so far as it is necessary for world peace," in the Middle East.[23]

During the first four months of 1947, *Life* also published color photographs of sixteen of Churchill's paintings, and bought the American rights to Churchill's *Secret Session Speeches*, to be published at the same time as the British edition. The London representative of Time-Life, Walter Graebner, kept the staff of *Life* informed of Churchill's progress on his war memoirs. In his first report he wrote of how Churchill did most of his work in bed, either at Chartwell or at his new London house, 28 Hyde Park Gate. While writing, Churchill often wore his "siren suit." He also wore it on what were otherwise more formal occasions. "Sometimes he'll work in bed all day up till midnight," Graebner

---

20. In the monetary values of 2005, this brought Churchill almost $10 million/ £5 million.

21. In the monetary values of 2005, this brought Churchill just over $2 million/ £1 million.

22. Letter of 19 February 1947, Churchill Papers, 4/25, Martin Gilbert, *Winston S. Churchill*, Volume 8, page 315.

23. *Life*, 14 April 1947.

wrote. "If he works out of bed it's always in his siren suit. (I don't think I've seen him out of it more than twice—and one of these times was at his daughter's marriage.) He keeps six secretaries busy; they work in shifts so that someone is on hand sixteen hours or more a day, seven days a week. One secretary drives with him to and from the country, as Mr. Churchill uses this time to dictate." Churchill told Graebner: "I can do about 1,000 words while motoring to Chartwell—never less than 800." [24]

While writing the prewar volume of his memoirs, Churchill frequently referred to the Anglo-American aspect in his public speeches: "War is not inevitable," he told a gathering of Scottish Conservatives in May 1947, "but it would be inevitable if Britain and the United States were to follow the policy of appeasement and one-sided disarmament which brought about the last war." [25] "It would have been very easy to prevent the last war," Churchill wrote to General MacArthur, "but it is not so easy to cope with the future. The peace and freedom-loving nations must not make exactly the same mistake again. That would be too hard." [26]

Throughout the autumn of 1947 Churchill worked on his memoirs. The return to the United States of the American Ambassador, Lewis Douglas, gave him the opportunity to send a handwritten message to Truman. The Marshall Plan was already bringing much needed aid to war-damaged Europe. "My dear Harry," Churchill wrote, "as our friend Lew Douglas is going home for a spell, I cannot resist sending by his hand a few lines to tell you how much I admire the policy into which you have guided your great country; and to thank you from the bottom of my heart for all you are doing to save the world from famine and War."

Churchill had not been in the United States for a year and a half. "I wish indeed I could come over & see you & many other friends in the Great Republic," he told Truman. "You have my warmest good wishes in yr

24. Letter of [   ] April 1947, Robert T. Elson, *"Time Inc": The History of a Publishing Enterprise,* volume 2, pages 214–15.

25. Speech of 15 May 1947, Winston S. Churchill, *Trust the People* (pamphlet); recording, BBC Written Archives Centre.

26. Letter of 23 August 1947, Churchill Papers, 2/153, Martin Gilbert, *Winston S. Churchill,* Volume 8, page 350.

memorable discharge of yr tremendous office, and you can be sure that all the strongest forces in Britain are & will be at yr side if trouble comes."[27] Truman replied in his own hand. The recent Soviet denunciations of him, he wrote, had "assured my re-election I think, although the voters would do me a very great favor if they retired me. No one man can carry the burden of the Presidency and do it right. But I have a good team now." Truman added: "Your Fulton speech becomes more nearly a prophecy every day," and he ended on a personal note: "You are very kind to me, and I think give me too much credit. But I like it—particularly from you. May you continue to enjoy health and happiness and a long life—the world needs you now as badly as ever."[28]

In the winter of 1947, at the studio he had built with his own hands in the garden of Chartwell, Churchill was copying a badly damaged painting of his father that had been sent to him by a well-wisher. While painting, he had had a vivid image. His father appeared and asked him about the events that had taken place in Britain and the world since his death in 1895. When he asked his son, "Which is the leading world power?" Churchill replied, "The United States." At this Lord Randolph remarked: "I don't mind that. You are half American yourself. Your mother was the most beautiful woman ever born. The Jeromes were a deep-rooted American family." Churchill then told his father, who did not realize that his son had pursued a political career: "I have always worked for friendship with the United States, and indeed throughout the English-speaking world."[29]

On 30 November 1947 Churchill was seventy-three. Among the letters of congratulations was one from General Marshall. "The years do fly by," he wrote, "but for you each year seems to offer more and greater

---

27. Letter of 24 September 1947, Truman Papers.
28. Letter of 14 October 1947, Churchill Papers, 2/158, Martin Gilbert, *Winston S. Churchill*, Volume 8, pages 351–52.
29. Randolph Churchill, "How He Came to Write It," *Sunday Telegraph*, 30 January 1966, the day on which the full text of "The Dream" was published in the *Sunday Telegraph*. It is also published in full in Martin Gilbert, *Winston S. Churchill*, Volume 8, pages 364–72.
30. Letter of 8 November 1947, Churchill Papers, 2/144, Martin Gilbert, *Winston S. Churchill*, Volume 8, page 372.

opportunities to serve your people and the world."[30] Two weeks after his birthday, having given a dinner to Marshall in London, Churchill flew to Morocco, where he stayed at the Hotel Mamounia in Marrakech, writing his war memoirs and painting. The money for his stay in Marrakech, and for the research assistants and secretaries who accompanied him, came from the American publishers of his memoirs. Writing the memoirs meant that the past was often at the forefront of Churchill's mind. Jock Colville recorded a conversation about the Anglo-American disputes over the Second Front, when Churchill told him: "No lover ever studied every whim of his mistress as I did those of President Roosevelt."[31]

Churchill intended to publish material in his memoirs that bore on current historical disputes. He told Earl Mountbatten that he would publish his instructions to Mountbatten in 1943, to prepare for a cross-Channel landing, "because our American friends all make out that I was the inveterate foe of any descent on the Continent."[32]

The Anglo-American dispute in the immediate aftermath of victory was another much-debated issue. "I must regard the giving up on the heart of Germany as a terrible event," Churchill wrote to the former Secretary of State, James Byrnes. "I think we were quite free to consider the matter in the light of the general situation, after the 'mockery' that was made by the Russians of our agreements at Yalta about Poland." As to the American failure to reach Prague in May 1945, "My recollection is that I did my utmost to persuade General Eisenhower to let his two armoured divisions roll into Prague, as they could so easily have done in a few hours. In this also great disasters have followed and no one can measure what will happen in the future."[33]

In the summer of 1948 the Soviet occupation forces in Eastern Germany imposed a road and rail blockade on all movement into and out of Berlin. In a letter from the White House, writing to Churchill to acknowledge receiving the first volume of Churchill's war memoirs, Truman commented that Churchill could "look with satisfaction upon

---

31. Diary entry of 2 May 1948, John Colville, *The Fringes of Power*, pages 623–24.

32. Letter of 4 August 1948, Mountbatten Papers.

33. Letter of 31 August 1948, Churchill Papers, 2/146, Martin Gilbert, *Winston S. Churchill*, Volume 8, page 428.

your great contribution to the overthrow of Nazism & Fascism in the World." Truman added: " 'Communism,' so called, is our next great problem. I hope we can solve it without the 'blood and tears' the other two cost." [34]

To Eisenhower, who had decided not to run for the Presidency that year, Churchill wrote: "I am deeply distressed by what we see now. There can be no stable peace in the world while Soviet Imperialism is rampant and Asia on the Elbe." He was strongly of the opinion that "waiting upon events to find the line of least resistance will not provide a means of escape for the poor world and the horrors which threaten it." What was needed was "a settlement with Soviet Russia as a result of which they would retire to their own country and dwell there, I trust, in contentment." It was "vital to the future," Churchill told Eisenhower, "that the moment for this settlement should be chosen when they will realise that the United States and its Allies possess overwhelming force. That is the only way of stopping World War Number Three."

Of Eisenhower's decision not to run for the Presidency, Churchill wrote: "My feeling is that you were right not to intervene on this occasion. Because if you had stood as a Democrat, it would have looked like going to the rescue of a party which has so long held office and is now in difficulties. On the other hand if you had stood as a Republican it would have been hard on the party whose President you served. However, luckily there is plenty of time." [35]

Churchill was especially distressed by two aspects of the contemporary political scene. "Anything that hurt Anglo-American relations drew a blast from Churchill," Walter Graebner recalled, going on to recount how Churchill "deplored the anti-American attitude" of the outspoken Labour politician Aneurin Bevan and some of his equally extreme left-wing supporters, and "felt even stronger" about the activities of Senator Joseph McCarthy. "One day, when McCarthy was reported as having said something particularly obnoxious," Churchill said to Graebner, "in a tone of deep melancholy, 'As if we haven't enough problems without that fellow McCarthy pigging everything up.' " [36]

---

34. Letter of 10 July 1948, Churchill Papers, 2/158, Martin Gilbert, *Winston S. Churchill*, Volume 8, page 421.

35. Letter of 27 July 1948, Eisenhower Papers.

36. Walter Graebner, *My Dear Mr Churchill*, page 122.

• • •

In September 1948, with the announcement that the Soviet Union was in the process of making its own atomic bomb, the Cold War intensified. Churchill did not despair. It had to be borne in mind, he told Anthony Eden, "that the American Air Force will be nearly double as strong this time next year as today, that the United States will have a third more atomic bombs and better, and far more effective means of delivery both by airplanes and the bases they are developing, the largest of which is in East Anglia." While Britain should not "surrender to Soviet aggression or quit Berlin," it might well be that "we and the Americans will be much stronger this time next year."[37]

The election of Truman in November 1948 gave Churchill much pleasure. "Of course it is my business as a foreigner or half a foreigner to keep out of American politics," he wrote, "but I am sure I can now say what a relief it has been to me and most of us here to feel that the long continued comradeship between us and also with the Democratic Party in peace and war will not be interrupted. This is most necessary and gives the best chance of preserving peace." Churchill added: "I wish you the utmost success in your Administration during this most critical and baffling period in world affairs. If I should be able to come over I shall not hesitate to pay my respects to you."[38]

That journey was not too long in coming. On 18 March 1949 Churchill and Clementine, their daughter Mary and her husband, Christopher Soames—a former Coldstream Guardsman and Assistant Military Attaché at the British Embassy in Paris—two secretaries, a detective and a valet boarded the 84,000-ton *Queen Elizabeth* for the transatlantic crossing. "It is now nearly fifty-five years since I first crossed the Atlantic in the 7,000-ton *Etruria,*" Churchill wrote that day to the Chairman of the Cunard White Star Line, "and came back in the *Lacania,* which is a long time as human lives go."[39]

---

37. Letter of 12 September 1948, Foreign Office Papers (Eden Papers).
38. Letter of 8 November 1948, Truman Papers.
39. Letter of 18 March 1949, Churchill Papers, 2/263, Martin Gilbert, *Winston S. Churchill,* Volume 8, page 463.

Chapter Thirty-Seven

᳇

THE INDEFATIGABLE TRAVELER

Churchill began his sixth peacetime visit to the United States in New York. Speaking there on 25 March 1949 he thanked the American people "on behalf of Britain and on behalf of Western Europe, of free Europe, as I have some credentials to do—for all you have done and are doing." The Marshall Plan, he told his audience, was "a turning point in the history of the world." As for the Atlantic Pact, it "was one of the most important documents ever signed by large communities of human beings and certainly indicates a very considerable advance in opinion as far as the United States of America is concerned." The Atlantic Pact—the North Atlantic Treaty—was about to be signed, creating the North Atlantic Treaty Organization (NATO).

Churchill then told his New York audience about a speech he had recently made in Brussels. If war came "Soviet armour" could reach Brussels in ten days. He had looked at the 30,000 people gathered to hear him—"good, faithful, decent people"—and while he was speaking to them he could feel their fear and anxiety, "but when I spoke of the United States being with us in this matter of European freedom, I felt a wave of hope in this great concourse and I know you will not let them down in regard to any matter in which you have pledged the word of the great Republic."[1] A few days later, in a private conversation with President Truman in Washington, Churchill urged the President to make public that the United States would indeed be prepared to use the atomic bomb to defend democracy.

From Washington, Churchill went by train to Boston, to speak at

---

1. Speech of 25 March 1949, Randolph S. Churchill, editor, *In the Balance: Speeches 1949 and 1950 by Winston S. Churchill*, pages 32–39.

the Massachusetts Institute of Technology. This was the invitation that had originally brought him to the United States. He began his speech by casting his mind and that of his audience back to the beginning of the century: "In 1900 a sense of moving hopefully forward to brighter, broader, easier days predominated. Little did we guess that what has been called the Century of the Common Man would witness as its outstanding feature more common men killing each other with greater facilities than any other five centuries put together in the history of the world. But we entered this terrible twentieth century with confidence."

Churchill then gave a survey of the years that followed the hopes of 1900. "We thought that with improving transportation nations would get to know each other better," he said. "We believed that as they got to know each other better they would like each other more, and that national rivalries would fade in a growing international consciousness. We took it almost for granted that science would confer continual boons and blessings upon us, would give us better meals, better garments and better dwellings for less trouble, and thus steadily shorten the hours of labour and leave more time for play and culture."

The vast expansion of scientific achievement as the century proceeded was not accompanied, Churchill noted, by any noticeable advance in the stature of man, "either in his mental faculties, or his moral character. His brain got no better, but it buzzed the more. The scale of events around him assumed gigantic proportions while he remained about the same size. By comparison therefore he actually became much smaller."

Churchill then spoke of the nature of man, and man's ability to rise above the dictates of science. His words were directed to the people of Eastern Europe and the Soviet Union: "Laws just or unjust may govern men's actions," he said. "Tyrannies may restrain or regulate their words. The machinery of propaganda may pack their minds with falsehood and deny them truth for many generations of time. But the soul of man thus held in trance or frozen in a long night can be awakened by a spark coming from God knows where and in a moment the whole structure of lies and oppression is on trial for its life. People in bondage need never despair. Let them hope and trust in the genius of mankind."

The only semi-independent Eastern European country after 1945, Czechoslovakia, had recently fallen completely under Communist control. Yet the British and American aim and ideal, Churchill declared, was friendship with Russians everywhere. "We seek nothing from Russia but goodwill and fair play." If Britain and the United States "persevere steadfastly together, and allow no appeasement of tyranny and wrong-doing in any form, it may not be our nerve or the structure of our civilization which will break, and peace may yet be preserved."[2]

On April 4, as Churchill was returning to Britain on board the *Queen Mary*, Ernest Bevin, who was then in Washington, signed the North Atlantic Treaty for Britain. This treaty, which Churchill had praised while in New York, joined the United States and Canada with eight European countries in a defense organization, the North Atlantic Treaty Organization, soon to be known by its initials as NATO. Two days after the treaty was signed, Truman, in an informal talk to recently elected members of Congress, said that he would "not hesitate" to order the use of the atomic bomb if it were necessary for the welfare of the United States "and if the fate of the democracies of the world were at stake." He added that he hoped and prayed it would never be necessary to do so: that the signing of the North Atlantic Treaty would prevent the United States from having to make such a decision.[3]

"I was very struck by Truman's remark about the Atomic Bomb," Churchill wrote to Baruch two weeks later. "This was indeed what I urged him to make in our short conversation at Washington. It will, I have no doubt, be a help to the cause of peace."[4] To Truman himself, Churchill wrote at the end of May: "I was deeply impressed by your statement about not fearing to use the atomic bomb if the need arose. I am sure this will do more than anything else to ward off the catastrophe of a third world war." Churchill added: "I have felt it right to speak, as you have seen, in terms of reassurance for the immediate future, but of course I remain under the impression of the fearful dangers which impend upon us. Complete unity, superior force and the undoubted readiness to use it, give us the only hopes of escape. Without you nothing can be done."[5]

------

2. Speech of 31 March 1949, Randolph S. Churchill, editor, *In the Balance: Speeches 1949 and 1950 by Winston S. Churchill*, pages 40–51; recording, BBC Written Archives Centre.
3. "America and the Atomic Bomb," *The Times*, 8 April 1949.
4. Letter of 28 April 1949, Baruch Papers.
5. Letter of 29 June 1949, Truman Papers.

"I am not quite so pessimistic as you are about the prospects for a third world war," Truman replied from the White House, and he added: "I rather think that eventually we are going to forget that idea, and get a real world peace. I don't believe even the Russians can stand to face complete destruction, which certainly would happen to them in the event of another war."[6]

In October 1949 Attlee told Churchill that the Anglo-American Combined Chiefs of Staff organization, which Churchill had so wanted to be continued after the war, was to be abolished. "It would have been much better to have preserved it," Churchill wrote, "and created an additional and larger organisation to cover the Atlantic Pact Powers. France, without a French army is a liability and not an asset to Great Britain, and there is no reason why our ties with the United States should have been weakened, in form at any rate, to please her."[7]

The only positive news from Churchill's perspective was Attlee's remark, when telling him about the abolition of the supreme Anglo-American planning body, that the government would do its utmost "to keep alive the spirit underlying the Combined Chiefs Organization and we know it is the Americans' intention to revert to this type of High Command in the event of hostilities."[8] Reflecting on the current crisis and the Second World War, Churchill told his research assistants that even if Hitler had not invaded the Soviet Union, "I still believe that we (US + GB) could have won single-handed."[9]

Clement Attlee having called a General Election, a vigorous campaign was under way at the beginning of 1950. During his own speeches Churchill praised the role of the United States in maintaining the security of the Atlantic alliance. He also noted, in a speech in Edinburgh, that Greece had been "rescued by the United States, carrying on the task which we began." Churchill urged a renewal of talks be-

---

6. Letter of 2 July 1949, Churchill Papers, 2/158, Martin Gilbert, *Winston S. Churchill*, Volume 8, page 468.

7. Letter of 11 October 1949, Churchill Papers, 2/81, Martin Gilbert, *Winston S. Churchill*, Volume 8, pages 491–92.

8. Letter of 30 September 1949, Churchill papers, 2/81, Martin Gilbert, *Winston S. Churchill*, Volume 8, page 492, footnote 1.

9. Note of 5 October 1949, Churchill Papers, 4/351A, Martin Gilbert, *Winston S. Churchill*, Volume 8, page 494.

tween the British, American and Soviet leaders, in order to lessen the global tensions. During his speech he coined a word to describe such a meeting: it would be a "summit." [10]

The Conservatives failed to be re-elected, but the margin between the two rival Parties had become so small that a new election would be inevitable within two years. In Parliament, Churchill was the main opposition speaker on defense. During a debate on the Cold War confrontations, he declared: "Do not, I beg the House, nurse foolish delusions that we have any other effective overall shield at the present time from mortal danger than the atomic bomb in the possession, thank God, of the United States." As for the earlier argument that a United States of Europe would be "resented" by the United States, with the Atlantic Pact "now we have the American people, with their own heavy burdens to bear, sacrificing themselves and using all their power and authority to bring about this very system." In this, Churchill believed, "lies the hope of the Western world." [11]

The memoir writing proceeded apace, with serialization in the *New York Times*. On April 16 Churchill received the first copies of the third volume. "My dear Harry," he wrote in his own hand to Truman that day, "Only our friendship entitles me to send you one of the earliest copies of my new Volume III on the War, and to warn you that you may have to face in future years IV, V and even possibly six. Forgive me." [12]

The NATO strategy that Churchill welcomed as an essential protection against Soviet threats involved the stationing of American bombers with nuclear bombs in Britain. He supported this, but recognized its burdens and even dangers. "We have quite rightly given the Americans a base in East Anglia for the obvious purpose of using the atomic bomb on Moscow and other Russian cities," he wrote to Attlee. "We are therefore a prime target for attack. Our defence against such an attack has been greatly weakened by our sale of jet-fighter airplanes to the Argentine and Egypt." [13]

---

10. Speech of 17 February 1950, Randolph S. Churchill, editor, *In the Balance: Speeches 1949 and 1950 by Winston S. Churchill*, pages 197–207.

11. Speech of 15 March 1950, *Hansard*, Parliamentary debates.

12. Letter of 16 April 1950, Truman Papers.

13. Letter of 24 May 1950, Premier Papers, 8/1160.

In a speech two months later, Churchill praised the Labour Government for having "fostered the closest relations with the United States."[14] Writing to Truman that August, he noted that the countries of Europe would, if the Communists had their way and secured a European neutrality pact, "be in a sort of no-man's-land between Britain and its American air bases, and the Soviet armies." That was why he favored a European Army, with France and Germany sharing the main burden; an army in which, he told Truman, "British, and I trust, Americans, will be strongly represented."[15]

At the end of the year Attlee visited Washington for talks with Truman. It was five years since the two men had last met. Churchill praised the visit, but commented: "it seems to me that five years is rather a long interval."[16]

The start of the Korean War on 25 June 1950, in which British and American troops fought side by side as part of a United Nations' war effort to protect South Korea from a sudden military attack by Communist North Korea, led to questions in Britain about the country's reliance on the United States. Churchill told the House of Commons: "It can only be justified and even tolerated because on either side of the Atlantic it is felt that interdependence is part of our faith and the means of our salvation."[17]

At the opening of Parliament that October, Churchill was critical of a British Government statement of policy that contained no reference to the American contribution in Korea. At one point in his speech, when he was praising Truman's "prompt initiative" at the start of the Korean War the previous June, a Labour Member of Parliament shouted out: "The right hon. Gentleman might give his own country some credit!" Churchill shot back his reply. "I have never been at all backward in defending the claims and considerations of this country," he said, "but I do not think that those claims are well sustained if they are based on a failure to recognize the overwhelming contribution which another country, the United States, has made." An "enormous

---

14. Speech of 27 July 1950, *Hansard*, Parliamentary debates.
15. Letter of 13 August 1950, Truman Papers.
16. Speech of 14 December 1950, *Hansard*, Parliamentary debates.
17. Speech of 26 June 1950, *Hansard*, Parliamentary debates.

proportion" of the whole burden had been borne by the United States. The least Britain could do would be to accord the United States some consideration. "We have quite enough real achievements in our record without endeavouring to minimize the legitimate and rightful contributions of great allies towards the common cause which we support."[18]

On November 30 Churchill was seventy-six. In a debate that day in the House of Commons, he contrasted American involvement in Europe after the two world wars: "Instead of retiring into isolation, instead of demanding full and prompt repayment of debts and disinteresting herself in Europe and even in the League of Nations, of which she had been one of the founders," he said, the United States in 1945 "has come forward step by step as the knowledge of the situation has dawned upon her and has made the great counterpoise upon which the freedom and the future of our civilization depends." This "fundamental change" in American policy constituted the best hope "for the salvation of Christian civilization and democracy from Communist and Russian conquest and control." For this reason, Britain's "first objective" should be "not to separate ourselves in action or in understanding or in sympathy in any degree, however slight, that can be avoided from the United States."[19]

At the beginning of 1951 the United Nations' troops in Korea were driven back by the North Korean Communist forces to a small perimeter around the port of Pusan. Churchill, who was working on the final volume of his memoirs in Marrakech, wrote to Eden: "The only point that seems urgent for me to make now is that we should on no account approve any separation between our policy and that of the United States on the measures to be taken against China."[20] To Governor Thomas E. Dewey of New York, Churchill wrote at the end of January: "You may be quite sure that whatever misunderstandings may arise from the petty by-play now going on between Mr Attlee's Government and the United States, the 'fraternal' association is unbreakable, and in this respect at least things have only to get worse to get better."[21]

------

18. Speech of 31 October 1950 (and interruption), *Hansard*, Parliamentary debates.

19. Speech of 30 November 1950, *Hansard*, Parliamentary debates.

20. Letter of 8 January 1951, Foreign Office Papers (Eden Papers).

21. Letter of 30 January 1951, Churchill Papers, 2/168, Martin Gilbert, *Winston S. Churchill*, Volume 8, page 590.

As the tide of war turned in Korea, Churchill sent Truman his European-based perspective. He had always hoped, he wrote, that the United States, while maintaining her necessary rights in the Far East, would not become too heavily involved there, "for it is in Europe that the mortal challenge to world freedom must be confronted."[22]

The publisher of Churchill's prewar biography of his ancestor John Churchill, Duke of Marlborough, was about to publish the memoirs of the former American commander in Italy, General Mark Clark. Churchill was not pleased by what he read. "I am sure the General wishes to be friendly in what he writes," he wrote to the publisher, but he noted that to English readers "much of his tales about his visits to Chequers will be considered vulgar: they are certainly vitiated by inaccuracy. I cannot accept many of the statements which he attributes to me, let alone the form in which they are expressed. I always say 'aren't' instead of 'ain't.' "

The bulk of the passages in which Churchill was mentioned constituted, he wrote, "an abuse of hospitality and intimacy in conversation." The stories in the book in no way represented "the manner in which Americans I received were accustomed to behave."[23] It was too late, the publishers replied, to make any changes beyond "ain't" to "aren't."

In March 1951 Ernest Bevin retired as Foreign Secretary, forced to do so by a terminal illness. In his tribute to Bevin, Churchill praised "his strengthening of our ties with the United States."[24] That month Churchill was invited back to the United States, to give a talk in Philadelphia at the bicentennial of the University of Pennsylvania. He was tempted to go, if only for a week. He would fly both ways "in one of the best BOAC special airplanes which is offered." As he explained to Clementine: "It is a week of one's life, but it might be a week well spent." Principal leaders of both Democrat and Republican Parties would be there, "and there is no doubt I could make a helpful speech."[25] In ad-

---

22. Letter of 12 February 1951, Truman Papers.
23. Letter of 21 February 1951, Churchill Papers, 4/333, Martin Gilbert, *Winston S. Churchill*, Volume 8, page 597.
24. Broadcast of 17 March 1951, Randolph S. Churchill, editor, *Stemming the Tide: Speeches 1951 and 1952 by Winston S. Churchill*, pages 29–34.
25. Letter of 25 March 1951, Spencer-Churchill Papers.

dition Truman had invited him to dine at the White House on either the night before his speech or the night after.

While making his plans to return to the United States, Churchill learned that Truman had dismissed General MacArthur, who had wanted to bomb air bases inside China that were being used in the Korean battles. Churchill approved what Truman had done. "I much look forward to a talk with you," he telegraphed to Truman on April 11. "May I also assure you that your action in asserting the authority of the civil power over military commanders, however able or distinguished, will receive universal approval in England."[26] Churchill's support for Truman's actions was sincere, but he was worried about speaking in Philadelphia while the controversy over the general's dismissal continued, and cancelled his visit. One of Churchill's secretaries explained the cancellation in a private letter. "Although Mr Churchill was careful not to admit it publicly," she wrote, "this was because of the MacArthur controversy which has been sweeping and splitting the country. He felt that the speech he will deliver at the University of Pennsylvania will be better received when these domestic Party political issues are over."[27]

That April, Churchill criticized Attlee for not having "put up a fight" to prevent the abolition of the Combined Chiefs of Staff. "Half the misunderstandings which have been so dangerous to Anglo-American relations during the Korean War," he declared, "would, I believe, have been avoided had there been a regular and constant meeting, as there were in the bygone years, between our two Chiefs of Staffs Committees. We cannot afford in the dangers in which we now stand to make mistakes like this."[28] Three weeks later, in the face of hostile interruptions from the Labour benches, Churchill supported the American argument in favor of a ban on raw material exports to China. The Americans knew, he said, that they were bearing "virtually the whole weight of the Korean war."

Britain's "great danger," Churchill warned, was in pursuing a policy "of girding at the United States and giving them the impression that they are left to do all the work, while we pull at their coat-tails and

---

26. Telegram of 11 April 1951, Truman Papers.
27. Jo Sturdee (later Countess of Onslow), letter of 24 May 1951, Churchill Papers, 2/174, Martin Gilbert, *Winston S. Churchill,* Volume 8, page 605, footnote 2.
28. Speech of 19 April 1951, *Hansard,* Parliamentary debates.

read them moral lessons in statecraft and about the love we all ought to have for China." Western Europe needed the United States "on the grounds of national safety and even of survival."[29] A week later, Churchill told the Scottish Conservatives in Glasgow how shocked he had been "to see how much anti-American feeling there was among the Left-wing Government supporters."[30]

A gift to Truman of one of his own paintings brought Churchill a swift response. "I can't find words adequate," Truman wrote, "to express my appreciation of the beautiful picture of the Atlas Mountains, painted by you. I shall treasure that picture as long as I live and it will be one of the most valued possessions I will be able to leave to Margaret when I pass on."[31] Margaret was Truman's daughter. On June 8 Churchill lunched with John Foster Dulles, Truman's special representative in Europe. Later that day Dulles wrote to Churchill about their exchange of views: "What you say always reflects the ripeness of experience and the vigor of a dynamic faith."[32]

Churchill was in the audience at an English-Speaking Union Dinner in London on July 3, when Eisenhower spoke about the danger of any neglect of the Western alliance, and the importance of a United Europe within that alliance. Churchill had been enormously impressed, writing to Eisenhower that it was "one of the greatest speeches delivered by any American in my lifetime—which is a long one." The speech carried with it "on strong wings the hope of the salvation of the world from its present perils and confusions." As to the future, Churchill wrote, "I think we ought now to be able to see the way forward fairly clearly, and I believe that events in the next two years are going to be our servants and we their masters."[33] One thing Churchill could not have predicted was that "in the next two years" he would again be Prime Minister of Britain, and Eisenhower would be President of the United States.

---

29. Speech of 11 May 1951, *Hansard*, Parliamentary debates.
30. Speech of 18 May 1951, Randolph S. Churchill, editor, *Stemming the Tide: Speeches 1951 and 1952 by Winston S. Churchill*, pages 80–89.
31. Letter of 28 June 1951, Squerryes Lodge Archive.
32. Letter of 8 June 1951, Churchill Papers, 2/114, Martin Gilbert, *Winston S. Churchill*, Volume 8, page 616.
33. Letter of 5 July 1951, Eisenhower Papers.

Chapter Thirty-Eight

✠

"I MARVEL AT AMERICA'S ALTRUISM, HER SUBLIME DISINTERESTEDNESS"

On 20 September 1951 Clement Attlee informed Churchill that he had decided to hold a General Election at the end of October. This election, Churchill wrote to General MacArthur, who had sent him his good wishes, "may be of great consequence to the future. I earnestly hope it may bring all of us on both sides of the Atlantic into the fraternal association for which I have so long worked."[1] Polling took place on October 25. The Conservatives were victorious, and on the following day Churchill became Prime Minister.

Two weeks later, in his first speech as Prime Minister, amid the glittering panoply of the Lord Mayor's Banquet in London, Churchill spoke forcefully of the place of the United States in the world. "The sacrifices and exertions which the United States are making," he said, "to deter, and if possible prevent, Communist aggression from making further inroads upon the free world are the main foundations of peace." But he could not resist referring, as he had done so often in the previous years, to the divisions of the prewar era. "A tithe of the efforts now being made by America," he said, "would have prevented the Second World War and would have probably led to the downfall of Hitler with scarcely any blood being shed except perhaps his own."

Churchill also spoke of the role of the United States in 1951. "I feel a deep gratitude towards our great American Ally," he said. "They have risen to the leadership of the world without any other ambition

---

1. Letter of 27 September 1951, Churchill Papers, 2/171, Martin Gilbert, *Winston S. Churchill*, Volume 8, page 640.

but to serve its highest causes faithfully." He also hoped to see a revival of Britain's "former influence and initiative" in the world.[2] To Clementine, who felt that her husband, at the age of seventy-six, was too old to be Prime Minister, he said he would only stay at Downing Street for one year. He just wanted, he told Jock Colville, "to have time to re-establish the intimate relationship with the United States, which had been a keynote of his policy in the war, and to restore at home the liberties which had been eroded by war-time restrictions and post-war socialist measures."[3]

On November 25 Churchill asked the Secretary of State for Air "what is being done to foster good relations between the US armed forces in this country and their English neighbours." He was told that there were 45,000 American servicemen in Britain, ten thousand wives and ten thousand children, and that such contacts as were made were "too frequently with the less admirable elements of our people." Churchill monitored what was to be done, stressing the need "to extend the provision of reasonable amenities."[4]

At a meeting of his Cabinet on December 11, less than two weeks after his seventy-seventh birthday, Churchill told his colleagues that he intended to visit the United States as soon as possible. It was not his intention, he explained, to ask for financial aid for Britain. He would ask the Americans instead for materials and equipment for the purpose "either of assisting our defence programme directly, or of assisting our exports and thus furthering the defence programme indirectly."[5] "I am sure you will have a success," his son, Randolph, wrote to him four days before he set off. "It is not in the interest of the Administration that any hint of disagreement should emerge. You have much to give & doubtless much to receive." Randolph added: "I foresee the British lion being a greater pet than ever!"[6]

On the last day of 1951 Churchill left London by train for

---

2. Speech of 9 November 1951, Randolph S. Churchill, editor, *Stemming the Tide: Speeches 1951 and 1952 by Winston S. Churchill*, pages 187–90; recording, BBC Written Archives Centre.

3. John Colville recollections, John Colville, *The Fringes of Power*, pages 632–33.

4. Premier Papers, 11/791.

5. Cabinet meeting, 11 December 1951, Cabinet Papers, 128/23.

6. Letter of 27 December 1951, Churchill Papers, 1/51, Martin Gilbert, *Winston S. Churchill*, Volume 8, page 671.

Southampton, then went on board the *Queen Mary* for his twelfth journey to the United States. Among those traveling with him was Earl Mountbatten, then Fourth Sea Lord. On the first night on board Mountbatten was Churchill's guest at dinner. It was an uncomfortable conversation, with Mountbatten questioning the wisdom of linking Britain irrevocably to American foreign policy, especially if it seemed that the course followed by the Americans was likely to lead to war. Churchill replied that the only security for Britain was to be found in linking its fortunes entirely with the Americans, and then—Mountbatten noted in his diary—turned to him with a rebuke. "I think you should be careful about your anti-American attitude," Churchill said. "You are one of the few commanders that they would willingly serve under. You will throw all that away if they think you are against them!"[7] At dinner that evening Churchill sang the whole of "Rule, Britannia!" followed by "It's All Quiet on the Potomac."

Reaching New York on 4 January 1952, Churchill flew in President Truman's plane to Washington, where Truman met him at the airport. That day Truman gave a luncheon party for Churchill at Blair House, which was being used as the Presidential residence while the nearby White House was being renovated. After the luncheon Churchill went to the British Embassy, where he was to stay. Five hours later the two men dined together on the Presidential yacht. "The last time you and I sat across the conference table was at Potsdam, Mr President," Churchill commented, and he added: "I must confess, sir, I held you in very low regard then. I loathed your taking the place of Franklin Roosevelt. I misjudged you badly. Since that time, you more than any other man, have saved Western civilization." Quoting this remark, Truman's biographer David McCullough comments: "In a dark period for Harry Truman, a winter of tawdry scandal, of interminable war in Korea and greatly diminished public confidence in his leadership, the gallant old ally had again, as only he could, served as a voice of affirmation."[8]

Churchill then gave Truman a survey of the international scene. There was, he said, "fear in the Kremlin." The Russians had earlier feared British and American friendship more than their enmity. This was beginning to change. At the time of the Berlin airlift in 1948, the

---

7. Diary entry, 31 December 1951, Philip Ziegler, *Mountbatten,* pages 502–3.
8. David McCullough, *Truman,* pages 874–75.

risks had been very great. Since then they had lessened. Churchill did not expect a deliberate attack by the Soviet Union in 1952. Since the end of the war, however, "they had gained half Europe and all China without loss." Churchill then praised Truman's "great decision" to commit American forces to Korea, and to pursue American rearmament. "Now the free world was not a naked world," he said, "but a re-arming world."

In recent months the Americans had been complaining in strong terms about British trade with Communist China. Truman reiterated these complaints. Churchill replied that he did not think China had gone permanently Communist, "but we had to deal with what was before us." He therefore "felt inclined" to give aid in resisting further Chinese aggression. At the same time he asked the United States to give Britain "moral assistance" in Iran (formerly Persia), where the Anglo-Iranian oil company had been nationalized: "We must both play one hand there." As to Egypt, Churchill told Truman that Britain's position there was not one of imperialism but of international duty. The recent American proposal for an international supervisory force on the Suez Canal was "an act of genius." He hoped the United States would be willing to back it up by sending troops, a Brigade perhaps, "as a symbol." If America would send such a force "everything would be cleared up quite quickly. Everyone else would fall in behind this." The British would then withdraw "a whole Division or more."[9]

As he was returning to the British Embassy, Churchill asked the Secretary of State, Dean Acheson: "Did you feel that around that table this evening there were gathered the governments of the world—not to dominate it, mind you—but to save it?"[10]

"Oh, I enjoyed it so much," Churchill told his doctor that night. "We talked as equals."[11] Those talks continued for two more days. At the first plenary session, held at the White House on the morning of January 7, Churchill pointed out that, despite rising defense costs and the need for economy at home, Britain intended "to make the maxi-

---

9. "Note of the conversation between the Prime Minister and the President," 5 January 1952, Cabinet Papers, 21/3057.
10. Memorandum of 6 January 1952, Truman Papers.
11. Moran diary, 5 January 1952, Lord Moran (Sir Charles Wilson), *Winston Churchill: The Struggle for Survival, 1940–1965,* pages 354–56.

mum possible contribution to common defence against aggression and Communism," and had put in hand a rearmament program for the common cause. To do this, however, there was an urgent need for steel; the United States had to help Britain on this.

Speaking of NATO, Churchill declared: "The great burden which the United States was bearing on behalf of the free world was a matter of universal admiration." The United Kingdom would continue to make "the biggest contribution of which they were capable." The Second World War had "swallowed up" Britain's reserves and resources to such an extent, however, that the Government would still have to impose "restrictions and restraint" upon the fifty million inhabitants of the British Isles.[12] For some items, including meat, rationing was still in force.

He was not in Washington, Churchill said, "to seek aid in order to improve the comfort and welfare of the British people." They would accept the necessary sacrifices required by their internal situation, and the Government would adopt the necessary measures. This, Churchill said, was Britain's "form of a declaration of independence."[13]

The second plenary session was held that afternoon to discuss Truman's proposal for the "standardisation of weapons for the free world." The Americans wanted their .30 rifle to become the standard rifle, replacing in Britain the British .303 rifle. Churchill disagreed. It was, he said "dangerous to change the calibre of a rifle unless a really long period of change was in prospect." During this discussion one of the British delegation, the Chief of the Imperial General Staff, Field Marshal Sir William Slim, is said to have remarked: "Well, I suppose we could experiment with a bastard rifle, partly American, partly British," to which Churchill replied: "Kindly moderate your language, Field Marshal. It may be recalled that I am myself partly British, partly American."[14]

Turning to naval matters, Churchill "declared," as the American note of the discussion recorded, "that he was not convinced of the need for a Supreme Commander in the Atlantic. He had lived through two world wars without any such arrangement. He insisted that he was

---

12. First Plenary Meeting, 7 January 1952, Cabinet Papers, 21/3057.
13. First Plenary Meeting, 11 A.M., 7 January 1952, Cabinet papers, 21/3057.
14. Quoted in Kay Halle, editor, *Irrepressible Churchill,* page 261.

not speaking lightly for, indeed, the Atlantic supply line was of vital importance to the UK and if naval affairs in the Atlantic were mismanaged, the UK 'would die.'" This was "not true" in the case of the United States, he added, "which later would still be in a position to land its armies in Europe."[15] Truman did not agree to the British proposal; three months later, when the Atlantic Command was formally set up, it was under an American admiral.

The third plenary meeting of the Washington Conference took place on the morning of January 8. Churchill, as the American minutes recorded, expressed his admiration for the manner in which the United States was carrying "virtually the entire load of the West" in the Far East. He paid special tribute to American fortitude in the Korean War, which had resulted in 36,000 American dead. He recognized the "peculiar difficulty" of prosecuting such a war when the nation as a whole did not consider itself to be directly threatened. Churchill then spoke of the United Kingdom's desire to help the United States in every way possible, but recognized that in the Far East there could be "no UK priority or equality of leadership." The role of leader there "squarely belonged to the United States, and the UK will do its utmost to meet US views and requests in relation to that area."

Churchill went on to tell Truman, Acheson and the other Americans present that, in his opinion, the President's decision to resist in Korea had done more than anything else "to reverse the tide in our relations with the Soviets in the post-war period." Indeed, he felt that 25 June 1950 marked "the turning point in the danger to the free world of communist aggression." Britain was profoundly grateful to the United States for its action. Had he been in power then "he would have broken relations with China when the Chinese attacked the UN forces in Korea." When he was returned to power, however, armistice talks had been initiated, and he did not think "that such a British action would be desirable now" because of its possible adverse effect on the negotiations.[16]

Not all went as smoothly as the official record appeared to show. One of the British officials present noted in his diary that Truman "was quite abrupt on one or two occasions with poor old Winston and had a

15. Second Plenary Meeting, 5 P.M. to 7 P.M., 7 January 1952, Truman Papers.
16. Third Plenary Meeting, 11 A.M. to 1 P.M., 8 January 1952, Truman Papers.

tendency, after one of the old man's powerful and emotional declarations of faith in Anglo-American co-operation, to cut it off with a 'Thank you, Mr Prime Minister. We might pass that to be worked out by our advisers.' A little wounding."[17]

The rearming of Germany, and the future of the European Defence Community, dominated the discussion at the plenary meeting on the afternoon of January 8. Churchill told Truman that Britain would do "everything possible" to further the formation of a European Army, although it would not participate in a European Federation. The European Army, he said, "offered the only method of integrating German forces in the defence of Western Europe." Without the support of the Germans he doubted if Western Europe could be "successfully defended." His one fear was that the "sacrifice of nationality," which the European Defence Community implied with its creation of a multinational force, would damage the loyalty of the soldiers.[18]

During the Washington talks, Churchill and Truman agreed that the atomic bomb would not be used from the American bases in East Anglia without British consent. This agreement set out in a formal manner what had earlier been a verbal and secret understanding between Truman and Attlee. The published agreement put at rest many fears that had arisen in Britain of a unilateral American action that might lead to fearsome reprisals. Churchill had shared those fears.

From Washington, Churchill went on January 9 to New York, by train. For two days he stayed at Bernard Baruch's apartment on East Sixty-sixth Street, where he continued the preparations he had begun during the transatlantic voyage for his address to Congress. On January 10, at Churchill's request, Baruch invited to lunch three of America's leading journalists: General Julius Ochs Adler and Arthur Sulzberger of the *New York Times* and Daniel Longwell of *Life*. Churchill's aim was to "get the feel" of American opinion before his address to Congress. "We had hardly taken our seats," his doctor noted, when Churchill said without warning: "What other nation in history, when it became supremely powerful, has had no thought of territorial aggrandizement, no ambition but to use its resources for the good of the

---

17. Diary entry, Evelyn Shuckburgh, *Descent to Suez: Diaries 1951–56*, page 32.
18. Fourth Plenary Meeting, 5 P.M., 8 January 1952, Cabinet Papers, 21/3057.

world? I marvel at America's altruism, her sublime disinterestedness."
As he said this, Churchill was in tears.[19]

From New York, Churchill went by overnight train to Ottawa,
where he spoke to the Canadian Parliament and was entertained by
leading politicians. Two days later he returned by night train to Washington, where he again stayed at the British Embassy, putting the final
touches to his speech to Congress on January 17. He began his speech
by assuring Congress: "I have not come here to ask you for money to
make life more comfortable or easier for us in Britain," and he added:
"Our standards of life are our own business and we can only keep our
self-respect and independence by looking after them ourselves."

During the war Britain had borne its share of the burden "and
fought from first to last, unconquered—and for a while alone—to the
utmost limits of our resources." America's "majestic obliteration" of all
it had given Britain under Lend-Lease "will never be forgotten by this
generation in Britain or by history." After thanking the United States
for bearing "nine-tenths, or more" of the burden in Korea, he went on
to welcome American patience in the armistice negotiations. The two
countries were agreed, he said, that if the truce they sought was
reached only to be broken, "our response will be prompt, resolute and
effective."

Churchill then spoke specifically of the atomic bomb. "It is my belief," he said, "that by accumulating deterrents of all kinds against aggression we shall, in fact, ward off the fearful catastrophe, the fears of
which darken the life and mar the progress of all the peoples of the
globe." His concluding words looked forward to healing wounds and
reconciling differences: "We must not lose patience, and we must not
lose hope. It may be that presently a new mood will reign behind the
Iron Curtain. If so it will be easy for them to show it, but the democracies must be on their guard against being deceived by a false dawn. We
seek to covet no one's territory; we plan no forestalling war; we trust
and pray that all will come right."

Many changes had taken place throughout the world since his address to Congress in 1941, Churchill commented. But there was one
thing "which is exactly the same as when I was here last. Britain and the

---

19. Moran diary, 10 January 1952, Lord Moran (Sir Charles Wilson), *Winston
Churchill: The Struggle for Survival, 1940–1965*, pages 361–62.

United States are working for the same high cause. Bismarck once said the supreme fact of the nineteenth century was that Britain and the United States spoke the same language. Let us make sure that the supreme fact of the twentieth century is that they tread the same path."[20]

That afternoon Churchill and Truman presided over the fifth and final plenary meeting of the Washington Conference. When the question of the Atlantic Command was raised again, there followed, Dean Acheson later recalled, "one of Mr. Churchill's greatest speeches." Acheson then gave the gist of it: "For centuries England had held the seas against every tyrant, wresting command of them from Spain and then from France, protecting our hemisphere from penetration by European systems in the days of our weakness." Now the United States, "in the plenitude of our power, bearing as we did the awful burden of atomic command and responsibility for the final word of peace or war, surely we could make room for Britain to play her historic role 'upon that western sea whose floor is white with the bones of Englishmen.'"[21]

Churchill's arguments were in part effective. The United Kingdom Home Command was extended westward to the hundred-fathom line. While not withdrawing his earlier objections, Churchill expressed his readiness to allow the appointment of a Supreme Commander, so that a command structure could be created, and could go ahead with the necessary planning in the Atlantic area. He reserved the right, the minutes of the meeting recorded, to bring forward modifications for the consideration of NATO at a later stage "if he so desired."[22]

That evening, at dinner at the British Embassy, in the presence of three senior American officers, the Chief of Army Staff General J. Lawton Collins, the Chief of the Air Staff General Hoyt S. Vandenberg and the Chief of Naval Operations Admiral Fechtler, as well as Averell Harriman, Churchill tried to reverse the American decision not to allow British officers to participate, as hitherto, in the National War College

---

20. Speech of 17 January 1952, Randolph S. Churchill, editor, *Stemming the Tide*, pages 220–27; recording, BBC Written Archives Centre.
21. Dean Acheson recollections, Dean Acheson, *Present at the Creation: My Years in the State Department*, page 602.
22. Fifth Plenary Meeting, 18 January 1952, Cabinet Papers, 21/3057.

and other American staff colleges. When General Collins said it was "quite impossible" as far as he was concerned "to let in the British again without letting in the French," and that Britain must wait until both could be let in together, Churchill expressed his disappointment at this line of reasoning, which, he said, "was not at all in harmony with his view of the relationship between the two countries."

General Collins and Admiral Fechtler, while agreeing that there should always be a "special relationship," said that "this should not be an open relationship." General Vandenberg added that "while he wished to maintain a special relationship" with the British Chiefs of Staff, it must be maintained "under the counter." When Harriman supported his military and naval colleagues, Churchill replied that he did not see why Britain "should be treated like other members of the alliance."[23] To his disappointment, he made no headway.

On January 19 Churchill left Washington by train for New York, where he again stayed. "I have just finished what seems to be the most strenuous fortnight I can remember," he wrote to Clementine, "& I am staying quiet here for 48 hours to recover. I never had such a whirl of people & problems, and the two speeches were very hard & exacting ordeals." About the talks he told her: "I am far from sure about the future in the Far East—or indeed elsewhere. No one can tell what is coming. I still hope we shall muddle along to greater strength. The Presidential Election is now going to amuse the Americans for the next nine anxious months."[24]

On January 22 Churchill had to cancel a civic reception at City Hall and a drive down Broadway because of "a feverish cold."[25] At ten that evening he went on board the *Queen Mary*, which sailed from New York just after midnight. Six days later Churchill was back in Britain. The lesson his visit had taught him, he told the House of Commons two weeks after his return, was that "the people of the United States realize today how grievous was the cost to them, in life and treasure, of the isolationism which led them to withdraw from the League of Nations which President Wilson had conceived and which British minds

23. "Record of Conversation," 19 January 1952, Premier Papers, 11/312.
24. Letter of 20 January 1952, Spencer-Churchill Papers.
25. "Programme of Events," Premier Papers, 11/161.

had so largely helped to shape."[26] In his next speech in the Commons, Churchill stressed that it was the design and intent of the Soviet Union and its satellites "and all its associates and fellow-travellers in many lands" to drive a wedge between the British and American democracies. Anything that secured Anglo-American unity must be considered a service "not only to freedom but to peace."

Churchill had continued to be concerned by anti-American feeling in Britain. But he was convinced that its extent was exaggerated. A delegation of American Senators who had visited several countries had come to London, he told the House of Commons, "and during their visit they asked to see me, and I received them in my home. I was impressed by the fact that this powerful body was greatly disturbed by the anti-American feeling which they thought existed in the House of Commons." Churchill had told the Senators: "Do not be misled. The anti-American elements in Parliament are only a quarter of the Labour Party, and the Labour Party is only a half of the House. Therefore, you may say that one-eighth at the outside give vent to anti-American sentiments. The Labour Party as a whole, and the Government of the day, supported by the Conservative Party in this matter, are whole-heartedly friendly to the United States, and recognize and are grateful for the part they are playing in the world and of the help they have given to us."[27]

---

26. Speech of 11 February 1952, *Hansard*, Parliamentary debates.
27. Speech of 26 February 1952, *Hansard*, Parliamentary debates.

Chapter Thirty-Nine

⌗

"WE MUST NOT CAST AWAY A SINGLE HOPE, HOWEVER SLENDER"

In May 1952 Churchill and his wife gave a dinner at 10 Downing Street for General and Mrs. Eisenhower, who were on their way back to the United States. Eisenhower, having given up his post as Supreme Commander of NATO, was to become one of the Republican contenders for the 1952 Presidential Election. "If I had been given a wish how I would spend my last night in England before saying farewell," he wrote to Churchill in his thank-you letter, "I could not have had it fulfilled in all respects so completely as I did at your dinner party last Thursday."[1] For Churchill the prospect of Eisenhower becoming President gave him hope for a final initiative, as his joint Principal Private Secretary, Jock Colville, recorded in his diary: "He told me that if Eisenhower were elected President, he would have another shot at making peace by means of a meeting of the Big Three. For that alone it would perhaps be worth remaining in office."

America was frequently at the forefront of Churchill's attention and imagination during his peacetime premiership. One idea he put forward echoed a concept he had first raised in the interwar years, of "the commodity sterling dollar"—an international medium of exchange based on the world prices of, say, fifteen commodities over a period of three years.[2] But Churchill was careful not to embrace every American link. When Truman suggested the appointment of a Briton

---

1. Letter of 22 May 1952, Churchill Papers, 2/217, Martin Gilbert, *Winston S. Churchill*, Volume 8, page 728.
2. Diary entry, 13–15 June 1952, John Colville, *The Fringes of Power*, pages 650–51.

as Deputy Chief of Staff for Korea, Churchill was wary, telling his Cabinet that the United Nations had entrusted the conduct of the Korean campaign to the United States, and that Britain would be "well-advised to avoid a position in which we shared responsibility without the means of making our influence effective." The Cabinet did not accept Churchill's advice.[3]

Throughout his second premiership Churchill encouraged arms sales to the United States. In a debate in the House of Commons he praised the new British Centurion tank both for its "high military value" to Britain, and because it "may also in time become a useful dollar-earning export."[4] Under his watchful eye two contracts were signed with the United States for eight hundred tanks, spare parts and ammunition for a total value of more than $140 million.[5]

On 1 July 1952 the Labour Party brought a motion of censure against the government for not opposing the American bombings on the Yalu River border between North Korea and China. In response Churchill praised the American achievement in Korea. "Due consideration should be given," he said, "to the monumental patience, breaking all previous human records, which has been displayed by the American Government and people in discharging their duty to the United Nations. I defy anyone to show any other historical example which can equal it."[6]

Not only foreign policy, but Britain's domestic needs, impinged on Anglo-American relations. In studying the proposed budget for 1952, Churchill looked for measures to curb the country's dollar spending. "No American tobacco should be allowed," he wrote to the Chancellor of the Exchequer, "and other luxuries should be cut. Please let me have the finance of American tobacco on a single page. You will surely get back some of your taxation on additional imports of non-dollar tobacco."[7]

That August, with the Anglo-American focus once more on foreign affairs, and on Britain's international monetary situation, Chur-

---

3. Cabinet meeting of 19 June 1952, Cabinet Papers, 128/25.
4. Speech of 5 March 1952, *Hansard,* Parliamentary debates.
5. In the monetary values of 2005 this was almost $1 billion/£2 billion.
6. Speech of 1 July 1952, *Hansard,* Parliamentary debates.
7. Letter of 9 July 1952, Premier Papers, 11/131.

chill persuaded Truman to make a joint protest to Iran, following the nationalization of the Anglo-Iranian Oil Company by the Iranian Prime Minister, Colonel Mossadeq. Churchill himself had negotiated the British majority shareholding in the company on the eve of war in 1914. "This is the first time since 1945," Jock Colville noted, "that the Americans have joined with us in taking overt action against a third power."[8]

Good relations with the United States were the basis of Churchill's foreign and defense policies. When Anthony Eden proposed supporting a United Nations' resolution on Korea that might lead to breaking off relations with China, Churchill wrote to him: "Proceed as you propose, but don't let us fall out with the US for the sake of Communist China."[9] Churchill also took steps to rebut Soviet charges that the United States was spreading plague germs throughout China. "People think they can deal with this by pooh-poohing it," he wrote to his Private Secretariat. "I thought it might be good perhaps for me to deal with it on behalf of the free world."[10]

When it came to history, Churchill was vigilant in seeking a fair presentation of Britain's war effort. An American television series on the war at sea, entitled *Victory at Sea*, did not please him. Having seen three of the thirty-minute films, he pointed out to the BBC, which was showing the thirteen-part series, that in the submarine war "British forces sunk 521 German U-boats compared to 174 sunk by the United States." The commentary had spoken of Britain's "feeble and pathetic" defense, but, Churchill stressed, "we did practically the whole work, not only of defending ourselves but of bringing in all American shipping after they entered the war, except their troop convoys."

The film on the Normandy landings, Churchill wrote, "gives the impression that only Americans took part in this, with occasional British units. In fact, however, we landed almost as many Divisions as they did, did four-firths of the transportation and naval bombardment, and quite a good share of the air." Until the spring of 1944 Britain "had more soldiers engaged and far more ships in the European

---

8. Diary entry, 22–25 August 1952, John Colville, *The Fringes of Power*, pages 653–54.

9. Minute of 3 September 1952, Premier Papers, 11/1074.

10. Minute of 21 September 1952, Premier Papers, 11/250.

scene, including Italy, than the United States. We even had, on a world wide calculation, plurality up to that date, after which they overtook us." The film as it stood, Churchill wrote, "would probably stir deep anger in British audiences."[11]

On 4 November 1952 Eisenhower was elected President of the United States. "I send you my sincere and heartfelt congratulations on your election," Churchill wrote. "I look forward to a renewal of our comradeship and of our work together for the same causes of peace and freedom as in the past."[12] Eisenhower replied on the following day: "Dear Winston, Thank you very much for the typically generous sentiments expressed in your cable. I shall look forward to receiving your letter and I too look forward to a renewal of our cooperative work in the interests of a free world. Ike."[13]

Churchill also wrote to the outgoing President Truman:

Dear Harry,

I have felt shy of obtruding myself on you while all this battle was on and all my best friends in the United States were fighting one another. We tried to follow with discerning eye all the movements of the troops in the field. It must have been very exciting for those engaged. Our island is unhappily too small for any really full-sized "whistle-stop" tour, but I am studying the plan with attention in case, which is unlikely, I should have a next time.[14]

I hope to come over again some time next year and look forward to seeing you again, if only in my capacity as an Honorary Doctor of Civil Law at Westminster College, Fulton, Missouri.

Let me however meanwhile express my gratitude to you for all you have done for our common show. I was very glad we had that final gallop together.

With kindest regards,

Winston[15]

---

11. Letter of 29 October 1952, Premier Papers, 11/408.
12. Telegram of 5 November 1952, Eisenhower Papers.
13. Telegram of 6 November 1952, Eisenhower Papers.
14. Churchill did not fight another General Election.
15. Letter of 7 November 1952, Premier Papers, 11/307.

"For your private ear," Churchill told Jock Colville about Eisenhower's election, "I am greatly disturbed. I think this makes war much more probable." [16] Such fears gave Churchill a new sense of mission: to stay on as Prime Minister until he could bring about, by his own exertions, a reconciliation of the United States and the Soviet Union. A sense of urgency was added to this when it was announced in mid-November that the United States had tested "thermo-nuclear weapons" on Eniwetok Atoll in the Pacific. Even Churchill was not informed at the time that this was a hydrogen bomb.

In Cabinet on November 25, discussing the American air bases in Britain, the Secretary of State for Air, Lord De L'Isle and Dudley, told his colleagues he was afraid that the creation of American communities in Britain, with their higher standard of living, might cause "criticism and discontent" in the neighborhood. Churchill urged his colleagues to realize that the presence of American forces in the United Kingdom "was an essential feature in the cold war." For that reason it was possible to defend the provision of "reasonable amenities" for the American forces. Churchill added: "Continuous effort should be made to preserve friendly relations between the United States forces in this country and their English neighbours and he would be glad to hear from the Secretary of State for Air what was being done for this purpose." [17]

Five days later Churchill was seventy-eight. "May your celebration be filled with joy and inspired devotion to your country and mankind," President-elect Eisenhower telegraphed.[18] A month later Churchill left London for Southampton and boarded the *Queen Mary* for New York. During the voyage, on New Year's Day 1953, Churchill told Colville that, with Eisenhower as President, he would have to cut things out of volume six of his war memoirs. He could no longer tell the story, he explained, of how the United States "gave way, to please Russia, vast tracts of Europe they had occupied, and how suspicious they were of his pleas for caution."

If Roosevelt had lived, Churchill reflected, and been in good health, "he would have seen the red light in time to check the Ameri-

---

16. Diary entry, 9 November 1952, John Colville, *The Fringes of Power,* page 654.
17. Cabinet meeting of 25 November 1952, Cabinet Papers, 128/25.
18. Telegram of 25 November 1952, Churchill Papers.

can policy. Truman, after all, had only been a novice, bewildered by the march of events and by responsibilities which he had never expected."[19]

On the morning of 5 January 1953 the *Queen Mary* docked in New York. After a short Press Conference Churchill and Clementine left the ship and went to Bernard Baruch's apartment, where Churchill had stayed the previous year. That afternoon Eisenhower arrived. It was fifteen days before he was to become President. He and Churchill spent two hours alone before attending a small dinner party in Baruch's apartment. Colville recorded some of the evening's conversation in his diary: "Winston said that a protoplasm was sexless. Then it divided into two sexes, which, in due course, united again in a different way to their common benefit and gratification. This should also be the story of England and America."[20]

On January 7 Churchill visited his mother's birthplace at 426 Henry Street, Brooklyn. Later that day, at a meeting with Eisenhower, he learned that the President-elect planned to announce in his inaugural speech that he would go anywhere to meet Stalin. Stockholm was mentioned. Churchill was deeply disappointed when Eisenhower told him he did not want Britain to participate in this meeting. Eisenhower's reason: It would involve "asking France and Italy." Alarmed at being excluded, Churchill asked Eisenhower whether it might not be wiser to keep to generalities in his inaugural speech, and wait until he could "survey the whole scene at leisure, and have all official information, before taking plunges." The election was over. Eisenhower had four years of certain power. "Why be in too great a hurry?"

On the evening of January 7, at dinner with Baruch at his home on Sixty-sixth Street, Churchill met for the second time the incoming Secretary of State, John Foster Dulles. Colville, who was present, noted a remark by Dulles, which Churchill found upsetting and unkind. Dulles commented that it would be "most unfortunate for Churchill to return to Washington" immediately after Eisenhower's inauguration. Dulles explained that the American public "thought Winston could cast a spell on all American statesmen," and that if he were directly associated with the economic talks that were scheduled at that time, "the

---

19. Diary entry, 1 January 1953, John Colville, *The Fringes of Power,* page 658.
20. Diary entry, 5 January 1953, John Colville, *The Fringes of Power,* pages 659–60.

fears of the people and of Congress would be aroused to such an extent that the success of the talks would be endangered."[21] During the discussion Dulles asked Churchill how he proposed to defend Hong Kong, to which Churchill replied, "by declaring war on anyone who attacked it."[22]

That night as Churchill went to bed, Colville noted that he said "some very harsh things about the Republican Party in general and Dulles in particular. . . . He said he would have no more to do with Dulles whose 'great slab of a face' he disliked and distrusted."[23]

On the morning of January 8 Churchill flew in President Truman's aircraft from New York to Washington, where he stayed at the British Embassy. That afternoon he called on Truman at the White House, and in the evening he hosted Truman at a dinner at the British Embassy. Then, on the following morning, he flew from Washington to Jamaica for a ten-day holiday. On his return to Britain he read a declaration by Eisenhower that China, which had been giving increasing support to the North Koreans in battle, could no longer be considered free from possible American counterattack. Churchill was concerned that Britain had not been consulted about this declaration. He at once wrote to Eisenhower to explain that, while he felt the distress of the "millions of Americans whose relations are under fire in Korea . . . I feel it in my bones, and it grieves and stirs me every day," he hoped that where "joint action affecting our common destiny" was desired, "you will let us know beforehand so that we can give our opinion and advice in time to have them considered."

Churchill also told Eisenhower that he and Anthony Eden were "resolved to make our co-operation with the United States effective over the world scene."[24] Eleven days later, following Egyptian demands that Britain leave the Suez Canal Zone, Churchill asked Eisenhower for a joint Anglo-American approach to Egypt. Eisenhower declined, explaining that he would only intervene if invited to do so by the Egyp-

---

21. Diary entry, 7 January 1953, John Colville, *The Fringes of Power,* pages 661–62.
22. "Note," 7 January 1953, Premier Papers, 11/433.
23. Diary entry, 7 January 1953, John Colville, *The Fringes of Power,* pages 661–62.
24. Telegram of 7 February 1953, Eisenhower Papers.

tian President, General Naguib. Churchill wrote back: "We therefore have to go on alone."[25]

On 5 March 1953 Stalin died in Moscow. Churchill hoped there would soon be an opportunity to revive his plan for a renewed Big Three meeting once Stalin's successors were in place. Six days after the Soviet leader's death he telegraphed to Eisenhower to encourage such a meeting. "I have the feeling," Churchill wrote, "that we might both of us together or separately be called to account," he wrote, "if no attempt was made to turn over a leaf so that a new page would be started with something more coherent on it than a series of casual and dangerous incidents at the many points of contact between the two divisions of the world."[26] Unfortunately for Churchill's hopes of a swift initiative, Eisenhower declined any prospect of a Three-Power meeting, arguing that it would be "another propaganda mill for the Soviet."[27]

For the next two years Churchill was repeatedly to challenge this view, and to urge upon Eisenhower the need, the urgency and the wisdom of a face-to-face meeting with the new Soviet rulers. In his search for a joint Anglo-American policy toward the Soviet Union, he made every effort not to undermine his relations with Eisenhower. In a letter to the Queen's Private Secretary he explained, with regard to the final volume of his war memoirs, that he had held the whole volume back from the printer until after the Presidential election in the United States, "and since then I have gone over it again and taken out any critical references to General Eisenhower which, now that he is President, might conceivably damage Anglo-American relations."[28] In sending the new volume to Eisenhower, Churchill asked the Cabinet Secretary, Sir Norman Brook, to draft a letter for him, in the first person.[29]

"I know that nothing which I have written will damage our friendship," the letter read. "But, now that you have assumed supreme political office in your country, I am most anxious that nothing should be

25. Letter of 5 April 1953, Premier Papers, 11/1074.
26. Telegram of 11 March 1953, Premier Papers, 11/422.
27. Letter of 12 March 1953, Premier Papers, 11/422.
28. Letter of 28 March 1953, Royal Archives.
29. Draft letter, Churchill Papers, CHUR 4/63A, David Reynolds, *In Command of History: Churchill Fighting and Writing the Second World War,* page 435.

published which might seem to others to threaten our current relations in our public duties or impair the sympathy and understanding which exist between our countries." He had therefore "gone over the book again in the last few months and have taken great pains to ensure that it contains nothing which might imply that there was in those days any controversy or lack of confidence between us." There was in fact, Churchill added, "little controversy in those years; but I have been careful to ensure that the few differences of opinion which arose are so described that even ill-disposed people will be unable now to turn them to mischievous account. I think therefore that you can be confident that the publication of this final volume will do nothing to disturb our present relationship." [30]

Churchill lost no time in renewing his appeal to Eisenhower to contemplate high level talks with the Soviet Union: "great hope" had arisen in the world, he told the President, "that there is a change of heart in the vast, mighty masses of Russia and this can carry them far and fast and perhaps into revolution." [31] Before Eisenhower could reply, Churchill telegraphed again. "A new hope has, I feel, been created in the unhappy, bewildered world," he wrote. "It ought to be possible to proclaim our unflinching determination to resist Communist tyranny and aggression and at the same time, though separately, to declare how glad we should be if we found there was a real change of heart and not let it be said that we had closed the door upon it." [32]

The President did not dismiss Churchill's concerns outright. "I agree with the tenor of your comments," he replied, and went on to tell Churchill he would certainly strive to make his forthcoming broadcast to the American people "one that will not freeze the tender buds of sprouting decency, if indeed they are really coming out." [33] Speaking in Glasgow four days later, Churchill referred to the possibilities opened up by there being "new men" in supreme power in Moscow. [34] From Washington, Eisenhower announced that he was willing to consider discussions with the Soviet Union on points of substance. It was,

---

30. Letter of 9 April 1953, Eisenhower Papers.
31. Telegram of 11 April 1953, Eisenhower Papers.
32. Telegram of 12 April 1953, Premier Papers, 11/1074.
33. Telegram of 13 April 1953, Eisenhower Papers.
34. Speech of 17 April 1953, Randolph S. Churchill, editor, *The Unwritten Alliance: Speeches 1953 to 1959 by Winston S. Churchill*, pages 28–35.

Churchill told the House of Commons, a "bold and inspiring initiative."[35] In sending copies of his exchanges with Eisenhower to the Queen, Churchill added: "I hope Your Majesty will feel that I have tried to save the spring-time buds—if any there be."[36]

Churchill wanted to expedite a summit, and feared Eisenhower would be tardy. "If nothing can be arranged as a result of the American initiative," he informed the President, "I shall have to consider seriously a personal contact. You told me in New York you would have no objection to this."[37] Eisenhower's reply was not encouraging. "We have so far seen no concrete Soviet actions which would indicate their willingness to perform in connection with larger issues," he wrote. "In the circumstances we would risk raising hopes of progress toward an accommodation which would be unjustified."[38]

Churchill would not give up. At the beginning of May he sent Eisenhower the draft of a letter he intended to send to the Soviet Foreign Minister, Vyacheslav Molotov, asking if he could come to Moscow "so that we could renew our own wartime relation" and also meet the new Soviet leader, Georgi Malenkov, for an informal meeting that might "restore an easy and friendly basis between us such as I have with so many other countries."[39] Eisenhower, supported by Dulles, did not want Churchill to send this message to Moscow. Churchill replied that except for Molotov, none of the new leaders in Moscow—Malenkov, Molotov, Lavrenti Beria and Marshal Nikolai Bulganin—had any contacts outside the Soviet Union. "I am very anxious to know these men and talk to them as I think I can frankly and on the dead level," Churchill told the President. "It is only by going to Moscow that I can meet them all and as I am only the head of a Government, not of a State, I see no obstacle. Of course, I would much rather go with you to any place you might appoint and that is, I believe, the best chance of a good result. I find it difficult to believe that we shall gain anything by an attitude of pure negation and your message to me certainly does not show much hope."[40]

------

35. Speech of 20 April 1953, *Hansard,* Parliamentary debates.
36. Letter of 14 April 1953, Royal Archives.
37. Telegram of 21 April 1953, Premier Papers, 11/422.
38. Telegram of 25 April 1953, Eisenhower Papers.
39. Telegram of 4 May 1953, Eisenhower Papers.
40. Telegram of 5 May 1953, Eisenhower Papers.

Eisenhower and Dulles were not convinced. Eisenhower explained to Churchill: "I still regard that area as one of potential disaster for the Western world."[41] Churchill took his appeal to the British public, indirectly rebuking the two Americans when he told the House of Commons on May 11: "If there is not at the summit of the nations the will to win the greatest prize and the greatest honour ever offered to mankind, doom-laden responsibility will fall upon those who now possess the power to decide. At the worst the participants in the meeting would have established more intimate contacts. At the best we might have a generation of peace."[42]

Churchill planned to advance his argument for a summit at an Anglo-American meeting in Bermuda, set for the end of June, with himself and Eisenhower as the principals. On June 24 he telegraphed to Eisenhower that he was holding three battalions of British troops and an artillery regiment "at short notice" to reinforce General Mark Clark's army in Korea "in any action that may be required of them by the United Nations."[43] That evening Churchill was the host at a banquet at 10 Downing Street for the Italian Prime Minister, Alcide de Gasperi. It was Churchill's last official function before leaving by ship for Bermuda a week later for talks with Eisenhower. But the meeting was not to be. At the end of the dinner Churchill suffered a severe stroke.

41. Letter of 8 May 1953, Premier Papers, 11/421.
42. Speech of 11 May 1953, *Hansard,* Parliamentary debates.
43. Telegram of 24 June 1953, Eisenhower Papers.

Chapter Forty

꙰

"NEVER BE SEPARATED FROM
THE AMERICANS"

Churchill's left side was partially paralyzed, but on 26 June 1953, three days after his stroke, he was able to dictate a telegram to Eisenhower, postponing the Bermuda meeting.[1] No news of anything untoward was made public; the only reference to Churchill in the *New York Times* on June 26 was news of the wedding of one of Churchill's cousins to a stockbroker.[2] On the following day, three days after his stroke, a brief statement from Downing Street announced that Churchill needed "a complete rest."[3] From General Marshall came "concern, affection and sympathy," and an added note: "Please do be careful, a patient in the full meaning of the word. You are too vastly important to the world to take any risks."[4]

Twenty-four days after his stroke Churchill dictated another telegram to Eisenhower, defending his desire for a summit. "Above all," he told the President, "I thought that you and I might have formed our own impression of Malenkov, who has never seen anybody outside Russia."[5]

---

1. Message of 26 June 1953, Eisenhower Papers.
2. "Churchill's Cousin Wed to Broker," *New York Times,* 26 June 1953. The cousin was Lady Rosemary Spencer-Churchill, daughter of the Tenth Duke of Marlborough. The stockbroker was Robert Muir.
3. "Churchill Delays Talks at Bermuda; Must Rest a Month," *New York Times,* 28 June 1953.
4. Letter of 1 July 1953, Churchill Papers, 2/144, Martin Gilbert, *Winston S. Churchill,* Volume 8, page 859.
5. Telegram of 17 July 1953, Eisenhower Papers.

Eisenhower's reply was negative. "I do not like talking informally," he wrote, "with those who only wish to entrap and embarrass us."[6] Churchill was not deterred. Three days after Eisenhower's reply, Colville noted that he was still "very wrapped up with the possibility of bringing something off with the Russians and with the idea of meeting Malenkov face to face." Colville added that Churchill was "Very disappointed in Eisenhower whom he thinks both weak and stupid. Bitterly regrets that the Democrats were not returned at the last Presidential Election."[7]

While Churchill recuperated, a secret Anglo-American plan that he had approved before his stroke came to a dramatic climax. On August 19 in Iran, Colonel Mossadeq was overthrown and the Shah reinstated. Eisenhower and Churchill had approved the plan, which stated bluntly, "Mossadeq must go."[8] Working together, the American Central Intelligence Agency and the British Secret Intelligence Service carried it out, using as their main agent Kermit Roosevelt, a grandson of President Theodore Roosevelt. Churchill had seen Kermit Roosevelt in London during the last months of Truman's presidency, when Churchill had spoken "with special vehemence" about the need for action.[9] But Truman had been averse to any such action.[10]

With the overthrow of Mossadeq, a new oil consortium was created, in which Anglo-Iranian Oil and a group of American oil companies each had a 40 percent stake. Churchill was later said to have called the Anglo-American enterprise "the finest operation since the war."[11] When Kermit Roosevelt returned through London, Churchill told him: "Young man, if I had been but a few years younger, I would have loved nothing better than to have served under your command in this great venture."[12]

---

6. Letter of 21 July 1953, Eisenhower Papers.

7. Diary entry, 24 July 1953, John Colville, *The Fringes of Power,* page 672.

8. National Security Archive, *Electronic Briefing Book No. 28,* "The Secret CIA History of the Iran Coup, 1953."

9. Kermit Roosevelt, *Countercoup: The Struggle for the Control of Iran,* page 107.

10. Stephen Kinzer, *All the Shah's Men: An American Coup and the Roots of Middle East Terror,* page 3.

11. Donald N. Wilber, *Overthrow of Premier Mossadeq of Iran, November 1952–August 1953,* CIA Special Report, *New York Times,* 16 April 2000.

12. Kermit Roosevelt, *Countercoup: The Struggle for the Control of Iran,* page 207.

As Churchill slowly recovered from the physical effects of his stroke, he invited Adlai Stevenson, Eisenhower's Democratic opponent in the 1952 Presidential election, to Chequers. At luncheon Churchill quoted to Stevenson by heart long sections of Bourke Cockran's speeches, with their constant refrain, "The earth is a generous mother." Over the Bank Holiday weekend, Churchill's mind was focused on a summit. "Winston is firmly hoping for talks which might lead to a relaxation of the Cold War," Colville noted, "and a respite in which science could use its marvels for improving the lot of man and, as he put it, the leisured classes of his youth might give way to the leisured masses of tomorrow." [13]

Churchill was well enough by September 8 to preside at a Cabinet meeting where the discussion was whether to support the admission of China to the United Nations. He did not want Britain to do anything that might upset the United States. "We should be well advised," he said, "to go to great lengths to avoid any further cause of Anglo-American misunderstanding at the present time." [14]

On October 10 Churchill addressed the Conservative Party's annual conference in Margate. During his speech he referred to his May 11 appeal for a summit. "I asked for very little," he told his listeners. "I held out no glittering or exciting hopes about Russia. I thought that friendly, informal, personal talks between the leading figures in the countries mainly involved might do good and could not easily do much harm, and that one good thing might lead to another." Churchill then referred, without naming the United States or its President, to Eisenhower's rejection of a summit. His "humble, modest plan," announced as the policy of Her Majesty's Government, had raised "a considerable stir all over the place and though we have not yet been able to persuade our trusted allies to adopt it in the form I suggested no one can say that it is dead."

Churchill was emphatic that a summit should be tried. "I still think that the leading men of the various nations ought to be able to meet together without trying to cut attitudes before excitable publics," he told his Margate audience, "or using regiments of experts to marshal

---

13. Diary entry, 31 July–4 August 1953, John Colville, *The Fringes of Power*, pages 672–73.

14. Cabinet meeting of 8 September 1953, Cabinet Papers, 128/26.

all the difficulties and objections." The important thing was to try to see "whether there is not something better for us all than tearing and blasting each other to pieces, which we can certainly do." [15]

On November 5 Churchill telegraphed to Eisenhower that before any approach to the Soviets, the two men should meet at Bermuda, as had been originally planned. [16] Eisenhower agreed. Four days later, at the Lord Mayor's Banquet in London, Churchill stressed that he did not share the anxieties of those who worried about too close a British relationship with the United States. "After all," he said, "we are both very free-speaking democracies and where there is a great deal of free speech there is always a certain amount of foolish speech. . . . It would be a pity if we thought about each other in terms of our local bugbears and matched one against the other."

Churchill's advice was clear: "Let us stick to our heroes, John Bull and Uncle Sam. They never were closer together than they are now; not only in sentiment but in common interest and in faithfulness to the cause of world freedom." It was, he stressed, "the growing unity and brotherhood between the United States and the British Common-wealth of Nations that sustains our faith in human destiny." [17]

On November 30 Churchill was seventy-nine. The following night at midnight, he left London by air for Bermuda, with refueling stops in Iceland and Newfoundland. On December 4, at the first plenary meeting, Churchill asked those present, "Is there a new Soviet look?" Had there been "a deep change in the mighty entity we call the Soviet Union?" He would not be "in too much of a hurry," Churchill told Eisenhower, "to believe that nothing but evil emanates from this mighty branch of the human family, or that nothing but danger and peril could come out of this vast ocean of land . . . so little known and understood." To the amazement of the British participants, Eisenhower replied, as Colville noted, "with a short, very violent statement,

---

15. Speech of 10 October 1953, Randolph S. Churchill, editor, *The Unwritten Alliance: Speeches 1953 to 1959 by Winston S. Churchill*, pages 57–67.
16. Telegram of 5 November 1953, Premier Papers, 11/418.
17. Speech of 9 November 1953, Randolph S. Churchill, editor, *The Unwritten Alliance*, pages 79–82.

in the coarsest terms," depicting the Soviet Union as "a woman of the streets."[18]

The official note takers captured Eisenhower's harsh mood. "If we understood that under this dress was the same old girl," the President said, "if we understood that despite bath, perfume or lace, it was still the same old girl, on that basis then we might explore all that Sir Winston had said. . . . Perhaps we could pull the old girl off the main street and put her in a back alley." But Eisenhower did not want to approach the problem "on the basis that there had been any change in the Soviet policy of destroying the Capitalist free world by all means, by force, by deceit or by lies. This was their long-term purpose. From their writings it was clear there had been no change since Lenin."[19]

Without waiting for Churchill's response, Eisenhower then adjourned the conference. When Eden asked when the next meeting should be, "the President replied, 'I don't know. Mine is with a whisky and soda'—and got up to leave the room."[20]

Churchill's hopes of a summit had been dashed. When the conference communiqué was shown to him he commented bitterly to Eden: "I can find nothing in this communiqué which shows the slightest desire for the success of the Conference or for an easement in relations with Russia."[21] Churchill flew back to Britain. At the first Cabinet meeting after his return, he advocated "determined efforts" to persuade the United States to adopt Britain's policy of increased trade with the Soviet Union.[22] Eisenhower rejected this, explaining that the British proposals "went further than public and Congressional opinion in the United States would be able to accept."[23]

Clementine Churchill felt that Eisenhower was "right about the Russian menace," but wished that her husband could see him again. If only America "were not so unsympathetic & indeed unhelpful to us,"

---

18. Diary entry, 4 December 1953, John Colville, *The Fringes of Power,* pages 685–87.

19. Meeting of 4 December 1953, Eisenhower Papers.

20. Diary entry, 4 December 1953, John Colville, *The Fringes of Power,* pages 685–87.

21. Minute of 7 December 1953, Premier Papers, 11/418.

22. Cabinet meeting, 18 January 1954, Cabinet Papers, 128/27.

23. Cabinet meeting, 24 March 1954, Cabinet Papers, 128/27.

she wrote.[24] Four days after her letter it was announced in the United States that for more than a year the country had possessed a hydrogen bomb. Churchill was indignant, telling the House of Commons five months later that he had been "deeply concerned at the lack of information we possessed" about the hydrogen bomb, and how it would affect civil defense, shelters, dispersion of population and anti-aircraft defense.[25] Britain had received no prior notice and no information at all.

A second American hydrogen bomb test at Bikini Atoll in the Pacific was made public at once. After being shown details of the impact of the explosion, which caused a 175-foot displacement of the ocean bed, Churchill again appealed to Eisenhower for a summit. Beginning his letter: "My dear friend," Churchill wrote: "Of course I recur to my earlier proposal of a personal meeting between Three. Men have to settle with men, no matter how vast, and in part beyond their comprehension, the business in hand may be. I can even imagine that a few simple words, spoken in the awe which may at once oppress and inspire the speakers, might lift this nuclear monster from our world."[26]

On March 27 Churchill again appealed to Eisenhower for a relaxation of American trade barriers with the Soviet Union, but he did not want a breach with the United States. Such a breach, he wrote to his friend Lord Beaverbrook, "might well be fatal to world peace and to our survival, for they could quite easily go it alone and we are far worse placed geographically."[27]

In the House of Commons, Churchill answered Labour criticisms that the British government should persuade the United States to abandon its hydrogen bomb tests or bring them under international control. The Government, Churchill replied, and he repeated this to the Cabinet the following day, "were not prepared to make any such representations to the United States Government or to take any other action which might impede American progress in building up their overwhelming strength in nuclear weapons, which provided the greatest possible deterrent against the outbreak of a third world war."[28]

24. Letter of 13 February 1954, Churchill Papers.
25. Speech of 12 July 1954, *Hansard*, Parliamentary debates.
26. Letter dated "March 1954," Eisenhower Papers.
27. Letter of 30 March 1954, Beaverbrook Papers.
28. Cabinet meeting, 31 March 1954, Cabinet Papers, 128/27.

In the House of Commons on April 5, Churchill reiterated his desire for a meeting between the Western and Soviet leaders. He also sought to answer Labour criticisms of the American hydrogen bomb. Nothing could be "more disastrous to peace," he declared, amid Labour interruptions, than for the House of Commons "to rouse needless antagonism in Congress or throughout America." Nothing could be more detrimental to the survival of Western Europe and the safety of Britain, he added, "than a grave dispute between Britain and the United States."[29]

An envoy from Eisenhower, Admiral Arthur W. Radford, sought Churchill's support for America's policy in South-East Asia. In talks with Admiral Radford, Churchill criticized the American concept of "war on the fringes." His policy "was quite different," he explained. It was "conversations at the centre."[30] To seek to bring about such conversations, and to persuade Eisenhower to join him in an approach to the Soviets, Churchill prepared to set off once more for Washington. "It seems to me," he wrote to Eisenhower, "that our meetings in the easy informal manner that we both desire may be a help in brushing away this chatter about an Anglo-American rift which can benefit no-one but our common foes."[31] The Americans, Churchill wrote to Clementine on the following day, "are the only people who can defend the free world even though they bring in Dulles to do it."[32]

Before leaving for the United States, Churchill spoke at a dinner given by the English-Speaking Union to welcome the American military commander of NATO, General Alfred M. Gruenther, to Britain. Churchill praised the "unwritten alliance which binds the British Commonwealth and Empire to the great republic of the United States," an alliance far closer than many that existed in writing, a treaty "with more enduring elements than clauses and protocols." The alliance between Britain and the United States was a special one: "We have history, law, philosophy, and literature; we have sentiment and common interest; we have a language which even the Scottish Nationalists will not mind me referring to as English. We are often in agreement on

---

29. Speech of 5 April 1954, *Hansard*, Parliamentary debates.
30. Record of a conversation, 26 April 1954, Premier Papers, 11/564.
31. Letter of 24 May 1954, Eisenhower Papers.
32. Letter of 25 May 1954, Spencer-Churchill Papers.

current events and we stand on the same foundation of the supreme realities of the modern world." [33]

Churchill and Eden left London for Washington by plane on the evening of June 24. Reaching Washington the following morning, after a refueling stop in Newfoundland, they were met by the Vice-President, Richard M. Nixon, and Dulles. At the airport Churchill spoke a few words into the barrage of microphones. "I have had a very comfortable journey," he said, "from my fatherland to my mother's land." [34] From the airport he was driven to the White House for lunch, after which, during a two-hour discussion, he asked Eisenhower to allow "the possibility of high level talks with the Soviets" to be added to their agenda. Eisenhower said he had no objection. Churchill then suggested an initial "reconnaissance in force" to the Soviet Union, perhaps by himself, to see "if anything promising developed." He would be interested in finding out "what sort of a man" was Malenkov, who, Churchill reiterated, had never been outside his own country. Churchill was convinced that "there was a deep underlying demand" on the part of the Russian people "to enjoy a better life, particularly after suffering oppression for more than fifty years."

Churchill then turned to the question of Egypt, hoping to secure American participation in a new Anglo-Egyptian agreement. The American minutes described his appeal as "prolonged and rather emotional." Churchill wanted the Egyptian Government to be told that it would receive neither arms nor aid from the United States until it reached agreement, "and that these would be cut off" if it broke the agreement. Dulles and Eisenhower agreed to work out some arrangement under which American aid to Egypt could be suspended if the Anglo-Egyptian agreement was violated. The discussion then turned to South-East Asia, with Churchill telling the Americans that he was anxious to take "some of the weight" off the United States in its presentation of an anti-Communist front, but stressing that England would never go to war in Indochina. Turning briefly to the Middle East, Churchill made the perceptive remark that it was "oilism and not colonialism which was evil in the world today." [35]

---

33. Speech of 8 June 1954, Randolph S. Churchill, editor, *The Unwritten Alliance: Speeches 1953 to 1959 by Winston S. Churchill*, pages 153–55.
34. *New York Times*, 26 June 1954.
35. Memorandum of conversation, 25 June 1954, Eisenhower Papers.

That evening, as Churchill was dressing for dinner to meet the American Cabinet, his doctor asked him when he would go to Russia. "It might be in July," Churchill replied.[36] On the following morning, Churchill spent several hours with Eisenhower, during which he told the President of the British decision to manufacture a hydrogen bomb, and to do so in Britain. During their talks Churchill asked Eisenhower how many Communists there were in the United States. The President replied that there were some 25,000 and that "we knew where they were, in emergency could pick them up." Eisenhower also told Churchill that "we had tried a number of Communists for conspiracy to destroy government by force."

The President then told Churchill he would not agree to a meeting anywhere under Soviet rule, but that he did not object to Churchill's suggestion of a meeting in either Stockholm or London. Later Eisenhower added The Hague as a possible meeting place. Eisenhower "tried to stress," the American notes of the meeting recorded, that no opportunity should be given to Malenkov to "hit the free world in the face."

Churchill told Eisenhower he could find out where the meeting could take place forty-eight hours after his return. As to the nations to be asked to the summit, "Two is company," Churchill said, "three is hard company, four is a deadlock." Eisenhower then told Churchill that he was "completely inexperienced" in that kind of negotiation. "I am not afraid to meet anybody face to face to talk to him," he said, "but the world gets in a habit of expecting a lot." At the end of the discussion Eisenhower told Churchill about the Anglo-American exchange of atomic information, adding: "We will give you everything we have got on that."[37]

At lunch that day Churchill met thirty leading members of Congress. Despite the increased complexities of the modern age, he told them, "a way could be found through the difficulties by the use of two important factors." One was time: "Do not throw away time," he said. "There are lots of things that seem impossible but can be worked out given time." The second was vigilance: "Eternal vigilance" was needed

---

36. Diary entry, 25 June–3 July 1954, Lord Moran (Sir Charles Wilson), *Winston Churchill: The Struggle for Survival, 1940–1965*, pages 560–74.
37. Meeting of 26 June 1954, Eisenhower Papers.

to guard the freedom of the world "against the intolerable philosophy of Communism." Every effort should be made by the free world "to keep it from being foisted, by force or ignorance, upon the human race." Churchill then told the American legislators that conferences with the Soviets were vitally important: "Meeting jaw to jaw is better than war."

It was "true perhaps," Churchill commented, "that America could stand alone in the world, particularly with its advantage in thermonuclear matters." Such a stand, however, would be unwise. The United States, even at the height of its present power, had not attempted to acquire territory, "and that made him very proud of his blood connections."

Churchill continued his remarks, as recorded by the White House stenographer, by saying that he and Eisenhower "had been talking for twelve years now about the problems of the day, that they had got to know each other, and that as far as he was concerned, the President was one of the few people from whom the Prime Minister derived pleasure in talking to him." Churchill added: "Thank God you have him at the head of your country and that your country is at the head of the world." There was yet more need "for forceful and valued service to show the way to peace with honour."[38]

The afternoon of June 26 was spent in conference at the White House. "Good progress," Colville wrote, "this time on Egypt." Churchill was elated by success, and in what Colville described as "a state of excited good humour." In the middle of the afternoon meeting he "suddenly emerged" from the discussions and summoned his son-in-law, Christopher Soames, and Jock Colville to go up to the White House solarium with him, "so as to look at a great storm which was raging." Colville added: "I can't imagine anybody else interrupting a meeting with the President of the United States, two Secretaries of State and two Ambassadors just for this purpose." The Russian visit project, Colville noted, had been expanded, by Eisenhower, to a meeting in London, together with the French and West German leaders, "at the opening of which Ike himself would be present."[39]

That night Churchill again dined with Eisenhower at the White

---

38. Congressional luncheon, 26 June 1954, Eisenhower Papers.
39. Diary entry, 26 June 1954, John Colville, *The Fringes of Power*, pages 573–74.

House. At eleven o'clock, he asked the President if he might be excused: He had to make up the six hours' sleep he had lost through the time zones. For Churchill and his party it was the London equivalent of five o'clock in the morning as they went to bed. Talks continued at the White House throughout the following day, a Sunday. "The Russian project," noted Colville in his diary, "has shrunk again as Dulles has been getting at the President." But Churchill was still determined, Colville noted, to meet the Russians himself, "as he has now an assurance that the Americans won't object."

Dulles also had a private talk with Churchill at the White House. His notes make clear just how wide the gulf was between his position and Churchill's. When Churchill told Dulles of the possibility of his having a high-level meeting with the Russians, "which might perhaps be preliminary to a three-power meeting," and that he had in mind possibly going to Stockholm to see whether there were "consenting minds," which would make it profitable to have a three-power meeting, Dulles replied that it was "extremely dangerous" to have such a meeting unless it would have positive results. "An illusion of success would be bad," he told Churchill, and an obvious failure would be bad "and might create the impression that the only alternative was war."

Dulles then pointed out that if Churchill made an exploratory mission alone, "it would not be looked upon well in this country, and also we might have to make it clear that Mr. Churchill was in no sense speaking or acting for the United States." Churchill replied that "he fully understood this," but that he would be going not in any sense as an intermediary between the United States and the Soviet Union, but representing the spirit and purpose of "our side." Dulles urged him to weigh the matter "very carefully" before making any positive decision.[40]

On the final day of the conference Churchill went to see Eisenhower to finalize a Declaration of Principles. In that declaration, he told the House of Commons after his return, Britain and the United States affirmed their "comradeship," offered the hand of friendship to all "who might seek it sincerely," reasserted their sympathy for and loyalty "to those still in bondage," proclaimed their desire to reduce armaments and turn nuclear power into peaceful channels, confirmed

---

40. Memorandum of a conversation, 27 June 1954, Eisenhower Papers.

their support of the United Nations and all organizations designed to promote and preserve the peace of the world, and proclaimed their determination to develop and maintain "the spiritual, economic, and military strength necessary" to pursue their purposes effectively. These were all principles, Churchill stressed, "which we share with our American friends."[41]

In addition to the Declaration of Principles, Churchill and Eisenhower announced their agreement that the German Federal Republic should take its place as an equal partner in the community of Western nations "where it can make its proper contribution to the defence of the free world." They added: "We are determined to achieve this goal."[42] After lunch that day at the British Embassy, Colville noted that Churchill became "jocular," telling the other guests "that if he were ever chased out of England and became an American citizen, he would hope to be elected to Congress. He would then propose two amendments to the American Constitution: (i) that at least half the members of the US Cabinet should have seats in Congress, (ii) that the President, instead of signing himself Dwight D. Eisenhower a hundred times a day should be authorised to sign himself 'Ike.'"[43]

On the afternoon of June 29 Churchill left Washington by air for Ottawa, seen off, as he had been welcomed, by Nixon and Dulles. After a broadcast to the Canadian people and dinner with the Canadian Prime Minister he flew back on the evening of June 30 to New York, reaching the city after midnight and being driven to the Hudson River docks, where he boarded the *Queen Elizabeth*. It was one o'clock in the morning. The ship remained that night moored to the quayside. In the morning Bernard Baruch was among those who came to see Churchill off. The *Queen Elizabeth* sailed at noon.

On the voyage back to Britain, Churchill told his doctor that he would not go to Moscow for the summit, but to Vienna, where he would try to persuade the Russians to sign an Austrian treaty. If that worked out, people would "whoop with joy," and he might travel on to Moscow for a "courtesy visit," perhaps staying forty-eight hours.[44] In his

---

41. Speech of 14 July 1954, *Hansard,* Parliamentary debates.
42. Declaration of Principles, Premier Papers, 11/667.
43. Diary entry, 29 June 1954, John Colville, *The Fringes of Power,* pages 573–74.
44. Diary entry, 4 July 1954, Lord Moran (Sir Charles Wilson), *Winston S. Churchill: The Struggle for Survival, 1940–1965,* pages 574–75.

cabin Churchill dictated a telegram to Molotov proposing talks with the Soviet leaders without Eisenhower being present.[45]

Churchill then informed Eisenhower of his telegram to Molotov. "I should be very glad if you would let me know," he had written to Molotov, "if you would like the idea of a friendly meeting, with no agenda and no object but to find a reasonable way of living side by side in growing confidence, easement and prosperity." Although his meeting with Molotov, wherever held, "would be simple and informal and last only a few days," it might, Churchill told Eisenhower, "be the prelude to a wider reunion where much might be settled."[46]

"You did not let any grass grow under your feet" was Eisenhower's comment when Churchill sent him the text of his message to Molotov. Eisenhower was angered, writing to Churchill that he had thought, "obviously erroneously," that when Churchill had left Washington, "you were in an undecided mood about this matter, and that when you had cleared your own mind I would receive some notice if you were to put your program into action." That was now past history, "and we must hope that the steps you have started will lead to a good result."[47] Alas, they did not. The members of Churchill's Cabinet were even more indignant than Eisenhower that Churchill had telegraphed to Molotov without consulting them.

Churchill did not give up his search for a summit. Even Eisenhower, while reasserting his doubts, sent his "prayerful hope that your mission, if you pursue it, may be crowned with complete success," adding that he was "not vexed" by Churchill's efforts. "Personal trust," Eisenhower explained, "based on more than a dozen years of close association and valued friendship may occasionally permit room for amazement but never for suspicion." Eisenhower's concern was Britain's reluctance to support the United States in its hard-line stance toward Communist China. "Frankly," he told Churchill, "I have no worries whatsoever about the ability of your Government and this one to keep Anglo-American relationships on a sound, friendly and cooperative basis as long as this one question which looms so importantly in the American mind does not rise up to plague us."[48]

---

45. Diary entry, 4 July 1954, John Colville, *The Fringes of Power,* pages 697–98.
46. Undated telegram, Eisenhower Papers.
47. Telegram of 7 July 1954, Eisenhower Papers.
48. Telegram of 8 July 1954, Premier Papers, 11/1074.

It was on a summit with the Soviets that Churchill focused his thoughts and efforts. "I cherish hopes not illusions," he telegraphed to Eisenhower on July 9, "and after all I am 'an expendable' and very ready to be one in so great a cause."[49] Eisenhower remained skeptical, so much so that on August 8, Churchill rebuked him. "Fancy that you and Malenkov should never have met," he wrote, "or that he should never have been outside Russia, when all the time in both countries appalling preparations are being made for measureless mutual destruction." Churchill went on to tell the President that even when the power of Britain was "so much less than that of the United States," he felt—"old age notwithstanding—a responsibility and resolve to use any remaining influence I may have to seek, if not for a solution at any rate for an easement."

"Easement" was the word Churchill used again and again in explaining to friends and colleagues what he had in mind with regard to the Soviet Union. Even if nothing solid or decisive were to be gained, he explained to Eisenhower, "no harm need be done." Even if realities presented themselves more plainly, "that might bring about a renewed effort for Peace." After all, Churchill told the President, "the interest of both sides is Survival and, as an additional attraction, measureless material prosperity of the masses."

Yet there were those, Churchill told Eisenhower, who said that the Heads of Governments "must not ever meet. Human affairs are too great for human beings. Only the Departments of State can cope with them, and meanwhile let us drift and have some more experiments and see how things feel in a year or two when they are so much nearer to us in annihilating power." Churchill rejected such arguments. "Now, I believe, is the moment for parley at the summit," he informed Eisenhower, and he went on to explain: "All the world desires it. In two or three years a different mood may rule either with those who have their hands upon the levers or upon the multitude whose votes they require." His aim was to help bring about "sensible and serious contact" between the Western and Soviet leaders.[50]

To Churchill's distress, the Communist leaders in Moscow refused to take up his offer of a meeting, even in a neutral capital. But Chur-

49. Telegram of 9 July 1954, Eisenhower Papers.
50. Letter of 8 August 1954, Eisenhower Papers.

chill did not give up, writing on his eightieth birthday, 30 November 1954, to Eisenhower: "I still hope we may reach a top level meeting with the new regime in Russia, and that you and I may both be present."[51] It was China, however, that loomed highest on the American agenda. The defense of Taiwan (Formosa) from Chinese Communist threats, and the need to support the Chinese Nationalist leader on Taiwan, Chiang Kai-shek, dominated Washington.

Churchill warned Eisenhower that he did not think it would be "right or wise" to encourage Chiang Kai-shek "to keep alive the reconquest of the Chinese mainland in order to inspire his faithful followers." Chiang Kai-shek deserved "the protection of your shield but not the use of your sword." Eisenhower must realize, however, Churchill added by way of assurance, that both he and Eden "desire to do our utmost to help you and our strongest resolve is to keep our two countries bound together in their sacred brotherhood."[52]

A possible summit with the Soviet Union still animated Churchill's hopes. In March 1955, after Marshal Bulganin replaced Malenkov at the top of the Soviet hierarchy, Churchill once again pressed Eisenhower to seek a summit. But the American Ambassador to Britain, Winthrop Aldrich, brought a message from the White House, "to the effect"—Churchill informed Clementine—"that Ike was not willing himself to participate in a meeting with Russia."[53]

On the following morning Churchill was present in Cabinet when a telegram from Sir Roger Makins, the British Ambassador in Washington was read out, making it clear that it was unlikely that either Eisenhower or Dulles was contemplating "an early Four-Power meeting with the Russians."[54] First a Soviet and then an American rejection had turned the summit project to nought.

For several months the eighty-year-old Churchill had been under continual pressure from his senior Cabinet colleagues to resign. That pressure intensified as the summit hopes receded. Forced to recognize that his two-year quest for a meeting with the Soviet leaders had failed, he bowed to the pressure of his colleagues, and agreed to lay down the

---

51. Letter of 7 December 1954, Eisenhower Papers.
52. Telegram of 15 February 1955, Eisenhower Papers.
53. Letter of 15 March 1955, Baroness Spencer-Churchill Papers.
54. Cabinet meeting, 16 March 1955, Cabinet Papers, 128/28.

burdens of office. In telling Eisenhower of his decision, Churchill wrote of "the causes for which we have both of us worked so long." Of these the first was "Anglo-American brotherhood," the second "the arrest of the Communist menace." These two causes, Churchill added, "are, I believe, identical."[55]

On March 31 Churchill spoke in the House of Commons for the last time as Prime Minister. During a debate on NATO, he was asked if he could arrange consultations between its European members and the North Americans. He replied: "Certainly, I think the closer the contacts between the United States and Europe the better."[56]

On April 5, the day before his resignation came into effect, Churchill held the final Cabinet meeting of his premiership, and of his career. When it was over he spoke to those members of his government who, while not in the Cabinet, were part of his administration: Junior Ministers and Under-Secretaries. One of them, Lord De L'Isle and Dudley, recalled Churchill's final words: "Man is spirit," and "Never be separated from the Americans."[57]

55. Letter of 3 April 1955, draft marked with a query "?not sent," Churchill Papers.
56. *Hansard*, Parliamentary Debates, 31 March 1955.
57. Lord De L'Isle and Dudley, VC, recollection, letter to the author, 13 July 1987.

Chapter Forty-One

⁂

FINAL DECADE:
"I DELIGHT IN MY
AMERICAN ANCESTRY"

Sixty years had passed between Churchill's first, youthful visit to the United States and his final exhortation, at the age of eighty, "Never be separated from the Americans." Retirement brought with it an end to the extraordinary, intense cycle of communications and visits, fears and hopes, disappointments and achievement. "I am glad," he wrote to his American friend Bernard Baruch a week after leaving Downing Street, "to be freed from responsibility, which was not in every case accompanied by power."[1] Lack of power—real power—had often inhibited and forestalled aspects of Anglo-American policy for which Churchill fought so hard. Whatever the disagreements—with Woodrow Wilson, Franklin Roosevelt, Harry Truman or Dwight Eisenhower—Churchill always made his case as best he could and fought his corner with determination.

The summit meeting Churchill had struggled so hard to bring about in his second premiership came to pass within two months of his resignation. His successor as Prime Minister, Anthony Eden, informed him: "The President has suggested that the top-level meeting should be held either around July 20 or towards the end of August."[2] Before leaving the United States for that first summit, Eisenhower wrote to

---

1. Letter of 4 April 1955, Baruch Papers.
2. Letter of 30 May 1955, Churchill Papers, 2/216, Martin Gilbert, *Winston S. Churchill*, Volume 8, pages 1141–43.

Churchill from the White House: "Soon Anthony and I will be meeting with the French and Russians at Geneva." Eisenhower added that Churchill's "courage and vision" would be missed at the meeting. "But your long quest for peace daily inspires much that we do."[3]

On 30 November 1955, Churchill's eighty-first birthday, Eisenhower sent him a gold medallion as "a token of America's enduring gratitude." The English-speaking peoples and "the entire world," wrote the President, "are the better for the wisdom of your counsel, for the inspiration of your unflagging optimism and for the heartening example of your shining courage. You have been a towering leader in the quest for peace, as you were in the battle for freedom through the dark days of war."[4] "Your letter has moved me more than I can tell you," Churchill replied on his birthday. "As you know, it is my deepest conviction that it is on the friendship between our two nations that the happiness and security of the free peoples rests—and indeed that of the whole world. Your eloquent words have once more given me proof, if it were needed, that you share my own feelings and reciprocate my personal affection."[5]

A week after his eighty-first birthday Churchill accepted the first Williamsburg Award, from the trustees of the preserved and reconstructed Virginia township and memorial known as "Colonial Williamsburg." In his acceptance speech at a ceremony in London, Churchill noted that "on my mother's side I have the right to enjoy the early memories of Colonial Williamsburg as much as anyone here. I delight in my American ancestry." He had been presented at the ceremony with a town crier's bell, modeled on one from colonial days. "Its silver tone is gentle," he said. "I shall ring it whenever I feel there is duty to be done."[6]

In a letter to Eisenhower in April 1956, Churchill commented on the earlier decision of the United States not to share its hydrogen bomb secrets with Britain. "This is past now so far as the main secret is

---

3. Letter of 15 July 1955, Churchill Papers, 2/217, Martin Gilbert, *Winston S. Churchill*, Volume 8, page 1151.
4. Letter of 26 November 1955, Churchill Papers, 2/217, Martin Gilbert, *Winston S. Churchill*, Volume 8, page 1170.
5. Letter of 30 November 1955, Eisenhower Papers.
6. Speech of 7 December 1955, Randolph S. Churchill, editor, *The Unwritten Alliance: Speeches 1953 to 1959 by Winston S. Churchill*, pages 280–81.

concerned," Churchill reflected, "but we have lost two or three years in having to work it out for ourselves." He was sending the President the first volume of his forthcoming book *A History of the English-Speaking Peoples.* "The whole thing is finished now," he wrote, adding: "I am afraid the Americans do not come into this volume, because it was only 'in fourteen hundred and ninety-two, Columbus over the ocean flew.'"

In his letter to Eisenhower, Churchill suggested that the horrors of nuclear war meant that the Soviet Union would not make war, knowing it would suffer millions of deaths among its own people.[7] Eisenhower disagreed. "You will remember," he wrote, "that in 1945 there was no possible excuse, once we had reached the Rhine in late '44, for Hitler to continue the war, yet his insane determination to rule or ruin brought additional and completely unnecessary destruction to his country; brought about its division between East and West and his own ignominious death."[8]

On 24 June 1956 Truman was Churchill's luncheon guest at Chartwell. Before a bronze bust of Franklin Roosevelt, and with drinks in hand, the two men "made what appeared to be a silent toast."[9] After the visit Truman wrote in his diary: "He showed me a large number of his paintings in the house and told me he had some 400 more in his studio in the valley below the house. . . . It was a very pleasant visit and a happy one for me."[10] That summer Churchill worked at Chartwell on the American Civil War section of his history. "I read four or five books on it," he told his doctor, "before I dictated anything."[11]

In October 1956, following the nationalization of the Suez Canal by President Nasser of Egypt, Britain, France and Israel launched a co-ordinated attacked on Egypt. That month Churchill had another stroke, but he was well enough after two weeks to issue a short statement on the crisis. The United States had refused to support Britain, and had forced a halt to the campaign, but Churchill was confident, he

---

7. Letter of 16 April 1956, Eisenhower Papers.
8. Letter of 27 April 1956, Premier Papers, 11/1690.
9. David McCullough, *Truman,* page 958.
10. Diary entry, 24 June 1956, Truman Papers.
11. Diary entry, 1 August 1956, Lord Moran (Sir Charles Wilson), *Winston Churchill: The Struggle for Survival, 1940–1965,* page 702.

wrote, "that our American friends will come to realize that, not for the first time, we have acted independently for the common good." [12]

Jock Colville, who visited Churchill that week, suggested he write a letter to Eisenhower "pointing out that the enemy are not the British but the Russians." Churchill asked Colville to put something down for him, and then asked his Private Secretary, Anthony Montague Browne, to polish it. The letter was sent, and Eisenhower replied, insisting that Britain's attack on Egypt was a "violation" of both basic principles and expediency. "Nothing saddens me more," Eisenhower added, "than the thought that I and my old friend of years have met a problem concerning which we do not see eye to eye. I shall never be happy until our old-time closeness has been restored." [13]

Churchill sent a copy of Eisenhower's letter to the Queen. "It is most interesting to learn his appreciation of the situation," she wrote in reply, "and I hope it means that the present feeling that this country and America are not seeing eye-to-eye will soon be speedily replaced by even stronger ties between us." [14] For Churchill the Suez crisis led to a resolve to act in a personal capacity in the Anglo-American sphere. "After Suez," Clementine explained to the Prime Minister, Harold Wilson, three weeks after Churchill's death, "he specifically set out to mend fences with the United States, and I believe that he had a marked effect in the ensuing years, both by his visits, speeches and talks with major American figures, and also by his public messages." [15]

At the beginning of 1957, Churchill learned that the United States was demanding an immediate and unconditional withdrawal of Israeli forces from Sinai, Israel having colluded with Britain and France in the attack on Egypt in October 1956. He wrote at once to the Chancellor of the Exchequer, Harold Macmillan: "I am astonished at Eisenhower and America's State Department." [16] Three months later he wrote to Clementine, who had lunched with Eisenhower's Democratic challenger, Adlai Stevenson: "His succession to Ike would no doubt be

---

12. *Manchester Guardian*, 5 November 1956.
13. Letter of 27 November 1956, Squerryes Lodge Archive.
14. Letter of 30 November 1956, Squerryes Lodge Archive.
15. Letter of 15 February 1965, Churchill Papers, 1/144, Gilbert, *Winston S. Churchill*, Volume 8, page 1225.
16. Letter of 24 February 1957, Squerryes Lodge Archive.

popular in England. But it is the Americans who have to choose!"[17] Stevenson failed in his challenge.

The storms of Suez passed. "I am so happy," Churchill told his constituents at Woodford the following summer, "to see that our relations with our American partner are being restored to their normal temperature." He added: "Make no mistake. It is in the closest association with our friends in the Commonwealth, America and NATO that our hopes of peace and happiness lie. Neither we nor they can afford estrangement."[18] Avoiding estrangement with the United States and seeking "easement" with the Soviet Union remained the twin pillars of Churchill's world view.

On 4 October 1957 the Soviet Union launched the first earth satellite, *Sputnik.* "The disconcerting thing," Churchill wrote to Clementine, "is the proof of the forwardness of Soviet sciences compared to the Americans." For the future, he told her: "We must struggle on; & looking to the Union with America."[19] That winter Churchill selected a dozen canvases for the first-ever exhibition devoted solely to his paintings. It was held in Kansas City, organized by Joyce Hall, the founder of Hallmark Cards. Reading about this in the *Daily Mail,* Clementine wrote to her husband, who was in the South of France: "1,221 persons visited your Exhibition in one day in Kansas City and that is a record."[20]

In February 1958, while still in the South of France, Churchill was taken ill with a high fever. A week later he recovered. This, wrote Richard Nixon from the office of the Vice-President in Washington, was "the kind of encouraging good news all of your friends want to hear!"[21] "How happy I am that you fooled the doctors, just as I did," Harry Truman wrote from his home in Independence, Missouri. The

---

17. Letter of 1 June 1957, Spencer-Churchill Papers.

18. Speech of 6 July 1957, Randolph S. Churchill, editor, *The Unwritten Alliance,* pages 296–99.

19. Letter of 11 October 1957, Spencer-Churchill Papers.

20. Letter of 25 January 1958, Churchill Papers, 1/55, Martin Gilbert, *Winston S. Churchill,* Volume 8, page 1251.

21. Letter of 24 February 1958, Churchill Papers, 1/60, Martin Gilbert, *Winston S. Churchill,* Volume 8, page 1262.

former President added: "I know that you will soon be back in Churchillian flying trim." [22]

As Churchill recovered, he made plans to return to the United States, invited to do so by Eisenhower. Clementine was concerned about the journey. "Of course I hope he won't go," she wrote to their daughter Mary. "If he does not make one or two speeches and television appearances, the visit will be a flop as regards the American People—who want to see and hear him. Then if he lets himself be persuaded to make public appearances it will half kill him." [23] Forced back to bed with an attack of jaundice, Churchill had to postpone his journey. "This is a great disappointment," he wrote to an American friend, "but it may come off later." [24]

In July 1958, during a crisis in the Middle East provoked by a coup in Iraq, the President of Lebanon appealed to the United States for support. Carrier-borne troops were sent. There was much criticism of this in Britain. Churchill, who did not share in this criticism, decided to speak in the House of Commons. He prepared four pages of handwritten notes. In them appeared the words: "It would be too easy to mock USA. We should refrain." And later: "What is really foolish is for two nations like England & USA to search for points of difference." And later: "The US have entered the Lebanon. They are in every way justified." [25]

A few days before the debate Churchill decided he was no longer up to speaking. He did attend, however, and voted with the government. The following spring he suffered another stroke. It was a small one, and a week later he fulfilled a long-standing engagement to speak in his constituency. The speech was prepared for him by Montague Browne. Churchill gave it, speaking clearly and steadily for more than twenty minutes, and then turned to Montague Browne with the words: "Now for America." [26]

---

22. Letter of 28 February 1958, Churchill Papers, 1/122, Martin Gilbert, *Winston S. Churchill*, Volume 8, page 1262.

23. Letter of 15 March 1958, Mary Soames, *Clementine Churchill*, page 465.

24. Letter of 11 April 1958, Reves Papers.

25. Handwritten notes, undated, Churchill Papers, 2/129, Martin Gilbert, *Winston S. Churchill*, Volume 8, pages 1271–72.

26. Diary entry, 20 April 1959, Lord Moran (Sir Charles Wilson), *Winston Churchill: The Struggle for Survival, 1940–1965*, page 702.

On 4 May 1959 Churchill flew to the United States. It was his fifteenth visit; his first had been almost sixty years earlier. Clementine was not well enough to accompany him, but Montague Browne was at his side throughout. Eisenhower, who had invited him, asked him to stay at the White House. On May 5, his first full day in Washington, he wrote to Clementine in his own hand, on White House notepaper: "My dearest Clemmie, Here I am. All goes well and the President is a real friend. We had a most pleasant dinner last night, and I caught up my arrears of sleep in (11) eleven hours. I am invited to stay in bed all the morning and am going to see Mr Dulles after luncheon."[27]

At dinner that night in the White House, Churchill read a short speech that Montague Browne had prepared for him. "To come across the Atlantic and to see so many friends and so many elements in the union of our peoples," he said, "has been a great and memorable joy to me." The fifty-two guests included his friend Bernard Baruch; the former Secretary of State, James Byrnes; the former American Ambassador to London, Lew Douglas; the head of the CIA, Allen Dulles (John Foster Dulles's brother); and the Senate Majority Leader, Lyndon Johnson, a future President.

Old and unwell though Churchill was, two of those whom he saw in Washington were far more ill. John Foster Dulles, whom he visited in the hospital, died of cancer two weeks later. General Marshall, having recently had a stroke, was unable to speak. He died on October 16.

On May 5 and again on May 6, Churchill lunched with Eisenhower at the White House. In a report to Sir Harold Caccia, the British Ambassador in Washington, Montague Browne set out what was discussed: The conversation, which was of "a very general nature, ranged much over personalities." During their talks Eisenhower recalled that when he had been appointed Supreme Commander of the cross-Channel landings in January 1944, Churchill had told him "that he could sack any British officer who proved difficult, but that he had not exercised this right in the case of Field Marshal Montgomery!"

Eisenhower had been upset by some cutting remarks by Montgomery in a recently televised interview on CBS. "Sir Winston succeeded to a great extent, I think, in smoothing the ruffled feathers," Montague Browne noted, "but it was surprisingly evident how affected

---

27. Letter of 5 May 1959, Spencer-Churchill Papers.

the President is by personal criticisms levelled at him from abroad. He also referred with asperity to attacks on him in the British Press, and for someone in his position seemed surprisingly thin-skinned."

As asked to do so by the Foreign Office, Churchill raised the question of discrimination against British contractors in the United States, and the trend toward protection to the detriment of British exports. The President appeared sympathetic, Montague Browne noted, but said he had "a difficult time in selling the desirability of a liberal American policy in this direction." Montague Browne's report continued: "During the three days we were in the White House the President showed an affectionate care and consideration for Sir Winston and spent a great deal of time with him."[28] Together Churchill and Eisenhower flew by helicopter to the President's farm at Gettysburg, a journey of just under an hour.

As a token of his visit to the farm, Churchill gave Eisenhower one of his paintings, *Valley of the Ourika and Atlas Mountains,* which Eisenhower subsequently put in the Oval Office in order, he explained, that "I may display it proudly to each and every visitor there."[29] Later, during a meeting with the British Embassy staff in Washington, someone asked Churchill about the animals he had seen at Eisenhower's farm. At that point, as one of those present, Lord Nicholas Gordon-Lennox, recalled, Churchill "was surprisingly able to say precisely how many of each had been shown to him. Except for the pigs: for some reason he had not (he said) been allowed to see these."[30]

Churchill flew back to Britain on May 10, the nineteenth anniversary of his having become Prime Minister. On the way to the airport he turned to the British Ambassador with the words: "I hope you will give the Prime Minister a good report of my visit; and say that I behaved myself."[31] At Andrews Air Force Base a small group of onlookers watched as he went up the steps to the plane. "He looks down on all of us," recalled one of those onlookers, James Humes, and said: "Farewell to

28. Report by Anthony Montague Browne, 21 May 1959, Churchill Papers, 2/298, Martin Gilbert, *Winston S. Churchill,* Volume 8, pages 1294–95.
29. This painting is now at the Dwight D. Eisenhower Library, Abilene, Kansas.
30. Recollections of Lord Nicholas Gordon-Lennox, letter to the author, 19 October 1987.
31. Remark by Sir Harold Caccia, communicated by Lord Nicholas Gordon-Lennox, letter to the author, 19 October 1987.

the land . . ." he paused ". . . of my mother. God bless you all. Good night."[32]

Back in Britain, where he was being advised on his circulatory problem by the Professor of Surgery at London University, Charles Rob, Churchill spoke of his American forebears. "I told him that I had just been offered a position in Rochester, New York, and I was thinking of going there," Professor Rob recalled. "He then said to me, 'You know some of my ancestors came from that area, you may not know it, but I am descended from a Seneca Indian squaw who was an ancestor of my mother' We then talked about the Indians in this area and I have a feeling that he thought he was descended from some enormous chief who had gone around scalping people and winning great battles against other tribes. Of course there was no evidence for this, but it made a nice fantasy for him to think about this Indian ancestor."[33]

When, toward the end of 1960, Churchill slipped in Clementine's room while saying goodnight to her, breaking a small bone in his back, among the messages of good wishes was one from Eisenhower, who telegraphed: "All the people of America are distressed to hear of your accident, none more than I."[34] Six days after Eisenhower's telegram Churchill suffered a mild stoke. A week later he was eighty-six years old. But he remained an indefatigable traveler. In the spring of 1961 he flew to Gibraltar and joined Aristotle Onassis's yacht the *Christina*— a former Royal Canadian Navy corvette—for a transatlantic and Caribbean cruise.

After visiting the West Indies, the *Christina* sailed up the Atlantic Coast of the United States to New York. Its first port of call was Palm Beach. Churchill did not go ashore, but his Private Secretary, Anthony Montague Browne, did, bringing back with him a copy of the *New York Times* for 7 April 1961. Churchill was photographed on board reading it.[35] The front page showed President Kennedy and the British Prime

---

32. Recollections of James Humes, "The Ideals of Democracy," *Finest Hour*, Third Quarter 1993, Number 80, pages 30–32.

33. Recollections of Professor Charles Rob, letter to the author, 17 November 1986.

34. Telegram of 17 November 1960, Churchill Papers, 1/61, Martin Gilbert, *Winston S. Churchill*, Volume 8, page 1316.

35. See photograph number 58.

Minister, Harold Macmillan, on board the Presidential yacht. From Palm Beach, the *Christina* sailed along the Atlantic coast through a fierce storm, reaching New York on the evening of April 11, and anchoring off Stapleton, Staten Island. On the morning of April 12 it sailed into the Hudson River, "amid whistle blasts from liners, freighters and other harbor craft." Police helicopters hovered overhead and a fireboat sprayed "geysers of water" in welcome.[36] The yacht then made fast at a mid-river buoy off the West Seventy-ninth Street Boat Basin. At midday Adlai Stevenson, then United States Ambassador to the United Nations, arrived by launch as one of the luncheon guests. After lunch Churchill sat on deck watching the *Queen Mary* leaving the Cunard pier for her voyage back to Britain. That night ninety-year-old Bernard Baruch was his guest at dinner. "It will be good to see my old friend again," Baruch told the reporters as he boarded the launch. "He's a wonderful young man at eighty-six."[37]

During dinner Montague Browne received a message to call "Operator 17" in Washington, to take "a top priority call." It was President John F. Kennedy, asking if Churchill would like to fly down to Washington in the Presidential plane "and spend a couple of days with me." Montague Browne had to make an immediate decision. He did so, explaining to Kennedy that Churchill could no longer undertake such a journey.[38] Churchill was due to fly back to London on April 13, but fierce winds made it impossible for him to be transferred from the *Christina* to shore. That night, with the *Christina* moored at the dock, Baruch was once more Churchill's dinner guest. On the following morning, the winds having abated, Churchill left the yacht for the airport, stopping briefly at Baruch's apartment so that the two men could drive together to Idlewild Airport (since December 1963 John F. Kennedy Airport). Eager to report every aspect of Churchill's life, the *New York Times* noted that "a special order" placed by Churchill for those traveling in his party had been transferred from the previous day's flight to the new one. It consisted of "two bottles of cognac, seven bottles of wine, one bottle of brandy and two pounds of Stilton cheese."[39]

36. "Churchill Sails In As Harbor Cheers," *New York Times*, 13 April 1961.

37. *New York Herald Tribune*, 13 April 1961.

38. Anthony Montague Browne, recollections, in conversation with the author, 14 July 1987. See also Montague Browne's memoir, *Long Sunset*, pages 288–90.

39. "Churchill Is Kept Here By Weather," *New York Times*, 14 April 1961.

Churchill reached London on the evening of April 14. He was not to see the United States again. That August at Chartwell, one of his lunch guests was Randolph's American friend Kay Halle. "During lunch," she later recalled, "I sat next to the Great Man, at his right, and he rose with his glass of hock and turning to me he said, 'Kay, let us drink to your great President, and—and ours.' I think it was his delicate way of expressing his fervent wish for a union of Great Britain and the United States as a beginning for a Union of all the Democracies."

Later that afternoon Churchill told Kay Halle that the British Commonwealth system was an example to follow. Each member country was completely independent, "but they are united under the symbol, the Crown." He hoped that soon the United States would follow, with Britain and America similarly united, "and that our symbol would be the Union." Churchill told Kay Halle that if all the democracies were to join together "it could become a great force in helping to solve our multiple world problems." Churchill also told his American guest: "You know I love your country—half mine—but I warn it from becoming stripped bare by the curse of plenty." [40]

It was from the United States that Churchill received his last high honor: honorary citizenship of the United States. Pressed for tenaciously by Kay Halle, a friend of both the Churchills and the Kennedys, it was proclaimed by President Kennedy on 9 April 1963. Because Churchill was not well enough to cross the Atlantic, Randolph received the honor on his father's behalf during a ceremony at the White House. Among the guests was ninety-two-year-old Bernard Baruch, with whom Churchill had worked closely in the First World War, and Averell Harriman, with whom he had worked closely in the Second. Kennedy's words encapsulated Churchill's achievement. "In the dark days and darker nights when England stood alone," Kennedy declared, "and most men save Englishmen despaired of England's life—he mobilized the English language and sent it into battle." [41]

Churchill, in London, watched the ceremony on television. In his message of acceptance, which was read out by Randolph, he referred to the Anglo-American theme that had been so much a part of his en-

---

40. Kay Halle, recollections, letter to the author, 12 June 1987.
41. John F. Kennedy, *Public Papers of the Presidents of the United States, 1963*, pages 315–16.

ergies for more than six decades: "I am, as you know, half American by blood, and the story of my association with that mighty and benevolent nation goes back nearly ninety years, to the day of my father's marriage." In "this century of storm and tragedy," he said, "I contemplate with high satisfaction the constant factor of the interwoven and upward progress of our peoples. Our comradeship and our brotherhood in war were unexampled. We stood together, and because of that fact the free world now stands." Of his new honor, the first honorary citizenship to be granted by the Congress of the United States to a foreigner, Churchill declared: "Mr President, your action illuminates the theme of unity of the English-speaking peoples to which I have devoted a large part of my life."[42]

The ceremony over, a message of congratulations came from the British Prime Minister, Harold Macmillan, who had just given a dinner for a number of senior American and British wartime generals. They had unanimously agreed to send him a message, Macmillan wrote, "recalling the days when we worked together under your leadership. We wished also to express our delight at your versatility, which allows you to combine being a loyal British subject with being a good United States' citizen."[43]

Old age and illness took their steady toll. On 30 November 1964 Churchill was ninety years old. Six weeks later he suffered a massive stroke. He died at his London home on 24 January 1965, the seventieth anniversary of his father's death. Six days later, at his funeral service at St. Paul's Cathedral, Eisenhower and Baruch were among the congregation. Later that day the BBC broadcast Eisenhower's tribute: "May we carry on his work until no nation lies in captivity, no man is denied opportunity for fulfilment."[44]

---

42. *New York Times*, 10 April 1963. In his lifetime the French soldier and statesman the Marquis de Lafayette (1757–1834) was made an honorary citizen of both Maryland and the Commonwealth of Virginia. It was not until 167 years after his death that he was made an honorary citizen of the United States (Public Law 107–209, 117th Congress, 2nd Session), passed into law by President George W. Bush on 6 August 2002.

43. Letter of 10 April 1963, Churchill Papers, 2/539, Martin Gilbert, *Winston S. Churchill*, Volume 8, page 1343.

44. "The Text of Eisenhower's Tribute on TV," *New York Times*, 31 January 1965.

Churchill was buried in Bladon churchyard, near Blenheim Palace, where he had been born, in a grave next to those of his English father and American mother. That same day, more than three thousand miles away, sixty people gathered in the rose garden of Franklin Roosevelt's home in Hyde Park on the Hudson, where Churchill had so often been a guest. They were there to mark the eighty-third anniversary of Roosevelt's birth. At that very moment, in Churchill's honor, the Liberty Bell in New York's Middle Collegiate Church, which had tolled the inauguration and death of all American Presidents since George Washington, tolled ninety-one times: ninety for the years of Churchill's life, and one more in recognition of his lifelong links and friendship with America and the Americans.

CHURCHILL'S AMERICAN VISITS

First: 2–18 November 1895
Second: 8 December 1900–1 February 1901
Third: 6 September–30 October 1929
Fourth: 11 December 1931–11 March 1932
Fifth: 22 December 1941–14 January 1942
Sixth: 17–25 June 1942
Seventh: 12–26 May 1943
Eighth: 12–14 August and 2–12 September 1943
Ninth: 16–20 September 1944
Tenth: 14 January–20 March 1946
Eleventh: 23 March–2 April 1949
Twelfth: 4–22 January 1952
Thirteenth: 5–9 January 1953
Fourteenth: 24–30 June 1954
Fifteenth: 4–10 May 1959
Sixteenth: 11–13 April 1961

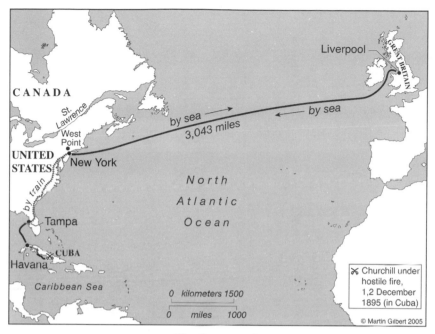

1. First Journey, 1895

2. First Lecture Tour, 1900–1901

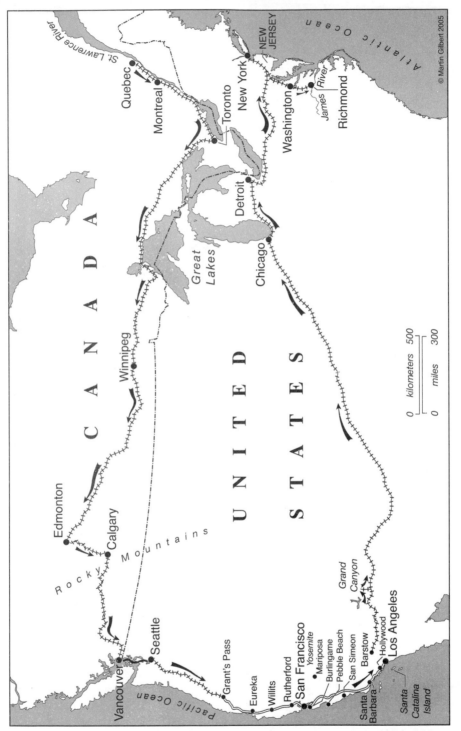

3. New World Journey, 1929

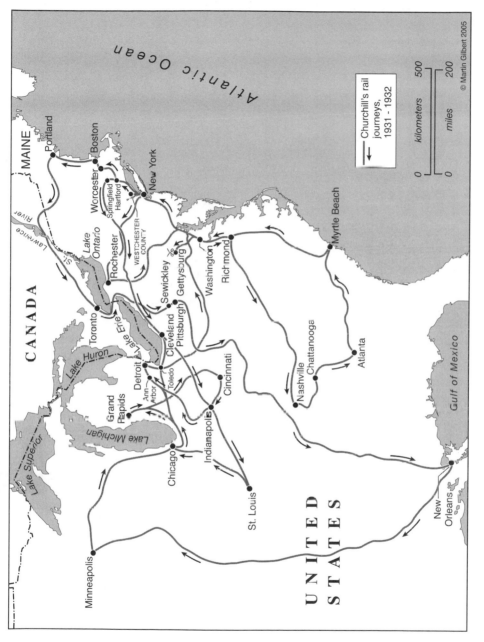

4. Second Lecture Tour, 1930–1931

5. Great Britain

6. The Lecture Tour That Never Was, 1938–1939

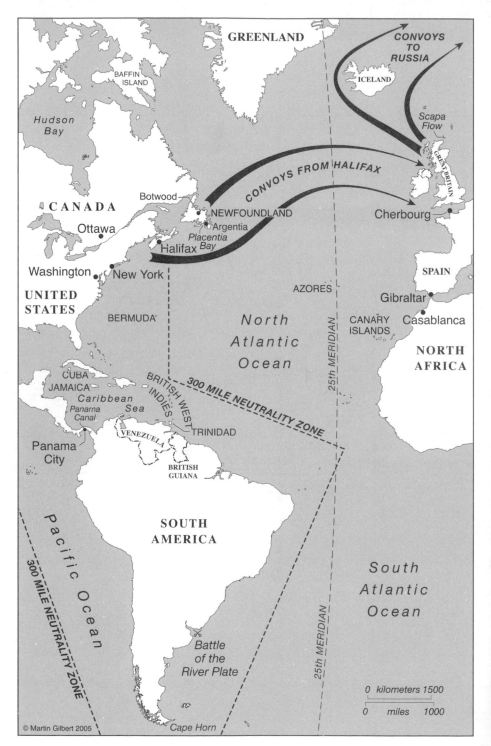

7. The Atlantic

8. The Mediterranean

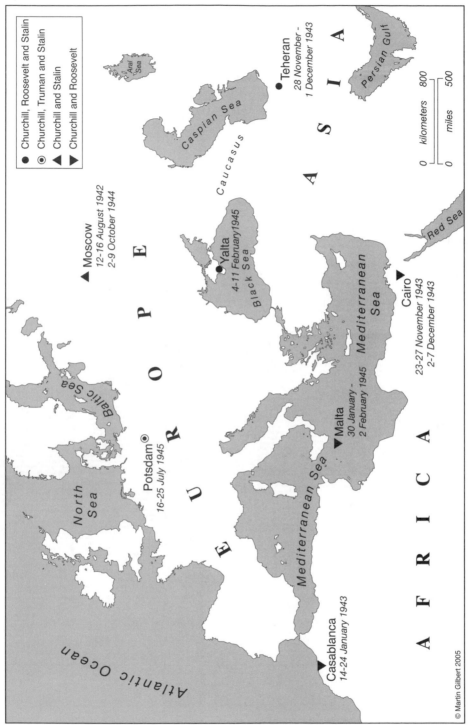

Legend:
- ● Churchill, Roosevelt and Stalin
- ⊙ Churchill, Truman and Stalin
- ◀ Churchill and Stalin
- ▶ Churchill and Roosevelt

Aral Sea

Caspian Sea

● Teheran
28 November -
1 December 1943

Persian Gulf

A S I A

Caucasus

▲ Moscow
12-16 August 1942
2-9 October 1944

E U R O P E

Black Sea

● Yalta
4-11 February 1945

Red Sea

▶ Cairo
23-27 November 1943
2-7 December 1943

Baltic Sea

⊙ Potsdam
16-25 July 1945

Mediterranean
Sea

▼ Malta
30 January -
2 February 1945

North Sea

Mediterranean Sea

A F R I C A

Atlantic Ocean

▼ Casablanca
14-24 January 1943

kilometers
0   800
miles
0   500

9. Wartime Conferences

© Martin Gilbert 2005

460

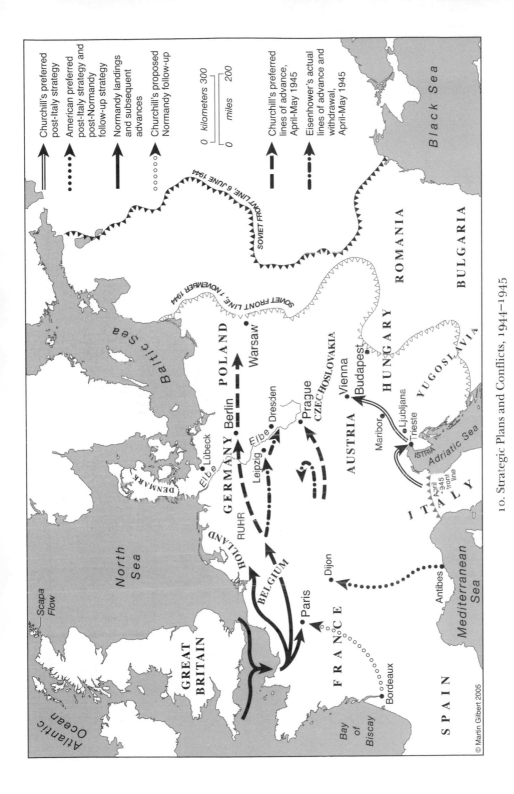

Churchill's preferred post-Italy strategy

American preferred post-Italy strategy and post-Normandy follow-up strategy

Normandy landings and subsequent advances

Churchill's proposed Normandy follow-up

Churchill's preferred lines of advance, April–May 1945

Eisenhower's actual lines of advance and withdrawal, April–May 1945

0 kilometers 300
0 miles 200

SOVIET FRONT LINE, 6 JUNE 1944

SOVIET FRONT LINE, 1 NOVEMBER 1944

Atlantic Ocean

Scapa Flow

GREAT BRITAIN

North Sea

Baltic Sea

DENMARK

Lübeck

Elbe

HOLLAND

BELGIUM

RUHR

GERMANY

Leipzig

Elbe

Dresden

Berlin

POLAND

Warsaw

Paris

FRANCE

Dijon

Prague

CZECHOSLOVAKIA

Vienna

AUSTRIA

Budapest

HUNGARY

Maribor

Ljubljana

Trieste

ISTRIA

Adriatic Sea

YUGOSLAVIA

ROMANIA

Black Sea

BULGARIA

April 1945 front line

I T A L Y

Antibes

Bordeaux

Bay of Biscay

SPAIN

Mediterranean Sea

© Martin Gilbert 2005

10. Strategic Plans and Conflicts, 1944–1945

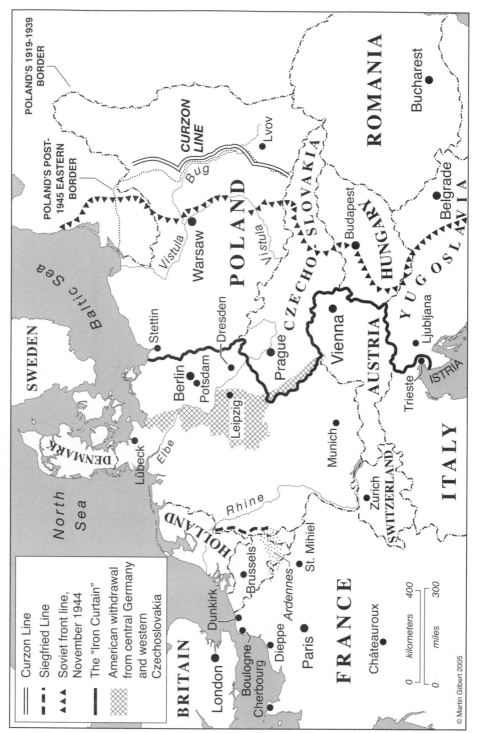

Legend:

- ═══ Curzon Line
- ▬ ▬ ▬ Siegfried Line
- ▲▲▲ Soviet front line, November 1944
- ▬▬▬ The "Iron Curtain"
- ▨▨ American withdrawal from central Germany and western Czechoslovakia

POLAND'S 1919-1939 BORDER

POLAND'S POST-1945 EASTERN BORDER

CURZON LINE

Lvov

Bug

Warsaw

Vistula

Vistula

POLAND

CZECHO-SLOVAKIA

Budapest

HUNGARY

ROMANIA

Bucharest

Belgrade

Y U G O S L A V I A

Ljubljana

Prague

Vienna

AUSTRIA

Trieste

ISTRIA

ITALY

Stettin

Dresden

Berlin

Potsdam

Leipzig

Munich

Zurich

SWITZERLAND

Elbe

Lübeck

DENMARK

SWEDEN

Baltic Sea

North Sea

Rhine

HOLLAND

Brussels

St. Mihiel

Ardennes

Dieppe

Dunkirk

Boulogne

Cherbourg

Paris

FRANCE

Châteauroux

BRITAIN

London

0   400 kilometers

0   300 miles

© Martin Gilbert 2005

11. Europe, November 1944–May 1945

462

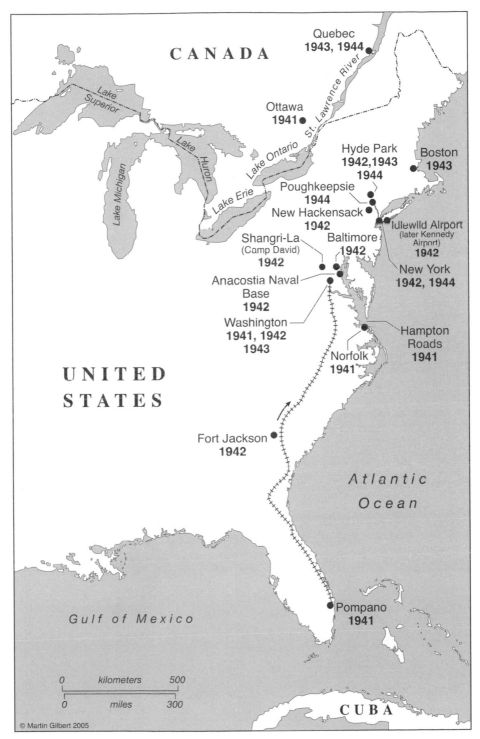

CANADA

Quebec
1943, 1944

Lake
Superior

Ottawa
1941

Lake Ontario

St. Lawrence River

Lake
Huron

Lake Michigan

Lake Erie

Hyde Park
**1942,1943
1944**

Boston
1943

Poughkeepsie
1944

New Hackensack
1942

Idlewild Airport
(later Kennedy
Airport)
1942

Shangri-La
(Camp David)
1942

Baltimore
1942

New York
1942, 1944

Anacostia Naval
Base
1942

**UNITED
STATES**

Washington
**1941, 1942
1943**

Hampton
Roads
1941

Norfolk
1941

*Atlantic
Ocean*

Fort Jackson
1942

Gulf of Mexico

Pompano
1941

| 0 | kilometers | 500 |
| 0 | miles | 300 |

© Martin Gilbert 2005

CUBA

12. Wartime Visits to the United States, 1941–1944

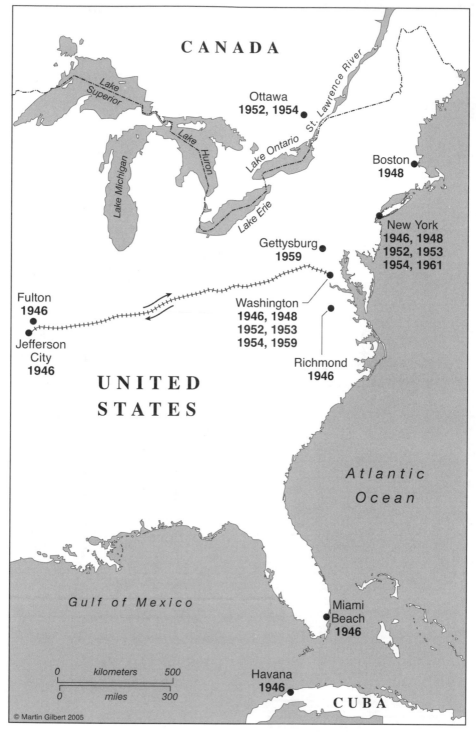

13. Postwar Visits to the United States, 1946–1961

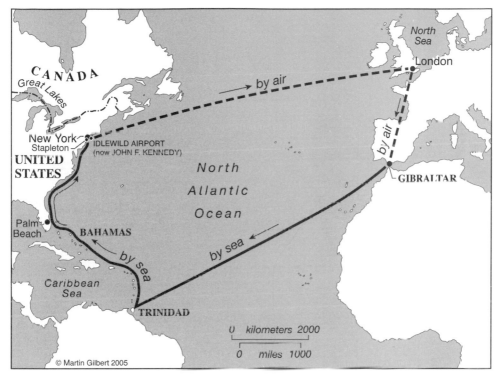

14. Last Journey, 1961

BIBLIOGRAPHY OF SOURCES
AND WORKS CITED

ARCHIVAL SOURCES

Royal Archives
Archives of *The Times*
BBC Written Archives Centre
German Foreign Office Archives
National Archives (formerly Public Record Office)
    Admiralty Papers
    Cabinet Papers
    Colonial Office Papers
    Foreign Office Papers
    Premier Papers
    Treasury Papers
    War Office Papers
Squerryes Lodge Archive (Winston S. Churchill Esq. Collection)

INDIVIDUAL COLLECTIONS

Louis J. Alber Papers
H. H. Asquith Papers
Earl of Avon (Anthony Eden) Papers
Lord Baldwin Papers
Bernard Baruch Papers
Lord Beaverbrook Papers
Lorraine Bonar Papers
Lord Butler (R. A. Butler) Papers
Lord Camrose Papers
Sir Austen Chamberlain Papers
Neville Chamberlain Papers
Randolph Churchill Papers
Bourke Cockran Papers
Sir John Colville Papers

Admiral Sir Andrew Cunningham Papers
Lord Curzon Papers
Sir Pierson Dixon Papers
Earl of Dundee Papers
President Dwight D. Eisenhower Papers
Felix Frankfurter Papers
Lord Hankey Papers
Averell Harriman Papers
Colonel House Papers
General Sir Ian Jacob Papers
Denis Kelly Papers
Walter Lippmann Papers
David Lloyd George Papers
Daniel Longwell Papers
William McAdoo Papers
Sir Edward Marsh Papers
Sir John Martin Papers
Earl Mountbatten of Burma Papers
Sir Harold Nicolson Papers
General George S. Patton Papers
Sir Richard Pim Papers
Emery Reves Papers
Franklin D. Roosevelt Papers
Theodore Roosevelt Papers
Lord Runciman Papers
Sir Philip Sassoon Papers
Sir Eric Seal Papers
Admiral William S. Sims Papers
Lady Soames Papers
General Sir E. L. Spears Papers
Baroness Spencer-Churchill papers
Marian Walker Spicer (Marian Holmes) Papers
Richard Storry Papers
Sir Colin Thornton-Kemsley Papers
Lord Thurso Papers
President Harry S. Truman Papers
Henry A. Wallace Papers
Lord Weir Papers
Field Marshal Sir Henry Wilson Papers

PRINCIPAL VOLUMES OF DOCUMENTS

Randolph S. Churchill, *Winston S. Churchill,* Companion (Document). Volumes
    1–2. London: William Heinemann, 1967, 1969.

Martin Gilbert, *Winston S. Churchill,* Companion (Document) Volumes 3–5. London: William Heinemann, 1972–82.

Martin Gilbert, *Churchill War Papers,* Volumes 1–3. London: William Heinemann, 1993–2000.

OTHER DOCUMENT VOLUMES

Peter G. Boyle, editor, *The Churchill-Eisenhower Correspondence, 1953–1955.* Chapel Hill: University of North Carolina Press, 1990.

Randolph S. Churchill, editor, *The Sinews of Peace: Post-War Speeches by Winston S. Churchill.* London: Cassell, 1948.

———, *Europe Unite: Speeches 1947 and 1948 by Winston S. Churchill.* London: Cassell, 1950.

———, *In the Balance: Speeches 1949 and 1950 by Winston S. Churchill.* London: Cassell, 1951.

———, *Stemming the Tide: Speeches 1951 and 1952 by Winston S. Churchill.* London: Cassell, 1953.

———, *The Unwritten Alliance: Speeches 1953 to 1959 by Winston S. Churchill.* London: Cassell, 1961.

Documents on Polish-Soviet Relations, 1939–1945, Volume 2. London: Heinemann, 1967.

Foreign Relations of the United States: Diplomatic Papers, 1944, Volume 3. Washington, D.C.: United States Government Printing Office, 1965.

John F. Kennedy, *Public Papers of the Presidents of the United States, 1963.* Washington D.C.: United States Government Printing Office, 1964.

Warren F. Kimball, *Churchill & Roosevelt: The Complete Correspondence.* 3 Volumes. Princeton, New Jersey: Princeton University Press, 1984.

J. W. Pickersgill and D. F. Forster. *The Mackenzie King Record, Volume 3, 1945–1946.* Toronto: University of Toronto Press, 1970.

Monte Poen, editor, *Letters Home by Harry Truman.* New York: Putnam, 1984.

United States Army in the World War, 1917–1919: Training and Use of American Units with the British and French, Volume 3. Washington, D.C.: United States Army Center of Military History, 1989.

B. D. Zevin, editor, *Nothing to Fear: The Selected Addresses of Franklin Delano Roosevelt, 1932–1945.* London: Hodder & Stoughton, 1947.

CHURCHILL BIBLIOGRAPHIES

Ronald I. Cohen, editor, *A Bibliography of the Published Writings of Sir Winston Churchill.* London: Continuum-Thoemmes, 2005.

Frederick Woods, *A Bibliography of the Works of Sir Winston Churchill, KG, OM, CH.* London: Kaye and Ward, 1969.

Curt J. Zoller, *Annotated Bibliography of Works About Sir Winston S. Churchill.* Armonk, New York: M.E. Sharpe, 2004.

PUBLISHED WORKS

Dean Acheson, *Present at the Creation: My Years in the State Department.* New York: Norton, 1969.

Earl of Avon (Anthony Eden). *The Reckoning: Eden Memoirs.* London: Cassell, 1965.

Sally Bedell Smith, *Grace and Power: The Kennedy White House.* London: Aurum Press, 2004.

Lord Birkenhead, *Halifax: The Life of Lord Halifax.* London: Hamish Hamilton, 1965.

Conrad Black, *Franklin Delano Roosevelt: Champion of Freedom.* New York: Public Affairs, 2003.

Charles E. Bohlen, *Witness of History.* New York: Norton, 1973.

Arthur Bryant, *The Turn of the Tide, 1939–1943.* London: Collins, 1957.

Oliver Lyttelton, Viscount Chandos. *The Memoirs of Lord Chandos.* London: Bodley Head, 1962.

John Spencer Churchill. *A Churchill Canvas.* Boston: Little, Brown, 1961; *A Crowded Canvas.* London: Odhams, 1961.

Randolph S. Churchill, *Twenty-One Years.* London: Weidenfeld & Nicolson, 1965.

———, *Winston S. Churchill,* Volumes 1 and 2. London: William Heinemann, 1967.

Randolph S. Churchill and Helmut Gernsheim, editors, *Churchill: His Life in Photographs.* London: Weidenfeld and Nicolson, 1955.

Sarah Churchill, *Keep on Dancing: An Autobiography.* London: Weidenfeld & Nicolson, 1981.

Winston S. Churchill, *The World Crisis,* Volumes 1–5. London: Thornton Butterworth, 1923–31.

———, *My Early Life.* London: Thornton Butterworth, 1930.

———, *Amid These Storms.* New York: Charles Scribner's Sons, 1932; published as *Thoughts and Adventures.* London: Thornton Butterworth, 1932.

———, *Trust the People.* London: Conservative and Unionist Central Office, 1947.

———, *The Second World War,* Volumes 1–6. London: Cassell, 1948–54.

———, *A History of the English-Speaking Peoples,* Volumes 1–4. London: Cassell, 1956–58.

Margaret L. Coit, *Mr. Baruch: The Man, the Myth, the Eighty Years.* Boston: Houghton Mifflin, 1957.

John Colville, *The Fringes of Power.* London: Hodder & Stoughton, 1985.

David Coombs with Minnie Churchill, *Sir Winston Churchill's Life Through His Paintings.* London: Chaucer Press, 2003.

Richard Harding Davis, *Real Soldiers of Fortune.* New York: Charles Scribner's Sons, 1906.

Geoffrey Dennis, *Coronation Commentary.* London: Heinemann, 1937.

David Dilks, editor, *The Diaries of Sir Alexander Cadogan, OM, 1938–1945*. London: Cassell, 1971.

Charles Eade, editor, *Secret Session Speeches by the Right Hon. Winston S. Churchill, OM, CH, MP.* London: Cassell, 1946.

Robert T. Elson, *"Time Inc": The Intimate History of a Publishing Enterprise*, Volume 2. New York: Atheneum, 1973.

Jack Fishman, *My Darling Clementine: The Story of Lady Churchill*. London: W. H. Allen, 1963.

Martin Gilbert, *Winston S. Churchill*, Volumes 3–8. London: William Heinemann, 1971–88.

———, *Second World War*. New York: Holt, 1989.

Walter Graebner, *My Dear Mr Churchill*. London: Michael Joseph, 1965.

Kay Halle, editor, *Irrepressible Churchill: Stories, Sayings and Impressions of Sir Winston Churchill*. London: Robson, 1985.

———, *Winston Churchill on America and Britain: A Selection of His Thoughts on Anglo-American Relations*. New York: Walker and Company, 1970.

W. Averell Harriman and Elie Abel. *Special Envoy to Churchill and Stalin, 1941–1946*. London: Hutchinson, 1976.

Richard Harrity and Ralph G. Martin, *Man of the Century: Churchill*. New York: Duell, Sloan and Pearce, 1962.

Albert Bushnell Hart and Herbert Ronald Ferleger, editors, *Theodore Roosevelt Cyclopedia*. Westport, Connecticut: Theodore Roosevelt Association and Meckler, 1989.

John Harvey, editor, *The Diplomatic Diaries of Oliver Harvey, 1937–1940*. London: Collins, 1970.

Herbert Hoover, *The Memoirs of Herbert Hoover*. London: Hollis & Carter, 1952.

Ralph Ingersoll, *Top Secret*. London and New York: Harcourt, Brace and Company, 1946.

Lord Ismay, *The Memoirs of General the Lord Ismay*. London: Heinemann, 1960.

Stephen Kinzer, *All the Shah's Men: An American Coup and the Roots of Middle East Terror*. Hoboken, New Jersey: John Wiley, 2003.

William L. Langer and S. Everett Gleason, *The World Crisis and American Foreign Policy: The Challenge to Isolation, 1937–1940*. New York: Harper for the World Council on Foreign Relations, 1952.

Anita Leslie, *The Fabulous Leonard Jerome*. London: Hutchinson, 1954.

———, *Jennie: The Life of Lady Randolph Churchill*. London: Hutchinson, 1969.

Henry Demarest Lloyd, *Wealth Against Commonwealth*. New York: Harper & Brothers, 1894.

David G. McCullough, *Truman*. New York: Simon & Schuster, 1992.

James McGurrin, *Bourke Cockran: A Free Lance in American Politics (The Right Wing Individualist Tradition in America)*. New York: Arno Press, 1972.

Harold Macmillan, *Tides of Fortune, 1945–55*. London: Macmillan, 1969.

———, *War Diaries: Politics and War in the Mediterranean, January 1943–May 1945*. London: Macmillan, 1984.

Sir James Marchant, editor, *Winston Spencer Churchill: Servant of Crown and Commonwealth*. London: Cassell, 1954.

Ralph G. Martin, *Jennie: The Life of Lady Randolph Churchill, The Romantic Years, 1854–1895*. Englewood Cliffs, New Jersey: Prentice-Hall, 1969.

——, *Jennie: The Life of Lady Randolph Churchill, The Dramatic Years, 1895–1921*. Englewood Cliffs, New Jersey: Prentice-Hall, 1971.

Jon Meacham, *Franklin and Winston: A Portrait of a Friendship*, London: Granta Books, 2004.

Phyllis Moir, *I Was Winston Churchill's Private Secretary*. Sydney, Australia: Angus and Robertson, 1941.

Anthony Montague Browne, *Long Sunset: Memoirs of Winston Churchill's Last Private Secretary*. London: Cassell, 1995.

Lord Moran (Sir Charles Wilson), *Winston Churchill: The Struggle for Survival, 1940–1965*. London: Constable, 1966.

Elting E. Morison, editor, *The Letters of Theodore Roosevelt*, Volumes 1–8. Cambridge, Massachusetts: Harvard University Press, 1951–54.

Nigel Nicolson, editor, *Harold Nicolson: Diaries and Letters, 1939–1945*. London: Collins, 1967.

Stanley Nott, *The Young Churchill*. New York: Coward-McCann, 1941.

Robert H. Pilpel, *Churchill in America, 1895–1961: An Affectionate Portrait*. New York: New English Library, 1976.

David Reynolds, *In Command of History: Churchill Fighting and Writing the Second World War*, London: Allen Lane, 2004.

Robert Rhodes James, editor, *Chips: The Diaries of Sir Henry Channon*. London: Weidenfeld & Nicolson, 1967.

Kermit Roosevelt, *Countercoup: The Struggle for the Control of Iran*. New York: McGraw-Hill, 1979.

Samuel I. Rosenman, editor, *The Public Papers and Addresses of Franklin D. Roosevelt*, Volume 9. New York, Macmillan, 1941.

Douglas S. Russell, *The Orders, Decorations and Medals of Sir Winston Churchill*. 2nd Edition. Washington, D.C.: Churchill Centre, 2004.

Percy Ernst Schramm, editor, *Kriegestagebuch des Oberkommandos der Wehrmacht*, Volume 3 (1943). Frankfurt-am-Main: Bernard & Graefe, 1965.

Robert E. Sherwood, *The White House Papers of Harry L. Hopkins*, Volumes 1–2. London: Eyre & Spottiswoode, 1948, 1949.

Evelyn Shuckburgh, *Descent to Suez: Diaries 1951–56*. London: Weidenfeld & Nicolson, 1986.

Philip Snow, *The Fall of Hong Kong: Britain, China and the Japanese Occupation*. New Haven and London: Yale University Press, 2003.

Mary Soames, *Clementine Churchill*. London: Cassell, 1979.

David Stafford, *Roosevelt & Churchill: Men of Secrets*. London: Little, Brown, 1999.

——, *Ten Days to D-Day: Countdown to the Liberation of Europe*. London: Little, Brown, 2003.

W. H. Thompson, *I Was Churchill's Shadow*. London: Christopher Johnson, 1951.

————, *Assignment Churchill*. New York: Farrar, Straus & Young, 1955.

Harry S. Truman, *Memoirs*. Volume 1, *Year of Decisions*. New York: Doubleday, 1955.

Warren Tute, *The Deadly Stroke*. London: Collins, 1973.

John W. Wheeler-Bennett, *King George VI, His Life and Reign*. London: Macmillan, 1958.

John G. Winant, *A Letter from Grosvenor Square: An Account of a Stewardship*. London: Hodder & Stoughton, 1947.

Philip Ziegler, *Mountbatten*. London: Collins, 1985.

PHONOGRAPH RECORDS

His Master's Voice ALP 1436 and 1554.
National Park Service, No. EDIS 39852

NEWSPAPERS

Atlanta Constitution
Baltimore Sun
Bath Daily Chronicle
Boston Globe
Boston Herald
Brooklyn Eagle
Chicago Sun
Chicago Tribune
Daily Graphic
Daily Telegraph
Evening Standard
Miami Daily News
Manchester Guardian
New Haven Morning Journal
New York Evening Journal
New York Herald Tribune
New York Times
New York Tribune
New York World
News of the World
Observer
Springfield (Massachusetts) Republican
Sunday Chronicle
The Times
Wall Street Journal
Washington Post

MAGAZINES AND JOURNALS

Collier's
Hansard
Imperial Review
Life
Michigan Quarterly Review
Nash's Pall Mall
The Nation
New York American
Saturday Evening Post
Saturday Review
Scribner's
Westminster Gazette

ARTICLES BY CHURCHILL (IN CHRONOLOGICAL ORDER)

"The Insurrection in Cuba: Letters from the Front." *Daily Graphic,* 13 December 1895.

"The Revolt in Cuba." *Saturday Review,* 15 February 1896.

"Officers and Gentlemen." *Saturday Evening Post,* 29 December 1900.

"The Chicago Scandals: The Novel Which is Making History." *PTO,* 16 and 23 June 1906.

"Mr Churchill's Tribute." *Observer,* 10 September 1916.

"Will America Fail Us?" *Illustrated Sunday Herald,* 30 November 1919.

"Shall We All Commit Suicide?" *Nash's Pall Mall,* September 1924.

"What I Saw and Heard in America." *Daily Telegraph,* 18 November 1929.

"Fever of Speculation in America." *Daily Telegraph,* 9 December 1929.

"Old Battlefields of Virginia." *Daily Telegraph,* 16 December 1929.

"Nature's Panorama in California." *Daily Telegraph,* 23 December 1929.

"Peter Pan Township of the Films." *Daily Telegraph,* 30 December 1929.

"Cartoons and Cartoonists." *Strand Magazine,* June 1931.

"My New York Misadventure" (Part 1). *Daily Mail,* 4 January 1932.

"I Was Conscious Through It All." *Daily Mail,* 5 January 1932.

"The Shattered Cause of Temperance." *Collier's,* 13 August 1932.

"Are We Too Clever?" *Collier's,* 27 August 1932.

"Defense in the Pacific." *Collier's,* 17 December 1932.

"The World's Great Stories Re-told: Uncle Tom's Cabin." *News of the World,* 8 January 1933.

"Land of Corn and Lobsters." *Collier's,* 5 August 1933.

"The Bond Between Us." *Collier's,* 4 November 1933.

"While the World Watches." *Collier's,* 29 December 1934.

"Every Working Man Will Be Affected If Roosevelt Fails." *Sunday Chronicle,* 10 February 1935.

"Why Not Dictatorship?" *Collier's,* 16 February 1935.

"Roosevelt and the Future of the New Deal." *Daily Mail,* 24 April 1935.

"Oldest and Richest" (John D. Rockefeller). *Collier's,* 11 July 1936.

"America Looks at Europe." *Evening Standard,* 31 May 1937.

"Tragedy of the Torpedoed Lusitania, Blunder Which Sealed the Fate of Germany." *News of the World,* 6 June 1937.

"Can America Keep Out of War?" *Collier's,* 2 October 1937.

"Europe's Plea to Roosevelt." *Evening Standard,* 10 December 1937.

"What Japan Thinks of Us." *Evening Standard,* 21 January 1938.

"The Union of the English-Speaking Peoples." *News of the World,* 15 May 1938.

"Influence the US May Wield on Europe's Destiny." *Daily Telegraph and Morning Post,* 4 August 1938.

"Can Europe Stave Off War?" *Daily Telegraph and Morning Post,* 15 September 1938.

"The Dream." *Sunday Telegraph,* 31 January 1966 (written in November 1947).

OTHER ARTICLES

Randolph Churchill, "How He Came to Write It." *Sunday Telegraph,* 30 January 1966.

Winston S. Churchill, "The Indian Blood That Fired My Grandfather." *Sunday Telegraph,* 24 October 1999.

James Humes, "The Ideals of Democracy." *Finest Hour,* Third Quarter, no. 80 (1993).

Cornelius Mann, "Two Famous Descendants of John Cooke and Sarah Warren." *New York Genealogical and Biographical Record* 73, no. 3, New York (July 1942).

John H. Mather, "Sir Winston Churchill: His Hardiness and Resilience." *Churchill Proceedings, 1996–1997,* The Churchill Centre, Washington D.C., 2000.

Fred A. McKenzie. "English War-Correspondents in South Africa." *Harper's Monthly Magazine,* New York, July 1900.

John P. Rossi, "Winston Churchill's Iron Curtain Speech: Forty Years After." *Modern Age,* Bryn Mawr, Pennsylvania, Spring 1986.

Dorothy Thompson, "Winston Churchill: He Inspires an Empire in Its Hour of Need." *Life,* 27 January 1941.

INTERNET SOURCES

Patrick McSherry, "Cruiser *New York.*" www.spanamwar.com.

National Security Archive. *Electronic Briefing Book No. 28,* "The Secret CIA History of the Iran Coup, 1953." www2.gwu.edu/~nsarchiv/NSAEBB.

Lawrence H. Officer, "What is the Relative Value in UK Pounds?" and "What is the Relative Value in US Dollars?" Economic History Services, 30 October 2004, EH.NET: www.eh.net.

Donald N. Wilber, *Overthrow of Premier Mossadeq of Iran, November 1952–August 1953.* CIA Special Report *New York Times,* 16 April 2000: www.nytimes.com.

ILLUSTRATION CREDITS

I am grateful to the following for permission to use photographs in their possession or in their copyright, and to have made photographs available to me:

Charles T. Mayer: 50
Chatto and Windus: 12
Churchill College Archive Centre: 21, 49, 52
Sir John Colville: 55
Daily Gleaner newspaper, Jamaica: 57
Dover Publications: 5
Harry S. Truman Presidential Library: 53, 54
Hutchinsons of London: 2
Imperial War Museum: 22, 23, 24, 25, 26, 27, 28, 30, 32, 33, 34, 35, 36, 37, 38, 40, 41, 42, 43, 44, 45, 46
J. E. Purdy: 8
John Lane, The Bodley Head: 12
Keystone Press: 39
Kustom Quality: 3
Library of Congress: 8, 31, 51, 57
Photo Helminger: 53
Richard M. Nixon Presidential Library: 56
Radio Times Hulton Picture Library: 29
Winston Churchill Memorial and Library in the United States at Westminster College, Fulton, Missouri: 18, 47, 48, 49, 58
Winston S. Churchill Esq: 1, 9, 13, 14, 15, 16, 17, 19, 20

INDEX

ABOUT THE AUTHOR

MARTIN GILBERT is Winston Churchill's official biographer, and a leading historian of the modern world. In 1962 he was elected a Fellow of Merton College, Oxford, and in the same year he began work as a research assistant to Randolph Churchill on the first two volumes of the official biography of Sir Winston Churchill. Following Randolph Churchill's death in 1968, Martin Gilbert was appointed Official Biographer, and wrote the other six volumes of the biography, the last of which, *Never Despair*, was published in 1988. He is the author of more than seventy books, among them the single-volume *Churchill: A Life*, twin histories of the First World War and Second World War, a comprehensive history of Israel, and the three-volume *A History of the Twentieth Century*. His book *The Holocaust* is one of the classic works on the subject. He is an Honorary Fellow of Merton College, Oxford (of which he was a Fellow until 1998), and a Distinguished Fellow of Hillsdale College, Michigan. In 1995 he was knighted "for services to British history and international relations," and in 1999 he was awarded a Doctorate of Literature by the University of Oxford for the totality of his published work.